THE LEAN TOOLBOX

A SOURCEBOOK FOR PROCESS IMPROVEMENT

Sixth edition

by

John Bicheno
University of Buckingham

and

Matthias Holweg
University of Oxford

PRODUCTION AND INVENTORY CONTROL, SYSTEMS AND INDUSTRIAL ENGINEERING (PICSIE) BOOKS

BUCKINGHAM, ENGLAND
2023

Published by:

PICSIE Books
15 Chandos Road
Buckingham, MK18 1AH
United Kingdom

E-mail: **bichenojohn@me.com**

Copyright © PICSIE Books, 2023
Publication date: January 2023
ISBN 978-1-7391674-0-0
British Library Cataloguing-in-Publication Data
A catalogue record for this book is available from the British Library

The greatest waste ... is failure to use the abilities of people, ...
to learn about their frustrations and about the contributions
that they are eager to make.

W. Edwards Deming

Table of Contents

1 HOW TO USE THIS BOOK 1

PHILOSOPHY, MINDSET & SCIENCE OF LEAN ... 2

2 THE LEAN PHILOSOPHY 2

  2.1 WHAT IS LEAN? 2
  2.2 WHERE DOES LEAN COME FROM? 2
  2.3 WHY DO WE CALL IT 'LEAN'? 4
  2.4 BEWARE OF A 'TOOL MINDSET' 6
  2.5 WHERE TO START YOUR LEAN TRANSFORMATION 7

3 THE LEAN MINDSET 10

  3.1 THE 'IDEAL WAY', 'TRUE NORTH', AND PURPOSE 10
  3.2 THE FIVE LEAN PRINCIPLES.................. 10
  3.3 SYNOPSIS: THE 25 PRINCIPLES OF LEAN.. 12
  3.4 VALUE AND WASTE 15
  3.5 THE ORIGINAL SEVEN WASTES 16
  3.6 THE NEW WASTES 19
  3.7 LEAN SERVICE................................. 21
  3.8 THE 3MS: MUDA, MURA AND MURI 23
  3.9 LEARNING: THE PDCA OR PDSA CYCLE . 23
  3.10 THE TOYOTA WAY 24
  3.11 THE DNA OF TPS 25
  3.12 LEAN AND ENVIRONMENTAL SUSTAINABILITY 27
  3.13 LEAN AND DIGITAL TECHNOLOGIES 29

4 THE SCIENCE OF LEAN........................... 31

  4.1 KEY DEFINITIONS 31
  4.2 THE KINGMAN EQUATION AND SCHEDULING DYNAMICS 32
  4.3 LITTLE'S LAW 36
  4.4 PARETO AND THE 80/20 RULE 37
  4.5 BUFFERS 40
  4.6 INVENTORY TRADE-OFF CURVES 41

  4.7 SCIENTIFIC METHOD AND EXPERIMENTATION 43
  4.8 BIAS AND SYSTEM1/SYSTEM2 THINKING 44
  4.9 VOLATILITY, VUCA AND CYNEFIN® 45

ORGANISING FOR FLOW 50

5 RESPECT AND HUMILITY 50

  5.1 RESPECT 50
  5.2 HUMILITY 50

6 GEMBA 52

  6.1 GEMBA AND GENCHI GENBUTSU 52
  6.2 GEMBA WALKS................................. 52
  6.3 RESPECT AND HUMILITY AT TOYOTA SA: A MINI CASE 54

7 QUESTIONING AND LISTENING 55

8 PSYCHOLOGICAL SAFETY 57

  8.1 MISTAKES AND IMPROVEMENT 57
  8.2 IMPROVING PSYCHOLOGICAL SAFETY...... 57

9 LEADING AND MENTORING 59

  9.1 LEADER STANDARD WORK 59
  9.2 LEAN COACHING AND MENTORING........ 59
  9.3 A NOTE ON INTERVENTION THEORY AND CHANGE 61

10 SOCIO TECHNICAL SYSTEMS..................... 62

  10.1 THE SYSTEMS CONCEPT........................ 62
  10.2 LEAN ORGANISATION AND SYSTEMS THINKING................................... 63

11 THE JOB CHARACTERISTICS MODEL.......... 66

  11.1 CORE JOB CHARACTERISTICS................ 66
  11.2 CRITICISMS AND EXTENSIONS OF JCM.... 68

12 MANAGING THE CHANGE PROCESS 70

  12.1 LEWIN'S CHANGE MODELS 70
  12.2 THE CHANGE ICEBERG 71
  12.3 VALUE STREAM MAPPING AS CHANGE CATALYST................................... 71

12.4   COMMON PROBLEMS WITH CHANGE PROGRAMMES................................. 72

13 ENGAGEMENT 74

13.1   THE CATHEDRAL MODEL OF ENGAGEMENT 75

13.2   THE ADOPTION CURVE AND KEY PEOPLE 76

PREPARING FOR FLOW................................ 78

14 5S.. 78

14.1   SORT 79

14.2   SIMPLIFY (OR SET-IN-ORDER OR STRAIGHTEN) 79

14.3   SCAN (OR SWEEP OR SHINE OR SCRUB) .. 80

14.4   STANDARDISE (OR STABILIZE OR SECURE) 80

14.5   SUSTAIN (OR SELF DISCIPLINE)............. 80

14.6   SAFETY 80

14.7   5S AS ROOT CAUSE 80

14.8   5S AND SUSTAINING IMPROVEMENTS 81

14.9   EXTENDING THE 5S CONCEPT 81

15 VISUAL MANAGEMENT............................ 82

15.1   CUMULATIVE FLOW DIAGRAMS 83

15.2   SINGLE POINT LESSONS 84

15.3   COMMUNICATIONS BOARD.................. 84

16 STANDARD WORK AND SOPS.................. 87

16.1   RACI CHARTS 90

16.2   WINDOW ANALYSIS AND STANDARDS 90

17 TRAINING WITHIN INDUSTRY.................. 92

17.1   JOB INSTRUCTION 92

17.2   JOB METHODS 93

17.3   JOB RELATIONS................................. 93

17.4   JOB SAFETY 93

18 TIME AND ACTIVITY............................... 94

18.1   TAKT TIME, PITCH TIME, PLANNED CYCLE TIME, AND CADENCE......................... 94

18.2   ACTIVITY TIMING, ACTIVITY SAMPLING AND WORK ELEMENTS............................. 95

19 CHANGEOVER REDUCTION (SMED) 96

19.1   WHAT IS A CHANGEOVER? 96

19.2   MAPPING THE CHANGEOVER PROCESS 96

20 QUALITY 100

20.1   UNDERSTANDING CUSTOMER NEEDS: THE KANO MODEL............................... 100

20.2   A FRAMEWORK FOR LEAN QUALITY 102

20.3   MISTAKES AND ERRORS 102

20.4   CHECKLISTS 106

20.5   VARIATION AND SIX SIGMA 107

20.6   COMPLEXITY 111

21 TOTAL PRODUCTIVE MAINTENANCE 114

21.1   OVERALL EQUIPMENT EFFECTIVENESS (OEE) 114

21.2   THE SIX BIG LOSSES 116

21.3   FOCUSING TPM ACTIVITIES 116

21.4   WILLMOTT'S 11-STEP MODEL............ 117

21.5   SOME SPECIAL FEATURES OF TPM 118

22 LAYOUT, CELLS AND LINE BALANCE 120

22.1   GENERAL LAYOUT: GOOD AND NOT SO GOOD AT THE FACTORY LEVEL........... 120

22.2   AREA LAYOUT................................. 122

22.3   MATERIAL HANDING: GOOD AND NOT SO GOOD AT THE FACTORY LEVEL........... 126

22.4   CELLS... 126

22.5   CELL OR LINE BALANCING 128

22.6   CHAKU-CHAKU CELL OR LINE............. 133

22.7   SERU CELLS 133

22.8   VIRTUAL CELLS 134

22.9   MOVING LINES AND PULSE LINES 135

22.10   ERGONOMICS................................. 136

22.11   3P: PRODUCTION PREPARATION PROCESS 137

CREATING FLOW 140

23 MAPPING 140

23.1   WHAT IS THE AIM OF MAPPING? 140

23.2   BEFORE YOU BEGIN MAPPING... 140

23.3   TYPES OF MAPS 141

23.4   ANALYSING MAPS: TOWARDS THE FUTURE STATE 154

23.5   SOME WARNINGS ABOUT MAPPING 157

23.6   VALUE STREAM MAPPING IN A DIGITAL AGE 159

24   DEMAND ANALYSIS AND VARIATION..... 161

24.1   LEVEL AND CHASE DEMAND 161

24.2   REDUCING UNNECESSARY DEMAND AND DEMAND VARIATION 162

24.3   DEMAND ANALYSIS 163

24.4   COMBINING VOLUME ANALYSIS WITH DEMAND PATTERNS........................ 165

24.5   SCHEDULING WITH CATEGORIZATION AND PLATEAUS 166

24.6   INVENTORY CONTROL OF PARTS ABC AND RRS.. 167

24.7   PART LEVELLING 168

25   SCHEDULING: GENERAL POINTS............ 170

25.1   IDENTIFYING STABLE AND UNSTABLE ZONES 170

25.2   DIFFERENT PROCESSES REQUIRE DIFFERENT APPROACHES TO SCHEDULING 172

25.3   BASICS OF LEAN SCHEDULING 173

25.4   ON MRP AND ERP 174

25.5   MASTER SCHEDULING AND FINAL ASSEMBLY SCHEDULING 175

25.6   SALES AND OPERATIONS PLANNING (S&OP) 175

25.7   CONSTRAINTS AND THEORY OF CONSTRAINTS 176

25.8   THE BUILDING BLOCKS 183

26   PULL SYSTEMS................................. 187

26.1   KANBAN...................................... 188

26.2   CONWIP 195

26.3   DRUM BUFFER ROPE (DBR) 196

26.4   POLCA...................................... 197

26.5   DEMAND DRIVEN MRP (DDMRP)..... 198

26.6   COMPARING KANBAN, DBR, CONWIP, POLCA AND DDMR 199

27   SCHEDULING LINE PROCESSES 201

27.1   THE LEVEL SCHEDULE 201

27.2   THE TEN VALUE STREAM SCHEDULING CONCEPTS 201

27.3   APPLYING REPETITIVE SCHEDULING...... 210

28   SCHEDULING BATCH PROCESSES........... 213

28.1   BATCH SIZING................................ 213

28.2   TWO APPROACHES TO BATCH SIZING ... 214

28.3   THE EVERY PRODUCT EVERY (EPE) CONCEPT 216

28.4   SPECIAL BATCH SIZE CONSIDERATIONS . 218

29   CREATING THE LEAN SUPPLY CHAIN 220

29.1   WHAT IS SUPPLY CHAIN MANAGEMENT? 220

29.2   UNCERTAINTY AND THE BULLWHIP EFFECT 223

29.3   MANAGING SUPPLY CHAIN RISK.......... 226

29.4   MANAGING SUPPLIER RELATIONS........ 227

29.5   SUPPLY CHAIN COLLABORATION.......... 232

29.6   LEAN LOGISTICS 233

IMPROVING FLOW............................... 235

30   IMPROVEMENT 235

30.1   HOW TO GET STARTED..................... 235

30.2   LEAN, THE S-CURVE AND INNOVATION.. 236

30.3   ORGANIZING FOR IMPROVEMENT 236

30.4   THE HIERARCHY OF IMPROVEMENT...... 237

31   KAIZEN.. 240

31.1   THE PHILOSOPHY OF KAIZEN.............. 240

31.2   THE KAIZEN FLAG 240

31.3   KAIZEN EVENTS............................. 241

31.4   THE KAIZEN EVENT PROCESS 241

31.5   RECORDING THE LESSONS 243

32   PROBLEM SOLVING 244

32.1   IMPROVEMENT TYPES 244

32.2   PASSIVE INCREMENTAL..................... 244

32.3   PASSIVE BREAKTHROUGH.................. 247

32.4	ENFORCED INCREMENTAL	247
32.5	ENFORCED BREAKTHROUGH	248
32.6	IMPROVEMENT CYCLES	248
32.7	ROOT CAUSE PROBLEM SOLVING	250
32.8	5 WHYS AND FISHBONE	251
32.9	A3 PROBLEM SOLVING	253
32.10	OODA LOOP	255

33 KATA **257**

33.1	TYPES OF KATA	257
33.2	KATA AND HOSHIN	258
33.3	WIDER AREAS OF APPLICATION	258

34 HOLDING THE GAINS **260**

34.1	BACKSLIDING	260
34.2	THE FAILURE MODES OF LEAN IMPLEMENTATIONS	261
34.3	SUSTAINING IMPROVEMENTS	265
34.4	KEEPING THE MOMENTUM	266

DESIGNING FOR FLOW **270**

35 LEAN PRODUCT DEVELOPMENT **270**

35.1	FOUR OBJECTIVES AND SIX TRADE-OFFS	271
35.2	WASTES IN NEW PRODUCT DEVELOPMENT	272
35.3	TOYOTA'S APPROACH TO PRODUCT DEVELOPMENT	273

36 TOOLS FOR LEAN NPD **277**

36.1	DESIGN THINKING	277
36.2	PHASE GATES	280
36.3	OBEYA	280
36.4	QUALITY FUNCTION DEVELOPMENT	281
36.5	VALUE ENGINEERING AND VALUE METHODOLOGY	282
36.6	DESIGN FOR MANUFACTURE (DFM) AND DESIGN FOR ASSEMBLY (DFA)	284
36.7	MODULARITY AND PLATFORMS	286
36.8	TRIZ	287

37 AGILE DEVELOPMENT **289**

37.1	THE IDEA OF AGILE DEVELOPMENT	289
37.2	THE AGILE MANIFESTO	289
37.3	SCRUM AND SPRINTS	290
37.4	KANBAN IN SOFTWARE DEVELOPMENT, SERVICE AND NPD	290
37.5	LEAN SOFTWARE AND DEVOPS	291

38 LEAN START-UP **292**

MOTIVATING AND MEASURING FOR FLOW . **294**

39 LEADING A LEAN ORGANISATION **294**

39.1	PEOPLE AND CHANGE IN LEAN	294
39.2	THE PEOPLE TRILOGY	295
39.3	CREATING THE LEAN CULTURE	302

40 HOSHIN KANRI OR POLICY DEPLOYMENT **304**

40.1	THE HOSHIN PROCESS AND CATCHBALL	305
40.2	THE HOSHIN MATRIX	305

41 MEASURING PERFORMANCE **308**

41.1	A GOOD MEASUREMENT SYSTEM	308
41.2	OKRS	310
41.3	DEMING'S AND SHEWHART'S COUNSEL	310
41.4	THE BASIC LEAN MEASURES	311
41.5	SHORT INTERVAL TRACKING AND CONTROL	312

42 LEAN ACCOUNTING **313**

42.1	WARNINGS AND DILEMMAS	313
42.2	THE BOX SCORE	316
42.3	TARGET COSTING, KAIZEN COSTING AND COST DOWN	316
42.4	SETTING UP A LEAN ACCOUNTING SYSTEM	319

DIGITAL TOOLS FOR FLOW **321**

43 MAKING SENSE OF THE DIGITAL TRANSFORMATION **321**

43.1	AMARA'S LAW	321
43.2	DIGITISATION OR DIGITALISATION?	322

44 THE DIGITAL TOOLBOX **324**

44.1	INDUSTRY 4.0	324
44.2	AI AND MACHINE LEARNING	324

44.3   Process Mining 325

44.4   3D Printing or Additive Manufacturing 326

44.5   Internet of Things, RFID and RLTS 326

44.6   Autonomous vehicles 327

44.7   Augmented, mixed and virtual reality 327

44.8   Digital twins 327

44.9   The Metaverse............................. 327

44.10   Cloud Computing 327

44.11   Quantum Computing.................... 327

45 WHAT'S NEXT? **328**

A LEAN CHRONOLOGY **329**

ABBREVIATIONS **333**

INDEX **336**

1   How to use this book

This book has a single purpose: to help you make Lean work in your organisation. It provides you with the key principles and tools needed for a successful and lasting lean transformation. It will guide your implementation and act as a reference guide for you to go back to as you advance on your lean journey.

No matter what context you are working in, the philosophy of Lean will always remain – yet as new challenges arise, different tools will be required. In this book we have assembled the main tools, systems and principles we have found to be useful when applying Lean in manufacturing or services, private or public services, product development, or and the office. We believe that Lean is particularly appropriate in a world around us with high levels of volatility, uncertainty, complexity and ambiguity.

It is important to understand that, from its beginnings at and before Toyota, Lean has been constantly evolving. It has reached many contexts by now, including healthcare, construction and software development. Thus, Lean is not 'what Toyota does', yet Toyota serves as the True North for Lean implementations by having defined the underlying philosophy of continuous improvement by reducing the 3M's – muda, muri and mura – in the process.

In that sense this book covers not just the manufacturing-related tools, but also the tools developed to apply outside low-variation, repetitive manufacturing operations. In essence, the philosophy is universal, the tools are not. This book serves as a reference guide for all lean implementations, so you will invariably come across sections that are not relevant to your specific context.

The general chapters in the first section on vision and purpose apply to all, the subsequent tools sections should be consulted as needed. To this effect we have organised the book in sections that follow the most common stages of a lean transformation:

1.   Vision, purpose and strategy

2.   Organising for flow

3.   Preparing and stabilising for flow

4.   Creating flow

5.   Improving and maintaining flow.

Then, we have three sections for concepts that support activities along all of these stages in your lean transformation:

6.   Designing products and services for flow

7.   Measuring and motivating for flow

8.   Digital concepts for flow.

We suggest you start with reading the first three chapters on philosophy, underpinning science, and mindset – even if you are a seasoned improvement professional – and then select the chapters you need as you proceed.

We wish you all the best in your lean journey!

John and Matthias

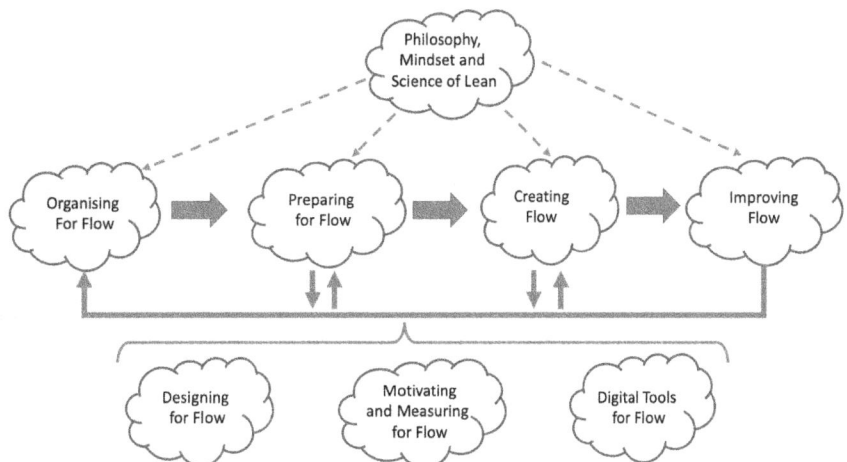

PHILOSOPHY, MINDSET AND SCIENCE OF LEAN

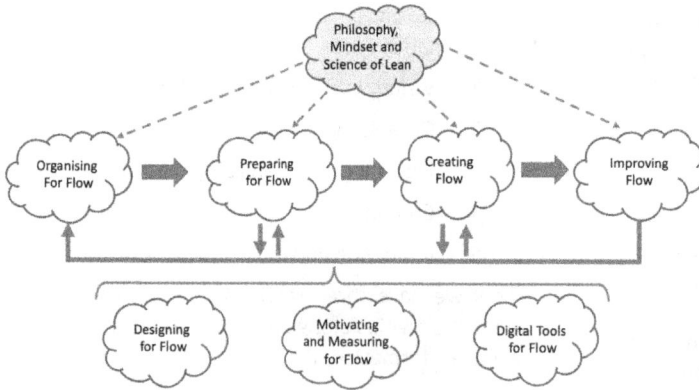

2 The Lean Philosophy

The Lean toolbox has evolved considerably over the past four decades as lean has been applied to wide range of contexts beyond automotive manufacturing. What has remained constant throughout is the underlying philosophy, which is foundational knowledge all lean implementations should be based on.

2.1 What is Lean?

Lean is about moving ever closer to uninterrupted flow in the sequence of operations that deliver perfect quality – in other words – becoming more of a time-based competitor. 'Flow' is not only of physical products and services but also the information and designs necessary to run operations. This requires continuous improvement in terms of removing *muda* (waste), *mura* (unevenness), and *muri* (overburden) from the process, in order to enhance the value-added content in the process. Especially important is that value must be defined in the eyes of the **customer**, in terms that are actually meaningful to the customer.

A 'quick and dirty' definition of Lean is 'doing more with less'. This is of course directly in line with the definition of productivity (the ratio of outputs over inputs). But this should be interpreted more widely as doing good for customers, employees, suppliers, community and society with less resources – materials, energy, pollution – to achieve ultimate sustainability.

The Lean Enterprise Institute states, 'The core idea is to maximize *customer value* while minimizing waste. Simply, lean means creating more value for customers with fewer resources.'

The ASQ defined Lean as 'the permanent struggle to flow value to each customer.' These definitions of Lean capture the essence:

- There is no end point; it is a journey.
- It is neither easy nor a quick fix: long term consistency is required.
- It is all about flow – and improving flow means understanding both customers and the system and reducing impediments to flow.
- The individual customer should be the focus. Not 'mass' but 'one at a time'.

Roger Schmenner, emeritus professor at Indiana talks about 'swift, even flow', which is also a neat and succinct summary. Masaaki Imai, pioneer of Kaizen, now thinks the core concepts are flow, synchronization, and levelling, or 'FSL'.

2.2 Where does Lean come from?

The foundation of the Toyota Motor Company dates back to 1918, when the entrepreneur Sakichi Toyoda established his spinning and weaving business based on his advanced automatic loom. He sold the patents to the Platts Brothers in 1929 for £100,000, and it is said that these funds provided the foundation for his son, Kiichiro, to realize his vision of manufacturing automobiles. The tale goes that Sakichi told his son on his deathbed: 'I served our country with the loom. I want you to serve it with the automobile'. At the time the Japanese market was dominated by the local subsidiaries of Ford and General Motors (GM), starting Toyoda's automotive business was fraught with financial difficulties and ownership struggles after Sakichi's death in 1930. Nevertheless, Kiichiro prevailed and began designing his Model AA – by making considerable use of Ford and GM components! The company was relabelled 'Toyota' to simplify the pronunciation and give it an auspicious meaning in Japanese. Truck and car production started in 1935 and 1936, respectively, and in 1937 the Toyota Motor Company was formally formed. World War II disrupted production, and the post-war economic hardship resulted in growing inventories of unsold cars, leading to financial difficulties at Toyota, leading to the resignation of Kiichiro from the company.

His cousin Eiji Toyoda became managing director– in what in retrospect bears considerable irony – was sent to the United States in 1950 to study American manufacturing methods. Going abroad to study competitors was not unusual; pre-war a Toyota delegation had visited the Focke-Wulff aircraft works in Germany, where they observed the 'Produktionstakt' concept, which later developed into what we now know as 'takt time'. Eiji Toyoda was determined to implement mass production techniques at Toyota, yet capital constraints and the low volumes in the Japanese market did not justify the large batch sizes common at Ford and GM. Toyota's first plant in Kariya was thus used both for prototype development and production, and had a capacity of 150 units per month.

While the simple and flexible equipment that Kiichiro had purchased in the 1930s would enable many of the concepts essential to TPS, the individual that gave the crucial impulse towards developing the Toyota Production System (TPS) capable of economically producing large variety in small volumes, was Taiichi Ohno (Ōno Taiichi). Ohno had joined Toyoda Spinning and Weaving in 1932 after graduating as mechanical engineer, and only in 1943 joined the automotive business after the weaving and spinning business had been dissolved. Ohno did not have any experience in manufacturing automobiles but brought a 'common-sense approach' without any preconceptions that has been instrumental in developing the fundamentally different Just-in-Time philosophy. Analysing the Western production systems, he argued that they had two logical flaws. First, he reasoned that producing components in large batches resulted in large inventories, which took up costly capital and warehouse space and resulted in a high number of defects. The second flaw was the inability to accommodate consumer preferences for product diversity. Ohno believed that GM had not abandoned Ford's mass production system, since the objective was still to use standard components enabling large batch sizes, thus minimizing changeovers. In his view, the management of Western vehicle manufacturers were (and arguably still are) striving for large scale production and economies of scale.

From 1948 onwards, Ohno gradually extended his concept of small-lot production throughout Toyota from the engine machining shop he was managing. His main focus was to reduce cost by eliminating waste, a notion that developed out of his experience with the automatic loom that stopped once the thread broke, in order not to waste any material or machine time. He referred to the loom as 'a text book in front of my eyes', and this 'jidoka' or 'autonomous machine' concept would become an integral part of the Toyota Production System. Ohno also visited the U.S. automobile factories in 1956, and incorporated ideas he developed during these visits, most notably the 'kanban supermarket' to control material replenishment. In his book, Ohno describes the two pillars of TPS as autonomation, based on Sakichi's loom, and JIT, which he claims came from Kiichiro who once stated that 'in a comprehensive industry such as automobile manufacturing, the best way to work would be to have all the parts for assembly at the side of the line just in time for their user'. In order for this system to work, it was necessary to produce and receive components and parts in small lot sizes, which was uneconomical according to traditional thinking. Ohno had to modify the machine changeover procedures to produce a growing variety in smaller lot sizes. This was helped by the fact that the much of the machinery Kiichiro had bought was simple, general-purpose equipment that was easy to modify and adapt. Change-over reduction was further advanced by Shigeo Shingo, who was hired as external consultant in 1955 and developed the SMED (single-minute exchange of dies) system.

The result was an ability to produce a considerable variety of automobiles in comparatively low volumes at a competitive cost, altering the conventional logic of mass production. In retrospect these changes were revolutionary, yet these were largely necessary adaptations to the economic circumstances at the time that required low volumes and great variety. By 1950, the entire Japanese auto industry was producing an annual output equivalent to less than three days' of the U.S. car production at the time. Toyota gradually found ways to combine the advantages of small-lot production with economies of scale in manufacturing and procurement. Thus, more than anything, it is this 'dynamic learning capability' that is at the heart of the success of TPS. As Fujimoto in his book on the evolution of TPS concludes:

'Toyota's production organization [..] adopted various elements of the Ford system selectively and in unbundled forms, and hybridized them with their ingenious system and original ideas. It also learnt from experiences with other industries (e.g. textiles). It is thus a myth that the Toyota Production System was a pure invention of genius Japanese automobile practitioners. However, we should not underestimate the entrepreneurial imagination of Toyota's production managers (e.g. Kiichiro Toyoda, Taiichi Ohno, and Eiji Toyoda), who integrated elements of the Ford system in a domestic environment quite different from that of the United States. Thus, the Toyota-style system has been neither purely original not totally imitative. It is essentially a hybrid'.

Astonishingly, TPS went largely unnoticed by the West – albeit not kept as a secret – and according to Ohno only started attracting attention during the first oil crisis in 1973, when Japanese imports threatened Western manufacturers.

TPS gained popularity in the Western manufacturing world through the studies of Robert 'Doc' Hall, and Richard Schonberger, and their hugely popular books 'Zero Inventories' and 'Japanese Manufacturing Techniques', respectively. These remain great reads today!

Further reading

Ohno, T. (1988), Toyota Production System: beyond large-scale production, Productivity Press, New York

Fujimoto, T. (1999), *The evolution of a manufacturing system at Toyota*, Oxford University Press, Oxford

Holweg, M. (2007), The genealogy of lean production. *Journal of operations management, 25(2)*, 420-437.

2.3   Why do we call it 'Lean'?

The first paper on TPS in English appeared in 1979, which was not published by academics, but by four managers of Toyota's Production Control department – including Fujio Cho, who in 1999 became president of the Toyota Motor Corporation. The Western world took notice: in 1979, the 'Repetitive Manufacturing Group (RMG)' was established to study TPS under sponsorship of the American Production and Inventory Control Society (APICS). The group held a meeting at Kawasaki's motorcycle plant in Lincoln, Nebraska, in June 1981 and exposed participants to Kawasaki's well-developed JIT system, a clone of Toyota's system. The group included Richard Schonberger and Robert Hall who, based on their experiences, published their books on JIT. In parallel, Yasuhiro Monden of Tsukuba University published his book on TPS in 1983. Up until this point, the debate in the Western world was largely based around shop-floor techniques, commonly referred to as 'JIT' or 'zero inventory' production.

The next step towards describing the Lean philosophy came with the International Motor Vehicle Program (IMVP) at MIT. The programme was based at MIT, but from the start the idea was to create an international network of faculty at other universities, with Dan Jones as UK team leader, Jim Womack, as research manager, and Dan Roos as programme director.

The programme was geared towards identifying what drove the Japanese competitive advantage. At the time a range of explanations were given. The most common explanations (and with hindsight, misperceptions) were:

1. **Cost advantage** – Japan was seen to have lower wage rates, a favourable Yen/Dollar exchange rate and lower cost of capital, elements that combine to an 'unfair playing field'.

2. **Luck** - Japan had fuel-efficient cars when the energy crisis came, or it was simply a fortunate effect of the 'business life cycle issue'.

3. **'Japan, Inc.**' – MITI, Japan's Ministry of International Trade and Industry, was suspected of orchestrating a large-scale industrial policy.

4. **Culture** – Cultural differences in Japan allowed for more efficient production, which cannot be replicated in other countries.

5. **Technology** – The use of advanced automation in Japanese factories ('It was all done with advanced robotics'). Some even suggested that the Japanese were acquiring Western technology, which they then exploited.

6. **Government Policy** – Trade barriers against the U.S., more lenient labour laws in Japan, and a national health care program lowered the overall labour cost.

The IMVP sponsor companies encouraged the research team to look into the issue of why Japan was getting ahead. The research remit was to not only describe the gap between the Western World and Japan, but also 'to measure the size of the gap', according to Dan Jones. A key challenge was to normalise the labour input that varies greatly by vehicle size and option content, as well as by the degree of vertical integration, i.e. to what extent the manufacturer produced components in house, or buys them in from suppliers. So, while there was a good understanding of the differences in manufacturing practices across regions, the way of executing a valid comparison was far less defined: as Dan Jones remarked, '[..] we had a method, but we did not have a methodology.'

The initial design of the benchmarking methodology was developed by Womack and Jones during 1985/86, and was tested at Renault's Flins plant in 1986. In May that year, John Krafcik went to see Jim Womack to discuss potential research opportunities if he were to enrol at MIT. Krafcik was the first American engineer to be hired by NUMMI, and joined MIT as an MBA student, and by summer 1986 Womack and Krafcik formally started the assembly plant study by visiting GM's Framingham assembly plant in Massachusetts.

Another MIT student, John Paul MacDuffie, also became involved in the programme at the time. MacDuffie was working as research assistant to Haruo Shimada from Keio University (a visiting professor at the Sloan School), who was interested in the Japanese transplants in the U.S., trying to understand how well they were able to transfer the Japanese human resource and production systems. Shimada was one of the first researchers allowed to visit and conduct interviews at the new transplants of Honda,

Nissan, Mazda, and NUMMI. Shimada used a benchmarking index according to which he classified companies on the spectrum from 'fragile' to 'robust' or 'buffered'. This terminology that was initially used by IMVP researchers, but 'fragile' later amended to 'Lean' which was seen to have a more positive connotation. The term 'Lean production' was first used by Krafcik in 1988, and subsequently, Womack et al. of course used the term 'Lean production' to contrast Toyota with the Western 'mass production' system in the 'Machine' book. The name 'Lean' was born!

Further Reading

Krafcik, J. 1988. The Triumph of the Lean Production System. *Sloan Management Review* (Fall), 41-52

Sugimori, Y., K. Kusunoki, K., Cho, F., Uchikawa, S. 1977. Toyota Production System and Kanban System; Materialization of Just-in-Time and Respect-for-Human System. *International Journal of Production Research*, 15 (6), 553–564

Womack, J.P., Jones, D.T., Roos, D. 1990. *The Machine that Changed the World*, HarperCollins, New York

See first two chapters of Jacob Stoller, *The Lean CEO*, McGraw Hill, 2015

2.4   Beware of a 'tool mindset'

For many, Lean started with 'tools'. Often, these were not even a set of tools but completely independent: 5S here, SMED there, kanban here and A3 there. But, like any set of tools, they are there for a purpose, not an end in themselves. Like Michelangelo chipping away all marble that was not David, so Lean tools are there to chip away everything that does not enhance value for the customer. For a while, a pure tools approach is not a bad thing. Like Michelangelo's original marble block, a lot can be removed with little skill. Then came Lean through Principles – often the 5 Lean Principles of Womack and Jones, or principles of self-help, respect, responsibility towards staff, customers and society. This is much better, and better still if systemically brought together.

To focus on tools is misguided. It risks not seeing the 'big picture' – a focus on overall customer satisfaction and flow. Åhlström and Modig talk about Flow Efficiency and Resource Efficiency. The former focuses on the customer and customer delays, the latter on resources. As an example, consider a hospital visit. Flow efficiency would seek to minimise delays for the patient, with the patient moving from stage to stage without intermediate waiting or queuing. Resource efficiency would seek to minimise delays to the doctor and staff and maximise the efficiency of equipment and operating theatres – the patient would just have to wait and queue. Hence, an exclusive focus on 'the tools' (5S, standard work, TPM, etc.) has the significant risk of downgrading customer needs. Of course, the ideal would be to minimise BOTH patient delays and achieve resource efficiency. Can this be done? Well, it can be approached – see the later section on Kingman's equation. Thus, one way of understanding Lean is to view it as a (proven) approach to dispense with increasingly inappropriate 'economies of scale' and to adopt 'economies of time'. Too often it is assumed that by aiming for resource efficiency, customer flow efficiency will simultaneously be achieved. Beware!

Most now realise that 'real' Lean is behaviour-driven. What everyone does every day without being told. But how to get to this state of nirvana? Behaviour is built through confidence and security – phycological safety. An example would be pulling the Andon chord when a problem occurs and doing this as a *habit*, in the confidence that this will be supported and expected. No 'lip service'. And the habit of using an experimental approach. Over time, with persistence, this builds a Lean mindset – the things we take to be self-evident.

The most important behaviour is that, at every level, leaders are teachers – continually reinforcing the correct usage of the principles and the tools. Not relying on a 10-day Lean course, or a book, or intranet for their staff to learn the principles and tools – but by self-demonstration and coaching every day.

In some ways the word 'Lean' is an unfortunate one, because it has connotations of being manufacturing only (but by no means is confined to it), as well 'mean-ness' or 'cutting back', generally in terms of headcount. On the contrary, Lean is about growth and opportunity. For example, Toyota has grown not cut back. They have grown because they have capitalized on the huge advantages that Lean brings. It is better to grow into profitability rather than to shrink into profitability.

This leads to another important idea – that of 'Lean Enterprise'. Womack and Jones have emphasized that Lean is concerned with enterprise not just with manufacturing. If you have already started on your Lean journey without involving design, marketing, accounting, HR, distribution, and field service, you will have to do so very soon or risk the whole programme. These functions have a vital role to play in answering what the organization will do with the improved flexibility, times, and improvement ability. If the answer is just 'reduce costs' management has missed the point. But the Lean enterprise also needs appropriate people policies, measures, accounting, design and new product introduction, supply chain activities, and service initiatives – perhaps even 'servitization'.

David Cochrane makes an excellent point: Lean, says he, is not what organizations need to do. Lean is what organizations *should become* by effective system design and implementation.

To conclude, take Ohno's Method:

1. Mentally force yourself into tight spots.
2. Think hard; systematically observe reality.
3. Generate ideas; find and implement simple, ingenious, low-cost solutions.
4. Derive personal pleasure from accomplishing Kaizen.

2.5 Where to start your lean transformation

Lean Transformation is the core topic of this book, yet if you are hoping to find a shortcut for your Lean journey here, we will have to disappoint you. While much of the modern management literature tends to propose the '3 steps to heaven', unfortunately all Lean transformations are different, and there is no one golden bullet recipe to follow.

As George Box the famous statistician said, 'All models are wrong, but some models are useful'. The same applies to lean transformation frameworks. Some tend to work well in most contexts, most notable value stream mapping (VSM), the 'House of Lean', and 5S (housekeeping).

It is possible to use VSM as guiding framework for Lean Transformation. But first, understand demand -customers, priorities, patterns, Then the basic idea is to go to 'gemba' (the workplace) and define the current state or 'as is' map. Accompany this with a thorough assessment of skills and resources. 'People' capabilities would be a must. In a next step, the future state or 'should be' process is defined. The gap between the current and future states becomes the implementation plan: what actions are needed - short term - to be taken for stability.

After improvements have been made, and the process is more stable, new current and future state maps are generated, and the cycle begins again. One will never reach the ideal state, but progressively move to an emerging vision of a lean process (See Chapter 9 for details on mapping).

Another option is to use the 'House of Lean' as guiding model. The original was developed at Toyota. An early version is shown below.

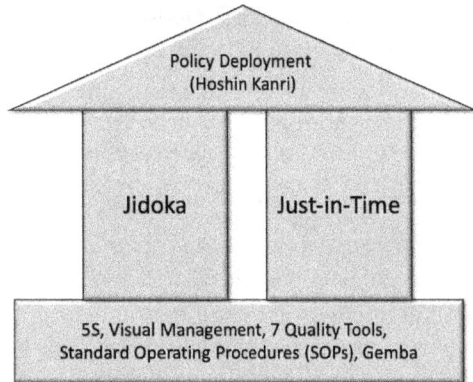

Note the two pillars: JIT and Jidoka (Flow and Quality or 'Go' and 'Stop'.) Note that having both pillars is a necessary regulating mechanism – you need both. Ohno noted that in the West, the preference was for Just in Time and he was dismayed that Jidoka and 'autonomation' (automation with a human touch) were frequently downplayed. Jidoka is a quality related concept concerned with prevention and not passing defectives downstream.

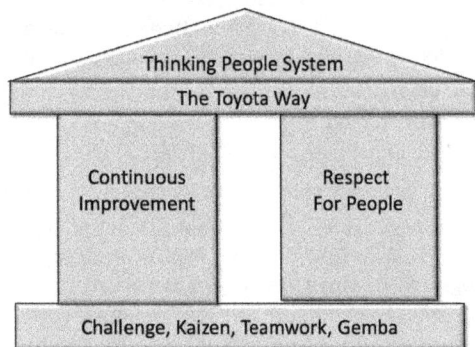

Later versions replaced the two main pillars of Just in Time and Jidoka with Continuous improvement and 'Respect for people', built on a foundation of Learning cycles. Even more lately Rother and Liker suggested that the Toyota system rests on a scientific way of thinking. But there is more. Scientific thinking is certainly needed for incremental improvement or kaizen. But

occasionally creative 'out of the box' thinking is needed to break through to the next level.

It is interesting to speculate on the change in the House between the two versions. One opinion, widely ignored, is that in early days Toyota suffered from quality and rework problems. Hence, Jidoka. These were largely solved. But if they are not solved, JIT flow will fail. A warning!

Here is the good news about such houses: They are familiar and easy to understand. They seem to make sense. They may have a proven record at organizations like Toyota.

Here is the not so good news: They suggest you need to build from the foundations up - irrespective of situation. The walls are not started before the foundations are complete – but often implementation is iterative. Several successful implementations have begun with the Policy Deployment roof. Moreover, the house is strongly tools oriented, rather than system oriented. Where does the customer come in? What happens if you are failing your customers due to poor delivery performance? How do you deliver value? These aspects require careful consideration if one chooses the House of Lean as a guiding model.

Recent versions of the house almost reversed mention of tools and became very strongly people-oriented. An example is shown, similar to a version used in Jeffrey Liker's 'The Toyota Way'. Liker's 2021 book shows a TPS house not unlike the version above, but adding culture and 'flexible, capable, motivated members' in the centre.

This version of the house is crucial for an understanding of Lean as it is perceived today. The two columns – continuous improvement and respect – are balanced and both are needed. The house falls if only one of these is present. This is exactly in-line with the Socio-Tech concept that is discussed in Chapter 10. Specifically, do not run-away with CI or 'tech' without balancing it with Respect (so often the case with early Lean). And do not focus too much on People and Respect whilst downplaying CI. (A tendency today in some organisations claiming to be Lean?). The two columns, together, enable a 'Thinking People System'.

The Lean Enterprise Institute (John Shook) has a related, excellent, version that covers the five areas of the house:

1. **Roof:** Situational: 'What problem are we trying to solve?'
2. **Left wall:** Process improvement – the way work is done
3. **Right wall:** Capability development – of all people
4. **Centre:** Leadership
5. **Foundations:** Thinking, mindset, and assumptions.

3 The Lean Mindset

Over the past four decades, much has been written about JIT, Toyota Production System, and Lean. They make a formidable list! In this chapter we present the foundations for understanding the Lean Management System.

We conclude this section with an outlook on how Lean can support project sustainability in operations, and how digital technologies can augment lean efforts.

3.1 The 'Ideal Way', 'True North', and Purpose

Perfection, as we shall see, is Womack and Jones' fifth Lean Principle. It could have been the first. So we need to ask, continually, 'Will that move us closer to the Ideal?'. And what is the ideal? It is perfect quality, zero waste, perfect customer satisfaction, zero environmental impact. (Is it so ridiculous to talk about 'Free Perfect and Now' as Robert Rodin did in transforming his company, Marshall Industries, pointing out that all the trends are going in those directions?) Indeed, think of Wiki and Google.

Toyota talks about 'True North'. Toyota Chairman Watanabe had a dream for the ideal state: A car that can improve air quality rather than pollute, that cannot injure people, that prevents accidents from happening, that can excite and entertain, and drive around the world on one tank of gas. (Perhaps the last should now be revised!)

Ohno had a vision too – of one at a time, completely flexible, no waste flow. In fact, that has been the driving force of Toyota for the past 60 years. Ohno did not have a Lean toolbox. He had in mind a vision of where he wanted to be. The vision first, **then** the necessary approach and tools. So look at every job, every process, and every system. What is the ideal way to do it? What is preventing us from doing that? How can the barriers be removed?

Another word that has become popular in Lean is 'Purpose'. The purpose of the organization from the customers' perspective. Of course, this is not 'profit' or the bonus of the CEO. Johnson and Johnson express this in their Credo: 'our first responsibility is to the doctors, nurses and patients, to mothers and fathers and all others who use our products and services. In meeting their needs everything we do must be of high quality….' (the credo continues about employees, communities and environment).

Moving towards perfection or true north is a repetitive process. Reducing the batch size moves you closer to the ideal, but you will need to come back and reduce it further. After you make the engine more fuel efficient, try it again then again and again. Perhaps change the engine type.

Likewise, Levitt maintained that Ford was not a production genius, but a marketing genius. His purpose was to make America, not only the rich, more mobile. He realised that if he could make and profitably sell a car for $500, millions of cars could be sold. That being the case, he had to find a way to make such a car.

Mike Rother, with the Kata approach, talks about the 'target condition' rather than True North. The target is where we want to be, but the path to get there is seldom clear in the detail. So we need to experiment, to see what works and what doesn't to get us nearer to the target. The word 'experiment' comes from 'ex' meaning from and 'periri' meaning try or attempt. This is the essence of PDSA, kata, kaizen – try it out and see. Whether succeed or fail, you learn.

3.2 The Five Lean Principles

In *Lean Thinking*, Womack and Jones renewed the message set out in *The Machine that Changed the World* (that Lean was, at least in automotive, literally 'do or die'), but extended it out beyond automotive. These reflective authors have given manufacturing, but to an extent also service, a vision of a world transformed from mass production to Lean enterprise. The five principles set out are of fundamental importance. Reading the Introduction to *Lean Thinking* should be compulsory for every executive.

Throughout *Lean Thinking*, Womack and Jones emphasized *Lean Enterprise* rather than Lean Manufacturing. In other words it was emphasising systems. But unfortunately the book became thought of as a manufacturing book, and the system message was missed.

In this section, whilst using Womack and Jones' 5 principles, some liberties have been taken, particularly in relating them to service. The point is vision: you may not get there within your lifetime, but try - others certainly will.

1. The first point is to **specify value from the point of view of the customer**. This is an established marketing idea (that customers buy results, not products - a clean shirt, not a washing machine). Too often, however, manufacturers tend to give the customers what is convenient for the manufacturer, or deemed economic for the customer. Womack and Jones cite batch-and-queue airline travel, involving long trips to the airport to enable big batch flights that start where you aren't and take you where you don't want to go, via hubs, and numerous delays. Recent work by Ariely and by Kahneman have revealed the myth of the economic rational man. So, what they value is uncertain – hence experimentation as for example in Ries' *The Lean Startup* (see Chapter on Designing Products and Services).

2. Then identify the **Value Stream**. This is the sequence of processes all the way from raw material to final customer, or from product concept to market launch. If possible look at the whole supply chain (or probably more accurately the 'demand network'). You are only as good as the weakest link; supply chains compete, not companies. Focus on the object (or product or customer), not the department, machine or process step. Think economies of time rather than economies of scale. Map and measure

performance of the value stream, not departments.

3. The third principle is **Flow.** Make value flow. If possible, use one-piece or one-document flow. Keep it moving. Avoid batches and queues, or at least continuously reduce them and the obstacles in their way. Try to design according to Stalk and Hout's Golden Rule - never to delay a value-adding step by a non value-adding step. Flow requires much preparation activity. But the important thing is vision: have in mind a guiding strategy that will move you inexorably towards simple, slim and swift customer flow.

4. Then comes **Pull**. Having set up the framework for flow, only operate as needed. Pull means short-term response to the customer's rate of demand, and not over producing. Think about pull on two levels: on the macro level most organisations will have to push up to a certain point and respond to final customer pull signals thereafter. An example is the classic Benetton 'jerseys in grey' that are stocked at an intermediate point in the supply chain in order to retain flexibility but also to give good customer service at low inventory levels. On the micro level, respond to pull signals as, for instance, when additional staff are needed at a supermarket checkout to avoid excessive queues. Attention to both levels is necessary. Each extension of pull reduces forecast uncertainty. Pull places a cap on inventory in the system.

5. Finally comes **Perfection**. Having worked through the previous principles, 'perfection' now seems more possible. Perfection does not mean only defect free - it means delivering exactly what the customer wants, exactly when (with no delay), at a fair price and with minimum waste. Beware of

benchmarking - the real benchmark is zero waste, not what the competitors or best practices are doing. In retrospect, perhaps a better phrase would have been 'continuous improvement'.

One quickly realises that these five principles are not a sequential, one off procedure, but rather a journey of continuous improvement. Start out today. Again, in retrospect, what is remarkable is that the original five make no reference to people.

3.3   Synopsis: The 25 Principles of Lean

The literature on Lean contains several seminal books, amongst them by Womack and Jones, Schonberger, Hall, Liker, and Imai. These built on the 'greats': Deming, Juran, and Ohno. To distil them is a daunting task, but certainly there are common themes. These 25 seem to be at the core:

1. **Customer**. The external customer is both the starting and ending point. Seek to maximise value to the customer. Optimise around the customer, not around internal operations. Understand the customer's true demand, in price, delivery, frequency, and quality - not what can be supplied. Understand demand patterns. Distinguish between value demand and failure demand.

2. **Purpose**. The 'big picture' question is 'What is the purpose?' This simple question is the way forward to reduce waste, complexity, and bureaucracy. And do the measures actually work for or against the purpose?

3. **Simplicity**. Lean is not simple, but simplicity pervades. Simplicity in operation, system, technology, control, and the goal. Simplicity is best achieved through avoidance of complexity, rather than by 'rationalisation' exercises. Think about ants that run a complex adaptive system without any management information system. Simplicity applies to product through part count reduction and commonality. Simplicity applies to

suppliers through working closely with a few trusted partners. Simplicity applies in the plant, by creating focused factories-within-a-factory. Beware of complex computer systems, complex and large automation, complex product lines, and complex rewards and bonus. Select the smallest, simplest machine consistent with quality and without compromising quality requirements.

4. **Waste**. Waste is endemic. Learn to recognise it, and seek to reduce it, always. Everyone from the chairman to the cleaners should wear 'muda spectacles' at all times. Seek to prevent waste by good design of products and processes.

5. **Process**. Organise and think end-to-end process. Think horizontal, not vertical. Concentrate on the way the product or customer moves, not on machine utilisation or layers of decision. Map to understand the process.

6. **Visuality**. Seek to make all operations as visible and transparent as possible. Control by sight. Adopt the visual factory. Make it quick and easy to identify when operations or schedules are diverging.

7. **Regularity**. Regularity makes for 'no surprises' operations. We run our lives on regularity (sleep, breakfast, etc); we should run our plants on this basis too. Seek out, by pareto, the top repeating products and build the schedule around regularity - this cuts inventory, improves quality, and allows simplicity of control. Regularity applies also with supply and new product introduction.

8. **Flow**. Seek 'keep it moving at the customer rate', 'one piece flow'. Synchronise operations so that the streams meet just in time. Flow should be the aim at cell level, in-company and along supply chains. Synchronise information and physical flows. If the

process cannot flow because of technical constraints, 'pulse' in small batches.

9. **Evenness**. 'Heijunka' or levelling is the key to reduced lead-time and quality. Seek ways to level both demand and the process - to level sell, to level buy, to level make. Seek to reduce waves. Be proactive – ask both customers and suppliers if they would not prefer smaller, more frequent batches.

10. **Pull.** Pull releases work depending on system status, thereby capping WIP inventory. Avoid overproduction. Have pull based demand chains, not push-based supply chains. Pull should take place at the customer's rate of demand. In demand chains this should be the final customer, not distorted by the intermediate 'bullwhip' effect.

11. **Postponement**. Delay activities and committing to product variety as late as possible so as to retain flexibility and to reduce waste and risk. This characteristic is closely associated with the concept of avoiding overproduction, but includes plant and equipment, information, and inventory. This is not the same as simply starting work at the last possible moment, but is about retaining flexibility at the right levels.

12. **Prevention**. Seek to prevent problems and waste, rather than to inspect and fix. Shift the emphasis from failure and appraisal to prevention. Inspecting the process, not the product, is prevention. Seek to prevent mistakes first through simplification, then mistake-proofing, and only then through inspection.

13. **Time**. Seek to reduce overall time to make, deliver, and to introduce new products. Use simultaneous, parallel, and overlapping processes in operations, design, and support services. Seek never to delay a value-adding step by a non value-adding step. Time is the best single overall measure. If time

reduction is a priority you tend to do all the right things: reduce wastes, improve quality and customer service.

14. **Improvement**. Improvement, but continuous improvement in particular, is everyone's concern. Improve though both small actions (kaizens) and larger actions (breakthrough). Improvement goes beyond waste reduction to include innovation and design. Improvement should include deliberate learning and experimentation.

15. **Partnership**. Seek co-operative working both internally between functions, and externally with suppliers. Seek to use teams, not individuals, internally and externally. Employees are partners too. Seek to build trust. Another way of saying this is Win-Win, which is one of Stephen Covey's principles of highly effective people. You must seek a win-win, never win-loose, solution and if you can't you should walk away.

16. **Value networks**. Great opportunities for cost, quality, delivery and flexibility lie with cooperating networks. Supply chains compete, not companies. Increasingly, value networks include 'co-opetition'. Expand the concept of the one-dimensional supply chain to a two-dimensional value network.

17. **Gemba**. Go to where the action is happening and seek the facts. Manage by direct observation. Implementation takes place on the floor, not in the office. Insist on Genshi Genbutsu (go see).

18. **Questioning (and listening).** Encourage a questioning culture. Ask why several times to try get to the root. Encourage questioning by everyone. As Bertrand Russell said, it is 'a healthy thing now and then to hang a question on things you have long taken for granted'. A manager who asks questions empowers. Listen actively, not passively. Restate the other's viewpoint. 'Seek first to

understand, then to be understood', said Covey. Coaching skills are required.

19. **Variation. ('Mura')** Variation is the enemy. 'Whenever you have variation, someone or something will wait'. It occurs in every process, product and person. Know the control limits, and learn to distinguish between common and special causes. Everyone should seek to reduce special causes, but managers should tackle common cause variation. Sometimes it is better to absorb variation with flexible systems (this is Ashby's Law of Requisite Variety) and sometimes better to reduce it.

20. **Avoiding overload.** Overloading resources **('Muri')** leads to inefficient people and long work queues. Because of variation, loading machines above about 85% or 90% utilization means both excessive lead times and to uncertainty in delivery. A Toyota 'secret' is slight excess capacity.

21. **Participation**. Give operators the first opportunity to solve problems. All employees should share responsibility for success and failure. True participation implies full information sharing.

22. **Thinking small**. Specify the smallest capable machine, and then build capacity in increments. Get best value out of existing machines before acquiring new ones. Break the 'economy of scale' concept by flexible labour and machines. Specify a maximum size of plant to retain 'family focus' and to develop thinking people. Locate small plants near to customer sites, and synchronise with their lines. Internally and externally make many small deliveries – runners or water spiders - rather than few big ones.

23. **Trust.** If we truly believe in participation and cutting waste, we have to build trust. Trust allows great swathes of bureaucracy and time to be removed both internally and externally. In supply chains, Dyer has shown how trust has enabled Toyota to slash transaction costs (that represent as much as 30% of costs in a company). Building trust with suppliers gives them the confidence to make investments and share knowledge. Internally, trust allows a de-layered, streamlined, and more creative organisation. A Deming maxim is his 90/10 rule: 90% of problems lie with the system, only 10% with the people.

24. **Learning.** Since Peter Drucker's original work on knowledge workers being the engine of today's corporation, the importance of deliberate and continuing learning has become increasingly important. Cultivate both explicit knowledge (such as tools in this book), but also tacit knowledge, involving softer or stickier skills. It is tacit knowledge that is hard to copy and gives sustainable advantage. Learning is built through the scientific method, through experimentation and PDSA.

25. **Humility and respect**. Last but by no means least. The more one strives for Lean, the more one realizes how little one knows, and how much there is yet to learn. Learning begins with humility. No humility means no learning. Respect should not be confused with 'being nice'. It is recognition of skills that others have that you do not. These skills need to be drawn out for the benefit of all. Look out for pseudo 'respect' – for example, asking for ideas but then not allowing time for their consideration. Not listening. Ohno was known to be a shouter at workers, but always fair. Shouting may not be acceptable today but constructive discussion will never be outdated. A thought: The African word 'Ubuntu' – a person becomes a person through other persons.

3.4   Value and Waste

Wally Hopp points out that concern for efficiency and reduction of waste is as old as civilisation itself. From the construction of the pyramids, to the Venetian Arsenal to Adam Smith's pin-making and on to Fred Taylor and Henry Ford– all have been striving for a better way.

A useful start is to classify activities as either value added (VA), non-value added (NVA), or necessary non-value-added (NNVA). The latter two wastes are a major focus for Lean.

Value-added activity is something that the customer is prepared to pay for and involves a transformation. In some types of service, for example, health care and holidays, the customer is certainly prepared to pay for experience-enhancing activities so VA, NVA and NNVA designations require situational awareness.

'Muda' is Japanese for waste. Fujio Cho, former President of Toyota, defined waste as 'anything other than the minimum amount of equipment, material, parts, space, and worker's time, which are absolutely essential to add value to the product'. (Toyota publications, by the way, always refer to the elimination of *unnecessary* wastes.)

One major maintenance organization simply says that waste is anything other than the minimum activities and materials necessary to get the job done immediately, right first time to the satisfaction of customers. They don't get into NVA and NNVA semantics. Another definition of waste is anything that does not affect Form, Fit or Functionality.

But consider:

- Value is the converse of waste. Any organisation needs continually to improve the ratio of value adding to non-value adding activities. There are three ways: preventing waste, reducing waste, and by value enhancement.

- Waste reduction is not the same as cost reduction. As Seddon has pointed out, cost reduction initiatives invariably lead to increases in cost! Why? Because cost related KPI's lead to unexpected behavioural outcomes and to failure demand. Ask BP about their cost reduction orientation at the Deepwater Horizon Well.

- Waste reduction without follow through is pointless. If, for example, movement waste has been reduced it needs to be followed through by, perhaps, reducing the number of kanban cards in the loop.

- All three types (VA, NVA, NNVA) are sources of variability. In a value stream these three are usually multiplicative, not additive.

There is almost always another level of resolution of waste. Within a 'value adding step' there are more detailed micro wastes, as in most assembly tasks or robot cycles. The production engineer shaving seconds off a machine cycle, when the end-to-end lead time is weeks is an example.

Prevention and Elimination of NNVA and NVA

NNVA activities create no value but are currently necessary to maintain operations. These activities do not do anything for customers, but may assist managers and meet legal requirements. Excessive bureaucracy and 'red tape' are unfortunate examples. NNVA should be reduced through simplification. It may well prove to be greatest bottom-line benefit of Lean. NNVA muda is the easiest to add to but difficult to remove, so *prevention* of NNVA muda should be in the mind of every manager in every function. As long ago as the 1960s Leslie Chapman in *Your Disobedient Servant* humorously described how bureaucracy and organisational levels grow, often by stealth, through self-promotion, and by fear of legal action and criticism. Hardly anyone gets fired for extra inventory, but people do get fired for out-of-stock. So, play it safe (?)

However, in some clerical activities, one may argue that the customer is never happy to pay. To call activities NNVA can then be both unhelpful (since everything is NNVA) or de-motivating to employees – How would you like to spend most of your life doing necessary non-value-added work?

Waste Elimination is achieved, as Dan Jones would say, by 'wearing muda spectacles' (a skill that must be developed), and by kaizen (both 'point' and 'flow' varieties), at the gemba. Elimination is assisted by 5S activities, standard work, mapping, level scheduling and by amplification reduction. Ohno was said to require new managers to spend several hours in a chalk circle, or on a chalk x, standing in one place and observing waste. Stay there until waste and variation has been noticed sufficiently well. Or, if not observed sufficiently well, 'Look more' and again 'look more', and yet again!

Waste Prevention is another matter. Womack and Jones talk about the ninth waste – making the wrong product perfectly – but it goes beyond that. Waste prevention cannot be done by wearing muda spectacles, but requires strong awareness of system, process, and product design. It is thought that perhaps 80% of costs are fixed at the design stage. Of that 80%, a good proportion will be waste. System design waste prevention involves thinking the movement of information, products and customers through the future system. For instance, questioning the necessity for ERP and the selection of far-removed suppliers and removing layers in a supply chain. Process design waste prevention involves the avoidance of 'monuments', the elimination of adjustments, and working with future customers and suppliers to ensure that future processes are as waste-free as possible. Prevention involves careful pre-design considerations including recycling.

Waste *prevention* is likely to assume a far greater role than waste elimination in the Lean organisation of the future – in the same way that prevention in quality is now widely regarded as more effective than inspection and fault elimination.

Finally,

A measure of the proportion of VA time is Process Cycle Efficiency (PCE)

PCE = VA time / (process lead time)

Some companies use this to prioritise which value streams to work on. But, take care:

- An apparently high PCE may be very inefficient because of a few long cycle operations.
- Does PCE account for rework, or failure demand? Some PCE analysis assumes right first time, which may be wildly incorrect!

Customer Waste and Resource Waste: Flow Efficiency and Resource Efficiency

Åhlström and Modig contrast Flow Efficiency with Resource Efficiency. As mentioned earlier, a unitary focus on Resource Efficiency would see idle resources as waste whilst ignoring the wastes that customers must endure. The medical doctor is the priority, not the patient. This would represent waste reduction as prioritised by the organisation not by the customer.

3.5   The Original Seven Wastes

Taiichi Ohno, father of the Toyota Production System, of JIT, and patriarch of Lean Operations, originally assembled the 7 wastes, but it was Deming who emphasised waste reduction in Japan in the 1950's. Today, however, it is appropriate to add to Ohno's famous list, presumptuous though that may be. The section after next begins with Ohno's original seven, then adds 'new' wastes for manufacturing and service.

Before we go further, we should remember that Ohno was critical about categorization. Categorization may blind you to other opportunities. As an example, our late colleague VS Mahesh who was once a senior executive with Tata Hotels, tells of Masaaki Imai visiting the Taj Hotel in Mumbai. Imai told the management that a room with one of the best views in the hotel was used as a laundry. What a waste!

You can remember the seven wastes by asking, 'Who is TIM WOOD?' Answer: Transport, Inventory, Motion, Waiting, Overproduction, Over-processing, and Defects. (We believe this idea came from the Lean Office at Cooper Standard, Plymouth, UK.)

Many will add the *waste of untapped human potential* (see below) as *wasted skills* to this, making it TIM WOODS. One can memorise this as 'Tiger Wood's little brother, Tim Woods' (he of course only has two half-brothers, none by the name of Tim).

An alternative is WORMPITS (Waiting, Overproduction, Rework, Motion, Processing, Inventory, Transport). Yet another is DOWNTIME (Defects, Overproduction, Waiting, No-value processing, Transport, Inventory, Motion, and Skills, employee brainpower that is wasted.)

In all these versions, the priority is to avoid, only then to cut.

The Waste of Overproduction

Ohno believed that the waste of overproduction was the most serious of all the wastes because it was the root of so many problems and other wastes. Overproduction is making too much, too early or 'just-in-case'. The aim should be to make or do or serve exactly what is required, no more and no less, just in time and with perfect quality. Overproduction discourages a smooth flow of goods or services. Categories of demand, and how to make it more uniform are discussed in the Demand Chapter.)

The Waste of Waiting

The waste of waiting is probably the second most important waste. It is directly relevant to FLOW. Waiting is the enemy of smooth flow In Lean we should be more concerned with flow of service or customers than we are with keeping operators busy.

In early days of Toyota, waiting for a machine was considered an 'insult to humanity' (people should have far better things to do than to require them to wait for a machine). In service many service companies 'insult' their customers by requiring them to wait – in effect saying 'your time is worth much less than mine'.

In a factory, any time that a part is seen not to be moving (or not having value added) is an indication of waste.. Although it may be very difficult to reduce waiting to zero, the goal remains.

The Waste of Unnecessary Motions

Next in importance is probably the waste of motion. Unnecessary motions refer to both human and layout. The human dimension relates to the importance of ergonomics for quality and productivity and the enormous proportion of time that is wasted at *every* workstation by non-optimal layout. A QWERTY keyboard for example is non-optimal. If operators have to stretch, bend, pick-up, move in order to see better, or in any way unduly exert themselves, the victim is immediately the operator but ultimately quality and the customer. 'Motion is not work' said Ohno – a useful distinction and reminder.

An awareness of the ergonomics of the workplace is not only ethically desirable, but economically sound. Toyota, famous for its quality, is known to place a high importance on 'quality of worklife'. Toyota encourages all its employees to be aware of working conditions that contribute to this form of waste. Today, of course, motion waste is also a health and safety issue.

The layout dimension involves poor workplace arrangement, leading to micro motion wastes These wastes are often repeated many, many times per day – sometimes without anyone noticing. In this regard 5S (see Chapter 14) can be seen as the way to attack motion waste.

The Waste of Transporting

Customers do not pay to have goods moved around unless they have hired a removal service! So any movement of materials is waste. It is a waste that can never be fully eliminated but it is also a waste that over time should be continually reduced. The number of transport and material handling operations is directly proportional to the likelihood of damage and deterioration. Double handling is a waste that affects productivity and quality.

Transporting is closely linked to communication. Where distances are long, communication is discouraged and quality may be the victim. Feedback on poor quality is inversely related to transportation length, whether in manufacturing or in services. There is increasingly the awareness that for improved quality in manufacturing or services, people from interacting groups need to be located physically together. For instance, the design office may be placed deliberately near to the production area. Zoom may help.

The Waste of Overprocessing (or Inappropriate Processing)

Overprocessing refers to the waste of 'using a hammer to crack a nut'. Think of a large central photocopier instead of distributed machines. But further, think of a large aircraft requiring passengers to travel large distances to and from a regional airport. Thinking in terms of one big machine instead of several smaller ones discourages operator 'ownership', leads to pressure to run the machine as much as possible rather than only when needed, and discourages general purpose flexible machines. It also leads to poor layout which, as we have seen, leads to extra transportation and poor communication. So the ideal is to use the smallest machine, capable of producing the required quality, distributed to the points of use.

How many have fallen into the trap of buying a 'monument' of a machine, that accountants then demand to be kept busy? The tail begins to wag the dog.

Inappropriate processing also refers to machines and processes that are not quality capable. An incapable process cannot help but make defects. In general, a capable process requires having the correct methods and training, as well as having the required standards, clearly known.

Note that it is important to take the longer-term view. Buying that large machine may just jeopardise the possibility of flow for many years to come, for both customers and employees. Think 'small is beautiful'. Smaller machines avoid

bottlenecks, improve flow lengths, perhaps are simpler, can be maintained at different times (instead of affecting the whole plant), and may improve cash flow and keep up with technology (buying one small machine per year, instead of one big machine every five years). Seru is an interesting concept here.

The Waste of Unnecessary (or Excess) Inventory

Although having no inventory is a goal that can never be attained, inventory is the enemy of quality and productivity. This is so because inventory tends to increase lead-time, prevents rapid identification of problems, and increases space thereby discouraging communication. The true cost of extra inventory is very much in excess of the money tied up in it. 'Push' systems almost invariably lead to this waste.

Buffers may be held to meet variation in demand and supply, but excessive inventory is waste. It also represents risk of obsolescence.

The Waste of Defects

The last, but not least, of Ohno's wastes is the waste of defects. Defects cost money, both immediate and longer term. In Quality Costing the failure or defect categories are internal failure (scrap, rework, delay) and external failure (including warranty, repairs, field service, but also possibly lost custom). Bear in mind that defect costs tend to escalate the longer they remain undetected. Thus a microchip discovered when made might cost just a few dollars to replace, but if it reaches the customer may cost hundreds, to say nothing of customer goodwill. So, central themes of total quality are 'prevention not detection', 'quality at source', and 'the chain of quality' (meaning that parts per million levels of defect can only be approached by concerted action all along the chain from marketing, to design, to supply, to manufacture, to distribution, to delivery, to field service.) A defect should be regarded as a challenge, as an opportunity to improve, rather than something to be traded off against what is ultimately poor management.

In service, 'zero defections' has become a powerful theme, recognising that the value of a retained customer increases with time.

3.6   The New Wastes

These may be added to Ohno's original list, and are appropriate in service and manufacturing:

The Waste of Untapped Human Potential

Ohno was reported to have said that the real objective of the Toyota Production System was 'to create thinking people'. So this 'new' waste is directly linked to Ohno. The 1980s were the decade of factory automation folly. GM and many others learnt the hard and expensive way that the automated factory and warehouse that does not benefit from continuous improvement and ongoing, innovative thought is doomed in the productivity race.

The Waste of Making the Wrong Product Efficiently

This is Womack and Jones' eighth waste. It is really a restatement of the first Lean principle, and closely related to the waste of overproduction.

Excessive Information and Communication

Ohno himself spoke about the dangers of this waste when he said that 'excessive information must be suppressed'. Think e mails (and maybe all those books about Lean!). If we are not to be submerged we need to think carefully before copying e mails to all in the office, to have team briefings for the sake of having them, to send staff on Lean and Quality courses the material of which is never used. But, Stephen Covey says, you need time to 'sharpen the axe' every day – beware of having no time to sharpen the axe because you are cutting down the tree – so prioritisation is important. This is closely related to the next waste.

The Waste of Time

Everyone suffers from this. Stephen Covey, referring not to Lean but to the 7 Principles of Highly Effective People, has a useful 2 x 2 matrix. The axes are important and urgent. Most people spend excessive time in the urgent but not important activity category. The not urgent, not important category is OK for relaxation but is otherwise waste. Urgent and important work may be fine, but could also indicate out-of-control conditions or firefighting. But everyone needs to prioritise time spent away from the urgent but not important to the important but not urgent category. This requires setting blocks of time aside. (See also the TPM Chapter on OEE applied to people.)

The Waste of Inappropriate Systems

How much software in your computer is never used – not the packages, but the actual code? The same goes for MRPII, now repackaged as ERP.

The Lean way is to remove waste before automating, or as Michael Hammer would say 'don't automate, obliterate!' The waste of inappropriate systems should not be confined to computers and automation. How much record keeping, checking, reconciling, is pure waste? It is frequently the order processing system, not the shop-floor that is the greatest consumer of time.

Wasted Energy and Water

This has become high priority! Although energy management systems in factory, office and home have grown in sophistication there still remains the human, common sense element: shutting down the machine, switching off the light, fixing the drip, insulating the roof, taking a full load, efficient routing, and the like. By the way, the JIT system of delivery does not waste energy when done correctly: use 'milk-rounds', picking up small quantities from several suppliers in the same area, or rationalise suppliers to enable mixed loads daily rather than single products weekly.

Several companies that have 'institutionalised' waste reduction, Toyota included, believe that a good foundation for waste awareness begins with everyday wastes such as switching off lights and printers. You get into the habit.

Wasted Natural Resources and Pollution

A most severe, and ever-more important waste is that of wasted natural resources. This vital topic is discussed below under Environmental Sustainability

The Waste of 'No Follow Through'

We began this section by saying that waste reduction is not the same as cost reduction. Further actions are generally required to reduce cost or to increase sales. If you don't do this, it is waste. So if you save walking distance, but don't do anything with the time saved, you have not really made a saving.

Waste of Knowledge

This waste results from simply letting knowledge disappear. It applies particularly in Design and Innovation, but also in many professional fields. So experience and knowledge that is gained when, for example, new products are designed, made, introduced, and marketed is not recorded and is simply forgotten about next time around. Such knowledge has to re-discovered all over again. 'Learning the hard way' is so silly when it already has been learned. Even if knowledge is re-used but not recorded, but instead is kept in the head of the person, there is the significant danger that it will be lost when that person leaves. So, have a procedure for recording lessons learned – even if this is as simple as a 'little black book'. Insist that it be done.

Allen Ward discusses Design Wastes in his book. Our own list of design wastes is given in the New Product Development Chapter of the book.

The Waste of Empty Labour

Empty Labour, is defined by Roland Paulsen, as 'everything you do at work that is not your work'. We all do this: take breaks, write private e mails, cell phone, discuss football, surf the web, buy on-line. The evidence is huge that empty work averages between 1.5 and 3 hours per office employee per day. Many or all break the rules. How much empty labour is there in factories? Plenty, it would seem. Parkinson's Law, proposed in 1958, was 'Work expands to fill the time available'. David Graeber caused a stir with his book on 'Bullshit Jobs'.

Empty labour is a complex and apparently growing problem of particular interest to Lean managers. There may be no 'answers'. Alienation and resistance play a role. 'Checking up' may make things worse, as per monitoring of key strokes. Involvement and empowerment may be a way forward. But the important thing is to realise how much potential there is, and how much growing temptation there is for non-involved employees.

Trade-off wastes and Buffers

We have considered the original 7 wastes. But are all these pure waste, to be eliminated over the long term? The truth is that some are 'trade-off' wastes that need careful consideration as to their optimal levels. Where 'excess' inventory and 'excess' waiting begin may not be simple.

Inventory: There are three cases, WIP inventory, buffer inventory, and pre-bottleneck buffer inventory.

WIP: Of course, inventory cannot be entirely eliminated if flow is to take place. Too little inventory will result in 'starvation' and loss of output. The minimum level may not be one piece per workstation. The true minimum is given by the 'critical WIP' the formula for which is (bottleneck rate x sum of process times).

For a production system with no variation, below the critical WIP starvation will result; above the critical WIP lead time will increase without any increase in output. This would be pure waste. With variation, the situation is more complex but a rule of thumb is that minimum WIP should be 1.2 x critical WIP.

Buffer Inventory: Inventory is one of the three types of buffer – inventory, time, and capacity. This is elaborated on in Chapter 3. There is a trade-off between these three types. One type may not be available. For example, a fire service cannot be inventoried so capacity or response time must be allowed. In a supermarket, the trade-off is between replenishment time and inventory. Reducing time should impact inventory. In a factory the trade-off is between capacity, time and inventory. To meet peak demands requires extra capacity, more inventory or more time.

Pre-bottleneck inventory. In the Drum-Buffer-Rope system, buffer inventory protects the bottleneck from running out of work. This is discussed in the section on Pull Systems.

Waiting. If customers are prepared to wait, inventory and possibly capacity can be reduced. Ferrari is presumably able to smooth production successfully, to use capacity very well and reduce inventories. This is not the case in a WalMart supermarket, although there might be quick response cross-docking that will help reduce inventories.

A Final Thought: Can You Go too Far on Waste Reduction?

The immediate response to this question from the Lean practitioner would be No! This is correct, but only if the bigger picture clearly is kept in mind. Consider…

For over 30 years Henry Ford drove out waste on the Model T line. Cars have never been produced as efficiently ever since. But, of course, in the end, customer dissatisfaction forced the abandonment of the line to less efficient mass production.

Thus waste reduction needs to be seen as the other side of the coin to innovation. Both are necessary.

In innovation and new product design, a no failure or no waste climate could be fatal. Since failures are inevitable in new and uncertain markets and

technologies, what is needed is experimentation, rapid evaluation, and then early abandonment or pivoting of under-promising projects. This methodology accepts waste as inevitable but stops big wastes from developing. This is a concept behind 'The Lean Startup' that is discussed in Chapter 38

Further reading

Taiichi Ohno / Japan Management Association, *Kanban: Just-in-Time at Toyota*, Productivity Press, 1985

George Stalk and Thomas Hout, *Competing Against Time*, The Free Press, New York, 1990

James Womack and Daniel Jones, *Lean Thinking*, revised edition, free Press, 2003

Roland Paulsen, *Empty Labour*, Cambridge, 2014

Wallace Hopp, *Supply Chain Science*, McGraw Hill, 2008

David Graeber, *Bullshit Jobs*, Allen Lane, 2018

3.7 Lean Service

Lean has been successfully applied to all types of service operations. What has been shown is that lean tends to work best for transactional services (high repetition, low involvement). This poses challenges for professional services, and for high-variety settings, like healthcare.

Much of the lean implementations in service are straight adaptations of lean manufacturing tools to service operations. For instance, TWI has been used in improving the packing of delivery vehicles thereby increasing load efficiency by 30%.

In other segments Lean *manufacturing* concepts may be problematical. For instance, a call centre operation might seek to standardise the call procedure in order to cut the average call length. In manufacturing this might be worthwhile but in service it misses the fundamental point about the *purpose* of a call centre: to resolve a customer's problem as soon as possible. To develop a true *lean service system*, one has to understand the concepts of purpose and failure demand.

Womack and Jones, in *Lean Solutions*, state the basic customer wants clearly. These are;

- Solve my problem completely
- Don't waste my time
- Get me exactly <u>what</u> I want
- Provide value <u>where</u> I want
- Solve my problem <u>when</u> I want.

Value and Failure Demand

In manufacturing we define 'waste' as all activities the customer is not prepared to pay for. In services, this approach is too simplistic. In particular in the public sector context the relationship between value and cost are much more complex. It is thus helpful to use the concept of 'purpose', and ask: what is the purpose of the service system from the customer's point of view? Purpose is an 'outside-in' view of the system, the reason you are doing the task. If a task is not a meaningful addition to the purpose of a system, it is most likely waste.

An important view, especially in service, is Seddon's concept of 'failure demand'. Failure demand occurs 'as a result of not doing something or not doing something right'. So, for example, the customer has to phone again to inquire as to progress. This multiplication in the demand signal (whereby one problem leads to multiple calls or requests) is called *failure demand*. We thus distinguish between two types of demand: value demand and failure demand, which when combined determine the load on the service system. Examples have shown that up to 60% of all demand in service settings can be failure demand. A hand-off is often a source of delay and service waste.

Failure demand is closely linked to the concept of purpose, as it occurs when a system is not operating in a purposeful way (from the customer's point of view). As Goldratt remarked, 'a busy resource is not necessarily a productive one'. The same applies to services.

An extension is unnecessary demand – for instance a hypochondriac, and the opposite – a person who fails to visit a doctor thereby leading to increased problems later. These and other types have been studied by Hartmann et al.

The Seven Service Wastes

Although the wastes discussed above begin with the customer, they are nevertheless applied from the organisations perspective. What about the customer's perspective? Perhaps an improvement programme should begin with Bicheno's service wastes:

1. **Delay** on the part of customers waiting for service, for delivery, in queues, for response, not arriving as promised. The customer's time may seem free to the provider, but when she takes custom elsewhere the pain begins.

2. **Duplication**. Having to re-enter data, repeat details on forms, copy information across, answer queries from several sources within the same organisation.

3. **Unnecessary movement**. Queuing several times, lack of one-stop, poor ergonomics in the service encounter.

4. **Unclear communication**, and the wastes of seeking clarification, confusion over product or service use, wasting time finding a location that may result in misuse or duplication.

5. **Incorrect inventory**. Out-of-stock, unable to get exactly what was required, substitute products or services.

6. **Opportunity lost** to retain or win customers, failure to establish rapport, ignoring customers, unfriendliness, and rudeness.

7. **Errors** in the service transaction, product defects in the product-service bundle, lost or damaged goods.

Note that a 'Complaints Department' is a good example of service waste, however efficiently it is run!

Further reading

James Womack and Daniel Jones, *Lean Solutions*, Simon and Schuster, 2005

John Seddon, *Freedom from command and control*. Vanguard Education Limited, 2003

Dieter Hartmann, John Bicheno, Bruno Emwanu, Teresa. Hattingh, 'Understanding System Failure in Healthcare', *SA Jnl. of Industrial Eng*., May 2021

John Bicheno, *The Service Systems Toolbox*, PICSIE Books, 2014

3.8   The 3Ms: Muda, Mura and Muri

Any discussion about waste (Muda) would be incomplete without a mention of the closely-related ideas of Mura (variability or unevenness) and Muri (overload or stress).

Ohno saw the three as being an integrated set. All three are necessary targets for improvement. Important drivers of Muda are Mura and Muri. This recognition is of foremost importance. The technical aspects of the interaction between the three are explored in the chapter on The Science of Lean, especially Kingman's equation.

It is unfortunate that many Lean implementations focus almost entirely on Muda, with scant attention to Mura and Muri. In fact, the reduction of Mura and Muri is a precondition for the success of kaizen and PDSA activities, simply because excessive overload and variation create unstable conditions. With unstable conditions kaizen and PDSA changes have no guarantee of reliability or reproducibility. The conclusions that are drawn are then a matter of chance.

Mura and Muri have both technical and human dimensions. Once again, this has often been downplayed.

The technical tools of Mura reduction are numerous and can be divided into external and internal variation reduction and are discussed throughout the book. Internal tools include 5S, standard work, TWI job instruction, statistical process control (SPC) and in fact the full range of Six Sigma techniques. Mura also results from a lack of synchronisation and poor scheduling.

External methods include working with suppliers, and smoothing both supply and demand. The human aspects of Mura reduction are just as important. They include skill training, monitoring, psychological safety in pulling an Andon cord and TWI job relations.

The tools of Muri reduction include most Lean scheduling concepts, such as pull systems, cell and line balance and heijunka . Human aspects include under-capacity scheduling, rob rotation and job enrichment.

Both Mura and Muri reduction are addressed by a Gemba management style, and by empowerment, engagement, team working, idea management, and information sharing. The three types of buffer – inventory, time, and capacity – have a direct impact on Mura and Muri. The three types of buffer need to be carefully sized and traded off – too much or too little would lead to Muda. Breakdowns are a source of stress and variability, resulting in Muda. So TPM is an enabler.

And, of course, product design impacts Mura, Muri and Muda. Unnecessary complexity is a cause, so value engineering is needed.

3.9   Learning: The PDCA or PDSA Cycle

First, virtually every improvement plan or suggestion is a hypothesis. It may or may not work. To learn if it works a learning cycle is required. PDCA or 'Plan, Do, Check, Act' or 'Plan, Do, Check, Adjust' cycle is without doubt the most widely used improvement cycle – but may just be the least understood. According to Peter Scholtes (who worked with Deming), Deming preferred the word 'study' to 'check'. Hence PDSA. But 'the Japanese have called it PDCA for decades'. Without 'Check' or 'Study' there can be no learning because hypotheses remain hypotheses. In the West many organisations are apt to just 'do' and neglect the P-S-A. Deming said that each of the four stages should be balanced. So not a 'quick and dirty' on plan, lots of attention on do, no check, and little on adjust or standardise. To truly learn PDSA requires mentoring, particularly in clarifying the hypothesis and check stages.

PDSA sounds simple and is easily glossed over, but if well done is a powerhouse for improvement. PDSA is considered a foundation of the Toyota Production System. Deming taught that one should think about change and improvement like a scientific experiment – predicting, setting up a hypothesis, observing, trying to refute it, and attempting to learn what if anything was wrong with the original hypothesis.

Plan or Hypothesis is the first step, but how do you plan when you don't yet know the facts or situation? Remember that PDSA is an ongoing cycle. So Check or Study will often be the first step, involving perhaps demand analysis, mapping, variation and delivery performance studies. If you start with check, then the cycle is identify problems, propose countermeasures, identify possible solutions, implement, test and sustain. Plan is not just about planning what to do, but about communication, 'scoping', discussion, consensus gaining and deployment. Begin with the customer - seek to understand their requirements. The idea of hypothesis is important: make a prediction of the desired outcome and later review to see if the hypothesis was correct. This is to help understand – one of Ohno's favourite words. The plan stage should also establish a time plan. It is claimed that leading Japanese companies take much longer to plan, but then implement far faster and more smoothly. Be clear about what the goals are, and plan how to get there. Attempt to identify constraints beforehand, so force field analysis is a good idea. Try to identify root causes.

Do (Try out possible solutions). This should be an easy stage if you have planned well. It is about carrying out the improvement, often in a test phase. This requires interpersonal implementation skills.

Study (Check, Observe, reflect, learn). A vital learning stage, but too frequently an opportunity lost. Is it working as you predicted? Did it work out as planned? If not, why not, and what can we learn for next time? The US Marines call this 'after action review' or AAR. Time needs to be set aside to Study - as at the end of a meeting, or at the end

of a 180 day future state implementation plan. Keki Bhote refers to B vs. C (Better vs. Current) analysis. This is to see if the improvement is sustained or as a result of the 'Hawthorne effect' which ceases when observation ceases. Six Sigma black belts would check the statistical significance – assessing the alpha and beta risks (accepting what should have been rejected, and vice versa). Once again ask about root causes. Also check if there are any outstanding issues.

Act (Adjust or Standardise). Adjust could also mean adjusting your thinking when your hypothesis turns out to be wrong. If check or study has worked out as expected, then standardise the important stages. As Juran says, 'Hold the gains'. A standard reflects the current best and safest known way, but is not fixed in stone forever. Think about improvement as moving from standard to improved standard. A deviation from standard procedures indicates that something is amiss. (See chapter 24). Consider if the new way can be incorporated elsewhere. Communicate the requirements to everyone concerned. Give thought to recurrence prevention - can both the people and the processes be made more capable? Finally prepare for the next round of the cycle by identifying any necessary further improvements. And don't forget to celebrate and congratulate if gains have been achieved.

Beware. If variability is excessive it is difficult to distinguish between real improvement and chance variation. See the section on Cynefin.

An extension: Honda uses a 3-stage cycle called DST to precede PDSA. D is 'Draw' or picture one's ideal state. S is 'See' – go to the gemba and observe, T is 'Think' – consider what needs to be done : What and where to focus, what to change, what to solve, what to improve. Only then, suggests Honda, do you move into PDCA.

A last word: Don't let the Deming PDCA cycle stand for 'Please Don't Change Anything'.

3.10   The Toyota Way

The 'Toyota Way' was launched by Fujio Cho, then President of Toyota, in 2001. The 'Toyota Way' is not fundamentally different from Lean, but it aims to take Lean beyond its traditional applications in manufacturing and product development, into the entire organisation. The Toyota Way is an attempt to translate Lean into all business processes within Toyota. It is worth noting that even after 50 years, Lean is still a journey for Toyota, where they continue to learn and expand their Lean efforts! The Toyota Way is based on five core values that employees at all levels are supposed to use in their daily work:

1. **Challenge:** to maintain a long-term vision and strive to meet all challenges with the courage and creativity needed to realise that vision.
2. **Kaizen:** to strive for continuous improvement. As no process can ever be declared perfect, there is always room for improvement.
3. **Genchi Genbutsu:** to go to the source to find the facts to make correct decisions, build consensus and achieve goals.
4. **Respect:** to make every effort to understand others, accepts responsibility and does its best to build mutual trust
5. **Teamwork:** to share opportunities for development and maximises individual and team performance.

Further reading

Jeffrey Liker, *The Toyota Way*, Second edition, McGrawHill, 2021.

3.11   The DNA of TPS

In a now classic article in *Harvard Business Review*, Spear and Bowen proposed the '4 Rules of the Toyota Production System'. Included in the article was the Four Questions. The article has become immensely influential. It was written following extensive research at Toyota. Stephen Spear claims that the four rules capture the essence or DNA of Toyota.

Rule 1: 'All work shall be highly specified as to content, sequence, timing, and outcome.' This simple sentence has enormous implications. It goes right back to the days of F W Taylor and his 'one best way'. There is a best way for almost everything. It is the basis of Plan, Do, Study, Act. Spear talks about 'highly' specified. We would rephrase as 'ALL work shall be appropriately specified'. In manufacturing, 'specification', or standard work, allows problems to be identified and reduced. In service, it requires tasks to be done in the current best known way to minimise error and maximise service. It also places the onus on management to see that specifications are developed. If there is a problem, it is not good enough to say 'you must try harder' or 'you must work more conscientiously', or 'we have a motivation problem'. Instead, the process needs to looked at to see why the problem arose in the first place and to prevent it happening again. If there is no standard method, this cannot be done. So 'why did the patient get the wrong medicine?' or 'why was there a part missing?' puts the emphasis on the process, not the person. This is pure Deming: system, not person.

Rule 2: 'Every customer-supplier connection must be direct, and there must be an unambiguous yes-or-no way to send requests and receive responses.' If there is a problem or issue the single, shortest path of communication must be clearly known and used. In the west we like to reward problem solvers. This is OK as long as the problem is communicated and its solution built in to the new standard. But, too often, the problem is solved but hardly anyone apart from the problem solver and perhaps his immediate manager knows about it. The next shift does not know, so when the problem recurs it is 'solved' in another way. Both shifts get rewards for 'initiative', but the fundamental solution remains in the head of the solver. In service, when a customer complains to the front desk, does the front desk person communicate it; does it get to the source? And, more likely, management sits in a fools-paradise thinking everything is great.

Sometimes the communication route is too long – most people have played the children's game of sending a message around a circle. Sometimes the problem is communicated to a 'CRM' or 'maintenance MIS' – leaving it up to someone else to follow up on. Sometimes, the problem is communicated through many informal networks – allowing distortion and mischief. Communication channels need to studied from top to bottom and from bottom to top. 'Every-ones problem is no-ones problem'.

Rule 3: 'The pathway for every product and service must be simple and direct.' This is about clear value streams. And it is about the minimum steps in the stream. We do not want the spaghetti of the job shop in either manufacturing or service. Do not leap into Theory of Constraints scheduling before untangling the spaghetti. Simplify the streams, the routings, the priorities. If at all possible, don't have a complex of shared machines and conflicting priorities (and then add insult to injury by requiring a complex finite scheduling package). Paying for a few extra machines can be more than worthwhile. In service, have you ever experienced multi-stage automatic telephone answering – and finally got through to a person (or worse, a machine) that cannot deal with your 'unusual' request? Try a human. Better still, try a highly knowledgeable human at the first stage. So, value stream map it *from the customer's perspective*. And remember Stalk and Hout's Golden Rule – 'Never delay a value adding step by a non value adding step.'

Rule 4: 'Any improvement must be made in accordance with the scientific method, under the guidance of a teacher, at the lowest possible level in the organization.' This is about all improvements being done under PDSA, even if it a small improvement. Without PDSA there is no learning. If there is no plan, no hypothesis there can be no surprises in the outcome. So all changes must be tested and reflected upon. The 'lowest level' means both place and organisational level. So improvement must be done at *Gemba* by *direct observation* probably using the *Socratic Method*. Direct observation is needed for understanding and to anticipate problems. The Socratic Method asks 'why'; it does not show 'how'.

Spear and Bowen suggest that the rules are not learned by instruction, but by questioning. The rules are not stated. The rules are absorbed over time. The manager is a teacher, not a 'boss'. And Socratic teaching is highly effective. Challenging questions involve going to Gemba and asking:

- How do you do this work?
- How do you know that you are doing it correctly?
- How do you know that the outcome is defect free?
- What do you do if you have a problem?

We would add a few:

- Who do you communicate with?
- How do you know what to do next?
- What signals cue your work?
- Do you do this in the same way as others?

In fact, it is learning by the ongoing use of (Kipling's) 'six honest serving men' – who taught me all I knew; their names are what and why and when; and how and where and who.'

This Socratic method encourages operators to think, question and learn. Persistent asking of the questions allows decentralisation to evolve.

Keep in mind that 'it is not the quality of the answers that distinguishes a Lean expert, but the quality of the questions' (source unknown), and as Yogi Berra said, 'Don't tell me the answer, just explain the question.'

To summarise: TPS is not rules or tools. It is not *instinct* (instinct can't be learned), but *instinctive* – like the unwritten rules of a society.

Further reading

Spear and Bowen, 'Decoding the DNA of the Toyota Production System', *Harvard Business Review*, Sept-Oct 1999, pp 97-106

Steven Spear, *Chasing the Rabbit*, McGraw Hill, 2009. The later edition, 2010, is called *The High Velocity Edge*. This remains of the best books on continuous improvement written to date.

3.12 Lean and Environmental Sustainability

Climate change is fact that every operations-based organisation is already facing. Welcome to the VUCA world.

Robert 'Doc' Hall, a highly respected 'godfather' of Lean / JIT in the USA since the early 1980s, has, over the past two decades, championed what he terms 'Compression'. Compression is based on ever-more-urgent environmental concerns and responsibilities, but asks for a total systems approach to economics, organisations and growth. Whilst acknowledging the many achievements of Lean, Doc believes there has often been a thinking failure to see the wider picture. Although energy audits and conservation have been in practice for decades, and water and air pollution is a limiting resource in many parts of the world, awareness of climate change together with increased energy shortages and pricing, air pollution, material shortages, floods, and food shortages seem all to have arisen within a short period of time.

As Rose Heathcote pleads, look up and down the value chain to spot opportunities and solve problems that matter:

- **Climate change**: Target greenhouse gas (GHG) emissions;
- **Biodiversity loss and land conversion:** Improve use of existing capacity and regenerate;

- **Energy:** Consume less, design products better and switch to planet-friendly alternatives;
- **Landfill:** Keep products and material in circulation and regenerate;
- **Air pollution:** Improve energy sources, reduce and capture pollution;
- **Chemical pollution:** Eliminate toxins from design and regenerate contaminated land;
- **Ocean degradation:** Target GHG's and eliminate ocean pollution;
- **Freshwater withdrawals and contamination:** Consume less, harvest more and keep it clean;
- **Ozone layer depletion:** Deal with residual chlorofluorocarbons and improve alternatives in circulation for less impact;
- **Deforestation:** Use less, keep materials in circulation and regenerate.
- **Nitrogen and phosphorous loading:** Protect soil and waterways from excess fertilizers and human waste and regenerate.

A systems view of the problems to be solved across the supply chain helps target the levers to a granular level, using lean problem-solving thought-processes such as A3 thinking and Kaizen. It begins by accepting the challenge and seeking worthwhile opportunities and then working on them every day, by everyone in a scientific (PDSA) way. Several business benefits emerge from this approach.

It makes business sense

There is a solid business case for lean thinking and equally strong case for sustainability thinking, building on a platform of cost and risk reduction, competitive advantage, reputation and legitimacy, and stakeholder value creation. Organisations can do well by doing good manifesting in top line growth, bottom line improvement and people and investor attraction.

- **Top line growth:** Consumers are more aware of the choices they make, migrating from companies that do not meet their values for sustainable offerings or are unwilling to change and solve their problems. Forward-thinking competitors move in and snap up this market share. It is only a matter of time before slow-to-change companies lose revenue over it. The sustainable enterprise stays ahead and relevant, producing sustainable offerings customers are prepared to pay for.

- **Bottom line improvement:** Wasting resources, energy, and capacity costs money. Consuming unnecessary materials or tolerating poor yields costs money. Paying fines and penalties for poor practices strains cash flow. Losing customers and employees costs money. If we look for sustainability problems prevalent in supply chain systems, we can identify improvements and associated cost benefits.

- **People asset attraction and retention:** Talent, particularly the up-and-coming generation, chooses to work for ethical, sustainability-conscious companies. Better employers attract and retain good people by caring for the well-being and futures of the employees and their families. It makes good business sense since there is a return for engagement. Research shows that highly engaged businesses bring 41% reduced absenteeism, 17% increase in productivity, 10% increased customer ratings, 20% more sales, 21% higher profitability and up to 59% less employee turnover. It costs to lose and replace skills.

- **Investor and finance attraction:** Doing right by stakeholders is good for shareholders and in 2020, 81% of sustainable indexes outperformed their benchmarks. Savvy investors are pressing companies to explain their climate strategies and approach to ESG issues. More financial institutions favour organisations with sustainable business models giving preference to applicants that pollute less and deliver positive impact. Companies that do not prepare will see their businesses and valuations suffer and it will become tougher to attract investment.

Capitalising on the gains takes a radical shift in mindset, a business model rethink and leader courage.

Andrea Pampanelli, Neil Trivedi and Pauline Found have taken a wider approach covering 'People, Planet, Profit' in what they term the 'Lean and Green Business Model'.

There are five key areas: Design for Environment, or design for ecological sustainability; Life Cycle Analysis, 'cradle to cradle', or reducing impact during the whole product or service life cycle; Cleaner production, or 'zero emissions'; Environmental management systems – ISO 14001, and policy deployment; and Environmental performance evaluation.

Throughout all of these not just CI, but 'green continuous improvement' should be everyone's focus by operating on all the following levels: Cell; Site; Supply Chain; and Office and Admin areas

At the value stream level (cell or factory) each of the level is looked at in detail, by a team (ideally comprising employees, customers, suppliers) in a kaizen workshop using:

- a '3P' approach (See Layout Chapter). Here, the alternatives for manufacture at each stage (for instance casting, turning, forming) are looked at through 'green' spectacles – seeking the best alternative over the life cycle.

- An input and output analysis. For instance, inputs may include the casting, rags, coolant, chemicals, electricity, tooling, degreasing. Outputs could be chips, spent tooling, oil, coolant, emissions, hazardous waste.

Large annual savings are reported. The approach would be to examine various pilot areas and then to roll out the lessons to 'sister' areas. Some examples at the site level include:

- Lights and machines that switch off automatically.
- Air instead of coolant, thereby saving purification and product cleaning.
- Pre-separation of metal swarf.
- Life-cycle investigation of pallet use for energy and cost.
- Machines on standby vs start-up costs.
- Cleaning by suck or blow – and with appropriate pressure.

Two final points:

- TPM (Total Productive Maintenance) is usually applied to a factory's machines. But there are frequently opportunities to apply TPM to the heating and ventilating systems in the company. In this case OEE could mean Overall Energy Efficiency, with the factors being availability x thermal efficiency x quality (here measured as the percentage of time outside of temperature control limits). MMTR and MTBF are, as in manufacturing, important measures.
- Six Sigma can be applied to reducing temperature variation in zones within the building or factory. The Six Sigma tool of Gage R and R is particularly

relevant. One hospital not only monitored the accuracy and performance of thermostat zones but introduced many more, each with appropriate settings, centrally controlled and monitored. Payback was measured in months.

Further reading

Robert Hall, *Compression*, CRC Press, 2010

Pampanelli, Andrea, Neil Trivedi, and Pauline Found. *The Green Factory: Creating lean and sustainable manufacturing*. CRC Press, 2015.

Raworth, K. *Doughnut Economics: Seven Ways to Thinking Like a 21st-Century Economist*. Dublin. Penguin Random House, 2022

Harter, H. and Mann, A, *The Right Culture: Not Just About Employee Satisfaction*, 2017

Polman, P. and Winston, A. *Net positive: How courageous companies thrive by giving more than they take*. Boston. Harvard Business Review Press, 2021

3.13 Lean and Digital Technologies

The digitalisation of all aspects of business has made great advances over the past decade. Often linked to concepts such 'Industry 4.0', a range of technologies have been developed that are very synergetic to lean transformations.

The main technologies of relevance are, first and foremost, related to the availability and analysis of data. As data is being captured through real-time sensor and location (RTLS) or Internet of Things (IoT), we are able to use that data to devise operational improvements.

Artificial intelligence (AI) methods, driven by advances in machine learning (ML), are now able to take over tasks in managing processes, such as outlier detection in quality management, or predictive maintenance. In addition, digital twins have emerged as a powerful tool for simulation and real-time planning. Last but not least, additive manufacturing (AM) or '3D printing' now allows for printing parts in small batches, avoiding the need for batch production due to costly changeovers.

We will explore the digital technologies and how they can support lean implementations in more detail in the final Chapter of this book. Across all of these, however, there are common mechanisms that are worth pointing out.

These include a cluster of mechanisms that *augment operational execution* in terms of speed and precision of execution, as well as flexibility in space and time. Furthermore, there is a second cluster of mechanisms that *augment decision-making* through visibility, feedback, engagement, and prevention.

These digital technologies are powerful, yet it always important to remember that technologies are a means to an end, not an end in itself!

Further reading

Cifone, F.D., et al. 2021. 'Lean 4.0': How can digital technologies support lean practices? *International Journal of Production Economics, 241*, p.108258.

4 The Science of Lean

This chapter aims to clarify and explore, basic definitions and eight central concepts. These will give a more complete, in-depth, understanding of Lean. Also included are the important related concepts of Scientific Method and Experimentation.

The sections below draw strongly on the seminal work of Factory Physics as developed by Hopp, Spearman and Pound, but also the work of Kingman and of Little.

4.1 Key definitions

In order have a meaningful discussion about a process and its performance, be it in manufacturing or services, it is important to define a couple of core concepts. Unfortunately, definitions vary across publications. Here we aim to give clarification with simplicity and will use these terms throughout this book.

Lead Time (LT): Externally, this denotes the time from customer order to delivery. Internally, it denotes the sum of waiting times for collection or processing, the actual run times, and any further wait for item collection, or delivery. Some of these may be zero, and most of these have variability.

Cycle Time: The time for an entity to traverse a system, including any rework or other delays. As such, cycle time is really a production rate, not a time per se. (Note that there is frequent misuse of the terms Lead Time and Cycle Time. See also *Planned Cycle Time* and *Station Cycle Time* below.)

Takt Time: The time actually available for value adding work during a period, divided by the average demand during the period. Like cycle time, takt time is a production rate. In this case, the process should not run faster than the customer demands items from it, in order to avoid overproduction.

Available time would exclude meeting time, maintenance time, kaizen time, etc. Note that the time actually available can be increased (by overtime, for example) or decreased (giving more time for kaizen) to stabilise takt time.

Takt time can be converted into *move speed* as in in a moving line, or a *pulse time*.

Takt time can also be a useful concept in design, new product introduction, service and hospitals but only if applied as an overall guide, not slavishly.

Pitch Time: Takt time x container quantity.

Note that container quantity can be the variable to determine the pitch. The pitch is frequently the interval between collections by the material handler.

Planned Cycle Time = Takt time/variation allowance.

Thus, planned cycle time should always be less than takt time. Typical variation allowance is 85% to 90% (.85 to .9). If no allowance is given large queues will result, schedules will be missed, and there will be no time for kaizen. See Kingman's Equation below.

Station Cycle Time (CT): Time between starting successive jobs or tasks.

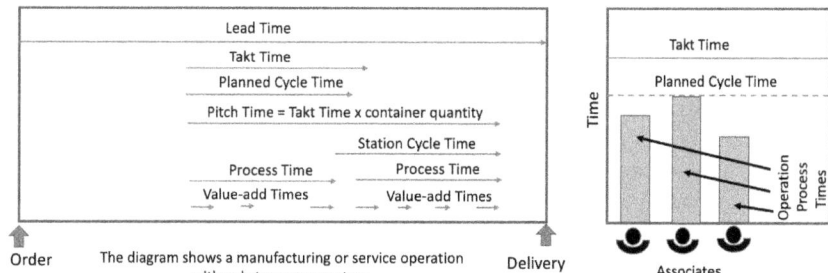

The diagram shows a manufacturing or service operation with only two process steps.

$$\text{Takt Time} = \frac{\text{Time available for work}}{\text{Demand in units during that time}}$$

Planned Cycle Time: Typically 90% of takt time

Process Time : Time to complete a process   Value add times: Process time – waste times

Station Cycle Time is the sum of move, queue, setup, run, wait to move times.
(the time between completion of two discrete units)

Operation Process Time (PT): Average time from starting a stage of work to finishing. Includes setup and other detractors from VA time, but does not include any time the resource is starved (upstream) or blocked (downstream).

Waiting times: there are two aspects of waiting that matter. First, it is the time a customer is ready for work to begin, but the resource is not yet available. This is the **Queue time**, CTq. Second, there is **Idle time** is the time the resource is ready to begin work but there is no work waiting to be done. Some idle time can be used for NNVA work such as paperwork. Note: CT=CTq+PT

Capacity: the maximum average rate at which entities can flow through a system.

Load: The amount of work to be done by a process within a particular period of time, or: Demand x Cycle Time. (Here, 'demand' is the average demand during a cycle.). This expresses the load in resource-minutes of the process.

Utilization: In the most simple view, it is Load/Capacity. Or Rate into a workcentre, divided by the capacity of the workcentre.

Note that resource utilization may not be stable because both demand and capacity may change in the short or medium term.

Productivity: Is the ratio of Output / Input for a process. In a broader sense, it can also be conceptualised as Efficiency x Effectiveness, where effectiveness is the customer's view; efficiency is the internal view.

Efficiency: standard time / actual time

Inventory Turns:

There are two ways to calculate inventory turns: Throughput units / work-in-process units, or cost of sales in $ / average inventory in $. The first one is more commonly used in operations, the latter in accounting.

Work in Process (WIP): The number of entities in a system. Entities may be products, parts, or people. This excludes raw material and finished goods.

Throughput Time (TT) = WIP x CT, or CT=TT/WIP. (This is Little's Law – see below).

Further reading:

Hopp, W.J. and Spearman, M.L., 2011. *Factory Physics*. Waveland Press.

4.2 The Kingman equation and Scheduling Dynamics

Kingman's equation leads to a deeper understanding of the factors and inter-relationships resulting in queues and lead time. (Queues are referred to a 'waiting lines' or 'lines in USA.)

But first, why should a Lean practitioner be interested in queues? Because, queues…

- Stop or delay flow
- Increase lead time. Queues are the major component of lead time.
- Work against quality – by delaying detection
- Take up space
- Annoy customers
- Decrease competitiveness.

For this reason, Lean focusses on the reduction of Mura, or unevenness, which is a major cause of queues. A good way to understand the linkage between variation and queues is given in Kingman's equation of the average waiting time in front of a process. There are three important variables involved in Kingman's equation: Arrival variation, process variation and utilization. Following Hopp and Spearman we can state Kingman's equation simply as L = VUT, where

- L is the average lead time or queue
- V is variation – made up of arrival rate variation and process rate variation.
- U is the process utilization
- T is the average process time.

Arrival Rate Variation

This is to do, externally, with the arrival pattern of customer demand, and internally the arrival pattern of work or demand at a workstation. Any system works better if the arrival pattern of work or customers is more even.

External demand variation is a significant type of variation. Yet it is very often the most ignored. For many organisations, reducing external demand variation can be a hugely cost effective activity. External demand variation is not fully controllable, but can be influenced. See Chapter 24 on Demand Analysis and Variation.

Process Rate Variation

Process variation results from numerous internal sources such as breakdowns, stoppages, absenteeism, material or parts shortage, inspection, instructions, and speed variation.

Internal process variation can be tackled by standardized work, TWI JI, Six Sigma, product design and simplification, poka-yoke, and the like.

Utilization

Utilization is Load divided by Capacity. Load is the work or demand coming onto the system; Capacity is best defined as the capability of a worker, machine, work centre, plant, or organization to produce output per time period. Alternatively, it is the rate of work into a station / the capacity of the station.

The classic queuing graph, reproduced in many publications, is shown below. The curve can easily be generated by a simple dice game. (See The Lean Games and Simulations Book.) It is of prime importance for a deeper understanding of Lean and Six Sigma. This graph is applicable in all service situations, and in any manufacturing situation where inventory cannot be built ahead of time, such as make-to-order. However, even in make to stock situations, queues often accumulate within the process.

Why does the queue build up like this? Because unused capacity is lost. Like a hotel, an unused bed one night cannot be recovered. But average demand is unaffected. Whenever demand exceeds capacity the queue builds. A queue only decreases when capacity exceeds demand. This is less and less likely with increasing utilization.

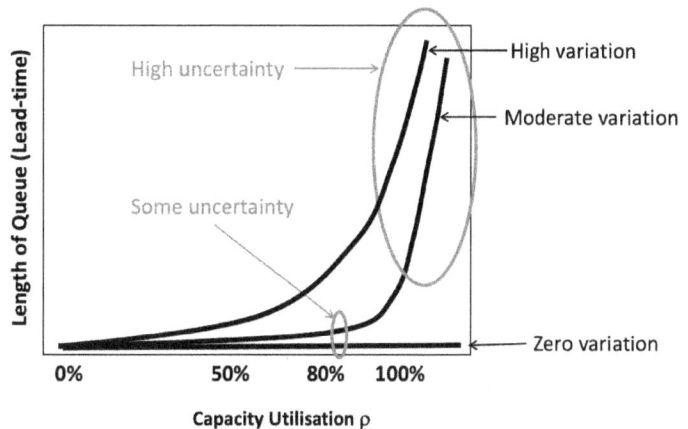

Notice, from the graph:

- There is an exponential (non-linear) increase in average queue (or lead time) with increasing capacity utilization.

- Queues really begin to 'bite' above about 80% utilization.

- At 100% utilization the queue is 'infinite', or would be very long if customers did not give up waiting.

- Job queues are very small when utilization is low.

- As utilization increases, so the range of uncertainty increases. Sometimes there is a huge queue, sometimes only a small queue. (Uncertainty is as bad as the queue itself. Customers hate uncertainty.)

- If there is no variation there is no queue as long as capacity exceeds demand.

- Variation makes little difference at low utilization but a big difference at high utilization. The greater the variation, the longer the average queue.

Kingman's Equation for the expected average waiting time *w* in a single-server queue is:

$$E(w) = \left[\frac{\rho}{1-\rho}\right] \times \left[\frac{Ca^2 + Cp^2}{2}\right] \times \tau$$

where:

Ca is the coefficient of arrival (or demand) variation; *Cp* is the coefficient of process variation; ρ is utilization (%); τ is the average process time. The time through a process is equal to w+τ. Or, as we defined it above, CT=CTq+PT.

The coefficients of variation (COV) measure arrival variation and process variation. COV is explored below.

Thus, from Kingman, there are three critical variables:

- Arrival variation (or levelling demand and supply). This is almost always greater than process variation.
- Process variation (reducing internal process variation)
- Utilization.

Variation in the order arrival rate and variation in the process is unevenness (Mura). Capacity is directly linked with overburden (Muri). The lesson is that unevenness and being overburdened are the big enemies. They are a major source of waste. To limit queues, you need to reduce the process variation and be very careful of order variations like promotional activity. And you need to run at comfortably less than 100% of capacity – if you don't your lead times will be both long and unpredictable. Muri and Mura lead to Muda.

Exploring Utilization, Load and Capacity

The formula for the utilization factor as used in the Kingman equation is $\rho/(1-\rho)$. The utilization, ρ, is expressed as a decimal between 0 and 1. Thus

- If utilization is 50%, the factor is 0.5/(1-0.5) = 1. The factor is effectively neutral.
- If utilization is 10%, the factor is 1/9. Variation is effectively dampened out, or makes little difference.

- If utilization is 90%, the factor is 9/1 = 9. Variation is massively amplified!

This is why utilization is such a powerful factor. 'Freed up' capacity will make a big difference to lead times and queues, especially at higher utilization levels.

Utilization is made up of two elements: *Load* and *Capacity*, both of which are also made of up two elements.

Load has two elements:

- Real (or 'value') demand. This is the first-time actual demand.
- Mistake demand (or 'failure demand' to use John Seddon's phrase). In manufacture this could be rework, incorrect quantities due to errors, or deliberate overproduction. In service, failure demand occurs when a customer has to revisit, enquire, chase up, on a previous call or demand. It can be very high – like 80% of calls in a call centre. The reduction of defects and failure demand should be a priority, especially at high utilization levels. In service, failure demand is often not measured or even recognised! Note that rework is a 'double whammy' in as far as it not only results in more work but also causes demand variation – often at the worst time!

..and *capacity* has two elements

- Base capacity. This is the capacity that would be available if everything worked perfectly. Perhaps an OEE of 100%. No breakdowns or stoppages.
- Wastes. All the wastes that detract from the capacity. Waiting (starvation), motion wastes, speed loss. The causes might relate to all of Ohno's 7 wastes. Note, however, that defects that cause rework are a waste category that results in extra load. (Hence OEE should not be used. Please refer to the Section on OEE. Better to use Mean time between failure and mean time to repair, and thus

utilization is MTBF / (MTBF + MTTR). Alternatively the 6 big losses can be used. See the Maintenance Chapter.)

But also note that, in some manual systems, there is a link between Load and Capacity. Recent research, but going back to 1954 and Parkinson's Law ('Work expands to fill the time available'), shows that Load and time pressure does indeed influence the rate of work or capacity.

Overall, we have:

$$\text{Utilization} = \frac{Load}{Capacity} = \frac{(\text{Value demand} + \text{rework})}{(\text{Base capacity} - \text{waste})}$$

Reducing rework or failure demand, reduces load, so utilization is reduced, and so queues are reduced – exponentially! Reducing waste increases capacity, so utilization is reduced, and so queues are reduced – exponentially!

The Coefficient of Variation (CV, also CoV)

Arrival variation and process variation is measured by a coefficient of variation:

$$CV = \frac{\sigma}{\mu}$$

where σ is the standard deviation of process time or arrival rate. μ is the average process time or arrival rate. So the coefficient is a relative ratio, not an absolute number.

Hopp and Spearman, in Factory Physics, suggest that:

- Low variability has a CV less than 0.75. Ignore?
- Moderate variability has a CV between 0.75 and 1.33. Provide extra capacity?
- High variability has a CV greater than 1.33. If possible, pull capacity as needed from less busy resources, or provide extra capacity.

Some observations:

- With long cycle-time work, absolute variation is not as important as with short cycle (process) time work. This makes sense. A 1 minute standard deviation is insignificant in a one hour cycle, but of huge significance where average cycle time is 1 minute.
- There are advantages to longer cycle operations. Two parallel lines each balanced with a planned cycle time of 2 minutes, will be more stable than a single line balanced to 1 minute. (But note that extra lineside inventory and tooling may offset this stability.)
- The CV is one reason why there is so much fuss about standard work in service operations. In service, most process times are longer than in manufacturing; some much longer. Why then risk over-standardisation that carries the risk of rework or 'failure demand'. Rework and failure demand have much more serious consequences.
- High CV schedule adherence is much more difficult. High inventory results. (Of course, this is right out of Kingman's equation.)

Exploring Muri and Mura

Muri or overburden: First, people: if people are to be partners in the process, they need to be willing participants in improvement. If they are to produce good quality work and be responsible for that quality, they cannot be expected to do so if they are stressed or overloaded. They must enjoy good 'quality of work life' at the workplace, so the ergonomics (temperature, lighting, vision, comfort, lifting, and risk of repetitive strain) must be as friendly as possible. Safety must be paramount. Improvement is not possible with 100% utilization.

Second, machines: machines also can be overburdened by working them beyond their limits – this is actually the basis of TPM.

Third, quality: For an Andon or 'line stop' system to work, there must be some slack in the system. A line should not be balanced to 100% of takt. If it is, any quality interruption cannot be rectified.

Fourth, schedule. As with quality, if there is no slack any interruption will cause the schedule to be missed.

In fact one reason why the Toyota system works as well as it does is because some slack is built in!

Mura or unevenness. Fast, uninterrupted flow is not possible with uneven demands. Queues and lead time will build up. Extra materials and inventory are required to meet peak demands. Of course, customer demands are not entirely even – but two points: First, do not amplify the unevenness by your own policies – such as end of month reporting, quantity discounts, and the like. Second, encourage both suppliers and customers to order and produce more evenly – often to mutual advantage. Does the supplier really want to deliver in bulk; does the customer really want six months' supply of toothpaste? Can you move closer to your customers to understand their true longer term requirements – thereby enabling your own operations to be smoothed in terms of working hours, leave and so forth? Buffering will often be necessary, but working together with your customers and suppliers smooths the overall flow! Also consider postponement as a way to reduce the risk of over- or understocking.

Perhaps Muri is the root problem. Overload causes stress to people and may cause lack of maintenance for machines. This in turn causes variation – Mura. Both then lead onto Muda.

Frequently, as in value stream mapping, Lean begins with a Muda hunt. Then, maybe, Mura is looked at and finally Muri.

A far better sequence is Muri, Mura, Muda.

4.3   Little's Law

Little's Law is the fundamental relationship between three critical variables in Lean operations. (John Little was an MIT Professor, who derived the mathematical proof and showed its robustness.) Simply stated, it is:

WIP = Throughput rate * Cycle Time

Or: Throughput rate = WIP / Cycle Time

Or: Entities = Entities/time x Cycle Time

But note that the variables are all <u>long-term averages</u>. The maximum may be quite different and, over a short period, say one day, the equation may not hold. Also, the process must be stable. So it is applicable to an established process but not during ramp up; patients in a hospital but not during an epidemic; inventory of drinks in a supply chain but not during a major sporting event.

WIP may be inventory, patients, calls in process (and in the queue) to a call centre, etc. Entities per time is the *throughput rate* or the rate of dealing with or completing an entity. Time is the cycle time as previously defined. (Beware of the misuse of Lead time).

Little's law is very robust. It holds where there is a range of jobs (or customers), each with its own process time, going through a process.

As Wally Hopp of Factory Physics fame says: *'It may be little, but it is the law*

Examples: If production rate is 500 units per day and WIP is 2000 units, then Average lead Time is = 2000 / 500 = 4 days.

If a call centre takes 1000 calls per 8 hour day and an average call takes 4 minutes, what is the average number of calls in the system? WIP = Cycle time x Throughput = 4 x 1000 / (8 x 60) or 8.3 calls.

To show the robustness, an example using both formula and Gantt chart is shown. (We assume this process is in a stable state.)

→ Consider a single machine over 20 hours, doing 4 jobs: A, B, C, D:

Job	Arrives at (hr)	Takes (hrs)
A	2	4
B	3	4
C	5	3
D	15	5

- Throughput: (λ): 4 jobs in 20 hours; TH=4/20 = 1/5 jobs per hour

- Cycle time(or W) : A is 4 hours in system; B is 7;C is 8; D is 5; Total 24 hours; average is 24/4 = 6 hrs.

- Average WIP = 24/20 = 6/5

- Little's Law: av. WIP = TH x CT or 6/5 = (or L=λW) = (1/5) x 6 = 24/20

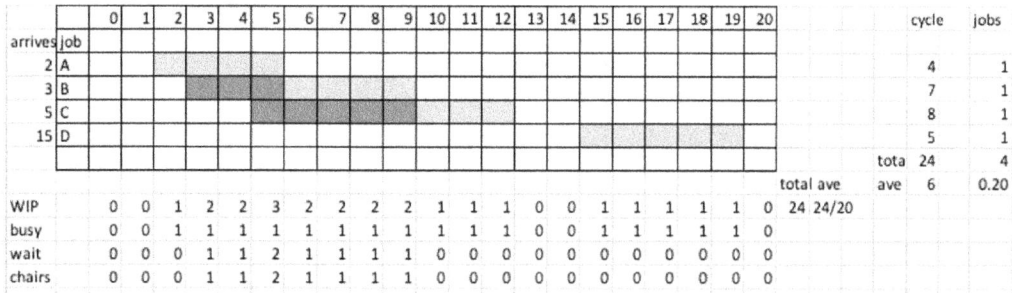

If a senior manager that says that cycle time must be reduced, she is, by Little's Law, saying that either inventory must be reduced or the rate must increase, or both. One can also check statements such as a manager claiming a WIP of 35 k assemblies when there is a throughput of 1500 assemblies per day and a cycle time of 30 days. So, quickly, WIP = 30 x 1,500 = 45,000. Something is wrong! (Inventory miscounted? Throughput wrong?)

In practice Little's Law is a useful because WIP and throughput are often easy to determine. Hence average cycle time can be calculated, and does not have to be tracked. In value stream mapping, this is a more accurate way of determining lead time than adding up value adding and non-value adding time.

4.4 Pareto and the 80/20 Rule

Pareto Analysis (or the 80/20 rule) has been called the single most important management concept of all time. Quite a claim! Pareto's Law, about the vital few and less important many applies to scheduling, quality, marketing, layout, warehousing – and much more! There are several essential Pareto analyses that every operations manager, and especially every aspiring Lean

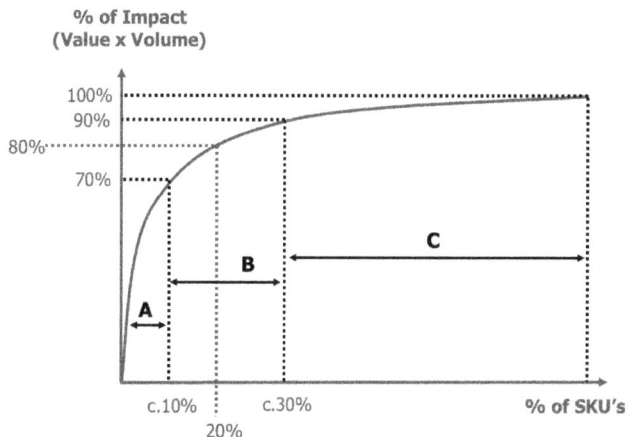

manager, should be aware of in relation to their own plant, these are: P-Q Analysis for layout and inventory, Contribution Pareto, and Parts and materials analysis.

P-Q (or Product Quantity) Analysis.

P-Q analysis is a Pareto procedure that simply ranks parts or products by volume, or quantity. It is an essential early step in deciding on layout. P-Q is also linked with the Runners, Repeaters and Strangers concept. Top end items (Runners) can justify dedicated equipment. Mid-range parts (Repeaters) may have to share cell facilities with other parts. Often some routing changes will be required. Parts in the tail of the Pareto (Strangers) are problematical for cells. The best case is that by clustering routings they can be brought into a few cells. The worst case is that these parts will have to go into a residual cell or job shop – or they are candidates for outsourcing.

An important issue is: at what level should you do a P-Q Analysis? A general answer is – the same level at which the Master Schedule is developed.

There are two types of Pareto P-Q analysis – value-based and volume-based – so the vertical axis may be value or volume. The value-based analysis may identify a small number of products where dedicated lines may be worthwhile irrespective of volume – for example a cosmetics line that is run on average one day per week, but thereby allows low inventories and extreme flexibility. A volume-based analysis may justify dedicated lines based on volume.

But not so fast! By rationalization methods (design, modularity, etc.) stranger parts can be made into repeaters. Whilst end items or products may be unique, their subassemblies or components may not be. Therefore, an upstream cell may be justified, even though a downstream cell may not be. Or, if you have a decoupling point in your supply chain, you can have part family cells upstream, but downstream the cells may be customer specific. The parts Pareto section below is of relevance.

Not so fast, part 2: the direction of movement should also be noted. In other words, a low volume product that is growing is more important than a slightly higher volume product that is declining.

Another derivative is P-Q-R, where in addition to product quantity you also consider routing. Here, the complexity of the routing for a product or item is used as a third decision variable what layout to use: the more standard the routing, the more likely a line or cell layout is justified. The more individual the routing, the more likely a job shop is appropriate.

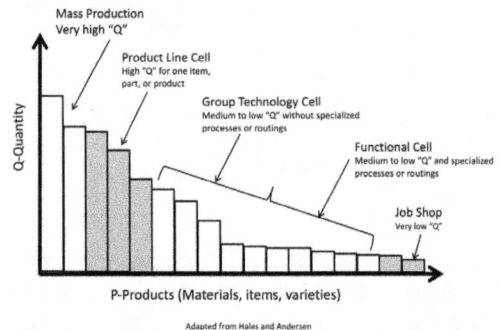

Adapted from Hales and Andersen

Contribution Analysis

Contribution is selling price minus direct costs (i.e. contribution to overheads). It is essential to know which products are making your money. A cumulative contribution analysis would look similar to the Pareto / ABC analysis shown above, except that the vertical axis would show the accumulated contribution. The analysis needs to be done for the current state and for the future state. Again, there are two sub-categories. The first is total contribution. Which products are making the greatest contribution, and which if any are making a loss? There may be strategic issues here – some products may have to be retained as loss leaders.

The second, and possibly more important, is 'contribution per bottleneck minute'. If you have a clear bottleneck process (where you could make more money if you had more capacity) or a stage that is a near bottleneck (or constraint), then you need to divide the unit contribution by the time spent on the bottleneck. Clearly, you don't want to have products that make small contribution *and* that tie up your precious bottleneck capacity. But take care with this type of analysis – if you cut products, be sure that all the 'direct' costs you have assumed will actually come down.

Contribution analysis is an essential early step in any Lean implementation. If it is not done you may waste your time improving streams that should be eliminated, or simply mis-prioritising.

Parts, Materials, and Tools Paretos

Parts, materials and to a lesser extent tool rationalization is a huge, and often untapped, field of opportunity in many companies. In fact, the potential often far exceeds taking out inventory as part of a scheduling, kanban, or value stream implementation.

Pareto is the way in. Where rationalization has not been done or specifically controlled for several years, part proliferation may be rampant. Getting after proliferation is big task, usually requiring a specific team, but with big payoff in inventory savings. But, more importantly, this activity allows the business to become much more flexible and in some instances literally to change the business model from long lead-time, high inventory build to stock to short lead-time, build to order.

For example, in one organization that one author was involved with, over 50 types of bar stock were reduced to just 5; in another 28 types of fastener were reduced to just 6. In a third case, implementation of NC laser fabric cutting in-house (on 4 material types) enabled a short-lead-time pull system to be introduced with one pacemaker, replacing large quantities of different material inventories (well over 100 part numbers), as well as forecasting, purchasing, MRP transactions, long lead-times, and part shortages - (as Zorba would have said,' the full catastrophe!').

Rationalization may involve upgrading existing specifications, and so appear 'uneconomic' but the payoff is in simplicity of control, in flexibility,

in inventory – but more importantly, in business opportunity.

Rationalization requires high-level support – and will typically meet resistance from both accountants concerned with unit costs (but not system costs), and from designers concerned with optimal product design and product 'waste' (Of course, whilst individual product waste may increase, overall system cost is slashed.)

The first step is to list the categories of major parts, components, materials, and tools. For example part categories may include fasteners, bushes, housings, and gears. Components may be motors, printed circuit boards, transformers, and containers. Materials may include coil steel, bar stock, plastic for injection moulding, fabrics, gloves, and packaging material.

The second step is to decide which categories to tackle first. Set up a multi-function group from the Lean promotion office, manufacturing, design, purchasing, accounting, and possibly marketing. Anticipate a stormy session, and get it chaired by a sympathetic system thinking, top manager.

The third step is to draw up usage Paretos for the chosen categories. Rank by annual usage and also by current inventory holding divided by annual usage last year. This second ranking will sometimes result in a few 'infinite' categories where usage has ceased. Examine the tail of the Pareto in the former case, and the head in the latter case.

Get the team to examine systematically each item from these two ends, always looking at the possibility of eliminating or combining items. This standardization and rationalization activity must be ongoing. Part proliferation slowly creeps in, in the Design office and via Marketing. These functions do need to appreciate wider system economics.

Further reading

H Lee Hales, Bruce Anderson, 2002 *Planning Manufacturing Cells,* Society of Manufacturing Engineers, Dearborn MI

4.5   Buffers

With variation in demands and process, buffers are a fact of life. Some Lean enthusiasts think that buffers are waste that can be eliminated. Sorry, they can be reduced, but not eliminated. There are three types of buffer:

- Inventory
- Capacity
- Time

An inventory buffer is inventory that protects against external demand uncertainty, supply uncertainty, and internal variations such as batching and rework.

A capacity buffer is extra capacity in the form of machines or people, that protect against both demand uncertainty and internal problems such as breakdowns or quality issues.

A time buffer adds to the lead time, so that customers or inventory must wait or queue. However a time buffer allows inventory buffers and capacity buffers to be reduced. If machines, particularly bottlenecks, break down, customers will wait or be forced to wait. If some customers cannot wait, such as in an emergency aircraft landing, other customers will be delayed, unless reserve capacity is held. If blood must always be on call, inventory will have to be held. But if there is reliable capacity for blood that can be called upon at short notice inventory can be reduced. Customers might be prepared to wait for a hairdresser or doctor or Ferrari, so capacity and inventory can be reduced. Some demand variation can be levelled by reservations. Reservations are a form of time buffer.

Toyota, in fact, reduces 'order to cash' time by employing extra capacity – in between shift time-buffers, time for problem solving, and lines balanced under takt time. (If lines were balanced strictly to takt, activating the 'andon' (line stop) system would often result in missing the schedule.) Six Sigma, TWI, standardized work all help to reduce variation, so buffers can then be reduced accordingly.

The selection, sizing, and management of these three types of buffer is a strategic issue in Lean, and in all operations. It is useful to think in terms of a **PORTFOLIO** of buffers. Like a financial portfolio the mix should change depending on perceived risk and opportunity.

Buffers must be matched to customer demand types and to variation. The sizing of each should be a deliberate decision, not left to chance. If demand variation can be reduced, all three types of buffer can be reduced. Demand variation should be a management priority. (See the Chapter on Demand management.)

A particular type of buffer may not be available. If customers require instant response to demand (as in a store), then there must be an inventory buffer. Many services (like a hairdresser or fire brigade) cannot be inventoried. For example, a fire brigade needs near instant response, so time buffers and inventory buffers are not available and reserve capacity must be kept. The question is, how much? It depends on how long customers are prepared to wait.

Sometimes capacity buffers can be reduced in the short term by, for example, moving people from shelf stacking to checkouts (as in Tesco), or by working into the maintenance shift (as at Toyota) – but then 'something else' (inventory or other customers) will wait. (Remember 'as soon as you have variation, someone or something will wait.')

In software development (or 'Agile'), or in design, and innovation – particularly where speed is everything – it makes sense to front load the process with extra capacity – a capacity buffer.

Finally, if variation is ignored – as in classic MRP, or if managers demand 100% utilization, then the price will be paid in longer lead times and more inventory. (See Kingman's equation above).

An observation: Lean and Agile: Some managers and academics like to distinguish Lean from 'Agile'. The phrase 'Leagile' has also crept in! Despite several academic papers, the distinction as to what exactly defines an agile operation is unclear. However, it may be useful to think in terms of the three types of buffer. Lean attempts to keep inventory buffers and lead times down. According to Kingman's equation, reduced lead times require lower variation or lower utilization. If we cannot tolerate lower utilization (i.e. capacity buffers) then we must reduce variation. 'Agile' would focus on flexibility and therefore larger capacity buffers are tolerated. This comes at a cost. The point is it is a strategic decision to select the appropriate mix of buffers, the appropriate focus on process variation, and the strategic response to demand variation. These must be considered specifically. It is not useful just to talk in vague terms about Agile and Leagile operations!

Location of Buffers

Where to locate and where not to locate inventory (and time) buffers is discussed in the Chapter on Scheduling. This is important if Lean is to achieve throughput nut with minimal inventories.

Supply Chain Buffers

Supply chain inventory buffers can be reduced by consolidation, known also as Pooling. By way of example, consider elevators installed in a building. Say the average weight of a passenger is 80 kg. with standard deviation 15 kg. If single person elevators were provided, they would each need to be able to carry 80 + 3 x 15 kg = 125 kg to serve 99% of users. (This is why 3 standard deviations is used.) But if elevators could take 4 passengers, they would need to be able to carry 4 x 80 + √4 x 3 x 15 = 320 + 90 = 410kg for the same service level. Compared with needed capacity of the 4 individual elevators (4 x 125 = 500kg), this represents a saving of 18%. How so? Because, as more passengers are added, it is less likely that all will be at the top range of weight. This is the square root law. Of course, more walking will be involved because the elevator location for 4 passengers will not be as convenient as 4 separate elevators. A similar situation arises in supply chains and in plant inventory 'supermarkets'. Inventory can be reduced by consolidating local

warehouses in distribution centres. There is a trade-off between reduced inventory and transport wastes.

The bottom line is that the three types of buffer are a portfolio in dynamic interplay between themselves and with variation and transportation costs. The three require adjustment as costs, customer variation and customer requirements change.

Example: The City of Chicago is subject to flash floods and is very flat. To prevent stormwater combined with sewage overflowing into Lake Michigan, the city has converted and extended a very large old quarry that serves as a buffer in front of the wastewater treatment plant. The cost of the whole system is apparently a cool $4 billion! The city could have built much larger treatment plants (that is, capacity) but finds it economical to level the demand into the wastewater plants with an 'inventory' buffer. A classic trade-off.

4.6   Inventory Trade-Off Curves

With the background of variation, buffers, and queues, the strategic issue concerning the inventory holding can be considered.

Fill rate is the percentage of time that the system is not in backorder. Another way of thinking about this is the percentage of customers (or orders) who get what they want. Stockout probability is the percentage of order cycles that have no stockouts.

Buffer and safety stock is often calculated by the stockout probability ($z * \sigma$) where z is the value corresponding to a particular probability in the one tail of the normal distribution (thus z=2.05 for 98%, and z = 1.64 for 95%), and σ is the standard deviation of demand. Although easy to calculate this is incorrect because it calculates the chance that, just before the next shipment arrives, nothing is left on the shelf. Very often a better measure is the fill rate.

Example: Consider the case where there are only three possible demands: 90, with 20% probability, 100 with 60% probability, and 110 with 20% probability. If 90 are stocked then on 20% of days there will be no stockout. (A manager may consider this, wrongly, as the service level, stockout probability or 'cycle fill rate'). But, nevertheless, on the other 80% of days 90 customers will get what they demand. So the fill rate is (90/90*0.2 + 90/100*0.6 + 90/110*0.2) = 90%.

This is a huge difference: 20% vs. 90%! The result is that using the short (safety stock) method is safe, but a lot more stock will be held if the planner confuses the stockout probability with the fill rate. If what is really required is a measure of the number of order cycles that are not met, then use the stockout probability formula. One other possible source of error in calculating the stockout probability whilst assuming a normal distribution of demand (mean and standard deviation) is that there may be the possibility of negative demand. (For example, if mean demand is 10 units per day and standard deviation is 5 units, then there would be negative demand beyond mean minus 2 standard deviations or on about 2.3% of days. Impossible!) Moreover, if the distribution is not normal but Poisson (as is more likely with low demand items) the calculation will also be incorrect. What is disturbing is that several MRP systems and current university textbooks confuse these concepts. The calculation for fill rate is longer, but can easily be done on a spreadsheet. Of course, the higher the item cost the more important it is to use the correct calculation.

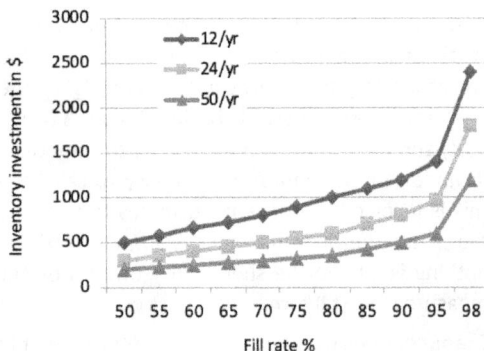

The inventory trade off curve shows the 'efficient frontier' trade-off between total inventory and fill rate. Inventory trade off curves should be calculated for every business having significant amounts of inventory. There will be a curve for each particular number of orders per year. The more orders, the less the inventory. This can link in with the EPEI (Every product every interval) calculation discussed in the Scheduling chapter.

Notice that:

- The curves show the Efficient Frontier for various order rates.

- There is a feasible and an infeasible region, for any frequency of replenishment. The infeasible region is below each curve because of uncertainty and variation.

- Like the graph of Kingman's equation, there is a steep exponential shape to the curve. Moving from 50% to 60% fill rate requires very little extra inventory, but moving from 88 % to 98% requires a great deal.

- The number of orders placed makes a difference. More orders mean smaller order quantities with greater frequency of delivery – so inventory comes down. But note the effect of more orders on inventory declines non-linearly. Moving from (say) 100 orders per year to 200 per year makes quite a difference. Moving from 200 to 300 orders makes less difference.

The frontier curve must be calculated by aggregating all SKUs together and then determining the fill rate for various levels of total inventory cost and the corresponding order rates.

The curve is a useful strategic tool because:

- The total current value of inventory, and the current order fill level, can be plotted on the graph. This generally shows a position far removed from the optimal frontier curve. Moving towards the frontier would usually represent a considerable inventory saving.

- The choice is then strategic. Reduce inventory but stay at the same fill rate. Stay at the same level of inventory, but improve the fill rate. Or, do a bit of both - improve fill rate AND reduce inventory.

- There is no right answer to this. Management must position its policies for the appropriate market offering.

- The inventory buffers have to be set against capacity buffers and time buffers.

- Remember, this is just inventory stocking policy. Savings can often be made simply by adjusting the inventory according to the appropriate policy.

Further reading

Wallace Hopp, *Supply Chain Science*, Waveland, 2008, reissued 2011

Edward Pound, Jeffrey Bell, Mark Spearman, *Factory Physics for Managers*, McGraw Hill, 2014

Wallace Hopp and Mark Spearman, *Factory Physics*, Third edition, McGraw Hill, 2008

John Bicheno, *The Lean Games and Simulations Book*, PICSIE, 2014. See the Kingman Equation Dice Game.

4.7   Scientific Method and Experimentation

This section provides caution about using PDSA in unstable situations. Due the strong influence of Deming, Plan Do Check Act (PDCA) or Plan Do Study Adjust is a widely quoted methodology for continuous improvement in a Lean context. In Lean, scientific method is most desirable, but alas, it is widely misused. Some PDSA cycles neglect the last two steps which in effect means that no valid learning can be made!

Closely related to PDSA is experimentation. Today, experiments are frequently used by, for example, Google and Amazon to determine effective marketing and web sites. 'Evidence based' is now demanded in most medical procedures and medicines. Experimentation is widely used in psychology to test theories.

Google, Amazon and others have literally millions of customers and are able to test web site designs by trying them out on very large samples. Likewise medical research demands closely controlled test procedures involving medicines and placebos.

In Lean operations, controlled experimentation is difficult or impossible. It may not be possible to have a control group, random selection of participants is not feasible, and sample size is often not large enough to attached confidence limits. In chaotic and complex situations (see the section on Snowden and Cynefin) repetition is unlikely. Nevertheless, valuable learning is possible by experimenting in Lean situations and a more rigorous approach should certainly be attempted and pitfalls avoided. Let us begin by stating that experimentation is an accepted way to establish a causal relationship between a circumstance and a behaviour.

The steps in Experimentation.

1. An independent variable must be established. For instance, this could be the balancing allowance in a cell or line for planned cycle time in relation to takt. (e.g. for a 60sec. takt, 90% would be balancing the cell for 54sec.) There must be two or more levels of the independent variable, say 60sec., 54sec., 48sec.

2. A dependent variable must then be selected. For the example, the number of good products produced in a shift. This is the variable that would be measured for each level of the independent variable.

3. Control variables must be established and maintained throughout the experiment. This could be the actual time worked during a shift, the product variety (if any), and the composition of the workforce in the cell.

4. Some variables might be allowed to be varied during the experiment, but should nevertheless be identified. For instance, the work day of the week.

5. Beware of confounding variables. These are circumstances that vary along with the independent variable. For instance, a team leader's response to andon calls may vary with the balancing allowance.

6. The experiment should be conducted over a length of time, or number of trials, to establish a degree of confidence. Statistical tests should be made if possible.

7. In larger experiments, say conducted by medical developers or web designers, the experiment should be conducted with a randomised sample and a control group. Randomised trials are difficult to do in many Lean operations environments. A control group may be possible – for instance, having two cells side by side with the experiment being conducted in one of the cells.

Further reading:

Stefan Thomke, *Experimentation Works*, Harvard, 2020

4.8   Bias and System1/System2 Thinking

A good way to illustrate the difference between System 1 and System 2 Thinking is a simple puzzle: A bat and a ball cost together $1.10, and the bat is $1 more expensive than the ball. How much is the ball? Many will respond quickly with the wrong answer of '10 cents', which stems from their System 1 bias that is, answering quickly and intuitively, without any deeper analysis.

Understanding Bias

Over the past two decades, thanks to work by Kahneman and Tversky, Ariely and others, much has been learned about people's biases and errors. These findings have significance for Lean.

We now know that managers and operators are not the entirely rational people that were once assumed. We all suffer from Cognitive Bias. For instance:

- We believe we have more influence over events than we actually do.

- The Sunk Cost bias means that we tend to hang on to initiatives well beyond their 'sell by' date. If it doesn't work, spend more money or time. An example may be MRP / ERP.

- The Overconfidence Bias means that we are often overconfident about ourselves and our projects, especially when the environment is favourable. This is why many projects (including this book!) are late. Lean implementation takes longer than you think.

- We are more averse to loss than to gain. Money and goods that we already have somehow acquire additional value.

- We are easily and unconsciously influenced by 'anchors' such as happy pictures or people, and by numbers and colours.

- In the excellent book, The Halo Effect, Phil Rosenzweig says that it is often assumed that culture contributes to success and performance. But the research does not support this. The reverse is true. Performance often drives culture. If there is success, people tend to report enthusiasm for change, great support, great teamwork, great management, a futuristic organisation and a 'hero at the helm'. But very quickly the same people in the same company with the same managers report negatively when performance, due perhaps to a change in the market, declines. The same managers are now said to lack vision, be complacent, and arrogant! Likewise there is a tendency to attribute success or failure to one thing – like culture or leadership - when there are almost invariably many forces at work. So, Rosenzweig takes issue with some of the major texts such as *Good to Great, Built to*

Last, and *In Search of Excellence*, warning that the 'lessons' may be a delusion.

- Other delusions that Rosenzweig warns about include 'Connecting the Winning Dots' – where characteristics of winners are identified, but how many losers also share those characteristics?. 'Timeless principles' often don't stand the long time test. And success stories are generally very poor at predicting future performance. So, in the authors' opinion, we need to study failures more than successes. Always ask managers from successful Lean companies about their failures….

Confirmation bias

What VS Mahesh calls 'Pygmalion' and Kahneman and many others calls 'Confirmation Bias' has long been known. We selectively seek out information that confirms our beliefs, and tend to ignore information that contradicts our beliefs. Margaret Heffernan calls this 'wilful blindness'. We all have 'filters' and build on flimsy evidence. So, for example, Israeli drill sergeants are told that one group comprises specially selected achievers and other group comprises the less able. The groups, however, unbeknown to the sergeants, were randomly selected. Nevertheless the superior group performs much better. Likewise, so do randomly selected maths students. A self-fulfilling prophesy.

Fixed and Growth Mindset

The distinguished psychologist Carol Dwek classifies people according to a 'fixed mindset' or 'a growth mindset'. (Actually a continuum.) People with a fixed mindset think their intelligence is static, a fixed trait. They avoid challenges, deflect criticism, and feel there is no point in effort. By contrast, those with a growth mindset embrace challenges, work hard to improve, and learn from criticism and feedback. Intelligence is not fixed, but can grow. Countless 'under-achievers' (Churchill, Branson, many sportspeople) have demonstrated this through

determination. As Henry Ford said, 'whether you think you can or whether you think you can't, you're absolutely right.' The growth mindset believes in 'Yet'. I or others can't do it yet, but will be able to with effort and support.

Now here is the point: A growth mindset can be learned! And taught. A good teacher motivates by giving constructive feedback, linking effort to achievement. Praising effort rather than success.

Of course, to give genuine constructive feedback one must believe in the potential of the mentee. One must know about confirmation bias.

George Davidson, former Manufacturing Director at Toyota South Africa, when asked about the aim of TPS simply said 'To create thinking people'. In other words, change their mindset.

4.9   Volatility, VUCA and Cynefin®

In the late 1980's Deming proposed what he called the 'System of Profound Knowledge', or SoPK. There are four elements, and Deming said that many managers have poor knowledge of these four.

- **Variation.** A need to distinguish common cause from special cause.
- **System.** The realisation that sub-systems are interconnected. Systems thinking is required to avoid 'whacking a mole'.
- **Knowledge.** Learning and Experimental Method. The PDSA cycle.
- **Motivation.** Intrinsic and Extrinsic motivation. Extrinsic motivation (pay and rewards) have only short term effect.

These four are the basic skills required of managers. They are critical for Lean success. They are also a useful checklist on why things go wrong. Four decades later, they remain highly relevant.

The VUCA Model

Particularly over the past two decades, the world of operations has moved relentlessly

	Explanation	Effects	Deming?
Volatility	Frequently changing, fluctuation of prices, demands, resource availability	Instability Risk	Variation?
Uncertainty	Not able to be accurately known or predicted. Surprises. Uncertainty of supply and demand	Indecisiveness Delay	Knowledge?
Complexity	Many interconnected parts influencing one another. Intricate. Feedback effects. Push down pop up.	Overload Mistakes	System?
Ambiguity	Vagueness of meaning or understanding. Lack of clarity about concepts	Doubt Distrust Misdirection	Motivation?

towards VUCA (volatility, uncertainty, complexity, and ambiguity). The acronym VUCA emerged in about 1987 but has since become widely accepted.

But many of the theories and concepts of what is now called Lean (and was previously known as the Taylor System, or Just-in-Time, and more lately 'Operational Excellence') relate to more stable, predictable environments. Dave Snowden named these as Clear (formerly called Simple) and Complicated environments as opposed to Complex (See Cynefin Model).

We believe that Deming' SoPK can mesh very well with VUCA. An explanation of the VUCA elements is given in the figure.

To quote from Bennett and Lemoine, 'Volatility, uncertainty, complexity, and ambiguity all require their own separate and unique responses. Each of the four is a distinct phenomenon with equally distinct appropriate responses that require different—and possibly difficult to reallocate—investments. Leaders face a pair of problems: If VUCA is seen as general, unavoidable, and unsolvable, leaders will take no action and fail to solve an actual problem. Alternatively, if leaders misread the environment and prepare for the wrong challenge, they will misdirect resources and fail to address the actual problem. '

Reference will be made to the VUCA concept in several sections of this book.

Snowdon's Cynefin® Model

The purpose of the Cynefin framework, as Dave Snowdon, its originator, says is for 'making sense of the world so we can act on it.' It is useful in 'sense-making' or helping to understand why approaches such as Six Sigma, and perhaps Lean, go haywire. Why 'Scientific Management' (Taylorism) works well in some environments but is a disaster in others. Why assuming you are in the complicated domain but are in fact in the chaotic domain could be a fatal mistake for the use of many Lean tools.

There are four domains in the framework, plus a central 'confused' domain. Some characteristics of the four domains and associated principles are briefly described below together with comments on their relevance for Lean problems and decisions. The domains are defined by the types of constraint – or no constraint in the case of chaotic. To move between domains requires energy. However, the reader should regard what follows as a brief overview and seek out fuller discussions – particularly as the framework is a developing one. The figure shows the Cynefin® framework superimposed with various Lean concepts.

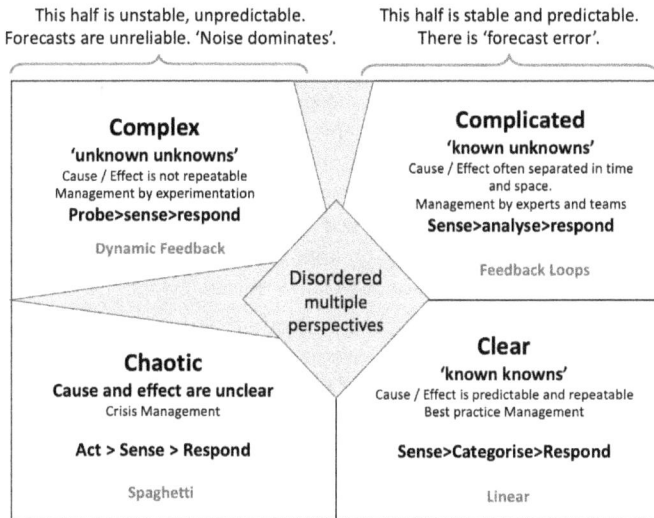

This half is unstable, unpredictable. Forecasts are unreliable. 'Noise dominates'.

This half is stable and predictable. There is 'forecast error'.

Complex
'unknown unknowns'
Cause / Effect is not repeatable
Management by experimentation
Probe>sense>respond

Dynamic Feedback

Complicated
'known unknowns'
Cause / Effect often separated in time and space.
Management by experts and teams
Sense>analyse>respond

Feedback Loops

Disordered multiple perspectives

Chaotic
Cause and effect are unclear
Crisis Management

Act > Sense > Respond

Spaghetti

Clear
'known knowns'
Cause / Effect is predictable and repeatable
Best practice Management

Sense>Categorise>Respond

Linear

Scott Page uses an excellent landscape analogy, although not directly related to Cynefin®. In the Clear domain there is one clear mountain peak. It is easy to identify. This is similar to FW Taylor's 'one best way'. In the Complicated domain the landscape is rugged. A mountain range with many local peaks. The overall highest peak may be very difficult to find, but advanced analysis techniques (Lean tools?) can get to a good or 'satisficing' solution. In the Complex domain, the landscape 'dances' – there are earthquakes and volcanoes, and the highest peak today may not even exist tomorrow. In Chaotic, it is jungle.

The Clear and Complicated domains can be regarded as Reductionist. (The parts can be studied separately; outcomes are predictable and repeatable experiments are possible.) Perhaps also these first two could be thought of as 'scientific' domains and the last two 'artistic' domains.

Snowden and Boone make the important point that most business education is focused on Clear and Complicated domains, but most leaders today actually work in the Complex and Chaotic domains.

Chaotic is a mess. Unpredictable. Here there is extreme sensitivity to conditions. One small change, and everything interacts. This is the domain of crisis management. The sequence should be '_Act, Sense, Respond'. To quote Snowden and Boone: '*In the chaotic domain, a leader's immediate job is not to discover patterns but to staunch the bleeding. A leader must first act to establish order, then sense where stability is present and from where it is absent, and then respond by working to transform the situation from chaos to complexity...*' Hence it is the domain of rapid response.

This is similar to the identification of stable and unstable zones in a value stream.

Clear: (previously 'Simple' or 'Obvious'). This domain has 'known-knowns'. We understand the relationships. The domain of Best Practice. The repeatable scientific experiment is possible and reliable. The sequence is Sense, Categorise, Respond. A single part in an engine. People are regarded as machines. Best or established practice holds sway. Lean focus might be on standard work and 5S.

Complicated. The domain of 'known-unknowns'. We know what we don't know. The domain of the Expert, and 'good practice'. The relationships between the parts are known, but there is uncertainty as to how they work together. Analysis can still be scientific but the many possible interactions between the parts leads to uncertainty. Mathematical modelling is possible, but will always be incomplete. Lean: An internal value stream. The sequence is Sense, Analyse, Respond. Judgment and expertise are necessary.

The next two domains fall into the 'Systems' area. Outcomes may not be reproducible.

Complex. Here there are unknown-unknowns. In this domain, solutions can 'emerge' (Snowden and

Boone quote Apollo 13 as an example. A solution emerged using the materials at hand in the spacecraft.) The sequence should be Probe, Sense, Respond. In the Complex domain, behaviour is unpredictable. Since the cause-and-effect relationships are uncertain, *experimentation is necessary to see what works*

Note: the phases known-knowns, known-unknowns, unknown-unknowns were made popular by controversial US Secretary of Defence Donald Rumsfeld, who died in July 2021.

Snowden, in his *Harvard Business Review* article, says that the Complex domain has the following characteristics:

- Non-linear interactions
- A large number of interactions
- Dynamic or emergent. Solutions arise rather than are imposed
- Hindsight does not lead to foresight, because the wider system constantly changes
- We cannot forecast or predict.

Scott Page says there are four characteristics of Complex systems: Interdependence, Connectedness, Diversity, and Adaptation.

In this Complex domain, non-linear relationships are common but unknown. Here, the best solution found today may not be the best solution tomorrow – because the other players or events may have changed. Because complex systems are in flux, adapting, and changing, this means that something that works today may not work tomorrow, and something that doesn't work today might work tomorrow. This is a problem for scientific method! There is a low probability of very high impact events – what Nassim Taleb calls 'black swans'. For instance, predictions of the financial crisis of 2007 were overlooked by the vast majority of analysts. An optimal solution to a supply chain problem may suddenly become non-optimal, or even poor. Such events are, according to some, becoming the norm. The impact for all organisations, but particularly for the Lean-aspiring, can be huge.

Sonja Blignaut has made the point that uncertainty is now the normal state. We used to think that stability was the normal state. But instability reigns: COVID, Brexit, Putin, Ukraine, Kim Jong, energy prices and climate change are examples. They interact. The more connected we become, the more complexity becomes apparent. She says complexity cannot be tamed, wished away, or simplified. Everything has risk and uncertainty. In this domain mutual consensus is an illusion – at best it is temporary. Also 'alignment' is difficult or impossible - because all relevant players have viewpoints that change. Hoshin?

Blastland offers another perspective which we have found useful. In the Clear and Complicated domains, forecasts and extrapolations are made but treating any small variation from the forecast as 'noise'. But in the complex area, noise dominates and the cone of uncertainty is huge. According to Kahneman, noise may well be more important than bias. Kahneman et al in their book *Noise* tell of two highly skilled insurance underwriters who, given the same information, are asked to suggest suitable insurance premiums. Their answers differed by 55%, not by the 10% that their managers predicted. A forecast elicits a response, so paradoxically as we have more data and better models, noise actually increases.

Further reading

W Edwards Deming, *Out of the Crisis*, Cambridge, 1986

Nathan Bennett and G. James Lemoine, 'What a difference a word makes: Understanding threats to performance in a VUCA world', *Business Horizons,* 2014

Michael Blastland, *The Hidden Half,* Atlantic Books, 2019

Daniel Kahneman, Oliver Sibony, and Cass Sunstein, *Noise*, Collins, 2021

Scott Page, *The Model Thinker*, Hachette Books, 2018

David Snowden and Mary Boone, 'A Leaders Framework for Decision Making', *Harvard Business Review*, November 2007, pp 68-76

David Snowden et al., *Cynefin – Weaving sense-making into the fabric of the world*, Cognitive Edge, 2021

ORGANISING FOR FLOW

This section covers the essential human aspects necessary for Lean transformation success. It includes chapters on job characteristics, managing the change process, and employee engagement – all essential aspects for a successful and sustained lean transformation!

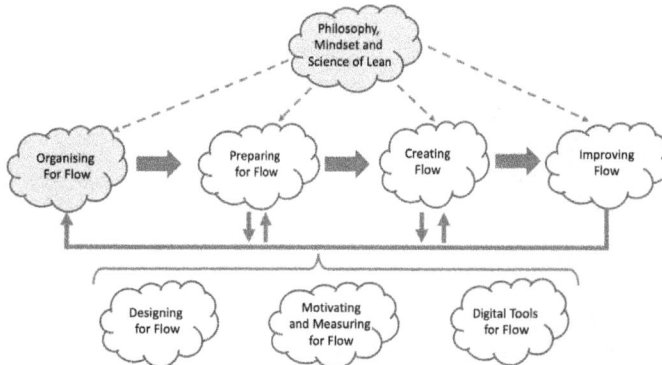

5   Respect and Humility

Perhaps THE baseline factors for organisation are Respect for workers and, Humility by managers. And the Gemba principle. They also are prominent in the Shingo Prize evaluation. Here we elaborate.

5.1   Respect

Amabile and Kramer say that **Respect** refers to either explicit or implicit recognition of another person's value. They also say that respect is gained by both catalysts (for instance, allowing autonomy, providing resources and time, helping with work, learning and listening), and nourishers (for instance giving encouragement and emotional support).

So respect is the extent to which a person's thoughts, opinions, and ideas are listened to and considered. Note, not necessarily implemented but seriously considered.

Humility and respect are the foundation of both Edgar Schein's book 'Humble Inquiry' and Gerald Egans 'Skilled Helper' approach (See Section 12.4) Both rely on sympathetic, carful listening and probing, open questions. Both are highly recommended. But for a quick and profound set, it is hard to beat TWI's four JR (Job Relations) guides. Please read the four in Chapter 17 on TWI.

These four guidelines should be followed by every line manager - with follow up. With practice and repetition such managers not only become more skilled but learn about themselves.

5.2   Humility

The more one knows about Lean, the more one realises how little one really knows. Dan Jones speaks about 'peeling the onion' to uncover waste – the same is true learning about Lean. A sure sign of impending failure is a manager who claims to 'know it all' or 'we tried that in 1990'.

Here we consider a few implications of these frequently misunderstood words.

- Deming spoke of the 94/6 rule. In his words: 'I should estimate that in my experience most troubles and most possibilities for improvement add up to the proportions something like this: 94% belongs to the system (responsibility of management) – 6% special.' So, don't blame the person...

- Respect is clear recognition that the worker at the workplace is highly likely to be the most knowledgeable person about the work. The opportunities, the barriers, the 'knack', the time.

- 'If the worker hasn't learned, the instructor hasn't taught'. TWI principle.

- 'Seek first to understand before seeking to be understood', says Covey

- Overload ('muri') of people shows no respect. They will have no time for kaizen. So don't expect improvements unless time is made available.

- Toyota team leaders have small spans of control to enable them to listen, take ideas forward, help solve problems, be aware of issues that might affect work. Respect.

- Outward signs of respect and humility: No reserved parking, same rules for all, uniforms, single canteen, who shows visitors around, chief executive pay and bonus, new managers begin work on the line.

- The 'Hot Stove Rules'. A hot stove gives warmth to the family. The family gathers around, supports and discusses. Parents use constructive, loving criticism. If the stove is touched, it burns instantly. But there is no memory of a misdeed, only continuing warmth being given out.

- Respect does not mean being nice. It does mean a deep seated appreciation of colleagues. One of the author's cousins was a miner. The environment is tough. Swearing and loud scolding is the norm, especially where safety is involved. But then, when one team member's wife fell ill, the team drove hundreds of miles to collect up the family. Not 'lip service' respect.

- In Africa, there is the word 'Ubuntu'. A person becomes a person through other persons.

- Loud mouth. Barely listening. Arrogance. My ideas are the most important. What do you know? Pretence consultation. I deserve a big bonus; you don't. The HiPPO (highest paid personal opinion.)

- Visitors to good Lean plants are invariably struck by the humility of their managers ('we have lots to learn') and their willingness to learn from others, no matter whom. Stephen Covey says that genuine listening is the most important of his 7 habits of highly effective people.

- If you keep employees or customers waiting you are saying to them 'your time is not as important as mine'. If you allow a worker to use a machine that results in defects, you are in effect saying 'your work does not matter that much'. Quality at source!

- Developing your people shows respect for them. Hansen and von Oetinger talk about 'T-shaped' managers. Toyota chairman Watanabe used this phrase also. But why only managers? T-shaped because they have a broad range of skills, but at least one in-depth skill. So Dell and Unipart, amongst others, encourage their people to improve their skills in non-strictly relevant areas such as history and cookery.

- Finally, John Seddon, a fan of Deming and Ohno but a critic of much of present-day Lean, caused a stir during a discussion with Jeffrey Liker (available on U Tube) when he said that 'respect is horsesh**'. What he meant was that respect needs to be earned through long-term actions. It is an outcome not a lip-service input.

Further reading

Peter Scholtes, *The Leaders Handbook,* McGraw Hill, 1998

Moreton Hansen and Bolko von Oetinger, 'Introducing T-Shaped Managers: Knowledge Management's Next Generation', *Harvard Business Review*, March 2002, pp106-117

Edgar Schein, *Humble inquiry*, BK, 2013

Gerald Egan, *The Skilled Helper*, 8th edition, Brooks Cole, 2007

See Graupp and Wrona, *The TWI Workbook*, Productivity, 2006

John Bicheno and Noel Hennessey, *Human Lean*, PICSIE Books, 2021

6   Gemba

(Note: Genba may be the more correct term, but here the usual 'Gemba' will be used.)

6.1   Gemba and Genchi Genbutsu

Gemba is the 'real place' or actual place where value is created... It is where you go to see first-hand and get information by direct observation. 'The gemba' could be anywhere – the factory floor, a customer site, a supplier's process, a front office or a design centre. It is where value is added. The Gemba way is to go to the place of action and collect the FACTS. The traditional way is to remain in the office and to discuss OPINIONS. Gemba can be thought of in terms of the 'four actuals':

First, understand that Gemba is part of a trilogy. Gemba is the real place. Genbutsu is the real part or object. Gemjitsu is the real or actual facts. Go to the Gemba. Observe genbutsu. Collect gemjitsu.

A Caution: Although Going to the Gemba is essential for first-hand observation, it is not that easy. Be aware that people's behaviour often changes when they are observed. Trust must be established first. A classic is changeover reduction in early stages of Lean: the standard time for the changeover often falls dramatically when observed even before any SMED (quick change-over) activity has taken place! Alternatively, it is the experience of many old-style Work Study officers that workers go into slow motion when the stopwatch comes out.

Let us remind ourselves that Gemba is not a 'Japanese thing'. They learned it from the Americans – specifically the famous Hawthorne experiments at General Electric. What was happening was that workers' productivity was responding not to the lighting levels but to the interest being taken in them by esteemed researchers. This became known as the Hawthorn Effect. But the West promptly forgot this lesson. The Japanese took it on. So, don't sit in the office looking at an excel spreadsheet and imagine that you are improving productivity – that is management by looking in the rear-view mirror. Instead, as was said by Union soldiers to General Burnside in the American Civil War *'Move your hindquarters from the headquarters.'*

6.2   Gemba Walks

A now popular approach in companies who implement lean principles is called 'Gemba Walks,' which denote the action of leaders going to see the actual process, understand the work, ask probing questions, and learning from those who do the work. This should become a routine activity – a habit. By so doing, leaders not only learn the issues first hand but demonstrate humility and that people are the critical value adders. The objective is to understand the value stream and its problems, rather than review results or make superficial comments from their office or conference room.

Since about 2005, 'Gemba Walks' have catapulted in popularity. They are now considered an integral part of 'Leader Standard Work'. The Gemba Walk concept applies to several levels of management. Thus a director might walk once per month, plant managers once per fortnight, a division manager weekly, and a value steam leader daily. Gemba walks are a good way to create visible leadership. It is desirable to have a Gemba Walk schedule showing who is to walk when and maybe where - the area, not the route.

However, the purpose and methodology of a Gemba Walk is sometimes not understood, so potential is lost. A walk may do more harm than good. What it is NOT is:

- A casual walk-through or tour.
- Management merely showing their face or flag waving on the shop floor or office.
- An inspection – demanding action on anything out of place that is spotted, or to catch people out.
- A routine walk-through, following the same route.

- Giving answers. Telling.
- Giving direct orders on the spot, rather than coaching front line leaders.

So, what are the characteristics of a good Gemba Walk?

- Purpose: teaching and supporting others and learning yourself
- Focus: on the work not blaming the person or issuing instructions.
- Time: allowing sufficient time for discussion and for follow up.
- Assignments: agree on what to do.
- Follow up: next time
- Objective: asking with curiosity. Seeking mutual understanding of issues. 'Can you show me…',
- Servant Leadership: Identifying obstacles that need to be removed by management so that flow can be improved.
- Communication and Trust: Building working relationships
- Emphasise the value stream, not vertical silos
- Follow up with line managers as to the agreed next steps.

There are two types of Gemba walks:

- **End to end walk** – development of the value stream
- **Area walk** – development of the area

Note that a Gemba Walk is different from MBWA 'Management by walking around' – a phrase made popular by Peters and Waterman in their book 'In Search of Excellence'. MBWA is unfocused and random. Not necessarily a bad thing – anything that gets senior managers to the Gemba has virtue – but MBWA lacks the follow through and relationship building that are features of Gemba walks. MBWA sounds more like a President's or King's visit, a special event that happens only occasionally.

Gemba walks typically involve beginning with a review of a performance board, with charts and measures, to identify actions relating to new and current problems.

A summary of Gemba Walks is the 7 G's:

1. **GO** to the actual place.
2. **GET** the facts from the actual situation by direct observation.
3. **GATHER** ideas and suggestions. Ask and listen – very little tell, unless asked.
4. **GIVE** credit where due.
5. **GRASP** the current condition and clarify the problem.
6. **GUIDE** the implementation through support, coaching, and feedback (Please see Feedback in Section 5.3).
7. **GENERATE** and agree improvement proposals together with the people at the gemba. (Establish the next target situation. This will often mean breaking down the problem into manageable chunks.)

A good Gemba Walk means that team leaders and workers get an opportunity to be heard, and to demonstrate pride in their work and achievements. Leaders, at all levels, learn respect, have the opportunity to coach, and better to understand people and process. As a leader visits the gemba, there is the opportunity to question, but certainly not to command. The choice of words is very important. Keep humility in mind. Never accuse. Swop 'you' for 'we' (for instance, instead of 'Why do you not keep to the schedule?' try 'What can we do to make hitting the schedule easier?'). Never try to boost your own ego ('I fully appreciate how difficult your job is.')

…and don't be afraid to say 'I don't know…', or 'That's new to me', or 'What a valuable insight that is.' Apparently, Amerigo Vespucci, after whom America was named, used a provocative map of the world with blank spaces thereby encouraging an age of exploration.

Of course, familiarity with the work, machine, or process leads to better questions. 'Are the stoppages on that dynamo still a problem?' and maybe as a follow up, 'Excellent! Tell me what was done to solve the problem?'

Further reading

Masaaki Imai, *Gemba Kaizen*, McGraw-Hill, New York, 1997

Jim Womack and John Shook, *Gemba Walks*, Expanded 2nd edition, LEI, 2013

David Mann, *Creating a Lean Culture*, third edition, CRC Press, 2014

Giles Johnston, *Kamishibai Boards*, Amazon Kindle, 2013

6.3 Respect and humility at Toyota SA: A mini case

On the morning of 12 April 2022 Durban, Natal-KwaZulu, South Africa has hit by intense rainfall and a resulting flood, estimated at one chance in 200 years. As a result of upstream dam sluices being automatically opened the Toyota plant, covering 87 hectares and situated in the area of the former international airport, found itself under up to a metre of water including huge quantities of mud. Electricity was cut off, meaning that use of cranes for recovery was not initially possible. Clean water was not available. Not only was the plant itself flooded but so too were several local suppliers and two dealerships. The extent of the damage was at least equal to Toyota's disruption following the Fukushima nuclear disaster.

The CEO at Toyota South Africa, Andrew Kirby, contacted TMC Japan who advised on a sequence of priorities: Employees first, local community second, plant restoration third.

Some employees' houses were extensively damaged and the company assisted with restoration. Not a single job was lost. Many employees took part in restoration activities. 50% of wages were paid to qualifying employees during downtime when there was no other work plus remuneration was given for employees who volunteered for community support. The programme was called Building Better Together. As a result, employee productivity and morale is now higher than pre-flood.

The quality status of 4000 completed vehicles affected by the flood was uncertain. To avoid possible future issues it was decided that all 4000 should be crushed rather than refurbished. Toyota Japan covered cash flows and eventually sent around 200 engineers to assist with plant restoration. Recovery involved careful machine restoration – including cleaning with toothbrushes. Although new machines were on order, delivery lead-times meant that many flood-damaged machines had to be restored in order to restart production. What amounted to a comprehensive TPM programme resulted in many learnings and employee engagement. A 7-phase sequence was decided – from emergency control, through cleaning, power up, equipment check, repairs and orders, equipment delivery and verification, to start-up. Logistics of parts already en-route from Japan when the flood hit required careful consideration.

A three-stage defence plan against possible future flood is in place – at site level, at factory level, and at machine location level – including locating some machines off the floor.

The plant reopened in stages. By August all production lines were again running but at reduced capacity. Some dealers, however, took the opportunity to increases prices at a result of delivery shortfalls.

7   Questioning and Listening

Sincere questioning, showing interest and follow through, is a positive feedback process.. Responses that illicit a punishment response will inevitably close down further dialogue. And vice versa - when associates learn that measures are there to expose problems and opportunities rather than to appropriate blame, the information itself is likely to be more genuine. Psychologists refer to this circular process as 'the norm of reciprocity'.

A question such as 'How is it going?' could get the response, 'OK', but a better reflective question would be 'What opportunities are there for improvement? – And then, of course, it is vital to follow up answers with further probes.

Listening could be one of the most important skills for ANY manager. Genuine listening shows respect, helps build trust, opens new possibilities, and gives the listener time to respond. Every skilled negotiating course emphasises listening as the prime skill. There are two types. **Passive listening** requires deep listening to understand the other person's perspective. What are the real underlying concerns? Listen for opportunities so that win-win can be achieved, not win-loose. Begin by asking open questions, that don't allow for yes-no answers. **Active listening** means clarifying what is being said by repeating the gist of what was said back to the speaker. 'If I have this correct, what you are saying is...' Active listening is the standard used in aviation, surgical ('scalpel', reply 'scalpel'), and security messaging. Repeating back can diffuse heated demands, simply because it demonstrates that an effort to understand is being made. This inverts the triangle of authority from top-down to bottom-up.

Spending time at the front line, call centre, or service counter listening to actual customer words is a great way to raise manager curiosity and motivation - far better than market survey, monitoring KPI's, or 'mystery shopping'. Ohno was famous for his 'chalk circle' approach - drawing a circle in chalk on the factory floor and requiring a manager to spend several hours inside it whilst observing operations, noticing variation, and taking note of wastes. The West too has its devotees. John Sainsbury who ran the supermarket chain could pass a shelf and see at a glance if prices were wrong. This is simply Gemba management as discussed in Chapter 6.

Warren Berger points out that, increasingly, answers are less important than questions. Many answers are to be found on the internet, in data bases, libraries, with experts, and with your people if you can only ask the right question. It was not always like this, but many managers still have the outdated mindset that, somehow, they must have all the answers. Schools, unfortunately, remain bastions of uni-directional instruction, and re-gurgitation during tests. That won't do in a Lean and changing environment. Levitt and Dubner say that three of the most powerful words a manager can use are 'I don't know'. Many times, managers don't actually know, but simply guess or put forward their opinion in areas outside of their expertise, thus stifling creativity and innovation. But, of course, questions need to be followed by action.

Rothstein and Santana from the Right Question Institute have designed a 'better way' to gain from questioning. Here we adapt from their ideas:

- Leaders design the Question Focus. 'We have a great opportunity to design this new layout. We know the product, and the required volume, but apart from that there is a blank sheet.'

- Operators write down the questions. No prompting from the leaders, and no discussion. 'Can it be done sideways?', 'Can it be done on one level?', 'Why in that room?' , 'Why in that order',
- Operators improve their questions. 'How many people will be required?', 'What would be the easiest sequence?'
- Operators prioritise their questions. Perhaps: Sequence, Orientation, Shape, People
- Operators and Leaders decide on the next steps. Maybe 'How are we going to do a trial on this proposal'?
- Reflection

Because of its wide relevance, the vital topic of Questioning and Listening is mentioned throughout this book. See, for instance, under Root Cause Problem Solving, Section 32.3

Finally, a great quote from Bertrand Russell as inspiration:

'It is a healthy thing now and then to hang a question mark on things you have long taken for granted.'

Further reading

Michael Marquardt, *Leading with Questions*, Jossey Bass, 2005

Warren Berger, *A More Beautiful Question*, Bloomsbury, 2014

Tracy and Ernie Richardson, *The Toyota Engagement Equation*, McGraw Hill, 2017 (Chapter 6)

8   Psychological safety

8.1   Mistakes and Improvement

We all make mistakes. We would like to prevent mistakes, but what happens when they occur – opportunity or suppression?   A fundamental requirement for continuous improvement is that problems are surfaced, or realised.

There is a famous story of Tom Watson, IBM founder, who said to an employee who had just made a $10m mistake and expected to be fired, *'You must be kidding. I have just invested $10m in your education!'* By contrast, during the 8-year Iran/Iraq war, Saddam Husain's field commanders were afraid of reporting reversals on pain of execution leading to a major loss in Basra. Literally, 'Don't shoot the messenger!'

There is the saying that bad news does not travel upwards. So Psychological Safety is more than 'speaking truth to power'. It is actively encouraging truth to be spoken to power.

This whole area, now called Psychological Safety, has been extensively studied by Amy Edmondson of Harvard Business School. Psychological Safety is the lack of fear that bringing bad news to the boss will be treated positively not negatively. As she explains, Psychological Safety is *'People are not hindered by interpersonal fear'* and where *'they fear holding back their full participation more than they fear sharing a potentially sensitive, threatening or wrong idea.'* So people realise that their job may be lost due to economic or company competitiveness, but are not threatened through highlighting defects and mistakes. It is vital for leaders and managers to cultivate the characteristics of trust, respect, humility, listening, and psychological safety in any Lean-aspiring organisation. *'Approach problems as a joint collaborator'* and *'replace blame with curiosity'*, says Laura Delizonna.

In her book, *The Fearless Organisation*, Edmondson quotes three case studies - Volkswagen, Wells Fargo bank, and Nokia phones – where a culture of fear worked against the transmission of bad news. In the case of VW, a domineering boss encouraged an elaborate scheme to defraud regulators by the development of software that allowed diesel emission regulations to be bypassed. (The engines passed static testing, but failed in roadgoing conditions.) The eventual outcome for the company saw a third of its market value vanish. To these cases, the case of the Boeing B737 Max could be added. The culture of a focus on the financials downplayed the fears of engineers leading to two fatal crashes and a huge fine.

Motivation by threat such as 'I want a 30% increase in sales or you will all be looking for another job' are not only incompatible with Lean continuous improvement but ultimately highly dangerous. Edmondson believes that many managers believe that motivation by fear is effective, but in fact it ensures *'that (the) creativity, good process, and passion needed to accomplish challenging goals in knowledge-intensive workplaces'* is eliminated.

8.2   Improving Psychological Safety

Deming spoke about driving out fear. But how to do this? Here we draw on the excellent work of Amy Edmondson for inspiration. Briefly, action to improve psychological safety is required for all of the following:

- Purpose. What, exactly, is the expected response with respect to mistakes, accidents, and safety?

- Structure. What needs to be reported and what doesn't? Study the ease and speed of communicating mistakes.

- Understanding, responding and not over-reacting, to mistakes that are predictable, preventable, complex, and an 'intelligent mistake'. Classify those that one can learn from, and those that need to be fixed. Standards that need to be followed, and standards that can be questioned. The time frames for expected responses require consideration.

- Personal security. Managerial attitudes to mistakes and to being wrong.

- Behaviour. Clarify the types of behaviour that will always be supported, and the types of 'mistakes' that will get you fired. (e.g. Sexist remarks). Whistleblowing policy?

- Active listening and Questions (See previous section.)

- Discouraging and surfacing workarounds. (A workaround may gain 'brownie points' but they result in problems and mistakes being overlooked – or, worse, encouraged.)

- Being Humble. See Ed Schein's excellent book, *Humble Inquiry*, and the section on Humility.

- Overcoming the 'Sounds of Silence' (to quote Simon and Garfunkel). Methods include round-robin speaking opportunity at meetings, and direct asking.

- Voice. The choice of words used in an organisation with respect to mistakes is influential to actions. Words need to be consistent and unambiguous within the organisation. A mistake or an error? A failure or an accident? A stoppage or an opportunity? A setback? A deviation or a defect? A nuisance and a 'screw-up'?

- Appreciation and acknowledgement of mistakes that have been surfaced.

Further reading

Laura Delizonna, 'High Performing Teams need Psychological Safety', *Harvard Business Review*, 24 August 2017

Amy Edmondson, *The Fearless Organization*, Wiley, 2019

9   Leading and Mentoring

9.1   Leader Standard Work

In his excellent book, *Creating a Lean Culture*, David Mann says that there are four principal elements of Lean Management. These are Leader standard work, Visual controls, Daily accountability process, and Leadership discipline. Of these, Leader standard work has the 'highest leverage' and helps consolidate the other three.

The concept of Leaders having standard work was given by Imai in his 'Kaizen Flag' concept. (See the Improvement Chapter). The concept turns out to be one of the most effective means for Lean transformation. It is simple to describe, but requires sustained determination for success.

Leader standard work involves drawing up a timetable of activities that each leader in the organization, from team leader to Vice President needs to follow. Times are set aside and rigorously adhered to. A typical sequence is a series of regular meetings that from team meetings to senior management.

At each level, there is two-way communication with those present. Issues are raised for upwards communication. Briefings allow downward communication. Escalation is incorporated – each level decides what to bring to the next level.

General agendas are fixed, but other items can be raised. Meetings are of fixed duration – typically 10 minutes, always start on-time, and may be stand-up. Team meetings take place around a board where daily performance and issues are shown. A standard problem-solving method, like PDSA, is shown and used. Non-production visuals, like training and news are also shown. Meetings are not missed for 'crises'.

The best examples include a visual display of the meeting timetables, and visual signals to indicate attendance and satisfactory outcomes of the meeting by each level of management. Policy deployment matrices specific to the area appear on the board.

The procedure is followed in all areas – from canteen to design.

What leaders at all levels are expected to do, regularly, in a Lean transformation is a vital but often neglected aspect. Drawing up the level-by-level agendas and procedures and training the leaders on how to do the task well, is a powerful unifying force.

Further reading

Phil Rosenzweig, *The Halo Effect*, Free Press, 2007

Stephen Spear, *Jack Smith (A), (B), (C)*, Harvard Business School Case Study, 2004, 9-604-060

Edward Lawler and Christopher Worley, *Built to Change*, Jossey Bass Wiley, 2006

David Mann, *Creating a Lean Culture*, Second Edition, CRC Press, 2010

9.2   Lean Coaching and Mentoring

One of the most critical tasks leaders at all levels in organisations face today is in assisting their subordinates to achieve their full potential. A key component in making this happen is the leader's ability to develop coaching skills that can release their employee's capability in a structured, safe environment. In fact, according to Mike Rother (*Toyota Kata*, 2018) coaching has become so critical in developing both individuals and organisations, that it is likely to become a significant factor in career progression and consequently a subject at business schools. Kata coaching is discussed in the Improvement Chapter.

While coaching encompasses many activities and techniques borrowed from other disciplines such as counselling, psychology, education, and consulting it is well defined by Whitmore (1992) who suggests that: *'Coaching is unlocking people's potential to maximise their own performance.'*

Lean coaching is a fundamental requirement in creating an environment where sustainable continuous improvement can take hold and thrive.   In   a Lean   coaching relationship, the coach will ask questions that stimulate critical thinking skills and reinforce systematic approaches for improving how leaders lead, and how work is done.

An important point is that coaching allows empowerment, participation, and delegation. Why? Because coaching your team, allows them to take on more responsibility. This is exactly in line with the Lean concept of 'creating thinking people' (TPS = Thinking People System). So, coaching should be done by every Lean manager, not by the HR function.

Lean coaches are often referred to as a sensei. A lean sensei is a master teacher of lean tools, systems and principles. While similar in experience to a Black Belt or Master Black Belt in the Six Sigma methodology, the sensei is more focused on facilitating and teaching lean than on the actual practice of it. A lean sensei typically stands outside of an organization, allowing him or her objectively to see what needs to be done and to develop a true continuous improvement culture without having to worry about internal politics or strong personalities.

In Michael Bungay Stanier's excellent book *The Coaching Habit* he gives 'seven essential questions' Briefly they are a series of open questions beginning with 'What's on your mind?', followed by 'and what else?'. The questions are not a strict series but often involve cycling back to probe further. Resist giving your 'solution' but instead ask about the challenge. Another question is particularly interesting for fans of the '5 Whys': Stanier suggests asking What instead of Why, particularly 'what' followed by 'did you...' (Of course, the 5Whys does have its place. See later in this chapter). Later comes 'How can I help? And, throughout, never underestimate the power of silence and listening.

Training with Simulations

The use of Lean Games and Simulations for training purposes has become widespread. Although frequently enjoyed by participants, the effectiveness soon fades unless the lessons are soon translated to meaningful actions.

More effective are real simulations using full scale artifacts sometimes called Learning Factories. A Learning Factory refers to a small scale factory which closely mimics a real factory where participants can learn by doing. Companies such as Vauxhall, Nissan and Toyota have set up full scale training lines. At the University of Dortmund, students and participants must design and make a limited number of simple but real products, including programming robots and devising the workstation layout. At the University of Witwatersrand, in association with Anglo American Corporation a Learning Factory for mining trainees was established. A three tier learning approach is used. A Foundation stage introduces Lean principles using a Learning Factory, simulating a manufacturing environment. Participants then progress to Application with authentic mining experiences such as maintenance and drilling to bridge the gap between theory and practice. Lastly, the participants are expected to apply their learning in their work environment doing site-specific projects where they receive coaching.

Further Reading

Michael Bungay Stanier, *The Coaching Habit*, Box of Crayons Press, 2016. Note: Access the web site www.boxofcrayons.com for several resources.

John Whitmore, *Coaching for Performance*, Nicholas Bearley, 2017

Sarah Makumbe, Teresa Hattingh, Neville Plint, Dewald Esterhuizen, 'Effectiveness of Using Learning Factories to impart Lean principles in Mining employees', *Procedia Manufacturing*, 23, 69-74, 2018

John Bicheno, *The Lean Games and Simulations Book*, PICSIE Books, 2015

9.3 A Note on Intervention Theory and Change

Gerard Egan's widely used and proven intervention theory (used in counselling) has three stages that are very similar to mapping stages: current picture, preferred picture, action plan. The first stage is about skilled, active listening, to help uncover blind spots. No advice or critique is given, but empathy is required. Use open, not closed, questions. Recognise past achievement and give respect. The task is to reframe the perspective. Points of leverage are discovered. The second stage is jointly developing the destination. This is about exploration and developing commitment. It has three sub-stages – possibilities, change agenda, and developing commitment. Stage three also has three sub-stages: possible strategies, selection of best-fit strategies, and plan – what, when, where, how. Patience is required. Think of the tortoise and the hare!

Further, in participating or leading a mapping project always be a 'Humble Enquirer' and an 'Appreciative Inquirer'. This is largely a question of respect and humility. Many find that participation in a mapping project brings out unexpected strengths – from the point of view of the person himself or herself and from the team. Management by asking positive questions. Recognising there are many 'best ways'.

Humble Inquiry is very much about listening – carefully and empathetically, putting yourself on the same level as the speaker. Appreciative Inquiry is a bottom-up approach recognising the many good things (people and process) that are already in place, and building on them.

Both approaches are 'the way to go' for mapping. They involve skills that are built up slowly over time, but are very effective.

Further reading

Gerald Egan, *The Skilled Helper*, (Eighth, or later edition), Brooks Cole, 2007

Val Wosket, *Egan's Skilled Helper Model*, Routledge, 2008. (Actually a book for counselling people with problems but, hey, we all have problems!)

Sarah Lewis, et al, *Appreciative Inquiry for Change Management*, Kogan Page, 2009

Edgar Schein, *Humble Inquiry: The Gentle Art of Asking Instead of Telling*, Berrett-Koehler, 2013

10 Socio Technical Systems

10.1 The systems concept

Manufacturing and service operations are socio-technical systems that consist of an interplay of machines, technology and people. Addressing a subset of these only will invariably mean that change efforts will fail. Why? Because any change to the physical process is likely to affect the people in some form, and people that do not cooperate with a new technology can become bottlenecks in the same way as machines can. Implementing change means making changes to the social system, in a variety of ways. All need to be managed. In short, Socio-Technical Systems

The concept of 'socio-tech', so central in Lean, was born out of experiences with the British National Coal Board during the 1950's. The new technology of longwall mining had been introduced but with disappointing results. Fred Emery, Ken Bamforth and Eric Trist from The Tavistock Institute, University of London, were called in to investigate. They found that the new technology had broken the supportive social structures of the miners who, informally, supported one another by sharing information and warning of safety issues.

Hence was born 'Socio Tech' theory which holds that both social systems (plural, including people, structures, skills) and technical systems (plural, including machines, information, layout) need to be considered together when implementing change. This led Fred Emery (linking with famous systems guru Russell Ackoff) to further develop Systems Thinking, and Eric Trist (linking with famous psychologist Kurt Lewin- he of force field analysis and unfreezing, freezing, refreezing) to develop Job Enrichment, Job Enlargement, Job Rotation and Work Design.

The pioneering work has been followed through by, for example Hackman and Oldham, by Weisbord on work design, and by Enid Mumford on socio technical organizations. All of these are now mainstream concepts not just in Lean but in the wider world of work. A concept diagram is given in the figure.

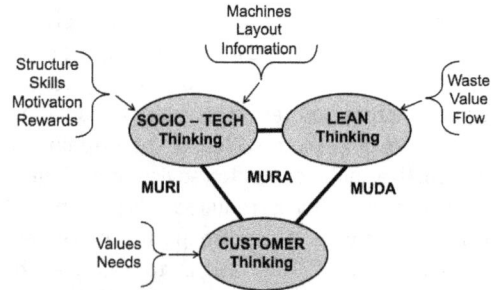

Socio-tech awareness is probably one of the most significant realisations relating to Lean over the past two decades. Toyota Japan has had to give recognition to socio-tech factors to counter alienation and recruitment difficulties with a younger workforce. Muda applies to the technical and human, and Muri (mental and physical overload) is highly relevant to the workforce.

Increasingly, customers are aware of the socio-tech situation of companies that they buy from. Witness the reactions to 'slave labour', child exploitation, and to the origins of some materials.

The key features that make up the 'social system' are:

Work organisation: team structures, shift patterns, hierarchies. What are the structures (formal and informal) around which work is organised? How are people grouped together, who is subordinate to whom? Are there natural work groups that can identify with a particular task outcome?

Responsibilities: line of reporting, scope for making changes. Here, the main question is the extent to which the responsibility for the process is devolved down to the team level. Giving the team members responsibility to improve the process is good practice, but this may mean effectively taking responsibilities away from the team leader or supervisor, who might see this as a demotion. The team leader's role will change. This was recognised in the 1940's with TWI's 'three legged stool' for the front line manager: job instruction (how to teach a job), job methods (how to assist improving a job), and job relations (how to work with the team).

Performance measurement: how are people rewarded, what incentives are given, what is the basis for promotion, etc. This is a critical point: 'what you get is what you measure'. People will try to look good on those performance measures that affect bonus, promotion, or status so make sure that the measures support the purpose. Use policy deployment to devolve measures down into the hierarchies of the organisation, using consensus building or 'nemawashi'.

It is very important to realise that making changes to any of the above means making changes to someone's working space and procedures, and not managing these changes will mean that the individual is likely to oppose, and in some cases even sabotage, the proposed changes.

Crucially, remember that extrinsic motivators ('carrots and sticks') such as pay lose their effect with time. Intrinsic motivators, self-drive, are more sustaining but require to be nurtured in the right environment. Dan Pink's excellent book 'Drive' is an important read for any Lean manager. Supported by much research, Pink explains that extrinsic motivators only are effective for those diminishing job categories where work is routine, unchallenging and directed by others. (Pink calls this 'algorithmic work'.) Surely this is not an aspiring Lean organisation! In a Lean organisation, what Pink calls 'Heuristic work' – experimentation and ideas - are required. Moreover, in job categories where the opposite is true, extrinsic motivators actually decrease creativity! Of course, this is true only beyond what Pink calls 'baseline rewards' and Herzberg called 'Hygiene Factors'.

10.2 Lean Organisation and Systems Thinking

Any Lean implementation needs to proceed from a systems perspective. But the tricky thing is how to integrate a systems (holistic) perspective with an experimental (reductionist) perspective.

An example: Manned flight was attempted unsuccessfully for hundreds of years. But Wilbur and Orville Wright realised that in order for manned flight to be successful, they needed to break the problem down into three sub-systems – lift, control, and thrust. Each of these required lots of separate experimental work – trial and error (or PDSA). A significant understanding of each was required before integrating. Then experiments had to be undertaken on the combined system. All previous attempts had failed due to treating the problem as a single problem without sufficient understanding of the sub-systems and how the sub systems needed to be combined.

So it is with Lean. Many Lean initiatives, as with manned flight, have failed because of insufficient identification and understanding of the sub-systems, but also have failed because the sub-systems have not been properly integrated. So there is a necessity for scientific (PDSA or kata-type) thinking as well as a necessity for holistic thinking.

Gestalt psychologist Kurt Koffa said that 'the whole is *other* than the sum of the parts', meaning that the whole takes on a different, independent identity. Thus, for example, the three elements of TWI (JI, JM, JR) become more powerful when joined together.

Deming, of course, was a great 'systems' advocate. The following system characteristics are all worthy of discussion and consideration:

- Seeking not to be *reductionist*.
- Systems: Wholes not Parts
- Understanding about relationships and interdependencies
- Feedback
- Engaging in multiple perspectives
- Reflecting on the *boundaries*

First, Systems Thinking is holistic. As Peter Checkland, UK Systems guru – a person who is more widely recognised in Japan than in his home UK – says, 'the systems approach seeks not to be *reductionist*'. 'Seeks' because it is quite hard to keep the end-to-end system in view when almost the whole business world, and the whole academic world, is organised by function. It is said that if you try to study a dog by taking all its pieces apart, the first thing you get is a non-working dog!

Lean is not about manufacturing or service but about the system that brings both of these together. Toyota learned their systems craft from, amongst others, Deming. Ohno saw economies of flow rather than economies of scale.

Believing that by optimising the individual parts will lead to optimising the whole represents, possibly, the greatest barrier to Lean. Thus, by buying a faster machine, automating the warehouse, or outsourcing a process step, may well look good from a departmental or vertical silo perspective, but may be a disaster from a Lean system perspective.

The systems approach means the focus should be on the organization or entity as *a whole before paying attention to the parts*. This is a very hard thing to do for most managers and other workers who have been brought up and educated in vertical silos. If we don't remain systemic we quickly get into the 'push down, pop up principle' whereby we solve one problem then another emerges because we have sub-optimised.

Sub-optimisation is very clearly visible when you look at the inventory profile across the

automotive supply chain. See the figure by Holweg and Pil. One can clearly see how JIT implementation has reduced inventories on site for the car manufacturers, yet this has only created an 'island of excellence' in the supply chain by pushing stocks into the component supply chain and the distribution system. As a result, stock is held at the most expensive level in the supply chain, accounting for three quarters of all capital employed in the supply chain. Remember to consider the Lean value stream, from raw materials to the end customer, to avoid such 'islands of (so-called) excellence'.

Water is a liquid at normal temperatures. Waters' constituents are the elements oxygen and hydrogen, which are gases. You can never understand the properties of water by studying oxygen and hydrogen. Likewise Lean and Lean tools. Like water, Lean is more than the sum of its components. Systems are in constant interplay with their environment – it is not obvious where the boundary is, what should be outsourced, the extent to which customers and suppliers are involved. Like ant colonies, systems adapt continuously when threatened. Systems evolve – like bugs combating insecticides. The question is how to recognise and kill off inappropriate tools whilst developing new and stronger ones.

Systems thinking recognises **relationships and interdependencies.** For example a sales force that takes orders without timing considerations can play havoc with lean schedules. And unilateral lean schedules can in turn play havoc with sales.

Hence **feedback**. This is an important distinction from unidirectional thinking that is unfortunately common in Lean. There are two kinds of feedback; positive and negative. Positive feedback loops are reinforcing like investment providing better service, in turn generating more funds through satisfied customers. Or good idea management encouraging yet more ideas. Or work overload (muri) that may cause errors leading to more

Inventory Profile of the Automotive Supply Chain

Source: Holweg and Pil 2004

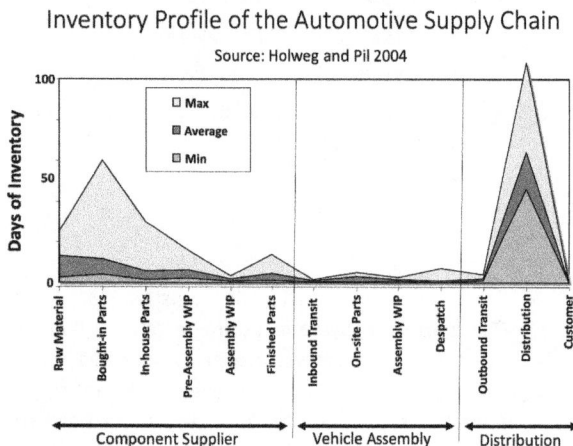

overload. Negative loops stabilise like a thermostat, or 'quality at source'. It is often helpful to draw out the connections between pairs of factors, showing if the link is positive (both factors move in the same direction like capital and interest) or negative where the factors move in opposite directions – like workload and attention to customers. Understand that there are many loops at work at any time. Some have 'lags', taking time to work through, such as building workforce commitment.

The great systems thinker C West Churchman was thinking about **multiple perspectives** when he said, 'the systems approach begins when you first see the world through the eyes of another'. In most Lean implementations there will be victims (maybe in status, pride, jobs, suppliers) and beneficiaries. Think of their viewpoint. In negotiation theory, this is known as Distributive Negotiation – how the pie is to be split. If the split is unfair it will not last. As Steven Covey said, 'seek win, win or walk away'.

Boundaries are, of course, central to both Lean and systems. Value streams rather than vertical silos.   But where should the value stream boundary be? Should some work be outsourced? What information flows are necessary for the value stream to work well, and who controls these flows? Boundaries, or focus, are a crucial consideration for effective problem solving – as in any A3. A problem boundary will often not coincide with an organisation function.

The great, and witty, systems thinker Russell Ackoff, Emeritus Professor at Wharton, talked about resolving problems (by discussion). Better is solving problems (incorporating a fact-based tools approach), but best of all is dissolving problems (by understanding the purpose of the system and using innovative thinking). Moving towards dissolving a problem often means redefining the problem boundary. Should you improve inventory control at a hospital by focusing on the dispensary or begin with the way in which medicines are prescribed, dispensed and distributed? Non-Lean practitioners resolve 'inefficiencies', beginning

Lean practitioners solve problems to remove waste, but the experienced Lean practitioner improves the whole system. Ackoff also said that a system is more about *interactions* than *actions* or *relationships and interdependencies*. In health care, for example, it is interactions between many professionals that count towards the success of a patient's recovery. In office systems it is the handoffs and rework loops that make the difference.

Remember, if you don't consider these systems insights, THE SYSTEM WILL BITE BACK. Is the Earth now fighting back climate change with fires, drought, and floods?

Further Reading.

Stafford Beer, *Diagnosing the System for Organisations*, Wiley, 1985

Peter Checkland, *Systems Thinking, Systems Practice*, Wiley, 1981

Robert Flood, *Rethinking the Fifth Discipline*, Routledge, 1999

John Gall, *The Systems Bible*, General Systemantics Press, 2006

Michael Jackson, *Critical Systems Thinking and the Management of Complexity*, Wiley, 2019

Barry Oshry, *Seeing Systems*, BK, 1996

Repenning and Sterman, 'Nobody ever gets credit for fixing problems that never happened', *California Management Review*, pp 64-88, Summer 2001.

Peter Senge, *The Fifth Discipline*, (Revised and Updated), Random House, 2006

Denis Sherwood, *Seeing the Forest for the Trees: A manager's Guide to applying Systems Thinking*,

Marvin Weisbord, *Productive Workplaces Revisited*, Jossey Bass, 2004

11 The Job Characteristics Model

Hackman and Oldham's Job Characteristics Model (JCM), developed in 1975 and expanded in 1980, continues to have great relevance for the design of effective jobs. An adapted version is shown in the figure. JCM applies equally to manufacturing and service.

The model can be linked to Expectancy Theory in as far as the underlying belief is that enriched jobs lead to job satisfaction, increased intrinsic motivation, and to improved work performance. Feedback is another link with Expectancy Theory. It is also linked to Herzberg's motivator-hygiene theory. Moreover, JCM is clearly in line with Organisation Development theory which proposes that to change a culture requires defining the desired actions and behaviours and then designing the work that reinforces such behaviours.

As shown in the figure there are three stages: Core Job Characteristics lead to improved Psychological States that in turn lead to good Work Outcomes. In 1980, 'moderators' were added. We have slightly modified and extended Hackman and Oldham's model following ideas from de Treville (2006) and Emiliani (2007).

Bob Emiliani made a useful distinction between what he called 'Fake Lean' and 'Real Lean'. Real Lean 'is the simultaneous deployment of both Continuous Improvement and Respect for People'. Respect is not the same as friendliness but does involve appreciation. Fake Lean is the employment of just one of these, typically 'the tools' of CI. Lack of respect for people, says Emiliani, is widespread and involves a focus, for instance, on 'earned hours, purchase price variance ...batch and queue thinking, firefighting, and the blame game'.

Importantly, all of the following core job characteristics can be influenced by management, particularly in a Lean environment.

11.1 Core Job Characteristics

- **Skill variety.** A good job requires having a variety of different activities and challenges, and would involve the use of several different skills. This can be achieved by job rotation, involvement in

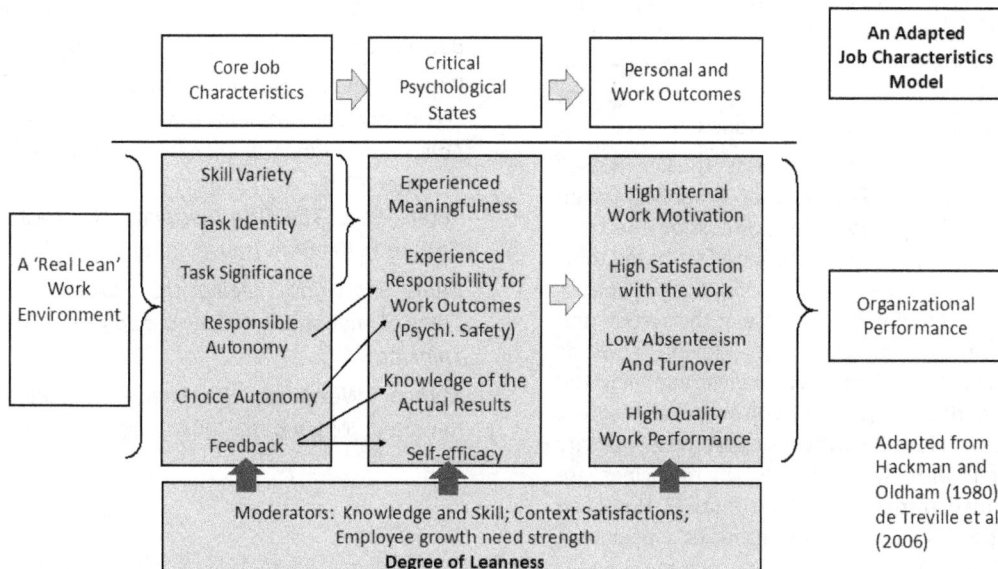

Moderators: Knowledge and Skill; Context Satisfactions; Employee growth need strength
Degree of Leanness

Adapted from Hackman and Oldham (1980); de Treville et al (2006) team meetings, 'quality at source', and participation in improvement.

- **Task Identity.** As far as possible a job should involve a complete job, start to finish. It is not necessary for a person to actually carry out all the tasks to make a product, but participation as a team member in a recognisable aspect or distinct stage is desirable. Manufacture of a subassembly, field maintenance, a class teacher, and customer support are examples. Unlike Charlie Chaplin in 'Modern Times', not a small, repetitive task with little link to the wider product or service.

- **Task Significance.** The job is seen as having substantial impact on success. Recall the story of the NASA toilet cleaner seeing his job as helping to get a man to the moon. The famous CEO of Scandinavian Airlines, Jan Carlsson, emphasised 'moments of truth' that involved every employee playing an important role in the customer journey. Carlsson emphasized that a single negative moment of truth could lose or win customer loyalty.

- **Autonomy** (here subdivided into Responsible Autonomy and Choice Autonomy) involves substantial own responsibility, for instance, for quality and meeting the schedule and timing – without close supervision. Standard work should not be limiting, but be seen as a platform for further improvement. For responsible autonomy there would need to be some flexibility perhaps with respect to buffer inventories, and recognition of inevitable variation. Utilization as a percentage of takt time (where used) should be less than (say) 90%, so as to avoid instability. (See Section 4.2 referring to Queues and utilization.) Choice autonomy would recognise a worker's variety of skills and allow sensible adjustment to changing circumstances, again without close supervision. Lateral task assistance, including the sort of mutually supportive team activities observed by Emery and Trist in their 'socio tech' studies, would be encouraged. The role of the supervisor or manager would be to facilitate flow and improvement, rather than act as 'controller'.

- **Feedback** on work carried out needs to be given to the worker from a variety of sources – the job itself, from supervisors, and from co-workers probably from further downstream. Such feedback needs to be constructive. Classic stories tell of Toyota managers thanking workers for stopping the line when a problem becomes apparent.

Critical Psychological States

- Experienced meaningfulness of the task stems equally from Skill Variety, Task Identity, and Task Significance. The three are equally weighted.

- Experienced responsibility for work outcomes stems from Responsible autonomy and Choice autonomy. We could add, following the Trilogy model (See Chapter 39), a climate of Psychological Safety as a Critical Psychological State.

- Knowledge of the actual results stems from feedback

- Self-efficacy is a worker's belief in the effectiveness or impact on him- or her-self of the work itself.

Personal and Work Outcomes

All the critical psychological states, when positive, together influence High internal work motivation, High satisfaction with the work, Low absenteeism and turnover and High-quality work performance.

Moderators

Hackman and Oldham later introduced Moderators as a recognition that there were other factors involved. Not all workers want the same levels of work outcomes. Perhaps there is a lack of resources or skill capability (knowledge and skill). Many stories tell of people whose real satisfaction lies outside of work, say with the kids' football team. Others perhaps are dissatisfied with salary, supervision, or working conditions. Note here Herzberg's 'Hygiene' factors. Stress and frustration? (Context satisfaction). Yet others have varying degrees of need and of interest and opportunities to learn (Employee growth need and strength). Note here links with Maslow's hierarchy or needs.

De Treville and Antonakis used the six job characteristics to derive what they called the Degree of Leanness. Thus, when all 6 are low the job is 'too Lean'; when the characteristics are a mix between high and low the job is 'somewhat right'; and when all characteristics are high the job is 'just right'.

The mix of Personal and Work Outcomes leads on to Organizational Performance. Lawler and Worley's concepts are relevant. They maintain that there are three primary organizational processes which contribute to organizational effectiveness. The sequence is important. First, Strategizing (a process which establishes 'strategic intent'). Second is Creating Value through competencies and capabilities. Third, Designing the structures and jobs that enable the organization to achieve effectiveness.

A note on Job Characteristic types

Job rotation is the process by which employee roles are rotated laterally in order to promote flexibility in the working environment.

Job enlargement is the process of allowing employees to determine their own work pace (within limits), to self-inspect the product, and be responsible for their own machine maintenance, their own workplace, including 5S, and the maintenance and improvement of standard work, all within certain limits.

Job enrichment allows a degree of autonomy in the planning and execution of work. This may include tasks formerly undertaken by people from higher levels. There is greater responsibility for the complete job outcomes. Participation in scheduling or TPM may be examples.

11.2 Criticisms and Extensions of the JCM

The criticisms of Hackman and Oldham's Job Characteristics model include ignoring organization structure, ignoring extrinsic rewards such as pay, as well as ignoring some intrinsic elements such as participation. Nevertheless, JCM remains probably the most significant and widely used model for job design.

More recently, in the light of changes in work organisation such as autonomy over work hours, service working, and emotional and social pressures, Parker reported that Morgeson and Humphrey added an additional 15 job characteristics covering knowledge motivation (e.g., problem-solving demands), social characteristics (e.g., social support), and contextual characteristics (e.g., work conditions). These additional factors explained 34%, 17%, and 4% respectively of the variance in job satisfaction. Other studies, reported by Parker showed that for a large sample of UK workers, individual autonomy was more strongly correlated with well-being and satisfaction than participation in a semiautonomous work group. But participation in a semiautonomous work group was better for learning.

There are other studies which reported that teams with high task interdependence perform better with high levels of team autonomy, whereas low-interdependence teams perform better with high levels of individual autonomy. Further, Parker reported that at Toyota NUMMI 'motivation arguably does not come from job autonomy; rather, employees are motivated by participative leadership, extensive training, employment security, engagement in continuous improvement, and other such positive features of the work context. The enabling context, combined with a clear understanding of the organization's mission, allows employees to experience identified motivation, that is, the internalization of values.' Further, de Treville and Antonakis similarly argued that 'a lack of autonomy over work timing and methods can be compensated for by other positive aspects of work design, including high levels of accountability (because employees can influence decisions), high skill variety and task identity (because employees are involved in repair and improvement), high levels of feedback (because employees have access to information), and high work facilitation (because lean production emphasizes the removal of obstacles to help performance).'

Further Reading

Bob Emiliani, *Real Lean*, Centre for Lean Business Management, 2007

Richard Hackman and Greg Oldham, *Work Redesign*, Addison Wesley, 1980

Sharon Parker, Beyond Motivation: Job and Work Design for Development, Health, Ambidexterity, and More, *Annual Review of Psychology*, 65:661-91, 2014

Suzanne de Treville and John Antonakis, 'Could Lean Production job design be intrinsically motivating? Contextual, configurational and levels-of-analysis issues', *Journal of Operations Management*, 24, pp 99-124, 2006

12 Managing the Change Process

There are several models how to implement change successfully. In this chapter we will focus on a select number of established models that we feel are useful in the context of a lean transformation.

12.1 Lewin's Change Models

At the most basic level, there is Kurt Lewin's famous 'unfreeze, change, re-freeze' model. The key point here is that each change process has three stages:

1. **Unfreeze**, whereby a situation is created that allows for changes to be proposed and discussed, and a stage that clearly communicates the objectives of the forthcoming change to the organization.

2. **Change**, where the actual changes are implemented. Again, clear communication about what is happening, and about the status of the project are crucial.

3. **Re-freeze**, whereby the status quo is 'frozen' and established as the new way of doing things. It is important to have a period of stability after every change, so that stability is regained. In the Deming cycle, this is referred to as 'holding the gains'. It is vital to create a stable process at the end of the change project, and to establish the new procedure as 'the way things are done' before embarking on a new change project. But, in today's dynamic environment, perhaps a better phrase is 'Remain slushy'.

Another seminal concept from Kurt Lewin is his **Force Field Analysis**, from the 1930's. It is a simple but powerful tool for change. Draw a vertical line on a board. List and explain the forces for change. Open a discussion on the forces working against change. Do this level by level. Listen genuinely. It is a method that incorporates humility and respect.

Consider the difference between *attitude* and *behaviour*: you can change behaviour in 10 seconds by setting the right incentives -- but changing attitude takes much longer. Thus it is key to firmly install the 'new way'. Remember the experience of Chrysler in the 1990s, when they implemented Japanese manufacturing techniques in their plants, and amongst others, installed Andon cords so workers could stop the line if a problem occurred. After four months the line had not been stopped a single time — not because there had not been any problems, but simply because workers were afraid of stopping the line, as this was a punishable offense prior to the 'change'!

Also make sure to measure the before and after process performance, to provide the empirical evidence that the new way is indeed the better way to go. On many occasions there will be a great temptation to go back to the old ways and having facts to show can help prevent that from happening.

There are 4 C's that underlie all successful change management programmes:

1. **Commitment:** empathy and support from the top level that signals that the change effort is serious and long-term.

2. **Communication:** change is often perceived as a threat, so clear and frequent communication is key to dissipate as much uncertainty as possible

3. **Co-production:** involvement of people concerned. Those affected by the change need to feel ownership of the new process, as otherwise there is a great temptation to revert back to the old ways.

4. **Consistency:** or 'sticking at it'. People need to understand that this is not just a

fad that will pass, but that you are serious.

These must be present at all times – and thought they might sound basic, if you manage to stick to these four simple concepts then you are halfway there!

Other changes models that might be useful include Ted Hutchin's, who usefully talks about five distinct stages (that he refers to as the Constraint Management Wheel of Change) – gaining consensus on the need, gaining consensus on the direction (of change), gaining consensus on the benefits of the solution, overcoming all reservations, making it happen.

12.2 The Change Iceberg

Several authors, Peter Scholtes (1998), Keki Bhote (2003), Bob Emiliani (2007), and Peter Hines et al (2008) use the analogy of the iceberg to explain Lean (and Six Sigma) change. Above the surface are the visible tools, layout, and processes. The official roles, responsibilities, plans, and standards. Below the surface lie the hard-to-see behaviours, leadership styles, and strategies. Scholtes makes the point that this informal organisation, having it's own styles, values and communication links (that are often a residual of history), is what largely determines the individual worker's experience or 'culture'.

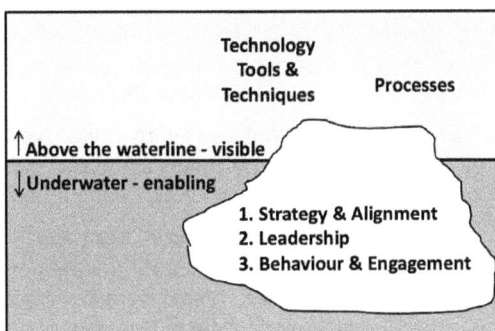

Technology Tools & Techniques

Processes

↑Above the waterline - visible

↓Underwater - enabling

1. Strategy & Alignment
2. Leadership
3. Behaviour & Engagement

Hines maintains that 'below the waterline' a vital part is alignment of policy and measures. This is done via Hoshin Deployment (See Chapter 40). The Hoshin Deployment procedure of by-in and consultation certainly helps with communication and alignment. And Policy Deployment relies on an appropriate policy actually being deployed.

12.3 Value Stream Mapping as Change Catalyst

In *Learning to See*, Rother and Shook discuss Current State, Future State and Action Plans as the trilogy in mapping and transformation. These three are also the basics of a change management programme, and is similar to Kurt Lewin's model.

Current State. The need for change must be recognised. The 'why'. This involves benchmarking current performance and identifying gaps.. Then the need to change must be communicated. Not just communicated, but explained and discussed in detail.

Future State. Where we are going must be explained. The vision. What must be changed. 'Without a vision the people perish' says the Bible. Great visions get everyone on board 'Getting a man to the moon and returning him safely to Earth before the end of the decade', said Kennedy (leading to even the toilet cleaner saying that his job was to help get someone to the moon). On the other hand, said Alice, 'Would you tell me, please, which way I ought to go from here?' 'That depends a good deal on where you want to get to', said the Cat. 'I don't much care where' said Alice. 'Then it doesn't matter which way you go', said the Cat.

Action Plan. The plan to get there must be agreed. The 'how' and 'when'. Another of Stephen Covey's habits is essential here: seek 'win win'. In this book we have emphasized identifying stable and unstable zones. The Action Plan should focus primarily on the unstable.

12.4 Common Problems with Change Programmes

The errors that can occur and severely hamper any major change programme are plentiful. While not exhaustive, John Kotter provides a very good list of common errors. Here, we list and comment:

1. **Not establishing a great enough sense of urgency.** Poor financial results get people's attention, but don't be paralysed by the wealth of options available on how to proceed. Getting a transformation programme started requires the cooperation of many individuals. Without motivation people won't help and the effort is likely to fail.

2. **Not creating a powerful enough guiding coalition.** Major change programmes need top-level support, but that in itself is not sufficient. In successful transformation, the chairman or CEO come together with a handful of divisional managers, plus middle management that will lead change in the respective departments, to develop a shared commitment to improvement through change.

3. **Lacking a vision.** The guiding coalition needs to develop a shared vision that is easy to communicate and appeals to all stakeholders, customers, shareholders and employees. Think about the next five years, and go beyond the numbers!

4. **Undercommunicating the vision by a factor of ten.** Transformation is impossible unless the hundreds or even thousands of employees affected are willing to help, possibly even making short-term sacrifices. However, no one will make sacrifices unless they believe that useful change is possible. Make sure your communication is credible and regular, and remember: you cannot overcommunicate!

5. **Not removing obstacles to the new vision**: transformations frequently hit large obstacles that middle management or employees are unable to move out of the way. Make sure that there is a communication link upwards, and that these 'elephants' are moved out of the way.

6. **Not systematically planning for, and creating short-term wins.** Large transformations take time, so in order not to lose momentum make sure you put in place short-term goals, and celebrate their achievement! People need to see compelling evidence of change with 12 months that the new journey is producing results, otherwise they will lose confidence.

7. **Declaring victory too soon.** After the first battles have been won, the results will come in, and there will be a temptation to declare the war over. But remember, it takes seconds to change behaviour, but years to change attitude. The changes need to sink in deeply in the company's culture in order to sustain!

8. **Not anchoring changes in the corporations' culture.** Change sticks when it becomes 'the way we do things around here'. New behaviours need to be rooted in social norms and shared values. The two ways to achieve that are to make a conscious attempt to illustrate how the new way of doing things has improved performance, and secondly make sure that the new generation of senior management embodies the new vision. Promote selectively based on criteria that support the new approach!

And specific to Lean transformations, Mike Rother, co-author of the *Learning to See* mapping book gives five pitfalls of implementing Lean:

1. **Confusing techniques with objectives.** This book has also made the point that Lean is not tools.

2. **Expecting training to make Lean happen.** Mike says this is 'pure bunk'. You need to change the system. (Recall here Deming's 94/6 rule whereby 94% of problems stem from the system – that only management can fix, and only 6% from operators).

Change cannot come purely from the bottom.

3. **Leading from the office, via plans, maps and charts.** Mike makes the point that Lean can only be achieved through Gemba (he does not use the word but means it).

4. **Relying solely on Blitz workshops.** Issues here are the lack of the big picture, sub-optimisation and sustainability. (Refer to the Kaizen Events section)

5. **Quitting after failures or too early.** As Zorba the Greek said, 'Nothing works the first time!'

To these five we can add a few of our own:

6. **Management commitment.** An old cliché perhaps, but it is difficult to think of a successful Lean transformation that has not had real commitment and involvement from the top. Sending out a clear signal helps – like insisting, as Koenigsaecker did, that directors participate in Kaizen events.

7. **Cherrypicking.** Pursuing a fairly random selection of tools in a fairly random selection of locations. Changeover reduction here, 5S there, mapping everywhere but with little follow through. Often these follow from the latest conference, book or meeting.

9. **The 'We are different' attitude** – so we need to re-invent our own system.

10. **The 'We can do it ourselves' notion.** Toyota did it themselves, but it took them two decades with some exceptional people. Ohno made almost no progress for a decade! Can you wait? Are you confident that you have the people, and that they will be around in a decade? Ultimately you can only do it yourself, but you will need guidance. A problem is that a fair proportion of Lean consultants have limited exposure outside of a small area. Even ex-Toyota people have crashed in environments that they know little about.

11. **Not thinking that '80% is greater than 100%'**, meaning that a set of decisions 80% correct but bought into by all will be better than an optimal 100% correct solution imposed by the 'experts'.

12. **Lack of full-time facilitation.** Most companies will need a Lean promotion office to keep the momentum going.

Further reading

Peter Checkland, Systems Thinking, Systems Practice, Wiley, 1973

John Kotter, Leading Change. *Harvard Business Review*, 2007, Vol. 85 Issue 1, p. 96-10

Peter Hines, Pauline Found, Gary Griffiths, Richard Harrison, *Staying Lean*, Second Edition, CRC Press, 2011

Daniel Pink, Drive: The Surprising Truth about what Motivates Us, Canongate, 2010

Peter Scholtes, *The Leaders Handbook*, McGraw Hill, 2008. (Scholtes was a friend of Deming who advocated extrinsic motivation decades ago.)

13 Engagement

Employee Engagement has emerged as a central concern for Lean Transformation success. A practical definition of employee engagement is given by MacLeod and Clark (2009) in their report to the U.K. government:

'Engagement is about creating opportunities for employees to connect with their colleagues, managers and wider organisation. It is also about creating an environment where employees are motivated to connect with their work and really care about doing a good job … It is a concept that places flexibility, change and continuous improvement at the heart of what it means to be an employee in the twenty-first century workplace.'

In practice, employee engagement levels have over the past decade remained disappointingly low in organisations worldwide. Gallup's 2017 report 'State of the Global Workforce' stated that '85% of employees worldwide are not engaged or are actively disengaged in their job', but 'in the best managed companies' as many as 70% of employees are engaged.

Dominic Bria has suggested five conditions for engagement:

1. Employee perceptions of the opportunities available for personal development in the form of cross-training and other learning that might lead to job variety, value to the company, and possible advancement.

2. Consistent publicly expressed appreciation from leaders and managers for ideas, work, and other contributions from employees.

3. Employee perceptions of the relative availability of the tools, training, direction and knowledge required to meet the work demands placed upon them.

4. The extent to which an employee is able to make meaningful decisions regarding their work.

5. Understanding of how their tasks help the organization accomplish its goals.

A research study carried out in Lake Region Medical by Noel Hennessay between 2014 and 2018 identified a significant link between

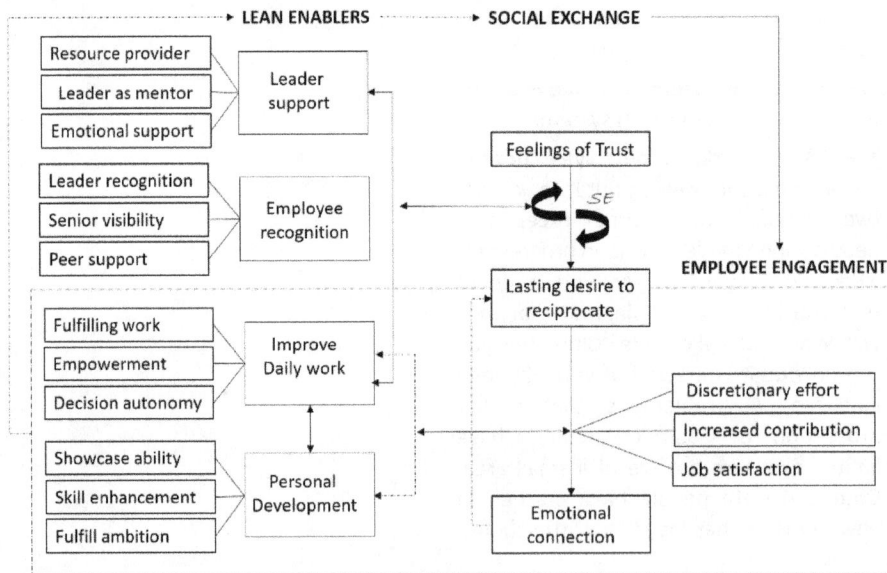

involvement in continuous improvement activity and employee engagement through a process of social exchange. Social exchange is typically demonstrated in both parties displaying a sense of loyalty, feelings of trust and a desire to reciprocate for real or perceived favours.

Within the CI process there are four key enablers which can become a catalyst for increased engagement. See the figure above.

The first and most significant of these is the role played by the leader in supporting the individual through the CI process which generates feelings of trust, loyalty, and a sense of obligation. The second revolves around the recognition that employees receive from their involvement in CI. This begins when the manager selects the individual from among their peers. Then, and as the project progresses, more recognition comes in the form of presenting updates at cell meetings or presenting the completed project to members of management and other visitors. The third relates to how the CI process can result in improvements to the employee's daily work, with social exchange developing as decisions and responsibilities are delegated to the employee. The final enabler is the opportunity for personal development that involvement in CI provides. This has special resonance for employees whose work is standardised. Consider for example a front-line assembly employee carrying out highly standardised work. That employee may have tremendous potential and great ambition, but no opportunity to display it.

When employees are involved in CI their job satisfaction levels increase significantly. This arises from the pride and achievement they get in their own personal development and the pride of completing the projects or initiatives. The organisation also benefits through the wider implementation of improvement and cost saving ideas. Another major benefit is the

shift in mind-set where engaged employees are now actively looking for opportunities to remove waste in the knowledge that their opinions are valued and will be listened to.

13.1 The Cathedral Model of Engagement

Frank Devine of Accelerated Improvement has had considerable success with his Cathedral Model for Lean culture development. The model has been used by several Shingo Prize winners (Gold, Silver, and Bronze.) in Europe.

As the name suggests the model is a sort-of House of Lean, but specifically about people. However, it is not a diagram but a set of practices that must be carried through. It is called the Cathedral Model after a bricklayer who is building a cathedral – not just building a wall that could be anywhere.

The model is generic and Devine adapts each implementation to the specific circumstances by involving large numbers of staff in a participative dialog. At its base are values and 'behavioural standards'. Values come from the organisation itself – for example Johnson and Johnson's Credo that is a one page statement beginning with 'our first responsibility is to the doctors, nurses and patients, to mothers and fathers and to all others who use our products and services'. The credo goes on to mention company responsibilities covering employees, communities and stockholders. Behavioural standards are then developed by employees at each site. They are

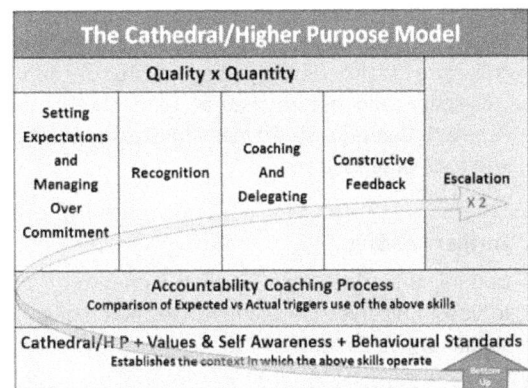

The Cathedral/Higher Purpose Model

Quality x Quantity

| Setting Expectations and Managing Over Commitment | Recognition | Coaching And Delegating | Constructive Feedback | Escalation X 2 |

Accountability Coaching Process
Comparison of Expected vs Actual triggers use of the above skills

Cathedral/H P + Values & Self Awareness + Behavioural Standards
Establishes the context in which the above skills operate

Bottom Up

concise statements that have to be bought-into by all. They are specifically 'bottom-up' not top-down, developed together with employees and unions, so are not 'lip-service' and become the daily expected behaviours. For example a standard such as 'Listen to people, involve them, and appreciate what they have done' is an outcome of mass participation, not by consultation or negotiation.

Upon this foundation is built the Cathedral's central pillars of Recognition, Coaching, and Constructive Feedback. In short, this puts specific meaning to the oft-used word 'Respect'. The outer walls are Expectations and Escalation.

Expectations are set, bottom-up, through behavioural standards and values, and top-down though managerial goals – perhaps through policy deployment. Leader standard work plays a role here. The employees themselves manage recognition, coaching, and feedback. Time needs to be set aside for each of these. Recognition involves primarily intrinsic rather than extrinsic motivation, as discussed by Pink in the last Chapter. Time should also be allowed for experimentation and initiative, or else improvement will not happen. All of these are managed visually where possible. Visual is the mechanism that drives continuous improvement. The other wall is Escalation, where an agreed procedure is in place where things go wrong. Note here the Deming 94/6 rule about problems most of which lie with the system rather than the person. But, occasionally, escalation may involve a problematic person.

Note: The inspiration for this section is from our colleague Frank Devine who, at Buckingham University, and before that at Lean Enterprise Research Centre, assisted many Masters students and their organisations.

Further Reading

Dominic Bria, 'Best Ways for Manufacturers to Boost Employee Engagement' posted on blog. shingo.org on 21 March 2018

Teresa Amabile and Steven Kramer, *The Progress Principle: Using Small Wins to Ignite Joy, Engagement, and Creativity at Work*, Harvard, 2011

Frank Devine and John Bicheno, 'Creating Employee Pull for Engagement', *Proceedings of the 6th European Lean Educator Conference*, Springer, 2020

Frank Devine, *Rapid Mass Engagement*, McGraw Hill, 2022

Noel Hennessey and John Bicheno, *Human Lean*, PICSIE, 2021, (Chapter on Engagement and Applications)

13.2 The Adoption Curve and Key People

Various writers have discussed an adoption curve covering the range of employees from early adopters to 'anchor draggers' This has merit in thinking about people aspects of Lean implementation. Here an adaptation is given, derived from the Rogers Curve, but based on the author's experience (and background) is given. The figure shows a notional distribution of a workforce. Areas represent approximate proportions.

The Lean Champion is a farmer not a hunter. *Farmers* take the long view, and win in the long term. *Hunters* take the short view, get early gains but ultimately die out. Farmers are shepherds. Early adopters are found on the right hand side of the figure. These people are 'gung ho' for change. They require very little convincing. But experience shows that there are two sub-groups here. *Dogs* are faithful, but are also intelligent. This valuable group will be the core of the change initiative. By contrast, *Lemmings* are easily up for change, any change, and, in a sense, are not the people you want. ('If he thinks it is a good thing, then it must be a bad idea.') They leap in just too quickly, without thought. *Horses* are the key group. They need guidance from a Lean champion. They require to be trained, to be broken in. Horses are also intelligent. Most horses work well in teams. The strategy to be adopted with horses depends on the situation. In normal circumstances the rider is in control, and the horse will take instruction except in emergencies. When there are fences and jumping is required, horse and rider act synergistically – the trick is the right balance between guidance by the rider and initiative and judgement by the horse. On a mountain hike, however, the best strategy for the rider is to let the horse take most of the control, relying on it to pick out the safest path. *Sheep* can be led by riders with horses and dogs.

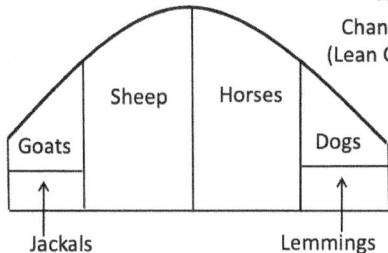

Change Agent
(Lean Champion)

Generally they cannot be relied upon to get there without considerable guidance. Shepherding is required. Sheep are multi-function providing wool and mutton. They are adaptive to a wide range of climates. Sheep can also be led to an extent by goats, either into the abattoir or into a lush field. (Note: Sheep is not a derogatory term – they are the backbone of much farming.) *Goats* are much more cautious. They have good reason to doubt, and some of those doubts are valuable insights. They climb trees and look around. But they can be made into valuable assistants. When they are convinced they are more useful than sheep. Goats lead sheep. Finally *Jackals* cannot be trained. They eat goats and sheep, and may scare horses. They are the true anchor draggers. Note that in this analogy, groups traditionally regarded as anchor draggers and early adopters both have sub groups. These sub groups need to be distinguished. Beware of lemmings. Listen to the goats – they may have good, thoughtful reasons for reluctance.

As an aside on what are here called Goats, Kegan and Lahey contend that a major reason why some people (and groups) are reluctant to change is 'competing commitments'. For example a manager is offered promotion but is committed to spending time with an aging relative. His superior then makes a 'big assumption' that the commitments are mutually exclusive. Destructive! To uncover this, Kegan and Lahey suggest that managers ask a series of questions. For instance, What would you like to see changed? Then, what commitments does your complaint imply? And, what are you doing that is keeping your commitment from being realised?, leading to working out a way to reconcile this big assumption with the change. Again, it's Covey – seek 'win-win, or walk away'.

Further reading

Robert Kegan and Lisa Lahey, 'The Real Reason People Won't change', *Harvard Business Review*, November 2001, pp 84-92. Reprint R0110E

Malcolm Gladwell, *The Tipping Point*, Abacus, 2000, Chapter 'The Law of the Few'

Everett Rogers, *Diffusion of Innovation*, Free Press, 1995

Edward Lawler and Christopher Worley, *Built to Change*, Jossey Bass Wiley, 2007

Mager and Pipe, *Analysing Performance Problems*, Pitman

Kurt Lewin, *Field Theory in Social Science*. New York: Harper and Row, 1951

PREPARING FOR FLOW

The topics in this section are the basic tools of Lean. All will be found to be essential over the course of a transformation and beyond. Together they help create stability. The tools in this pathway form a mutually reinforcing set. Their power grows exponentially as they become integrated. All are open-ended in as far as there will always remain further opportunities and improvements.

Takt time and activity times are basic building blocks for Lean flow. 5S provides the housekeeping basis, but also should encompass visual management. Visual management should be part of 5S, and this makes TPM and standard work more effective. One of the 5S's - perhaps the most important - is Standards. The 5Ss and particularly standards are closely related to the TPM methodology. 5S, standard work, and TPM are also the basis for fast, consistent changeover operations. Finally, demand smoothing allows all the others to be more effective. Together, the topics are the foundations for fast, flexible flow. In combination these topics are an effective attack on Muda (waste), Muri ('overburden' or difficult work), and Mura (unevenness). Beware: making 5S or TPM an end in itself! Implementation of the concepts below is never ending. Improvement is always possible.

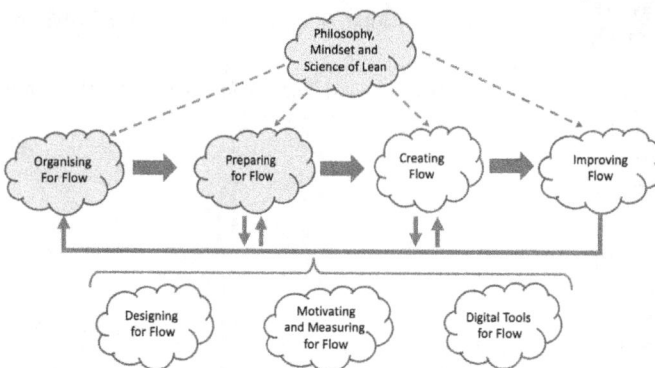

14 5S

5S is probably the most popular tool in Lean. But, should you start your Lean programme with 5S? Probably not!

There is the good news and the bad news: The good: it is apparently easy to do, usually has a positive impact on quality and productivity and sends out a powerful message that Lean 'has arrived' and is for everyone. The not so good: 5S, when too narrowly interpreted, can be a diversion from real priorities, can be seen as merely tidying up, and can give Lean a bad name though over-zealousness.

First, be clear of the motivation for 5S. If the place is a mess, and needs a clean-up, please don't say you need a 5S program. Say that you need to tidy up! Why? Because if you establish in the minds of your people that '5S equals clean-up' (and that is it), then you risk misunderstanding a very powerful concept, you risk project sustainability issues, and you may even risk that Lean is seen as something rather trivial – or worse – just a silly set of activities. (As indeed has happened in several companies, but spectacularly in various government offices.) Then, later, when the real needs for 5S (like reduction in variation, meeting the schedule, exposing problems, improving machine availability and performance, etc.) are recognised, THEN do 5S as a 'pull' activity.

The real objectives of a 5S program should be:

- To reduce waste
- To reduce variation
- To improve productivity

5S programs that work well are in situations where the need to achieve these three are well known and 5S is seen as the way to do it.

But 5S is also a mindset thing – changing attitudes from 'I work in an unorganised, messy office' to 'I work in a really well organised office where everyone knows <u>and can see</u> where everything is supposed to be and what when and how to do it.'

The classic 5S's are: **S**eiri, **S**eiton, **S**eiso, **S**eiketsu, **S**hitsuke. Most commonly these are translated into **S**ort, **S**implify, **S**can, **S**tandardise, **S**ustain, but many other synonymous terms have been used, see below.

A common alternative for 5S is the CANDO pneumonic – **C**lean-up, **A**rrange, **N**eatness, **D**iscipline, **O**ngoing improvement.

	Inventory	Suppliers	Computer Systems	Costing Systems
Sort	Throw out all dead and excessive stock	Select the best two suppliers in each category. Scrap the rest.	Delete all dead files and applications	Do you need all those costs and variances? Prune them!
Simplify	Arrange in the best positions	Cut all wasteful, duplicate transactions	Arrange files in logical folders, hierarchies	Cut transactions. Review report frequency. Incorporate o/head directly
Scan	Regularly review dated stock and ABC category changes	Improve supplier performance by supplier associations & kaizen	Clear out inactive files regularly	Audit the use made of costing reports and transaction size & frequency
Stabilize	Footprint, standard locations	A runner system, payments	Systems, formats	Adopt reporting standards
Sustain	Audit ABC, frequency of use.	Audit performance	Audit perform & response	Review and reduce.

14.1 Sort

Throw out what is not used or needed. The first step is to decide, with the team from the area, the sorting criteria – for example the team may decide that items that can kept at the workplace are

- items that are used every week
- items that are needed for important quick customer response
- items for health and safety

whereas less the frequently used are kept firstly in cupboards, and secondly in the storeroom.

Then the team needs to classify according to the sort criteria. Touch every item systematically. If it can be kept at the workplace, is the quantity correct? If never used, or in doubt, then red tag or throw out. A Red Tag is a label with the date; if no

one accesses it within a specified period it should be thrown out, recycled or auctioned. The sort stage should be done regularly – say once every six months, but as a regular activity not a re-launch of 5S. You know a 5S program is not working when it is really a frequently repeating sequence of 2S or 3S activities.

Be careful of over-zealousness and over-the-top. Within reason, permit some personal items to be kept at the workplace. Also permit personal discretion and location choice. (Readers may recall the laughable situation rightly reported with some ridicule in *The Times* of December 2006 showing a taped-up location for a banana on a desktop. If that is your manager's idea of what Lean is about, resign immediately!)

Some offices have been known to use Feng Shui to get the 'vibes' right. Is this OTT?

14.2 Simplify (or Set-in-Order or Straighten)

Locate what remains in the best place. A place for everything (using shadow boards, inventory footprints, trolleys, locating at right height, and colour matching equipment to areas – or simply good sensible locations.) Like a kitchen where the family knows the location of cutlery and plates and do not have to be told. Are drawers and doors really needed? The best location is the place where it is silly to put it anywhere else. And everything in its place (if not in place and not in use, a problem is indicated). The standard is The 'Dental Surgery'. Why? Because all can relate to that standard of excellence, and know the consequences of failure. Locate items by frequency to minimise stretching and bending. Repeat this stage whenever products or parts change. Use a spaghetti diagram for analysis. Ergonomic principles should play a role here, and an ergonomic audit may help. (There are many excellent, inexpensive books on office ergonomics – there is no excuse not to use them.) This stage starts the journey towards visual management: 'Galsworth's 6' : See next Chapter.

14.3   Scan (or Sweep or Shine or Scrub)

Keep up the good work. This includes physical tidy up, on an ongoing basis, and 'visual scanning' whereby team members are always on the lookout for anything out of place, and try to correct it immediately. Some companies adopt a 5 minute routine whereby operators work out a 5 minute clean-up routine for each day of the week such that by week end everything has been covered the required number of times. Designate exactly who is responsible for what and what the standard is. The stage will require suitable cleaning equipment to be suitably located and renewed. There may be a sign-off chart for routine cleaning. (By the way, have a standard procedure for the 5 minute clean-up routine.)

'Cleaning is checking,' means that these are integrated. You don't just clean up, you check for any abnormality and its root causes. The garage analogy is first clean up – this enables oil leakage to be identified. Continue to clean up any leakage that occurs. But then ask 'why is leakage occurring?' and decide what should be done for prevention. On your car you don't check oil, water, tyres, and tyre pressure every time you drive, but you do check them when you clean your car. Same principle.

Scan may also include calibrating, keeping track, observing, monitoring, looking out for wastes, lubricating, dusting, computer monitor cleaning, and routine servicing.

It would be good to engender the:

- 'Mary Poppins' effect – making clean-up fun, (lots of scope here, like cartoons), and the
- 'Tom Sawyer' effect – demonstrating to others that they are really missing out by not tidying up (!)

14.4   Standardise (or Stabilize or Secure)

Only now is it possible to adopt standard procedures. This is the real bottom line for 5S. See the sections on Failsafing and Standard Work. But 5S standards also need to be maintained. So develop standards for the first 3 S's. Standardising also includes measuring, recording, training, and work balancing.

Here, visual management becomes the norm. Without it is not proper 5S! (For more on this see the Chapters on Visual Management and Standard Work below.)

14.5   Sustain (or Self Discipline)

Everyone participates in 5S on an ongoing basis. Sustaining is about participation and improvement about making the other 5S activities a habit. Carry out audits on housekeeping regularly. Some award a floating trophy for achievement. Others erect a board in the entrance hall with current 5S scores. Yet others have a weekly draw out of a hat and then all first line managers descend on the chosen area to have a close look.

14.6   Safety

Some companies add a sixth S – SAFETY. Although good to emphasize, a good 5S program should stress safety as an aspect of each of the five stages. It may confuse to list safety separately. Safety procedures and standards should also be developed, maintained and audited as part of the programme. The removal of unsafe conditions should certainly be integral to 5S.

Some companies adopt regular walk about audits and competitions. The first line supervisor audits daily, the area manager weekly at random times, the section manager monthly and so on.

14.7   5S as Root Cause

5S lies at the root of many issues in service and manufacturing. All staff need to be sensitised to this fact, and be encouraged to make improvements as soon as possible – not to have to wait for some kaizen event. For example, in service, it is a 5S issue when:

- a nurse arrives at a patient in bed, or a repairman arrives at a site, and discovers that there is something missing,
- a document cannot be found,
- a surgeon encounters an unfamiliar layout in an operating theatre,
- customers ask for the location of an item in a supermarket or shop (or visual management) issue
- lecturers don't find working flip chart pens,
- a stationery store runs out of paper,
- ...and so on....

In all these cases it is no good just to correct the error. Management by sight is required. The situation must be highlighted and a simple non-bureaucratic procedure put in place to permanently solve the problem.

14.8   5S and Sustaining Improvements

Many companies now claim that they are doing 5S but are in fact doing 2S sporadically. Having no 5S sustainability is a waste, and the programme requires increasing effort to re-energise. The real productivity and quality benefit of 5S are in the later S's, particularly standardisation, not the relatively easy-to-do first two.

Hirano suggests a host of 5S activities, carried out at various frequencies: Amongst others:

- A 5S month, once a year(?), to re-energise efforts
- 5S days, one to four per month including evaluations
- 5S seminars by outside experts – with lots of photos.
- 5S visits to leading outside companies
- 5S patrols, following a set route
- 5S model workplaces (this has become popular in NHS hospitals)
- 5S competitions

- 5S award ceremonies
- 5S exhibits
- 5 minute 5S each day

Doing all this sounds like overkill, but putting a few in place has proved helpful in sustaining 5S.

14.9   Extending the 5S Concept

Perhaps less recognised, the 5S concept can be powerfully applied to information and information flow. Sort and simplify the information transactions that flow around the organization. Of course, it is appropriate to ask about e mail flow and to establish standardised rules about cc's and when to expect answers. But even more potent is to examine the decision processes. What is the minimum necessary information that is required for planning, scheduling, orders, invoicing, staffing, recruiting, and more? This overlaps with Lean Accounting (as opposed to Accounting for Lean), and with A3, but goes far beyond these. The saving and streamlining potential will often make physical 5S seem trivial. Sort should include not only wasted communication, but the time-accuracy trade-off (is 90% accurate in half the time not far better?). Simplify should include the best means of communication. (One Danish company uses data projectors to continuously project current progress into both factory and offices).

Scan includes the best way of updating. Standardise should cover all information flows.

Sustain: X% physical audits are OK, but what about auditing all transactions?

Further reading

Productivity Press Development Team, *5S for Operators*, Productivity, 2002

Hiroyuki Hirano, *5 Pillars of the Visual Workplace*, Productivity, 1995

Gwendolyn Galsworth, *Work That Makes Sense: Operator-led Visuality*, Visual Lean, 2011

15 Visual Management

Visual management, 'visuality' or 'control by sight', is a key theme in Lean operations. Visual management is the 'litmus test' for Lean – if you go into any operation and find that schedules, standard work, the problem-solving process, quality and maintenance are not immediately apparent, and up to date, there is an excellent chance that the operation is far off Lean.

Visual management should not be a topic in itself, but should be integrated into every Lean activity: 5S, cell design, inventory control, scheduling, design, to name just a few. Moreover, although visual is the prime focus, please don't ignore audio or even feel, such as vibrations (like your iPhone). Audio useful: At Toyota each robot cell has its own unique tune, which gets played over loudspeaker when there is a stoppage or problem. Maintenance engineers learn to listen out for the tunes they are responsible for. Tunes change with urgency.

Gwendolyn Galsworth, probably the world authority on the topic, defines a visual workplace as one that is '...self-ordering, self-explaining, self-regulating, and self-improving; where what is supposed to happen does happen on time, every time....because of visual devices.' And a 'visual device is a mechanism or thing intentionally designed to influence, guide, direct, limit or even guarantee our behaviour by making vital information available as close to the point of use as possible to anyone...who needs it without speaking a word'. Note the word 'behaviour'. 'Visuality', as Gwendolyn refers to it, begins with the prime question 'what do I need to know to do my (or the team's) work?'. She then uses 'six core questions' (similar to 'Kipling analysis'):

- visual where (correct locations, as in shadow boards, footprints)
- visual how (as in standardized work or single point lessons – including pictures)
- visual when (tasks need to take place, as in a Heijunka box or Kamishibai board)
- visual what (to be made or done, including dimensions, stages in idea boards, problems)
- visual who (as in tool responsibility, or Yamazumi boards)
- visual how much (as in kanban or a supermarket).

All of these help cut wastes in the form of time, paperwork, errors, miscommunication as well as encouraging detection of problems and idea generation. 'A picture is worth a thousand words'.

Galsworth uses an excellent analogy to a railway crossing to illustrate different levels of visual control:

- Visual indicator. Warning sign. No control. Labels.
- Visual signal. Flashing lights. Some power. Lights and sound when machines stop.
- Visual control. Automatic barriers. Significant power. Andon.
- Visual guarantee. Separation of road and rail track. Absolute power. Poka-yoke.

Visibility fits in well with several other Lean themes:

- Speed (no waste of time having to look for information), Improvement (progress should be for all to see, and celebrated).
- Up to date and clear schedules (via kanban, progress boards, automatic recording).
- Making problems apparent (via overhead Andon boards or lights).
- Involvement (clarity on who is doing what and who can do what).
- Teamworking (making visible the good work of teams, and skill matrix)
- Standardisation (keeping standards up to date by locating them at the workplace).
- Responsiveness (requiring quick response to maintenance and quality problems via for example a line stop chord or a red tag maintenance board).

Design is a fruitful area for good visuals. Donald Norman's classic text is a masterpiece, covering products, psychology, errors, and learning – to name just a few. Please read – an education!

A few examples of visual management follow. However, note that visual management should never succumb to 'visual clutter'. Too much will detract, so selectiveness is required.

- Machines: Transparent plastic guards and covers used wherever practical to enable operators and maintenance people to see the innards of machines.
- OEE charts placed next to machines or at team meeting areas; there should be four graphs – one for overall OEE and one each for the three elements of OEE. Below each graph should be kept a fishbone diagram with the contributing factors.
- Changeover times should be graphed routinely, to prevent slippage.
- The Heijunka box is a visual display of the status of the day's schedule.
- Kanban priority boards used where there is changeover (triangle kanban) give a continually updated display of the urgency of the next products to be made.
- Lights to indicate status, with the overhead Andon Board linked to computer to record stoppages for later analysis (not blame!)
- Management: Is it possible to have the production control and scheduling office on the shop floor?
- Cost, Quality, Delivery performance should be a central trio on display, possibly joined by Safety, Lead-time, and Days of Inventory.
- Line rebalancing charts showing planned cycle time, and with magnetic strips for each work element, kept in the team area.
- People: A skills matrix (or I L U O chart) indicates achievement from beginner to instructor. Operators shown on rows, tasks on columns.
- Employee suggestions board (note: not box!) – and showing progress of each idea

(submitted, considered, accepted, in progress, implemented).

- Mirrors with slogans such as 'You are looking at our most important source of ideas'
- Methods: Keep those standards and methods at the workplace!
- Materials: Don't forget to keep footprinting up to date.
- Maintenance: A maintenance 'red tag' board, showing all outstanding concerns.
- Money: There is a welcome tendency towards displaying company financial and sales data on the shop floor.
- Improvement: Keep a flipchart handy to note problems (which accumulate Pareto style)
- Storyboards, showing the standard stages in kaizen events, recent successes and current progress.
- 5S: Display area responsibilities and 5-minute clean-up plans. Use shadow boards. Label and organise. Use kitchen organisation, not 'garage' organisation. Display audit results and winners.

Galsworth makes the important point that visual management extends beyond the shop floor to the design of forms, to the presentation of information, to office layout, and to the home, together saving countless hours of waste spent searching and clarifying.

15.1 Cumulative Flow Diagrams

These have been used for many years in production control. The cumulative number or items, tasks or features is shown on the vertical axis against time on the horizontal axis. In Production Control the bottom line indicates cumulative demand and the top line indicates cumulative production. The vertical distance between the lines indicates inventory and the horizontal distance indicates lead time. An example is shown in the Demand Analysis chapter. In Agile software or project management, three or four cumulative lines are drawn: tasks added, in progress, completed, and sometimes tasks under review. The vertical gaps between the lines is a good indication of problems. Watch out for vertical line jumps (unexpected new tasks?) and plateaus (no progress? bottleneck?). There are many software versions.

15.2   Single Point Lessons

A useful and widely adopted procedure is the Single Point Lesson. These are found on the factory floor and:

- Focus on one single point for improvement
- Are highly visual – containing the steps, key points, and invariably a diagram or photograph
- Contain content that can be delivered in 15 minutes or less

- Address the main stages of learning – awareness, understanding, competence, ability to train others.

Note: See also the sections on Training within Industry (TWI) concepts that should be the foundation for Single Point Lessons.

Problem (Trouble shooting) Cards. These are 'what if' cards to cope with relatively rare but important contingencies. (What to do if the chuck breaks..) Most air force pilots are used to the idea of consulting a card in an emergency – so as to avoid potentially disastrous mistakes in a time of stress and crisis.

15.3   Communications Board

In virtually all Lean transformation situations, a Communications Board is a major device for improvement. It links directly with Lean philosophy, as it is a means of

- Communicating purpose, and ensuring consistency

Communications Board

- Problem surfacing and resolution
- Waste reduction
- Team-working

The Communications Board becomes the focal point for communication, review and problem solving. Every morning there is a meeting around the Communications Board. Communication is two way – from the group leader to the group and from the group to the group leader. A meeting should take less than 15 minutes – frequently 10 or less.

Charts that are shown on the board may include:

- **The Policy Deployment matrix**. This shows the aims, projects, measures and results for the area. It will also show how the area's activities relate to the wider organizational aims and projects,

- **Concern, Cause, Countermeasure (3C) chart** – any concerns should be raised and entered, and all outstanding concerns discussed at the daily meeting. Each stage of each concern should be dated. A standard methodology such as A3 could be used with the Communications Board showing the overall status. A3s relating to concerns could be in an area next to the board.

- **SQCDP (safety, quality, cost, delivery, productivity) boards** - with graphs, pareto analysis, and countermeasure trackers for each section

- **Short interval schedule control** - day by the hour with reasons for non-attainment

- **Idea boards** - showing progress with submitted ideas

- **Project progress boards** - showing activities started and complete against a movable vertical line indicating today's date

- **Yamazumi boards** - showing actions that must be done. Green is done, red is not.

- **Performance charts** – linked to productivity measures such as throughput. It is important that these are a source of problem identification and NOT a means of blame or competition.

- **Quality charts** – tracking problem areas, complaints, errors. Also as a means for improvement not blame.

- **Management audits** – where different levels of management are expected to visit the area at appropriate frequencies – for instance CEO once per year, appropriate director quarterly, departmental managers monthly, section managers weekly, team leaders daily. Each turns over a magnetic counter from red to green when the visit is complete. The re-set dates (green to red) are stated. The set of activities that each is supposed to cover is kept on clipboard next to the board.

- **Total Productive Maintenance / OEE charts**. See the separate section on this topic.

- **A skills matrix** – showing stages of development, learner, can do under instruction can do working alone, instructor - against each skill category. These are often shown in a PDCA format cycle with the quadrants coloured in as the skill level is attained. A skills matrix is not just a 'factory thing' – it has many uses in professional environments, from lecturer to engineer, to accountant.

- **A task allocation chart** – who is working on what projects. Often done with post its in a Design or Agile software environment. The post its are kanbans, preventing overload as well as highlighting problems.

- A leave roster

- General company notices

Each chart would have a designated person responsible for chart maintenance and updating. This needs to be done by a designated time, before the daily meeting.

Don't forget simple things like having a marker attached to a string.

Note: All of these boards should indicate current status by means of prominent red and green dots.

Rules for Visual Management Team Meetings

Rules should be established and displayed for daily meetings held at the boards. Typical rules include:

- Standing, no sitting
- Attendance
- Stick to time
- Time limit for any speaker
- Priorities must be fixed and made clear
- Boards must be updated before the meeting
- One speaker at a time
- Specific actions – 'Do' not 'Try to'.

Further reading

Michel Grief, *The Visual Factory*, Productivity, Portland, OR, 1991

Gwendolyn Galsworth, *Visual Systems: Harnessing the Power of a Visual Workplace*, AmaCom, New York, 1997

Gwendolyn Galsworth, *Work That Makes Sense: Operator-led Visuality'*, Visual Lean, 2011

David Sibbert, *Visual Meetings*, Wiley, 2011

Eric Johnson, The Elements of Choice, One World, 2022

Donald Norman, *The Design of Everyday Things*, MIT Press, 2013

16 Standard Work and SOPs

Standard work aims at creating processes and procedures that are repeatable, reliable, and capable. It is the basis for improvement.

Three useful quotations set the scene:

'To standardise a method is to choose out of many methods the best one, and use it. What is the best way to do a thing? It is the sum of all the good ways we have discovered up to the present. It therefore becomes the standard. Today's standardisation is the necessary foundation on which tomorrow's improvement will be based. If you think of 'standardisation as the best we know today, but which is to be improved tomorrow' - you get somewhere. But if you think of standards as confining, then progress stops.' (Henry Ford, Today and Tomorrow, 1926).

'In a Western company the standard operation is the property of management or the engineering department. In a Japanese company it is the property of the people doing the job. They prepare it, work to it, and are responsible for improving it. Contrary to Taylor's teaching, the Japanese combine thinking and doing, and thus achieve a high level of involvement and commitment' (Peter Wickens, Former HR Director, Nissan UK). But note, the team leader or coach still has a very active role to play.

'A proper (standard) procedure cannot be written from a desk. It must be tried and revised many times in the production plant. Furthermore, it must be a procedure that anybody can understand on sight. For production people to be able to write a standard work sheet that others can understand, they must be convinced of its importance.' (Taiichi Ohno).

Ohno believed that only by preparing their own job instructions could operators together with team leaders comprehend the details of their work and know why they should have to do things that way, and only then would they be capable of pondering better ways to do the work. This is the basis of kaizen. In other words actually making operators and supervisors write work instructions means that they have to think about the way that the work is done. This sentiment has much in common with TWI job breakdown analysis.

From the first quote we learn that a standard is not static, but improves over time. From the second we learn that a standard is not imposed from on high. From the third we learn that standards are inherently practical. A good standard comes out of a bottom-up questioning culture – ever seeking a better, simpler, safer way to do a task – not a top-down imposed way of working. If you have no standard you cannot improve, by definition. So standards are part of PDSA.

There is sometimes confusion over standards, standard work, standardized work, and standard operating procedures (SOPs). Arguments about standards – yes or no – are simply fatuous.

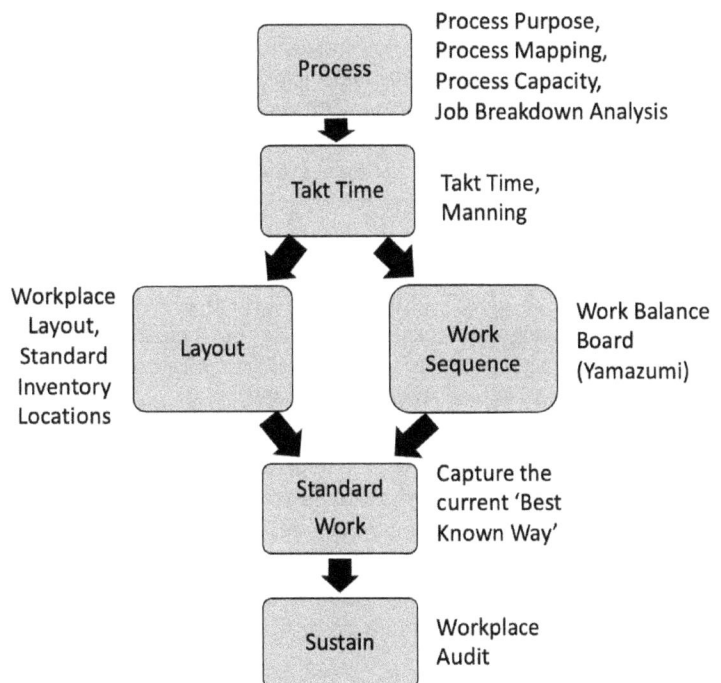

Process → Process Purpose, Process Mapping, Process Capacity, Job Breakdown Analysis

Takt Time → Takt Time, Manning

Layout → Workplace Layout, Standard Inventory Locations

Work Sequence → Work Balance Board (Yamazumi)

Standard Work → Capture the current 'Best Known Way'

Sustain → Workplace Audit

We all have standards. Frequently these are not written down. A standard is the way you want it to be. A standard might be an expectation of behaviour, of good service, a desired condition or a visual appearance. These are 'soft' standards. A problem here is that people have different soft standards, and these change with time and place.

Generally, engineering standards, safety standards, and process standards are 'hard' - subject to limits. Some may have a degree of tolerance. There are many types: standard containers, standard inventory, standard time. A standard, then, is a norm of expected activity. In a process, a detailed written standard may be called a 'standard operating procedure' or SOP.

A work standard is a description in fairly general terms about how a job should be done – the what, where, when.

When the work is actually being performed as in the standard, it is 'standardized work'. Therefore, most work is not yet standardized work but an aspiration towards standardized work. Standard Work is a proven, more precise description.

An excellent type of SOP is the Job Breakdown Sheet described in the next Chapter on Training Within Industry under Job Instruction (TWI JI). A Job Breakdown sheet has wide application in both service and manufacturing, with special emphasis on the 'Key Points' and 'The Reasons for the Key Points'. An example of a Standard Operations sheet with respect to a Cell is given in the Layout Chapter.

It is useful to think of standardized work as a spectrum. Some situations are inherently more variable so detail can be counterproductive. But, not having any guideline would be equally unsatisfactory. At the other extreme some safety situations demand precise instructions.

Standards should not be there to 'catch you out', but to enable. This is like a tennis or golf lesson. You don't hide your weaknesses to the coach, you bring them out because you want to improve.

Here is an important point: A problem is a comparison between the actual situation and the desired standard be it a hard or a soft standard.

Hence, if there is no standard there can be no problem.

Beware of a 'standard' that becomes confused with a target. This may generate silly behaviour such as improving OEE by making bigger batches. Another poor use of a standard is where it becomes confused with an accounting or costing standard – especially with absorption costing where failing to meet the budgeted rate of work leads to under-recovery of overhead and hence pressures to over-produce to 'recover' the overhead. This is plain nonsense in the context of Lean. Likewise requiring office workers to tape standard locations for pens and folders on their desks is absurd.

Also, do not believe that having standard work means that anyone can just read the sheet and do the work. Much job instruction and coaching is usually necessary. (See the section on TWI).

'Premature standardizing practice before it has reached stability can be as inefficient as not standardizing practice once it has reached stability' (says Hopp in *Hospital Operations*, p 470).

So, a balance needs to be sought.

At the outset it should be said that by 'standards' is not meant the rigid, work-study imposed, job specification that is associated with classic mass production. Such standards have no place in the world of Lean. For such 'jobs' industrial sabotage and absenteeism are to be expected. Beware of the human-relations based reaction against 'work standards' that are often confused with work-study. On the other hand, allowing standards that are too loose on critical aspects may lead to no standards, which in turn lead to decreased safety and productivity.

Also, beware of thinking that standards have no place in non-repetitive work such as maintenance, service, design, or senior management. Good, flexible maintenance and service work is built by combining various small standard work elements. Good design comes out of creativity combined with standard methods and materials, adhering to standard procedures and gateways. At Disney Florida, for example, visitors to Universal Studios walk through section by section. Within each section, the time is divided into blocks and in each block certain loosely scripted material must be covered by the artist. Do visitors notice this? No, they enjoy the professional but personalised delivery.

Far from thinking of a standard as something that confines (as in adversarial work methods of old), one should think about a standard that enables and empowers. This is like the 'rules of engagement' in the military – where a modern soldier has to be free to make decisions, but under an umbrella of guidance as to what can and can't be done.

Deming, in proposing the PDSA cycle, saw improvement moving from standard to standard. Juran emphasised the importance of 'holding the gains' by establishing standards following a process improvement, rather than allowing them to drift back to the old ways. Supervisors should have prime responsibility for maintaining and improving standard work.

Spear and Bowen in a classic article discuss the apparent paradox of TPS that activities, communications and flows at Toyota are at once rigidly scripted yet enormously flexible and adaptable. They conclude that that it is the specification of standards and communications that gives the system the ability to make huge numbers of controlled changes using the scientific method. Without standards and the scientific method, change would amount to little more than trial and error. (See Section 3.11)

Despite what some people think about Frederick Taylor, there remains 'one best way', with available technology, to do any task that will minimise time and effort, and maximise safety, quality and productivity. A task does not have to be fully detailed end-to-end, but has 'key points' and 'reasons for key points' that are the result of experience. This is the TWI job instruction lesson. See the next Chapter.

Recently the 'Learning Organisation' has become fashionable, including 'knowledge harvesting' from everyone in the organisation. How is this to be achieved? By documenting experience; in other words by establishing key points or standards from which others may learn.

Management standards should exist for meetings, communications, budgets, and many other activities. Strike the right balance of detail.

Leader standard work is very powerful. Establish a routine that requires different tasks, audits, or visits to be done at regular intervals. Perhaps, at director level once per quarter, manager level once per month, team leader level every day. Team members are expected to do a problem review every morning. That is the standard.

But Leader Standard Work should never become a tick box exercise. See the section on Gemba Walks for good practice (Chapter 6) and Leader Standard Work (Chapter 9).

Building Culture through Standard Work. How do you build 'culture'? Though management standards! By regularity. It becomes 'the way we do things around here'. We hold a problem review meeting every day. We discuss better ways to do tasks. We hold after action review meetings. We build checklists. We try to never let a customer go home dissatisfied. Culture emerges out of the standard practices. But standard practices are not left to chance – the what and the why (and the 'will do') comes down from the top, but the 'hows' are developed locally, sometimes with expert help.

Be aware, if you are a manager, that standards begin at the top but are carried out at all levels. The day you walk past an unacceptable practice and don't enquire (note: do not impose), is the day that quality and culture begins to slip back.

Since SOPS often run to many pages, they are often difficult to monitor. Far better is to use TWI type **Job Breakdown Sheets** that are far more compact. These highlight key points and reasons for key points. Team leaders should monitor the key points. If they are not being followed either there is a problem or a better way has been found. See the next Chapter on TWI.

16.1 RACI Charts

RACI charts (Pronounced 'racey') are good practice for establishing SOPS. (These have wide application outside of SOPS.) RACI denotes who is R = responsible, A = accountable, C = needs to be consulted, I = needs to be informed.

	Supervisor	Operator	Facilitator	Area Manager
Prepare standard	C	C	R	A
Write standard	C	R	I	A
Approve standard	R	I	C	A
Audit standard	R and A	I	I	A

It is good practice to use PDCA for standards and develop a set of standard questions for each stage. For instance: PLAN: What characteristics are important? How stable is the process? Who are the stakeholders, and how should they be engaged? Who is likely to know the best known method (BKM)? How will it be piloted? How will be process be monitored? DO: Who will prepare, write, approve, audit (RACI). CHECK: What checks are needed to make sure the SOP has been written and implemented correctly? ACT: Who will train, implement, verify? How much time is needed?

In a McKinsey newsletter DeSmet and Hughes criticise traditional RACI charts saying that, often, there is no clear decider, poor orchestration of stakeholders, poor delegation and ineffective meetings. Instead they suggest a DARE Chart for Deciders, Advisors, Recommenders, and Execution Stakeholders. An advance!

16.2 Window Analysis and Standards

Window analysis is a framework used to confirm that standards are being followed, and to identify potential problems. It is particularly appropriate for assembly operations where following standard work is critical to quality. The method helps to establish the reason for the failure of a standard – whether caused by establishing the standard, communicating the standard or adhering to the standard. The method is used by, for example, Sony.

The method seeks to understand whether the issue identified is confined to one person or group, or is more widespread. In the figure 'Party X may be a manager, Party Y an operator.

The categories are: 'Known' or 'Unknown' – whether the correct methods are established and known – and 'Practised' or 'Unpractised' – whether the correct methods are practised 100% of the time.

There are then four conditions – refer to the figure:

A – only if methods are known and practised by both parties 100% of the time.

B – an adherence problem, when a method is established and understood, but not practised by all parties.

C – a communication problem, when the method is established, but some individuals are not informed about it.

D – a standardisation problem, where the right method is not established.

To explain further:

Take two parties: This could be a team leader and worker; the quality dept and a supervisor; a senior manager and a middle manager, a supplier and customer.

There are several possible standards. For instance quality, job, leader, specs, management, company, behavioural.

Each of the two parties has a viewpoint on the standard. There are three possibilities by each party: Unknown, Known but not practised, Known and practised. Hence the matrix diagram. This allows a root-cause diagnosis of the problem - or no problem in the case of known and practised by both parties.

The question is how to find out the situation. This might be by questioning, by audit, by results, etc.

Standard Work: Management Obligations; 6T

Standard work can only be successful if the conditions are in place. By 'conditions' is meant the assumptions that were made when the standard work was set up. Management, not the worker, is responsible for meeting these conditions. These can be termed the 6T, and should be audited or checked.

They are applicable in both manufacturing and service. Of course, the first check if standards are not being met is to ask about the wider conditions.

Task: Is what is required absolutely clear, including the 'reasons for the key points'? Recall the TWI phrase, 'If the worker hasn't learned, the instructor hasn't taught'. Is the standard up to date?

Tell: Is the worker always informed? For instance, there may be a new worker upstream, a new answer procedure in a call centre, or variations with delivery. (Tugger is another 'T': Are line deliveries consistent?)

Tech or Tools: Are these (both hardware and software) in a good condition and available when needed? Have the product parts changed?

Time: is there sufficient time available to meet the expected standard? The cell or line might have been balanced for takt (or planned cycle time), but is that the current condition? Has time been allowed for any extra requirements?

Target: If there is a target, can it be met under current conditions? There may be situations that are outside of the worker's control. Has the target changed?

Temperature or Environment: Too hot, too cold, too humid, not enough light, etc.? Has anything changed?

Further reading

Robert W Hall, 'Standard Work: Holding the Gains', *Target,* Fourth Quarter, 1998, pp 13- 19

Taiichi Ohno, *Toyota Production System*, Productivity Press, Portland, OR, 1988

Spear and Bowen, 'Decoding the DNA of the Toyota Production System', *Harvard Business Review*, Sept/Oct 1999

John Bicheno and Philip Catherwood, *Six Sigma and the Quality Toolbox*, PICSIE, 2005

Mike Rother, *Toyota Kata*, McGraw Hill, 2010

Joseph Niederstadt, *Standardized Work for Noncyclical Processes*, CRC Press, 2010

Timothy Martin and Jeffrey Bell, *New Horizons in Standardized Work*, CRC Press, 2011

Aaron DeSmet and Caitlin Hewes, 'The limits of RACI – and a better way to make decisions, *McKinsey and Co Newsletter*, July 25, 2022

17 Training Within Industry

Training Within Industry (TWI) originated in WW2 in the USA in response to the need to train vast numbers of new workers – mainly women. Some of the best industrial engineers and psychologists were used to develop the concepts. TWI migrated around the world, including to Japan, following WW2. The UK government became a strong advocate. TWI has had long-term links with Toyota. Ohno made use of TWI concepts, and the TWI legacy remains at Toyota today.

We are GREAT fans of TWI. We believe that many a Lean implementation has failed due to inadequate attention at the front line, that TWI would have addressed.

The original TWI thinking was (and still is) that Knowledge is specific to the organisation or area and much of it is acquired externally but developed internally. For example, chemical engineering or computer programming have their own specific bodies of knowledge relevant within an organisation. They form the foundation of what the enterprise does. But there are also skills or capabilities that are more widely applicable. These skills are the TWI focus.

TWI is arguably the most effective and influential industrial training programme ever developed. The thought was, and is, that it is the front-line supervisor who has the greatest impact on day to day productivity and process stability by using three linked concepts: how to instruct a job (JI, job instruction), how to improve a job (JM, job methods) and how to deal with people issues (JR, job relations). The package of skills is what makes team working effective This became known as the 'three-legged stool' to emphasize that all three are necessary. Today, many Toyota team leaders still carry quick reminder cards based on TWI. Those three skills are, still today, considered the essential tasks for any team leader at Toyota. The original TWI names 'Job Relations' and 'Job Methods' ceased to be used at Toyota in 2000 – but the essential steps form the backbone of the 'people' expectations of team leaders and supervisors

Each of the three has a four-step standardised procedure, summarised below. These are closely allied with PDSA (Plan, Do, Study/Adjust, Act), and there is a detailed instruction procedure, available free on the web.

Note: In the UK, TWI may be confused with the long-established 'The Welding Institute'. No connection, except that Training Within Industry certainly applies in welding.

17.1 Job Instruction

The 4 steps are:

1. **Prepare the worker.** Put the person at ease and in the correct position.

2. **Present the operations. (**Here the important steps, key points, and reasons for the key points must first be identified and then demonstrated.)

3. **Try out performance.** Here the trainee demonstrates his understanding by repeatedly going through the steps, key points, and reasons. 'Continue until YOU know that THEY know'

4. **Follow up.** Check the person frequently. Encourage questions.

And always remember: 'If the worker hasn't learned, the instructor hasn't taught' (!!)

Job Breakdown Sheet: In order to teach TWI JI, a Job Breakdown Sheet must be developed. This requires careful observation of the job, and of experienced workers, in order to develop the sheet which contains main steps, key points, and reasons for key points. The resulting sheet can then be used as an audit tool. Toyota regularly requires very senior managers audit jobs according to the sheet.

Some may argue that a detailed Job Breakdown Sheet is not appropriate in a service context where personal interaction is required. We would argue that EVERY job has key points, but that slavish adherence to all main steps is often inappropriate.

17.2   Job Methods

JM is the basis of Kaizen. Although the name has changed, the essential very detailed steps remain. The four steps are:

1. Break down the current job. (List all the details covering material handling, machine work, hand work.)
2. Question every detail. (Use why, what, where, when, how, who.)
3. Develop the new job. (Eliminate, combine, rearrange, simplify)
4. Apply. (Get final approval, write up the new standard, give credit where due.)

17.3   Job Relations

JR addresses one of the most challenging parts of a supervisor's job – establishing and maintaining good supervisor–employee relations and dealing with problems when they arise. Job Relations is aimed at giving supervisors basic skills in behaviour in organizations, motivation, and communication. The Four 'Foundations of Good Job Relations' are 'solid gold' for every person in a management position. They are:

1. Let each worker know how he/she is getting along.
2. Give credit when due.
3. Tell people in advance about changes that will affect them.
4. Make best use of each person's ability.

The TWI four steps on JR (job relations) are:

1. Get the facts. ('Be sure you have the whole story.' Find out what rules and customs apply. Talk with the individuals concerned. Get opinions and feelings.)
2. Weigh up and decide. ('Don't jump to conclusions.' Fit the facts together. Check practices and policies. What possible actions are there? – note plural 'actions' not 'action'. Consider the effect of possible actions on the individual, the group, and on

production. Sometimes a period of reflection is helpful.

3. Take action. ('Don't pass the buck.' Consider if you are going to handle the problem yourself, whether you need help, and whether the actions should be referred to others. Consider the timing of the action.
4. Check the results. (Did your action help?) How soon and how often should you check? Watch for changes in output, attitudes, and relationships.

A TWI Job Relations mantra is 'People must be treated as individuals'.

17.4   Job Safety

JS was added later to the TWI trilogy. Safety is incorporated into each of JI, JM, JR but was considered sufficiently important to include a specific fourth aspect. The steps are:

1. Spot the causes of danger or risk
2. Decide countermeasures
3. Enforce countermeasures
4. Check results.

Today, however, there are many risk and hazard assessment templates – linking frequency with consequences that are usefully employed together with TWI JS.

In recent years strong links have been established between the TWI and Toyota Kata communities. (See later section on Kata)

Further reading

Patrick Graupp and Bob Wrona, *The TWI Workbook*, Productivity, 2006

For a detailed case study on the Lego Group, see Patrick Graupp, Gitte Jakobsen, John Villema, *Building a Global Learning Organisation*, CRC Press, 2014

18 Time and Activity

18.1 Takt Time, Pitch Time, Planned Cycle Time, and Cadence

Takt time is the fundamental concept to do with the regular, uniform rate of progression of products through all stages from raw material to customer. Takt time is the drumbeat cycle of the rate of flow of products. It is the 'metronome' (from the German origins of the word). Understanding takt time is fundamental to flow and mapping of repetitive Lean Operations.

Takt time is the available work time (say per day) divided by the average demand per day. Note that there are two variables – one to do with the customer, the other to do with the plant manager. Therefore, if demand changes a manager could maintain the same takt time by adjusting the available work time. The available time is the actual time after allowances for planned stoppages (for planned maintenance, team briefings, breaks). Demand is the average sales rate (including spare parts) plus any extras such as test parts and (we hope not) anticipated scrap. It is expressed in time units: e.g. 30 seconds (or 30 seconds between completions). Where there are multiple parts going down a line, the overall takt time is calculated by dividing the available time by the total number of parts. Please refer to the Scheduling Chapter

Where demand is seasonal or variable, selection of the period over which demand is estimated is important. Selecting a longer period will stabilize build rate but at the expense of more supermarket inventory to smooth out the bumps. Moving towards build to order may mean having more frequent takt time changes.

For machines and processes, working to takt time may mean slowing down. Strangely and counter-intuitively, slowing down to achieve synchronization may lead to a reduction in lead-time. This is because queues build up after machines that run faster than the takt time. This simple realization of synchronisation, to try to get all machines in a plant running at the constant takt time, can have dramatic results. It changes the job shop into a pseudo assembly line. Takt time should drive the whole thinking of the plant and the supply chain. In a plant it is the drumbeat. Consideration needs to be given to the number of parts per product sold. Thus if there are four wheels per trolley sold, and wheels are all made on the same machine, the wheel machine needs to have a takt time of approximately one quarter that of the main assembly line. (Approximately because there may be special demands for additional spare wheels). So takt times in a plant leads to overall synchronization.

Several takt times can be set for a line – and the line balanced for each takt time. Then, depending on demand, the appropriate takt and manning can be used.

Likewise, takt can be calculated daily in warehouse order-picking operations, to calculate the number of pickers. Here, there may be a morning takt and an afternoon takt.

Pitch Time is the takt time multiplied by the container quantity or a convenient multiple of parts. Instead of thinking the time to make one part, think of the time required to fill the standard container. The analogy of the ski lift is particularly appropriate – a constant rate of movement delivering 4 different people at a regular spacing.

The pitch increment is the basic time slot used in heijunka. The material handler in a heijunka system should fit in with the pitch time. In that sense, pitch time is the vital drumbeat of the whole system, forcing regularity, visibility and flow.

Planned cycle time is the more practical unit, used for instance in line balancing. Planned cycle time is always a percentage of takt time, typically 80% to 90%. If takt time were used to balance a line, then any stoppage would result in missing the production target.

Cadence is the term used in design or new product introduction. This is not related to takt time but has similar philosophy. Example: A Phase is completed every three weeks, or a new version introduced every 6 months.

18.2 Activity Timing, Activity Sampling and Work Elements

Activity timing is the long-established industrial engineering (or time and motion study) task of determining the duration of work elements. This is an essential input into cell balance ('Yamazumi') boards, value stream maps, scheduling, and costing. In Lean, timing is best done by operators rather than by I.E.s – thereby encouraging ownership and avoiding the pitfalls of suspicion and 'slow-motion' work. In time and motion studies, the rule is to do motion study before timing. Standard work or TWI job breakdown before timing.

Preferably, make a video of the tasks. (This is better than live recording, because it allows backtracking, and slow motion. It also avoids the stress of several people with stopwatches standing over an operator.) Be sure to video at least 10 cycles on each shift. If several operators are used, film each of them. A very useful learning experience is to get operators from different shifts together to see if there is variation between operators, and to agree on the best method. This should be an essential step in determining standard work. If you are an outside observer, it will take time to familiarize yourself with the exact tasks – best of all is if you can do the work yourself. This is another good reason for using operators themselves to do the timing.

With the correct methods established, begin the timing. If necessary, re-video. It is good to video several operators, from different shifts. First, break down the work sequence into work elements each with a clear start and end point. Agree on these points. Keep manual (work) times, walk times, and wait times separate and record each of these under separate columns. Machine cycles should be separately recorded. Make a list of the sequence of activities that an operator goes through in a complete sequence. Some of the manual times will turn out to be non-value adding, or non-value adding unavoidable. When balancing the cell, try to reduce or eliminate wait and walk times. Critically examine the possibility of reducing NVA or NNVA steps.

Time at least 10 good cycles of each – by a 'good' cycle is meant a cycle where nothing goes wrong. Discard 'outliers'. Time to the nearest whole second. For each work element time, take the lowest more frequently occurring time. In other words, in 10 observed cycles of 4, 5, 6, 6, 7, 7,8, 8, 8, 8 take 6.

Note: In traditional time study, the time used is the observed time plus an allowance for 'PR&D' – personal, rest and delay. Do not add this allowance. Rather, give operators more frequent breaks.

A Note on Activity Sampling

Activity Sampling is a quick, effective way to establish data on wastes and how people, or machines, are spending their day. Often, people don't know this about themselves! The method involves taking perhaps 250 random observations of each operator in the area over a representative period of time, perhaps a week, certainly a full day. If days are similar sample a day. If days are different, sample over a week or longer.

There are formulas for calculating the number of observations to yield a certain desired confidence level, but generally 250 observations is satisfactory to gain a good impression. A random observation is just that – at random times over the day or week. Decide how many observations to take in a day, and spread the observations more or less (but not exactly) evenly across the day. One way of avoiding bias is for the observer to turn his back on the subject and count down from say 20. Then turn and observe in that instant. With each observation note down what that person is doing at that instant – value adding, or non value adding by category – for instance walking, recording, watching, talking, etc. Simply then calculate the percentage in each category.

Beware, however! This should not constitute 'spying' or subversive data collection but rather as an analysis activity aimed at improvement. It is best done by operators themselves. This must be explained to those being observed.

Note: 'Big Data' and Process Mining may outdate some activity sampling. See page 160.

19 Changeover Reduction (SMED)

Changeover reduction is a pillar of Lean operations. The late Shigeo Shingo produced the classic work on 'SMED', and until recently very little has been added to what he said. A significant advance was made by a group at the University of Bath (McIntosh et al, 2001). Also Six Sigma methods have added useful dimensions on variation. Generally, for Lean, the reason to do changeover reduction is to allow for small batch flow and improved EPE performance.

(By the way, Shingo did not invent quick changeover. He codified it. It had already been known at Toyota before Shingo, and at Ford before that. In *Workplace Management*, (Gemba Press, 2007) Ohno tells a story of how workers from Toyota Japan went to Toyota Brazil to learn about forge changeover that the Japanese did not believe could be done.)

Changeover also applies in the office and in service. Every time a new piece of work is started or returned to, there is both physical and mental time lost. Several studies on multitasking have shown mental readjustment times of up to 15 minutes. This is hidden waste. There is a story of three ships being loaded in port by one crane. Each ship has a loading time of a week. If all three are loaded together (multitasking) all three will release together in week 3. If the ships are loaded sequentially, ship 1 will be released after week 1, ship 2 after week 2, and ship 3 after week 3. And that is optimistic, ignoring inter-ship crane movement. Sequence is important. (This is, of course, batch vs mixed-model.)

19.1 What is a changeover?

There are three views. The first, narrow, view is the time that a machine is idle between batches (the 'internal' time). The second, and widely held, view is that it is the time from the last piece of the first batch to the first good piece of the second. A third view, is that it is the time from the standard rate of running of the first batch to the standard rate of running the second. This view therefore includes rundown and ramp-up times.

The classic Shingo methodology is:

- Identify and classify internal and external activities. Make a video?

- Separate 'internal' activities from 'external' activities. External or preparation activities should be maximized. Cut or reduce waste activities such as movement, fetching tools, filling in forms.

- Try to convert internal activities to external (for example by pre-heating a die).

- Use engineering on the remaining internal activities. There are many tricks, from quick release nuts, to constant platform shims, to multiple hole connections done together. Both Shingo and McIntosh are an excellent source of ideas.

- Finally, minimize external activity time. (Why? Because in small batch production there may be insufficient time to prepare for the changeover during a batch run.)

The Formula 1 pit-stop analogy is useful. Actual stop time is now a remarkable 2.5 seconds. But note this is a high-cost changeover with minimum time virtually the only goal. Safety is important but again costs big money. The wheel is held in place by only one nut. 13 people are involved. Would this be cost effective for you?

19.2 Mapping the changeover process

Mapping is a standard tool for SMED. Begin by chunking the changeover into major stages – these will be, at least, preparation, actual changeover, and re-establishing speed and quality. Then divide each stage into steps. Use a brown paper chart with all the steps in the changeover going along the top of the chart. Then construct rows along the chart. The rows are as follows: Total time for the step. People involved, internal time, external time, and then three further rows – one to note whether the step can be reduced, simplified, eliminated, or done in parallel; another for other ideas and sketches, and the third row for photos. Use post-it stickers for the last three rows.

To standardize, the work combination chart and job breakdown chart are useful. See separate sections on these. (Chapter 17)

Adjustment is an important consideration that can consume much time. List all adjustments on a separate sheet. Categorise into three: Adjustments that should not be made – here think of ways in which the setting can be fixed or welded. Second, adjustments that have a limited number of standard settings – each of these should be indicated or marked on the machine or jig, or ways thought of to achieve 'one touch' adjustment. And third, adjustments that truly need adjustment: for these try to devise a standard one best way.

Poka-yoke or mistake proofing should be made integral to every changeover reduction exercise. See the section on Mistakes under Quality (20.3)

Variation in changeover time is almost as important as the changeover time itself. If a changeover has large variation, then good scheduling practice is made difficult. Therefore, track the major elements of changeover and determine which stages have greatest variation. Then tackle variation as a separate exercise.

Changeover is part of OEE, so changeover reduction may be done under the auspices of TPM. The very thorough 11-step TPM approach will always be effective, but the effort to go through all 11 steps is significant. TPM will also help highlight the importance of the changeover in relation to other losses, particularly when changeover is being done for capacity reasons. (See TPM Chapter.)

To derive the target changeover time for mixed model flow, please refer to the Batch sizing section. Essentially, this involves working out how much time is available in a day (or week) for changeover, after making the standard set or 'campaign' of products. Then divide the available time by the number of changeovers that are required in that period. This will give the target changeover time. This process is iterative. If there is insufficient time to make all changeovers in a day, try two days, then three, and so on until a realistic changeover target time is found. Then, after a time, reduce the period. And so on.

It is useful to think strategy: Is the changeover to reduce time, to reduce cost, to improve quality, to reduce manpower, to limit maintenance, or a combination. Is the aim to increase capacity or to improve flow? Generally you can't have them all.

McIntosh et al say there are four elements to successful changeover: Attitude, including workplace culture and receptiveness to change; Resources including time, money, personnel, training, tools; Awareness, including the contribution of changeover to (flow), flexibility, inventory, capacity and awareness of different possibilities of achieving quick changeover; and Direction, including leadership and vision, priority and ranking, (and presumably impact on the value stream). McIntosh usefully divides changeover reduction into three phases.

The table below has been developed from their work. McIntosh et al make a strong case that there are two general approaches, organization-led (i.e. SMED) and design-led. For each, there are four areas to address:

1. 'Online activities' (by internal and external task reallocation, or by designs that allow the sequence to be altered – for example simultaneous rather than sequential steps);

2. Adjustment (by reducing trial and error by for example indicators and shims, or by design which allows 'snap-on' adjustment),

3. Variety (by standardization and standard operations or by design which reduces the possibilities of variation – poka-yoke) , and

4. Effort (by work simplification and preparation or by design which incorporates simplification – for example fixing multiple hoses by one fixture).

The choice between organisation-led and design-led, depends on objectives, on how much is willing to be spent, and on sustainability – design-led locks in improvements much more than organization-led. McIntosh at al suggest that a 'reference changeover' be developed. This is what Lean practitioners would call a 'paper kaizen' activity. It involves collecting data (e.g. by video), identifying and cutting all waste, rearranging activities, and doing the changeover as efficiently as possible. This establishes the theoretical benchmark.

Phase	Tasks	Issues
Strategic	Identify opportunities Focus priorities Identify the approach to use (Organisation led or design led)	Internal team? Consultants? New equipment? Dedicated equipment? TPM / OEE approach?
Preparatory	Existing performance records Variation in times? Postponement? Fix targets (e.g. via VSM)	5S of tools and dies Sequence dependencies? Use blitz? Involve different shifts?
Implementation	Video SMED technology Engineering changes Poka-yoke? Regularity and sequencing	Records Incentives? SOPS Sustainability

Six Sigma methodologies have also been attempted on changeover. It is now clear that the SMED methodology is much more effective at reducing time, and should always be done first. But then Six Sigma analysis can be useful to examine the causes of time variation. If the changeover is important enough, building the distribution of changeover times seeking root causes of, for example, bi-modal time distributions can be worthwhile.

Design-led changeover involves a whole tranche of possibilities some of which are: First breaking task interdependencies and automating adjustments (for example incorporating a measuring scale); Making parts more robust or lighter; Second Poka-yoke, incorporating built-in tools (e.g. welded spanner), improving access, and mechanization and robotics. Clearly there is overlap with TPM.

Finally a few tips:

- Measure and record changeover times. Many changeover times have fallen by doing this alone…..

- Involve the team in analysis. Do not rely only on Industrial Engineers.

- Make a video, and get operators to record and critique. The video must remain their property. When making a video try if possible to use two or even three teams. One team to video the big picture, one team to record hand movements, and one team to record any information that the operator must follow or complete. Ideally, each team should have a cameraman, a recorder to make notes, and a commentator to speak about what is happening. Put their ideas up on a board at the workplace.

- Consider a financial incentive for consistent improvement in changeover, whilst discouraging incentives for more production.

- Remember the equation: Changeover time x no of batches = constant. In other words as changeover time comes down, this must be converted into smaller batches. Resist the temptation just to gain extra capacity.

- Q: 'How do you get to Carnegie Hall?' A: 'Practice, man, practice'. It's what grand prix teams do.

- Use trolleys onto which all tools and equipment are placed, and which can be wheeled to the changeover machine

- Regularity in the schedule helps. If everyone knows that Machine A is changed over every day at 9 a.m., then everyone from forklift driver to setter will be on hand.

- Tool and die maintenance is a vital, but sometimes overlooked, part of setup reduction. Don't compromise.

- At bottlenecks, use a team for the changeover, bringing in operators from non-bottleneck machines.

- The optimal sequence of changeovers should be incorporated into scheduling.

Further reading

Shigeo Shingo, *SMED*, Productivity Press, Portland, OR, 1985

R I McIntosh, S J Culley, A R Mileham, G W Owen, *Improving Changeover Performance*, Butterworth Heinemann, London, 2001

20 Quality

The goal of Perfection, the last of the Five Lean Principles, covers quality, delivery, flexibility, and safety. The (earlier) Toyota Temple of Lean had two pillars, JIT and Jidoka (Jidoka being closely associated with quality, especially poka-yoke). Jidoka is strongly associated with the 'Quality at Source' principle – don't pass on defects even if it takes longer to complete the task. The two pillars are mutually supportive. For instance, improving quality improves Just in Time performance through less disruption and smoother flow. And improving JIT improves quality. Reduced batch sizes allow faster detection and less rework. Pull systems could be regarded as a quality tool. Layout influences quality through improved communication. Postponement reduces variation. Jidoka is a major way of exposing waste and improving quality through surfacing problems, by for example pulling the Andon cord. Quality is one of a family of five inter-related concepts which together make up a foundation stone for Lean stability. The others are standard work, TPM, 5S, and visual management.

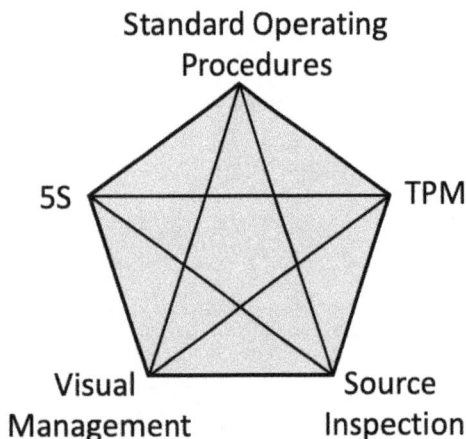

Standard Operating Procedures — TPM — Source Inspection — Visual Management — 5S

20.1 Understanding Customer Needs: The Kano Model

Noriaki Kano is a Japanese academic who is best known for his excellent 'Kano model'. The Kano Model has emerged as one the most useful and powerful aids to product and service design and improvement. The Kano model relates three factors (which Kano argues are present in every product or service) to their degree of implementation or level of implementation, as shown in the figure. Kano's three factors are Basic (or 'must be') factors, Performance (or 'more is better') factors, and Delighter (or 'excitement') factors. The degree of customer satisfaction ranges from 'disgust', through neutrality, to 'delight'.

A Basic factor is something that a customer simply expects to be there. If it is not present the customer will be dissatisfied or disgusted, but if it is fully implemented or present it will merely result in a feeling of neutrality. Examples are clean sheets in a hotel, a station tuner on a radio, or windscreen washers on a car. Notice that there may be degrees of implementation: sheets may be clean but blemished. Basic factors should not be taken for granted, or regarded as easy to satisfy; some may even be exceptionally difficult to identify. One example is handouts that a lecturer may regard as trivial but the audience may regard as a basic necessity. If you don't get the basics right, all else may fail - in this respect it is like Maslow's Hierarchy of Needs: it is no good thinking about self-esteem needs unless survival needs are catered for. (In fact, the Kano model is based partly on the Herzberg Motivator-Hygiene theory of motivation.) Market surveys are of limited value for basics (because they are simply expected). Therefore a designer needs to build up a list by experience, direct observation and organized feedback.

To test if a characteristic is basic, performance or delighter, ask two questions:

1. How do you feel if (the characteristic) is absent?

2. How do you feel if (the characteristic) is present?

→If 1=bad, 2=neutral, it is a basic

→If 1=neutral, 2=good, it is a delighter

→ If the answer is 'It depends', it is a performance factor.

Notice the non-linear shape of the curve. This is in line with economic theory that suggests that most people have such non-linear responses. (See Kahneman). If you had a 50/50 chance of winning or losing $1 million would you do it? Most people would not accept a bet with a 90% chance of winning $1 million if they had a 10% chance of losing $1 million, but for $10 there would be more takers.

THE KANO MODEL

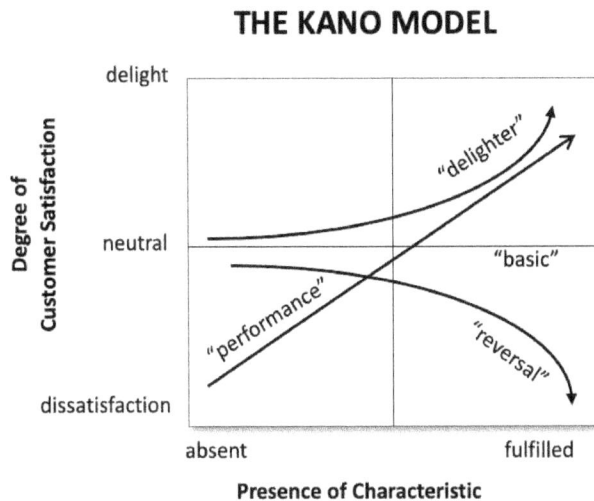

Presence of Characteristic

A Performance factor can cause disgust at one extreme, but if fully implemented can result in delight. This factor is also termed 'more is better' but could also be 'faster is better' or 'easier is better'. Performance factors are usually in existence already, but are neutral, causing neither disgust nor delight. It is not so much the fact that the feature exists; it is how it can be improved. The challenge is to identify them, and to change their performance. Examples are speed of check in at a hotel, ease of tuning on a radio, or fuel consumption. Performance factors represent real opportunity to designers and to R&D staff. They may be identified through market surveys, but observation is also important, especially in identifying performance features that cause dissatisfaction. Creativity or process redesign is often required to deliver the factor faster or more easily, and information support may play a role as in the 'one minute' check in at some top hotels.

Finally, a Delighter or Excitement factor is something that customers do not expect, but if present may cause increasing delight. Examples are getting a bottle of water from a hotel doorman when you return from a jog, or a radio tuner that retunes itself when moving out of range of a transmitter. By definition, market surveys are of little use here. Once again, it is creativity, based on an appreciation of (latent) customer needs that can provide the breakthrough. But we need to be careful about Delighters also: a true Delighter is provided at minimal extra cost - it would certainly cause customer delight to give them all a complimentary car, but would be disastrous for company finances. Therefore, perhaps a more appropriate hotel Delighter would be to give guests a choice of sheet colour, pillow type (English or Continental), and sheet type (linen, satin, or cotton). There are risks with providing Delighters – customers may come to expect them – as may have happened with Ford and GM car discounts.

Kano factors are not static. What may be a Delighter this year may migrate towards being a Basic in a few years' time. Also, what may be a Delighter in one part of the world may be a Basic in another. Thus it is crucial to keep up to date with changing customer expectations. Benchmarking may be a way to go. From Kano we also learn that a reactive quality policy, reacting to complaints, or dissatisfiers, will at best lead to neutrality but proactive action is required to create delight.

The Kano Model works well with Quality Function Deployment. (See p258) Basics should be satisfied, and delighters can be explicitly traded off in the 'roof' of the QFD matrix (for example fuel consumption may suggest a lighter car, but safety suggests a stronger one - so the quest is to find a material that is light, strong, and inexpensive.)

Further reading

Special Issue on Kano's Methods: *Center for Quality of Management Journal*, Vol 2, No 4, Fall 1993 (Several articles, including administering Kano questionnaires).

Joiner, B.L., *Fourth Generation Management*, McGraw Hill, New York, 1994

Lou Cohen, *Quality Function Deployment*, Addison Wesley, Reading MA, 1995

20.2   A Framework for Lean Quality

Perfection in Quality should be approached in three ways, according to Hinckley.

- a reduction in **complexity** in product design and in process design.
- the prevention and reduction of **mistakes**.
- a reduction in **variation.**

Each of these three has particular tools that are most applicable. This is shown in the table.

	Product	Process
Complexity	GT, DFM, DFSS, QCC tools, Kano Model	DFM, Layout, SOPs, 5S, SMED, Mapping
Variation	Six Sigma, Shainin tools	Six Sigma, visibility, SPC, TPM, 7 quality tools, 5S, SOPS, Shainin tools, Successive inspection
Mistakes	Pokayoke, DFM	Pokayoke, 5S, SOPs, visibility

For each of these three approaches, complexity, mistakes, and variation, there are six possible sources of problems – man / people, machine, material, methods, and measures / messages , mother nature. This gives a table, with examples, as shown. All of these need to be tackled for a comprehensive attack on poor quality.

Hinckley makes the point that process variation is much less of a problem than it once was. This is because of machine consistency and automation. For that reason mistakes are increasingly important. In Lean, and particularly Lean Six Sigma, there has been huge attention given to variation. This is sometimes misplaced. The 'big one' is now mistakes. Hinckley states that the most effective

order to tackle quality problems is first to address the product, then the process, and finally the related tools and equipment. Within each category, first simplify, then mistake proof, then convert adjustments to settings (i.e. one stop rather than fiddling back and forth), and finally control variation.

20.3   Mistakes and Errors

Many mistakes go un-noticed or the costs are disregarded. In manufacturing, although mistakes are rare, they can be significant when compared with Six Sigma levels. A 1962 study found that 1 in 10k to 1 in 100k assembly omissions go undetected. 1 in 10k is 100 ppm (or 5 sigma) with omissions alone. Take healthcare costs: From missing taking a pill (consequences zero to huge), onto the 26 useless tests that, according to Harvard surgeon, Atul Gawande, are given to millions of Americans each year – not only costing direct money but also causing stress and anxiety. And to the thousands of 'avoidable deaths' in UK hospitals that former Health Minister Jeremy Hunt calls 'the biggest scandal in global healthcare'. Margaret Heffernan says that in US healthcare mistakes cost between $17bn and $29 bn per year! Even worse, is unreported or suppressed information on mistakes. (See Psychological Safety Chapter 8).

The source of mistakes is important. Often a 'mistake' is made here – assuming that standard work or more training will eliminate the problem when if fact the problem lies deeper with the design of the product or the system. The latter includes boring, highly repetitive work. Hence Deming's 94/6 rule and job rotation.

There are six prime sources of mistakes:

Machines: If these give early warning (say with vibration or age) then TPM can make an impact. But if random and predictable (what but not when) then a poka-yoke device may be good option. See Reliability Centred Maintenance.

	Man (People)	Machine	Method	Materials	Measurement	Mother Nature
Variation	Training, Experience	Tool wear, Vibration	Execution methods, standard work	Material variation	Gage accuracy	Temperature, humidity
Mistakes	Omission	Incorrect setup, software	Wrong method	Wrong material or part	Wrong instructions	Ignoring this type
Complexity	Individual differences, motivation	Difficult setup or adjustment	Difficult task, assembly complexity	Difficult to work or assemble	Unclear information	Interaction effects

Employees: Poka-yokes and checklists may help in routine situations. Employees themselves are the major route to developing effective poka-yokes and checklists. Note that, as Atul Gawande has discussed in the case of surgeons and nurses, an attitude change may be necessary for the lower status employee to use checklists with higher status employees. The same applies to of much quality control. Speed of feedback is vital, as in the andon system. (Note: Andon is not a poka-yoke. A poka-yoke requires 100% automatic detection.)

Some employee 'mistakes' can be addressed by creative methods such as asking employees to give the eye colour of customers, thereby (perhaps) ensuring eye contact.

Employee-Customer interactions cause much of 'Failure Demand' (Seddon's phrase) that can add significantly to the volume of work.

5S and visuality are part solutions to reducing employee mistakes. Of course, they are not poka-yoke.

Information, includes miscommunication and documentation. The former could include information cascades (as in Hoshin), listening and respect. The latter could include inaccurate bills of materials and lot sizing in an MRP system. Some

reasonableness checks can be built in, as in a control range.

In scheduling, the Pareto and levelling approaches towards regularity, help to prevent what Phil Crosby says is 'making the same old mistake for the 500th time'.

Customers: Chase and Stewart say that customers cause one third of mistakes. Francis Frei's customer variability also applies to mistakes: Arrival (when they arrive); Request (volume and time), Capability (of customers to perform instructions themselves); Effort (how much will they try); Preference (mismatch of expectations). Mapping customer journeys against 'Moments of Truth' has been a reasonably successful way to reduce these mistakes. (See Bicheno's book *The Service Systems Toolbox*.)

Attitude or Cognitive Bias. A classic story here is of Dr. Semmelweiss who, in 1847 collected huge evidence relating the washing of hands to baby survival rates. For decades, doctors around the world refused to accept the evidence, citing a slur on their professional competence. It couldn't happen today, could it? Yes, it could – as at Bristol Royal Infirmary where a whistleblower revealed that mortality was 5 or 6 times the average – and was forced out. There have been sad cases where people have been sent to prison for rape having been identified clearly, only to be released years later when DNA evidence proved the accusation to be false. There are also Solomon Asch's amusing, yet worrying, experiments with persons who are persuaded by a (planted) group that all 6 lines in a set are the same length when one of the lines is clearly longer.

Bias is a major cause of mistakes. Kahneman, in his book 'Thinking, Fast and Slow', has shown the extent of bias that everyone has. His 'System 1' thinking (quick and automatic, but sometimes wrong) is a warning. Irving Janis who studied 'Groupthink' mistakes at Bay of Pigs and Peal Harbour says that Groupthink blinds us to mistakes and encourages greater risk taking. Groupthink is 'going along to get along'.

Design simplicity is paramount. The more parts, the more assembly steps, the greater the possibility of mistakes. Obvious? Yes, but practised? In the wonderful book 'The Design of Everyday Things', Donald Norman shows how good design – through elegant simplicity - not only reduces mistakes but also captures customers. Ask Apple Computer. Donald talks about physical, cultural, semantic, and logical 'constraints' that need to be considered in achieving good and elegant design: Physical – only fits one way; Cultural – different cultures notice written messages in different ways; Semantic – ('Bill Posters will be prosecuted.' But Bill Posters is an innocent man!) ; Logical – the design of intuitive computer screens.

Self-Inspection, Successive Inspection, and Source Inspection.

Self-inspection is where an operator performs an inspection immediately after the manufacturing step is made. Successive inspection is where the next operator checks the previous step or steps. These types of judgement inspection are worthy of consideration because they provide immediate or short-term feedback and (in the case of successive checks) are capable of a high degree of reliability. For instance, if an inspection has 90% reliability, 100 out of 1000 defects would remain after the first inspection, 10 would remain after the second, and 1 (or 0.1%) after the third. This is a higher reliability and often faster than SPC. However, a problem is attitude: 'I won't bother because someone else will catch it'. Another problem is that they are both 'after the event' and are not prevention. Hence, Shingo's focus on 'source inspection' – the root cause of the mistake – or process design. Source inspection aims for 'work that is done correctly, completely, and at the right time' (Hinckley). To achieve that, one needs in-depth understanding of customer requirements – whether internal or external.

Poka-yoke

(alternative spellings: pokayoke and poke-yoke)

The late Shigeo Shingo developed and classified the poka-yoke concept, particularly in manufacturing. Shingo's book *Zero Quality Control: Source Inspection and the Poka-yoke System* is the classic work. More recently C Martin Hinckley made a significant contribution through his work *Make No Mistake!*

We all make mistakes. Hinckley says a mistake is a rare, random event. Chase and Stewart define a mistake as being the 'result of an activity, either mental or physical, that deviates from what was intended'.

'Poka-yoke' literally means you must prevent (yoke) inadvertent mistakes (poka). (If you don't like the Japanese term, try mistake-proof, fail-safe or even 'goof proof')

A poka-yoke (or mistake-proof) device according to Shingo uses '100% automatic inspection together with warning or stop'. Here, key words are 100% and automatic. Note that a poka-yoke is not a control device like a thermostat or toilet control valve that takes action every time, but rather a device that senses abnormalities and takes action only when an abnormality is identified. Interestingly, a poka-yoke can apparently also mean 'distraction–proofing' in Japanese – with implications for using a mobile phone when driving or e-mail interruptions.

Shingo distinguishes between 'mistakes' (which are inevitable) and 'defects' (which result when a mistake reaches a customer). The aim of poka-yoke is to design devices that prevent mistakes becoming defects. According to Shingo there are two categories – those that warn, and those that prevent or control. There are three types: 'contact', 'fixed value', and 'motion step'. This means that there are six categories, as shown in the figure with service examples.

Pokayoke Types		
	Control	**Warning**
Contact	Parking height bars Armrests on seats	Staff mirrors Shop entrance bell
Fixed Value	French fry scoop Pre-dosed medication	Tray with indentations
Motion step	Airline lavatory doors	Spellcheckers Beepers on ATMs

Adapted from : "Failsafe Services" by Richard Chase and Douglas Stewart, OMA Conference, 1993

The contact type makes contact with every product or has a physical shape that inhibits mistakes. An example is a fixed diameter hole through which all products must fall; an oversize product does not fall through and a defect is registered. The fixed value method is a design that makes it clear when a part is missing or not used. An example is an 'egg tray' used for the supply of parts. Sometimes this type can be combined with the contact type, where parts not only have to be present in the egg tray but also are automatically correctly aligned. The motion step type automatically ensures that the correct numbers of steps have been taken. For example, an operator is required to step on a pressure-sensitive pad during every assembly cycle, or a medicine bottle has a press-down-and-turn feature for safety.

Shingo further developed failsafe classification by saying that there are five areas (in manufacturing) that have potential for mistake-proofing: the operator (Me), the Material, the Machine, the Method, and the Information (4 M plus I). An alternative is the process control model comprising input, process, output, feedback, and result. All are candidates for mistake-proofing.

According to Grout, areas where poka-yoke should be considered include areas where worker vigilance is required, where mispositioning is likely, where SPC is difficult, where external failure costs dramatically exceed internal failure costs, and in mixed model and production.

Shingo says that poka-yoke should be thought of as having both a short action cycle (where immediate shut down or warning is given), but also a long action cycle where the reasons for the defect occurring in the first place are investigated. John Grout makes the useful point that one drawback of poka-yoke devices is that potentially valuable information about process variance may be lost, thereby inhibiting improvement.

Hinckley has developed an excellent approach to mistake proofing. He has developed a classification scheme comprising 10 common categories: omitted operations, omitted parts, wrong orientation, misaligned, wrong location, wrong part, misadjusted, prohibited action, added part, mis-read instruction. For each category, various mistake proofing solutions have been developed. Thus, having identified the type of mistake, one can look through the set of possible solutions and adapt or select the most suitable one. See his excellent web site: assuredquality.com

There is a continuum of poka-yokes. Take seatbelts: A weak poka-yoke would require a driver to use a checklist, including fastening a seatbelt before setting off. A slightly stronger version would require any car passenger to go through the checklist with the driver. A medium strength poka-yoke would give an audio or display warning when a seatbelt is not fastened. A strong poka-yoke would prevent the car from starting unless the driver's seatbelt is fastened. The seatbelt example illustrates that the choice of poka-yoke needs to consider both risk and user acceptance.

20.4   Checklists

A checklist is not a true poka-yoke, but nevertheless is important in reducing mistakes. A checklist is not automatic, relies on human conscientiousness, and often requires a change in culture or attitude to be effective. Note that this is not a question of training or competence but a problem of the human brain just having too much to think of, particularly in stressful situations. (Surgeons are highly trained but occasionally might leave an instrument inside a patient.)

Checklists have received long overdue attention recently due to the work of Atul Gawande's book 'The Checklist Manifesto'. Gawande is a Harvard surgeon. The number of errors made in hospitals is truly astounding. From cutting off the wrong limb, to leaving instruments inside a patient, to administering the wrong medicine. Thousands of such cases occur each year in the UK, tens of thousands in USA. Checklists have had remarkable success in reducing such errors, but they require a change in culture – allowing a nurse to go through a checklist for a surgeon (previously a no-no). This is not seen as a reflection of competence, but as a life-saver in a highly stressful, pressurized environment. In the UK, 1 in 16 hospital patients get an infection. This situation has led the deputy head of the health service to encourage patients to carry out their own check: ask the nurse or doctor if they have washed their hands!

Gawande points out that checklists have been hundreds of times more cost effective than many new drugs. In fact, new drugs are part of the problem – which one to select?, and is the most effective one known to the doctor? And addiction.

Of course, checklists have long been used in aircraft, starting with the B-17 bomber in World War II. There are the three important points:

1. The checklist must not be too long. (Only the 'key points' in TWI terms.) Perhaps 10 points or less. (A case in point was the crash of an airliner taking off from La Guardia, New York. When the engines failed, the pilot used a checklist but it was too long to complete. He nevertheless ditched the aircraft safely in the East River.)

2. The checklist is not a reflection of incompetence, but a recognition that in a focused, stressful situation, important points can be missed. (Recall the 'Invisible Gorilla' experiment, where many people counting ball throws simply do not see a man in a gorilla suit walking past!)

3. A checklist is best administered by a second person, again not as a reflection of competence but in recognition that the first person may have many simultaneous things on his or her mind. The second person is therefore helping not hindering.

Given these characteristics, checklists have a great future in service and manufacturing.

There are links between checklists and TWI. First, key points are picked up in TWI Job Instruction.

1. Ask, can each key point be failsafed? If yes, then it would no longer necessarily be a key point.

2. Key points should be audited using the TWI Job Breakdown chart. In complex work, and repetitive manual work this is especially important. Of course, only periodically. Without this, defects and failure demand are inevitable. Not a policeman, but a helper, as above.

3. Note the TWI mantra that not every step has a key point or points. But there are a few critical key points that have to be done correctly. This is NOT over-standardising work that some critics of Lean cite as a major drawback.

4. TWI Job Methods, in questioning every step through 'Kipling analysis', brings out the key points and checklist possibilities.

See also the section on Performance Improvement: Errors, Insight, Blindness in the Managing Change Chapter

Our thanks to our friend Martin Hinckley for great inspiration.

Further reading

Shigeo Shingo, *Zero Quality Control: Source Inspection and the Pokayoke System*, Productivity Press, 1986

C Martin Hinckley, *Make No Mistake*, Productivity Press, Portland, 2001

See Hinckley's extensive web site: AssuredQuality.com

An award-winning web site on poka-yoke is by John Grout: www.mistakeproofing.com

Joseph Hallinan, *Why we Make Mistakes*, Broadway, 2009

Richard Chase and Douglas Stewart, *Mistake-Proofing: Designing Errors Out*, John Grout Publishing e book, 2007

Atul Gawande, *The Checklist Manifesto*, Profile, 2011

Daniel Kahneman, *Thinking, Fast and Slow*, Allen Lane, 2011

Frances Frei and Anne Morris, *Uncommon Service,* Harvard, 2012.

Frances Frei and Anne Morris, *Unleashed,* Harvard, 2020.

Carol Tavris and Elliot Aronson, *Mistakes Were Made (But not by me)*, Harcourt, 2007

Donald Norman, *The Design of Everyday Things*, Revised edition, MIT Press, 2013

John Bicheno, *The Service Systems Toolbox*, PICSIE, 2012

20.5   Variation and Six Sigma

A principal approach for the reduction of variation is Six Sigma. In essence, Six Sigma is a tool to assess and improve the capability of a highly repetitive process. It can work in conjunction with the foundation tools for the limitation of variation that also includes TPM, 5S, Standard work and changeover reduction. Tools for the control of variation include SPC and Pre-Control.

Before starting out on a sophisticated Six Sigma programme, a Lean company should ensure that they have made reasonable progress with 5S combined with visuality, standard work and, in many environments, with TPM. This is akin to sending in the public health engineers before the medical specialists. The medics will have point impact, but it is unlikely to be sustained. The public health engineer working to achieve clean water and pollution from sewage is likely to have far greater and lasting impact. Then the medics take over to do their valuable specific work.

Statistical Process Control (SPC) is a good technique for variation monitoring and control, provided that its limitations are recognised. SPC is concerned with monitoring the process, not the product. If the process is in control, and capable, then the products that are produced by the process will consistently conform to specification. However, SPC is probably not reliable for monitoring or controlling at levels of five or Six Sigma – below perhaps 1,000 parts per million (0.1%).

Although Lean and Six Sigma sometimes compete, in more enlightened companies they are seen as partners. Phrases such as 'Lean Sigma', 'Lean Six Sigma' have emerged. This is both good news and bad news. Good news because Lean has often tended to downplay variation, and because it is less strong at detailed problem solving (as opposed to problem surfacing). Together they make for a powerful combination. They share a common heritage in the teachings of Shewhart, Deming, Juran and Feigenbaum.

But it can also be bad news if each is defined too narrowly – as the second section of this chapter sets out there are complexity, variation, and mistake issues in a comprehensive approach to quality. Just as Lean has sometimes downplayed variation, Six Sigma has sometimes downplayed mistakes and complexity. (For example, some Six Sigma studies only consider poka-yoke in the Improve stage of DMAIC.) Gary Klein reports the case of the famous innovator company 3M that became so obsessed with Six Sigma detail that they lost some of their innovation capabilities. Klein suggests that a suitable balance must be found between errors and Uncertainty on one side and Insight on the other.

A starting point for Six Sigma is the belief in *process*. An organisation is characterised by processes, frequently cross-functional. The SIPOC (Supplier, Input, Process, Output, Customer) model makes clear that a process has suppliers, inputs, the process itself, outputs, and customers. It is useful to go through these systematically.

The fundamental assumption in Six Sigma is that everything is a process, and that every process can be measured. The main purpose is to identify and eradicate sources of undesired variation. Six Sigma has a specific methodology: Define, Measure, Analyse, Improve, Control (**DMAIC**) - in essence similar to the Deming (PDSA) cycle. Six Sigma progresses on a 'project by project basis', and is process-oriented. These projects are generally fairly narrow and have definite start and end points. It takes customer requirements into account at an early stage. A strong feature of Six Sigma is its bias towards data – measuring the variation of the process, and trying to both narrow the variation and to shift it within customer requirements – with 3.4 parts per million being the (frequently unattained) Six Sigma goal. Another feature is its strong financial bias – the benefits of every project are expected to show up in the financials, and are certainly costed. (Many a Six Sigma Black Belt will say that Six Sigma is not about defect reduction, but about making or saving money.)

Note: The DMAIC Cycle is discussed under Improvement Cycles, Section 32.2; Failure modes involving Lean and Six Sigma are discussed in Section 34.2.

Six Sigma is strongly based on statistics. Insistence on hard data is indeed a great strength. But Shingo warns, 'When I first heard about inductive statistics in 1951, I firmly believed it to be the best technique around, and it took me 26 years to break completely free of its spell'. Shingo's journey away from a statistics-based approach to quality should be required reading for every black belt and helps explain Toyota's lack of enthusiasm for Six Sigma (see below).

GE's version of Six Sigma revolves around six key principles. These are:

1. **Critical to Quality**. The starting point is the customer, and those attributes most important to the customer must be determined.

2. **Defect.** A defect is anything that fails to deliver exactly what the customer requires.

3. **Process Capability.** Processes must be made capable of delivering customer requirements.

4. **Variation.** As experienced by the customer. What the customer sees and feels.

5. **Stable Operations.** The aim is to ensure consistent, predictable processes to improve the customer's experience.

6. **Design for Six Sigma.** Design must meet customer needs and process capability.

The term 'Six Sigma' derives from the spread or variation inherent in any process. Essentially, the Sigma level will tell you how many defects you can expect, on average, for that process. This is a powerful way of describing performance, as it can be applied to any type of process – irrespective of whether it is in manufacturing or services. It is also limiting, as it only captures 'defects' as in deviation from the prescribed bounds of tolerance, and it assumes a normal distribution (the Central Limit Theorem is the foundation for this assumption.) The following table puts the Sigma level into context by translating it into a percentage (how many results of your process will be within tolerance), and finally, how many parts per million do they Sigma levels relate to.

So why choose such a stringent performance level of **Six Sigma**, if **four** sigma already only returns 0.6% defects? Because of 'process drift' or 'process walk' (see figure below). The originators of Six Sigma, Motorola, allowed for a 1.5 sigma drift. Thus, a 3 sigma process could in the long term become a 1.5 sigma process corresponding to 93,32% within the tolerance area or 6,68% outside (66.800 PPM).

However, with a 6-sigma process, a 1.5-sigma drift will result in only 3.4 defects per million opportunities! So, even with a 1.5 Sigma process drift, a Six Sigma process would be close to perfection. Of course, for some process such as airline flights, Six Sigma is not good enough. (In fact, measured by fatalities per sector flown, commercial aviation consistently performs better than 7 sigma.)

Applying this to Shewart's original definition of a capable process (that could place 3 standard deviations either side of the process mean), would be a 4.25 Sigma process using this logic. This point often confuses people, and there is no empirical or mathematical justification for the 1.5 Sigma shift.

Whether or not a process can achieve 3.4 defects per million, is in a sense not the point. The point is the rigorous process that moves one towards the goal. It is probably true that today most manufacturing firms are achieving 3 or 4 sigma performance, and most service firms achieve around 2 sigma. So Six Sigma is better thought of as a structured problem solving methodology rather than a measurement standard.

Process Walk

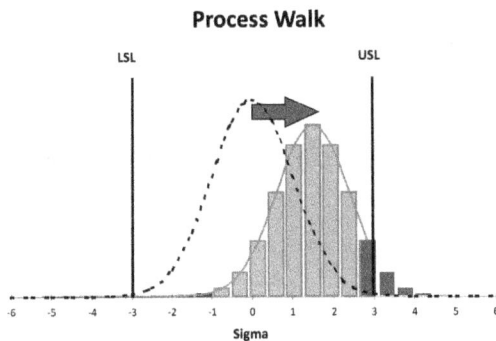

Green, Black and Master Black Belts

Six Sigma is driven by people qualified in the methodology. A useful innovation has been to recognise Six Sigma expertise by judo-type belts. A black belt typically requires four weeks of training held over four months and requires a practical project. The four weeks correspond to Measure, Analyse, Improve, Control in the DMAIC cycle. Black belts often work full time on Six Sigma projects and typically aim at savings exceeding $250k per year. Master black belts are more experienced black belts who act as mentors. There

are also Six Sigma 'Champions' who define the WHAT (a very important role, requiring cross functional and cross process knowledge), whereas Black Belts are concerned with the HOW. Some companies retain their Black Belts for between two and three years, and thereafter move them into line management positions or Champion positions. Green belts go through less rigorous training. Some companies, for instance Allied Signal / Honeywell have set goals of 90% of the workforce becoming green belts within 5 years. In a Six Sigma project there is typically a process owner, team leaders, a black belt, perhaps several green belts, and team members. Implementation and human issues are considered to be as important as the Six Sigma tools themselves.

Design for Six Sigma (DFSS) addresses design of product issues. This aspect is discussed in the New Product Introduction chapter.

How to calculate the Sigma Level of a Process

The sigma level of a process refers to the average percentage you would expect to fall outside the specific tolerance. So in order to calculate the Sigma level of a process, you first need to define the process and its tolerance levels, and then measure it (with n>>30 measurements, ideally).

The calculation of a 'sigma level' is based on the number of defects per million opportunities (DPMO). An 'opportunity' is essentially every time a customer interacts a process, so DPMO tells you how many times you let the customer down due to poor performance.

In order to calculate the DPMO, three distinct pieces of information are required: the number of units produced, and the actual number of defects uncovered.

DPMO = [Number of Defects / (Number of measurements taken * Number of units produced)] * 1,000,000.

Once you have the DPMO figure, one can convert that into a Sigma level by using the standard Six Sigma conversion table.

Example: A manufacturer of computer hard drives would like to measure their Six Sigma level. Over a given period of time, the manufacturer creates 180,000 hard drives. The manufacturer performs 8 individual checks to test quality of the drives. During testing 4,302 are rejected. Overall, there were n=4,302 defects in 8 x 180,000 opportunities, which gives a DPMO = 2,987.5. This gives a Sigma level between 4.2 and 4.3.

Warning: Note that any 'sigma' calculation is based on the normal distribution, which bears the danger of missing mistakes (low frequency) since these are generally not picked up by sampling methods. Such low-frequency events can easily be 1 in 1,000.

Integrating Lean and Six Sigma

The integration of Lean and Six Sigma has become fashionable. Beware – many Lean Six Sigma courses (even 'black belt' qualifications) are overwhelmingly about Six Sigma, with little Lean content beyond 5S, the wastes, and basic value stream mapping

It may be argued that Lean and Six Sigma both have strong Deming connections. Deming placed emphasis on two main themes during his life – removal of waste and reduction of variation (see Deming, 1982).

Waste reduction is central to Lean, and variation reduction is central to Six Sigma. Several large multinational manufacturing companies, for example Ford and Honeywell, have had separate Lean and Six Sigma programmes. Inevitably, these two powerful and widely used approaches have clashed and merged with titles to indicate this fact. The authors have identified Lean

Sigma, Fit Sigma, Six Sigma plus, Power Lean, Lean Six Sigma, and Quick Sigma. Some of these are trademarked. There are likely to be others.

The term Lean Six Sigma has emerged as most common. Here, Lean is used to remove the waste and non-value adding activities whilst Six Sigma is used to control the variation within the value adding portion of the process – thus attempting to produce a comprehensive improvement programme.

Drickhamer (2002) discusses how the adoption of Lean techniques prior to the application of Six Sigma projects can provide real benefits, removing the elitist strain from Six Sigma through teamwork whilst tackling the low hanging fruit with Lean.

Martin Hinckley's useful framework for comprehensive quality improvement has been adapted, below, as a proposed framework for suggesting the most effective approach – Lean or Six Sigma – and with some tool examples.

This has a double benefit of removing much of the process noise that is the 'bug bear' of Six Sigma projects. In two key insights he notes firstly from the Six Sigma perspective on blitz events, *'The solution to many complex and long-standing*

Area	Lean	Six Sigma
Objectives	Reduce waste Improve value	Reduce Variation Shift distribution inside customer requirements
Framework	5 Principles (not always followed)	DMAIC (always followed)
Focus	Value Stream	Project / Process
Improvement	Many small improvements, a few 'low kaizens'. Everywhere, simultaneous	A small number of larger projects - $0.25m cut-off? One at a time
Typical Goals	Cost, Quality, Delivery, Lead Time Financials often not quantified. Vague?	Improved Sigma Level (Attempt six Sigma, 3.4 DPMO) Money saving
People involved in improvement	Team led by (perhaps) Lean Expert. Often wide involvement on different levels.	Black Belts supported by Green Belts
Time Horizon	Long term. Continuous, but also short-term Kaizen	Short Term. Project by project.
Tools	Often simple but complex to integrate	Sometimes complex statistical
Typical Early steps	Map the value stream	Collect data on process variation
Impact	Can be large, system-wide	Individual projects may have large savings
Problem root Causes	Via 5 Whys (weak)	Via e.g. DOE (strong)

| Combining Lean and Six Sigma | | | | | |
Man / People	Machine	Method	Material / Product	Measures	Mother Nature
Variation	Lean (teams involvement, policy deployment) Kaizen	Six Sigma (CpK) Lean (SMED)	Lean (5S, SOPS) Six Sigma (SPC, DOE, DMAIC)	Lean Supply Six Sigma (SPC, DOE)	Lean (policy deployment) Six Sigma (DPMO, Gage R&R)	Six Sigma DOE
Mistakes	Lean pokayoke	Lean pokayoke	Lean pokayoke	Lean pokayoke	Six Sigma Lean	Six Sigma (DOE?)
Complexity	Lean (cross training, waste removal)	Lean (TPM, 5S)	Lean (waste removal)	DFSS Lean (GT, design)	Lean (policy deployment)	Six Sigma (DOE?)

problems can't be resolved using intuitive methods in less than a week' and secondly from the Lean perspective '*If you go and make everything a Six Sigma problem, you are going to constipate your system and waste a lot of resources*'.

With this background, a comparative table is shown on the next page.

A Note on Shainin Methods

Shainin's approach to defects has not received the attention it deserves. Here, there are a family of tests and experiments that reveal the 'Red x' or true problem. These include multi-variate analysis, swopping components, paired comparisons, B vs C (new against current) and the 'Tukey test'. See Keki Bhote's book.

Toyota and Six Sigma

The classic Lean company is Toyota. But, thus far, Toyota appears not to have employed Six Sigma in any way. Why? Frankly, the authors do not know but have held informal discussions with a number of Toyota staff. There appear to be at least seven reasons, possibly more. These are:

1. The preference for poka-yoke. See the earlier Shingo quote. At Toyota there are reported to be between 5 and 10 poka-yoke devices for each process step!

2. The idea that problems and defects need to 'surfaced' immediately, not studied at length. TPS is packed with concepts that are designed to highlight problems as soon as

possible. The systems include line stop, andon board, music when a machine stops, Heijunka (which can highlight non attainment of schedule within minutes), and of course a wide awareness of 'muda'. The thought seems to be to 'enforce' short term and continuous problem solving. Moreover, when problems are identified, the '5 whys' are employed to try to get to the root cause.

3. A worry about the elitism of Six Sigma, especially the 'black belt' image. The TPS way is for everyone to be involved in improvement, and hence a great reluctance to identify specialist problem solvers – however good. This is also reflected in policy deployment.

4. A 'Systems Approach'. Although Six Sigma would claim to use a systems approach, Toyota would use Six Sigma tools in conjunction with value stream mapping, A3, and policy deployment. Hence, it avoids the sub-optimisation that is a risk in Six Sigma projects.

5. A belief that many quality problems lie in design.

6. Toyota has a significant improvement organization in place that undoubtedly extends the Six Sigma master black belt/black belt/ green belt organization. Refer to the improvement section of the book.

7. The preference for using TWI-type approaches: JI, JM, JR.

20.6 Complexity

Complexity is an interesting concept – although everyone understands the word, as well as its negative impacts on any type of operation, virtually no one can define it properly!

Of course, complexity overlaps with mistakes. Apple computer has shown the way with elegance and intuitive simplicity leading to one of the largest companies in the world by market capitalisation.

What complexity does is to increase the need for management control – the more complex a system becomes, the more effort is needed to control it. Nobel laureate Herbert Simon distinguishes between *static* and *dynamic* complexity. Static complexity refers to those the elements or 'nodes' in the system that add to the complexity by being there, i.e. the more suppliers or product variants, the more complex the system becomes. Dynamic complexity on the other hand refers to the dynamic interaction between nodes, for example, the more volatile demand patterns are, the more complex managing the supply chain becomes (See bullwhip effect in the Supply Chain Chapter).

Complexity can also refer to both product and process. Product complexity refers to both the number of components and the difficulty of assembly. Process complexity refers to both the number of operations and the difficulty of each operation. Hinckley, following on from Boothroyd and Dewhurst, has shown that product defect rates are strongly related to assembly complexity.

Quality Control of Complexity (QCC)

Hinckley has developed a method called Quality Control of Complexity. The frequency of mistakes increases with increasing assembly complexity. The QCC method begins by constructing a tree diagram for assembling a product. Then the time required to complete the assembly is estimated from a set of tables covering alignment, orientation, size, thickness, insertion directions, insertion conditions, fasteners, fastening process, and handling. Alternative designs can then be evaluated based on the ratio of times to the power 1.3 (a value which has been found to be widely applicable). The results can be dramatic both for quality and for cost – perhaps a 50% reduction over the full lifetime. The power and simplicity of this technique should not be ignored.

Group Technology (GT)

Group Technology is a set of procedures aimed at simplifying products without compromising customer choice. It identifies similarities in function to reduce product and process proliferation. Thus a part designer would not start from a blank CAD screen, but would first search a database for products with similar functions. Similarly, for instance in selecting fastenings, she would make the selection from a pre-defined set rather than from an unlimited choice. The impact on part proliferation, on inventory, on manufacturing routings, and of course on quality can be dramatic.

Various GT coding and classification systems exist to assist both product designers and process designers. A part is described by stringing together a set of digits that cover for example material, usage, shape, size, machining, and forming. For cell design, particularly for complex machining cells, GT may be an early port of call to examine alternative methods and routings. Generalised classification systems can be complex, but frequently companies develop their own much simpler version which serves adequately.

Design for Assembly

Design for assembly, design for manufacture, and more generally DFx, are a key set of techniques for Lean processing simplicity. They impact time, cost, inventory, and quality. Design for manufacture is discussed in the Design and New Product Introduction section of this book.

Process complexity may be independent from product complexity. A range of tools can reduce process complexity. The tools include:

- Part presentation
- Dividing work into tasks that can be completed in one or two minutes
- Using standard operating procedures
- 5S with visual management
- Simplified material flows and layout
- TPM

- SMED
- Visual controls.

Further reading

Keki Bhote, *The Ultimate Six Sigma*, AmaCom, New York, 2002

Keki Bhote, The Power of Ultimate Six Sigma, AmaCom, 2003

Howard Gitlow and David Levine, *Six Sigma for Green Belts and Champions*, FT / Prentice Hall, 2005

Frank Gryna, Richard Chua, Joseph DeFeo, *Juran's Quality Planning and Analysis*, Fifth Edition, McGraw Hill, 2007

John Bicheno and Philip Catherwood, *Six Sigma and the Quality Toolbox*, PICSIE Books, 2005

Martin Hinckley, *Make No Mistake*, CRC, 2001

Gary Klein, *Seeing what others Don't*, Nicholas Brearley, 2013

For a wonderful book on statistics in Quality, including SPC, see Don Wheeler, *Understanding Variation*, SPC Press, 2000

21 Total Productive Maintenance

TPM is integral to Lean. It is concerned with process stabilization. Certainly no Lean implementation can be a success with a high level of stoppages. TPM goes well beyond breakdown issues to cover availability, performance, quality, as well as safety and capital investment through making best use, and extending the life, of equipment.

TPM can be viewed in relation to the classic 'Bathtub Curve', below:

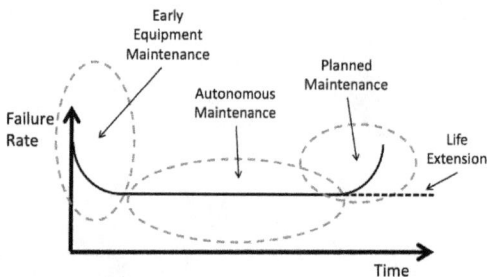

Not all machines have a full bathtub curve, but most equipment has a characteristic shape.

In addition to the types shown in the figure, there is also Condition-based maintenance and Maintenance elimination.

TPM has much in common with Total Quality. Both are concerned with the life cycle. Both aim at prevention. Both aim to 'spread the load' by getting front line staff to take over as much responsibility as possible thereby directing resources to where it is most effective and freeing up specialists to do more complex tasks (thereby creating a positive feedback loop).

Failures are reduced in the burn-in period by early equipment maintenance and by improved understanding of equipment usage. During the plateau period the failure rate is reduced by autonomous maintenance and by the 11-step programme. (See below.) The steps also extend the life of equipment. The wear-out stage is managed through predictive and planned maintenance, thereby minimising unexpected disruptions.

Generally, TPM activities are either EVENT BASED or TIME BASED. Think about driving your car. Do you check every time, when you clean, or every Sunday? Often, both are required.

Peter Willmott says there are 5 aspects to TPM:

- Increase OEE or equivalent measure
- Improve existing planned maintenance systems
- Make routine front-line asset care part of the job
- Increase skills (hand and operations, team working and problem solving)
- Early involvement in new equipment specification.
- Make performance visible. (This last is considered an aspect often ignored.)

21.1 Overall Equipment Effectiveness (OEE)

OEE is Availability x Performance x Quality, expressed in percentage terms. Availability is actual run time / planned run time. Performance is actual quantity produced / theoretical (or target) quantity produced. Quality is quantity produced right first time / total quantity produced.

An example: A shift takes 9 hours. Working time is 8 hours – planned maintenance and meeting time is one hour. Breakdowns take 20 minutes. Changeovers take 40 minutes. The standard machine cycle time is 1 minute. At the end of the day 350 parts have been produced of which 50 are scrapped, 30 of them during adjustment.

- Availability: (8 x 60 – 20 – 40)/480 = 420/480 = 88%
- Performance: actual quantity is 350 out of possible 420 in 420 minutes, so 350/420 = 83%
- Quality: 300/350 = 86%
- **OEE = 88% x 83% x 86% = 63%**

For non-process industry world class OEE is in the range 85% to 90%. Beware, however! There is no such thing is a universal world-class OEE figure. For process industry 85% would often be much too low. Note that figures in the 90's may indicate that insufficient time is being given to changeover, so batches may be too large. Each of the elements of OEE should be graphed as well as the overall figure. Keep these at Gemba. Also, below each chart, it is good to have a fishbone diagram showing possible causes. Even better, keep a CEDAC (cause and effect with addition of cards) where progress is recorded on coloured cards (red still to do, yellow done, notes on the back).

Some authorities (Willmott, McCarthy and Rich) extend the OEE concept:

- Equipment OEE includes the Six Big Losses (see below). This is also known as 'Floor-to-Floor OEE).

- Door-to-Door OEE extends the loss concept to the cell, or line or even to the plant. This would include preparation losses, such as supply failures (waiting for materials), co-ordination losses, such as transportation delays and double handling, and adherence losses, such as schedule adherence and material losses.

- Supply Chain OEE would further extend the door-to-door losses to the supply chain. Usually with just one supplier at a time.

Cautions on using OEE

Some words of warning on the use of OEE:

- OEE says nothing about schedule attainment. It is useless having a high OEE if you are making the wrong products! OEE should not be used alone, but alongside schedule attainment

- The OEE formula gives equal weight to quality and availability. But, usually, quality is far more important because rework and rejects result in greater load, and more instability.

- You can improve OEE in good and bad ways. Good ways are to reduce minor stoppages and decrease the length of a changeover. A bad way is simply to do fewer changeovers.

- Availability is made up of MTTR (mean time to repair) and MTBF (mean time between

failures). The formula is: **Availability = MTBF / (MTBF + MTTR)**

- Thus we can have two machines with the same availability but very different breakdown intervals and repair times! Machine A has short MTTR and a short MTBF. Machine B has long MTTR and a long MTBF. A and B have the same availability, but machine A is far preferable because flow will be more uniform and less buffer inventory will be required.

- There is a cost factor – reducing changeover at great cost may be counterproductive.

- Do not measure OEE plant-wide. Combining the performance of more than one machine is meaningless. Target only critical machines. Pareto!

- There are other ways to cook the books – simply don't make products with higher defect rates or more difficult adjustments.

- A boast like 'We have improved OEE by 20%' should be greeted with extreme caution: Is it overproducing? Is it a bottleneck? Is it appropriate? Is it because bigger batches are being made?

- Should OEE be calculated shift-by-shift? Yes, because the principle is that you should only measure what you can do something about.

- A serious drawback with OEE is that no measure of variation is included in the standard OEE calculation. In other words, two machines may have similar OEEs over (say) a week, but very different variation. Consider two machines with the same overall OEE of 80%. One oscillates between 20-100%, the other between 78-82%. The results, in terms of impact on the system, will in turn be very different. Of course, this is predicted by Kingman's equation. (See Chapter 4 on the Science of Lean.)

21.2 The Six Big Losses

The three factors of OEE are further broken down into the six big losses, as shown in the figure. The usefulness of the six losses is to target improvement activities.

1. Breakdowns are often defined as unplanned stoppages of 10 minutes or more. Note that some organisations consider planned maintenance as an availability loss.

2. Set-up and adjustment. Setup time can be reduced by SMED activities (See separate section), but it is adjustments that frequently go unnoticed, unmeasured, and are a huge source of loss.

3. Idling and Minor Stops. Minor stops are often defined as stoppages of less than 10 minutes. Again, they are frequently unmeasured but their accumulation results in this category being the largest loss category of the six.

4. Reduced speed. Sometimes machines are set to run at lower than design speed.

5. Quality losses (scrap, rework, yield) not only involve loss of capacity but also materials, energy, and schedules. They should include both mistakes and variation. Mistakes are often the big, but the less recognised, one.

6. Start-up. Can be huge in some industries where the process never achieves the target rate. Frequently occurs at the beginning of every shift.

The Six Big Losses in relation to OEE

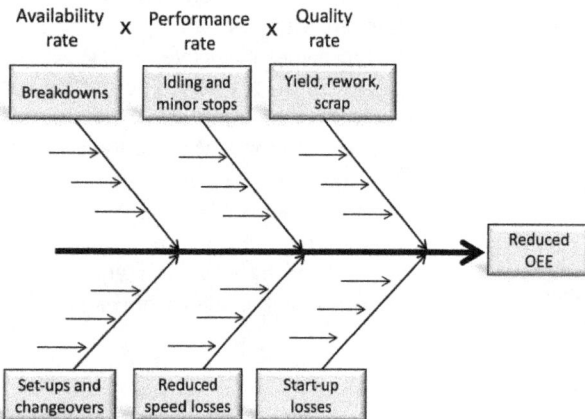

Overlap with adjustment requires careful definition.

21.3 Focusing TPM Activities

An excellent way to focus TPM activities is to graph performance as follows:

To construct: Start with the working day. Determine planned maintenance, break time, and planned idle time. Split the remaining time into the six big losses and actual effective working time. Divide by typical planned production in units. The result is a stacked bar chart as shown.

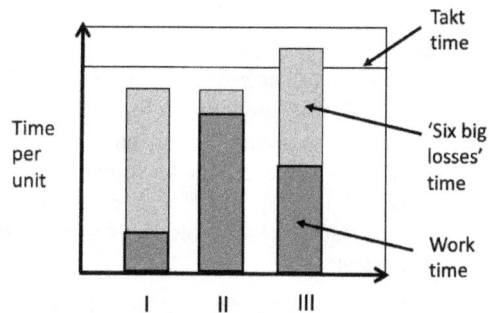

Consider the three machines shown: Machine 1 has the worst OEE. Machine 2 is closest to takt time. Machine 3 has a comfortable machine cycle but losses mean that total work cycle exceeds takt. Which to target? To target by worst OEE may be to miss the point. The question is, is this serious? To focus on machine cycle (as has been suggested in various value stream mapping publications) is not relevant as long as total time is below takt time. Machine 3 is the machine to focus on, even though it has moderate OEE and comfortable machine cycle time. And what to focus on, on Machine 3? Look at the 6 big losses. To take this analysis further, it would be good to repeat the analysis by days of the week, using a run diagram. And monitor OEE using SPC principles.

Standards

Every asset category (for example coolant, belts, pneumatic, electrical) needs to have a maintenance 'judgement standard' together with the frequency and the reason for the standard. On display, updated, and reviewed.

Improving Availability: MTBF and MTTR

If the goal is 100% overall availability, mean time to repair and mean time between failures must both be tackled – preventing breakdowns and taking quick action – if and when breakdowns occur. This involves:

- Maintenance training (including TWI style job instruction JI)
- Maintenance job analysis (including TWI style job breakdown)
- Maintenance facilities (correct tools, equipment, measurement tools, dies, inventories and spares, including shadow boards)
- Quick response (lights, red cards.)
- Refurbishment schedule (see below)

- Asset care plan (see below)
- Machine selection, testing, installation
- Visual and feedback signs (Kamishibai, OEE tracking, Single Point lessons, A3 problem solving, record boards.)

Most important, however, is the involvement of the operators and team leaders to give them the opportunity, responsibility, recognition, and incentives, for improving availability. This can be hugely motivational. Use small wins with feedback.

MTBF and MTTR can be looked at as a decision tree, together with possible actions and tools, as in the figure. (This figure is adapted from one used at Lake Region Manufacturing, Ireland.)

21.4 Willmott's 11-Step Model

Peter Willmott, UK TPM guru, has proposed a widely used 11-step model. The process is a long and thorough one. Absolutely not a quick fix.

1. Collect Equipment History and Performance Analysis. This step focuses the project and sets measurement objectives (e.g. cost, OEE, manning, material savings).

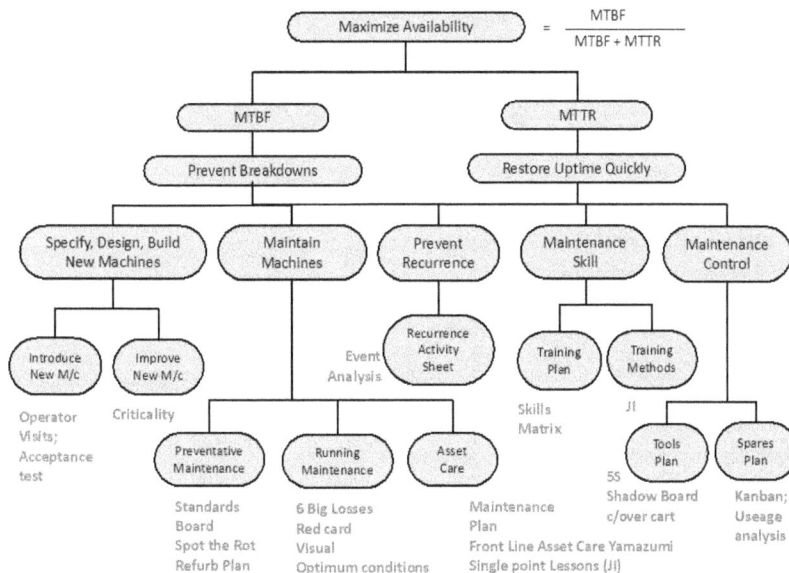

2. Define and Calculate KPIs and OEE. Clarify the meaning and interpretation amongst team members. Set up an OEE display board at Gemba. Brainstorm out possible causes and display on a chart.

3. Assess Six Big Losses and Set Priorities. This will involve an analysis such as shown earlier. Agree and sign off the priorities with management.

4. Critical Assessment. Produce a list of all components of the relevant machines. Discuss and understand the role of each component and their interdependencies – not superficially, but in detail. Discuss the optimal conditions for the operation of each critical component (e.g. temperature, lubrication, cleanliness, sharpness). Then define the normal operating conditions. Finally discuss the sources of accelerated deterioration for each component – equipment based, operator based, environment based.

5. Initial Clean-up and Condition Appraisal. Agree the cleaning areas. Source all necessary and specified cleaning equipment. Photograph the current state. Systematically inspect every part of the machine in detail. Clean and inspect, capturing all problems found. Develop a cleaning and inspection programme ('Cleaning is checking'). Identify sources of contamination (internal and external) and develop a plan to eliminate, isolate, and prevent contamination. Develop a phased refurbishment schedule – covering item, labour hours, planned completion, and PDCA cycle stage. Look into poka-yoke and quick changeover and undertake this where necessary.

6. Develop Future Total Asset Care. Clearly define the role and the tasks of the operator. Produce a clean and check list, with appropriate frequencies. Develop a Kamishabi Board (see Visual Management, Chapter 15), covering the phased and daily activities of maintenance, safety, quality, and operator checks. Identify, mark and colour code, all gauges, pipework, lubrication points, levels and sight glasses, nut positions.

7. Root Cause Analysis of problems. This is an improvement cycle. OEE leads to the particular loss being identified leading to the issues that are tackled by the 5 whys, and often by A3 analysis.

8. Develop Best Practice Routines and Standards. Taking all that has been learned in previous steps, assemble a best practice manual. Develop Single Point Lessons (See separate section under Visual Management) where necessary. Review Standard Operating Procedures and maintenance instructions.

Review equipment spares – what needs to be kept, where, how much. Index the spares and cross reference with manuals and SOPS. Develop a spares catalogue associated with each machine. Locate the manuals appropriately.

Many good routines can be developed by using 'your God-given senses' to quote Willmott. Again, think of your car. At least 30 checks are possible without any mechanical knowledge. They will make a difference to the car, and maybe to your life!

9. Individual and team skill development

10. Leadership and behaviours

11. Audit and review

These last three steps have much in common with other Lean practices, but the hands-on experience of the earlier steps builds a huge amount of stimulation and motivation. It is real Action Learning.

Peter Willmott uses excellent analogies in the form of owning and using a motor car, football team management, and daily care of the human body to link TPM practice with everyday experience. In particular, the use of human senses – eyes, ears, nose, touch is powerful.

21.5 Some Special Features of TPM

'At its worst when new'. This provocative statement goes to the heart of TPM. Why should an item of equipment be at its worst when new? Because, it may not yet be quality capable, standard procedures not yet worked out, mistake proofing (poka-yoke) devices not yet added, operating and failure modes not yet known, 6 big losses not yet measured or understood, and vital internal elements not yet made visible (through transparent covers) or monitored by condition monitoring.

Visibility. Like Lean, TPM aims to make what is happening clear for all to see. This means maintenance records need to be kept next to the machine, problems noted on charts kept next to the machine and, following a 5 S exercise, vital components made visible by replacing (where possible) steel covers with transparent plastic or glass. Also, any leaks or drips are more easily seen.

Red Tags. Red tags are a common form of visible TPM. Maintenance 'concerns' are written on red tags and hung on a prominent board on the shop floor. They remain there until action is taken. Red tags usually cover concerns that cannot be dealt with by operators.

Reliability Centred Maintenance (RCM)

RCM was developed during the 1960's when it became apparent that scheduled maintenance has little effect on complex equipment, and fixed interval maintenance can be ineffective. Complex equipment often gives an indication of impending failure. As a result RCM uses condition-based and predictive methods rather than time based methods. RCM often begins with prioritising assets, and then identifying failure modes, identifying risk reduction tasks, and developing failure finding tests.

Condition Monitoring

Condition monitoring is a specialist function in RCM, but in some environments (for example heavy and rotating machinery) an important means to reduce cost. Methods include vibration detection, temperature monitoring, bearing monitoring, emission monitoring, and oil analysis. Often the sequence is vibration, sound, heat, then failure. Today, there are hand-held, and computer linked, devices to assist.

Information Systems. Information systems were always an important part of PM, and remain so with TPM. However, their scope is extended from machines to include operator, safety and energy issues but also to allow for workplace data recording.

Maintenance Elimination through Design

This approach involves a detailed examination of parts and systems with the idea of eliminating those with low reliability or low maintainability.

A related approach in design involves subjecting items to Noise, Vibration, and Harshness (NVH) tests to reduce or eliminate fatigue-driven reliability issues. This is widely used in automotive, aircraft, and machine tool design. An example NVH software is LMS, part of Siemens.

Design and Administration, and Benchmarking. Today, TPM is beginning to be seen in administrative and white-collar areas. Willmott calls this Total Productive Administration. Of course, there are computers, photocopiers, and fax machines but there are also tidy (?) desks, filing cabinets, and refreshment rooms.

Further reading

Denis McCarthy and Nick Rich, *Lean TPM*, Butterworth Heinemann, *Second edition, 2014*

Seiichi Nakajima (Ed), *TPM Development Program*, Productivity Press, Cambridge MA, 1989

John Campbell and James Reyes-Picknell, *Uptime*, Second edition, Productivity, 2006

Peter Willmott, *Total Productive Maintenance: The Western Way*, Butterworth Heinemann, Oxford, 1994

Peter Willmott, John Quirke, Andy Brunskill, *TPM: A Foundation of Operational Excellence*, SA Partners, 2019

John Moubray, *Reliability Centred Maintenance*, (Second edition), Butterworth Heinemann, Oxford, 2001

Edgar Bradley, *Reliability Engineering*, (Second Edition), CRC Press, 2022

Our sincere thanks to Peter Willmott for his help and inspiration.

22 Layout, Cells and Line Balance

'We shape our buildings; thereafter they shape us.' Winston Churchill

Lean Layout sets the framework for any Lean transformation. It is important because you live with the results of poor layout day in and day out for, maybe, years.

Layout is usually approached as a hierarchy

- Plant Location. (See Supply Chain Ch 29)
- Area Layout (See Mapping Chapter 23 and The Building Blocks in section 25.9)
- Cell Layout (This Chapter)
- Socio-Technical considerations (Ch 10)
- Workstation Layout and Ergonomics

In the Flow Chapters the Product Process Matrix is discussed. This is highly relevant to layout, the thesis being that a major influence on layout is volume and repetitiveness. The major types of layout are shown again in the next table.

22.1 General Layout: Good and Not so Good at the Factory Level.

Before you start....

An opportunity to do a major layout is an opportunity not to be missed. It will help or hinder your Lean direction for a long time. So, visit extensively. Read all you can. And think: Is this an opportunity to redefine the business? For example, you could compete on lead time instead of cost – like some in-mall opticians that deliver a pair of glasses in one hour, or by Seru cells. You might rationalise the product line. You may outsource processes that are not key to your business). Or you may in-source for lead-time reasons. You may decide to trade inventory for machines – having excess machine capacity allowing quick response and make to order rather than make to stock with bigger inventories.

Rajan Suri has pointed out that there are two approaches to cells – the technical and the managerial. The former involves calculations and waste elimination and the latter involves understanding the market and where competitive advantage lies. This is most appropriate.

Later in this Chapter the 3P process is described. 3P is a participative methodology for building cells and processes for new products.

Size is important. Schonberger suggests a general cut-off point at around 50k square meters or half million square feet. Why? Because plants above this size are in danger of becoming unfocused. The workforce becomes too large. Lines of communication are stretched. Gemba walk by managers become impractical. Of course, there are exceptions like car plants. But can the plant be broken down into sub-plants, each preferably end-to-end, and each with its own order entry, production control, dispatch, meeting areas, and so on?

Bad: Square Functional / Job Shop Layout: In the Lean world traditional functional layout is seldom justifiable. It invariably involves batch and queue, significant transport, and long lead times. Poor quality often accompanies this because of failure to detect problems quickly. Complex scheduling routes and floating bottlenecks are often a feature. (Finite scheduling is not the answer- it is a bit like adding insult to injury.) But even worse is where this type of layout occurs on multi-floors. Demolish and start again!

A Little Better: Rectangular end-to-end flow, with receiving at one end and dispatch at the other end. Although the main lines may flow well, invariably there are long transport distances to workstations far from the receiving dock.

Sometimes Better: Spine layout is a good choice for fast changing situations. HP are enthusiastic users. Here there is a central material handling spine with cell areas along the spine, sometimes on both sides. Automatic guided vehicles may run along the spine. A warehouse may be situated at one end of the spine. Cells along the spine can be added or subtracted. Two-way flow is made possible. Even better is where there are also outside doors giving direct access to the cells.

	Project	Job Shop	Cell	Line	Flow
Also known as		Process layout		Assembly line	
Examples	Civil engineering, large turbines	Custom manufacture	Component assembly, robotic welding	Car or electronic end item assembly	Chemical works, flows between vessels
Volume	One-off, low	Low, batches	Moderate	Moderate to high	Continuous or batch flow
Traditional Characteristic		Flexible not efficient		Efficient not flexible	
Scheduling	Critical path	MRP, Finite scheduling	Heijunka	Broadcast	Optimization software
Evolution	Lean construction	Modularity, pulse line	Longer cycle teams	Global body line	Smaller vessels; 'base' and 'flex' plants
Issues	Coordination, learning	De-skilling	Boring, repetitive tasks, acceptance from former job shop people	Boring, repetitive tasks	Becoming high tech, skill shortage
Lean challenges	Standard work for repetitive elements	Standard work	Pace of improvement, value streams or linked cells	Mixed model	Down-sizing

The bad news comes from locked-in material handling along the spine that often involves wasteful travel.

Much Better: Rectangular layout – perhaps on a 60:40 ratio and with numerous delivery doors along one of the longer sides and numerous dispatch areas along the other long side. Direct delivery to cells is made possible. This also allows parallel processing along short, dedicated value streams and the possibility of sharing labour resources between the parallel streams.

In the sections below we look at some Layout Innovations:

Innovative (1): Star-shaped or Fishbone shaped building design. The arms of the star are sub-assembly lines but having numerous outside access points. One of the arms is final assembly.

Innovative (2): Assembly at Toyota's Tahara Plant follows a 'doubling back' or spiral concept – starting out and working towards the centre. It also incorporates breaks in the line that are there to facilitate 'line stop' creating a buffer between sections so that one section can stop without the whole plant stopping. (How many stops should there be per day? How about over 1,000! 'We stop for or mistakes; others ship their mistakes!') This shape allows immediate feedback of problems.

Innovative (3): Volvo's Kalmar plant is arranged in hexagonal areas, one of which is used for team based assembly.

Innovative (4): According to Michel Baudin Toyota's Miyagi plant features mixed model final assembly with cars moving along sideways rather than end to end. This saves space and operator movement. Energy also is saved by cars being moved on low friction platforms rather than by traditional chain-pulled conveyor.

All these cases are even better where suppliers are located on-site right around the parent site.

Modern design incorporates good height and big windows. Floors should be thick enough to support changing machine locations, and may also contain numerous fibre optic cable points. But also think one-level ergonomic flow – this may mean having to locate the bases of some machines below the nominal floor level so that the level of the workpiece is maintained. On the other hand, tilting or changing the workpiece height for worker access and ergonomics, is also found.

Innovative (5): In the 1990's, Sony and Canon began their cell implementation, calling it Seru Production. A central idea is the supporting socio-technical aspect of team working. Gradually this has extended to self-managing teams to include devolved decision-making, scheduling, materials management, and packaging. As well as offering greater flexibility, Seru cells also deliver significant energy savings.

Both Sony and Canon have realised huge cost-savings in inventory, machines, floor space, lead-time and people by changing to a Seru system. To quote from Yin et al: *'Seru is differentiated by its singular focus on responsiveness as a strategy, with efficiency gains as a secondary priority…. Rather than explaining Seru as a combination of lean and agile approaches, understanding its effectiveness requires that we explore the trade-off between responsiveness and efficiency that Seru illustrates.'* (See the later section on Seru).

Designing **Layout for flexibility** is increasingly being attempted. In automotive, mixed model lines now send both cars and vans down the same line. Services (electricity, air, information) are designed for flexibility. Many plants incorporate socio-tech considerations such as natural light, meeting and relaxation areas on the factory floor, and integration of several disciplines into value streams near to assembly.

Architects are now integrating with operations people much earlier. The new buildings at a world renowned teaching hospital were completed a few years ago. Prior to moving in, many kaizen events were held with doctors, nurses and other staff. But in some cases walls and rooms were in the wrong place, and could not be moved. The hospital will have to live with this for decades. If only the events

could have taken place with architects using simulated spaces or virtual reality!

22.2   Area Layout
Starting Out on Area Layout

The starting point for area layout should be the P-Q (Product – Quantity) Analysis and Runners, Repeaters, Strangers. These give an initial clue to organization. When looking at the P-Q profile, routings are also relevant (Hence Hales and Anderson prefer P-Q-R). High volume suggests assembly lines or production line cells (a production line cell is used for one product family and its variants having common routings). Moderate volumes suggest traditional cells that can cope with a variety of products that share common characteristics but share most routings. Low volumes suggest functional cells, with like machines grouped together, and some specialised routings or off-cell processes, or a job shop.

Contribution analysis is important for possible product line rationalization or design modification. Contribution per bottleneck minute is important for products that share constrained resources. (See the Contribution section in Chapter 4 on The Science of Lean.)

Area or Value Stream Analysis

The task here is to group parts into cells is a similar but more detailed procedure to Value Stream identification. There are several approaches.

Inspection (or 'Eyeball'). Perhaps the most common procedure is to group by inspection or by customer. For example, two cells to make automotive components – one for Ford the other for Toyota. Such cells are often run according to the customer's methodology – FPS for Ford, TPS for Toyota. Alternatively group by product or family that 'everyone knows' has similar characteristics.

Matrix Approach to Identify Product Families: Where routings are complex, draw up a table of products against process steps. Do not include minor process or processes that are visited by all products.

A straight-forward tool for family identification is King's' rank order clustering algorithm. This does not always yield clear product family identification but is always worth trying in any situation where a variety of products (or services) visit a variety of processes.

Small example. Four products through 7 processes. Are there families?

The solution sequence is shown in the Figure.

- The Xs represent necessary processes for each part. (Ignore circles for now.)

- The first stage is to assign weights to each process column. This should be done right to left in powers of 2 ($2^0, 2^1, 2^2$, etc.) Hence 1,2,4, 8 etc

- Total weight is calculated for each product row, adding the weights for each applicable process. For example, Row 1: 16+8+1=25

- Rearrange the rows, top to bottom, according to the total weights, to give the next matrix.

- Assign weights to each product row, in powers of 2 from bottom to top. Calculate total weight for each column. For example for process 1 column: 8+4=12.

- Now rearrange the process columns left to right to give the final matrix.

- Two non-overlapping cells or value streams are indicated. In this case establish two cells or map two value streams.

- If the original matrix contained Xs where the circles appear, no non-overlapping cells are possible. In this case, repeat the above calculation sequence.

Eventually a solution as shown in the final matrix will emerge.

- What to do with the overlapping processes C3 and D1? Possibilities include:

- If a process is not suitable for incorporation in a cell (for example a paint line in a factory or a Cat scanner in a hospital) simply locate this in a common area as a shared resource.

- If it economic, have two machines – one in each cell. (This is one of the great advantages of the Lean policy of 'small machines')

- Redesign a product so that the shared resource is not used.

- Split the cells. In the example, one cell for processes 5,6 and another for processes 4,7,2. These are fed by or into processes 1 and 3.

Note the outliers, D1 and C3. Can these be re-routed? Common processes (Paint lines? Tool maintenance?) should then be located to enable flow to be as easy as possible. Likewise supermarkets, which should be grouped together so as to allow convenient runner or material handling routes.

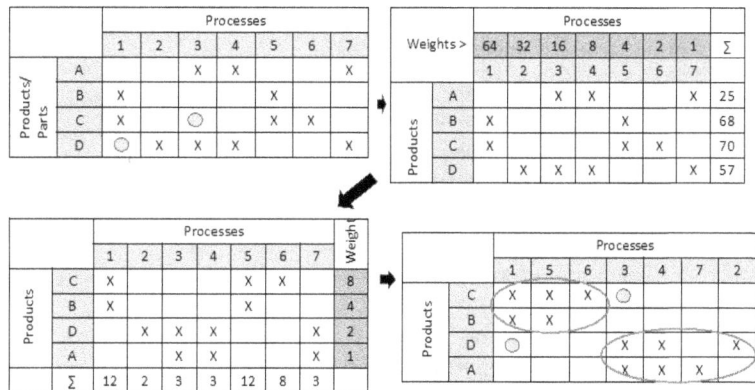

After: J.R.King, 'Machine component grouping.....', IJPR, 1980, v18, n2, 213-232

Further reading

J.R. King, 'Machine-component grouping in production flow analysis: an approach using a rank order clustering algorithm', *Int. Jnl. of Production Research*, Vol18, n2, 213-232, 2007

Note: Today there are several approaches available for more complex cases, including Artificial Intelligence. These are discussed in the following reference:

Shafer, S. M. (1998) 'Part machine labour grouping: the problem and solution methods' In *Group Technology & Cellular Manufacturing: updated perspectives*, Eds. Nallan C. Suresh E. John M. Kay, Kluwer Academic Publishers

Area Analysis by SLP

Systematic Layout Planning (SLP) is a robust procedure developed by Richard Muther Associates, and useful for area layout of offices and factories. It can also be used for micro workstation layout. It is quick and effective. (For a more detailed explanation see Lee Hales, Hyer and Wemmerlov, or Tompkins et al.) The procedure involves:

- Establishing the desirable closeness relationship between all major sections and departments, according to the vowel sequence AEIOUX – absolute, essential, important, ordinary, unimportant, and undesirable. All the relationships can be shown on a triangle matrix as below.

- Then, a 'space relationship diagram' is drawn with an initial layout or the current layout. The desirable closeness obtained from the triangle matrix is drawn in using multiple lines: 4 lines for A, 3 for E, 2 for I, 1 for U, and a zig-zag line for X. Then, simply using an inspection approach, the departments are rearranged so as to minimise the total length of all lines together. Place departments with most line connections close together. Alternatively, the lines can be coloured from red for A, through orange, yellow, black, blue – and

rearranging with the idea of making the diagram 'cooler'.

- Lastly, the relative locations are fitted into the actual space available.

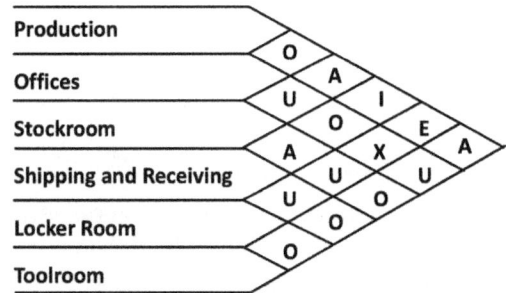

The Cell Flow Diagram

Incorporating quantities and routings: Vertical or Horizontal?

Once the broad value streams have been established, another technique derived from Richard Muther Associates is useful for more complex value streams where products or assemblies within the stream vary in quantity and routings, and where the issues are whether to split the value stream into a series of linked cells, to have one continuous cell, and which processes should be incorporated into the main cells. This involves drawing a 'cell flow diagram'. This is simply a schematic of the sequence of processes, with the intensity of the volumes of assemblies or components shown by numbers of lines from 4 for high to 1 for low. As shown below.

This useful diagram is a provocative aid. One can see a main line and a support line – but the question is should this be in one cell, two parallel cells or a two sub cells leading into one operation.

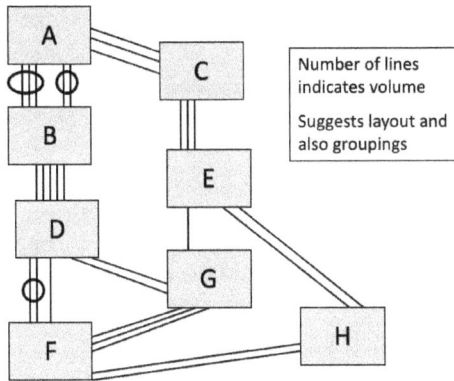

Number of lines indicates volume

Suggests layout and also groupings

Other general points to consider:

- The grouping of inventory into supermarkets is critical for Lean. Supermarkets provide the basic framework. They should be stable, whilst cells come and go. Try to have a few supermarkets, rather than inventory all over the place in little stores or in one central warehouse. See the Lean Scheduling Building Blocks section.

- Break up the value steam map into pull segments or loops, often separated by supermarkets. Then use these as building blocks for layout design.

- Be cautious about a big warehouse – especially an automated warehouse or automatic storage and retrieval system. There will always be a temptation to fill it. If you have an AS/RS already, set in place a plan to reduce usage then close it down.

- Establish a series of specific 'waterspider' (runner) routes – with material handlers making regular circuits. This powerful concept paces the work and flows information regularly via pull systems.

- Think three dimensions. Can deliveries be made from below or above? For example, can plastic be fed into injection moulding machines from the floor below thereby allowing a high state of cleanliness and separation of operators and forklifts?

- Don't get hooked on using old facilities. Better to demolish and move. Costs will

quickly be recovered. Like Dell. Many plants grow like topsy, locating new work in any available space. They pay the price over many years.

- Locate design and engineering areas close to manufacturing. Make them share common break areas. Even better make engineers walk past production areas to get to their work area.

- Locate production control in the middle of the plant floor. If possible, manager's offices also. Don't make supervisors offices too comfortable.

- Foster communication and visibility in the office by open plan layout, and common meeting areas

- Share information by visual displays. One idea is to have a data projector permanently on display and linked to current performance status and company news. Gather around Communication Boards. (See Leader Standard Work in Chapter 9.)

Operator Considerations

There would seem to be a slow but steady movement away from short cycle jobs towards longer, more interesting jobs. In other words there is a move away from long-thin layout to short-fat layout or one single line with short cycle tasks and takt time to several parallel lines with longer cycles and takt time. Job rotation is one solution to repetitive boring jobs, but is only a marginal improvement. Volvo tried parallel groups for job turnover reasons. Job turnover did reduce, but the additional problems were multiple inventory locations, hence more complex transport, multiple tooling, and group work norms some of which were high but others low. Training is also an issue. But this experience is no reason to reject longer cycle work. Longer cycle work is potentially more efficient because there is less balancing loss with fewer, longer cycles. So, what can be done to get the 'best of both worlds'?

- Group operators into tight groups, perhaps having several cells that share a common supermarket. Group takt = takt time x number in the group.

- Give each operator a long cycle job (like assembling a complete photocopier) but get the group to work in parallel and start and stop together. They pace one another. This is often better than the whole group assembling one product at a single location, with reduced cycle time, because they get in each others' way (called work interference).

- Get the operators to govern their own rate over (say) half a day. As long as they meet target by the end.

There is much to be said for combining operations rather than specialization in a series. Think about a supermarket checkout. Would you rather progress through a series of checkouts, each one specializing: the first on fruit and vegetables, the second on drinks, the third on dairy etc. Life would be a pain! (See Seru, below)

22.3 Material Handing: Good and Not so Good at the Factory Level.

Bad: Long conveyors, especially powered conveyors. Why? They lock-in the waste of movement, and worse they get forgotten about as waste. Because they are barriers around which much travel has to take place. They work subtly against communication and quality. There is always the danger that they become another unofficial store.

Also bad: Forklifts. These may be inevitable depending on the size of the product. But they also subtly encourage material movement in big batches by stillage. They take up space and are dangerous.

Better: FIFO lanes, if short, can be effective in encouraging flow. If too long, they can become inventory traps. A long FIFO lane should always be questioned but, if found to be necessary, one long lane should be replaced by two short side-by-side lanes to reduce double handling. Good FIFO lanes are marked with warning colours to indicate if inventory is building up.

Better: Tugger trains. These go around a regular route, calling at 'bus stops' at regular intervals. The best are low-bed on which human-movable wheeled containers are placed. Human-movable small containers are good if carried at ergonomically friendly heights. Standard stopping locations should be part of the concept. A balance needs to be struck between the size of the tugger and the frequency of routing.

Much Better: Gravity feed, short conveyors, linking closely located machines. FIFO lanes, should include coloured inventory accumulation warnings or even poka-yoke light-beam warnings.

Best: Generally, are hand trolleys or small AGVs. These need to be moved by material handler or runner, not by cell operators. Cell operators can activate AGVs. These give maximum flexibility, at minimum cost with no risk of breakdown. They encourage small batch flow. Beware, however, of kitting trolleys. Sometimes justifiable, but kitting is often double-handling waste.

22.4 Cells

Why Cells?

Cells have become almost universal so there is no need for long debate. Compared with a traditional job shop the advantages are massive reduction in lead time through one-piece flow, big reductions in inventory, simplified control, early identification of quality problems, improved possibilities for job rotation, identification with the item, and volume flexibility by adjusting the number of workers. The type of cell, however, remains an issue. Two basic types: long and thin, with short repetitive work content, or short but fat, with longer work content. Although the former may be more efficient (less inventory stocking locations, less tool variety, less training), it is also more boring so job turnover may be an issue.

A Cell is Not a Cell: The Cell Ideal.

Although cells are widespread, many do not conform to the cell ideal. The ideal cell has one piece flow, good visibility, minimal inventories between stations (not zero), an organization that matches – cell supervisors and identification of workers with the cell, support functions – quality, maintenance, ideally scheduling – that are focused on the cell not the wider enterprise, supporting supermarkets and runner routes, and incorporated poka-yoke devices.

Moving to one piece flow has huge advantages – most dramatically a cut in lead time. Consider 4 machines with a cycle time of 1 minute per part, each sequentially producing a batch of 10 parts. The batch emerges after 40 minutes. With one piece flow, the first part emerges after 4 minutes! The former case is called 'fake flow'. But lead time is only one aspect – dramatic changes in transport (moving away from forklifts?), space, and in early problem detection are also big advantages.

Cell Working Arrangements

In this section we consider various working arrangements in a cell. Cell balancing is considered in the next section.

There is wide agreement of the virtues of U shaped cells. These include ease of balancing, improved communication and feedback for quality and other issues, improved visibility, and ease of control where one operator does the first and last operation.

But a cell need not be U shaped. Straight-through has flexibility and material handling advantages particularly for large artefacts. L shape may be chosen for storage considerations.

There are several possibilities for working in a U cell. Volume, activity times, quality, and boredom alleviation are the major considerations.

For Assembly Cells:

- At it most basic, a cell can be manned by a single operator who moves (walks) between workstations, usually in a counter-clockwise direction for ease of hand movement (Toyota believes counter-clockwise is the natural way – think athletic tracks, horse racing.) Of course, the operator needs to be trained to do all jobs. This is ideal for low volume work.

- As volume increases more operators are added. There are several alternatives:

- Two or more operators 'chase' one another around the cell, doing all the tasks at all workstations. This is known as 'rabbit chase'. This is good where operators work more or less at the same pace. It facilitates low inventory. It is good for job interest and health. Operators pace one another, and can take breaks without coverage. No detailed task timing or balancing is required since all operators do all jobs. Only the total time to do all jobs is required. The number of operators required is the total cell work content (minutes) / required completion rate (or takt time). Thus is the time for one operator to complete all tasks in the cell is 10 minutes, and one job is required every 5 minutes, then 10/5 = 2 operators are required.

- Two or more operators chase one another around the cell but move in a direction opposite to the material flow. This is the 'reverse rabbit run' gives slightly more time flexibility. Try it and see!

- Two or more operators move around different but set routes in the cell. Here operators do not have to know all tasks. It is easier to include accurate or detailed tasks where sitting is required. Often, buffer (decoupling) inventory is held between worker routes. Timing and balancing will be required. See next section.

- Multiple cells or cells in series. Here a decoupling inventory or FIFO lanes are found between cells. One of the 'cells' may be an outside contractor for a special purpose.

- Split cells. Where an operation takes longer than the takt time, a cell can be split into parallel paths.

For Machine Cells: Here, either the operator's cycle time or the machine cycle time will be the determining factor. The operator may have to load, start, and unload machines. An operator can also walk, inspect and move inventory during the machine cycles. Cell balancing becomes more complex.

The Cell Trade-off

As more operators are added the capacity of the cell increases, but in a non-linear, asymptotic way. Operator costs increase linearly. Thus there is an optimal level of operators where unit cost is minimised. However, minimum cost may not correspond with demand or with synchronising the value stream. Flexibility rather than cost may be an overriding concern.

Also, consider different demand rates. It is good practice to configure a cell or line so as to run at several rates, and to change over quickly between rates, by for example quick change part presentation.

22.5   Cell or Line Balancing

First, note that there are a range of algorithms available for assembly line balancing. Several have been around for 40+ years and include:

- Helgerson-Birnie: Ranked positional weight
- Kilbridge-Webster
- Hoffman Analysis.

All of these require an assembly precedence diagram detailing the logical sequence of assembly steps. A precedence diagram is similar to a project network diagram except that there are usually several possible starting activities and several possible ending activities. For a complex assembly line, involving several hundred activities, it is now usual to use simulation, stochastic balancing, or Artificial intelligence. (AI).

Cell balancing or less complex line balancing is best done by operators themselves working with industrial engineers. Of course, for participation, there must be no threat of job loss. The steps are:

- Establish the takt time – derived from customer demand and work hours. Note that demand may be able to be levelled, and work hours changed to stabilise the takt time.

- Consider different target rates. A good Lean cell should be able to adjust easily from one rate to another. Normally, then, the cell is balanced for (say) three rates. This enables a rate change to be rapidly done.

- Establish the target cycle time. This will be less than takt time – normally 90% of takt, lower for high variation work, higher for very low variation work. (If you balance to 100% of takt, one little problem and you will miss the target. Remember that any stoppage is time lost that can never be recovered, so balancing to 100% of takt means inevitable overtime. (See Kingman's equation in the Science of Lean Chapter.)

- Remove obvious wastes and establish good practice. Do this without timing. If it is an existing cell, make a video and ask operators to critique. Look out for movement wastes, poor ergonomics, signage, and inventory footprinting. If there are multiple shifts, compare the same operation across all shifts with operators from each. Ask the operators to come up with the 'best of the best' or the ideal way.

- Consider the best layout as if one operator was running the cell. This will give the most efficient layout.

- Then establish work element times. Ideally get operators to work out the times themselves. Use a video (?). Time at least 10 cycles. Get the operators to select an appropriate cycle time for each work element. This will not be the average, minimum, or longest time but at the pace for a good, steady rate. (We are not talking work study here; that is anathema to many.) Generally synthetic time standards such as MTM are not satisfactory – not because they give the wrong answers but because they send out the wrong message. Don't add in an allowance factor. Rather factor in breaks into the takt time calculation.

- Be particularly aware of non-repetitive work. For example:

- Does an operator go to fetch parts every so often?

- Are there interruptions? Why?

- What documentation or records are needed?

- Is there a break in the normal rhythm of work? Why?

- What happens when material is delivered? Is there a break to sort out documentation, orientation, container placement, etc.

- In all these cases, what can be done to make the work more smooth and less wasteful?

- Inventory in a Cell. Remember the ideal is usually one-piece flow.

A cell is not a cell if batches continue to be run. That is, if there is a batch between each stage. Merely changing the locations of machines so as to create a U-shape does not constitute cell manufacture. If batches continue to be run, this is what is called 'fake flow'. But wait. Although one-piece flow and not batches is the way to go, this does not mean having one piece per workstation! At least initially. Start with a few parts between stations as a buffer, and then remove them as flow becomes more established and problems are ironed out.

- Focus on detailed work station ergonomics and movement. Operators should stand and move, not sit, except for accurate work and hand assembly. Avoid the need to bend or reach. Use standard laws of ergonomics.

- A word on automation: Lean is not anti-automation in cells, but is cautious about it.

Good reasons for automation is quality and 'dull, dirty, dangerous' or 'hot heavy hazardous'. A bad reason is to same people – for two reasons. First, robots don't improve. Don't lock in waste. Automation is not as flexible as people. Automating to allow machines to run unattended is good. So is auto-eject.

- An activity sample can be a useful supplementary exercise to collect data on wastes that may be occurring.

- For a new cell, do a 'cardboard kaizen'. Here, use full scale cardboard boxes to represent the machines and have operators walk around as if they were running the cell. Make adjustments. This is PDCA.

Timing and Cell Balancing

Most time studies of repetitive manual work reveal that the distribution of times for a work element is skewed to the right – that is with a short tail to the distribution on the left and a long tail on the right. This is also similar to the Poisson distribution observed in many service transactions – most transactions take a short time but a few take a very long time. It is the long tail on the right that is the 'killer' for line balancing. The long tail is usually caused by quality or part problems rather than operator problems. If variation can be reduced – to cut the tail, then (strangely?) the average time for a job can be increased. This is a feedback loop – take longer over a work element and thereby reduce problems at that or subsequent elements which in turn means that time for those elements can be increased! Of course, there are limits to this. This is a consequence of the non-linear queuing curve discussed in The Science of Lean chapter. It is also common experience when sitting in a holdup on the highway and finding that the 'fast' lane has become the slow lane. The 'fast' lane has greater variation. Think about the tortoise and the hare.

- After all the work time elements, value add and non-value- add, have been accumulated, the approximate number of operators needed can be calculated from the sum of all the operator work elements divided by the cycle time. This would be the case for manual assembly work. Where there are machines, a machine cycle may govern if the machine cycle plus load and unload times is greater than the required cell cycle time. In this case two parallel machines or even complete parallel cells may be required. Where a machine cycle is less than the required cell cycle time, normally, activities can be found for the operator to do while the machine is running. An operator should not stand and watch a machine run through a cycle. Sometimes an unoccupied operator is unavoidable for part of the machine cycle. This is where the Work Combination chart is particularly useful. See below.

- If there is a very long cycle work element in the process, say a batch process or where work needs to go out for a subcontracted stage, it is still possible to run a one-piece flow cell. Here, simply have an output and an input buffer at that stage but otherwise run the cell as usual.

- Think whether the cell or team leader should be included as an operator or in a full-time support role. On a complex inter-dependant assembly line it is a good idea to have the team leader as a floater – to assist with problems and to cover for short absenteeism (minutes for toilet) or longer term (days for leave). The size of each team will then be a consideration – Toyota uses around 6 on its lines, more in less complex areas. In a less tight cell, the team leader may well be one of the regular operators.

- Make up a Yamazumi or work balance board. Preferably use magnetic strips for the work elements cut to scale so as to represent the work element times. Green for value add work, red for all others. The strips are then fitted in and accumulated on the board up to the planned cycle time line to represent the work of each operator. See

the figure on accumulating the full level for all but the final operator.

- Repeat the cell balance exercise for the appropriate number of work rates, or takt times. As different numbers of operators will be used, it may be necessary to incorporate additional buffers between operator routes. Also, work out the changeover procedure from one line rate to another. Quick changeover principles are relevant here. A hint: When adding a new operator to a cell, add him in the middle, not a beginning. The latter will cause increased variation in output.

- Decide on the standard inventory quantities, containers and footprinting.

- Incorporate 'poka-yoke' failsafe methods where possible. This is not only for quality

- Decide on the 'what if' or andon signals and communications that will be needed. Establish the procedure for what happens when there is any sort of problem.

- Establish the production control system for the cell. Maybe Heijunka (See separate section) or a work by the hour board. In any case, include a conveniently located problem board where the reasons for failures to attain the required rate are noted as they occur. This, of course, is not 'blame and punishment' but problem surfacing. Far from blame, operators should be commended for writing perceptive reasons on the board.

- Establish the start-up procedures and checks for the beginning of the shift. Remember to deduct this time from the takt time calculation. Likewise, if there are regular maintenance or check activities that need to be performed after every (say) 10,000 cycles, establish these procedures and allow for their time.

- Prepare standard work charts – the Work Combination Chart and the Cell Layout chart, completes the design. See the figures. The best people to prepare these are the cell operators working in conjunction with industrial engineers. Having operators participate in the preparation of standard work encourages their questioning work methods and helps with sustainability. The work combination chart is a Gantt-type chart showing how the sequence of activities and times that each operator follows. Note that movement activities are not recorded but shown as wavy lines connecting the activities. The cell layout chart shows the geography or plan view of the cell, the routes that each operator follows in the work sequence, and very importantly the locations and quantities of the standard inventories. You will notice that the example shows operators moving back and forth. This is not desirable if operators can walk around the cell in a circle, either in the direction of material flow, or in a direction opposite to flow.

- Then implement and verify the standard work charts. (See job breakdown sheets in Chapter 17).

Cell Balancing Alternatives: Bucket Brigade

Bucket brigade balancing has become popular because it often increases productivity, improves flexibility, and avoids the problems of timing of work elements. The method is suitable where all operators know or can learn many of the tasks.

First, estimate the required number of operators. The example below will be given for 3 operators doing 8 tasks.

Line up the three operators next to the first three tasks. Operator 1 starts work at task 1, then passes the piece to operator 2, who passes it to operator 3 for the third task. Operator 3 then progresses the work through all the remaining tasks until she completes the last task. She then starts walking back downstream. In the meantime, Operators 1 and 2 have been working on the second piece. When Operator 2 completes task 2, she moves to task 3 and so on until she meets Operator 3 walking

back after completing task 8. When they meet, Operator 3 then takes over the partly completed piece, turns around, and completes the remaining tasks to task 8. Again Operator 3 walks back downstream. Meanwhile Operator 2, having handed the piece to Operator 3, turns around and walks back downstream until she meets Operator 1 who is progressing the third piece. At that point Operator 2 takes over piece 3, turns around, and continues to work downstream. When Operator 1 met Operator 2, Operator 1 turns around, walks back to the first task and then begins piece 4. This is carried on until the cell settles down to a natural balance of work between the three operators. No detailed balancing or Yamuzumi board is needed.

The three operators will establish a natural output rate, not a pre-determined rate as with time study. If the output is not sufficient, an extra operator will have to added or extra time worked.

Bucket brigade line balancing has the following significant advantages:

- No time study required.
- Greater productivity in comparison with a line balanced against takt time or target cycle time. This is because a target cycle time line can hardly ever be perfectly balanced. There is no time wasted with bucket brigade.
- Flexible. The line adjusts automatically when adding or subtracting an operator (for output or toilet reasons).
- Slower or faster operators are automatically adjusted for.

Note that bucket brigade line balancing has application in transactional office situations. Sequential office processes are sometimes ignored, for several reasons including difficult-to-see, manager ignorance or having other priorities, and 'it's a factory thing'. Yet bucket brigade is a non-threatening method that avoids timing as well as overcoming the problem of task variability.

Standard Operations Combination Chart

	Process:	Block assembly	Required output		Takt Time:		Operational Takt (90%):		Date:	Mar-05
	Part Name:	R2D2-block	1,160 units/day			55 secs		49 secs	Updated By:	COR

OPERATOR	Sequence	WORK ELEMENT OR DESCRIPTION	MANUAL VA	MANUAL NVA	AUTO.	WALK	Operation time shown in one-second units
1	1	Pick-up @ store "a"		2		2	
	2	Unload/oad "B"		10	35	5	
	3	Unoad/Load "Test"		10	35	2	
	4	Unload/Load "C"		10	35	2	
	5	Drop-off @ store 'b'				6	
		Return to store 'a'					
		Total		30		17	
2	1	Pick-up @ store "b"		5		2	
	2	Unload/Load "D"		10	35	2	
	3	Unload/Load "E"		10	35	2	
	4	Unload/Load "F"		10	35	2	
	5	Drop-off @ store 'c'				6	
		Return to store 'b'					
		Total		30		14	
3	1	Pick-up @ store "c"		5		2	
	2	Unload/Load "G"		10	35	2	
	3	Drop-off @ end of cell				8	
	4	Pick-up @ start of cell				2	
	5	Unload/Load "A"		10	35	2	
	6	Drop-off @ store 'a'				8	
		Return to store 'c'					
		Total		20		24	

Standard Operations Chart

Line Name:
PG U-shaped cell

Standard WIP:
11

Symbols:
Standard WIP △
Quality checkpoint ☆
Safety checkpoint: ✚

Quality/Safety Points:
Operator 1:
Step 2: Check manifold
Step 5: Avoid touching rod (hot)
Operator 2:
Step 2: Check tolerance
Step 6: Inspect sleeve

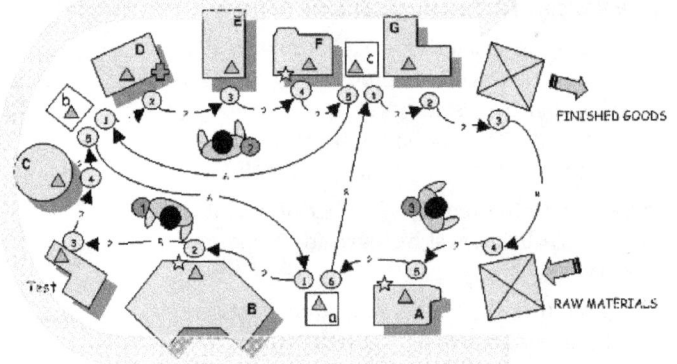

FINISHED GOODS

RAW MATERIALS

Balancing Mixed Model and Multi Model Lines or Cells

Balancing complex mixed model lines can be complex. Mixed model production interchanges products on the same line. Multi model lines usually run in small batches on the same line but with changeover operations between the various products. Each type can be paced unbuffered (like a mechanised line) or unpaced buffered (with operators moving pieces between stations). Paced unbuffered balancing can be calculated deterministically, other types generally require simulation. Readers are referred to the 'bible' and 'guru' on this topic, Armin Scholl.

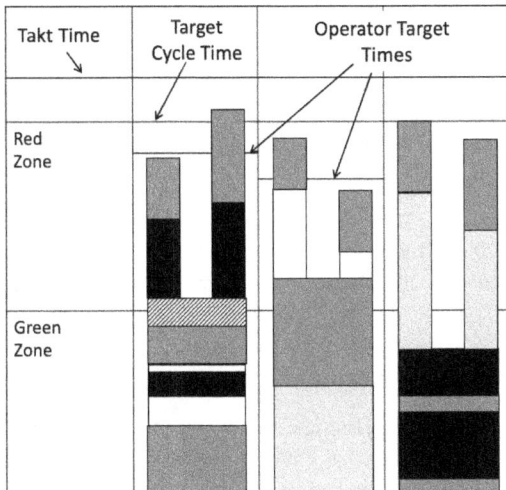

A simple case is illustrated in the figure, which shows a line balance board for a mixed model line with two products. Time is on the vertical axis. First, takt time is established. Then the target cycle time is set below the takt time to allow for general operator variation. A third line is the operator target times. These individual station times allow for relative complexity and uncertainty at each workstation. In the example, operator B has a much more difficult or variable task than the other operators. In the Green Zone activity times for the common elements are assembled. These activities are done for every product. Of course, the Green Zone is variable for each workstation, so the zone

limits are approximate. In the Red Zone the work elements unique to each product are accumulated. In some cases, for instance A, a total product assembly time can exceed the operator target time, so long as the weighted average time reflecting the product mix, does not exceed the target time.

22.6 Chaku-Chaku Cell or Line

A chaku-chaku (or load-load) line (such as at Boeing) is the name given to a very compact and partly automated cell. It invariably includes one piece flow, automatic load and unload, and multiple poka-yoke devices. The various machines are linked by gravity conveyors or chutes. Very often a chaku-chaku is used by one operator on an as-and-when needed basis, such as when feeding into a larger assembly.

22.7 Seru Cells

The first Seru Cells were established at Sony and Canon in the mid 1990's as response to highly variable and short-term demands, particularly in the electronics industry. Conventional Lean Cells were established to cope with the flexibility required where stable repetitive production (the assembly line) is not suitable. Seru cells take this a step further. However, the boundary between conventional cells and Seru cells is blurred. (The word Seru means cell in Japanese.) If there is a difference, it is to do with the aim: Conventional cells aim to efficiency; Seru cells aim for flexibility with the short-term cost having a lower priority. A Seru cell would not be cost-competitive against a higher volume assembly line. Flexibility is achieved by operators and by machines. In other words, more training is required and machines are selected for versatility, not necessarily speed. They are also usually designed to cope with a wider range of products or parts, often customised. As such, Seru cells are probably better aligned to more a modern, changing environment – in both manufacturing and service. Assemble to order would be prime territory. Job enrichment and enlargement comes with the territory.

At Canon, a single operator assembles (assembled?) most of an entire photocopier, drawing on sub-assemblies and inventories placed close to the cell. Several single operators work in parallel each making a customised copier. They may share common feeder inventories. Of course, such operators are highly trained.

One can think about Seru cells as falling along a spectrum from medium volume repetitive cells to low volume customised cells. Outside of the spectrum, at the high end, is the conventional assembly line. Along the spectrum, from high to low, the number of operators would fall, ending with a single operator at the low end. Likewise, utilization would fall across the spectrum. Probably, one could classify a Chaku-Chaku line as Seru. A Pulse line could also be regarded as Seru. Both these are discussed in this Chapter. Detailed timing and complex line balancing is usually not needed. The bucket-brigade approach would be more suitable. Where there is a single operator in a cell there is no balancing waste. Where there is more than one seru cells become less efficient as variety (and hence different cycle times) increases. Some academic work has gone into balancing low volume, high variation seru cells – but is this needed?

We are aware of cases of Seru-type cells in organisations even though the word Seru is unknown. In one case a manufacturer of electronic sub-assemblies supplies the aerospace, marine, construction, and machine tool industries with a lead time typically of one or two days. Here, several cells are unmanned most of the time but when needed a single operator makes the assembly usually to customer requirements. If design is required this is carried out usually by a single engineer in under a day. The 'seru' operators normally work in medium volume cells, but are called off as and when required. Visitors to the plant, 'wearing

Lean spectacles', frequently remark on unused capacity and inventories. But that is not the point. The point is lead time flexibility and competitiveness. Keeping detailed tabs on assembly progress with a single operator over an extended cycle is difficult – but who cares as long as the work is finished within the shift. Andon May be used in a Seru cell.

In another case, a medical equipment supplier only runs certain cells when there is demand. These low-tech cells use several operators, depending on the level of demand. In yet another case, all assembly benches are on wheels and are simply moved to form temporary cells as and when required.

Is this the real Agile? Is a Benihana restaurant a good example of a Seru cell?

Further reading

Yong Yin, Stecke K. E., Swink M. and Kaku I, 'Lessons from seru production on manufacturing competitively in a high cost environment', *Journal of Operations Management*, March 2017, vol. 49–51, pp. 67–76.

22.8   Virtual Cells

Sometimes it is impossible to create a cell in one area due to size or environmental conditions such as a clean room. Stages may have to be separated. In this case a virtual cell may be a possibility. Instead of two areas with say four similar machines each being managed as a process job shop, consider changing to four virtual cells of two different machines each, managed as four distinct lines or cells. Operators move with the parts from area to area without intermediate buffers, so creating the effect of one piece or small-batch flow. The advantage is vastly reduced lead time and reduced scheduling complexity, against the penalty of greater transport and the need for cross training. This is really creating and running a value stream but in a traditional type of layout.

Operators identify with the line rather than with the process job shop. In the simple case cited, each operator would have to have the skills to run both types of machine and would move from one area to the other 'flowing' the product one piece at a time as far as possible. The old way would involve batch and queue; the new way would frequently involve setting up both machines as a flow line, albeit in separate locations.

22.9 Moving Lines and Pulse Lines

Henry Ford's original line was a 'pulse' line – in other words cars spent time at a fixed location before moving on to the next fixed location. This principle is now being rediscovered for a variety of large, slow moving, complex items such as aircraft engines, wings, aircraft and vehicle maintenance, remanufacturing, large transformers, electrical switching gear, earthmoving equipment, and ship and boat sections. Moreover, the principles may be applicable in areas as diverse as hospitals, construction, even education. The Lean principles of (relatively) fast, flexible flow fully apply. As with much of Lean a big issue is believing that a moving line is possible in the first place – traditional ways (batch and queue, project management, complex scheduling, bottlenecks etc.) have been in place for decades.

As Henry Ford found a century ago, such lines are a revolution in productivity when compared with static build. As well as huge productivity and time gains, there is invariably a big reduction in space, a big improvement in quality (through improved standardization and visibility), and big gains in training and apprenticeship.

Historically, the American railroads were built with a type of moving line system, progressing 50 miles per

day, and today track maintenance is just beginning to adopt moving line concepts.

A pulse line is used where station cycle times are long – say several days, and a moving line is used for shorter station cycle times – say several hours. A moving line moves very slowly (perhaps in mm per minute) but continuously, using a track or conveyor. One or several products are on the moving line at a time, depending on complexity. A pulse line uses a platform, such as 'hovercraft' cushion, to move between fixed stations at a regular takt time. Typically a small number of items are on the pulse line at a time. It is essentially a CONWIP system. Boeing has used a moving line for two decades.

Pulse or moving lines may be fed by supporting cells from which parts are pulled, or automotive style using a broadcast schedule to synchronize several lines.

The steps to set up a pulse or moving line are broadly the same as those used for a cell. Many of the steps are similar to the previous section. A few differences are given below.

1. Establish the product families. A line can be used for a class of products, like helicopters, even though there may be considerable customization between individual units, but not for mixed products such as helicopters and aircraft.

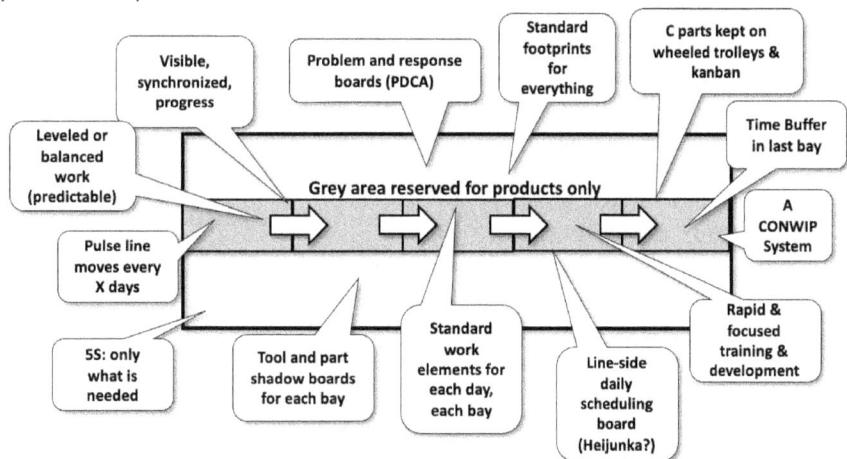

2. Calculate takt time. This will determine the number of stations in a pulse line, and the total time in a moving line. Takt time is often long – say a day. The design question is how much work can be packaged together in a takt time, leading to the number of stations.

3. Develop standard work packages. Even in high variety lines there will be much fully standard work, and some semi-standard as for example in maintenance. Identify, time, and document. These are the essential 'Lego bricks' for such lines.

4. Accumulate and determine the standard work packages against the takt time. In moving lines, first determine the number of operators as for cells, but bearing in mind simultaneous operations, then balance the operators' work against the takt time. In pulse lines determine the number of operators per station – this will depend on simultaneous operations as well as technical considerations. In both cases, earlier stations could be more fully loaded whilst later stations are more lightly loaded to retain catch-up capability. Make allowance for uncertainty and complexity.

5. Establish standard locations and footprints for tools, and part trolleys. Each station should have its own shadow board. This is one of the great advantages of such lines, so try for low-waste ergonomic micro-layouts. At each station, get operators to participate in developing their own part and equipment handling systems. Keep frequently used tools and parts line-side. Get a 5S system established. Over time, work on rationalizing tools and parts.

6. Establish pull systems for required parts. Try to pull as much as possible. Use a demand classification system (see separate section). Establish priority kanban systems and supermarkets for supporting cells feeding the line. A and B parts should be stored on specifically designed wheeled trolleys, and moved to the exact location just-in-time. (See section on PFEP Chapter 27.)

7. Establish a progress signalling system. Visibility is another great advantage of lines, so capitalize on this aspect. In a moving line signalling is typically by marks on the floor corresponding to time and a light system so operators can report and display completions. In a pulse line, each day's work standard work elements are loaded via cards on a card slot board, and turned around when complete. In both types, it is necessary to pre-consider contingencies resulting in delays – transfer to next day or station (limited possibility in a moving line), floating labour, stop the line, work overtime (not desirable?). Develop a board on which unforeseen problems are displayed, and an action sequence determined – perhaps like a TPM red card system.

8. Establish the planning system. For mixed model or variable time lines such as maintenance, the work packages in each cycle may vary. The work packages and manning will then have to be pre-planned subject to the constraint of the takt time. This planning is probably best done by a Heijunka-like manual capacity board that loads up the individual standard work elements.

Big and exciting opportunities lie in this concept being applied in maintenance, hospitals, and construction. 100 Years after Henry Ford, we are only just beginning.

22.10 Ergonomics

Good ergonomics – of both products and processes – should be essential for any manufacturer – Lean or otherwise. What makes Lean Ergonomics an extension to conventional ergonomics? This brief section does not deal with ergonomics per sé (there are many excellent text available), but comments on the Lean perspective on Ergonomics.

- Working to Takt or Rhythm. A regular rhythm can assist good blood circulation. By contrast, 'static' effort (for instance where a moderate rate of work persists for 1 minute or more, or slight effort lasts for 5 minutes or more, can obstruct the flow of blood. (Kroemer and Grandjean 1997)

- Lean favours standing rather than sitting (except for intricate work) – for flexibility to move between workstations, but also for posture and to help avoid lower back problems. Ergonomists recommend a combination of sitting and standing. Certainly standing or sitting without movement is poor practice. Sitting can lock-in an operator and inhibit movement. A good compromise is to have standing and moving operators but also frequent breaks with comfortable chairs in team areas. This fits in with 'standard work rate or stop' philosophy discussed under balancing. Some sitting can be accommodated in lines and cells – as per Toyota's 'raku raku' seats which swing inside a car to allow a sitting operator to assemble. Some cell workstations are amenable to the best of all – allowing the operator to adjust between sit or stand.

- There is an inverse relationship between force exerted and duration of muscular contraction (See Kroemer and Grandjean, p 11). Toyota has developed an ergonomic evaluation system based on this relationship – a maximum force for each particular duration – exceeding the line calls for workstation redesign.

- The best workstations (both sitting and standing) allow for height adjustment both for the height of the operator and the type of work (higher for accurate, lower for heavier). Seats should be adjustable for height and backrest inclination. Look up the recommended heights of seats, work surfaces, and inspection surfaces for your own size operators in an ergonomic text. See readings.

(Likewise, in an office, one should not sit all day. Standing work desks are becoming popular. Winston Churchill used one. You can see it at his house, Chartwell.)

- 5S. Take the opportunity to do 'Ergonomic 5S', not just 5S. Shadow boards for tools and parts need to be correctly located ergonomically. Try to maintain a natural posture at all times. The 5S principle of avoiding personal toolboxes can make sense both ergonomically (located at correct height and reach) and for standardization reasons. Every course on 5S should at least say a few words on work heights and ergonomic workstation layout, lifting, lighting, controls, vibration and noise. Visibility principles should extend to ergonomics – for example seeing the progress of a moving line clearly marked by lights or time markings on the floor. Can a tool shuttle be used on a line to keep pace with the line? Every 5S exercise should incorporate visual management.

- TPM and Quality related gages, dials and displays should also be designed using ergonomic principles. Operating ranges should be colour marked so normal conditions can be seen at a glance, lubrication levels made visible without bending, needle orientation aligned on dials, etc. (see Kroemer and Grandjean, chapter 8)

- Use visual warning devices. An example is coloured stickers placed on all containers to indicate if they are human movable, human movable with care, or only machine movable.

22.11 3P: Production Preparation Process

Toyota's '3P' (Production Preparation Process) is a powerful participative methodology at the interface of the 'Double Diamonds' of Exploration and Execution. (see Chapter 35). It is used to design or redesign a process layout or cell. This should always be done for new product families, when a facility is planned, and where a process needs overhaul. Originally found in manufacturing, 3P is now appearing in office and hospital settings. Distinctive features are participation, alternative generation, and physical modelling. The aim is to try out and test various approaches before committing to full scale implementation. Also, of course, workers will be much happier if they work in an environment designed by themselves.

3P should always be undertaken by an open-minded, participative team of operators from the area, and from any other appropriate area such as quality, engineering, design, and scheduling. The steps are as follows:

1. Establish the aims. This may include productivity, space, defect rates, workstation reduction. Determine envisaged production rates, and calculate takt time where appropriate. List the design criteria.

2. Draw a flowchart or fishbone of how the product or family is currently made or envisaged. Add photos. Add 'kaizen bursts' of current problems.

3. List the function steps, not the process steps. ('Removing material' is a function step; 'Milling' is a process step.) Use verb plus noun.

4. Collect the parts, material and tools for each function step. Set these out on a table for all to see.

5. Make a preliminary work balance (Yamazumi) board using takt (planned cycle time.) Return to this board and modify as work proceeds. This may involve timing various activities.

6. At this stage, some 3P exercises are split into sub teams each of which generates solutions. This is to foster a greater number of ideas and to prevent idea domination by strong personalities.

7. Generate alternatives to make or assemble the product. The classic Toyota approach is to require at least 5 ideas. Never accept only one solution! This can be done on two levels – broad concept design, and detailed steps. For instance assembly may be done by pressing together, clipping together, screwing, welding, bolting, moulding, even 3D printing. Remember to incorporate poka-yoke, quick change over, safety, ergonomics, material handling. Quick change parts presentation is desirable for multiple products. The whole idea is a low cost, flexible solution

8. Evaluate against the aims. Select the most appropriate solution or solutions.

9. Take the more promising ideas and construct a small scale model. Use simple materials – cardboard, toilet rolls, Lego. Use the model for 'simulation'. Consider part and operator movement. Discuss with input from various team member viewpoints. Modify and adjust.

10. Return to steps 7 or 8 until a preferred solution emerges. Return to Step 5.

11. Now build a full scale mock up using cardboard boxes, wooden tables. Modular tubing is ideal. Get operators to move around, simulating making the product. Use a flipchart and record ideas.

12. Finally, build the actual cell, perhaps still retaining modular tubing and flip chart.

Further reading

Allan Coletta, *The Lean 3P Advantage*, CRC Press, 2012

Michael Baudin, *Working with Machines*, Productivity Press, 2007, and *Lean Assembly*, Productivity Press, 2002

Nancy Hyer and Urban Wemmerlov, Reorganizing the Factory: Competing through Cellular Manufacturing, Productivity, 2002

James Tompkins et al, *Facilities Planning*, Third edition, Wiley, 2003

H Lee Hales and Bruce Andersen, *Planning Manufacturing Cells*, SME, 2002

Mike Rother and Rick Harris, *Creating Continuous Flow*, LEI, 2001

Kevin Duggan, *Creating Mixed Model Value Streams*, Productivity, 2002

Armin Scholl and Christian Becker, 'State of the Art exact and heuristic solution procedures for simple assembly line balancing', *European Jnl of Operational Research*, 168 (3), 2006

Richard Schonberger, Best Practices in Lean Six Sigma Process Improvement, John Wiley, 2007.

K. Kroemer and E. Grandjean, *Fitting the Task to the Human*, 5th edn., Taylor and Francis, 1997 (Perhaps unavailable, so try...)

Steven Shorrock (ed), *Human Factors and Ergonomics in Practice*, Routledge, 2016

John Nicholas, *Competitive Manufacturing Management*, McGraw Hill, 1998, Chapters 9 and 10.

Yong Yin, Kathryn Stecke, Morgan Swink, Ikou Kaku, 'Lessons from Seru production on manufacturing competitively in a high cost environment, *Journal of Operations Management*, 49-51, pp 67-76, 2017

CREATING FLOW

Creating Flow is central to Lean. Creating Flow involves many considerations, building on the preceding Preparing for Flow Chapters. Creating Flow is dealt with in the following Chapters:

- Mapping
- Demand Analysis
- General Comments on Lean Scheduling
- Pull Systems
- Line processes. (Repetitive, more stable, no shared resources – the classic Lean value steam)
- Batch processes (Less repetitive, shared resources, batching, greater variation in demands).

Mapping enables the identification of Stable and Unstable Zones. The Identification of Stable and Unstable Zones, together with Demand Analysis and Queueing Dynamics form a trilogy of basic requirements for successful Lean Flow Scheduling. Together these concepts allow for effective pull scheduling, both internally and along the supply network.

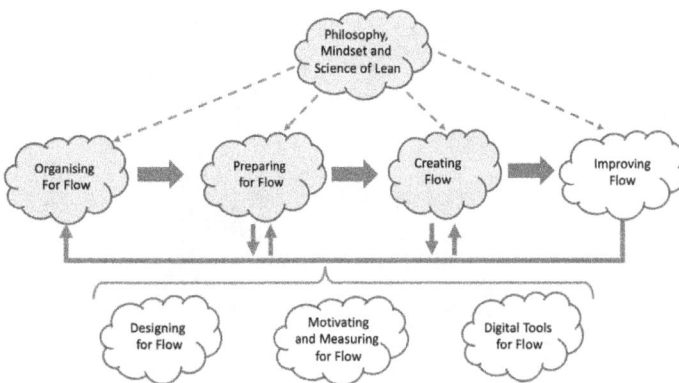

23 Mapping

Mapping and associated assessments are major analysis tools in Lean. Mapping is the 'Meta Tool' in the Lean Toolbox because the mapping tools should guide the use of many other tools.

Remember that all mapping and analysis is waste unless it leads to action. Doing mapping is not the same thing as doing Lean. Do not fall for Paralysis by Analysis.

23.1 What is the Aim of Mapping?

The real purpose of mapping is to design the future state. It is a visualization exercise – a vision of the current state and of the future state. This is done by establishing priorities for Lean implementation, both short and medium term. Mapping is also an excellent vehicle for involvement and participation. For many, participation on a mapping exercise is their first practical exposure to Lean outside of a classroom or after a 5S exercise. Mapping is also a great tool for idea generation.

Although maps should be on display, mapping is not for decoration, it is for action – obvious, but beware of framed or laminated maps.

Like Lincoln at Gettysburg maps should be by the people for the people.

23.2 Before You begin Mapping...

Mapping is a powerful tool, but is not the universal answer.

First, clarify the aim, and the implementation period. 'If you don't know where you are going any road (map) will get you there'. What are the essential issues that a mapping exercise aims to achieve? Is it short term cash flow, longer term productivity, survival, or is it simply that 'mapping is such a usual thing to do in Lean that 'I suppose we better do an exercise ourselves'?. An important aim should be the identification of zones of stability and instability, in order to prioritise improvement.

Second, is scope. Defining the value streams is discussed later, but there is an immediate issue of scope. Where does it start and where does it end? Is it to be a local exercise, a pilot, or will it be end-to-end across the site with an idea of extending out to the supply chain in the future. Why start in the factory? Why not with customer service? (Many companies are far better with their internal operations than they are with field service, or delivery, or installation.) Or, start with administration – the factory has been worked over many times but seldom the office. Often, the biggest problems are in the information flows that support physical operations. So, one might need to do some preliminary high-level maps to help answer these and similar questions.

Third is performance. A value steam map is also a snapshot in time, so is not usual to pick up vital variation information. In other words, a value stream map is good for muda, less good for muri and mura. One will want to understand what is:

- The delivery performance, and the variation thereof – not one average figure!
- Demand management. (Read the Chapter!)
- Customer satisfaction, and reasons for dissatisfaction.
- Lead time variation

Remember that a mapping exercise should be at least as much about the information flows as about the physical flows. It is tying the two together that is the real benefit.

23.3 Types of Maps

There are 7 basic map types: Brown paper, 'Learning to See', Information flow, Spaghetti, Quality filter, Demand amplification, Financial map.

Outline Physical Map (or Brown Paper Chart or Big Picture)

A Brown Paper Chart is a high-level diagram showing the main product flows and stages. An example of a brown paper chart is shown above, taken from an automotive metal pressing

company. It serves to clarify the overall logic of the plant. A supply chain version would show the main suppliers, service centres, supply routes, distribution routes, distribution centres, and main customers. Often products and percentages going through different channels would be shown.

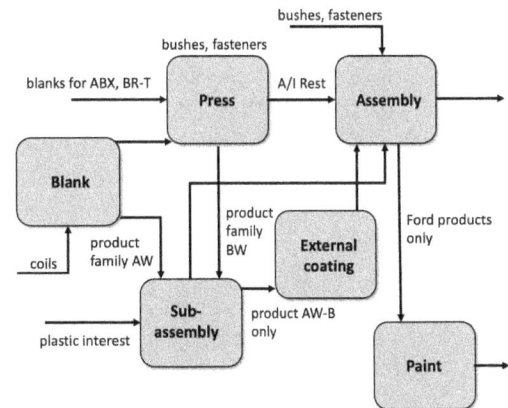

The chart can become a focus in the 'war room' showing, by means of frequently updated photographs, graphics, and 'post it' notes, the progress and highlights. A 'Master Schedule' can go alongside – showing the Gantt chart of progress towards implementation. The team should gather around the Master Schedule at regular (weekly?) intervals to check progress.

Physical Flow 'Learning to See' Maps

The 'Learning to See' map has emerged as the most popular and clear way to illustrate the current and future state of a value stream. The method maps both material and information flows. It is quick to learn because it uses simple boxes to indicate stages, and other obvious symbols such as trucks, factories, and kanban cards. The tool is suitable for repetitive operations, especially where a single product or family is made. A powerful feature is that it 'closes the loop' from customer order to supply to manufacture ending with the delivery of the product. (This closed loop is not shown on most detailed activity charts.) An example is shown below, with the main mapping icons.

The point about these diagrams is that they give a clear overview that can be used for planning and participation meetings, from shop floor to top management. As a reference tool they can be placed on boards in meeting areas, and ideas can be added by Post-it stickers.

Progress can be charted.

Unlike the Brown Paper or Big Picture map shown above, where sequences were aggregated together, here draw out the actual processing sequence steps – for example 'assemble', but not the detail of how assembly is done.

- Link the steps with push or pull arrows.

- Add a data box below each step. The data box will contain the changeover time, and the process time for a typical product. (Note: the process time is the time taken by the machine or process. If a batch is made together on a machine, do not divide the process time by the batch size – doing so could mislead as to the actual time taken. But if the batch comprises discrete items that are individually made, then the process time is the individual cycle time.)

- In the data box, include the batch size and make notes if batch sizes vary. Also include the number operators. Use full time equivalents (FTE's).

- Rejects and rework. Include notes in the data box on the occurrence at each step. For rework, indicate the rework loop. Show the locations and quantities of any safety stocks.

- Estimate the variation, especially at shared and critical resources. The coefficient of variation CV would be ideal (See 'Science of Lean' Chapter), but for most purposes simply estimate process variation time as low, medium, high.

- Make notes in the data box with regard to reliability of the process, ideally mean time between failures (MTBF), and mean time to repair (MTTR). Note that OEE is a less useful figure. (See under TPM Chapter 21.)

- Add the current inventory that is found between the process steps. Show this below an inventory triangle symbol.

- Identify any supermarkets or stores.

- Buffer stocks. Show the locations and quantities.

- Draw in the means of physical replenishment of inventory, such as a kanban loop or 'runner' frequency.

- Calculate takt time. See Chapter 18 on this. Takt time = Available time / Average Demand. Note: For shared resources, takt time may not be useful, but for downstream operations it can be a powerful concept that sets the overall drumbeat rate.

To create the future state and ideal state diagrams requires two steps.

First, incorporate short-term improvements from the seven basic maps discussed below. This includes waste reduction ideas. Show these as 'Kaizen bursts' on the diagram. The second step requires more in-depth knowledge of Lean possibilities. These are the subjects of Layout and Scheduling. However, it is useful to break up the value steam map into pull segments or loops, often separated by supermarkets. In particular make an assessment of stable and unstable sub-loops. Then use these as building blocks for layout design.

Time Line: In a 'Learning to See' map, a time line is added at the base of the map and derived from processing times and inventory consumption times. (The latter is constructed from inventory x takt time). Be aware that this can be highly misleading because delays between inventory movements are ignored, and inventory holdings will often vary with time in the month and with seasonality. Inventory movement often takes place with a particular frequency – like twice per day or in response to a pull signal. Of course, such delays will impact the lead time.

Current State Map

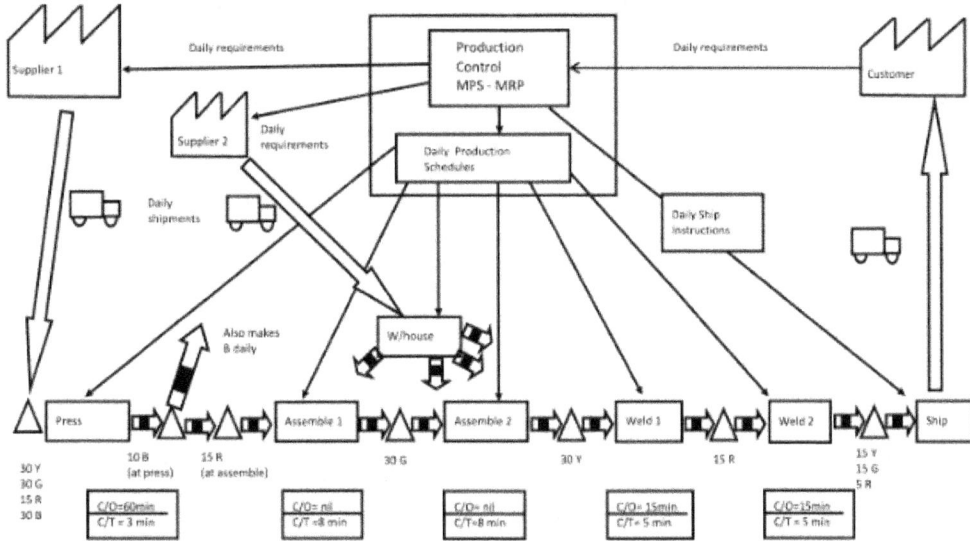

Container Size = RM: 20 or 10; WIP & FGI: 10

Future State Map

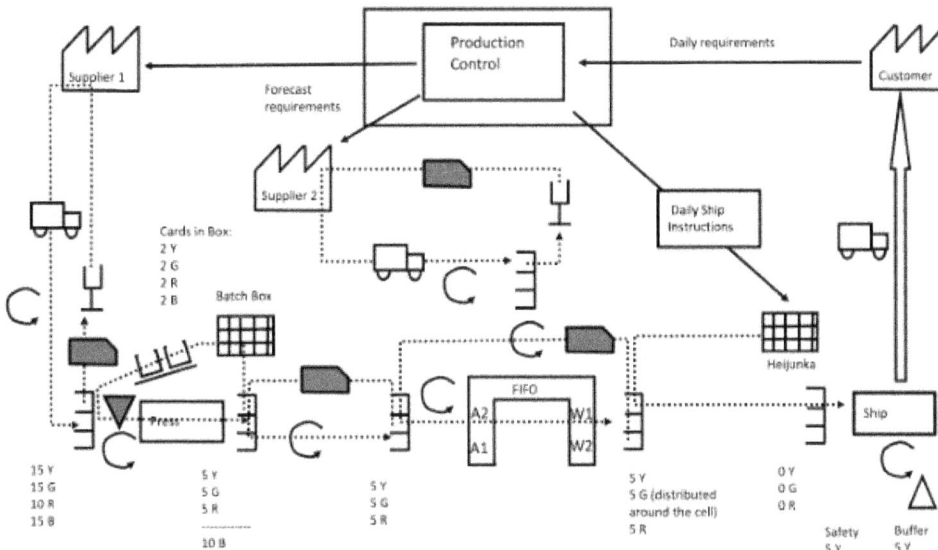

Container Size = 5 (Products)
Container (cup) Size = 10 (?) (Components)

Likewise, inventory holdings will often fluctuate, perhaps running down near month end or with the reporting period, and increasing in anticipation of seasonal demand. Therefore, of course, lead time will vary. Make a note on the time line to indicate these additional times and the variation in lead time.

A recommended alternative is to use Little's Law. (See 'Science of Lean' Chapter 4). The form of the equation here is:

Average lead time = Inventory/(Throughput rate)

Both WIP and throughput rate are generally easier to obtain than average lead time. So merely count up the WIP (of main products, including part-assembled but not components) – including raw material converted to equivalent products and FGI) and obtain the usual shipment rate. Say inventory is 5000 (RM+WIP+FGI) and an average of 500 products is shipped per day, then average lead time is 10 days.

Limitations: *Learning to See* mapping has limitations that one needs to be aware of. Firstly, it usually considers only one product (or family) at the time, and does not consider impacts on capacity of shared resources. Secondly, it is a static picture only. It does not capture variation. Therefore it can make only a preliminary (and sometimes misleading) statement about capacity or loading. Be aware!

Further reading

Mike Rother and John Shook, *Learning to See*, The Lean Enterprise Institute, Brookline, MA, 1998

Karen Martin and Mike Osterling, *Value Steam Mapping*, McGraw Hill 2014. A useful reference particularly on organising the mapping team.

Mark Nash and Sheila Poling, *Mapping the Total Value Stream*, CRC Press, 2008. A useful reference particularly on mapping mechanics.

Information Flow Map

The Information Flow Map is the partner of the Physical Flow map that together enable to complete closed loop from order receipt to delivery to be shown. In some businesses it is all about information flow – there is no physical flow.

The map is constructed by tracing an order from receipt, through preparation of schedules, capacity considerations, material planning, to issuing of individual work orders or production signals, and onto dispatch information. Invoicing, inventory receipt and control, accounting, and quality control information may also be included although these latter categories are unnecessary in first pass mapping.

If there is a S&OP (Sales and Operations Planning) process, this must be understood to the extent of knowing about frequency, attendance, inputs and outputs, and priorities.

In addition to drawing the map, it is often useful to collect and display samples of the important forms and computer screen dumps. This adds to the depth of understanding.

Since information flow is mainly intangible the team will have to rely on tracing an order, tagging, and questioning various staff. It is desirable to have members from relevant support functions on the mapping team.

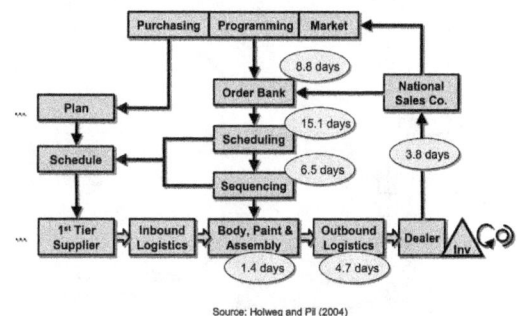

Source: Holweg and Pil (2004)

A balance must be struck on detail, particularly with scheduling, ERP / MRP, and spreadsheets. This is not easy. (Many managers are unaware of how decisions on batch sizing, capacity, and sequencing are made and feel happy to hand over control of these vital functions to a 'black box' or a middle manager who takes decisions by default. Our experience is that this is dangerous.)

A separate diagram showing the modules of the operations planning process is useful. For example how Master Scheduling, MRP, Capacity Planning, and Sequencing, work together and what formal systems (e.g. ERP) and informal (spreadsheets) are used. An example is shown above.

It is also useful to ask about the education and training of people involved in production planning. For example do they have a CPIM or a degree?

The Figure above shows a simplified map of the order fulfilment process in the car industry, which takes (on average) 41 days to complete an order. Most of this delay happens in the information flow, at the various stages of scheduling.

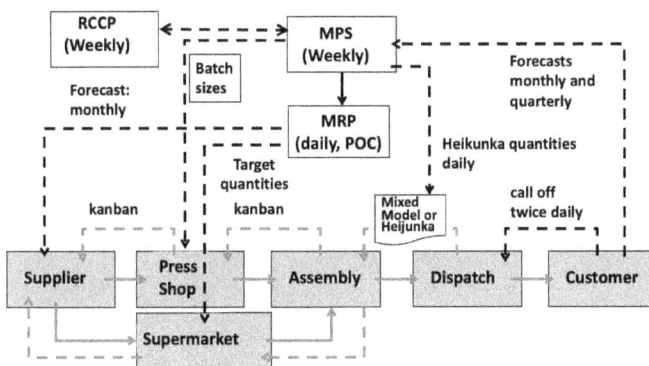

The following questions will need to be clarified:

- How are forecasts made?
- How are orders received, and do the orders 'consume' the forecast?
- Record the sequence of steps that an actual order goes through from receipt to start of manufacture. Construct a sub-map of these steps.
- How long does a new order take from receipt to beginning of manufacture? Of course, this will be subject to urgency and to regularity of the orders. Take samples of

orders, noting receipt and launch date, and make an estimate.

- How is the MPS constructed?
- What are the order priorities and how are emergency or rush orders dealt with?
- What are the actual working hours after meetings etc., and what are the rules with regard to overtime and not meeting the schedule?
- How is capacity calculated?
- How is load calculated, especially at critical and shared resources?
- What level of utilization is considered appropriate, especially at critical resources and in assembly operations? (Please refer to the chapter 'The Science of Lean', Chapter 4)
- How is the detail schedule constructed and revised? (This can be a complex issue. It is discussed in detail in Chapters 25 through 28.)
   - How much decision making is done by front line staff? For instance, can a team leader change the manufacturing sequence?
   - How are materials planned? Perhaps MRP and the MRP rule used– for example period order quantity? Or kanban?
   - How is inventory replenished to the various resources? This should include the decision rules, quantities, runner frequency, and signalling system.
- How is labour allocated?
- How is rework scheduled? What happens about rejects? (For example, does the batch size decline or is buffer stock used?)
- Find out about buffer stocks and safety stocks. Sometimes these are kept separate, sometimes not. How are they replenished?
- How frequently is the schedule status checked, and what happens when the schedule is missed?

- It is useful to look at both the formal system (say ERP) and the informal systems (perhaps off-line spreadsheets, calculations, verbal communications that over-ride the system.)

- What are the KPI's? What happens when the KPI's are missed?. It is important to discuss whether the KPI's are the right KPI's: Do they support the purpose? There are many pitfalls here (See the Measures chapter 41).

Just a few of the information flow improvement considerations are:

- Can any activities that delay a physical value adding activity be simplified or rescheduled?

- Are there any activities, particularly non-value adding activities, which can be done in parallel with the sequence of value adding activities?

- Can activities that have to be passed from department to department (and back!) be reorganized into a team activity?

- What preparations can be made before the main sequence of information steps is initiated so as to avoid delays? (e.g. preparing the paperwork.)

- If orders or jobs are done in batches, can the batches be split so as to move on to a second activity before the whole batch is complete at the first activity?

- Can staff flexibility be improved so as to allow several tasks to be done by one person, thus cutting handing-on delays? (What training and backup would be required?)

- How are decisions made? Can decision making power be devolved to the point of use? Can the routine decisions be recognized so that they can be dealt with at the gemba?

Michael Hammer has some useful suggestions concerning assumptions. The following is based on his 'Out-of-the box thinking'.

- Are you assuming a specialist must do the work? (People).

- Are you assuming that purchasing will pay only after receiving an invoice? (Time).

- Are you assuming that record keeping must be done in the office? (Place).

- Are you assuming that inventory is required for better service? (Resources).

- Are you assuming that the customer should not be involved? (Customer).

Further reading

Benson Shapiro, Kasturi Rangan, John Sviokla, 'Staple Yourself to an Order', *Harvard Business Review*, July-August 1992, pp113-122

George Stalk and Thomas Hout, *Competing Against Time*, The Free Press, New York, 1990

John Bicheno, *The Service Systems Toolbox*, PICSIE, 2012. See Part 3: Service Analysis and Mapping

Beau Keyte and Drew Locher, *The Complete Lean Enterprise: Value Stream Mapping for Administrative and Office Processes*, Productivity, 2004

Michal Hammer and James Champy, *Reengineering the Corporation*.

Robert Jacobs, et al, *Manufacturing Planning and Control for Supply Chain Management*, McGraw Hill, 2011. Not on mapping and far more comprehensive than needed for an information map, but useful for comparison.

Spaghetti Diagram

The Spaghetti Diagram (or String Diagram) is a long established tool for more effective layout. It tracks the waste of transport and the waste of motion. It could not be simpler. Merely get a layout diagram of the plant and trace the physical flow of the product in question on the diagram. Mark on the diagram the locations of inventory storage points. Do not forget rework loops, inspection points, and weigh points. Calculate the total length of flow. Show component delivery flow paths in another colour. Again calculate the length of travel. Wasteful movement and poor layout become clearly apparent. Do get the mapping team to walk the distance, rather than just to draw it. While the team is walking, get them to take note of variations in vertical movements – the more constant the vertical level, the better.

A spaghetti diagram can also be used to map collection routes for parts, and external processing travel paths. Many plants have, for shock-tactics purposes, worked out the equivalent annual distance travelled in terms of, for instance, number of times around the world. Jim Womack once related the average speed of travel of an aerospace part to the speed of an ant!

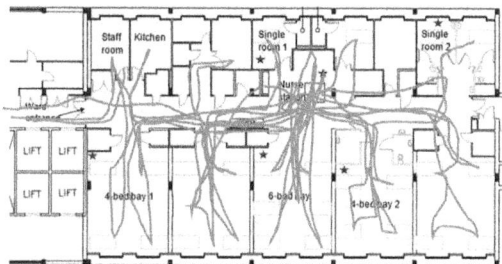

The *Learning to See* map gives the logic of the main steps, the information flows, and the time line. The Spaghetti Diagram gives the geography. So they form a set. Strangely, this simple but powerful tool gets little or no mention in some mapping publications. At least two flows should be traced – the product flow and the regular (or irregular) material handling routes.

Lean layout groups inventory into supermarkets from which parts are pulled. Parts should not be scattered around in many locations. Parts are delivered to the line and products collected from the line by a material handler (water spider or runner) following set routes. The spaghetti diagram is the prime tool for establishing the best routes. The spaghetti diagram can also be used at the workplace level, for instance for changeover reduction analysis.

Quality Filter Map

Quality filter mapping aims to track the locations and sources of defects along a process route. The Quality Filter Map is a graph showing the parts per million (ppm) rate against process stage. Although this information may be collected and shown as part of a *Learning to See* current state map, a quality filter map adds emphasis. Two bars should be shown, Scrap and Rework.

Note that scrap and rework should be recorded not only at points where the company records defects, but also at all operation steps. This is to ensure picking up what Juran refers to as 'chronic' wastes (the underlying defects, reworks, or inspections that have become so routine that they are not recognized as a problem). An example is the 100% manual touch-up welds done at the end of a robotic assembly line, which enjoyed zero priority for improvement but which, upon analysis, proved to be one of the most costly quality problems in the plant.

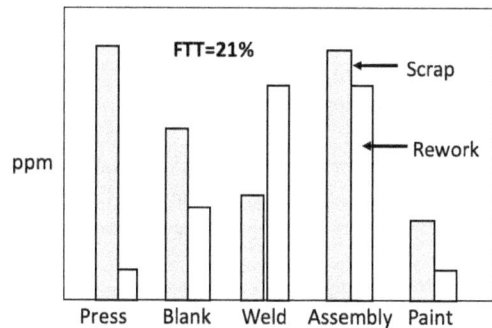

First time through (FTT) is often calculated as part of the Quality Filter Map. FTT is expressed as a percentage: 100 x (parts shipped - (parts reworked+parts scrapped)) / parts shipped. Note that if parts are reworked at several workstations the FTT figure can be negative.

An alternative to FTT is OTIF (on time in full) – the percentage of parts that are delivered both on time and in full. This percentage figure can be compared with the days of finished goods inventory. The more the days of finished goods inventory the higher the OTIF should be. (For example, if there are 10 days of finished goods inventory why is OTIF not 100%?). See Fill Rate / Inventory curve in 'Science of Lean' chapter 4.

Quality filter mapping can highlight defects that are passed over long distances along a process route or supply chain only to be rejected beyond the point at which return for rework is not economic. Also, beware of parts that are passed onto constraint machines, thereby wasting capacity.

Alternatively, the **Yield** (output/input) percentage can be calculated at each stage. This can be useful in process industry and in offices.

Beware of accepting the official defect figures. 5 ppm at final dispatch may be the result of excellent process control, or of numerous inspections and reworks. In 1995 the story was told of a famous German car whose average time for rectification exceeded the total time required to build an entire new Toyota. The final build quality of the German car was, however, superb.

Demand Amplification Mapping

This tool maps what is termed the 'Forrester Effect' after Jay Forrester of MIT who first modelled the amplification of disturbances along the supply chain and illustrated the effect in supply chain games. It is also a form of the well-known run diagram used in quality management. Amplification happens in plant and in supply chains, but the latter has enjoyed more attention. It is about linearity of flow and arrival variation. Amplification is the enemy of linear production and Lean manufacturing, and results from batching and inventory control policies applied along the supply chain. For instance, fairly regular or linear customer demand is translated into batch orders by a retailer, then subject to further modification by a distributor adjusting safety stocks, then amplified further by a manufacturer who may have long changeovers and big batches, and then further modified by a supplier who orders in yet larger batches to get quantity

discounts. The result is that, further along the chain, the pattern of demand in no way resembles the final customer demand.

An amplification map is plotted usually day-by-day across a month. There will be a line for each stage. For example, from purchasing, receiving dock, order entry, from completions at various stages, and from dispatch. In a supply chain, an amplification map shows orders, shipments, and inventory levels at each company in the chain over a period that matches the cumulative lead-time in the chain. It is quite a big job to get this data – but the results are often startling.

The figure shows an example from the grocery sector, which was collected by David Simons and Barry Evans from Lean Enterprise Research Centre. The chart shows how the EPOS (electronic point of sales) demand, which essentially is what customers pay for at the till, is amplified as it is passed back to the supplier. Some distortion occurs when the store orders from the RDC (regional distribution centre), but then manual intervention by the purchasing function at the supermarket chain causes major amplifications in the signal. This is by no means malicious, but is an effect that occurs when final demand is not transparent to the decision-makers, and forecasting takes over. The advantages of stable, regular orders from the customers are being destroyed. Life is being made very difficult for the supplier, and overall much more stock is held in the system. What is going wrong, and what should be addressed?

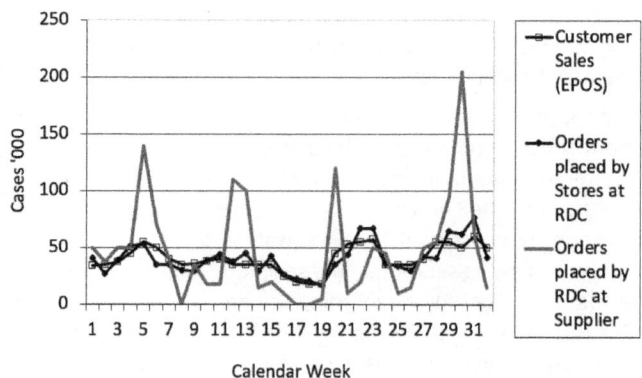

The amplification map is a great tool for getting at the heart of scheduling issues. It is also a good evaluation tool that forms part of a periodic report to management or as a tool for evaluating the process of Lean implementation. The amplification issue and its possible solutions in the supply chain context are discussed in the Supply Chain chapter.

Note: in order to create a meaningful demand amplification map it is important to pick a volume or runner product and a representative time horizon (generally 3+ months, avoid Christmas and summer periods). Also make sure that the components and materials you map only go into the final product you are looking at so that you can show direct correspondence of the demand patterns.

(Demand amplification is further covered in Chapter 29 on Supply Chain.)

Further reading

Jay Forrester, 1961, *Industrial Dynamics,* MIT Press, Cambridge MA

Lee, H. L., V. Padmanabhan, et al. , 1997. 'The Bullwhip Effect in Supply Chains' *Sloan Management Review* Vol. 38 No. 3, p. 93-102.

Financial Maps

It is possible to combine *Learning to See* maps with financial aspects to see where money is tied up – and how often is money turned around. This grabs senior manager's attention more than stock turns! Financial maps are also necessary to give the Lean enterprise viewpoint, rather than just Lean operations. Two maps are useful – the Cash Flow map and the Cost map.

The Cash Flow Map traces cash flows into and out of the company. This is important because this is 'real money'. Cash is king. Most are aware that a profitable company can still go out of business due to cash flow problems. How fast cash is turned over is the prime concern.

The Cash Flow Map highlights the gap in financing between paying for raw materials and components and receiving payment from customers. The gap

has to be financed by the company. So, where are the opportunities to reduce the gap: payment lead time to suppliers, lead time due to internal operations, delivery, or waiting for payment?

The Cost Map is simply an extension of the Current State map, and shows a snapshot of the main direct costs relating to the value stream. Inventory costs are shown with respect to the raw material costs and do not reflect the cost accumulation of value added work as a part progresses. There are two reasons: First, the accumulated value is a matter of judgement and in any case takes time to calculate with little benefit. Second, it may be argued that a part-completed product is of no value to the customer until completed. The stage-by-stage costs show the direct costs – certainly labour, but maybe machine charge out rates or depreciation. (There is argument about this, because machine cost is sunk. Perhaps show with and without. But, in any case, a consistent method should be used.)

There are two requirements:

- The money: Estimate the value of each inventory point in money terms. Also estimate the daily variable costs of running each manufacturing process or segment. Variable costs mainly will be people, including supervision. Exclude overheads.

- The time: Estimate the days to be financed. This map is an important one for senior management. To calculate the days, convert each inventory holding along the manufacturing sequence to days of demand. This is inventory holding x takt time. Base the calculation on demand at the time when the Sequence map was drawn up, but note the comments on Time Line above. Then separate into raw material (RM), work in process (WIP), and finished goods (FGI). Display these on a map. Then add the credit period that your company grants to customers. These four items (RM days, WIP days, FGI days, Credit days) constitute the total financing period for the operation. But suppliers may also grant payment terms, so this time should be deducted to give the net operation financing time.

Note in the figure that a contribution profile is also shown. Contribution (See the Contribution section in the Chapter on The Science of Lean.) is important because the contribution (sales price – direct costs) of all parts made in the value stream influences what products should be made.

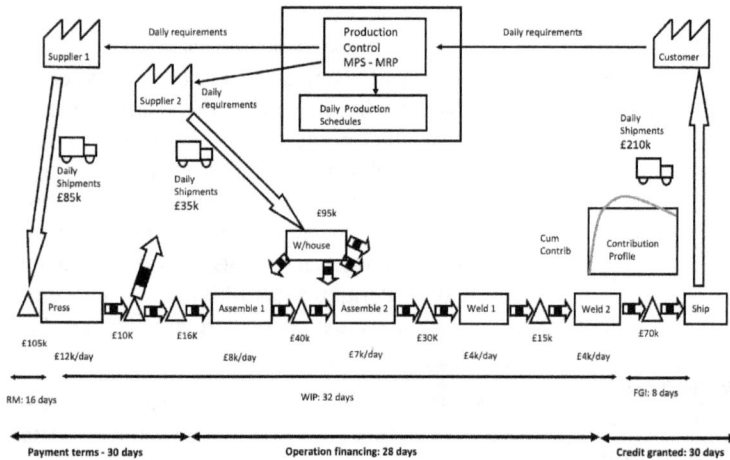

Note also that any shared resource should be highlighted. The cost of a shared resource should be apportioned between the sharing value streams, based on the time spent on the resource.

Human Resource 'Maps'

The future state map will carry with it requirements for the future required skill set. These skills should be determined. A human resource skill inventory or 'map' will begin at a high level and will list, for each level from manager to operator, skill requirements and what will need to be known and standardized. The gaps between present and required skills will form the human resource development plan. Here, the TWI framework will be useful. (See also TWI Chapter 17.)

TWI has five categories of needs for supervisors (a 'supervisor' is widely defined as anyone who is in charge of people or who directs the work of others.) The five are: Knowledge of the Work –

specific to the company or process; Knowledge of Responsibilities – again specific to the company; and then the three TWI skills of Job Instruction (JI) – how to instruct; Job Methods (JM) – how to problem solve and improve; and Job Relations (JR) – how to work effectively with people. List these out as a matrix- similar to the skills matrix.

We now look at two related 'maps' or analysis tools for looking at the crucial question of lead time.

The Lead Time Map and Pareto

The Lead Time Pareto is not a map per sè, but is an estimate of the length of time of each of the elements of total end-to-end lead time – order to delivery. It is way to focus attention on the most time consuming elements.

Draw out a Gantt chart or critical path network from the time that an order is received to the time of delivery (for a make to order item) or the time from planning a new batch to its delivery into finished goods (for a make to stock item). As a preliminary exercise, estimates will do. You may well have to get finance and manufacturing planning in a room together to agree. The various elements typically comprise many of the following:

- Order entry time: paperwork. The time from receipt of order to entry into the manufacturing and planning system.

- Credit verification

- Manufacturing planning time.

- Schedule assembly time – needed to consolidate orders into balanced assembly sequences.

- Configuration time: the time from entry into the system to completion of the configuration. In assemble to order or make to order this could involve design or CAD time and configuration checks. This time may be zero in make to stock environments, and may be zero or near zero in repetitive operations.

- Procurement or material acquisition time: the time taken to procure materials and components, to kit (if done) and to bring the materials from the store to the point of use. In repetitive operations some elements of procurement time could be regarded as zero where they are done routinely or in parallel with order entry time or configuration time.

- Non-specific manufacturing time: the time taken for 'variety as late as possible' manufacturing stages, where components or subassemblies are not specific to a final product or order. Note that this time element may overlap or be done in parallel with order entry time and configuration time. See DDMRP (Section 26.5) for an alternative view.

- Order-specific manufacturing time: the time taken in those manufacturing stages which are order- or customer-specific. This time may be zero in make-to-stock.

- Order launch

- Wait, move, queue, changeover, run times (For each stage, although some of these elements may be zero if there is a cell. Also tackle the longest subassembly sequence, not minor non-critical path subassemblies.)

- Time spent as WIP or semi-finished, between stages
  - o Inspection / quality control time
  - o Finished goods store time
  - o Delivery time
  - o Invoice time
  - o Payment time.

Of course, some of these will overlap or be done in parallel. The important thing is – which of these or other stages takes the most time and is on the critical path? So, don't work on the physical flows if it is the office stages that take the most time.

Lead Time Map

...arranged as a Gantt chart

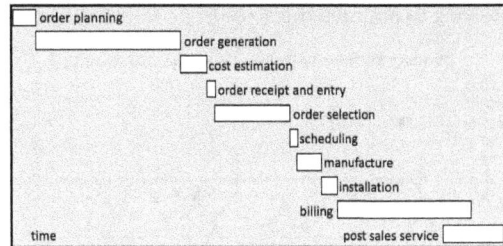

...and as a Pareto

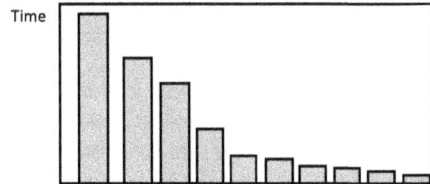

Lead Time Variation and Inventory Days of Cover

Lead time variation is important – perhaps as important as the overall lead time. We have already looked at the Lead Time Pareto, now look at variation.

Be sure to track the customer's order to delivery time, not the organization's internal times. See the graph below. Note that control limits have been added. This is to identify 'special causes' or 'out of control' situations or times.

When mapping, it is important to look at 'end-to-end' performance, not just some minor subsystems. Measuring subsystems gives little indication of overall system performance. As Ohno was saying, 'all we are interested in doing is reducing the lead time from order to completion.' In the 3DayCar programme, the information flows for the entire Order-to-Delivery (OTD) process of major car companies was mapped.

While most people in the car industry are focused on improving the vehicle assembly operation, it only accounts for 4% of the overall process delay the customer experiences!

When you map a system, look at end-to-end performance. Then look at outliers first, before starting to improve the system.

Product X: Order-to-Delivery Lead-time, by Month

Throughout the following analysis it is frequently (always?) more useful to express inventory in terms of 'days of cover' rather than inventory units. Days of cover should relate to Sales units, not to money. You will need to get the total unit sales for a typical month and then to divide by the number of working days in the month – excluding weekends and holidays – to give the average daily sales rate. You may want to check this for several months, and also to get the normal range – upper and lower.

Then, in subsequent mapping, convert each accumulation of inventory to days of sales cover by dividing the inventory at that stage by the average daily sales rate. This is a more meaningful figure. It is generally more robust than calculating the time line by multiplying the inventory at the stage by the takt time - especially where there are shared resources or where takt is not very meaningful as in the case of some process industries.

Thereafter, group the days of inventory into the appropriate main stages of raw materials, work in process, and finished goods. Of these, WIP is solely under the value stream's control whereas raw material may have to be held due to erratic supply and finished goods may have to be held to meet uncertain demands.

The next five maps are best regarded as the core set for plant mapping. They should be used together. Together they give a powerful picture of Lean status.

Gantt Charts

Gantt Charts, originally developed by Henry Gantt over a century ago and widely used in project management, are a useful supplement to mapping and to analysis. They should enjoy as wide a use in Lean as in project management.

A Gantt Chart example: Patients arrive *on average* every 20 minutes as shown. Average times for Check-in is 10 minutes, Operation time is 15 minutes; Clean-up is 5 minutes. The operating theatre is used for both operation and clean-up. Draw a Gantt chart showing patients in the system and chairs needed while patients wait. From the chart we can see that the theatre is fully utilised but because patients arrive unevenly some must wait considerable times.

Where there are several resources, say in the above case surgeons, nurses, and administrators, additional rows can be added for each. Usage is simply transferred down. In this example (courtesy of Simon Dodds) a resource of interest is the number of waiting chairs to be provided. It can be

Legend:
- is check in / prep
- is operation
- is clean
- is patient wait

arriv	0	5	10	15	20	25	30	35	40	45	50	55	60	65	70	75	80	85	90	95	100	105	110	115	120	125	130	135	140	145	150	155	160	165
0																																		
20																																		
40																																		
50																																		
75																																		
85																																		
95																																		
100																																		

WIP	1	1	1	1	2	2	1	1	2	2	1	2	2	2	1	2	2	2	3	4	4	3	3	3	3	2	2	2	1	1	1	1		
chairs	0	0	0	0	0	0	0	0	0	0	0	1	0	0	0	0	1	0	1	1	2	1	2	2	2	1	1	1	0	0	0	0		
checkin	1	1			1	1			1	1						1	1	1	1	1	1	1	1											

seen that two chairs are required between times 105 and 125 minutes.

'Seeing the Whole' Supply Chain Mapping

Seeing the Whole Mapping is very similar to Value Stream Mapping described later. Only the scope is greater – the inter-company value stream rather than the in-plant value stream. A seeing the Whole map looks just like a Value Stream Map, except that plants replace process stages. Of course some intermediate stages may be warehouses or cross-docks. Information flows are in the top half, physical flows in the bottom half. The more detailed principles will be described in the Supply Chain Chapter; here the special features with respect to mapping are mentioned.

The main benefit of Seeing the Whole mapping is to gain an understanding of the complete supply chain and to identify major co-ordination opportunities, rather than detailed kaizen implementation activities.

To this end, assembly of the mapping team from multiple companies is easily the most difficult and important issue. It has to be seen as a mutual benefit exercise – no hidden agendas. The team will be high level, because the issues are high level. The core of the mapping team should be schedulers from participating companies.

What is a complete supply chain – how far upstream should you go? Answer: Pragmatically as far as cooperation from participating companies will allow. Even linking two companies is a worthwhile exercise.

Since the focus is on the complete value stream most in-plant stages can be aggregated. In general, most plants will be drawn as single process boxes or stages. An exception is where there is a mix of shared and dedicated resources within a plant – for example a common press shop feeding a dedicated assembly line. These will often have separate scheduling systems. Ideally, each company in the complete supply chain will first have done an internal 'Learning to See' map. But there are plenty of opportunities to go after even if Learning to see maps have not been developed. For example, in

the 3 Day Car study it was found that by far most of the 6 week delay between placing an order and receiving a new car was due to information delays along the chain. Forget the internal physical changes and work on the information flows.

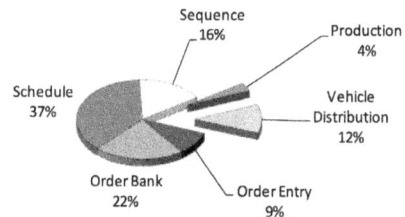

Source: Holweg and Pil (2004)

As with Value Stream maps, the main supporting maps are valuable – in particular the 'Demand Amplification Map', for which data should be collected alongside the 'Seeing the Whole' map. The focus should be more on the information flows rather than the physical flows. Do show the physical flows along the bottom of the map, but concentrate on the information flows. The physical flows can be 'black boxed', but real benefits accrue when getting into the details of the supply chain scheduling decisions, and the associated delays. When mapping the information flows, also record how often IT systems or databases are updated, or scheduling systems run: if a system runs only once per week, the average delay caused here is 3.5 days!

Keep the end customer in mind throughout the exercise. Intermediate customers (other companies) are important, but the supply chain exists for the end customer. Thus waste identification and opportunities are focused on the end customer.

A weakness of both Value Stream maps and Seeing the Whole maps is the way they deal with shared resources. There will likely be several shared resources in a complete supply chain. The way they are scheduled is key. What other supply chains are served, and how much capacity is devoted to the particular supply chain are important questions. For instance in one supply chain studied, a mid-chain participant could originally only devote one day a week to the particular supply chain. So, could changeover be reduced or buffer (supply chain supermarket) added to allow a more stable EPE (every product every) cycle – and who would pay for this? A detailed understanding of the scheduling assumptions and constraints is one of the great pay-offs. The scheduling building blocks (see section 25.9) are relevant in supply chains also. See later section on Shared Resources.

Yet another weakness is ignoring variation – which is even more of a problem in a supply chain than in a plant. So do consider the vulnerability of the future state chain to disruptions, breakdowns, variation on delivery times, and quality problems. Consider the strategic location of supply chain supermarkets.

Further reading

Dan Jones and Jim Womack, *Seeing the Whole: mapping the extended value stream*, Lean Enterprise Institute, Boston, 2002

Darren Dolcemascolo, *Improving the Extended Value Stream*, Productivity, 2006

Holweg and Pil, *The Second Century,* MIT Press, 2004

Feedback (System Dynamics) Diagrams

Many of the maps discussed reflect a snapshot situation. However, it is frequently useful to attempt to capture the inherent dynamics and feedback loops. Merely drawing these out, even without quantification, can lead to much improved understanding. (Remember Ohno's favourite word – understand.)

An example is shown. This concerns a never-ending spiral that a company found itself in. Schedule instability drove short term line performance variation. This caused schedule over-runs that in turn reduced planned maintenance time. Reduction in planned maintenance produced quality problems that fed straight back to schedule over-runs. Short term line performance affected OEE that was also affected by long and variable changeover times. Poor OEE, in turn encouraged

bigger batches. Bigger batches led to high inventory which produced shelf life issues – customers would not accept products with too short a shelf life. This waste and customer demands led directly to a fire-fighting schedule, a basic cause of schedule instability.

This example illustrates that 'root causes' are sometimes part of a feedback loop. Prioritising time for planned maintenance, even in the face of short-term customer demand failure, together with tacking changeover time turned out to be a good solution. See figure below.

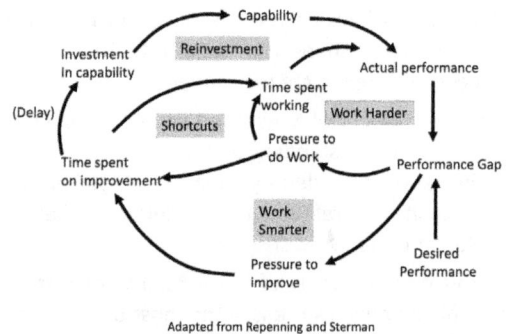

Adapted from Repenning and Sterman

Further reading

Peter Senge, *The Fifth Discipline*, (revised edn.), Random House, 2006

Repenning and Sterman, 'Nobody ever gets credit for fixing problems that never happened', *California Management Review*, Summer 2001, pp 64 - 88

23.4 Analysing Maps: Towards the Future State

Value Stream Analysis is often presented as a four step sequence: Identify Streams, Current State, Future State, Action Plan. That is an unsuitable over-simplification for most cases. A central point is that there is no point, indeed it may be misleading, to attempt to construct a Future State map where there is considerable instability. You may do your Kaizen improvements on just the wrong thing – creating further instability. You haven't a hope of doing good kaizen if many people are running around expediting, addressing workforce problems such as absenteeism, reworking products, or suffering demand and supply instability. Moving to future state implementation too early tempts failure and could be bad for morale. Sceptics are vindicated!

Value Stream Analysis is best seen as an evolving set of steps that are never complete. Strategy, products, technology, people all change with time. So should your value streams.

Now the questioning begins. The aim is to reduce time and waste. It is essentially a creative process. Preferably the people involved in the process should be used in its analysis and improvement. Bold thinking is a requirement, not piecemeal adjustment. The title of the classic article in Harvard Business Review by Michael Hammer gives the clue: 'Reengineering Work: Don't Automate, Obliterate!'; that is the type of thinking that is required. Competitive benchmarking may be useful, as may the creativity encouraged by value engineering. The same Harvard Business Review article tells how Ford used to have 400 accounts payable clerks compared with just 7 people at Mazda at a comparable division.

Begin with Value Stream Identification.

Follow through with Current State mapping each value stream (product family), or the most important value stream. ('Important' could mean financial contribution, important customers, or excess waste, or market potential.). After Current State mapping, do not progress to a Future State map- YET.

The important next consideration is to question the stability of the current State. A team discussion is required. Pointers are given in a section below.

Stability, and Identification of Stable and Unstable Zones

Many, perhaps most, value streams have stable and unstable zones. An unstable zone is a process or series of processes that are unpredictable or unreliable due to a host of factors – high process time variation, breakdowns, quality issues, part supply, rework. A cell may be unstable in an otherwise stable value stream, as might be a dispatch bay. In service, a particular stage in (say) insurance claim processing may be unstable. Unstable zones are particularly relevant in high variety, make-to-order manufacturing. A job shop would be a classic case.

A principle aim of Lean is steady, reliable FLOW (or swift, even flow according to Roger Schmenner). When flow is interrupted by unstable processes, Lean advantage is lost.

An important route to improvement is to begin by recognising, identifying and then tackling unstable zones instead of a 'blizzard' attack on waste across an entire value stream much of which effort will yield marginal results. In the worst case, stable zones are targeted first thereby delaying effectiveness.

The aim is to determine **zones of stability and instability**. For this, more detailed observation and questioning is required. Ask the operators for their experience of problems. Often the unstable processes are well known to operators who work with them every day.

To enable flow, unstable stages need to be buffered by inventory, and possibly by capacity and time buffers while the instability is tackled. See the Scheduling Chapters, particularly Chapter 25. See also the next section on coping with Shared Resources.

There are several pointers to stability, most of them requiring additional data. However, the judgement as to stability is not a formula but a cautionary management go/no-go judgement based on the factors below. If the factors are severe, they need to addressed before proceeding to the Future State.

- How frequently do breakdowns or stoppages occur? High repetition of breakdown stoppages will lead to frequent re-scheduling. No lean system can tolerate this. Breakdown and stoppage data may be available from TPM or by questioning operators.

- Determine typical variation in demand (both quantity and product type). Obtain data from scheduling or sales. How stable, and how much instability is self-caused? Supplier problems in timing and quality make a Lean system difficult. A short-term non-lean, but necessary, response could be higher buffer stocks.

- Rework adds to the load, hence to higher utilization, hence to unstable queues. See Chapter 4 on the Science of Lean.

- Variation and utilization: Be particularly careful if a system has both high utilization and high variation.

- The basic VSM will have identified potential bottlenecks, but here ask about shifting bottlenecks. There may be one bottleneck for a particular product, but another bottleneck in the same value stream for another product.

- Starvation and blockages cause instability. Starvation is waste resulting from upstream problems. Blockages is waste resulting from downstream problems. Note that a bottleneck may be disguised by starvation and blockages. Blocked and starved resources can mislead as to where the true bottlenecks lie. See Section 25.1

- Poor on time in full measures are indicative of several problems.

- If Bill of Material accuracy is poor the system will always be battling against shortages. Shortages are a major source of instability in non-line operations.

- Supply issues need to be noted – quantity, quality, type. (Quality or receiving may have such data.)

- Last but by no means least: Are employees capable? Lean requires devolved authority and problem-solving skills.

Some of the remedies leading to greater stability are briefly summarised below, but in general, see the Chapters on Preparing for Flow. Some of these remedies can take several months to carry out but, as mentioned, don't waste time attempting to implement future state action plans that involve zones that are already stable.

- 5S: Without 5S, or at least without 3S, workstations will have excessive waste, leading to wastes of time.

- TWI, especially Job Instruction (JI) and Job Relations (JR) are long-established, highly practical, methods. The 'four foundations' of JR should be ingrained in everyday people management.

- Standard Work: Is standard work in place and being followed?

- Andon or line-stop helps to reduce rework and helps to build a culture of participation and trust.

- Demand and production smoothing concepts are often quick and low cost. Perfect smoothing is a long way off, but aim to remove the sharp peaks.

- Visual management: Are schedules, procedures, problems on display?

- Layout and buffers will be addressed in the Future State action plan, but silly layouts and movements can often be addressed at short notice.

- Total productive maintenance (TPM) is an extensive and ongoing concern, but frequent stoppages and long changeovers destroy Lean initiatives.

In addition, it will be necessary to obtain rough ideas on process times by product type. (This may be available from MRP data or from layout data.).

The outcome will be a refined map with approximate zones of stability and instability identified. Identifying and responding to unstable zones is further considered in the Scheduling chapters 25 to 28.

Shared Resources

Many value streams in both manufacturing and service have shared resources. Here we are discussing fixed physical resources not workers who may move between value streams. So, for instance, a press operation may feed into several subsequent value streams, or a blood analysis may be used for several patient conditions. Some publications on VSM, for example 'Learning to See', ignore shared resources. Subsequent analysis will then be misleading.

A matrix analysis, such as described under Identifying Product Families is a starting point. Typically, it is found that a small proportion of products account for a large proportion of total demand. Consider first the question of creating dedicated, or near-dedicated, resources for those small number of products that account for a large proportion of demand. In any case, these top-demand products should be scheduled more frequently than the many low-demand products. This is particularly relevant where there is more than one resource of the same type where, instead of several shared resources, one or more is dedicated. Perhaps even purchase an additional resource that can be dedicated. The results for lead-time and simplification of scheduling can be dramatic.

In general, a shared resource means more buffer inventory and increased lead time. So, wherever there is a shared resource, one should always calculate the cost-benefit of the alternative of dedicated machines set against reduced inventory, lead time and flexibility. Decisions should be based upon the impact on throughput, inventory, and operating expense.

Some shared resources simply cannot be dedicated to a value stream. Here a shared resource needs to be specifically identified on a VSM. Often there are both WIP and changeover considerations. WIP in front of the resource should be split into two, being that used in the particular value stream being mapped and by all other value streams.

Value-add total process time shown in the timeline would be calculated based on the particular VSM's WIP, being WIP X unit process (or run) time. Non-value-add time is more complex. Here the complete EPEI (every product every) cycle needs to be considered. See the formula for EPEI in Chapter 28. The EPEI will give a good approximation of the realistic lead-time through the shared resource.

A VSM with no shared resources typically uses FIFO lanes between stages. However, a shared resource with changeover will typically require a priority kanban system. This is also discussed in Chapter 28.

Further reading

Kevin Duggan / Institute for Operational Excellence, 'Designing Value Stream Flow Through Shared Equipment'. Monograph, 2018.

Christoph Roser, *All about Pull*, All About Lean, 2021

23.5   Some warnings about mapping

When used appropriately, VSM is a powerful tool. When used too early by the unwary, it may mislead or even lead to scepticism. Why the cautions in early stages of using VSM? Remember that VSM is essentially a snapshot. How representative is the snapshot? The following points deliberately repeat earlier mentioned considerations.

- Demand uncertainty: Arrival variation can destabilise any system, but can be reduced. See Demand Analysis Chapter.

- Process uncertainty: Process variation - times and inventory variation. See Science of Lean : Mura

- Utilization: High utilization leads to high sensitivity to variation and instability. See Science of Lean : Muri.

- Stability: Quality, rework, breakdowns. If any of these are critical, the system will fail.

- Supply: is it reliable?

- Bottlenecks, buffers, shared resources. How critical are the bottlenecks and do they shift? Are they protected by buffers? Blocking and starvation from and to a bottleneck? See Scheduling Chapter

- Choice of the product to map. See Identifying Product Families in the Layout Chapter 22.

- Information flows. Sometimes the problem in a value stream is not the physical flow but

- the information flows – including accuracy and timing. See earlier.
  - Scheduling decisions. How is the schedule constructed?
  - Operator and team leader competence. This should always be a consideration.

VSM is best thought of an iterative, learning tool – not as a one-off exercise. Early attempts at VSM should be regarded as awareness raising but not used the basis for Future State design. Then, later, as stability and knowledge grows, VSM evolves into a powerful guide to change initiatives.

Probably, the misuse of VSM stems from the original book on VSM – Rother and Shook's 'Learning to See'. This classic book is superb on the mechanics of drawing a current state map but is based on a large number of assumptions that are not found in many situations. The assumptions include characteristics that are found amongst Toyota suppliers including stability of demand, a small number of products, no shared resources, precisely known times, and no quality issues. Variation is not mentioned, nor is layout. To be fair, Rother and Shook emphasise that VSM is a macro tool, used for big picture appreciation.

To be sure, the classic VSM book *Learning to See* by Rother and Shook is a great introduction. If the assumptions above are realistic for you, then *Learning to See* should be your VSM bible. For most, however, this is unrealistic. What to do? Three courses of action: the first stage is a conventional *Learning to See* mapping combined with the other mapping tools and considerations mentioned above. This should lead to several small-scale improvements and adjustments. The second is breaking the value stream into zones of stability and non-stability. A developing third stage would make use of digital data collection and the internet of things (IoT). See below.

It should be noted that Toyota does not do much value stream mapping internally, but tends to use the tool to assist suppliers. Second, nearly all mapping publications assume clear value streams with little or no branching, no shared resources, and fairly stable, ongoing, repetitive demand. In addition, information flows are often treated fairly superficially. These are unrealistic for many real world situations.

A common fist stage mistake it to get the team to add kaizen bursts that are ideas rather than solutions coming out of analysis. This is jumping to conclusions before the full facts are known! Another is that scheduling, buffers, and information flows are downplayed. If such an approach is adopted there will be benefit in early days particularly where there is lots of 'low hanging fruit'. But the real potential will not be realised.

A good lean analyst will add questions to the map; an inexperienced mapper will add random ideas.

The Action Plan: Future State Development

If you are reasonably confident about system stability, now progress to developing the Future State. This is a creative process not a mechanical process. The focus will be on manufacturing and transactional service. (For non-transactional service - interactive processes, custom processes, or project or design type processes the reader's attention is drawn to the book 'The Service Systems Toolbox'.)

McKinsey's Lisa Christensen, Jake Gittleson, and Matthew Smith suggest a 3 X3 approach: Focus on a maximum of 3 changes, within 3 months, with a development team of at least 3 people.
Prioritise improvements in the Unstable Zones. There will be a long list of minor changes, but knowledge of scheduling concepts is required. Please refer to the Scheduling and Pull Chapters.

The 4N Chart

A very useful, and fun, aid in developing the future state map is Simon Dodds' 4N chart as shown below.

The team starts at the bottom-left and focuses on current negative feelings. These are the Niggles. Apply 5 Why to these Niggles. Then focus on the positive feelings that are generated by the current situation. These Nuggets are features that should be retained. Then come the No-nos that the team would certainly like to be rid of. Finally, the Nice ifs are features that the team would like more of – aspects that generate positive feelings.

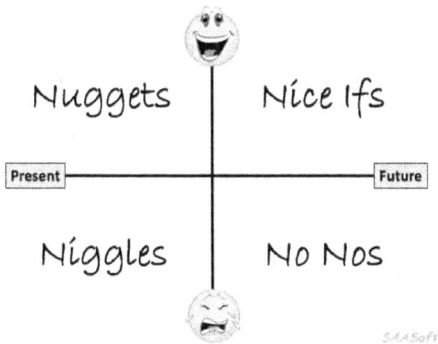

Copyright SAASoft. Used with Permission.

23.6 Value Stream Mapping in a Digital Age

In both service and manufacturing, collecting data for VSM has long been a purely manual process. This has had the considerable side benefit of getting middle, or even senior, managers to the Gemba to observe the process first-hand.

Data collected on a VSM exercise has sometimes been entered digitally into spreadsheets or by using VSM specific software. The latter requires variation to be incorporated, both of arrivals and of individual processes. Some VSMs have even been examined using simulation software. The good news here is improved clarity of documentation and greater insight. The not-so-good is possible intimidation by participants who may not be familiar with the software or a reluctance to contribute ideas when the VSM is presented digitally instead of manually drawn.

For some years workflow data collection, and even more recently internet of things (IoT) has become available. This enables even greater insight. The issue with manual VSM is that it is a snapshot. Insight depends, to an extent, on the luck of the draw when the mapping was done. Representative or not? There are no feedback loops (or rework), no shifting bottlenecks, no shared resources, no

variation with time, no shocks such as breakdowns. And of course, no people aspects.

What is ideal is to incorporate both manual and digital insights. Following the flow by direct observation is invaluable, as are manual displays of current state and team-based participation around improvements and future state.

Service: The example in the figure shows an outline of a digital (data mining) and a manual VSM for the same transactional process. The digital data-mining version shows the number of transactions collected automatically by workflow. An even better version would automatically collect process time variation, and arrival time variation across the day. This allows numerous forms of analysis. Variation is now much more easily collected automatically. Demand data requires special analysis. An important point here is to differentiate value demand from failure demand. (And in hospital settings, the possible addition of delayed demand and discretionary demand.)

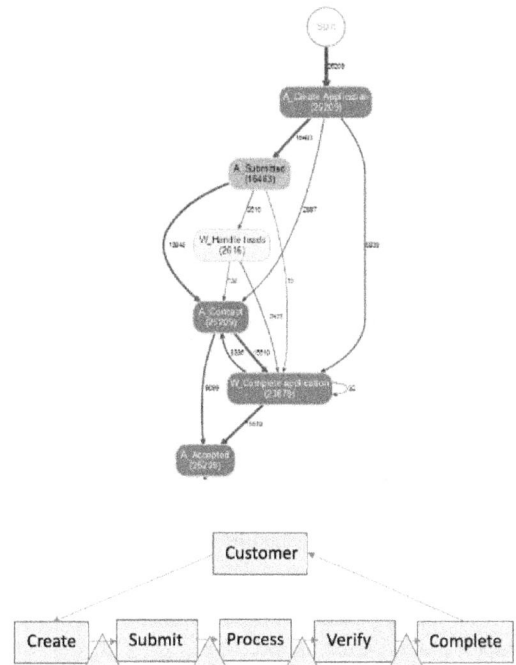

Digital mapping allows much more detailed insight into how a process actually works, including the variants. Every 'event' is tracked automatically, typically sourced from ERP. (An event has a case identifier, activity, and time stamp.) In the digital figure above, the activities are shown. The number in the activity node shows the frequency of the activity and the number between nodes shows the frequency of movement between nodes. An illustration is shown in the figure above. Time durations can also be shown. By contrast, in manual transactional service VSMs, inventory is shown in triangles. But physical inventory may not exist or be difficult to see and to record.

Manual mapping usually follows only the main sequence of events or how managers think the process should normally work. But in practice there are invariably special cases, 'short-cuts', new stages, reworks – to name just a few of the many variants that actually occur. In some settings, for example healthcare, insurance claims or purchasing, the variants can run into hundreds! Of course, such variants cause delays and customer dissatisfaction, not to mention cost. Variants may result in unrecognised bottlenecks and consume unplanned-for resource usage. This means that a manual value stream mapping exercise may be misleading. However, a manual analysis still retains the great benefit of getting those involved to visit the gemba. Therefore, as stated, both manual and automated data collection would be beneficial.

A data mining analysis helps to identify wastes, where standardization is required, and which stages are suitable for automation (RPA?) and which are not suitable.

(Note: if the process is Interactive – involving face-to-face interactions with customers – data mining alone will probably be insufficient.)

A developing requirement is good, accurate and rapid status information flow from digital or internet of things (IoT) monitoring. The identification of stable and unstable zones will enable a much more insightful, and up-to-date, analysis.

Thus we move mapping into the digital age with IoT, real-time simulation and eventually the Digital Twin. We can address dynamic changes as they occur and make schedule adjustments. (Note: A Digital Twin would make process decisions automatically but today there are Digital Shadows which monitor and advise.)

Although much attention has been given to the IoT, there is also the Internet of Content, the Internet of People, and the Internet of Places. The sources of data (or 'Big Data') is ever-expanding from ERP systems, phones, vehicles, machines, credit cards...the list goes on and on. With all of these, data can be captured automatically and analysed.

Examples:

IoT: Maintenance, RCM and TPM, Inventory management, Process control, Customer and demand understanding.

Internet of Content: Transactional events in office, service, healthcare. Costing.

Internet of People: Who is working on what? Idea and creative sources, training, coaching and HR. (Beware: Ethical and trust issues will surface.)

Internet of Places: Where activities are happening. Internal spaghetti, External transport, traffic.

Note: Please also refer to the section on Process Mining. Section 44.4, page 325.

Further reading

Web links are not given because they are apt to change. Please search the web and UTube for process mining and mapping providers. Examples are UiPath, Celonis, and RapidMiner. Demo software is often available.

24   Demand Analysis and Variation

Demand Analysis is one of the trilogy of concepts that have a major influence on effective lean scheduling. (The others in the trilogy are queuing dynamics and zones of stability and instability.)

'In the beginning, there was need', said Ohno. Understanding demand should be the first, or at least a very early, tool to use with Lean implementation.

Demand management has the objective of levelling demand as far as possible. This makes flow easier with implications for lead time, quality, and cost.

We Maasaki Imai, of Kaizen fame, has recently started using a new word to reflect the importance of taming or levelling demand and supply. It is 'Baratsuki'.

24.1   Level and Chase Demand

A classic stalwart in operations management is the distinction between Level and Chase scheduling. See the figure. As the names suggest, level scheduling maintains a constant production rate throughout the planning period – typically several months. Chase scheduling tracks the forecast of actual demand. In the figures, showing cumulative demand forecast and planned production, the vertical distance between the production and demand lines represents the inventory holding. The horizontal distance between the lines would show the average age of inventory.

Inventory optimisation. Lean favours reduced inventory – un-necessary inventory being one of the classic wastes. But customers have service lead-time expectations so 'Extra' safety inventory may be an order-winner. Generally, it is better to have a little more inventory, to avoid shortages, than to have too little, thereby risking customer satisfaction and stopping the completion of expensive products. (Recall the automotive microprocessor shortage.)

The Level plan minimises rate changeover and line rebalancing costs but the penalty is large inventory holdings that may exceed shelf life. The Chase plan leads to less inventory but involves rate changes. Of course, a hybrid is plan is possible. (For a simple product family the optimal solution is made possible by Linear Programming (LP) given forecasts, holding costs, changeover costs, and constraints such as minimum and maximum inventory holdings and age.)

For assembly, the costs of rate changes (requiring re-balancing) may be high. This explains why some manufactures prefer to run a lengthy level schedule. For Lean operations it may be possible to get the best of both by, for example:

- Balancing the line for (say) three rates thereby enabling rapid changeover.

- Employing smaller, more flexible machines- and flexible labour

- Dedicating lines that are only used only periodically, when needed. (Seasonal demand?) or Seru cells.

- Independent stand-alone assembly stations, employing multi-trained labour, into which kits are pulled.

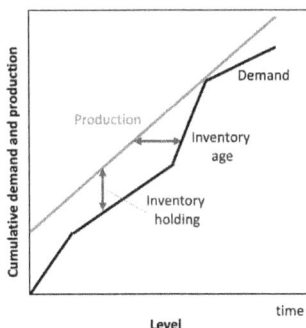

Level

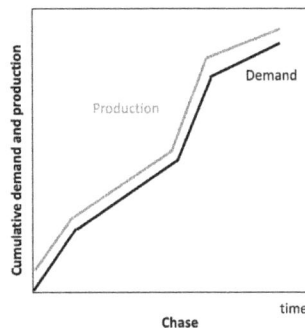

Chase

24.2 Reducing Unnecessary Demand and Demand Variation

We have learned from Kingman's Equation (See 'Science of Lean' Chapter 4) that there are three factors causing queues and lead time: demand variation, process variation, and utilization.

Of course there is demand (arrival) variation. But how much variation is self-imposed and avoidable? And how much demand should simply not be there? The following examples are highly cost-effective steps. Most lie within the power of planning staff and policy rather than with shop floor execution. Examples:

- End on month sales reporting and incentives leading to 'hockey stick' demand patterns.

- Quantity discounts rather than discounts for regular orders.

- Period order quantity and other batching algorithms in a MRP / ERP system that can transform level demands into lumpy demands.

- Un-coordinated supply chain activities resulting in the 'bullwhip' effect.

- Un-coordinated sales promotions and management inventory adjustments. There are trade-offs between promotions and 'everyday low prices' (as Proctor and Gamble were surprised to discover).

- Simply questioning customers (or planners) as to their exact needs. (In a classic case, monthly batches had been delivered for years. The real requirement was for weekly batches. Revealing this previously unquestioned situation led to significant improvements for both manufacturer and customer.)

- Are there incentives for distributors to work towards smooth demand? Toyota is known for the considerable influence placed on Japanese distributors to help smooth demand across the year.

- Seasonality? The authors have come across cases where assumed seasonality is found to be a myth caused by marketing, budgeting, or habit. Medicine tablets and diapers are examples.

- Can 'Yield Management' or 'Revenue Management' concepts be used – like hotels and airlines? Book ahead and get a discount; book late and pay more. Yes, this can work with products as well as service.

- Can customers be offered upgrades? For instance Dell offers customers free or bargain upgrades thereby helping to smooth variety and to shift ageing inventory. Both the customer and the manufacturer benefit.

- Failure Demand or 'Mistake Demand' How much demand is failure demand – 'demand resulting from not doing something or from not doing something correctly'? In other words, rework, recalls and returns but also work resulting from incorrect information and from not understanding customer requirements. This can be huge, especially in service, repair and overhaul business. Moreover such demands are often not only 'lumpy' but tend to come at peak times. Ignore at your peril!

- Of course, in healthcare and in other services, how much demand can be avoided by prevention?

Looking at factors such as these should be the starting point for any Lean scheduling project. Simply to use demand data without questioning the causes of demand fluctuation is a huge waste.

Reducing Process Variation

The standard ways to reduce process variation is through 5S and Standard Work. TWI Job

Instruction has a very important role. However, don't neglect :

- TPM and particularly breakdown stoppages. A breakdown not only affects capacity but there is also disturbance recovery time.
- Workstation layout and ergonomics.
- Delivery of parts by a runner, and kanban operations. A runner (material handler) should place parts in their correct position ready for assembly. An operator should not have to undo packaging or move containers of parts. Likewise, handling of kanban cards should be by the runner.

Reducing Utilization

Two routes to reducing utilization are reducing unnecessary demand and improving capacity. Unnecessary demand can result from over-ambitious forecasts – this is really a question of understanding customers better. 'The waste of overproduction'. An important source of unnecessary demand results from rework and defects. In service, reducing failure demand must be a priority (see above). Reducing rework calls for a range of quality tools and methods including Andon, TWI job instruction, poka-yoke, SPC, self- and successive inspection as well as feedback from subsequent processes and from customers. Toyota North Wales has a wonderful display of actual failures and their consequences. All operators see the display.

Reducing Variation or Reducing Utilization?

Of course, it depends. Usually however, reducing utilization (or, in effect, adding or freeing up capacity) is usually more effective. Also, of course, you should do both.

Refer to the figure:

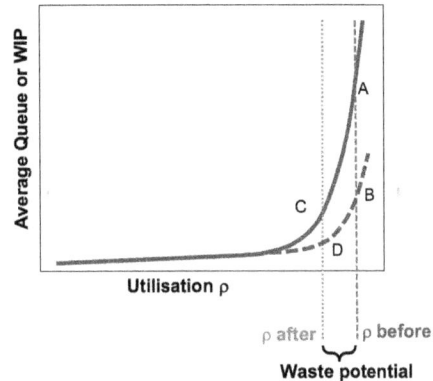

Assume your starting point is position A. By reducing variation whilst maintaining utilization will move you to position B. By reducing utilization alone will move you to position C on the original curve. Generally, because of the steepness of the original Kingman curve, there is a dramatic reduction in queue length by reducing utilization. Reducing variation alone creates a new curve which is less steep than the original curve.

Point D is reached by reducing both utilization and variation.

Also, importantly, reducing utilization is generally easier and faster than reducing variation.

24.3   Demand Analysis

Demand Analysis is an essential concept for Lean scheduling, recognising the fact that, inevitably, products have different demand patterns and volumes. The idea is to capitalise on repeatability and stability where possible and to manage other demands appropriately. This leads onto the possibility of maximising level scheduling, one of the most powerful yet under-used ideas in Lean.

Demand analysis is linked with Pareto quantity analysis and with frequency pattern analysis. See below.

First, product contribution analysis should be done to identify any products that should be phased out or treated with special care. (See the Contribution section in the Chapter on The Science of Lean.)

Second all demand data over a representative period should be manually scanned to detect and cleanse unusual events and data errors. An unusual event may be a part recall or a special event such as The Olympics.

Third, demand should, over time, be smoothed as self-induced and unnecessary variation is eliminated. Methods were discussed above..

The implication is that the three above steps will have to be repeated periodically.

Do not attempt to use the demand classification procedure below before these three steps (particularly the third) have been completed.

Study the demand patterns. What is the variation of demand over time? (Perhaps by hour, day, week, month, year. What is an appropriate horizon for capturing demand? How stable is demand when plotted by day, week, month, quarter?

Draw control charts of demand volume over appropriate time horizons. Draw the control limits. See if demand is 'in control'. If there are 'out of control' peaks try to find out why.

Then, early on, measure end-to-end response time. This is the time taken to actually meet customer demands, end-to-end. Not promised, or shipped, or first time delivery but measuring what customers actually want. (See Scion 23.4)

Demand Categories

The Runners, Repeaters, Strangers (RRS) concept originated in Lucas Industries perhaps four decades ago. 'Runners' are high volume products or components sometimes justifying dedicated resources. They should be run frequently, perhaps every day, and form the backbone of the schedule. Repeaters are lower volume but occur regularly. They should occupy regular slots in the schedule – perhaps weekly or fortnightly. The quantity may vary but the time slot should be maintained as far as possible. Strangers are low or intermittent volume, fitted around the runners and repeaters in the schedule.

Michael Baudin's RRS approach is different, interesting, and useful. This is an approach to parts rather than for scheduling. His classification is based on the percentage of products that use a particular part. If it is 100% (or the part is used in all products) then it is a runner. Below 100%, but above a particular chosen percentage, then it is a repeater. Finally, if the part of used in a small percentage of products, it is a stranger.

First, an analogy on scheduling: the Runner, Repeater, Stranger (RRS) scheduling principle is much like the way we run our lives. We have runners, for example heartbeat that goes on all the time, and we don't plan for these. But nevertheless, good practice is keeping your heart in good condition through exercise. Then repeaters: we sleep every night perhaps not for the same length of time but every night. You know, without being told, not to telephone your friends at 3 a.m. Likewise you have breakfast every day. You use the opportunity to talk to the family, because they are all there without having to arrange a special meeting. What you don't do, even though it may appear more efficient, is to have one big breakfast lasting three whole days at the beginning of the month (one 'setup'). You organise your food inventories around these regular habits. Then strangers: you do different things each day, but these different activities are slotted in around the regular activities.

Once again, Quality Guru Phil Crosby talks about running your business 'like ballet, not hockey'. In ballet you rehearse, adjust and do it the same for each performance. In (ice) hockey, each game is different. Runners, repeaters, and strangers allow ballet style management. Too often, it is hockey style - we collapse exhausted in our chair at the end of the week, feeling satisfied but having solved the same old problem for the 500th time!

Categorization

A useful categorization is used Boylon et al and by John Darlington. Refer to the figure. Note that these demand patterns may apply to end items (products) and to repeating sub-assemblies. In the descriptions below words such as high and low variance, 'regular', and 'random' need to be determined locally rather than through some statistical test.

Note that an end item may fall into more than one pattern. For instance, an end item may be normal variance, high demand but a lumpy pattern may also occur due to a special event and a policy demands pattern may occur due to stock adjustments.

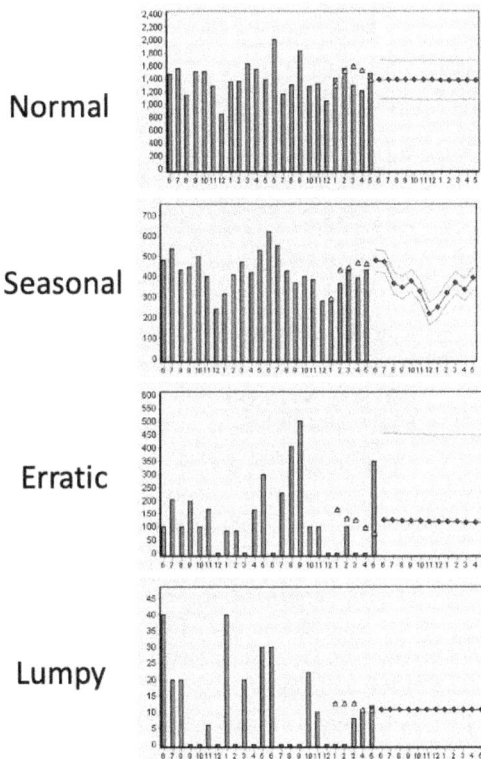

Normal

Seasonal

Erratic

Lumpy

The pattern illustrations are from John Darlington, with permission.

The 'Glenday Sieve' is classic Pareto analysis by volume, named by Ian Glenday. 'The Sieve' uses four categories of sales volume: the top 50% (accounting for perhaps 6% of SKU's) are referred to as GREEN. The next 45% by volume (accounting

for perhaps a further 45% of SKU's) are GREEN. The next 4% of volume (accounting for perhaps 20% of SKU's) are BLUE. The last 1% by volume account for perhaps 30% of SKU's are RED. An alternative name is PHIL for Prime, High, Intermediate, Low.

24.4 Combining Volume Analysis with Demand Patterns

Our experience is that a powerful approach to scheduling uses BOTH the Demand Pattern AND the Glenday Pareto analysis. This is shown in the Figure below. Notice a number of points:

- Some categories are inherently more suitable for Make-to-Stock (MTS) production others for Make-to-Order (MTO) or Build-to-Order (BTO)

- Normal, high demand GREEN category can be made regularly with little risk. This is because, with high demand, there is the 'pooling' effect (or Central Limit Theorem)- where low demand from one customer is likely to be offset by high demand from another. The greater the number of demand sources, the greater is the pooling effect. This large category by volume should form the basic, underlying frequently repeating schedule.

- Normal YELLOW and BLUE category SKU's will be scheduled periodically. Normal demand GREEN category is a prime target for cells. Investigate!

- DO NOT allow Seasonal, Erratic, and Lumpy demand orders to disrupt the repeating, regular schedule. Establish schedule time bands, the most important band being for GREEN NORMAL. Always question Erratic and Lumpy demands – are such demands required to be delivered or shipped in large batches – or would the customer really prefer more spread-out delivery?

- BLUE and RED category SKUs (particularly Erratic and Lumpy) should be examined by contribution analysis. Phase them out if demand is declining or contribution is small.

	Green/Prime	Yellow/Hi	Blue/Int	Red/Low
Normal, high	The basic,regular repeating, mixed model, Line?	Repeating schedule, Cell?	MTS, scheduled periodically	n/a
Normal, low	A repeating schedule, Is a Cell possible? Mixed model		Fit around Green & Yellow	n/a?
Seasonal	Base forecast? Season adjust. Postponement? MTO extra shift		Overtime or temps for specials	
Erratic	MTS if forecastable or predictable, else MTO/ ATO lead time dependent	MTO, ATO fit these around Green	fit around, but why erratic?	Why erratic? Question!
Lumpy			fit around	Why lumpy? Question!
Mgmt C	Frequent, small adjustment; better than infrequent large		Infrequent	n/a

MTS

MTO or BTO or ATO

Dedicate if possible; Regular, Repeating Schedule

Examine contribution; Increase price? Growth or decline? Design change?

Monitor if demand is increasing – these may become GREEN or YELLOW later.

- Seasonal demand pattern SKUs should be treated differently for scheduling purposes from Erratic and Lumpy pattern SKUs. Scheduling plateaus should be considered, where demand can be levelled for a particular season.

- Management Control SKUs are inventory adjustments made by management (or the S&OP function) in relation to special circumstances. Examples: New products, sales promotions, replacement for defective items, etc. Depending on shelf life and changeover costs, it is preferable to make these in smaller batches.

24.5 Scheduling with Categorization and Plateaus

The concept is to run the top demands at a constant rate for as long as possible, whilst minimising finished goods (or near finished goods) inventories.

Before considering scheduling categories, be remined that

- Queueing Dynamics implies that attention is given to arrival and process variation and that a process utilization 'cap' of perhaps 85% is established.

- Zones of stability and instability are known. Zones of instability need to be buffered by inventory to reduce problem overspill.

GREEN NORMAL is usually the 'top' band, accounting for perhaps 50% of total demand. This should be level scheduled. This schedule band should be prioritised and defended from change. Many of these demands could be MTS, using the pooling principle. Dedicated resources should be investigated.

Next, the top demands (GREEN, YELLOW with NORMAL OR SEASONAL Patterns) should be (manually?) scanned for plateaus or seasonality. This is an attempt to get the best combination of Level and Chase demand. Split the year into plateaus of stable demand. This may mean building up inventory at times and drawing on inventory at other times whilst maintaining a level schedule.

One company refers to this as their 80/20 schedule – meaning that 80% of their SKU's are run with level schedules, and 20% run irregularly but fitted around the top band

Likewise any BLUE NORMAL demands could be scheduled around the top two bands.

Thereafter, GREEN and YELLOW, ERRATIC and LUMPY demands could go into another band which is fitted around the remaining NORMAL and SEASONAL demands. Possibly MTO, BTO, or ATO.

Finally, any BLUE ERRATIC or LUMPY are fitted into any remaining capacity.

Techniques for achieving schedule stability include:

- Use the 'variety as late as possible' concept. Do not add variety until the last possible moment. Design has an important role. Upstream stability; downstream flexibility. Upstream, before the postponement point, there is less variation and greater stability. In cars this is body in white – at this stage MTS is converted to ATO

- Use control limits, much like an SPC chart. As long as demand stays within these limits, don't change the plan. Or, use a CUSUM chart to detect changes to underlying demand. A CUSUM is one of the most effective ways of detecting shifts in demand patterns.

- Remember takt time is derived from customer demand and available production time – so it is partly under your own control. Don't over-react to changes in customer demand.

- Use the 'available to promise' logic found in most Master Scheduling packages.

- Move to 'milk round' deliveries – whereby several small batches are delivered on a single vehicle more frequently, rather than a big batch less frequently, meaning that total number of loads remains unchanged.

24.6 Inventory Control of Parts ABC and RRS

A useful way to think of Lean inventory control and control of parts is the table below. Note that here runners, repeaters and strangers refer to component parts not to end products. A component part may be used in several end items, whether the end items are runners repeaters or strangers.

The supply of parts or sub-assemblies to an assembly line (or even to batch production) should be levelled as far as possible. This is to enable the material handling activity to work at a consistent rate. Hence the thoughts of Michel Baudin are useful. (See Demand categories 24.3 above.)

First, however, note that ABC analysis based on ranked (unit cost x annual volume) and quoted in many textbooks (and MBA programs!) is simply wrong and outdated. It would mean that 1000 x $1 items should have equal priority as one $1000 item! Moreover, as MRP guru Joe Orlicky pointed out in 1975 (yes, 1975!) 'with a computer available...the (traditional) ABC concept tends to become irrelevant'. (Because Demand Categories, as discussed above are much superior.)

By value NOT by usage!		Runner	Repeater	Stranger
	A	Tight kanban	Tight kanban	Manual Adjustment
	B	Tight kanban	'Loose' kanban	MRP / Forecast-driven
	C	Two-bin	Two-bin	Two-bin 'Go see'

The columns are runners, repeaters and strangers The rows are the A, B, C inventory classification. A parts are expensive, B intermediate, C are low cost commodity parts.

The entries in the cells indicate the broad options. The table is not intended for every company but is a broad guideline. Each company should develop its own matrix. An A class repeater is likely to be a candidate for tight kanban (that is, kanban with small safety stock). A class strangers require careful monitoring and may be candidates for MRP or some forecast-based system. Lack of repetition makes kanban less feasible. B class repeaters are probably candidates for kanban with more safety stock. Generally C class items should be managed by a simple procedure such as a two-bin system or reorder point system – perhaps periodic review for runners and continuous review for strangers.

A further dimension is lead-time, shown in the table below.

		Runners	Repeaters	Strangers
A	Short L/T	Tight kanban	Tight Kanban	Signal kanban
	Long L/T	Kanban + SS	Loose Kanban	Adjustment SS
B	Short L/T	Kanban	Tight Kanban	Signal kanban
	Long L/T	Kanban + SS	Loose Kanban	Forecast-driven MRP
C	Short L/T	VMI	VMI	Two-bin / ROP + SS
	Long L/T	Two-bin + SS	Two-bin + SS	Two-bin + SS

Volatility / reliability of supplier may be another dimension
SS = safety stock; VMI = vendor managed inventory; ROP = reorder point

Here, VMI is vendor managed inventory and signal kanban is a launch-activated signal system such as used for Ford engines or Johnson controls seats.

Note that there should always be efforts to convert stranger parts into repeaters and repeater parts into runners, thereby reducing and eventually eliminating the need for MRP. This rationalisation should begin with product design.

Of course, demand for parts varies with time. A runner may evolve into a stranger or vice versa. So it is necessary to keep tags on this. There is software on the market that will do this automatically, and flag up when a part has shifted significantly between categories. Alternatively, the position of each part should be reviewed manually whenever a major change in demand mix of end products occurs.

24.7   Part Levelling

A further consideration is levelling the delivery of parts to the line. This aids runner (material handling tugger) and picking routines. The aim is a steady flow of parts to workstations.

Even though the assembly sequence may have been levelled (using categorization analysis above, and mixed model scheduling as described in the Scheduling Line Processes Chapter below), this does not necessarily mean that parts flow will be levelled. This is because different products may use different quantities of the same part.

Consider the example shown in the figure.

Here there are two sequences for four products. Each sequence involves a tugger delivery of parts. The number of parts varies by product. The mixed model sequence has been levelled according to takt time. Notice that in the 'before' situation the number of parts delivered in each tugger visit varies considerably. By changing the mixed model sequence (whilst, of course, maintaining takt and products), the deliveries are considerably improved.

The calculation for a simple mixed model case can be worked out by spreadsheet trials, but for a complex assembly process involving hundreds of parts computer routines are required. See Monden for a calculation method.

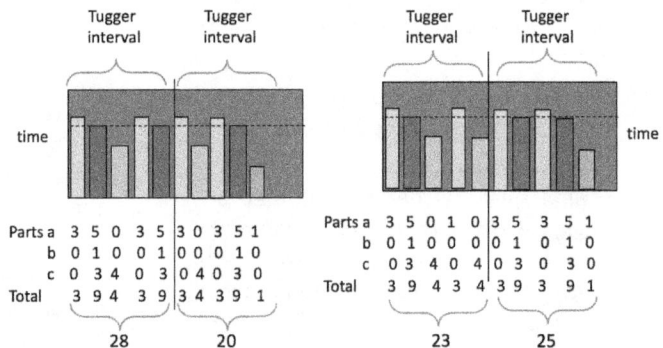

	Tugger interval				Tugger interval					Tugger interval					Tugger interval			
time																			time
Parts a	3	5	0	3	5	3	0	3	5	1	3	5	0	1	0	3	5	3	5	1
b	0	1	0	0	1	0	0	0	1	0	0	1	0	0	0	0	1	0	1	0
c	0	3	4	0	3	0	4	0	3	0	0	3	4	0	4	0	3	0	3	0
Total	3	9	4	3	9	3	4	3	9	1	3	9	4	3	4	3	9	3	9	1
			28					20					23					25		

Further reading

Matthias Holweg and Frits K. Pil, The Second Century: Reconnecting Customer and Value Chains through Build-to-Order, MIT Press, Cambridge MA, 2004

John Darlington, *MSc Lean Enterprise Notes*, DCAF Module, University of Buckingham, 2015

Ian Glenday and Rick Sather, *Lean RFS*, CRC Press, 2013

Yasuhiro Monden, *Toyota Production System*, (Second edition), Chapman and Hall, London, 1998

Yashiro Monden, *Toyota Production System*, 4th edition, CRC / IIE Press, 2012 (esp. Chapter 21 for the (complex) methods for assembly line smoothing.)

25 Scheduling: General points

Scheduling is at the heart of Lean. All the other tools described in the book, can be seen as contributing to better schedule performance. Scheduling directly impacts lead time, delivery performance, cost and quality. Yet, for several managers, incredibly, scheduling is not high priority. Nor is the position of scheduler or master scheduler a high-status job.

As stated, the 'Flow' package of Chapters comprises Mapping, Demand Analysis, General Points, Line Processes and Batch Processes.

A successful schedule requires the integration of a trilogy of concepts: Demand Analysis, Queueing Dynamics, and Identification of Stable and Unstable Zones. See the figure.

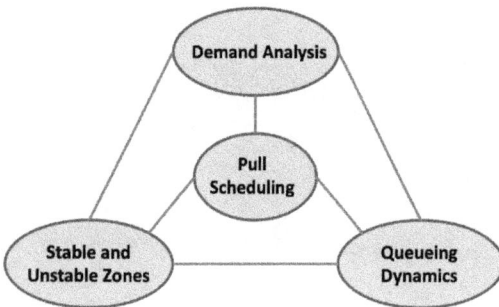

Demand Analysis and Queueing Dynamics were each discussed in separate earlier Chapters.

In the Chapter on Value Stream Mapping, attention was given to differentiating stable and unstable zones. Here we add detail.

25.1 Identifying Stable and Unstable Zones

The following sections apply in both service and manufacturing.

First: Indicators. Unstable zones usually have several problems that are known by people working at the processes. A prime indicator is an inability to meet the schedule, thereby affecting overall value stream performance. The causes are many, as mentioned earlier, but their frequency is

their determining factor. Simply asking front-line staff where problem areas lie can be confirmed with data. Of particular note is process time variation as a result of product variety. (A particular process may have wildly different process times between products or options. Therefore a changing schedule may be the cause of an unstable zone.)

Second: Measurement: The Chapter on The Science of Lean described the Kingman equation for queues and lead time. There are two causes of long queues and instability: variation and utilization. Utilization above 85% or 90% results not only in a severe escalation of queues (except where there is very low process variation) but also considerable uncertainty of queue length. Therefore a clear candidate for an unstable zone is a process with high utilization. The related factor is process variation, measured by the coefficient of variation CV_p. CV measures the standard deviation of process time divided by the average. A high CV would be above about 1.3 – an excellent indicator of an unstable process. (Reminder: utilization is load / capacity. Capacity needs to consider availability, which is measured by MTBF/(MTBF + MTTR)).

Third: Starvation and Blockage. A bottleneck may occur with relatively low utilization due to starvation and or blockage. Therefore determining bottlenecks by examining utilization alone may mislead. Starvation is waste resulting from upstream problems. Blockages is waste resulting from downstream problems.

The figure below illustrates a hospital stream where utilization is an imperfect indicator of a bottleneck. By combination, Resource 6 is the bottleneck. Note that utilization alone is NOT the sole indicator of a bottleneck.

Fourth: Propagation. To quote Don Reinertsen, 'It is important to go beyond the popular but simplistic idea that the capacity of the bottleneck controls system flow. In fact, flow through a bottleneck is affected strongly by the process that precedes the bottleneck. The upstream process determines the variation in the arrival rate at the bottleneck, and thus affects the queue. Managing the process upstream of the bottleneck is a valuable tool for improving flow at the bottleneck.' From *The Principles of Product Development Flow*, Celeritas, p 67:

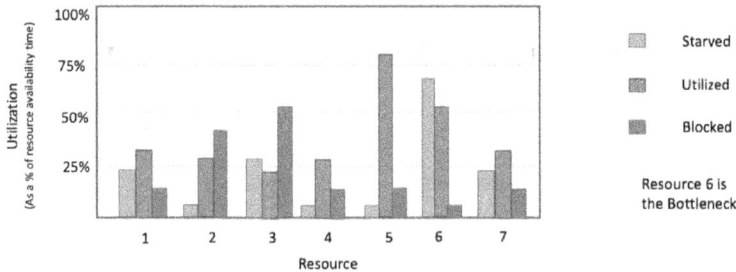

Hopp and Spearman have described, and formulated, the propagation of flow variability. Here we will not consider the formulas (Se, Chapter 8). There are two factors involved – utilization and variability. (As with Kingman equation mentioned above.) A high utilization workstation with high variation will increase downstream arrival variability thereby increasing problems and possibly creating or extending an unstable zone. On the other hand, a high utilization workstation with low variation will have no effect on (or even reduce) downstream arrival variability. Wally Hopp gives the example of a crowd leaving a football match (high variability) overwhelming the downstream parking area exit (limited capacity). Although this might be unavoidable at sporting matches, in manufacturing (or service) this can be avoided 'Machines with long setups or failures, schedules that run products in batches, and staffing policies that periodically idle certain operations …serve to feed work to downstream processes in uneven waves'.

Improving Flows in Unstable Zones

Let us begin with two quotes:

'The key for thinking like a true scientist is the acceptance that any real-life situation, no matter how complex it initially looks is, once understood, embarrassingly simple.'

from Eli Goldratt, *The Choice, and* author of *The Goal*

'The more rationalization efforts progress, the more it appears that they were only doing things that are obvious….When something looks fantastic there must be something bad about it…When you see a factory and think 'There is nothing worth seeing here', they may in fact be doing a lot better. ….The simpler it is, the harder it is to do.'

from Taiichi Ohno, *Workplace Management*, Chapter 21

Continuous Improvement activities should prioritise unstable zones in value streams. The full range of Lean tools are applicable, from standard work to kata, and including layout. A Toyota example was the focus on reducing rework at NUMMI by giving particular encouragement to Andon. (Rework is an important source of instability.) Product and process design have an important role. A Toyota example has been the move towards 'New Global Architecture' which rationalises platforms and parts, as well as stabilizing flow, and gaining economies of scale and flexibility. A service example would be targeting the causes of failure demand.

Buffers: It may sound counterproductive but adding buffers to unstable zones can improve overall flow. Buffers – whether inventory capacity or time, bring stability. They should however be regarded as temporary measures. Inventory is not always waste. It is a shock-absorber held before and or after an unstable zone. Capacity buffers can be achieved by (in descending order) TPM, working additional shift time, or deliberate over-sizing. Time buffers merely add to promised lead times. (Beware, however, of the self-fulfilling *lead time syndrome* as described by the late MRP Guru,

George Plossl. (Adding inventory increases lead time which in turn results in more problems.)

Blocked and Starved Resources: The reasons for a blocked or starved resource may lie within or outside of the unstable zone. Outside reasons include upstream or downstream process variability. Classic cases occur regularly in hospitals with regard to operating theatres. Outside upstream reasons include availability of staff, medicines or test results. An outside downstream reason is availability of post-operation beds. Inside reasons include equipment availability and lack of Check Lists as described by Atul Gawande. Eli Goldratt's 4 improvement stages (Identify, Exploit, Subordinate, Elevate) are, as usual, great advice. (See the section on the Synchronous Rules in the Scheduling: General Chapter.)

Monitoring by Internet of Things (IoT) and Digital Twin

The Internet of Things combined with the Digital Twin allows real-time monitoring and schedule adjustment. A worthwhile consideration for high product variety, high process variability manufacturing. The Digital Twin and IoT may sound good, but should not be started until some of the above approaches have been started. For now, this is a high-tech, high cost solution.

Who should do the work?

Stable zones are prime areas for operator team involvement. Unstable zones require different types of attention. Work content, batch sizes, product family grouping, buffer selection and sizing, balancing and sequencing, part shortages, and tool and machine selection are all tasks where the lead is taken by engineers, analysts and managers. Of course, operators need to be consulted. Leader standard work needs particular focus on unstable zones. However, this is not to deny participation by everyone in improvement activities such as 5S and 5 Why, A3 point analysis, standard work, layout and movement, quality variability and rework reduction.

A Hierarchy of Stages for Stable and Unstable Zones

Richter et al, in working with German high-tech manufacturer Bosch, suggest a cycle of review and action stages

Yearly: A PDCA cycle that focused on the identification of stable and unstable zones to be tackled in the following period as part of policy deployment targets. (Hoshin?)

Quarterly: A focus on the 'reduction of 'value added variability, since this requires extensive activities like restructuring, re-balancing or re-sequencing'

Monthly: A focus on 'the effectiveness of daily activities, reducing non value added variability and capacity constraints.'

Further reading

Ralph Richter, Jochen Deuse, Peter Willats, Marius Syberg and David Lenze From 'Creating Lean Value Streams *through proactive Variability Management*', *International Journal of Production Research*, 2022

25.2 Different processes require different approaches to scheduling

A basic point to note about Lean scheduling is that most manufacturing situations are essentially two or more linked stages, or loops (as discussed in the Mapping section), each of which should have their own appropriate scheduling system. Typically, downstream, this is fairly repetitive assembly using a value stream with heijunka or day by the hour, a single pacemaker, small or no changeovers, and pull. Upstream, there are shared resources (resources that are shared between two or more value streams), where batch sizing is important. In the intermediate situation, cells (traditional or Seru) are found.

Hence, these situations are dealt with in three Scheduling chapters – General, Line and Batch. The situations often overlap, as shown in the figure.

The figure aligns different types of Layout against volume (this is known as the 'Product Process Matrix').

The Product Process Matrix

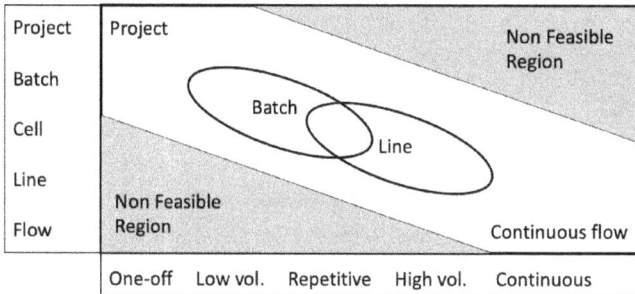

Laid out in this way, there are non-feasible regions (for example it would be folly to set up an assembly line for very low volume operations) and a feasible region that is in line with conventional thinking. Note, however, that the feasible region is quite broad.

The feasible region implies that the process or layout must evolve as the volume increases. Failure to adjust leads to a system that is out of alignment. Moreover, there are appropriate, but overlapping, scheduling systems for each region. In the one-off project management area (e.g. new product introductions, large construction) critical path analysis, or 'Last Planner' is an appropriate tool. For job shops with shifting bottlenecks Finite Scheduling packages may be appropriate. A slow-moving pulse line is often an appropriate form of layout for low volume, but regular production. Drum Buffer Rope (DBR) or CONWIP is often an effective scheduling tool for intermediate volume, particularly where there are bottlenecks. (See the Chapter 28 on Batch Processes.)

Note, once again, most facilities have both of these situations occurring along a product stream.

Some Lean literature (including some Lean accounting literature) gives the impression that all Lean scheduling is done end to end, with a single downstream pacemaker. This is desirable, but rare. Even Toyota, after 60 years, still has some shared resources and two stage scheduling. Of course,

every opportunity should be taken to create end-to-end value streams with a single pacemaker.

25.3   Basics of Lean Scheduling

Of course, Scheduling applies in both manufacturing and service contexts. Some of the words change, but the concepts remain. Here both contexts will be referred to as 'production'.

In some organisations, Lean concepts like 5S, kaizen, waste, standardisation, or Six Sigma, have become so prominent in the minds of senior management that production planning systems and procedures have been ignored. They are 'less sexy'. This is a serious mistake.

Some pointers or warnings:

- The **purpose** of the production planning and control function should evolve as Lean is implemented. There are three forms of evolution. First, the planning department should be less and less involved with execution and monitoring. Planning, though, remains important. Second, the role should evolve towards analysis and decision support rather than routine planning. (Exactly the same comments apply to Accounting). By decision support is meant appropriate advice on current bottlenecks, demand analysis, appropriate buffer and safety stocks, changeover priorities, maintenance priorities, appropriate kaizen activity and, vitally, on capacity and demand policy. Sales and Operation (S&OP) participation, is, of course, vital. Third, it should advise on appropriate supply chain decisions – where, when and how much inventory to position. The placement and sizing of the three types of buffer is important. All this means a much higher level thoughtful role. Planning should in no way be threatened by Lean – quite the reverse. Only the best people will do.

With the Digital Twin concept coming into prominence there is the temptation to move scheduling to more centralised functions. Beware! As General Stanley McChrystal described, the coalition forces in Afghanistan had all the tech, but the Taliban were running rings around them.

- **Bills of Material accuracy and structuring** is fundamental. Without good BOMs, material requirement planning – whether via an MRP/ERP system or not – is difficult or impossible. This information is needed for sizing of buffers, supermarkets and kanban quantities, and for planning runner routes. If BOMs are inaccurate, incorrect parts will be ordered and Lean will fail. BOMs should be restructured to reduce the number of levels as cells are introduced. Planning and modular bills, though emanating from classic MRP practice, are extremely useful in Lean

- **Safety Stocks.** When was the last time safety and buffer stocks were reviewed? Simply, it is necessary whenever demand changes, or changeover is reduced, or lead times change, or OEE improves. In short, in a Lean programme, continually!

- **Batch Sizes.** Same comments as for safety stocks.

- **Routing files.** Routings are essential for cell design, for capacity analysis, and for resource planning. If your routing file deteriorates, so will your Lean programme.

Sometimes the Production Planning office is not seen as having a part in Lean. 'Lean is for the operations floor but we need to get on with Planning' What a mistake to make! Visual management boards and improvement events, including cyclic reviews of batch sizes and zones of instability, safety inventories, planning lead time assumptions, lead time verification, and reviews of planning measures should be integral to Lean. In some enlightened companies, the best and brightest spend a period in manufacturing planning and control. But likewise planners should spend time on the shop floor. It was not for nothing that

George Plossl, manufacturing planning and control guru, made statements like 'The Master Schedule should be management's handle on the business' and 'lead times are what you say they are'.

Scheduling is the apex of 'System'. For a good, flow schedule, many aspects have to come together in harmony – quality, standards, pull systems, delivery, material handling, and of course people aspects.

25.4   On MRP and ERP

MRP (and wider ERP) is essential for most manufactures. Why? To keep track of inventory, for ordering inventory via bills of materials and MRP logic, for rough cut capacity planning, for order entry. MRP is near essential in that it provides a single data base for operations, sales, and accounting data. So much for the good news. But Lean users should be aware of the assumptions and downsides that can seriously disrupt a Lean implementation:

1. MRP ignores variation. Throughout this book, the importance of allowing for the effects of variation is emphasized.

2. Most MRP systems assume fixed lead times and infinite capacity. A finite scheduling module in MRP is supposed to correct for this by finite scheduling that takes capacity into account. Some of these algorithms are poor. As a result, many manufacturers resort to spreadsheet solutions.

3. ERP is more of a financial and costing aid than a scheduling system. As an accounting tool it is reasonable. (But note remarks on Lean accounting in the later Chapter).

4. Most MRP systems 'regenerate' daily or weekly. The reason is that schedules get out of date, often as soon as they come out. The result is changing schedules and instability. But why so often? An MRP system should rather use SPC type logic where, within the control limits, no changes are necessary. In fact SPC teaches that over-reaction will increase variation, making things worse!

5. Rework affects capacity and utilization. It can even create a bottleneck that would not be revealed in many capacity modules (CRP). Rework also increases variation, thereby (via Kingman's equation) increasing lead time and inventory. Rework is, of course, a 'big deal' in many service organisations.

6. Scrap is often treated in MRP by a 'scrap factor'. But, as pointed out by Hopp and Spearman, the problem with scrap is variation in the scrap rate. A 10% average rate may mean 1 unit in 10, or 1 batch in 10. A huge difference! The consequences are in customer service, throughput (via possible starvation of bottleneck), and extra un-needed inventory.

7. Process variation: There is a huge difference between a resource with low rate variation and one with high variation. If an average is used in MRP, Lead-time and throughput will suffer.

8. Supplier lead time variation: Again, there is a huge difference between a supplier with low variation and one with high variation. If an average is used in MRP, throughput and customer service can suffer. Extra inventory is a likely consequence.

9. Too often, MRP is used blindly by planners who let the computer make the decisions without recognizing the impact of built in parameters and assumptions. For example, batch sizes, ordering policies like period order quantity, and standard lead times are built in.

10. Although not confined to MRP, the classic Lead-time syndrome may result from an unthinking use of MRP. The syndrome is : shortages happen > lead times are increased for safety sake > more inventory is released into production > lead times increase > schedule changes are more likely > more shortages occur.

So, bottom line: Use MRP only for inventory planning and control, not for execution. For scheduling and execution most MRP modules are (as yet) unsuitable. DDMRP is a possible exception – a partial solution. See under Pull Systems.

25.5 Master Scheduling and Final Assembly Scheduling

In many organizations it is appropriate to have both a Master Production Schedule (MPS) and a Final Assembly Schedule (FAS). The use of these depends on the ratio of manufacturing lead time to customer expected lead times. Obviously the most desirable situation is to reduce total manufacturing lead times so that they are less than customer expected lead time. This reduces dependence on forecasting, cuts WIP and eliminates FGI. An intermediate milestone, now being routinely achieved in automotive first tier, is to reduce final assembly time to less than customer expected lead time. In this case forecasting is only necessary so as to ensure sufficient buffer at the postponement point. MRP might still be necessary for long lead time parts and raw material. Ideally, MRP is only used for planning – issuing call-off expectations to suppliers.

25.6 Sales and Operations Planning (S&OP)

S&OP has evolved substantially over the past decade with increased use of the Cloud, analytics, and AI. But a more important driver has been the recognition that effective S&OP should involve not merely a meeting between sales and marketing staff and operations and supply chain people. S&OP is a vital integrating set of activities, led by senior management, involving sales, marketing, operations, supply chain, finance, IT, Design, and HR, as a prime means of achieving the goals of the business. Purchasing needs to be included. If Purchasing does not understand Lean flow concepts, or acts independently, buying large batches of components at low cost – but putting the supply chain at risk through delivery or quality failure, puts the whole value stream at risk. Acquisition is also important as the chip shortage has demonstrated.

Perhaps S&OP should better be termed 'Executive S&OP' (as used by Wallace and Stahl) to indicate its importance as being the link between strategy and detailed planning and execution. Classically adversarial departments work together for both customer satisfaction and reduced cost. Lean, of course, has an important role here since it overlaps with most or all of these functions. S&OP is a company-wide, collaborate process undertaken on a regular basis. Historically, 'regular' would mean a monthly cycle. Although this would still represent good practice at many organisations, sometimes a more frequent process, perhaps triggered by the converging needs of planning and execution and by developing events, is now being seen.

Now there are beginning to be other topics included in the S&OP agenda: Project Sustainability and IT/AI/robotics/ additive manufacturing.

There is the gradual movement away from spreadsheet-based S&OP towards cloud-based applications with integration of ERP and supply-chain systems and that include AI, data analytics and machine learning as well as statistical software such as SPSS. S&OP integrates forecasts, sales, planned and actual production, and planned and actual inventory for (typically) families of products on a rolling horizon of several months. Advanced systems integrate with financial, marketing, and logistics planning. Under S&OP, there are no separate plans for these functions. Instead, good S&OP would include challenging discussion between production, marketing, finance, and HR.

S&OP takes into account and makes decisions on both volume (capacity and quantity) and mix (relative mix and financial contribution). Volume and mix are monitored and adjusted against changing demands, forecasts, and new product introduction. Make to stock, Make to order, Assemble or Build to order, Postponement should all be regularly discussed as customer preferences, technology, capability, supply, and cost structures change. Lean plays an important role here as improvement initiatives impact lead-time, variation, capacity, quality, and rework. In this respect, S&OP should be seen as in a two-way conversation with Lean helping to prioritise Lean

initiatives, and responding to achieved Lean initiatives.

Wallace and Stahl propose a 5-step monthly rolling process for S&OP: Data gathering, Demand planning, Supply planning, Pre-meeting, and Executive meeting. Today, all these steps would involve multi-function inputs, analytics, and discussion – perhaps triggered by external events – resulting in the final top-level decision meeting. The pre-meeting should highlight any areas or developments that require attention. Demand and supply planning should consider all the factors outlined in the earlier relevant sections of this chapter. Decisions are usually made in terms of families of products – getting the right balance of the number of items or family groupings for decisions would be an important judgement call. Too many items reduce effective consideration. As the monthly plan rolls forward, a Planning Time Fence is crossed within which the schedule is firmed. The planning time fence may be as little as one week for a mature Lean organisation.

Appointing the right members of the S&OP team, representing various functions, is critical. Not necessarily full-time. But certainly the days of a single person with S&OP preparation responsibility, or even of a single 'Demand Planner' are over.

Further reading:

Thomas Wallace and Robert Stahl, *Sales and Operations Planning: The How-to Handbook*, 3rd edition, T.F. Wallace and Co., 2008

25.7 Constraints and Theory of Constraints

First, some definitions. According to APICS / Assoc for Supply Chain Management a **constraint** is 'any element or factor that prevents a system from achieving a higher level of performance with respect to its goal. Constraints can be physical, such as a machine centre or lack of material, but they can also be managerial, such as a policy or procedure.' A resource with the highest utilization is a possible candidate. APICS defines a **bottleneck** as 'a facility, function, department or resource whose capacity is less than the demand placed upon it. For example, a bottleneck machine or work centre exists where jobs are processed at a slower rate than they are demanded.' As noted earlier, a bottleneck may move due to breakdowns or a change in product mix. A **constrained critical resource** (CCR) is a resource that has the potential to become a bottleneck – by, for example, periodic overload or sufficient unreliability. A constraint can be called a bottleneck but a bottleneck is not always a constraint.

In plant scheduling it is constraints that determine the throughput of the plant. Note that there is generally only one constraint, like the weakest link in a chain. A 'balanced' plant should not be the concern of management, but rather the continuing identification, exposure, and elimination of a series of constraints.

Throughput, Inventory, Operating Expense

The late Eli Goldratt, the developer of TOC, advocated the use of only three performance measures for operations: Throughput ('the rate at which the system generates money through sales'), Inventory ('the money invested in purchasing things that it intends to sell'), and Operating Expense ('the money that the system spends to turn inventory into throughput') as the most appropriate measures for the flow of material. We should note some important differences with more conventional usage of these words. Throughput is the volume of sales in monetary terms, not units. Products only become 'throughput' when sold. Inventory is the basic cost of materials used and excludes value added for work in progress. Again, building inventory is of no use unless it is sold, so its value should not be recorded until it is sold. And Operating Expense makes no distinction between direct and indirect costs, which is seen as meaningless. The aim, of course, is to move throughput up, and inventory and operating expense down. Any investment should be judged on these criteria alone. This cuts decision making to the bone. All three have an impact on the

essential financials of business (cash flow, profit, and return on investment), but in varying degrees.

Goldratt said that throughput is the first priority, then inventory, then operating expense. Why so? Because throughput has an immediate positive impact on the three financials, whereas one can afford to *increase* inventory and operating expense provided throughput improves. Decreasing inventory has a one-off effect on cash, and can reduce lead-time but unless one is careful, reducing inventory may reduce throughput. Likewise operating expense, but with the possibility of removing the inherent skills of the business. Note that many businesses, when faced with a crisis, adopt just the opposite priorities – first cut people, then inventories, then perhaps try to improve throughput.

Dependent Events and Statistical Fluctuations

Eli Goldratt believed that pure, uninterrupted flow in production is rare if not impossible. This is because of what he termed 'statistical fluctuation' - the minor changes in process speed, operator performance, quality of parts, and so on. Average flow rates are not good enough to calculate throughput. (Note similarities with Kingman.)

Even with very large buffer inventories between operators, part shortages may develop. Lean, according to Goldratt, aims at attacking statistical fluctuation so as to enable flow - so it does. But Goldratt believed that this is both very difficult and a waste of resources - which should be better directed at bottlenecks. Hence the TOC rules in the next section.

TOC thinking is particularly applicable in batch environments that are moving towards flow manufacturing. The more you reduce changeover times, the more you smooth demand, the more you reduce variation, the more you tackle waste, the better.

Constraints, Bottlenecks and Non-Bottleneck Resources: The Synchronous Rules

In this section, the 'Synchronous Rules' or 'laws' of TOC are summarised. Some insights from Factory Physics (Hopp and Spearman) have been added. In the next section Goldratt's Improvement Cycle is given. Both of these are applicable in Line and in Batch operations.

Whilst working on the alleviation of the constraint, the schedule should be organised around this constraint. The principles (often referred to as the TOC or Synchronous principles) follow. (Note that here the word 'bottleneck' is used, but it is often a constraint rather than a bottleneck).

1. Balance flow, not capacity. For too long, according to Goldratt, the emphasis has been on trying to equate the capacity of the work centres through which a product, or service, passes during processing. This is futile, because there will inevitably be faster and slower processes. So, instead, effort should be made to achieve a continuous flow of work. This means protecting bottlenecks, eliminating unnecessary queues of work in front of non-bottleneck work centres, and splitting batches so that work can be moved ahead to the next workstation without waiting for the whole batch to be complete.

2. The utilisation of a non-bottleneck is determined not by its own capacity but by some other constraint in the system. A non-bottleneck should not be used all the time or overproduction will result, and therefore the capacity and utilisation of non-bottleneck resources is mostly irrelevant. (Traditional accountants have choked on this one!) It is the bottlenecks that govern flow. There are implications for OEE measurement.

3. Utilisation and Activation are not synonymous. This emphasises the point that a non-bottleneck resource should not be 'activated' all the time because overproduction will result. Activation is only effective if the resource is actually producing work that can be sold. Notice that this differs from the conventional definition of utilisation.

4. An hour lost at a bottleneck is an hour lost for the whole system. Since a bottleneck governs the amount of throughput in a system, if the bottleneck stops it is equivalent to stopping the entire system. The implications of this for maintenance, scheduling, safety stocks, and selection of equipment are profound!

5. An hour saved at a non-bottleneck is merely a mirage. In effect it is worthless. This has implications for many Lean and Six Sigma improvement activities. It also has deeply significant implications for cost accounting.

6. Bottlenecks govern both throughput and inventory in the system. A system's output is the same as the bottleneck's output, and inventory should only be let into a system at a rate that the bottleneck is capable of handling. (Note with DBR).

7. The transfer batch may not, and many times should not, equal the process batch. A transfer batch is the amount of work in process inventory that is moved along between workstations. Goldratt said that this quantity should not necessarily equal the production batch quantity. Instead batch splitting should be adopted to encourage flow and to minimise inventory cost. (Hence Toyota's use of both production and move kanban.)

8. The process batch should be variable, not fixed. The optimal schedule cannot, or should not, be constrained by the artificial requirement that a product must be made in one large batch. It will often be preferable to split batches into sub-batches. On true bottleneck operations, and on CCR's, batches should be made as large as possible between setup (changeover) operations (thereby minimising setup time) but on non-bottlenecks, batches should be made as small as possible by changing over as often as possible so as to use the time available. So the batch size may change from stage to stage. This statement is also a rejection of formulas such as EOQ (economic order quantity). It also has implications for MRP and Lean systems.

9. Lead times are the result of a schedule, and cannot be predetermined. Here Goldratt disagrees with the use of standard pre-specified lead times such as one usually finds in MRP.

10. Schedules should be assembled by looking at all constraints simultaneously. In scheduling, constraints may be machines, labour, material. Look at all. In a typical operation, some products or services will be constrained by production capacity, others by labour, and yet others perhaps by management inaction.

The Theory of Constraints Improvement Cycle

Theory of Constraints (TOC) and the related Thinking Process (TP) was developed by Eli Goldratt as an extension to his classic work *The Goal*. Goldratt claims wide applicability for TOC, not limited to manufacturing management. At the heart of TOC is the realization that if a company had no constraints it would make an infinite profit. Most companies have a very small number of true constraints. From this follows Goldratt's five step TOC process of ongoing improvement.

The TOC Improvement Cycle has broad similarities to PDSA, but is more focused. It is an exceptionally powerful cycle for Lean, but sometimes ignored by Lean practitioners.

1. **Identify the constraint.**

2. **Decide how to 'exploit' the constraint.** A constraint is precious, so don't waste it. If it is a physical bottleneck, make sure you keep it going, protect it with a time buffer, seek alternative routings, don't process defectives on it, make it quality capable, ensure it has good maintenance attention, ensure that only work for which there is a confirmed market in the near future are processed on it. Here the batch size should be maximised consistent with demand requirements. Use supermarkets that facilitate flow into the constraint.

3. **'Subordinate' all other resources to the constraint.** Encourage flow to the constraint to be as regular and uninterrupted as possible. This will allow buffer protecting the constraint (Drum) to be reduced, thereby reducing lead time. Reduce variation in resources immediately upstream of the constraint. Make everyone aware of the constraint's importance. For instance move inventory as fast as possible after processing on the constraint, reduce changeover time on non-constraints so as to reduce batch size and improve flow to the constraint, make sure that the constraint is not delayed by a non-constraint (a non-constraint can become a constraint if it is mismanaged). The right batch size at a non-constraint is derived from doing the maximum number of changeovers that time will allow – in other words minimize the batch size and maximise flow.

4. **'Elevate' the constraint.** Break it, but only after doing steps 2 and 3. Buy an additional resource or work overtime on the constraint. If it were a true constraint, this would be worthwhile. Beware, however. It is seldom necessary to break a constraint if steps 2 and 3 are taken. Knowing the constraint is often a valuable piece of information around which planning and control can take place. If you break the constraint, it will move – possibly to a hard-to determine location.

5. **Finally, if the constraint has been broken, go to step 1.** Otherwise continue. Be careful that you do not make inertia the new constraint, by doing nothing. Hutchins makes the useful point that there are five stages for each of these five steps. They are (1) gaining consensus on the problem (2) gain consensus on the direction of the solution (3) gain consensus on the benefits of the solution (4) overcome reservations, and (5) make it happen.

Further reading

H. Wiiliam Dettner, *Goldratt's Theory of Constraints: A Systems Approach to Continuous Improvement*, ASQC Quality Press, Milwaukee WI, 1997

Lisa Scheinkopf, *Thinking for a Change: Putting the TOC Thinking Processes to Use*, St. Lucie, APICS, Boca Raton, 1999

Eli Goldratt, *The Theory of Constraints*, North River Press, New York, 1990.

Robert E Stein, *The Theory of Constraints: Applications in Quality and Manufacturing*, (Second edition, Revised and expanded), Marcel Dekker, New York, 1997

Ted Hutchin, *Constraint Management in Manufacturing*, Taylor and Francis, 2002

Bottlenecks: Blocking, Starving and Location

The importance of Blocking and starvation was discussed in Section 25.1. Utilization is often used to identify bottlenecks, but this is not always wise. A bottleneck may move and the true bottleneck may be obscured by being blocked or starved. Blocking refers to an obstruction at a downstream station that prevents production at the earlier station. Starvation refers to an obstruction or waste at a workstation upstream that literally starves a downstream workstation of work.

If there are stoppages at important resources, data on three factors need to be collected – utilization, starvation, and blockages. Monitoring only utilization whilst ignoring starvation and blockages can be misleading.

The table below gives some clues as to possible causes and solutions of bottleneck problems.

Problem	Location/wrt bottleneck	Possible Causes	Solutions?
Blocked	Downstream	Process	Job Methods; standard work
		Schedule	Batch sizing; quality
		People	Job relations; visual management
Starved	Upstream	Process	Job Methods; standard work
		Schedule	Pull; inventory buffer; batch; rework
		People	Job relations
Overload	At bottleneck	Process	Goldratt's 5 steps
		Schedule	Batch sizing; demand management
		People	Job relations; teamwork

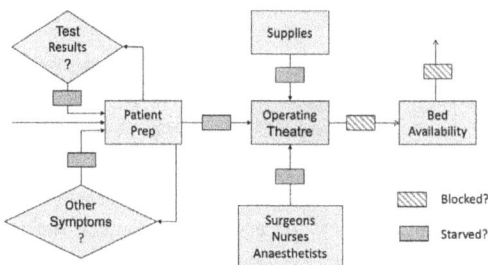

As an example, blocking and starving is a common problem. See the figure above for an example from a hospital, where the operating theatre is subject to both blocking and starving.

Identifying Shifting Bottlenecks

What are some clues for the identification of shifting bottlenecks? Keep a look out for changes in inventory levels, as shown in the figure. This figure is adapted from Christoph Roser who has several guides for identifying shifting bottlenecks.

Today, some organisations are adopting a 'digital twin' that, through using IoT, enables shifting bottlenecks to be tracked electronically. Others may use sensors and light signals. As ever, humans should retain an important role for appropriate response.

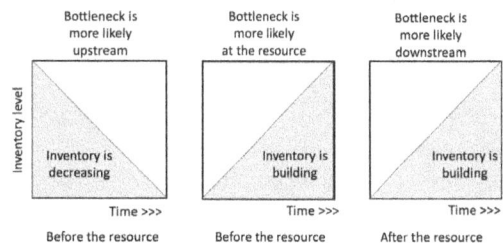

Conflicts between Lean Thinking, TOC and Factory Physics

For the most part, in our opinion, there is little conflict and much to be gained, by treating TOC, Factory Physics and Lean as fully compatible, particularly where there are shared resources between value streams. This is particularly the case regarding the Product Process Matrix presented earlier.

Synergy and similarities: In an excellent paper, Moore and Schienkopf contrast Lean with TOC. But their comments apply equally, perhaps more so, to Factory Physics. So we will use TOC/FP below. TOC/FP are logical and pragmatic. Both share the goal of flow and throughput. Both, but particularly FP are good at identifying that handful of potential improvements that will make a real difference. In fact, the main criticism of Lean that Moore and Schienkopf identify is that Lean is less able to prioritise where to start with improvements, although value stream mapping prioritization into zones enables one to understand the system and its dependencies more clearly. TOC/FP helps to identify and quantify the opportunities without taking the 'leap of faith' sometimes associated with some Lean implementations. TOC and FP encourage pull rather than push. However there are some philosophical differences:

Each of the concepts below have been discussed in earlier sections. These concepts are here presented for consolidation purposes and as a reminder.

First, **shared resources:** Lean, in general, tries to set up clear value streams with no shared resources and adequate capacity. Bottlenecks should be avoided. Spear and Bowen's third rule, ('The pathway for every product and service must be simple and direct.'), discussed in the Value and Waste section, make this clear. TOC/FP accepts bottlenecks and shared resources, and schedules around them.

In real systems, even highly repetitive, there are often shared resources such as paint lines and press shops. So the reality is that, often, TOC/FP concepts will be very useful in many Lean environments, but the goal of clear, simple, unshared value streams should be the ideal, desirable state. To help with this, the small machine principle (use the smallest possible capable machine) should always be used.

Second, is **utilization**. There are still those that think that maximum utilization at every resource is not only a good thing, but leads to a global optimum. TOC/FP teaches the opposite. Maximising utilization at all resources will lead to excessive inventory, and waste. Traditional accountants, beware! See Kingman equation.

Third, is **Inventory between processes**. The classic Lean way is to have inventory between stages and to pull, stage-by-stage, with Kanban. TOC/FP rejects this, in favour of Drum Buffer Rope (DBR). The Factory Physics version is CONWIP (or Constant Work in Progress). With DBR and CONWIP inventory is allowed to fluctuate between workstations. This is more robust to variation. Classic in-process kanban, however, can highlight problems at intermediate stages faster than DBR or CONWIP. We favour splitting value streams into stable and unstable zones.

Fourth, is **Line balancing**. You don't balance a line in TOC/FP. You control through the bottleneck or CONWIP. In fact, balancing to equalise work is considered positively harmful because 'statistical fluctuations and dependent events' together lead to a fall in output well below the balance rate. This does not happen with DBR or CONWIP.

Fifth is the **question of waste**. It is important to know which constraints are affecting performance in any part of an enterprise. If, for example, you have a marketing constraint, it would be foolish to expend more effort on production. The thought that a constraint governs throughput of a plant has massive implications for investment, costing, and continuous improvement. Essentially, an investment that only targets a non-constraint is waste. Likewise, many continuous improvement efforts are waste. Waste walks may themselves be waste. This could be in conflict with standard Lean Thinking, and Six Sigma, but in fact exposes a weakness in both. Hopp and Spearman talk about 'free waste' or bad waste and 'trade-off waste' or potentially good waste. Removal of good waste involves no penalty. Space and most transport savings are examples. Removal of trade-off waste may have consequences for money Lead-time or customer service. Examples are some safety inventories, some over-processing, some 'inefficient' transport.

Sixth, **Costing** has also had a shake-up. 'Throughput accounting' uses the equation Revenue – direct materials - operating expenses = Profit. Here, there is no 'variable overhead'. Direct labour is treated as a fixed (or temporarily fixed) cost, and inventories and products are not revalued (that is, they do not accumulate cost) on their path through the plant. More is said on this topic in the Measures and Accounting section.

Further reading

Richard Moore and Lisa Schienkopf, *Theory of Constraints and Lean Manufacturing Friends or Foes?* Chesapeake Consulting Inc., 1998 (Supplied by Goldratt Institute).

Wallace Hopp and Mark Spearman, *Factory Physics*, (Third edition), McGrawHill, 2008

Wallace Hopp, *Supply Chain Science*, 2008

Ed Pound, Jeffrey Bell, Mark Spearman, *Factory Physics for Managers*, McGraw Hill, 2014

Kevin Duggan, *Creating Mixed Model Value Streams*, Second edition, CRC Press, 2013

Art Smalley, *Creating Level Pull*, LEI, 2004

Christoph Roser, *All About Pull* Production, All About Lean, 2021

25.8   The Building Blocks

In this section the intention is to provide a set of building blocks that can be slotted together 'Lego' style to construct the framework for almost any Lean scheduling system. The building blocks provide the skeleton of supermarkets and stores around which the scheduling system is built.

The idea is that the blocks can be combined to make up any system. Note that the blocks identify the *stages* at which inventory buffers should be located, but the actual *locations* may differ. For instance, where a building block identifies that a buffer is required between stages A and B, the location may be immediately after A, mid-way between A and B, or next to B.

Block 1: A is a constraint or bottleneck feeding **B** a non-constraint.

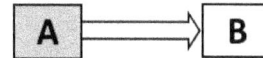

Q: Where should buffer be placed?

A: In front of A, (to ensure that it is able to keep working) but not in front of B (that can easily catch up lost time). Beware, however, if B is sufficiently starved it may become the constraint.

Q: How much buffer in front of A?

A: A little, but sufficient to ensure time coverage for frequent upstream disruption, but not for unusual events. May also include replenishment time for parts on a pull system, plus safety stock.

Block 2: B is a non-constraint feeding **A** that is a constraint or bottleneck.

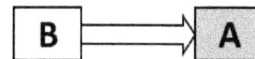

Q: Where should buffer be placed?

A: Not in front of B, except if B has high variation. Also, where B is at the beginning of a line, buffer before B is required to protect against delivery fluctuations.

Block 3: A is a constraint; **B** and **C** are non-constraints. To make a part at B requires a part from A and a part from B.

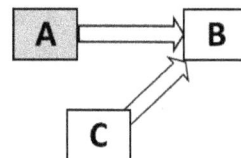

Q: Where to place buffer inventory?

A: In front of A and not in front of B on line A to B, (as before). But also in front of B on line C to B. Why? Because after the product has passed the valuable constraint, it should be delayed as little as possible, for instance waiting for a part from non-constraint C. If C goes down this will unnecessarily hold up the completion of B. permanent inventory held between A and B would simply increase the lead time.

Think of an assembly line making cars – you would not want to delay the main line whilst waiting for a minor part. So definitely in front of B on line C to B if it is a 'C' part. However, if from C is an 'A' category part it may be too expensive to hold a buffer in front of B, so synchronisation must be arranged.

Block 4: A, B, C, D are sequential operations.

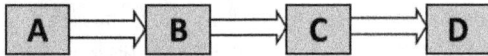

Q: What are relevant questions here?

A: First, is there a constraint or near constraint in relation to overall takt time? If yes, split into pull loops, separated by supermarkets. Second, can the process be flowed, especially one-piece flow or pitch-time flowed. (Pitch flow means moving products every pitch increment.) If it can be flowed, then the processes can be treated as a cell and controlled by one pull signal, possibly with a supermarket or buffer in front of A.

Block 5 has three processes each having changeover time. Arm A is a bottleneck. This occurs in 'V' type plants, for example process plants such as steel. Resource A, of course, needs to be protected by inventory. But, because changeovers occur, resource C needs to make batches for A that will be sufficient to keep A running whilst C changes over and makes a batch for resource B, and then changes over again to make a new batch for resource A. Also, inventory must be kept in front of A to protect against downtime failures by C. Changeover times and reliability for the non-bottleneck resource C are very important so as to

limit the otherwise large inventories that need to be kept.

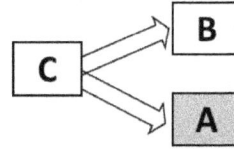

So, in this case, a long changeover at a non-bottleneck is as important as at a bottleneck.

Block 6 occurs in situations where there are powered conveyors, such as bottling plants. Here, not only is sufficient inventory needed in front of bottleneck A (so as to protect against starvation by B), but also sufficient space to prevent A becoming clogged or blocked.

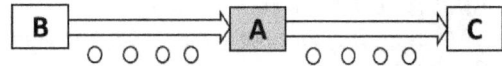

Block 7: A Fishbone Layout is shown in the Figure below. Many assembly lines have this configuration. Here, buffers must be located at points at which the supporting (or subassembly) lines meet the main line. This is to prevent the main line from being stopped due to a shortage of (typically) much lower cost parts. Shortage of parts is a significant problem in convergent plants. (They are known as 'A' plants in TOC).

The supporting or subassembly lines should be CONWIP lines. A 'piggyback' card or 'broadcast' sheet should be set up so that parts or subassemblies reach the pre-assembly line in good time. The actual time that a new part or subassembly is started is determined by the subassembly lead time. Authorisation to begin the next part is by CONWIP pull signal. The sequence or type of part comes from a piggyback card (released from the main product) or from a 'broadcast sheet'. The way it works is: when a product (car?) going down the main line reaches a particular point, a broadcast signal is sent ahead to the appropriate line to begin the sequence. When the CONWIP signal is received, the next subassembly in the sequence is started. The buffer is a time buffer or an inventory buffer if parts are similar.

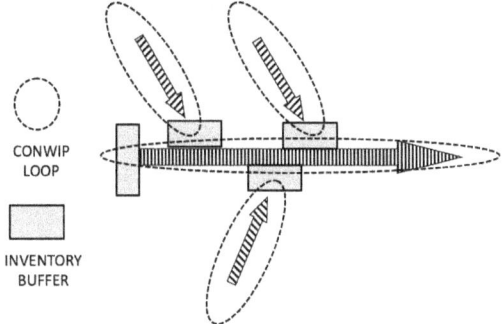

CONWIP
LOOP

INVENTORY
BUFFER

Block 8: The figure below shows **a Window Layout.** This is a common configuration, with shared resources (such as casting) early on, followed by several parallel lines or streams that eventually share a common packing area. The shared resources feeding multiple lines are scheduled by pull. The parallel lines are each CONWIP loops. The shared resources fed by multiple lines are scheduled by another method as discussed below.

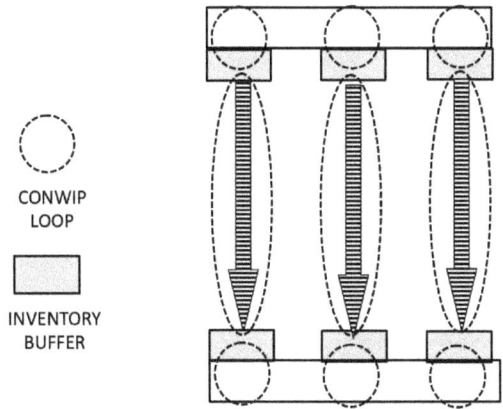

CONWIP
LOOP

INVENTORY
BUFFER

Buffers (Supermarkets or FIFO lanes, as appropriate) are located at the beginning and end of each parallel line.

The configuration is known as Window layout. Actual cases may be full Window, or T type (as described in TOC).

In the section below two further Blocks are considered. These involve a shared resource – that is a machine or process that is shared between more than one value stream.

Block 9: Where subsequent multiple lines are fed from a supermarket between the shared resource and the lines. A supermarket would be used for repetitive, higher volume parts. A figure is shown below. Here...

- Parts are pulled by subsequent cells or lines from the supermarket located after the shared resource.

- As parts are pulled, production kanban cards are released so that the part can be replaced.

- The kanban cards accumulate in columns in a vertical batch box. A virtual queue.

- There is a pre-determined batch quantity for each part. The batch quantity would be split into a number of kanban cards.

- When sufficient production kanban cards have accumulated to reach the pre-determined batch processing quantity, the batch can be made.

- The kanban cards making up the batch will usually have to go into a queue whilst other parts are made on the shared resource.

- When a batch is completed by the shared resource the next batch is selected from the queue. (In other words there is a CONWIP loop around the shared resource.)

- Selection from the queue of the next part to be made on the shared resource is determined by sequence and priority.

- The batch is started on the shared resource. When completed the batch goes into the supermarket with a kanban card attached to each container making up the batch.

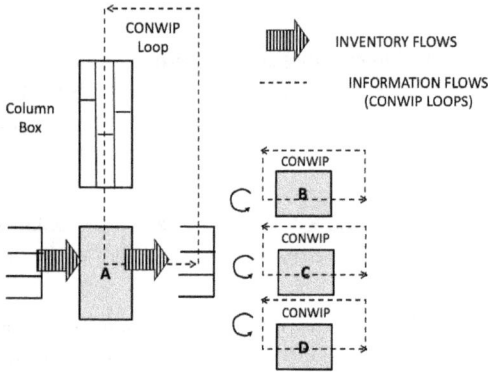

- When a batch is started at the shared resource, parts or materials are pulled from the supermarket immediately upstream of the shared resource.
- There is one CONWIP loop around the shared resource, and a CONWIP loop for each supplier and upstream resource

Block 10: Shared resource fed by a supermarket, perhaps from multiple lines or suppliers.

Here several types of jobs from various lines (B, C, D) are processed by a single shared resource. For example, an autoclave or paint line. There is uncertainty of subsequent use after resource A, so a supermarket is used. See the Figure below.

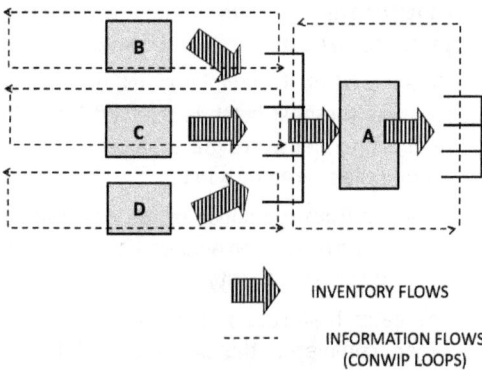

- The shared resource A may require parts from B, C and D to complete the process
- As parts are pulled from the downstream supermarket, kanban cards are released.
- The released cards authorise the next batch to be pulled (started) on shared resource A.
- Kanban cards are then released to the upstream lines (B, C, D) authorising them to replace the pulled parts.

26 Pull Systems

Good pull scheduling systems are built on the trilogy of Demand Analysis, Queueing Dynamics, and the concept of Zones of stability and instability.

A quote to begin: *'Flow if you can; pull if you must'*.

Here, 'flow' means a balanced line or cell, or a moving conveyor.

APICS (Assoc for Supply Chain Mgmt) says that a pull system is, 'In production, the production of items only as demanded for use, *or to replace those taken for use* (our italics). In material control, the withdrawal of inventory as demanded by the using operations. Material is not issued until a signal comes from the user.'

We prefer the concise and accurate definition of a pull system from Hopp and Spearman in *Factory Physics*:

'A pull system is one in which work is released based on the status of the system and thereby places an inherent limit on WIP.' This is an excellent definition, but we go further: a pull system is also a signalling system that notifies when replenishment should begin and also quickly identifies areas where urgent attention is needed.

By contrast, 'A push system is one in which work is released without consideration of system status and hence does not inherently limit WIP.'

Therefore, immediately, we see that an MRP system is a push system. Nor is pull a make to order system. Kanban is one method of pull.

According to Hopp and Spearman, the main advantages of pull are reduced WIP and cycle time (as pull systems limit the amount of WIP), smoother production flow, improved quality (as systems with short queues quickly reveal high levels of yield loss), and ultimately, reduced cost due to all of the above.

Pull is the scheduling *principle*, kanban is one form of pull *mechanism* albeit a prominent one. (Some others are CONWIP, Drum Buffer Rope, 2-bin, eban, faxban, and audio-based call),

To expand on the foundation trilogy mentioned above, pull systems are not a universal panacea. There are cautions and pre-requisites:

- Demand Analysis: A levelled schedule is, in most cases, a powerful facilitator for pull. A stop-start process is not suitable. Referring to demand types, erratic and lumpy demand patterns may be more suitable to a Master schedule-driven system. Very low demand items may spend excessive time as WIP with a pull system. Short shelf life – where the replenishment interval is longer than the remaining shelf life – is not suitable.

- Queueing Dynamics: Kingman's equation (once again!). Beware of the three variables, and their interaction: very high utilization, high arrival or demand variation, and high process variation. Pull is an effective way to reduce Muda (waste), Mura (unevenness) and to achieve Muri (unreasonableness).

- Zones of Stability and Instability: High levels of rejects, rework or breakdown stoppages will play havoc with a pull system. Stability is a pre-requisite. Remember that pull is the fourth of Womack and Jones' Lean principles. That is deliberate – there is a lot to do before introducing kanban – reducing demand amplification, reducing changeover, creating more stable work through standard work, reducing the defect rate, and reducing disruptions through breakdowns.

Pull System Types
- Kanban types
- Re-order point
- CONWIP
- Drum Buffer Rope (DBR)
- Hybrid (using a combination of kanban, CONWIP and perhaps DBR)
- POLCA
- Demand Driven MRP (DDMRP)

- Re-order point (ROP)

26.1   Kanban

The Rules of Kanban

These are the fundamental rules of a Kanban system, irrespective of its type and application:

- Downstream operations come to withdraw parts from upstream operations.
- Make only the exact quantity indicated on the kanban
- Demands are placed on upstream operations by means of cards or other signals
- Only active parts are allowed at the workplace. Active parts should have specific locations.
- Authorisation to produce is by card (or signal) only.
- Each kanban card circulates between a particular pair of workstations, or a workstation and a supermarket, only.
- Quality at source is a requirement. Only good items are sent downstream.
- The number of kanbans should be reduced as problems decrease.

Types of Kanban

A basic classification is:

- Production kanbans
  - Product (single or dual)
  - Signal or triangle
  - Generic (capacity)
- Move or withdrawal kanbans
  - In-plant
  - Supplier
- Other Forms of Kanban

Simply put, a production kanban authorises production. A move kanban authorises movement from a store or between workstations. The distinction however is not important except in the case of dual card systems.

Production Kanbans

Product Kanban

A product kanban is the simplest form of pull system. With this type, whenever a product is called for it is simply replaced. If there is no call, there is no authorisation so there is no production. In practice, the variations of this type include kanban squares (a vacant square is the authorisation to fill the square with another similar part), cards (which are returned to the feeding workstation to authorise making a replacement quantity as specified on the card), and other variations such as 'faxban' or 'e-ban' (which operate in exactly the same way as cards, except that the pull signals are electronic not physical).

Single-Card Kanban

Traditional kanban is suitable in all stable manufacturing environments where there is repetitive production. In practice, the single card kanban category is by far the most popular type. It is easy to understand, easy to see, and reasonably easy to install. Single card kanban means that a single card (or pull signal) operates between each pair of workstations, or between a store and a workstation. Although there are usually several single-card kanbans in a loop between a pair of workstations, each kanban is the authorisation to both make a part or container of parts and to move it to a specified location.

Product Kanban with Multiple Products

(a) Sequential Operations

In sequential operations having several different products, product kanban can be used between stations provided there are not too many products. Here, usually, one partly completed product of each type is placed as buffer between each workstation. If product A is called for at the end of a line, triggers are activated sequentially along the line to make a replacement A. Similarly for B, and so on. Other products do not move until they are called for. This system allows a quick response build from a limited selection of products, but has the penalty of holding intermediate buffers of part completed products of each type. Hence this system becomes impractical for more than a handful of products. The generic kanban type should then be used, as explained below.

(b) Assemble to Order Operations

A variation that is employed in several assemble-to-order operations (for instance, personal computer 'make to order') involves simply having shelves with at least one or two of all parts and subassemblies surrounding the final assembly area. When an order comes in, it is simply configured from the appropriate shelves. This then creates a blank space on the shelf that is the signal for subassembly areas to replace that subassembly. Subassembly areas are themselves arranged into cells that pull parts from the store. In this way, literally millions of different configurations can be made under a pull system.

(c) Product Kanban with Synchronised Operations

Where there are several legs in a bill of material or assembly structure, synchronisation can be achieved by variations of so-called 'golf ball' kanban. Here, as the main build progresses, signals are sent to areas producing supporting assemblies to warn them to prepare the appropriate assemblies 'just in time' to meet up with the main build as it progresses along the line. Different colour 'golf balls' are moved (often blown by air or sent electronically) to the subassembly stations to signal them to prepare the exact required subassembly. This form of kanban can be used internally (say to prepare different windscreens or coloured bumpers) to go onto particular cars, or externally (for instance when sent to external seat suppliers to prepare the exact sequence of seats to meet up with a particular sequence of cars).

(d) Emergency Kanban or 'Red Box'.

Emergency kanban is a 'special event' kanban that is inserted in kanban loops to compensate for unusual circumstances. Such kanban cards are usually of a different colour so that they may be distinguished easily. Such kanbans automatically go to the head of the queue so their requirements are dealt with as soon as possible. Having produced the additional quantity, emergency kanbans are then withdrawn.

Instead of different coloured kanban cards, a Red Box is placed lineside. Here, if there is any problem with a kanban batch (defects? shortages, wrong timing, etc.) the kanban card is inserted in the red box instead of the usual out box. Any such cards require priority attention usually by upstream processes. Without a red box kanban risks failure!

The procedures for kanban cards placed in a red box need to be carefully worked out in advance. For instance:

- Make up shortfalls at end of shift.
- Draw on safety stock.
- Team leader to go to problem source and rectify immediately, etc.

To cope with special circumstances such as seasonal demand, compensation for transport disruption or poor weather, additional kanbans are inserted in the kanban loop sequence by team leader working with production control These cards are then withdrawn when the normal situation is restored.

Dual-Card Kanban

Dual card kanban, long established at Toyota, and increasingly elsewhere, uses both production and move (or conveyance) kanban cards. Production (or signal) kanbans stay at a particular workcentre and circulate from input board through the workstation to finished goods and back to input with production kanban attached. Production kanbans authorise the workstation operator to make parts. When parts are withdrawn from finished goods, the kanban is detached and moved back to the input board where it waits in the queue.

Move kanbans circulate between a particular pair of workstations. Move kanbans authorise the material handler to move parts (with attached move kanban) from the finished goods area of a workstation to the input area of a second workstation. When the workstation operator at the second workstation removes parts from the input area, the move kanban is detached and authorises the material handler to fetch the next quantity. Note that the move distance and time may be very long.

The dual cards, working together, mean that the move quantity does not have to equal the make quantity. This is good for linking several operations using a pacemaker or Heijunka system. Also, production kanbans generally have short lead times because they stay at the workcentre. This means quick response and lower inventory.

The figure below illustrates a simple dual-card Kanban system:

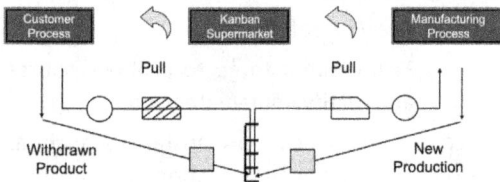

Signal (or Triangle) Kanban

Where there is changeover, a signal (or triangle or priority) kanban is used. As parts are withdrawn, at a second (downstream) workstation, so kanbans are hung on the board at a first (upstream) workstation under the appropriate product column. (See figure)

A batch box or board is used where there are long changeover operations and several products requiring a priority to be determined. By 'long changeover' is meant a changeover taking longer than a pitch increment. Where a changeover is shorter than a pitch increment, a FIFO lane is preferable.

A target batch size is calculated for each product (see Batch Process Chapter 28), and the target is marked on the board. Triangle (signal) kanbans accumulate on the board from the base card upwards until the target batch size line is reached. The accumulated set of triangle kanbans for a particular product would be the batch size of that product to be produced, and are placed in a box. The box joins the FIFO lane of other product boxes. The FIFO lane (queue of boxes) is located just in front of the changeover operation. The FIFO lane could indicate the wait delay before processing. In other words the boxes accumulate in the FIFO lane that is painted by coloured zones – first green (soon to be produced), then yellow and then red. If the accumulation is in the red zone, special action or overtime is required.

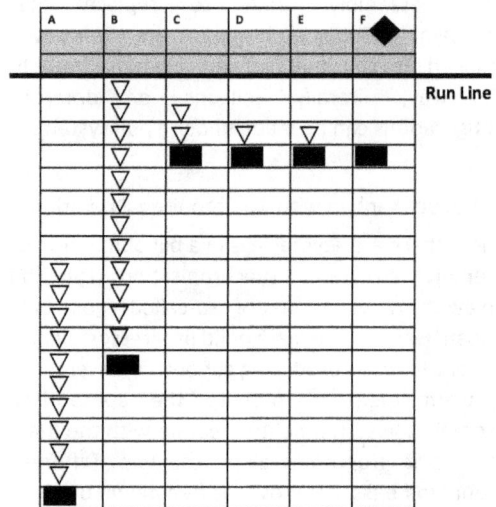

The batch box is a visible, up-to-date warning of an impending changeover. In normal circumstances the batch is made when the target level is reached. If there are problems kanbans may accumulate beyond the target level. This would indicate higher priority. Normally, a batch is made to cover all the kanbans in the product column. In very slack periods, a smaller batch may be made to cover only the cards on the board.

In the figure, part B is authorized to be run, having reached the target batch size. Part F is currently being run. Other parts are accumulating but with different batch sizes.

Capacity or Generic Kanban

Generic (or 'capacity') Kanban authorise feeding work centres to make a part, but do not specify what part is to be made. The part to be made is specified via a manifest or a 'broadcast' system. It is therefore the preferable pull system where there are a large number of products, all of which have similar routings and fairly similar time requirements at each workstation. Generic kanban has less WIP than product kanban, but the response time is slower. Note: This is similar to the CONWIP system – see below.

The SMART Kanban System

SMART (for Synchronous Material Availability Request Ticket), is used by Ford and others.

One version of SMART cards is for repetitive, small or inexpensive parts, particularly where a part is used in several workstations or processes. These are collected by the material handler on the regular route and returned to the SMART office where they are scanned by bar-code reader. Flashing lights indicate to the material handler the priority for replenishment. This is a 'loose kanban' or slow response system.

SMART call is for fast moving or heavy or expensive parts or where space is limited on the line. The operator presses a button lineside when a re-order point is reached. This is a 'tight kanban' or fast response system.

E SMART gives pull signals directly from the line to external suppliers. Such parts bypass the warehouse / supermarket.

SMART squares painted on the floor indicate the exact stopping point for the front wheel of a forklift or tugger vehicle, to optimise unloading.

There are other forms of kanban, for example:

- A kanban carousel is a storage rack on wheels that is rotated. The back is filled while the front is being used. This is good for kit parts.
- A sequenced in line storage (SILS) is a sloping gravity feed rack for mixed model heavy parts moved between next-door supplier and consumer.
- A slowly rotating table moves between a group of assembly operators. On one vertical level are components and on another level are part-completed products. One station is the load and unload point for parts, another is the point of use.
- Some automotive plants use a shuttle with a kit of parts that travel along with a car over a set of workstations. Used for custom options.
- A gravity container system. This is a container that slides along a slope attached to a weight and pulley. When the container is empty the weight and pulley pulls the container up the slope to the upstream station. When the container is full, gravity moves the container down the slope to the downstream station, and the weight up. (Nifty, eh!)

An example using Kanban and Mapping:

Here a press operation replenishes the material for an assembly cell. The steps below relate to the Figure below.

- 1. The customer or cell draws from a supermarket. When a container becomes empty (or sometimes when the first part is withdrawn)....
- 2. A Move card is sent to the post press supermarket
- 3. The Production card (triangle) is detached, and the Move card is attached to the container
- 4. The container with the Move card is returned to the cell.

- 5. The Production card (triangle kanban) is sent to the Batch Board

- 6. The number of Production (triangle) kanbans accumulates and eventually reaches the target batch size target line.

- 7. When the target line is reached, the set of kanbans for the product are placed in the press queue.

- 8. When the set reaches the beginning of the queue, the product is made.

- 9. The raw material kanban is detached and moved to the kanban post

- 10. The Production (triangle) kanban is placed in the finished goods container, which is moved to the supermarket. The cycle is complete.

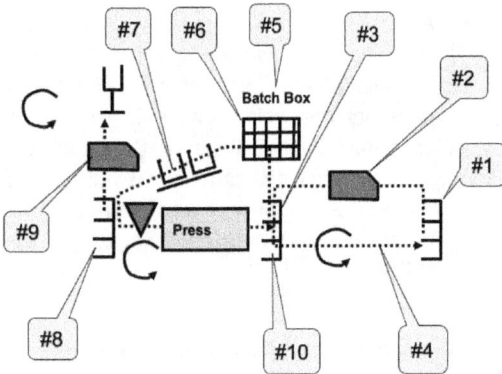

Setting the Number of Kanban Cards

In line with Lean Manufacturing, the correct answer to the question of the number of kanban cards should generally be 'less than last time!' The well-known water and rocks analogy applies. That is, reduce the inventory levels by removing a kanban (or by reducing the kanban quantity) and 'expose the rocks'. Note that the philosophy of gradually reducing inventory by removing kanbans is 'win-win' approach: either nothing will happen in which case you have 'won' because you have found that you can run a little tighter or you 'hit a rock' in which case you have also 'won' because you have hit not just any old rock, but the most pressing rock

or constraint. This is what Toyota has done for decades.

The general rule on kanbans is therefore to start 'loose', with a generous amount of safety stock, and to move towards 'tight kanban' gradually, but steadily. However, Ohno warned about an excessive number kanbans – thereby losing the responsive 'feel' of a pull system. If you really want to use a formula, try what follows.

Kanban formulas (and there are many variations) are all imprecise estimators. The variables are quite difficult accurately to determine (and their times vary!), so that is why 'Estimating' is used rather than 'Calculating'.

In general, kanban works like the traditional two-bin system. In the two-bin system when the reorder point ROP is reached another batch is ordered. The ROP has sufficient inventory remaining to cover usage during the replenishment period. ROP is calculated thus:

$$ROP = D \times LT + SS$$

where D = demand during the lead-time LT between placing and order and receiving delivery, and SS is the safety stock expressed as a number of kanbans. This familiar formula is the basis for all kanban calculations. If the container or stillage quantity is Q, then the number of kanbans is simply

$$N = (D \times LT) / Q + SS$$

where N should be rounded up.

A better formula, more akin to Lean, adapted from Roser, follows. This is for a particular part, whether internal or external from a supplier.

N = ((Replenishment time X Demand frequency) / No of parts per container)) + Safety number + Buffer number

Where:

- Demand frequency is parts used per time. This could be directly related to takt time. For instance, 2 parts used every takt time.

Or, a part may be used only in custom products on average (say) 3 per shift. Where batches are moved, the demand frequency should be the number of batches consumed during a replenishment time x the batch size.

- Replenishment time applies for each particular part under consideration and is the time from when a replenishment order is first signalled from an operation to the time that the replenishment part arrives in the buffer at the operation. This time would include:

- Kanban collection time (Time between initiation and collection. i.e. placing a kanban in the slot or box and it being collected by the material handler.). Could be zero if electronic, or related to the runner cycle, or collected by the upstream workstation.

- Card move time. (Time from collection to arrival at the upstream make point.)

- Batch size accumulation time. (The time for the accumulation of cards to reach the batch signal quantity. See the earlier Signal kanban section.) If no batch, this time is zero.

- Queue time for production. (Waiting for production to start.) If there are several products in the queue, it is the usual time to complete all products ahead in the queue. This can be substantial.

- Process time. (Time to setup and make the batch.) For assembly with no setup this could be the time to make one unit, or to fill the container. If a batch has to be made, the batch process time must be included. However, sometimes a batch is placed in several consecutive containers in which case the time to fill the first container MAY be used.

- It might also be the case that the pull signal is sent to the beginning of a sequence of processes all of which need to be completed before arriving at the move

point. If so, all of these times need to be accumulated. (Better in this case to call it process lead time.)

- Product move time. Time from completion at the immediate upstream process and the arrival at the initiating work centre. The delivery time and collection time would be linked with the material handling (or runner cycle)

- Safety Quantity is a judgement call, dependent on supplier reliability, breakdowns, and quality issues.

Buffer and Safety Inventory and Numbers

Ignoring these two factors in the kanban estimation would be fatal unless demand was absolutely stable and uniform and everything worked perfectly!

The numbers of cards to cover these likelihoods are estimated based on the risk of occurrence for every part. Do you want to cover worst case or average case? It is a management decision. The cost of the part would also be a factor. Play it very safe with low cost parts.

It is often good to distinguish between buffer and safety inventories. Buffer inventory protects against internal variation caused by process variation, breakdowns or quality issues. Safety inventory protects against customer demand variation and uncertainty. Safety inventory is usually held only in customer-facing situations such finished goods or at postponement points. The appropriate type of inventory is drawn on depending on the issue. Of course, the two types can be lumped together but the reason for distinguishing between the two is to help surface problems. Where they are combined visibility is more difficult even though some saving in inventory is possible.

It will be appreciated that determining or estimating all these times and quantities is an estimating art, not a science. Therefore, be generous with the estimates and then observe if too much inventory is held in front of the initiating work centre. Also, the number of cards should be reviewed regularly – certainly when any major change affecting the above times is implemented, and particularly for A (more expensive) parts. Some organisations track the times for important parts. For B and C items, be generous. See the section on Inventory Control of Parts ABC and RRS in Section 24.6.

Estimating the number of kanbans is usually not an independent calculation but is tied in with batch sizing and with the design of the runner (or 'tugger') routes. The design of runner routes is discussed in the next Chapter on Scheduling Line Processes.

Notice that the number of kanbans depends on demand, or demand frequency, or takt time. This means that when demand changes, the number of kanbans should change. In an unstable environment there could be quite a bit of adding and subtracting kanbans.

Example: Demand for X is 32 parts per day, fairly level. The operation works 8 hours net per day. This means 32/8=4 parts per hour on average are pulled. 2 parts is also the container (move) quantity. The runner (material handler) has a cycle every hour. (This means kanban move time to the feeder station and move time of parts from the feeder is a total of 1 hour, and there is a maximum wait of 1 hour before card collection and 1 hour after production at the feeder). The feeder usually has a queue of 2 hours for other parts. The batch quantity at the feeder is 16 parts, or 4 hours of usage. (This means that 8 cards must accumulate before the batch can be made.). At the feeder there is a half-hour setup and a half-hour run time for the 16 parts. 6 parts (three containers) is the allocated buffer quantity. Zero safety quantity.

Demand frequency = 4 parts per hour.

Replenishment time:

> 1 hour max wait for card collection
>
> 0.5 move card to feeder
>
> 4 hours for batch accumulation at feeder

2 hour wait in feeder queue

1 hour setup and run at feeder

1 hour max wait to move

0.5 hour move batch to workstation

= total 10 hours

Then N = (10x4)/2 + 3 = 20+3 = 23 kanbans in the loop. Often these would be 'Triangle' kanbans to indicate that a changeover operation is part of the loop.

Of course if parts are supplied 'instantly' from the feeder (no setup + run, and accumulation time and no queue) all these could be zero: a reduction of 7 hours, then N would be (3 x 4)/2 + 3 = 9 kanbans.

It may be helpful to draw out a diagram such as shown to estimate the number of kanbans for particular cases. This may aid discussion since the estimation should best be done by a group.

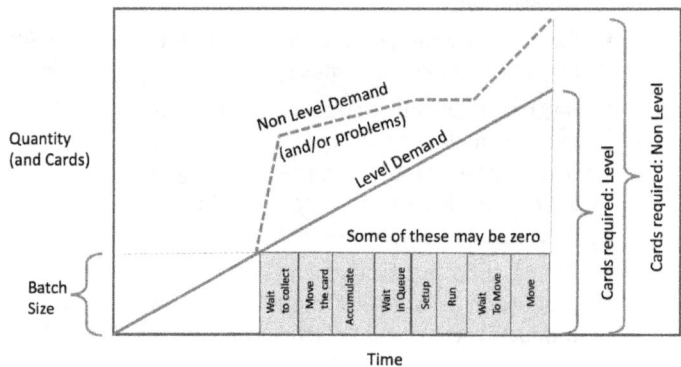

Kanban limitations

A weakness of kanban is that it assumes repetitive production (even where generic kanban is used) and a fairly level schedule. So there are problems with erratic and lumpy demand. If so, buffer inventories between the various stages may be idle for lengthy periods, waiting to be pulled. This is of course 'muda'. Further complications are routings (and LT) that may vary significantly between products, and variation in processing times resulting in imbalanced lines and temporary bottlenecks. In such circumstances traditional kanban systems may have more inventory than MRP push systems.

Kanban cards (physical or electronic) require strict discipline. Cards need to be numbered and the sequence maintained. If lost – problems!

Kanban in the Office

In project management, agile software, and design situations kanban has become widespread. This type is not the same as the pull type as found in manufacturing, but rather reverts to the translation of the word kanban being a sign or a signal.

Kanban in the office is a non-threatening, visual aid, best introduced by the team themselves allowing for their own modifications. Although there are software versions, probably the best type uses a simple board.

Post-it notes are used to show work elements. They are moved across the board following the stages. Each stage has a column. The stages might include New Tasks, Tasks Ready to Go, Tasks in Process, Tasks Delayed, Tasks Complete. Each post-it note names the task, and perhaps has a start date and a process owner. Some choose to have different coloured notes perhaps for different projects that the team is concerned with.

The board is a visual display of progress, including capacity issues and problems. A weekly or daily team meeting is held at the board.

Various rules have to be established. For instance, no movement ahead before completion and maximum number of tasks in a column. Resource availability by stage may also be shown.

26.2   CONWIP

A CONWIP loop is a multi-stage pull system. When a time quantity of work (say an hour's worth of demand) is completed at the last stage, an hour's quantity of work is begun at the first stage. Hence a CONstant Work in Process system).

So the pull signal comes from the end of the line, but the sequence is given at the beginning of the line. Work is released from a virtual queue. The pull signal may be a card, but the card would not be specific to a particular part but rather to release capacity to begin work. In a cell, a blank space at the start of the cell could be the CONWIP signal to start another job. Therefore, kanban is an inventory system but CONWIP (and POLCA and DBR) are capacity systems.

A CONWIP system has the great advantage of stabilizing lead time. This is because the inventory in the loop, (or strictly the total inventory processing time) from beginning to end of the loop, remains constant. What is let in is what is let out.

With CONWIP, inventory accumulates automatically at the most heavily utilized workstation – or constraint. Of course, this is just where you would like it to accumulate. And, if the constraint shifts (as a result of a change in product mix or breakdowns) the inventory accumulation point (or buffer) will shift.

So there are two advantages of CONWIP: stable lead time and automatic relocation of buffer.

However, orders usually accumulate in a random fashion. So whilst production time is a constant, the overall lead time, including queue time before entering the CONWIP loop, may not be. To respond to this, Hopp and Spearman recommend a 'virtual queue' in front of the release point. The virtual queue is the sequence of orders waiting to be released. The virtual queue has the advantage that queue jumping has little consequence whilst in the virtual queue. Once released, however, the sequence of jobs should not change. This facilitates low inventory and predictable lead times.

In planning the schedule a variation allowance (say 85%) should be applied to avoid capacity overload. The 85% figure makes allowance for variation, in line with Kingman's equation, but execution would use all available capacity up to 100%. So, promise orders to 85%, but work to full capacity. If things go well orders will arrive early. If things don't go so well, most will arrive on time. Quoted lead time can be given using Little's Law, slightly modified, as:

$$QLT = (WIP\ /\ (throughput\ rate)\ *\ 1/0.85$$

The virtual queue should be monitored against control limits. Where the virtual queue builds up beyond a certain level, capacity must be increased by, for example, working overtime.

The figure shows a CONWIP examples in a hospital setting:

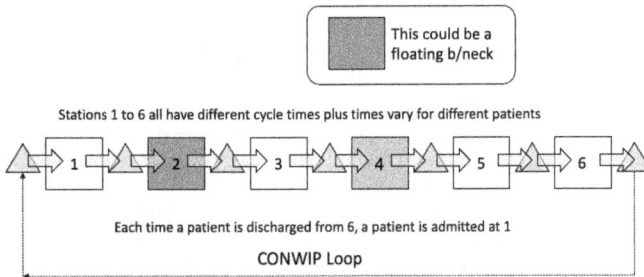

Stations 1 to 6 all have different cycle times plus times vary for different patients

Each time a patient is discharged from 6, a patient is admitted at 1

CONWIP Loop

There are two issues with CONWIP:

- Time to detect problems downstream is slower than with kanban, particularly if the loop is long.

- CONWIP has problems with large and variable process industry batches. For instance a brewing batch cannot easily be split. Here, partial completion stages can be used.

26.3   Drum Buffer Rope (DBR)

DBR is the methodology employed with Theory of Constraints (TOC). (Please refer to Section 25.7 on TOC.) DBR is a multi-stage pull system. What is let out at the constraint (Drum) is let in at the first workstation (or 'gateway'). The Buffer contains inventory that protects the constraint from starvation. To quote the late Eli Goldratt, 'An hour lost at a bottleneck is an hour lost for the whole system..'. The Rope is the multi-stage pull mechanism connecting the constraint and the gateway. Because of what Goldratt termed 'statistical fluctuations and dependent events' the DBR system is much more robust than kanban when used in production. Total inventory is constant between gateway and constraint. Downstream of the constraint, however, things can go wrong and un-noticed.

Pre-constraint buffers in DBR.

To ensure that the bottleneck (or Drum) always has work available, a buffer is established immediately upstream of the bottleneck. There may or may not be inventory between other processes, but there should always be inventory in this buffer. Note that this buffer is best thought of as a time buffer not an inventory buffer. In other words, there may be two hours of product A (say 10 parts) in the buffer on Monday, and two hours of Product B (say 5 parts) in the buffer on Tuesday, depending on unit process time at the bottleneck.

At the bottleneck a FIFO lane buffer may be used – this could be physical or electronic. It is coloured Red, Yellow, and Green. Refer to the figure.

When there is sufficient inventory (that is, time) in the buffer, there is inventory in all Red, Yellow and Green zones. With variation and possible upstream problems, the Green zone buffer might be depleted to expose the Yellow zone. This is a warning. With further depletion inventory may only remain in the Red zone. Now there is a danger that the bottleneck may be starved and have to wait. If this situation is reached, the upstream workstations must work harder or longer (or 'sprint') to restore the buffers.

A second FIFO lane buffer may be established at the entry point of the line. This inventory is waiting to be released into the line by a 'Rope' signal from the bottleneck or Drum. Here, orders accumulate, first in the Green zone then in Yellow, then in Red. This is an indication of unacceptable lead time.

The size of the buffer at the bottleneck is related to upstream uncertainty in stoppages and quality problems. This is an issue relating to MTBF (mean time between failures) and MTTR (mean time to repair), rejects and rework and stockout probability.

Sizing of the buffer at the bottleneck can be established by simulation. In practice, however, sizing is done by trial and error – starting with a generous quantity, monitoring, and then reducing excess inventory.

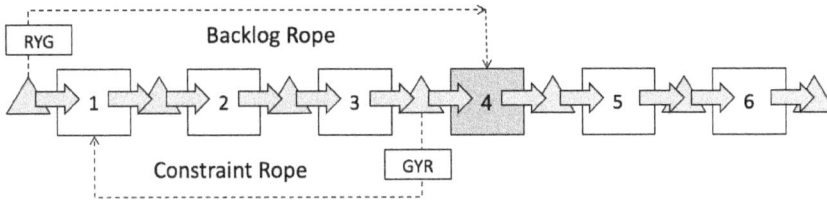

Note that an inventory buffer extends lead time because additional WIP is used. There is a trade-off between the cost of additional inventory and the cost of lost throughput. Throughput usually dominates. There are diminishing returns for buffer inventory in front of a bottleneck. Eventually extra buffer makes no difference to throughput but simply adds to lead time. If inventory is expensive, less buffer should be held.

Therefore, in Theory of Constraints, beyond a certain limit, it becomes more effective to hold an additional inventory buffer at a workstation immediately upstream of the bottleneck, particularly if an upstream workstation has capacity just below that of the bottleneck. If the capacity of the upstream workstation is similar to the capacity of the bottleneck, then with variation the actual bottleneck may shift and it would be a good idea to hold permanent buffer inventory in front of both locations. None is needed if the upstream workstation has ample capacity.

Often the location of the bottleneck is clear-cut, but not always. A workstation with a slightly lower utilization than the apparent bottleneck but having a higher coefficient of variation (CV) may in fact be the true bottleneck. A higher CV may result from process instability or breakdowns.

Also note that downstream of the bottleneck things can go wrong – like stoppages and rejects. A DBR line without an end-of-line FIFO type monitoring system would not detect stoppages downstream of the bottleneck. Thus, end-to-end lead-time may not be stable.

26.4   POLCA

POLCA (for **P**aired-cell **O**verlapping **L**oops of **C**ards with **A**uthorization) is an unusual system principally aimed at the for job shop, and low-volume high-mix manufacturing. It was introduced by Rajan Suri in 1998 as the pull system for quick response manufacturing (QRM). QRM principles have significant overlap with Lean for both tools and people. POLCA has few followers but those few are enthusiastic. Here we will give a brief overview but the reader is referred to Suri's work.

Refer to the figure below.

First, every pair of production sequences, or loops, must have a set of cards. The number of cards in a loop is determined by a calculation similar to that for kanban cards.

For a job to start at a process, a capacity authority card from the next process must be available (sent back after completion of the previous job) AND a dispatch list authorization. The dispatch list comes from ERP/MRP giving a 'not before' date (or priority) that will allow sufficient lead time for on-time completion. The dispatch list must also show material availability – a job cannot be released until material is available. Authority cards go to the front of the previous (upstream) stage, unlike kanbans which go to the front of the next stage. This means that an operation is not started until the next stage is ready.

There are two analogies: A private pilot explained his POLCA system to Bicheno by saying that he would not take off before knowing he could land. This is the POLCA capacity authorization. In India some train timetables state *'The times below are not departure times. Rather they show times before which the train will not depart'* (!) This is the dispatch list authorization.

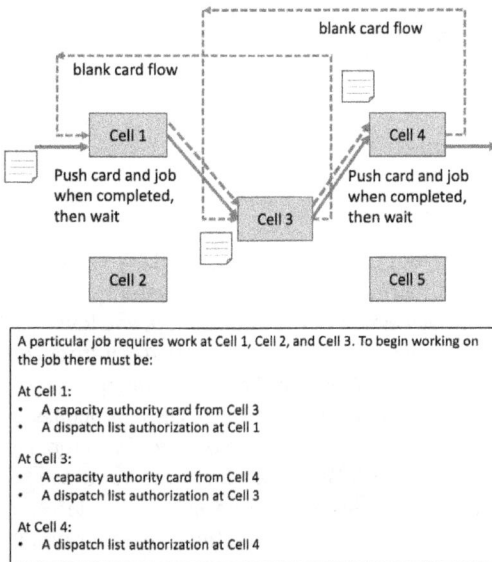

A particular job requires work at Cell 1, Cell 2, and Cell 3. To begin working on the job there must be:

At Cell 1:
- A capacity authority card from Cell 3
- A dispatch list authorization at Cell 1

At Cell 3:
- A capacity authority card from Cell 4
- A dispatch list authorization at Cell 3

At Cell 4:
- A dispatch list authorization at Cell 4

26.5   Demand Driven MRP (DDMRP)

Demand Driven MRP (DDMRP) has come into prominence since about 2015 with the publication of a book by Ptak and Smith. DDMRP is strictly not a push system in terms of the definition given at the start of this Chapter, but can be used to supply pull supermarkets and support the pull systems mentioned above, particularly in non-repetitive situations. (We have seen DDMRP used in this way at an aerospace sub-system manufacturer.)

DDMRP is push-pull system that overcomes some of the limitations of conventional MRP. In conventional MRP or ERP there is a master Production Schedule or MPS, and a bill of material (or BOM) for each product type. Each leg of the BOM has associated lead times. The MPS 'explodes' the BOM to generate the material requirements. These features are found also in many Lean systems,

MRP is much like baking cakes. The BOM is the recipe for all the ingredients. If you want to make 100 cakes, you need 100 times the recipe ingredients. So you multiply it out. This is called 'explosion'. Then you look at what you already have, and deduct this quantity. This is called

netting. And you need to order the ingredients ahead of time, allowing at least the longest time to acquire any ingredient. This is called 'lead time offset'. So the MPS drives inventory acquisition to all levels of the BOM.

DDMRP claims that it is built upon the best of MRP, DRP, Lean, TOC, Six Sigma, and Innovation.

There are 5 components to a DDMRP system. 1. Strategic Decoupling; 2. Buffer Profiles and Levels; 3. Dynamic Adjustment; 4. Demand Driven Planning; 5. Visible and collaborative execution.

In conventional MRP a product can only proceed to the next stage of manufacture if all parts (in the BOM) are available. If any part is not available the schedule will be missed. So shortages are a major problem with many production systems -as well as some Lean pull systems. In DDMP, decoupling points (buffers) are established at critical converging points in a BOM. These buffers are replenished in a separate exercise involving three levels of safety (green, yellow, red). With these decoupled points established, lead times can be determined for any part to be manufactured, based on the lead time to the decoupling point, and not the full cumulative lead time as in MRP. A great advance!

The location and sizing of these decoupled buffers (and where no buffers are necessary) are established by a fairly involved procedure. A prime consideration is part commonality - the latest point in the BOM at which flexibility can be maintained However, this may be useful in locating and sizing supermarkets in non-repetitive Lean systems (non-normal demand patterns and green and yellow frequency – as discussed in Demand Analysis.)

Decoupled inventories are in effect postponement points, an idea that is well established in car manufacture. In car manufacture the decoupling point is the bodies in white stage. Materials can be ordered and body pressing and welding can take place in anticipation of actual orders because of commonality. The actual customer spec is built on the final assembly line with a comparatively short lead time. Lead times for raw material acquisition and for pressing and welding operations are irrelevant for customer lead time and for the preparation of the final assembly schedule. The only considerations are fixing, monitoring and

value stream and are an attractive proposition where there is high variety, differing cycle times or

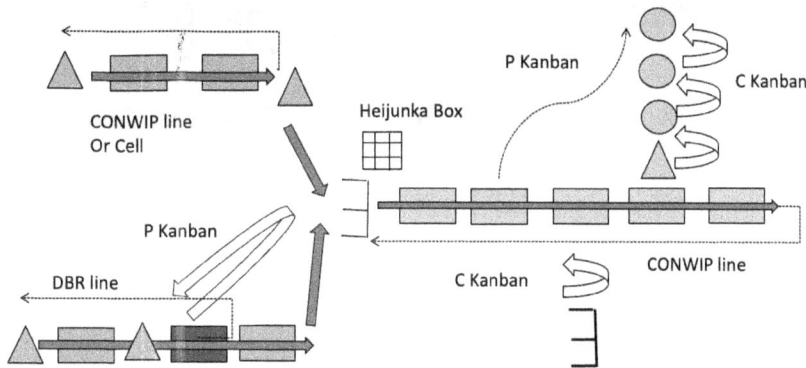

adjusting the body in white inventories, and the final assembly time. This is essentially what DDMRP does. Instead of one decoupling point as in car assembly, there will be numerous decoupling points in a DDMRP implementation.

Further reading

Carol Ptak and Chad Smith, *Demand Driven Material Requirements Planning (Version 3)*, Industrial Press, 2019

26.6 Comparing Kanban, DBR, CONWIP, POLCA and DDMR

Kanban, DBR and CONWIP can be combined and tailored to the requirements of many systems. For instance, one might have a CONWIP feeder line for a variety of parts where there is considerable process time change between part types, and a DBR line where there is a stable but long changeover. Another feeder sequence might use kanban triggered by a particular product passing a particular point in final assembly. The final assembly line may be a CONWIP line controlled by a Heijunka box system drawing on a supermarket.

For job shop, high variety systems there is a case for combining with DDMRP.

CONWIP and DBR systems are less sensitive to process interruptions in the middle stages of the

product mix, or where there is good probability of disruption due to quality or breakdown.

This is a powerful advantage over Drum Buffer Rope (where inventory is stable between the gateway and the constraint, but anything can happen downstream of the constraint).

Simple kanban is not suited for erratic, lumpy or highly seasonal demand patterns, or else inventory will sit for ages between usage. This drawback can be overcome but will require much adjustment to the number of replenishment cards.

Kanban: When used in production along a line, between stations, kanban needs to be treated with caution. For example, using kanban squares between stations does highlight problems quickly, but with high variation tasks, throughput often falls. This is because production can only happen when the next square authorizes production by a pull signal AND the previous square has inventory available.

As noted in the Science of Lean (Chapter 4), one-piece flow is sometimes not the ideal, but depends upon cycle time differences between resources. This is particularly relevant for more complex streams. Starvation and blocking are particular considerations where bottlenecks are involved. This is discussed in Chapter 25.

A comparison between systems is given in the table on the next page.

Further reading

Christoph Roser, *All About Pull,* All About Lean, 2021. (A highly detailed explanation, covering most situations.)

	Kanban	Drum Buffer Rope	CONWIP	POLCA	DDMR
Outline	Stage by stage cards; production and move types.	Bottleneck protected by buffer; pull from B/neck to gateway	Multi-stage pull linking end to beginning	Dual card. Release by both MRP & next stage availability	Replenish strategic b_ by MRP. M_ from orders
Analogy	Supermarket	'Herbie' on the hike; bottleneck determines.	Swimming pool circular lanes - one in one out.	Don't take off before you can land; Indian railway	Two stage holiday. Ta_ different cl_ and then decide.
Applicable	Repetitive low variation fixed path; component supply	Fixed path; limited variation	Fixed path; more variation	Towards job shop. High variation	Repetitive lead time p_ with uncer_
Additions	Capacity kanbans; e-bans, golfball	RYG queue monitoring at b/neck and gateway	Multiple loops separated by buffers	Lead time costing and thinking	Buffer sign_ system
Strengths	Problems apparent fast	Focus on b/neck thruput	Fixed lead time; Shifting b/necks auto	Fairly flexible routings	Reduces o_ lead time
Limitations	FIFO routing; for a line variation destroys thruput; no of cards often changes	FIFO routing; loose control downstream of b/neck; expensive inventory at buffer? Data dependent	FIFO routing in a segment; when b/neck shifts thruput may be lost.	MRP dependent. Two cards for each pair of stations may mean complexity	Permanent_ buffers for repetitive l_ lead time p_ Buffer forecasting
Heijunka, level scheduling?	Yes in a cell or line	Maybe	Probably	No	Maybe
Pareto, RRS Glenday Sieve	Yes	Yes	Yes	Maybe	Maybe
One piece flow/ batch?	One piece flow; container	One piece or batch	One piece or batch	Batch	atch

27 Scheduling Line Processes

27.1 The Level Schedule

Even after years of Lean activity, many still think that the level schedule is an automotive Lean concept and hence not applicable. This is simply wrong! The level schedule can almost always be applied to a good proportion of products. The word 'Heijunka' is a Japanese term for levelling.

Here we consider the 'why' for a schedule to be as level as possible. In the section on the Eleven Lean Scheduling concepts below, the 'how' will be discussed.

Why is a level schedule such a worthwhile aim, and such a potent driving force:

- Muri and Mura are often cited as the root causes of Muda. Mura (unevenness) is directly related to level scheduling. Muri (overburden) causes instability and leads to instable schedules. Recall the Kingman Equation section in 'The Science of Lean' Chapter with graph of queue against utilization. With unevenness, as utilization increases towards 100% of capacity, so delays build exponentially and the uncertainty of schedule attainment increases.

- Level scheduling extends to suppliers and to customers – end to end along the supply chain. Suppliers appreciate regular orders and delivery schedules – this enables them to become Lean themselves. Likewise, if customers place regular orders, flow is made much easier, and inventory is reduced.

- Internally, delivery schedules are smoothed. A tugger (or runner) can be set up. Material handling is much more efficient. Perhaps the plant can stop using those fork lift trucks for big batches.

- Fast problem identification is facilitated by level schedules. Visual management is made easier. As soon as a schedule deviates from plan it is noticed, and the root cause sought.

- The level schedule facilitates lean or cell layout, the small machine concept, and value streams.

- Everyone works better with no surprises.

- And how about level schedules for management? This is the essence of what David Mann says about Lean Leadership – standard work for managers with meetings held at standard, regular times. In short, predictable level schedules.

- In Design, Intel and others level their Design process, bringing out new generations of chips on a regular cycle.

Complete levelling of operations may not be possible. However, there are many actions that can be taken towards levelling. This is discussed in Chapter 24 on Demand Analysis

27.2 The ten value stream scheduling concepts

The ten concepts presented in the following section form a set that enable most repetitive value streams (or loops) to implement a successful Lean scheduling system. Here we deal with a value stream having minimal shared resources. Shared resources and batch sizing is considered in the next Chapter. The set of ten can be applied within repetitive loops. Several loops, separated by buffers or shared resources, may form a value stream. Of course, each concept can be applied individually but in a full Lean scheduling system most or all are used together. The ten given below, together with the shared resource, batch sizing and buffer locations in the next Chapter are the essential tools and concepts used to convert a current state to a Lean future state. The ten are:

1. Demand Smoothing
2. Demand Analysis
3. Takt and Pitch Time
4. The Pacemaker
5. Mixed Model Scheduling
6. Kanban, Pull and CONWIP

7. Material handling routes and Plan For Every Part, and Presentation

8. Heijunka (or similar) for levelling and capacity management.

9. Supermarkets and FIFO Lanes

10. Sales and Operations Planning (S&OP)

Demand Smoothing and Demand Analysis

The smoother and more regular demands can be, the easier and better the schedule should be. Demand smoothing is a particular case of the Level Scheduling concept, the advantages and methods of which were discussed above and in the Demand Analysis Chapter. Also discussed were ideas on how not to 'unsmooth' demand by self-inflicted actions such as uncoordinated sales actions.

Takt Time and Pitch Time

The takt time is the drumbeat, and the pitch time is the repeating increment within which containers (or regular batch sizes) are moved. Takt is the available work time divided by demand over that period. Pitch is takt time x container quantity, and frequently used as the interval in a heijunka system. Takt and Pitch are discussed in greater detail in the Preparing for Flow, Chapter 18.

The Pacemaker

The single pacemaker is the stage around which the whole value stream within the plant is scheduled. One pacemaker per value stream or loop. Having one pacemaker avoids amplification problems (see the mapping Chapter) and creates synchronisation. If the pacemaker is the heart, the material handler is the circulation.

A pacemaker can work with Kanban, heijunka, CONWIP and DBR. In many situations it is desirable to select a process well downstream as the pacemaker, so that upstream operations can be pulled. The pacemaker need not be a constraint or bottleneck, though it often is if a DBR system is used. After the pacemaker, you would like flow to be first in first out (FIFO).

A pacemaker in a repetitive system works better with a levelled schedule. The pacemaker should send out a production authorisation signal every pitch increment, or at least at a regular rate. It is common to use a Heijunka box, or 'Day by the hour' board at the pacemaker as the actual scheduling point.

Mixed Model Scheduling

First, a warning: Mixed model scheduling and the heijunka box are for more mature Lean systems. A lot of stability work is a pre-requisite. See the Chapters on Preparing for Flow.

Mixed model scheduling means scheduling **ABC, ABC, ABC**..... in a repeating sequence rather than in three separate large batches of A, B, and C. There are several reasons for this: it is a powerful aid to cell and line balancing (by placing long cycle items next to short cycle items), it reduces WIP inventory and sometimes finished goods inventory, it may lead to better customer service, and (a big one) results in a constant rate of flow of parts to the line or cell by material handling, rather than at different rates for different products.

In assembly operations with no changeover, mixed model operations are most desirable. It is particularly advantageous when products with different assembly times come down a line, such as in a car plant. Here a 'complex' car is followed by a 'simple' car. This is much better for flow and material handing than having all 'complex' cars followed by all 'simple' cars.

Mixed model sequences are derived from the product mix demand. So if there are two products, A with 66% demand, and B with 33%, then the best mixed model sequence is **AABAABAAB**. The best sequence is calculated from the nearest lowest common denominator. Thus if demand for A, B and C is in the ratio 10, 5, 2 the sequence could be **AABAABACAABAABABC.** The actual sequence would be dependent on process times – this can be quite complex, requiring computer algorithms.

In practical terms, the degree of mixed model scheduling depends upon order sizing, shipment frequency and changeover. For example, if the usual customer pack or container takes 20 product A's and 10 product B's, and average demand is for 40 A and 20 B per hour, it may not be sensible to make in a **AABAAB** repeating sequence but rather 20A, 10B, 20A, 10B. (But 40A, 20B once per hour has dangers). The pack size would be used to establish the pitch time. The pitch and sequence would then be used in setting up the heijunka box. See later. If the company ships twice per day, the best policy would be to make every product at a minimum of twice per day in the appropriate shipping quantities.

Caution: Moving directly into the optimal mixed model sequence could be asking for trouble. Instead, evolve into the sequence by, for instance, halving the batch size, sorting out problems, then halving again until the optimal sequence is reached.

The choice of the repeating mixed model sequence – for example 20A 10B 20A 10B or 40A 20B - could be influenced by the frequency with which a tugger vehicle or runner comes around to replenish parts. The idea is for the tugger to deliver approximately the same mix of parts on every circuit, thereby establishing flow.

Where there are short changeovers, the minimum feasible batch can be calculated with the formula:

Changeover time + assembly cycle time x batch size = takt time x batch size.

Solving this equation for the batch size will give the minimum number of like products that need to be made together in a batch within a mixed model run sequence. For example, if changeover time is 10 minutes, cycle time is 3 minutes and takt time is 5 minutes, then 10 + 3b should equal 5b, so b or (batch) is 5. So, at least 5 of a particular product need to made together before changing over to make another product.

In a heijunka box the mix model sequence is arranged in pitch increments. Some companies use standard pitch increments, and vary the length of the work day; others derive the pitch increment directly from takt.

Either way, first, the mixed model batch size or container size decides the pitch increment, and second, the number of pitch increments and the product mix decides the mixed model sequence. Thus if there are 48 10- minute pitch increments in the heijunka and the lowest common denominator demand mix is 6A, 3B, 2C, 1D then the day would be divided into 4 12-pitch increment repeating slots, each of **ABABACABACAD** – provided that there is no changeover.

That is the basic story. But sometimes it is not quite as simple. What happens when cycle times vary a lot (more than one third), or where there is high demand or mix variation, or all three?

- First, differentiate between repeater and stranger items. It may be necessary to establish different safety stock policies for each category. Repeater items can be held in inventory and replenished in off demand periods. Strangers need to be built.

- A 'Glenday Sieve' allows for maximum advantage to be taken from high demand, but low SKU count, items.

- For high cycle time variation between products, first ensure that long cycle products (or containers) are placed in sequence next to short cycle products. Then make use of FIFO lanes between assembly stations.

- If the mix or demand varies, ideally a cell will have been balanced separately for different rates. This will usually mean changing the labour requirements. Some companies are able to run two or more rates within a single shift.

- Lead time to make the product is a factor. If the lead time is long, use a supermarket to buffer (i.e. hold safety stock) for make-to-stock items (or repeaters), and give priority to make-to-order items (or strangers). If lead time is short, it may be possible just to use FIFO lanes between stations. WIP in the FIFO lanes accumulates and depletes as assembly times vary.

Kevin Duggan suggests developing a 'Mix Logic Chart' to establish the policies in advance of the situation developing, rather than just working out what to do 'seat of the pants style' at the morning meeting. He gives several examples in his book. (It's back to 'ballet rather than hockey' style management!)

		Demand Change	
		No	Yes
Mix Change	No	Standard operations	Change labour? Overtime?
	Yes	Employ safety stock? Use FIFO lanes?	Labour and inventory changes

Kanban and Pull

Kanban and pull are two central topics that are too extensive to be covered in this overview of the Ten Value Stream Scheduling Concepts. Please see the separate Chapter on Pull Systems.

Material Handling (Runner) Routes, Plan For Every Part (PFEP) and Presentation.

A runner (or material handler or tugger) plays a central role in a Lean repetitive system. Far from being a dreary job, the runner acts like the information system holding the whole system together, noticing problems, and levelling flow.

The runner often starts and ends his or her regular cycle at the Heijunka box – perhaps every few pitch increments. Certainly, he or she will come around at regular intervals, typically once per hour, visiting standard locations or 'bus stops'. During the regular cycle, the runner collects kanbans, picks parts, moves parts, and delivers parts pulled from the previous cycle. A constant route is followed. The runner may also collect finished products and issue Heijunka cards to the beginning of the cell. A runner should always be carrying either parts or cards, often both.

Plan for Every Part (PFEP)

PFEP means just that – developing a plan for how every part will end up at the point of use at the right time in the most efficient way. This means having an internal supply chain from receiving dock to assembly point that is most appropriate to the frequency of use, weight, size, and cost of every part. The material handling routes need to be designed according to all of these together. The aim is to smooth the flow of parts to the lines or cell throughout the shift. This is a form of Heijunka, but for parts not products. (See section 24.7).

The location of bus stops should be designed: serving individual workstations, cells, or an area?

The runner route is a fixed time, variable quantity route. In other words although the interval is fixed the drop-off quantities may vary. The aim is levelled deliveries. It would not be good if the runner was delivering many parts during one run and few in the next. Mixed model scheduling helps, as does using small containers. (See Section 22.3)

Kitting is a possibility. Will parts be delivered as a kit (relating to a particular product) or individually. Part presentation on the line is also an issue, affecting the amount of actual value added assembly time available within a takt time.

(Note: The word 'pick' is used below. This may be an individual part but more likely is a box of components or fasteners, a stillage of metal pressings or a kit to make up a subassembly.)

The calculation of the number of runners and routes is iterative. First, the number of runners or material handlers needs to be calculated. One consideration is whether the runners will do the picking or whether dedicated pickers are used. If dedicated pickers are used the replenishment interval is extended because pickers get kanban cards one cycle and then must pick from a supermarket during the cycle so that parts are ready for collection by the runners during the next cycle. Another consideration is how many lines or cells need to served together. (For example, are runners dedicated to cells; or cells per runner?)

Then comes the times – for getting pick tickets, picking, travel, unloading, return.

A bill of materials for every workstation every day is needed. This is not the general BOM used for example by MRP, but a more detailed breakdown of daily picks required for all products at each workstation. The total number of parts (or picks) to be delivered to the complete line is then calculated by aggregation.

When combined with the capacity of the tugger vehicle, the number of runners can be calculated:

No of runner trips per day = no of picks per day/ no of picks per trip;

No of runners per day = no of trips per day x time per trip / (time per day * 0.85)

Note: the 0.85 figure is an allowance figure for variation.

Example: Effective working time per day (after meetings etc) = 450 minutes, 1200 picks per day; 40 picks per trip; 50 minutes per round trip

No of trips required = 1200/40 = 30/day

No of runners = 30 x 50 / (450 * 0.85) = 3.9 or 4 runners; Each runner will distribute 1200/4 = 300 picks per day; each of the 450/50 = 9 trips per runner per day distributing 300/9 = approximately or ideally, 35 picks per trip.

Then comes cost: Expensive parts would only be permanently stocked on the line if they are frequently used. Low frequency, expensive parts require special delivery, often triggered only and each time the product requiring the part is launched onto the line. By contrast low cost items can be stocked for longer periods on the line.

Then comes size and weight. The material handling tugger has finite capacity, so weight and size of parts for delivery need to be evenly distributed through the shift.

In the example, the 35 picks per trip is an average that needs to levelled according to cost, size, and weight; regular parts spread evenly, low cost parts infrequently, high cost, large, heavy as required.

Buffer stock and safety stock will be required for some or all parts.

A reminder: We are discussing a pull system, where picks are pulled from workstations. These are the picks that need to be levelled.

The Heijunka system (or day by the hour) can be used. In other words, the deliveries are monitored and if behind (or ahead) problem-solving action is

taken. If the runner experiences a shortage he draws on the buffer or safety stock as appropriate. He (or the team leader) should write up the reason for the occurrence immediately.

PFEP in Warehousing: The PFEP Heijunka system can be used in warehousing. Basically the same calculations are made (often daily) but instead of distributing to lines or cells, the process feeds delivery vehicles or staging points. The same powerful problem highlighting and improvement methodology is used.

Heijunka (or Level) Scheduling

The Heijunka box is the classic method of Lean scheduling in a repetitive value stream or cell environment. It simultaneously achieves a level schedule or pacing, visibility of schedule, and early problem highlighting. It is usually used at the pacemaker process, and as such controls and paces a whole loop within a value stream. Moreover it can be used as a form of short-interval synchronization tool. Heijunka can be used for production scheduling, for warehouse order picking, and in the office. And finally, Heijunka encourages schedules to be developed and controlled by supervisors at the Gemba.

Heijunka can mean either level scheduling or level capacity. Levelling the schedule means moving ever closer to a repeating mixed model sequence. Levelling capacity means having a pre-determined planned capacity each day and then releasing work so as to fill, but never over-fill, the daily slots. The resulting regularity of flow of materials and of information is a major advantage.

There are several forms:

- The classic heijunka box
- Day by the hour boards
- Sequence wheel
- Virtual queues with CONWIP

The Heijunka box is a post-box system for kanban cards that authorizes production in pitch increment-sized time slots. A typical pitch increment is between 10 and 30 minutes. The box is loaded at the cell level by supervisors or team leaders. It is in effect a manual finite scheduler. As with kanban, a Heijunka system is always visible and up to date. You can see at a glance how far behind schedule you are.

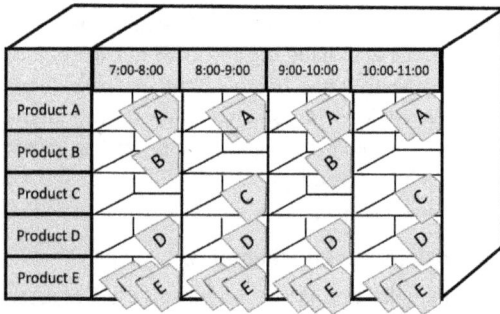

A Heijunka Box has columns from left to right for each pitch increment (or time slot), and rows for each product or family. For each pitch increment – except break increments – a Heijunka card is placed in one of the product rows to authorize production of one pitch increments' amount of work. A pitch increment normally fills a (small) container of parts, so deviations, when planned work is not completed, are clearly apparent. The cell is authorized, kanban style, to produce only that amount at the specific time. (A variant is that a cell may be allowed to produce the next pitch increments' quantity, but no more.) Therefore, loading up the Heijunka box levels the schedule and withdrawing the cards paces production during the shift. Should any item fail to be ready for collection, or the cell is unable to start work, this is immediately apparent. The worst case of undetected production failure is one pitch increment.

A simple example:

- There are three products A,B,C where daily demand over a levelled time period is A:60; B:40; C:20. (total 120)
- The mixed model sequence would be ABABAC. See the figure below.
- Available time (after rest allowance) is 4 hours per day (240 minutes)

- Takt is 240/120 = 2 min or 120 seconds;
- Container quantity is 10 products; so pitch is 10x2 = 20 minutes
- The Heijunka box achieves levelling across the day in pitch increments.
- If a 10-product sequence cannot be made in 1200 seconds, (20 min) then the reason is shown on the Heijunka board.
- Planned cycle time would be (say) 85% of 2 min, or (say) 100 seconds. This is what would be used to distribute the work and determine the number of operators in the cell.

Each column gives the authority to START work on those products. If previous pitch work is not completed, give the reason

In the example:

Start	20m	40m	60m	80m	10m rest	110 m	130 m	150 m	etc
A	5	5	5	5		5	5	5	
B	4	3	3	4		3	3	4	
C	1	2	2	1		2	2	1	

In a 20 minute pitch interval, cell operators could make AAAAABBBC or ABABABABAC. Depends on relative times.

Heijunka becomes the pacemaker of the material handling system. A material handler is authorized to collect the specific quantity at that time slot. A regular material handling route should be regarded as an integral part of Heijunka the frequency of which should ideally be a whole multiple of the pitch time.

Where heijunka is used with a finished goods store, the material handler takes the Heijunka card for the slot as authorization to withdraw from finished goods. He detaches the production kanban on the container and sends it to authorize making the next batch. The used heijunka card is placed in a box to be used the next day.

If demand cannot be met as per the heijunka schedule, (i.e. there has been a stoppage), the material handler draws on buffer stock but raises a flag to show that he has done so. At the end of the shift, the buffer must be replaced. Some users differentiate between buffer stock to cope with line stoppages, and safety stock to cope with customer surges in demand.

Mixed model scheduling is usually, but not necessarily, incorporated in Heijunka. The Heijunka box is loaded mixed-model fashion – not **AAAAAABBBCCC** but **ABACABACABAC**. See the earlier section on Mixed Model.

Heijunka is not a tool for the job shop or for highly variable production. Having said that, Dell Computer uses a 'sort of' Heijunka (but not called that), by loading up work into two hour increments which are issued to the factory floor. It can be adopted for maintenance and long cycles.

A basic issue is whether to maintain a constant pitch time increment and derive the batch or pitch quantity as the takt time changes or to maintain a standard container quantity and derive the pitch increment as the takt time changes. The former seems most popular, leading to stability of material handling routes and rate of work. In this case, when the takt changes the container quantity should change and the number of pitch increments changes to meet the demand. The shift may end with idle time or overtime.

In a warehouse one simply accumulates the required number of picks to fill the slot.

Where there are very long work cycles or takt times such as with large items (Refer for example to the section on the Pulse Line in The Layout Chapter), the pitch increment can be made a fraction of the pitch time – normally a convenient time increment such as 30 minutes or 1 hour. This is referred to as 'Mini Pitch' or 'Inverse Pitch'. The heijunka is then built around longer (say 30 minute) standard blocks of work. The great advantages of levelling and pacing remain.

Heijunka cards may also be 'piggybacked' to achieve the effect of a 'broadcast sheet' as found in automotive plants. In this case a slot may contain several cards, each of which goes to a different subassembly cell thereby synchronizing several streams automatically. This avoids having a separate schedule for each cell or line.

Location of Heijunka Box

Ideally a heijunka box (or pacemaker) is located at the end of a value stream nearest the customer. This is the case with repetitive products - typically make to stock or parts that are ordered very frequently. The small percentage of SKU's that make up a large percentage of volume, form the basis of the schedule. If parts are ordered several times per day, as in first tier automotive, the box should be located well downstream. Repetition allows pull to take place all along the value stream. Sequence and pull initiation are at the same place.

However, where there is large proportion of non-repetitive products or parts – typically make to order, 'strangers', erratic, lumpy and management control type demands, and Pareto B, C and D parts – the Heijunka box or pacemaker should be located at the beginning of a value stream or CONWIP loop. This beginning point may be located after a postponement point, or in other words where final assembly begins.

The reason why the heijunka box is located upstream in this case is that there are few similar parts and highly variable process time so conventional kanban is not suitable. Parts must be pushed through the process but a CONWIP system linking end and start points ensures inventory control.

Release of Heijunka production authorization cards.

A heijunka card should only be released when a part (or pitch quantity) is completed. This means that the authority to begin work is given every pitch increment, but the heijunka card is only released when work actually is completed. This ensures that inventory along the line never accumulates. In other words, it is a CONWIP system. If a heijunka production authorization card were to be released every pitch increment irrespective of completions, then this would be a push system not a pull system. In this case, if there was a stoppage half way along the line, parts would still be started and would accumulate.

Releasing production cards only when a completion occurs has the advantage of reasonably quick problem detection. If a card cannot be released during the planned pitch increment, the fact that the line is behind schedule – and by how much – can be clearly seen.

A **Day By the Hour** scheduling board plans and executes like a Heijunka box, but with hourly pitch increments. Performance tracking is simply by accumulating completions against plan. This is suitable where products are fairly similar or where there are long runs. Although simpler than a Heijunka box, the lack of cards means that over- and under-runs are less apparent.

The **Rotating Wheel** fixes the sequence of order releases. One rotation of the wheel is an EPEI cycle. The cycle depends on the EPEI calculation (see next Chapter) and may be any length of time, so whilst the sequence is fixed what happens on (say) each Monday will usually be different. Mixed model can be incorporated in a cycle by (say) making 'runners' more frequently and 'strangers' less frequently.

A **Virtual Queue** is a flexible system usually working with CONWIP. The queue of jobs for release is 'virtual' because queue jumping and priorities can change up to point of release. Release is triggered by CONWIP. Unlike classic Heijunka, a virtual queue is established at the beginning of a line or loop – upstream rather than downstream. Mixed model logic is still used for the basic sequence, but make-to-order and rush orders are accommodated by moving them ahead in the virtual queue.

Finally, a Heijunka box should be regarded as the final Lean tool. Why? – because so much must be in place for it to be a real success – cell design, mixed model, low defect levels, kanban loops and discipline, changeover reduction, and operator flexibility and authority. But Heijunka is the real 'cherry on the top' – it is the ultimate tool for stability, productivity, and quality.

Supermarkets and FIFO Lanes

A Supermarket is an inventory store where the runner 'goes shopping' to collect needed parts. Parts are pulled as needed, and there is uncertainty of sequence. Flow should take place between supermarkets. Supermarket areas should be grouped together to enable the material handler to visit on his or her regular routes.

With reference to value stream maps, often supermarkets are established at the boundary between loops of pull - say between a press and a group of cells, or where two value streams converge or diverge, or where two CONWIP loops meet.

It is permissible to have work in process inventory between workstations only when it is under visible kanban control (or CONWIP or drum buffer rope). All other inventory should be located in relatively few supermarkets.

The finished goods supermarket is sometimes called the 'wall of shame' to indicate that demand management and schedule stability still require further development. In a finished goods supermarket the inventory should be continually reviewed. For example, use a marker system that shows if there is too much inventory in circulation because inventory below the marker is never called upon. A marker can be used for each container or location of a part in the supermarket, and then removed when the container is moved. If the container never moves for (say) a month the marker will remain, indicating excessive inventory.

Sizing of supermarkets and their associated kanban loops is discussed on a following section.

A (by now hopefully) obvious point: do not use an automatic storage and retrieval system as a supermarket. They encourage more inventory, prevent visibility, and have slow response for a material handler or runner. And they may break down. However a small AS/RS (or carousel) can be used for consumables and slow response parts, if space and security are issues. Generally, though, they are things to be avoided!

FIFO Lanes are dynamic buffers of inventory between stages having different cycle times but a set sequence. Inventory accumulates in the FIFO lane whilst waiting for the next operation. The maximum inventory in a FIFO lane depends upon the time delay at the next stage – for example whilst waiting for a changeover. They may also be used to link physically separated processes whilst maintaining the schedule. A FIFO lane should have a clearly marked maximum quantity. A FIFO lane should never be used as a work in process store, having permanent inventory. If the inventory in a FIFO lane never goes down to near zero, there is probably too much inventory in the lane. Good practice is to paint colours on the FIFO lane to indicate to the preceding operation when more parts are needed. Thus it is a form of kanban square. Where the green section of the lane is exposed replacement may take place. If the red is exposed, replacement should take place.

Merely setting up an in-process FIFO lane instead of an interim buffer point where the schedule can change, can bring large advantages for lead time, simplicity and lead time reduction. It is a way of achieving Spear and Bowen's third rule of the Toyota DNA. (Forgotten that? Read it again – it is highly relevant to Lean scheduling!)

A FIFO lane should have a definite maximum inventory. Typical would be where a second process is involved in a changeover whilst the first process continues to manufacture. Here, inventory queues in the FIFO lane between them. The minimum size of the FIFO lane needs to be able to sustain the rate of production of the first process during the time the second process changes over. You would probably add some contingency. Another case is where the first operation works a double shift whilst the second works single shift. The FIFO lane should then hold at least one shift of material from the first shift plus contingency. In both cases, the contingency should include the likelihood of breakdown in the next operation, and if the second operation is a bottleneck, the likelihood of breakdown in the first operation.

A FIFO lane should be filled from one end and emptied from the other end. A flag can be added where there is date sensitive material. For small part stores this can be a gravity rack for containers. For FIFO lanes used for large containers, two shorter side-by-side lanes is often preferable to one longer lane. This helps avoid double handling when the lane is emptied from the front necessitating moving up all the containers in the queue. With two shorter side-by-side lanes, pull takes place from one lane while the other is being filled. A signalling system (light? sign?) may be necessary for the material handler to indicate which lane to fill, thereby maintaining FIFO integrity.

Alternatively a FIFO lane can be controlled by a CONWIP signalling system – only letting in work at the start of a sequence of processes when work is let out at the end.

In mixed model production, a FIFO lane can be seen as a method to claw back time where the operation cycle time (on the next stage) varies around takt time. Time is lost on the next operation where the cycle time is longer than takt, so inventory accumulates in the lane. Inventory then decreases when products having a cycle shorter than takt go through the next operation. See the calculation below.

In a supply chain a FIFO lane equivalent is the cross dock. The supply chain equivalent of a supermarket is a warehouse.

Sizing a FIFO lane:

In the formulas below, LS is the lane size, but ignoring safety considerations due to breakdown etc. (Note if B has a shorter cycle time than A, no lane is necessary.)

- For the size of a FIFO lane after a changeover operation A, feeding an operation B with longer cycle time than the changeover operation, use the formula:

  (c/over time at A) + LS (cycle time A) = LS (cycle time B). Solve for LS.

- For the size of a FIFO lane before a changeover operation A, being fed by an operation B, use: LS = changeover time on A / cycle time of B

- For the size of FIFO lane needed where one or more cycle times are greater than takt, but average time for the mixed model sequence is less than takt. Consider only those products having a cycle time greater than takt in a repeating mixed model sequence. Use: LS = (accumulated times in the sequence that are greater than takt) / (takt time).

Example: A mixed model sequence is ABCDE repeating. Takt is 25 seconds. Cycle times are 15, 30, 40, 20, 10 respectively.

Average cycle time = 23 secs.

Accumulated times greater than takt = 30+40 = 70

Lane size is 70/25 = 3, but rearrange so that sequence is A, B, D, C, E repeating. Probably have a stop trigger if there more than (say) 5 in the lane.

However if a batch of products, each exceeding the takt time, is run together, then the accumulated time must be for all of those products together. For example if 10 C's are frequently run together in a batch, then then each C exceeds takt by 15 seconds, and accumulated times greater than takt is 10 x 15 = 150 seconds. The FIFO lane should accommodate 150 / 25 = 6 products.

Sizing Supermarkets

The sizing of a supermarket is integrally associated with the design of the runner (or tugger) route.

The supermarket symbol adopted here has an extra box. This is useful to remind one of the four inventory elements in a supermarket:

- buffer stock
- safety stock
- batch or container quantity
- workstation demand during the replenishment time.

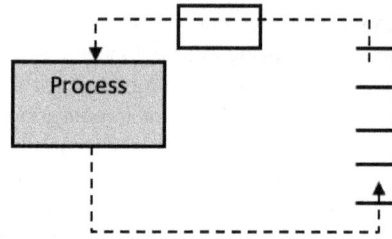

Supermarkets are part of a kanban loop. Estimating the number of kanbans (and the associated inventory) was discussed in the Pull Chapter. Buffer and safety quantities need consideration – usually moving from generous to tightened.

What remains is to decide how much of the inventory is to lineside and how much is to be kept in the supermarket.

For level demand, Safety stock is calculated from the service level, and associated number of standard deviations (z value), and from standard deviation of demand during the forecast horizon. So, buffer stock = average demand during lead time x z x standard deviation of demand.

Note, however, the difference between service level and fill rate. Fill rate may be more appropriate.

Sales and Operations Planning (S&OP)

S&OP was discussed in the General Scheduling Chapter. It is an essential concept for repetitive scheduling.

27.3   Applying Repetitive Scheduling

Good repetitive scheduling draws on all three of the trilogy of Demand Analysis, Queuing Dynamics, and splitting a value stream into Stable and Unstable Zones.

Glenday maintains that repetitive scheduling positively impacts improvement, motivation, service, and supplier relationships.

This section incorporates many ideas from Demand Analysis. See sections 24.3 to 24.5.

To use these ideas to create effective Lean schedules requires the following:

- The universal Pareto phenomenon – in this case, demand against SKU. It will invariably be found that a very small number of SKU's account for a very large proportion of demand. Glenday refers to these as 'Green', claiming that 6% of SKU's account for 50% of volume. In any case it is ESSENTIAL to do such an analysis.

- Understanding Pooling. The example of elevators was given in Section 4.5. Here, the greater the volume of customer demands for a SKU that can be pooled, the less will be the percentage variation (or coefficient of variation). This is simply because a high demand by one customer has a good chance of being balanced against a low demand by another.

- Stability. As a result of pooling, the top runners will have large demand stability – or at least there will be regular demand for a fair proportion of total demand for the top SKUs. The same is not true for the bottom (perhaps) 80% of SKU's that constitute (perhaps) 20% of volume demand. These analyses must be done.

- Postponement. There may well be a process stage after which product variety expands. These principles and analyses are even more effective when applied at the postponement point.

- The Base Schedule. Maximum use must be made of the stable proportion of SKU's. This applies both to make-to-stock and make-to-order items. In make-to-order, there will be very small risk of overproduction of a base schedule in anticipation of demand.

- Regularity. The base proportion (the stable proportion of a small number of SKU's, but which constitute a large volume) should form a regular schedule that is repeated for a considerable period – weeks or even months. This regularity gives huge advantages for continuous improvement, motivation and morale, maintenance, and supply.

- EPEI (Every Product Every) calculations should not necessarily be done for EVERY product, but are very useful for the top SKU's. See next Chapter.

- Control Limits. For the small proportion of top SKU's, upper and lower control limits need to be established. For make to stock there should be control limits for inventory. For make to order the control limits are for demand. Only when the control limits are breached, does the regular schedule need to be changed.

- Plateaus. The idea is to run the stable schedules for as long as possible. Here, forecasting and historic demand plays a role. Perhaps two or three plateaus per year are established for top SKU's. There may be short periods when no plateau can be established.

- Lumpy, Erratic, Management Control demands. The Boylon / Darlington categorization is useful here. Scheduling these types should be handled at an S&OP meeting, with the aim of not disturbing the regular schedule.

- Run to quantity or run to time. 'To quantity' means that the run size is the prime aim. 'To time' means that time stability is important – day to day, week to week, etc. Each has advantages that will need to be discussed. Quantity regularity may be more important with make to order. Time regularity for make to order.

- Fitting other demands around the regular schedule. All other SKU demands are fitted around the regular schedule. Policies to avoid overload are required – scheduling less than capacity. Policies to cope with unusual demands or stoppages are also required – overtime, subcontracting, or between-shift time-buffers.

Further reading

Kevin Duggan, *Creating Mixed Model Value Streams*, Productivity, 2002

James Vatalaro and Robert Taylor, *Implementing a Mixed Model Kanban System*, Productivity, 2003

Art Smalley, *Creating Level Pull*, LEI, 2004

Don Tapping and Tom Fabrizio, *Value Stream Management*. (Video series), Productivity, 2001

Tom Luyster with Don Tapping, *Creating Your Lean Future State*, Productivity, 2006

Ed Pound, Jeffrey Bell, Mark Spearman, *Factory Physics for Managers*, McGraw Hill, 2014

Shaun Snapp, *The Real Story Behind ERP*, SCM Focus, 2014

Tim Conrad and Robyn Rooks, *Turbo Flow: Using Plan For Every Part to turbo charge your Supply Chain*, CRC Press, 2011

Tom Wallace and Robert Stahl, *Sales and Operations Planning*, 3rd edition, TF Wallace, 2008. (Useful for a review against the S&OP process.)

28 Scheduling Batch Processes

In this Chapter we consider the scheduling of more complex value streams. Although it is highly desirable to have uninterrupted value streams with no shared resources, many organizations have a legacy of 'monuments', complex flows, and an SKU range with a long tail of low demand. Every aspiring Lean organization should work towards eliminating such complexity, but for many it will remain an aspiration for years to come.

28.1 Batch Sizing

This section gives an introduction to batch sizing and scheduling in situations where changeover remains a significant factor. Of course, one should still continue to attack changeover times, since any reduction improves the flow and reduces batch sizes.

First, a few words on the economic batch quantity (EBQ / EOQ) : from a Lean perspective, this approach should be totally rejected. Major criticisms include:

- no account is taken of takt time or flow rate
- classic 'batch and queue' thinking
- changeover cost has to be given as a cost per changeover, but changeover teams are usually a fixed resource
- inventory-holding costs are often understated
- capacity is assumed to be infinite.

The EOQ formula ($\sqrt{(2DS/(IC)}$) is theoretically sound but practically useless for process batch sizing. The formula MAY still be useful in independent demand purchasing. The four variables in the formula are Demand D (uncertain), Setup (or Order) cost S (Use the average cost or marginal cost or zero if no additional resources are used?), Inventory holding cost (we know that, in Lean, this is much higher than cost of capital because of quality, space, and lead time considerations – but by how much?), and the Cost of the item C. (The accumulated cost at the point of changeover or the initial cost? Is overhead included? What happens with make to order?) And finally the '2' in the formula derives from the unlikely situation of constant level demand. Average holding is half the order quantity – highly unlikely in batch processes! So if you still want to use it.....

Of course, if changeover can be reduced batch size reduction should follow. Solve the problem by physical change not mathematics!

The general Theory of Constraints batch sizing guideline is to increase batch sizes on capacity constrained machines, whilst reducing batch sizes on non-constrained machines. If after tackling bottlenecks, changeover teams are available they should be used to carry out more changeover reduction on non-constrained machines, with corresponding reduction in transfer batch sizes, so that such machines become more fully utilised in either changeover or running. The resulting reduction in WIP can be used to justify employing more resources on changeover. All this makes good sense, and is compatible with Lean thinking. Be careful, however: We should <u>first try to reduce batch size before tackling changeover reduction!</u> Use creativity. Be careful of Goldratt's 'Herbie' hiking story: Could the troop be broken into sub troops? This would be much more effective than offloading Herbie's pack and/or using the 'rope' to link the troop together! Also, Herbie had no rework or 'failure demand'.

Some truths about batch size

The following ideas draw on Don Reinertsen's insights. Don wrote points in relation to product development, but they apply equally in production.

Reducing batch size...

- reduces cycle time. The leading pieces can move ahead; they don't have to wait for the complete batch to finish
- smooths the flow, thereby reducing variability – possibly with dramatic results. (See Science of Lean chapter). Small, decoupled batches allow next stages to be worked on in parallel.

- Improves quality. Faster detection and feedback. And a whole batch may be judged by one element.

- Reduces risk. The time between batch completions reduces the forecast horizon and error

- Improves motivation, by improving feedback frequency.

- Toyota uses production kanban and move kanban. This is clever because each may have its own appropriate batch size.

Further reading

Donald Reinertsen, *The Principles of Product Development Flow*, Celeritas, 2009

28.2 Two Approaches to Batch Sizing

We are concerned here with batch sizing necessitated by changeover and sometimes by shared resources.

Two approaches to batch sizing will be described. The first is for variable demand where there is mix of demand patterns – stable, erratic, lumpy, management control. The second or EPE approach is suitable where demand is much more stable, and plateaus of stable demand could be developed.

A starting point for each is to examine the historic demand pattern and to classify each item that will be processed by the resource.

See Chapter 24 for Demand Analysis.

Variable Demand Lean Batch Sizing

1. An analysis of demand may reveal a pattern of regular repeating demands. If so, capitalize on this by using the EPEI formula in a section below. In this section we are concerned with general batch sizing suitable for variable, changing situations as well as for more irregular demands.

2. A part may appear in several demand categories. For example 'normal' and 'lumpy'. Whilst the part will frequently be made in one batch, necessitating both types

of demand to be added together. For subsequent supermarket safety stock purposes the two types should preferably be kept separate.

3. The detailed batch size procedure is given in the section below.

4. The batch resource should not be overloaded. According to Kingman's equation (see Science of Lean Chapter), queues escalate sharply above (say) 85% of utilization. 85% is a good rule of thumb figure to use as the maximum capacity, but this should be reviewed. Above 90% certainly risks failure. This percentage is to allow for variation, not breakdown.

5. A batch size should be linked with the downstream usage rate and delivery frequency. If a part is delivered once per day, ideally the batch size should match or be less than the daily delivery. In this case, for long changeovers there would be no point in making a batch smaller than the daily requirement.

6. A batch size should be a multiple of the container or pack quantity used. The container could be the move quantity

7. It is important to question any non-uniform demands. Why is that lumpy demand occurring? Will a customer accept several smaller orders? Is lumpy demand due to self-inflicted factors such as 'end of month hockey stick'?

8. For expected or forecasted orders, use the principle of 'consuming the forecast'.

9. Products or assemblies for which there is a definite sales order should enjoy priority. The next priority is for the small percentage of SKU's that make up a large percentage of volume. (See the Demand Analysis Chapter.) Make to stock items have lower priority, but their priority increases as stocks run down.

10. There is clearly an advantage for schedules to be as stable as possible over a number of periods – weeks or months. To air this,

safety stocks (against demand variation) and buffer stocks (against process contingencies) may be held.

11. Whilst the EPEI calculation gives the time required to make every product, big demand products can be made more frequently, compensated by low demand items made less frequently. Note: Using Glenday Sieve analysis, you will usually find that a small proportion of SKU's account for a large proportion of total demand. As noted through pooling, aggregated demand for these top SKU's will be much more stable than for other SKU's.

The batch size procedure for Variable Demands

1. Examine demand for the immediate period ahead. A period should be the normal schedule period – say weekly or fortnightly. Rank demand according to actual orders, regular orders, make to stock demands with declining urgency. Note that a particular part (or SKU) may appear in more than one category – for example a lumpy order but also as a make to stock part. For the calculation these should be combined. Here both will be referred to as a SKU.

2. Round up the demand for each SKU to bring it in line with the container size or pack quantity for the item.

3. Assuming one changeover per SKU, calculate the total time to do one changeover for each item. (To be even smarter, allow for the best sequence of setups to minimize total setup time.)

4. Calculate run times for all SKUs together. Run time for an SKU = demand for the SKU during the period * process time for the SKU

5. Subtract total run times for all items from total work (or shift) time to give gross available time. Net available time should take into account planned maintenance time, uptime availability, and also make an allowance for variation – say 85%. Thus,

Gross available time =

total work time − ∑ planned run times.

Net available time = Gross Available time x (1 -MTTR / (MTBF + MTTR)) x variation allowance.

6. Calculate number of possible changeovers. Is there time for one changeover for each SKU during the period? (i.e. Net available time - ∑ (changeover times for each SKU))

If yes go to next step.

If no, increase the period. Go to step 4. (Total work time and total run times will increase, but total changeover will be unchanged.) Recalculate then return to the beginning of this step.

7. It is now possible to make a batch of each SKU during each planning period. Batch sizes are, of course, equal to the demand during the planning period.

If you wish, you can stop here. Further improvement may be possible by following the next steps.

8. Calculate the remaining net available time during the period after subtracting the total changeover time for all SKUs up to this point from the previous net available time.

Is there time for an additional changeover during the period? If no, go to step 10 below. If yes, proceed.

9. Select the biggest demand quantity. Do the additional changeover on this SKU, and halve the demand quantity.

Go to step 8.

10. Stop if you wish, or investigate the pairwise swop procedure. See later in this Chapter.

Simple Example: There are four SKUs: A, B, C, D with demands during the period of 150, 100, 30, 10 respectively. Each SKU has an individual run time of 1 minute, and a 30 minute changeover. There is a daily shift with work time (after start-up meetings) of 480 minutes.

MTTR is 20 minutes; MTBF is 480 minutes. Utilization allowance is 85%

Gross available time = 480 - $\sum$ run times = 480-280 = 200 minutes

Net available time is 200 x (1-(20 / (20+480))) x 0.85 = 163 minutes

No of possible changeovers = 163/30 = 5.4 (i.e more than 4)

So we can have at least one changeover per SKU during the shift, with batch sizes of 150,100,30,10.

4 changeovers will take 120 minutes

Remaining time is 163-120 = 40 minutes. So another changeover is possible.

Select SKU A. During the shift there will be 2 batches of A, and one batch of B,C,D. Batch sizes will be 75, 100, 75, 30, 10 for A,B,A,C,D

Further improvement is possible using Pairwise Swop between SKUs B and D. See later section.

28.3 The Every Product Every (EPE) Concept

The EPE concept is an important Lean idea that establishes a regular repeating cycle. EPE regularity has big advantages for standard work, quality, predictability, suppliers, changeover time, and regular time for improvement. 'A good Lean schedule is a boring schedule' is a good maxim. An EPE cycle is often referred to as a 'campaign'. A Lean ideal is to run every product every day. This would be excellent for service and inventory but is seldom feasible.

The basis of batch EPE is to make the batch as small as possible by doing as many changeovers as possible in the available time. This is similar to the previous section, but a short cut formula is used.

By the way, the 'available time' may be with the machine process or the setting crew. Likewise, the critical changeover time is likely to be 'internal changeover time'.

The EPE formula is: EPE days = $\sum$ (changeover time per campaign)/ (Total available time per day - $\sum$ (demand run time per day))

Example: Three SKUs are run on a bottleneck process. Assume that each product is run once in each campaign. The effective workday is 8 hours. Using the data from the table below, total changeover time for all products together is 5 hours. Production time to make an average of one days' demand of all products together is 6 hours.

Then EPEI = 5 / (8-6) = 2.5 days. This means that there should be a repeating cycle every 2.5 days.

Batch sizes are A: 3 x 2.5 = 7.5 hours run time; B = 2 x 2.5 = 5 hours run time; C = 2.5 hours run time. The batches will however need to be rounded to match the container size.

Different processes will of course have different batch sizes – necessitating a FIFO lane between them.

Strict EPE would imply running a batch of every SKU in an EPE cycle. Every SKU would have the same interval between runs. This is not always sensible because, as was discussed in the Demand Analysis Chapter, there is often a pareto distribution of SKU's (with a few big runners and a long tail of other SKU's.) Moreover, there is also erratic, lumpy and 'management control' demand.

Part	Daily Demand	Run time req'd per day (hrs)	Change-overtime (hrs)	Batch size (hrs)	Batch Size (units)	Contain-er size	No of contain-ers/batch
A	300	3	1	7.5	750	100	8
B	400	2	2	5	1000	100	10
C	50	1	2	2.5	250	50	5
Total		6 hrs per day	5 hrs per campaign				

Therefore, following the Demand Analysis Chapter, it is possible to establish a dual scheduling planning procedure whereby the top (say) 50% of SKUs (i.e. Green and Yellow categories, Normal Demand pattern) are run according to EPE and the remainder are run as required using the procedure from the last section, 28.2.

The EPE should be re-calculated whenever there is significant change in demand. Use a SPC-type control chart to monitor total demand. Often, total demand will be much more stable than individual SKU demands.

EPE and sequence dependent changeover times.

Where there are significant differences in changeover time depending on sequence, use the above calculation with average changeover times to get the approximate batch size. Then make the products in the correct sequence that will minimise total changeover time. However, use 'constant sequence, variable quantity' batches – that its, when a batch is due to be made, make all current demand – up to (say) a maximum of twice the EPE batch size, and a minimum of (say) half the EPE batch size.

EPE with Fairly Uniform Demand

Example: ACME makes 6 products A,B,C, D, E, F in a press shop. All changeovers take 30 minutes. Demand for the products translates to daily actual run time of 3, 2, 0.5, 0.5, 0.5, 0.5 hours respectively. Net available working time per day (after breaks, routine maintenance, MTTR/MTBF, team meetings) is 8 hours per day.

Total run time per week = 7 hours

Total changeover time for all products = 3 hours

EPE interval	Run time	c/over time	Total time	Available hours	Feasible?
1 day	7	3	10	8	No
2 days	14	3	17	16	No
3 days	21	3	24	24	Just!
4 days	28	3	31	32	Yes (1 spare)
5 days	35	3	38	40	Yes (2 spare)

A 3-day cycle is feasible, but makes no allowance for problems. The 4 day EPE cycle seems attractive.

The 5-day EPE has 2 hours spare that could be used to do an extra 4 changeovers per week.

EPE with a Strong Pareto of SKU's: Dual scheduling planning

If the SKU range has a strong Pareto shape – in other words some SKUs have very high demand but there is a long tail of very low demand SKUs consider the following procedure can be adopted. (Some may consider this not worth the effort!)

The procedure is essentially a two-at-a-time trade-off whereby products at the high-demand end of the pareto are scheduled more frequently (thereby reducing the batch quantity and WIP) with a corresponding decrease in the frequency of scheduling of products at the low-demand end of the pareto (thereby increasing the batch quantity and WIP). Total changeover time remains approximately the same because each additional batch (and reduction in batch size) and an additional changeover among the high-quantity products is matched by a corresponding increase in batch size and one less changeover time among the low quantity products.

As a simple example, consider 12 'Green' and 'Yellow' SKUs scheduled in a repeating cycle of 10 days. Changeover time between products is assumed constant. For a 20 day cycle the sequence below would be repeated twice, giving 24 scheduling buckets:

Product	A	B	C	D	E	F	G	H	I	J	K	L
Batch size	120	60	48	21	21	18	18	18	15	15	12	6

Now take the outer pairs, A and L. In 20 days there would be two changeovers for each SKU. This would mean an average inventory for A and L as follows:

A: 0.5x120x2cyclesx10 days=1200 SKU-days;

L: 0.5x6x2x10=60; Total 1260 SKU-days

First, double the batch size of L, but schedule an additional batch of A. In 20 days L would be scheduled once but A would be scheduled 3 times, giving batch sizes of 80 and 12 respectively. Total changeovers remain, but average inventory is then 800 for A and 120 for L. A saving of 340 SKU-days.

Then take the next outer products B and K, and calculate. And again, for C and J. And yet again for

D and I. Continue until the SKU-day saving goes negative. The results are shown in the table. (This can be calculated with a simple spreadsheet.)

pair	Average inventory over 20 days SKU-days						Saving in SKU-days
	2 c/o by left-most	2 c/o by right-most	Total SKU days	1 c/o by left-most	3 c/o by right-most	Total SKU days	
A&L	1200	60	1260	800	120	920	340
B&K	600	120	720	400	240	640	80
C&J	480	150	630	320	300	620	10
D&I	300	150	450	200	300	500	-50

Therefore, adjusting the first and last three SKUs would be worthwhile, not more. This would result in the following sequence over 20 days with 24 slots.

Product	A	B	C	D	E	F	G	J	A	B	C	H
Batch size	80	40	32	21	21	18	18	30	80	40	32	18

Product	I	D	E	K	A	B	C	F	G	H	I	L
Batch size	15	21	21	24	80	40	32	18	18	18	15	12

This sequence, compared with the original, saves 340+80+10=430 SKU-days of average inventory, but more important gives a more level schedule – reducing the standard deviation of batch sizes from 31.5 to 20.6. There may be positive implications for subsequent assembly operations and for material handling.

EPE Batch Sizing and Non-Constant Demand: Scheduling Bands

The standard EPE calculation works well for constant demand. What happens when demand is not constant? The following is one good practical solution. This splits scheduling into bands – typically three: stable, small variation, large variation. (See also the Demand Analysis Chapter.)

- Begin with SKUs falling within Glenday 'Green' and 'Yellow' categories that also have normal demand patterns. There is a good chance that a proportion of demands for each of these SKU's will persist throughout the year or at least for a season. A small allowance can be tolerated. If so, these should form the stable band of the repeating schedule throughout the year, consuming (say) 30% of capacity. The EPE calculations will apply and will repeat every period throughout the year. This will bring great stability.

- The next band will comprise perhaps 'Yellow' and seasonal SKUs. Possibly some erratic and lumpy demands? Here, the task is to look out for 'plateaus' – periods during which overall demand for the SKU is fairly constant. EPE calculations can be applied during each plateau period.

- The final band would cater for all other demands.

- In one agricultural machinery case known to the authors there is highly seasonal demand for 4 months that can be anticipated. A level EPE schedule for 80% of SKUs is run with no variation for 8 months to build the anticipation inventory. During the remaining 4 months, customisation, specials and any shortfalls are built.

28.4 Special Batch Size Considerations

We know that a better way to calculate batch sizes is to use the available time to do more changeovers and to drive down the batch size. However, there are situations where the approach needs modification.

- Where there is lots of time available for extra changeovers but the cost of inventory is significant. Continue doing more changeovers until the marginal cost of changeover exceeds the cost of inventory saved.

- Where quality requirements (or process uncertainty) means that scrap almost inevitably results from more changeovers. A changeover should result in an inventory (batch size) saving. If the inventory saving from doing an additional changeover is less than the scrap cost, then the additional changeover should not be done.

Another way of saying this is that batch size reduction (and changeover reduction) has diminishing returns. There will come a point where it is not worth doing an additional changeover. Beware, however, of using this as an excuse. Very quick SMED changeovers can be a huge benefit for flexibility – even if there is adequate capacity.

EPE and Target Changeover Time

Another approach is to calculate the target changeover time that will allow an EPE of (say) one day. For example if there was an average of 7 hours of demand for 6 SKUs run time during an 8 hour per day, would leave 1 hour for changeover. 6 changeovers are required for an EPE of 1 day, so the target changeover time would be an average of 10 minutes. For a 2 day EPE the target would be 20 minutes per changeover. This is a very useful calculation since changeover times below 10 minutes will not yield further inventory or lead time reductions, but could give more free time for other improvement activities.

29 Creating the Lean Supply Chain

29.1 What is supply chain management?

Supply chain management is relatively new discipline: only in the early 1980s did firms realise that their competitiveness was just not determined by what they do, but also what their upstream suppliers and downstream suppliers were doing. Out of that insight came the notion that is it is equally important to manage your supply chain, as it is to manage your own operation. (This is also reflected in Kingman's equation where one of the three influential factors on lead time is arrival variation.)

Having a fast cycle-time in manufacturing is great, but when you have a slow distributor, the customer does not enjoy the overall benefit. In fact, for most manufacturers, their products are a function of their suppliers' processes as much as those of their own processes. Vehicle manufacturers for example will buy about 60-80% of the value of their product ex-factory from suppliers. The actual assembly plant only accounts for about 12% of the cost of manufacturing a vehicle. On top of that comes the cost for distribution, retail and marketing operations, which can account for up to 30% of the list or retail price. In electronics, the actual assembly generally only accounts for 2-5% of the actual of the total product cost. So it is important to note that:

- Supply chain capabilities are a significant determinant of competitiveness since the final product is not the sole achievement of the OEM, but the customer experience is co-determined by the supply chain in terms of quality, cost, delivery
- A significant proportion of the value of the final product is generally sourced from suppliers
- The performance of one tier in the supply chain is a function of the supply and distribution functions, i.e. surrounding tiers. Or put in other words, the supply chain is only as strong as its weakest (poorest) supplier.

Think of the cases of Cisco that had to write off $2.5 billion worth of inventory during the dot.com crash, as it was too slow to adjust its supply chain to a slowing demand in the marketplace. Or of Airbus, that had to delay the delivery of its new A380 flagship product for almost two years as it was not able to deliver correct product specifications to its suppliers – and ended up with cables that were too short. Back to the drawing board as the first aircraft was already in production!

As Martin Christopher says, *'Value Chains compete, not individual companies'*. In traditional Operations Management, you optimise the processes with a single factory, and the assumption is that by linking these local optima, you get a global optimum at the supply chain level. That of course is wrong. In fact, some very costly dynamic dysfunctions can develop in supply chains (the Bullwhip effect is one of them), which lead to amplified orders, demand variability, poor capacity utilisation, stock-outs of some items, and overstocking on others.

The key trick in supply chain management is to consider the entire *system* of suppliers, manufacturing plants, and distribution tiers, and to aim for synergy: the whole is more than the sum of its parts. In other words, to analyse the system by looking at the connections or interfaces between firms, and then manage the system *as a whole*. The differential benefit of supply chain management then is the value you derive by not simply managing individual pieces, but the entire system. According to Martin Christopher, the goal is

'..to manage upstream and downstream relationships with suppliers and customers in order to create enhanced value in the final market place at less cost to the supply chain as a whole.'

There are many supply chains: for new products, we talk about the 'forward supply chain'. For recycling, reuse and remanufacturing of goods after they have ended their economic life we talk about the reverse supply chain. We also talk about external supply chains that cross boundaries of firms, and internal supply chains within the boundaries of a firm. Value streams, the lean name for supply chains, encompass all activities from raw materials to finished product, i.e. both external and internal supply chains.

In this section we will show the basic design of supply chains, show the root causes for the costly distortions that can occur, show how to work with supplier and logistics firms, how to deal with customer orders and the need to customize products, and finally, some general frameworks for designing Lean supply chains. Much of the communication in the supply chain is done electronically (using barcodes, EPOS and RFID and other tools), yet the basic functionality of the supply chain remains the same. It is important to understand these first. Technology can support improving a lean supply chain, yet it cannot create a lean supply chain in the first place!

Who actually manages the supply chain?

The need for, and benefits of, managing the supply chain are obvious: well-managed supply chains should deliver goods in less time, at a better quality, at overall less cost. What is less clear is *who* actually manages the supply chain.

The fundamental problem with supply chain management is that any supply chain is composed of independent businesses – each responsible to their respective shareholders. So there is not a single entity capable of defining and implementing a given supply chain strategy.

Once you have identified that the supply chain does not run optimally, how do you persuade the various companies in the system to change their behaviour? How do you motivate a firm to compromise (sub-optimise) their own operation, for the greater good of an overall more efficient supply chain? Essentially there are only two mechanisms at hand: *power*, and *shared rewards*.

In the first, the more powerful entity in the system simply dictates the changes, and punishes the supplier on non-compliance. This is (or was) common in the automotive industry, where few car makers buy from many smaller suppliers. This approach is not Lean. It does not respect the supplier, and creates bad feelings that in the long run will hurt the car maker.

A better approach is to share rewards, as is common in other sectors. In the grocery retail business for example, Coca-Cola or Unilever are equal to a Tesco or Wal-Mart in power, and shared rewards are needed to motivate partners to change the supply processes. Here, both parties collaborate and either directly share the savings from the process improvement, or the long-term lock-in (essentially the prospect of a renewed contract) persuades suppliers or retailers to comply. This is known as Distributive Negotiation and is discussed in most texts on negotiation.

Narayanan and Raman outline four steps how to go about aligning supply chain processes:

1. **Acknowledge that an incentive misalignment exists**. Use demand amplification mapping to show the current dysfunctions, and highlight the waste.
2. **Diagnose** the cause for the misalignment, using root-cause analyses.
3. **Change incentives** (contracts, performance measures) to reward partners for acting in the supply chain's best interests.
4. **Review periodically**, and educate managers across tiers, so that they understand the implications of their decisions on the other partners in the system.

Further reading

David Simchi-Levi, Philip Kaminsky, Edith Simchi-Levi, *Designing and Managing the Supply Chain*, Irwin McGraw Hill, Boston, (Second edition) 2003

Martin Christopher, *Logistics and Supply Chain Management*, FT Prentice Hall, 5th edition, 2016.

Narayanan, V.G., Raman, A. 2004. Aligning incentives in supply chains. *Harvard Business Review* 82 (11), p.94-103

The three supply chain 'enemies'

Before we get into the more detailed concepts of supply chain management, there are some basic principles that apply to all supply chains alike. There are three main causes for waste in the supply chain:

Variability, as it causes uncertainty that needs to be covered with buffers – in terms of excess capacity, inventory or time. Variability also forms the trigger for the infamous 'bullwhip effect' (see below).

Delay, as the longer the lead-time for the system to respond to a change in demand, the more drastic its reaction will be. Hence, reducing the reaction time also means that the 'ripples' caused in the system will be less severe. Ideally, if all partners in the system have visibility of changes in demand, there should not be any ripples at all. This is the approach behind EPOS, VMI and CPFR discussed below.

Decision-points, as more people 'second-guess' or create forecasts of forecasts, the worse the demand signal will become. A rule of thumb is that every unmanaged hand-off in the supply chain will lead to a doubling of the variation in the demand signal.

In short, the same principles of 'swift, even flow' also apply to supply chains. These simply work best when there is a little variation in the demand signal as possible, quick reaction to (and visibility of) changes in demand, and as few points of interference as possible. Most of the concepts in supply chain management aim to reduce one or several of the three supply chain enemies.

So what makes a supply chain lean?

Supply chains are connected manufacturing processes, so there are two types of wastes that occur: (1) the traditional wastes in each manufacturing operations along the way, and (2), wastes that occur because of poor coordination and scheduling across tiers in the system. It is the second part that is the focus of creating a lean supply chain, namely how to avoid wastes occurring due to poor coordination across tiers in the supply chain. These wastes generally occur because many production planning systems, like MRP, were not designed to consider the implications of their decisions on the wider supply chain. Thus, by default, decisions made at firm level will lead to interface losses, or wastes, in the supply chain. The lean supply chain seeks to eliminate these wastes where possible, by coordinating decisions across all tiers of the system, or value stream.

There are some basic frameworks that summarise the concepts introduced in this chapter. These should serve as simple mental models to remember the key aspects of supply chain management.

3 T's

First is Richard Wilding '**3 T's** of highly effective supply chains', which are **Time**, as any lead-time in the system worsens the bullwhip and causes excess inventory, **Transparency**, as a lack of forward visibility creates uncertainty and ultimately stock or unused capacity, and **Trust,** as long-term collaborative supplier relationships by far outperform short-term adversarial ones.

Triple-A Supply Chain

Another framework that is powerful and easy to remember is Hau Lee's **Triple-A** supply chain, which features **Agility** to respond to changing customer needs, **Adaptability** to long-term changes in markets and technology, and **Alignment** of incentives to enable cooperation and coordination across tiers in the chain. See the table below for details.

Triple-Characters	Objectives	Processes
Agility	Respond to short-term changes in market demand and supply quickly; handle external disruption (such as technological and industrial changes) smoothly	• Promote flow of information with suppliers and customers • Develop collaborative relationship with suppliers • Design for postponement • Build inventory buffers by maintaining a stockpile of inexpensive but key components. • Have a dependable logistics system or partners • Draw up contingency plans and develop crisis management teams
Adaptability	Adjust structure of supply chain network to meet market and/or technology changes, in particular to modify supply-chain network alignment with product architectures/developments	• Monitor market/industrial environment to spot new supply bases and technology changes. • Use intermediaries to develop supplier-chain and logistics activities • Be aware of needs of ultimate consumers not just immediate customers • Create flexible/modularity of product development/architectures • Determine where companies product stand in terms of technology cycles and product life cycles
Alignment	Create incentives for better a firm's performance	• Share information and knowledge openly with suppliers and customers • Lay down roles, tasks and responsibilities clearly for suppliers and customers • Equitably share risks, costs and gain of improvement initiatives

Source: Lee, H.L. (2004), The Triple-A Supply Chain, Harvard Business Review (October), p105.

4V's of Toyota

In their book on Toyota's supply chain, Iyer et al. point to four practices used by Toyota:

Variety: Determine your variety of offerings based on operational efficiency and market demand

Velocity: Maintain a steady flow through all processes of the supply chain

Variability: Manage inconsistencies carefully to reduce cost and improve quality

Visibility: Ensure the transparency of all processes to enable continuous learning and improvement.

These closely overlap with the 'three supply chain enemies' and '3T's', but add the adversarial effect of unnecessary product variety to the picture.

Further Reading

Hau Lee (2004) Creating the Triple-A supply chain, *Harvard Business Review,* October, p.105.

Richard Wilding (2003) The 3Ts of Highly Effective Supply Chains, *Supply Chain Practice*, Vol. 5 Issue 3, p.30-39

Iyer, A. V., Seshadri, S., and Vasher, R., *Toyota supply chain management: A strategic approach to Toyota's renowned system*, (2009), McGraw-Hill

29.2   Uncertainty and the Bullwhip Effect

Think of dynamic distortions as waves on the ocean – the smoother the waves, the less energy the ship loses going in one direction. Supply chains are the same: the more volatile the demand and delivery patterns, the more inventory, expedited shipment and under- or over utilised capacity one can expect. In a study of the grocery retail sector, Kurt Salmon and Associates found that there was 12.5%-25% excess cost in supply chain, with a $30bn cost saving potential in the US grocery sector alone (on a $300bn turnover). Key to understanding these 'ripple effects' is to distinguish the root causes, and the system reaction that follows. Let's start with the most important root cause, uncertainty.

Types of uncertainty

There are three basic types of uncertainty that can have a negative impact on any process, factory of supply chain:

1. **Demand uncertainty.** This type is related to the marketplace - what the customer orders. This can be variable because of weather (e.g. ice cream sales), seasonality (e.g. sales of lawn mowers), or follow a general trend (e.g. customers buying more flatscreen OLED TVs, rather than older types). Other factors that impact on the demand are sales promotions (which general cause temporary upswings, but also downswings for related products), new product introductions or new technologies (see section on disruptive technologies), and competitor action (sales promotions, new products). Apart from promotions and dynamic pricing there is generally little that can reduce demand uncertainty. But beware of assuming that demand is uncertain, before you have explored all the root causes, and be aware of self-caused variation. (See also Chapter 24 on Demand Analysis.)

2. **Conversion or throughput uncertainty.** This is any type of process uncertainty that hits throughput, such as producing defects, machine stoppages and breakdowns, long change-overs, as well as unpredictable lead-times for a given process. These can all be reduced with Lean, TPM and Six Sigma.

3. **Supply uncertainty.** Any type of uncertainty related to the delivery of materials and components. This could be in the form of variable quality, poor on-time delivery performance, and variable lead-times. Supplier co-operation is relevant,

As discussed in the Demand Analysis Chapter it is important to distinguish between **actual** (i.e. caused by the end customer) and **self-created** (i.e. created by poor coordination in the supply chain) uncertainty. For example, when a promotion increases sales for a certain product, generally consumers will pull purchases forward to make good use of the low price. Thus, the high demand during a promotion is generally followed by an artificial and self-created slump in demand. Wal-Mart uses this argument not to have any promotions at all, and instead runs a stable supply chain using 'Everyday low prices' (EDLP). They successfully avert the negative consequences of promotions, and instead lower all prices equally based on the savings from running a stable supply chain.

Further Reading

Davis, T., 'Effective supply chain management', *Sloan Management Review* 34 (4), 35-46, 1993

The 'Bullwhip Effect'

The Bullwhip effect is a supply chain phenomenon in which fluctuations (uncertainty) in orders amplify as they move along a supply chain (see also section on Demand Amplification in the Mapping Chapter). The 'bullwhip' is an increase in order variance as the signal is transmitted from one tier to the next tier in the supply chain.

There is a vertical dimension to do with instability and growth in magnitude and a horizontal dimension to do with fluctuations over time. The Bullwhip effect can seriously damage the performance of a supply chain, however lean an individual player in the chain may be. The effects are the need to keep excess capacity, and to keep fluctuations between control limits (even when there is little fluctuation at the customer end!). Yet another effect is poor customer service.

How does it happen? The basic problem applies to any system that has a *delay* in responding to *variability* in the input signal: as the system takes some time to respond and adjust the output upwards or downwards, there is a slight over- or undershoot that is eventually passed on to the next tier. Here, the reaction tends to be even greater. Have you ever wondered why traffic on the motorway sometimes comes to a complete stop, for no apparent reason? The answer is the bullwhip: as the cars are driving too close to one another, the reaction time for drivers to reduce speed is insufficient, so eventually the 'reaction' of the system amplifies up to the point where traffic comes to a halt. The same effect happens in the supply chain, which we are showing here as a set of two linked water tanks: one representing the retailer (downstream), the other one the supplier (upstream). The amount of water represents the inventory in the system, the valves that control the water flow into and out of the tanks are the ordering decisions.

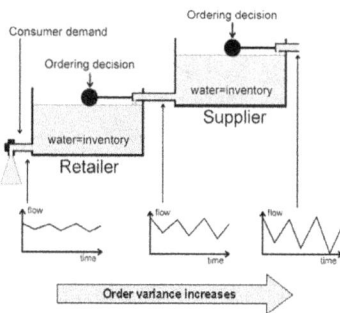

As there is a delay in the information flow, the preceding tier (the supplier in this case) has to react even more strongly to a change in demand: overall, the variance of the order increases. (See figure). (This is similar to Kingman's equation.)

Thus, the demand signal is perceived to be more variable, the higher up in the supply chain one goes. Research has shown that on average, the order variance increases by a factor of 2 for each tier in the supply chain!

What is important to remember here is that 'structure drives behaviour' (as shown very nicely by Jay Forrester and John Sterman at MIT in the 'Beer Game' simulation). That is, many of the elements that cause demand amplification or the bullwhip effect are built into the system, and are not driven by the end customer!

At a fundamental level, the bullwhip effect is a systems effect that cannot be avoided: it will by

default occur in any multi-tiered system that features both variability in the demand signal, and a delay in responding to that variability as the signal moves from tier to tier.

There are several further contributing factors: Lee et al. (1997) identify five inter-related factors as causes, building on the earlier work by Forrester and Burbidge:

1. **Demand forecasting and signal processing**. This is one element of the so-called Forrester or amplification effect. Forecasters at each stage of the supply chain try to hold and adjust safety stocks to buffer against variation. A chain reaction takes place as a result of a minor disturbance leading to greater variation and hence more safety stock all along the chain. Signal processing amplification also results from the way orders are interpreted, so is linked to batching discussed below. Improving the forecasts and reducing uncertainty by sharing information is an effective counter.

2. **Lead times.** The other element of the so-called Forrester effect, results directly from the fact that safety stocks and order quantities are calculated from lead times and variability. Reducing the lead-time improves performance.

3. **Batching.** Also known as the Burbidge effect this results from orders being placed in batches – a large batch followed by no orders, in a repeating cycle. Batches may be ordered for transportation or order cost reasons. The EPE and milk round concept can help here. (See Batch Scheduling.)

4. **Price fluctuations and promotions.** Supply chain players may try to anticipate price increases or take advantage of quantity discounts. Information sharing and coordination of response to increases can help. Elimination of inappropriate quantity discounts in favour of 'every-day low pricing' (EDLP) is effective.

5. **Rationing and inflated orders.** Also known as the Houlihan or 'Flywheel' effect, this results from supply chain partners trying to anticipate shortages or distributors rationing supplies in the interests or fairness. Over ordering can lead to a vicious cycle where the increase is interpreted as an increase in ultimate customer demand rather than a safety stock policy change. Orders lead to shortages leading to higher orders and so on until extra capacity is installed, leading to a collapse in orders. Again, sharing of information is a way to go. Note that these bullwhip factors are usually thought of in a supply chain context but may also occur internally within a plant.

See three enemies of a stable (and Lean) supply chain mentioned above.

Always remember Michael Hammer's quote: 'Inventory is a substitute for information' – where you have perfect information, you do not need any buffer stock. The less reliable information you have, the more inventory you need to hold.

Finally, it is worth pointing out that MRP systems can act as 'triggers' for the bullwhip effects, as they (1) plan on batches, (2) use algorithms such as EOQ or period order quantity that favour larger batches, and (3) tend to group but not to synchronise component material demand signals across multiple products. As a result they tend to produce uneven batch-driven demand signals that often act as trigger for the bullwhip upstream.

Further reading

David Simchi-Levi, Philip Kaminsky, Edith Simchi-Levi, *Designing and Managing the Supply Chain,*(Second edition), McGraw Hill, 2003

Steve Disney and Denis Towill, 'Vendor-managed inventory and bullwhip reduction in a two-level supply chain', *International Journal of Operations and Production Management*, 23: 5/6, 2003

Sterman, J.D. *Business dynamics: systems thinking and modeling for a complex world*, Irwin McGraw-Hill, Boston, 2000

29.3   Managing Supply Chain Risk

We have seen many shocks that have affected supply chain operations in recent years, from the global pandemic, to wars, and of course, climate change. See VUCA in Chapter 4. All of these events threaten the operations of a supply chain, causing the risks of supply failure. So a key ability in management is to assess risk, and to devise strategies for mitigating or hedging against it. There are several stages to risk management: **prevention,** which aims at lowering the odds of the risk occurring, **control**, which reduces the damage if it does occur, **transfer via insurance,** where you pay someone else to take on your risk, **diversification,** whereby you aim not to put all your money on one card, and finally, **hedging**, where you contract for a future price (which prevents both a loss, but also any extraordinary gain). In addition to these, there are also operational means how to reduce risk, called **risk pooling**.

With regards to supply chain management, the risk pooling idea is to redesign the supply chain, the production process, or the product to either reduce the uncertainty the firm faces or to hedge uncertainty so that the firm is in a better position to mitigate the consequence of uncertainty. The basic ways in which this can be done are:

1. **Location pooling**, whereby the inventory from multiple territories and locations is combined into a central or regional facility, which minimizes the risks of stock-outs or overstocking. The square root calculation is a guide. Thus by combining two facilities safety inventory for the same service level can be reduced from $2\bar{v}$ to $\sqrt{2}\bar{v}$ (i.e $1.42\bar{v}$).

2. **Product pooling** or **postponement** or **late configuration**, whereby product configuration is delayed using a modular design, which can serve overall demand with fewer products variants. HP implemented this approach very successfully within its printer division to counter demand uncertainty across markets.

3. **Capacity pooling**, whereby each production facility produces several models, in order to

counter any peaks or troughs for individual models. Volvo uses so-called 'swing models' that are produced in both of its plants to counter any demand fluctuations over the life cycles of its other models.

Overall risk pooling uses the basic principle that pooling several sources of variability, on aggregate, leads to less variability overall. It follows the two rules of forecasting: postponement (and aggregation) increases the quality of the demand signal, and a reduction of lead-time (or forecasting horizon) increases the quality of the signal. Risk-pooling strategies are most effective where demands are negatively correlated (i.e. as demand for one product goes up, the demand for another one goes down). The uncertainty with total demand is much less than the uncertainty with any individual item.

When do you use which approach?

The central two questions in risk management are: (1) how likely is the event, and (2) in case that event takes place, how severe are the consequences? Events like earthquakes will have serious ramifications, but fortunately are very rare. So buffering against this risk (by holding months of inventory, for example) is not feasible. Instead, contingency planning is needed. On the other hand, the risk of losing a container on deep-sea shipping routes is moderate, yet the ramifications are generally not severe. Here, holding safety stock may be an option. (In 1997 a container holding 5m Lego bricks fell overboard off Cornwall. Bricks are still being washed up in 2022! In 2021 a container ship went aground in the Suez Canal causing knock-on effects for container deliveries throughout Europe.)

The approach taken to managing such risks needs to differ. Hopp provides a very useful framework in this regard. Refer to the figure. (Reprinted by permission of Waveland Press, Inc., from Hopp 'Supply Chain Science', Long Grove IL.,Waveland Press, Inc., © 2008, (reissued 2011), All rights reserved.)

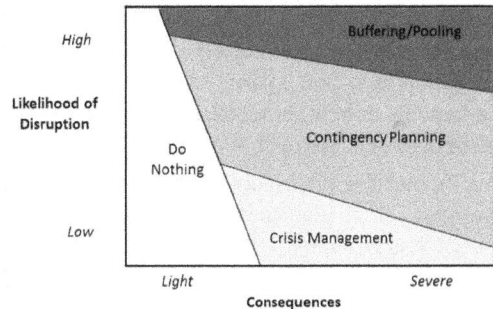

Buffering refers to holding excess resources in terms of capacity, inventory or time to cover against possible fluctuations in demand or supply,

Pooling refers to sharing buffers across multiple sources of variability (such as demand from several markets),

Contingency planning refers defining a set of actions in case the event takes place, so that the response can start without delay, and

Crisis management is a reactive strategy (as distinct from the above proactive options) for events that are so unlikely or unforeseeable that none of the above options apply.

Further reading

David Simchi Levi et al., *Designing and Managing the Supply Chain*, MacGraw-Hill, (2nd ed), 2003

Wallace Hopp, *Supply Chain Science*. Waveland Press, 2011

29.4 Managing Supplier Relations

There are essentially two basic and opposing models how to relate to suppliers: the cost-driven adversarial model, and the long-term collaborative model. The former is the traditional Western model where you aim to negotiate hard, to get the best unit cost. And if next year another supplier offers a better price, you switch. The Japanese model is very different: here the relationship is built on trust, and long-term commitment. In Japan this was further cemented by cross-ownership (the *keiretsu* in Japan, or *chaebol* in South Korea).

However it would be a mistake to assume that there is no competition in a Japanese-style relationship. In fact the reason the Japanese supplier relationship model is so much more successful (for A- and B-parts), is because it merges the benefits of long-term collaboration and trust, with a persistent element of market-pressure.

The Partnership philosophy is that, through co-operation rather than confrontation, both parties benefit. It is a longer-term view, emphasizing total cost rather than product price. Cost includes not only today's price of the part or product, but also its quality (defect / ppm rate), delivery reliability, the simplicity with which the transaction is processed, and the future potential for price reductions.

But partnership goes further: long-term, stable relationships are sought rather than short term, adversarial, quick advantage. The analogy of a marriage is often used. It may have its ups and downs, but commitment remains. In a partnership, contracts will be longer term to give the supplier confidence and the motivation to invest and improve. Both parties recognize that the game whereby low prices are bid and then argued up on contingencies once the contract is awarded is wasteful and counterproductive. Instead, it may be possible for both parties to co-operate on price reduction, sharing the benefits between them. Such co-operation may be achieved through the temporary secondment of staff. See the next section on Supplier Associations.

The features of a Japanese-style supplier partnership are:

1. **Long-term collaborative relationship**, where trust and commitment, as well as respect of the right of mutual existence are the prime directive. There is no opportunistic behaviour ('screwing the supplier') for a short-term advantage. The focus is long-term.

2. **Dual sourcing**: Each component will have few, but at least two, sources. The proportion of the volume is adjusted every year according to supplier performance. So there is a long-term commitment and security, but also an element of market pressure in the relationship.

3. **Joint Improvement activities**: There is a strong collaboration with suppliers on operational improvement; for example Toyota has a dedicated Supplier Support Center (TSSC) in Kentucky to educate suppliers in Lean. Also, while Toyota demand annual cost reductions, these are realised in collaboration, not isolation.

4. **Operations and logistics:** Level production schedules are used to avoid spikes in the supply chain. Also, milk-round delivery systems that can handle mixed-loads, and small-lot deliveries needed for Just-in-Time or Just-in-Sequence supply. The disciplined system of JIT delivery windows at the plant means that suppliers deliver only what is needed, even if this compromises load efficiency in transport.

The Supplier-Partnering Hierarchy

The collaborative supplier relationship model is essential for supporting a Lean supply chain, and can be applied in the Western world as much as it has been used in Japan. The argument that the Eastern keiretsu (Japan) or chaebol (Korea) structures are essential to support long-term relationships have long been disproven, as the Japanese vehicle manufacturers are working as efficiently with Western suppliers, where they do not own parts of the company.

Liker and Choi illustrate how the Japanese manufacturers have built equally strong supply chains to support their US plants. They illustrate a set of principles of building 'deep supplier relations': This works as follows:

Conduct joint improvement activities.

1. Exchange best practices with *suppliers*.

2. Initiate kaizen projects at *suppliers'* facilities.

3. Set up *supplier* study groups.

Share information intensively but selectively.

4. Set specific times, places, and agendas for meetings.

5. Use rigid formats for sharing information.

6. Insist on accurate data collection.

7. Share information in a structured fashion.

Develop **suppliers'** technical capabilities.

8. Build **suppliers'** problem-solving skills.

9. Develop a common lexicon.

10. Hone core **suppliers'** innovation capabilities.

Supervise your **suppliers**.

11. Send monthly report cards to core **suppliers**.

12. Provide immediate and constant feedback.

13. Get senior managers involved in solving problems.

14. Turn *supplier* rivalry into opportunity.

15. Source each component from two or three vendors.

Create compatible production philosophies and systems.

16. Set up joint ventures with existing **suppliers** to transfer knowledge and maintain control.

17. Understand how your *suppliers* work.

18. Learn about **suppliers'** businesses.

19. Go see how **suppliers** work.

20. Respect **suppliers'** capabilities.

21. Commit to co-prosperity.

Trust, Partnership and Dedicated Assets

Another view on the collaborative supplier relation model was given by Jeffrey Dyer in his seminal book in 2000 in which he identified three key characteristics that make the Toyota US supply chain so effective. Although much has changed since Dyer's analysis - for instance Ford has hived off Visteon, GM has hived of Delphi, and Mercedes acquired and subsequently disposed of Chrysler, the points made remain valid and important in many industries. The three interrelated characteristics are:

The critical role of Trust. Trust is where each partner builds confidence in its promises and commitments and does not exploit the vulnerabilities of its partners. Building trust takes time (for example in selecting and favouring suppliers) but then allows fast, flexible flow in new product introduction and in the supply chain. Bureaucracy and waste in the form of transactions can be dramatically cut. Dyer gives impressive evidence of the extent of transaction costs, and the cost of mistrust. He points out that trust also encourages investment, innovation, and stable employment. Dyer shows Toyota in the USA well ahead in trustworthiness.

Investment in dedicated assets. Building on trust allows investment in dedicated assets. Dyer shows that Ford and GM during the 1990s internally manufactured about twice as much as Toyota, had approximately the same proportion of arms-length suppliers, but had approximately one fifth the proportion of supplier partners as Toyota. (Things have changed, since.) Dedicated assets are possible with partners, and in turn allow better productivity, quality, design, and speed.

Incidentally, Dyer points out that the advantages of dedicated assets and partnership are much more important in complex industries - (it is here where Japanese industries are much more efficient), but are far less important in simple product industries where arms-length relationships may be beneficial.

The development and transfer of knowledge throughout the network. Again, made possible with trust and dedicated assets, knowledge transfer (of both explicit and tacit knowledge) is a key factor in improvement in productivity and quality. In our experience Toyota cells in the UK are often far more productive than cells run for other manufacturers within the same supplier site. This is because they enjoy more assistance, get more stable schedules, have more confidence in the future, have more simple procedures, often get better terms, enjoy better coaching, and are less fearful about visits from Toyota improvement experts and engineers than most other customers.

In Japan, and increasingly in the rest of the world, supplier partnership is now expanding down from relationships with first tier suppliers, to second and even third tier. Larger firms in the car industry have been leaders, but other industries and smaller firms are following. The thought, in common with TQM, is that quality is only as good as the weakest link.

Further reading

Jeffrey Dyer, *Collaborative Advantage*, Oxford University Press, 2000

Liker, J.K., Choi, T.Y. 2004. Building Deep Supplier Relationships. *Harvard Business Review* (December), 104-113

Kereitsu and Chaebol

The term 'kereitsu' ('chaebol' is the equivalent in South Korea) refers to a group of companies that are interlocked via cross-shareholding. Generally kereitsus will span across many industry sectors, and include banks and other service providers. Kereitsus have dominated the Japanese manufacturing sector, or even the entire economy, and remain a major aspect of Japanese manufacturing. The main kereitsus are Mitsui, Mitsubishi, Sumitomo (Mazda) and Mizuho (Nissan) and Tokai (Toyota).

Relationships in the kereitsu are traditionally of high mutual trust, collaboration and have a long-term outlook. The term used here is 'anshin', piece of mind, which captures the supplier's confidence that as long as it makes genuine effort, the supply relationship will be sustained.

A common misunderstanding here is that car firms like Toyota will only source from their kereitsu suppliers. This is not true. Firms like Toyota will generally have several sources for each part, and will compare component cost on the open market.

Another common misunderstanding is that the kereitsu supplier relationship always outperforms traditional arms-length relationships. The case of Nissan is instructive here: its suppliers were 'over-embedded', and became complacent and lagged on innovation, which contributed to Nissan's bankruptcy in 1999. After Renault's takeover, it transpired that Nissan was paying up to 20% more for identical parts. Supplier links can also become 'too close', in as far as collaboration can unduly shield from market pressures to remain cost competitive.

Supplier Selection

For Lean supply to work there must of necessity be few or even single suppliers per part. The idea is to work with a few good, trusted suppliers who supply a wide range of parts. During the last decade drastic reductions in many a company's supplier base have taken place. An objective is to remove the long tail of the supplier Pareto curve whereby perhaps 10% of parts are supplied by 80% of the suppliers.

Generally, collaborative long-term supplier partnerships make sense for 'A' and possibly 'B' parts; less so for commodity items, where commodity purchasing via internet auctions may be developing. Part criticality and risk also influence the rationalization decision; you would not risk partnership with a company having poor industrial relations, or weak finances, or poor quality assurance. This means that a team approach is necessary in supplier selection. The Purchasing Officer may co-ordinate, but throughout the partnership Design would talk to their opposite number in Design, Quality to Quality, Production control to Production control, and so on.

There should be little risk of 'being taken for a ride' (also referred to as 'opportunistic behaviour') because the supplier has too much to lose. But there are ways around this too: having one supplier exclusively supplying a part to one plant, but another supplier exclusively supplying the same part to another plant. This spreads the risk whilst still achieving single supplier advantages.

Alternatively there is the Japanese practice of cultivating several suppliers simultaneously but then awarding an exclusive contract to one supplier for a part for the life of the product, and selecting another supplier for a similar part going into another end product.

There are at least four models for thinking about supplier selection and sourcing that should be considered by Lean supply chain managers. Several logistics managers make use of more than one of the following to help structure their selection and rationalization process.

1. The Demand analysis The Demand ABC inventory model, discussed in the Demand Chapter is relevant. Clearly there should be a difference in sourcing policy between runner parts (close partnership?) and stranger parts (loose partnership?). And a difference in policy between expensive and low cost SKU's.

2. Part complexity and logistics supply chain complexity. Consider a two by two matrix with part or process complexity along one axis and logistics supply chain complexity along the other axis. Logistics complexity may also refer to the needs for flexibility and responsive lead times. Long lead time in itself does not indicate logistics complexity. High-High (both process complexity and logistics complexity): here close partnerships are a possibility. The 'low-low' segment may suggest global low cost purchasing via perhaps E Bay. Complex parts and processes but with low logistics difficulties may suggest partnership sourcing on a worldwide basis. Finally, high logistics difficulties but with low part or process complexity suggest local sourcing but from arm's length suppliers.

3. Jeffrey Dyer suggests three categories – internally manufactured, partner suppliers, and arms-length independent suppliers. His analysis shows the huge advantages gained by Toyota in sourcing approximately half its component costs from partner suppliers. But the other two categories each make up approximately one quarter of total component costs. Dyer refers to this mix as the governance profile. But the ideal profile differs by industry favouring a higher proportion of partners in high-tech adaptive industry.

Note however that Toyota does not seem to have joined the web-based purchasing revolution, preferring to deal with a limited number of suppliers in a traditional way. One of the reasons may be the way in which the Internet-based purchasing platforms have evolved: the much-praised COVISINT platform launched by several OEMs in 2000 never delivered on its grand promise of saving $1,000 per car, and soon was abused by vehicle manufacturers for auctions that were entirely decided on by the lowest price, and were rules were frequently bent to the advantages of the OEMs. Not surprisingly, suppliers were reluctant to join, and soon came up with their own purchasing portal, SupplyOn, which assures fair rules and is used successfully by the automotive industry.

The late Clayton Christensen has a concept based on his **'disruptive technologies'** thesis. This is not a supplier selection concept, but more to do with sourcing strategy. The performance of a product type (such as a PC) or major subassembly type (such as hard disk) improves with time. The needs of customers also grow, but generally at a slower rate. In early days in the life cycle, when the needs of customers are above the product performance curve, Christensen calls this 'not good enough'. But as performance grows, the product or subassembly outstrips the needs of customers, even demanding ones. PCs are now in this category for most customers. Christensen calls this 'good enough'. When a product is strongly good enough it is vulnerable to disruptive technologies. Christensen believes that a sea change occurs as products or assemblies move from the not good enough to the good enough category. In the former case, integration is critical to success, with integration of R&D, design, and manufacture. The integrators make the money. But in the good enough category, a company must compete on new dimensions of speed and flexibility. Modules and interfaces are more clearly specifiable. In this case disintegration is required - being able to source the current best components from the appropriate suppliers. Here, power shifts to those that are able to supply the needed modules with the required flexibility. But the OEMs have power also – forcing suppliers to develop more innovative components; in fact saying to them that they are 'not good enough'

Further reading

Jeffrey Dyer, *Collaborative Advantage*, Oxford University Press, 2000

Clayton Christensen et al, 'Skate to Where the Money Will Be', *Harvard Business Review*, November 2001, pp72-81

29.5 Supply Chain Collaboration

Much of the communication (such as forecasts, orders, call-offs, shipping and delivery notifications, as well as location data) is submitted digitally these days. Key mechanisms include dedicated electronic data interchange (EDI) systems, but also barcode and web-based systems are being used. The main advantage is the ability to reduce delays in communication, and to create visibility of inventory and orders for all parties. Both aspects greatly reduce the bullwhip effect and other dynamic distortions. See the three 'supply chain enemies' above!

Vendor Managed Inventory (VMI)

A centralized information system, with actual demand forecasts provided by the first stage to all players in the chain is an effective method of significantly reducing the bullwhip effect. Not quite as good is where each player determines target inventory levels determined from moving averages from the next stage downstream, and uses this target as the basis for orders to the next stage upstream. Disney and Towill suggest that the appropriate use of VMI (vendor managed inventory) may be a solution (see also section below). Here the customer passes inventory information to the supplier instead of orders. The actual inventory at the customer is compared with a pre-agreed reorder point (ROP), set to cover adequate availability. Both parties also agree an order-up-to level (OUP). When actual inventory is at or below the ROP the supplier delivers the difference up to the OUP level. This system can work well between each tier in a supply chain, and is made more effective using milkrounds.

The water-tank model below is an illustration. In VMI the supplier takes over the ordering decision from the retailer. This is beneficial, as it provides the supplier with direct visibility of 'what is going on' at the retailer in terms of stock levels, and most importantly, it also eliminates one decision-tier from the supply chain. As we have seen earlier, the bullwhip effect is driven by lead-times, uncertainty, and hand-offs or decision points. VMI is a powerful tool in reducing the bullwhip effect: it reduces uncertainty by allowing additional visibility of consumption at the retail tier, it cuts lead-times as the supplier does not have to wait for a formal order, and it eliminates a decision point.

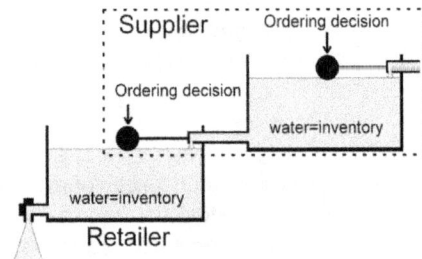

Information Sharing

Information sharing can happen in two ways: the retailer or manufacturer can share its actual sales data ('EPOS', or electronic point of sale data, that retailers generally share with their suppliers), or they can share and align their forecasts with their suppliers (collaborative forecasting). These two types serve very different purposes: EPOS data can be very useful to plan short-term execution and to drive the replenishment signal (where it works like a kanban: sell one, replenish one); shared forecasts have little value in the short term, but are essential to align capacities and avoid bottlenecks and overproduction in the future. Also, sales promotions need to be communicated well in advance, so that the entire supply chain is aware of the likely short-term increases, but does not overreact when the spikes go through the system.

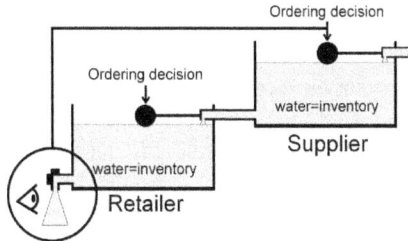

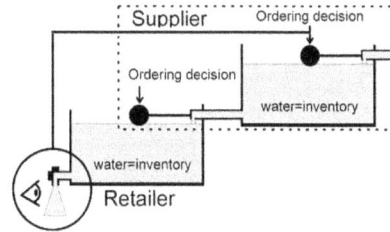

Collaborative Planning, Forecasting and Replenishment (CPFR)

The collaborative planning, forecasting and replenishment approach (CPFR) was piloted by the grocery retail sector (see vics.org), and effectively merges the VMI and collaborative planning elements, to form a model of close supply chain collaboration. Shown below in our water tank model, CPFR uses tools to increase the demand visibility (collaborative forecasting), EPOS data to drive continuous replenishment, as well as reduced decision tiers for inventory and order management (VMI). Thus, it is a powerful tool to manage high-volume supply chains in the fast-moving consumer goods arena. The CPFR model has also been used in many other sectors, but remember these points:

- There is a cost for setting up these systems, so do use a Pareto analysis of suppliers to determine whether it is worth worthwhile

- The system only works where you can include close to 100% of the demand. When some suppliers or customers do not collaborate, the value derived for a SKU from CPFR will be considerably less

- Make sure to use the additional information gained not just for sales planning, but also communicate this to production. Link the production schedule to the customer forecasts. A common mistake is to have the information, but not to use it!

Further reading

Matthias Holweg et al., 2005, Supply Chain Collaboration: Making Sense of the Strategy Continuum, *European Management Journal*, Vol. 23, No.2, p. 170-181

29.6 Lean Logistics

The term 'lean logistics' can mean two things: firstly, the application of lean thinking to improving logistics operations, but more commonly, the changes that need to be made to traditional (full-truck-load based) logistics to support lean manufacturing. In the latter case, two concepts are important: milk-round collection and the waterspider/runner concept.

The long-established milk-round concept is widely applied, across many industry sectors. The idea is that a vehicle travels frequently around a set route starting and ending at the plant, and visiting several suppliers en route. At each supplier a small (daily?) batch of (several?) parts are collected in a particular window slot – typically a half hour. A milk-round may also be found in distribution.

The milk-round concept is similar to the waterspider or runner concept within a plant. Runners have proved a hugely effective concept within plant. Likewise milk-rounds are proving a hugely affective way to reduce amplification and to encourage steady flow between supply chain members. The runner is the internal drumbeat; the milk-round is the external drumbeat. The greater the degree of mixed model, or the lower the 'EPE', the better it will all work. Milk-rounds are also an aid to problem surfacing and improvement. See the separate section on runners and waterspider (Section 27.2).

Milk-rounds can reduce the waste of transport, improve fast, flexible flow and reduce lead-times. It encourages confidence, and as a result reduces buffer inventories and encourages synchronized scheduling. Perhaps a small batch of several parts is collected every day rather than a large batch of one SKU every week. Moreover, an efficient routing calling at several suppliers can reduce total distance. If the company is really clever it can deliver finished products, return totes or even move parts from one supplier to another. Some milk-rounds include cross docking, whereby parts are picked up on a milk-round from more distant suppliers, perhaps using smaller vehicles that consolidate into a larger vehicle.

Synchronization is needed to minimize the length of time inventory spends on the cross dock. The marginal cost of joining a milk-round circuit may be small. This idea should be sold to supplier meetings. The more suppliers or distributors that join, the less the cost to everyone. Today, milk-rounds are 'owned' by either OEMs or first tier suppliers, although the vehicles may be owned by a third-party contactor.

Further reading

Martin Christopher, 'Logistics and supply chain management'. Pearson, 2023.

IMPROVING FLOW

Lean is certainly about Flow – not only creating flow but improving flow and holding the gains. Lean is a never-ending journey. The methodologies for achieving these opportunities are discussed in this section.

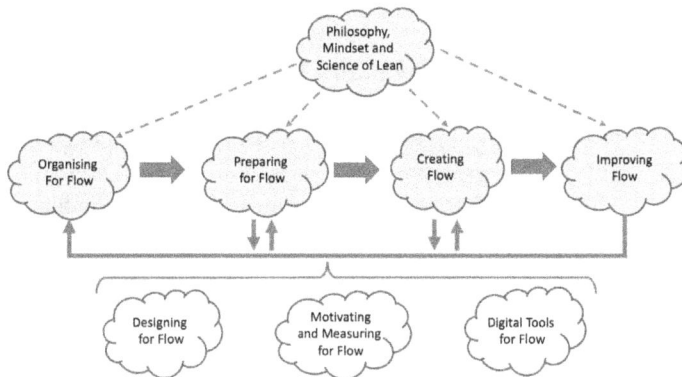

30 Improvement

The essence of Lean is continuous improvement, or kaizen. Without improvement, any organization will fail. To be pervasive, improvement needs to reach all levels and involve all value streams or processes, internally and along the supply chain. For improvement there needs to be a problem – and seeing the problem is the first problem. Problems are not necessarily big things. Since virtually nothing is perfect there is almost always an opportunity – a problem – to which an improvement cycle can be applied. People are often astounded when they hear (as in the Harvard Jack Smith case) that even at Toyota Kamingo plant that had been doing Lean for 50 years, a new manager was tasked to find, on average, one improvement every 20 minutes. These are mainly small adjustments. But each one counts and they accumulate. Peter Willmott, UK TPM guru, does a 'spot the rot' exercise where participants can easily spot 100 potential improvements within an hour at even the most developed plant. It is a matter of 'learning to see'.

30.1 How to get started

The starting point of any process improvement is to aim for a stable, dependable (or predictable process). Unless you have this, any further improvement you make may be a mirage (as effectively the outcome is still random). Thus, the very first step is to create a dependable process that delivers predictable outcome. In SPC terms, the process needs to be 'in control'. Upon this foundation you can then start to improve quality, to create a process that is 'capable'. Only then do you go after speed improvement. Cost reduction is the outcome of all these activities, not the focus!

This sequential approach to process improvement is called the 'sand cone' model and was proposed by Ferdows and De Meyer in 1990. Their sequence is:

Quality → Dependability → Speed → Cost efficiency, as shown in the figure.

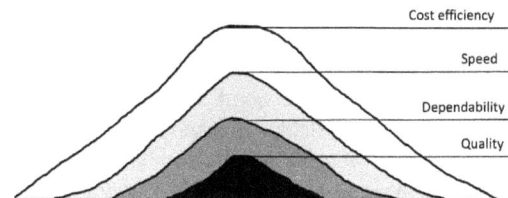

A common assumption is that '5S' is the best starting point for process improvement. This is true – in parts! As just pointed out, you need a stable and predictable process to make meaningful improvements. So those elements in 5S, sorting, straightening and sweeping, make perfect sense early on in a process improvement project. The latter stages of 5S, however, may not be needed, or may not *yet* be needed. Thus it is good to start with tidying up mess, so do a '2S' or '3S', but 5S should involve Standardise and Sustain -- on a pull basis, and not push! See Chapter 14.

Further reading

Ferdows, K., and De Meyer, A. (1990). Lasting improvements in manufacturing performance: in search of a new theory. *Journal of Operations Management*, 9(2), 168-184.

30.2   Lean, the S-curve and Innovation

Throughout history, every innovation has gone through an S-curve. Slow start, take off, fast growth, slowing growth, and maturity. Lean is no different. Neither is Six Sigma.

In the mid 1960's the Olympic record for the high jump was progressing slowly. The dominant approach was the 'Western Roll'. Enter Dick Fosbury with a radically new approach, initially scorned by his coach. But persistence won out and the 'Fosbury Flop' triumphed in the 1968 Olympics. From that moment other approaches were instantly outdated. The Western Roll could be improved upon continuously, but will never again win gold.

So it is with Lean: Kaizen and Breakthrough (or Kaikaku) need to work together. Breakthroughs often come from outside. As Steven Johnson has pointed out in 'Where Good Ideas Come From', they almost invariably involve 'the adjacent possible'. Innovations are imported from adjacent areas. So Henry Ford used ideas from cattle slaughter disassembly, from 'scientific methods' and from the electric motor that enabled high consistency of parts and movement. Toyota built on Ford, but added ideas from the loom, from Juran's quality ideas and Deming teaching, and from American supermarkets and trams.

Within each big S-curve there are little s curves – smaller innovations that accumulate through time. These are necessary, but not sufficient. Without the occasional breakthrough, Lean will invariably stagnate.

A great danger in Lean, as in other fields, is Groupthink. Lean people always talking to Lean people. Always taking only one company as the role model. As the late Harvard Business School professor Clayton Christensen showed, 'disruptive' innovations classically come from the outside and are seen as irrelevant until they too improve and cross the line to become 'good enough'. Perhaps the future of Lean lies with frugal innovations from India, from additive manufacturing, from service concepts, and from IT and AI.

30.3   Organizing for Improvement

There are two aspects of improvement organization. The first is the improvement organization itself centred on the Lean Promotion Office, champions and steering groups. The second aspect is the improvement structure itself comprising five levels from individual to supply chain project.

The Lean Promotion Office, and Lean Six Sigma

When an organization grows beyond perhaps 100 people, certainly 200, it becomes necessary to institutionalise improvement and sustainability. The Lean Promotion Office is a good name, but alternatives are a Kaizen office, a continuous improvement (CI) office, or even a Lean Six Sigma (LSS) Office A rule of thumb is that the Lean Promotion Office (LPO) should comprise 1 to 2% of the workforce full time during a major implementation, and 0.5 to 1% thereafter. These are the internal Lean consultants.

Many organizations, including Toyota, have found that implementing and sustaining Lean requires full time expert facilitators. They are the repository of expertise and should have general responsibility for Lean momentum. Note that the LPO cannot have authority for Lean implementation – that will always lie with line managers. So the ideal head of the LPO is a respected Lean believer, and an influential individual who works through line managers, helping them to achieve their Lean goals. But the LPO is strictly a facilitating function – in no way should it be seen as 'the guys who do Lean around here'. Lean enthusiasts or Lean disciples, irrespective of age or position, should of course, staff the LPO.

Remember the wise words of Sun Tzu, in *The Art of War*, 'Go to the people. Live amongst them. Start with what they have. Build on what they know. And when the deed is done, the mission accomplished, of the best leaders the people will say 'We have done it ourselves''.

The LPO has specific responsibility for developing the general roadmap or Master Schedule for Lean implementation. Specific tasks that the LPO undertakes include assistance with mapping and the development of future state maps, advice on specific aspects such as number of kanbans, tailoring 5S and Lean audit assessment tools for specific value streams, preparing waste questionnaires, running short courses on specific topics such as Lean accounting, coaching on facilitation and presentation skills, and preparing a newsletters and videos. Coaching and mentoring is a major responsibility – often using A3's. Several larger organizations, for instance Ford, have established libraries and on-line information. Dell has packaged on-line training into two hour modules that can be taken in slack periods.

The LPO is a facilitating office, not a doing function. Toyota refers to 'Jishuken' (or 'fresh eyes') groups – this is what a LPO should facilitate and encourage – to look at things in a fresh way, from a different viewpoint.

In addition to the LPO, some organizations have appointed various line managers as expert internal consultants on relevant aspects such as Lean accounting, changeover, poka-yoke, pull systems, and demand management. These people have the responsibility of keeping up with developments on their topic.

The question of the relationship of a Six Sigma function to the LPO is controversial. Today often Lean and Six Sigma have merged into a Lean Six Sigma (LSS) function. However, whilst the Lean Promotion Office is a support role, not doing projects themselves, the Six Sigma function, with Master Black Belts and Black Belts may actually be engaged in more difficult improvement projects, requiring statistical expertise. Both functions, Lean and Six Sigma, should be engaged in training. But beware – some LSS training is mostly about Six Sigma, and only superficially about Lean. In the author's recent experience, some LSS Black Belts have very limited Lean knowledge, although they may be excellent Six Sigma practitioners. The question of elitist-type 'Black Belts' remains controversial.

30.4   The Hierarchy of Improvement

Kaizen, or Lean improvement needs to be organised on five levels in most, if not all, organizations aspiring towards Lean.

Level 1: The Individual

The individual needs to be recognised as the expert of her own process. As such, she needs to understand not only the process itself in great detail but also why the process is necessary and how it fits into the wider value stream. So, not only inserting a car's trunk (boot) seal in the best possible way, but knowing the necessity for keeping out damp and dust. Shingo suggested that the 'know why' or underlying philosophy is the most important stage of learning. So both improvement and project sustainability begin with the individual at the workplace, an aspect that is covered by TWI job breakdown sheets. ('Reasons for key points'.)

At the individual workstation level there are always opportunities for waste reduction – work piece orientation, inventory and tool location, work sequence, ergonomics, poka-yoke, and on and on. Toyota South Africa calls their individual program 'Eyako' – the Zulu word for 'my own'. The team leader has an important role to play here – encouraging, facilitating and recognising achievement – and bring individual improvements to the attention of others. Individual 'thank you' notes carry much weight.

At Toyota's North Wales plant there is an excellent walk-through exhibit showing examples of good and bad quality – and the consequences. All employees take the tour.

Level 2: The Work Team or Mini Point Kaizen

Groups or Teams of perhaps 6, that work in a cell or on a line segment undertake improvement projects affecting their collective work area. Examples include work flows, cell layout, line re-balance, 5S, footprinting, and cell-level quality. Some activities may result from 'point kaizens' identified during wider current state mapping. These initiatives may be done 'on the fly' as a result of team meetings, or short kaizen event activities. They may be facilitated or assisted by the section leader or LPO. Many of the initiatives would arise as a result of issues being surfaced at daily team meetings or as a result of TWI job method (JM) analysis. Recognition is crucial, so the team needs to present improvements to a wider audience. Do not make the mistake of using a level 3 kaizen event when the team can comfortably do it themselves.

Scholtes recognises that there is a difference between 'teams' and 'teamwork'. He describes that 'Teams' refers to small groups of people working together towards some common purpose. Teamwork refers to an environment in the larger organisation that creates and sustains relationships of trust, support, respect, interdependence, and collaboration'. This understanding recognises that it is relatively easy to establish a team, but to establish an environment for teamworking is a lot more difficult. He quotes Petronius Arbiter in what would be well recognised within many organizations:

'We trained hard, but it seemed that every time we were beginning to form up into teams, we would be reorganised. I was to learn later in life that we tend to meet any new situation by reorganising; and a wonderful method it can be for creating the illusion of progress while producing confusion, inefficiency and demoralisation.'

Kata methodology (both improvement and coaching type) seeks to overcome this, by taking small, tentative, experimental steps and learning.

Level 3: Kaizen Groups

A Kaizen Event is carried out in a local area, but involves both more time (typically 3 to 5 days full time) and outsiders. These events address more complex issues than the work group can handle comfortably. Examples include more substantial layout changes, the implementation of a single pacemaker-based scheduling system together with runner route, and integrating manufacturing and information flows. For many companies, event groups are the prime engine for improvement. Unlike the level 2 improvement teams, this type of group forms for the specific purpose of the event, and disbands thereafter.

Level 4: Value Steam Improvements: Flow Kaizen Groups.

Flow kaizen groups work across a full internal value stream, taking weeks to 3 months for a project. Today in some organisations they may be labelled as Lean Six Sigma projects. They are the prime engines for creating future states. Their targets would be those set out in a future state and action plan exercise. (Refer to the mapping Chapter). Value Stream groups are normally not full time although some members may work uninterrupted for a number of days. They would be led by a project manager, often assisted by the LPO, and sometimes mentored by consultants. The group would be a multi-disciplinary, working along a complete process or value stream and across several areas and functions. Flow kaizen projects would address process issues, system issues, and organizational issues.

Level 5: Supply Chain Kaizen Groups.

Similar to Flow Kaizen Groups, these groups work in the supply chain. They will invariably comprise part-time representatives from each participating organization. A respected project manager, typically from the OEM company would be appointed, and there is a greater role for consultants. A 'Seeing the Whole' value stream map would typically be the centrepiece.

Further reading

John Bicheno and Phil Catherwood, *Six Sigma and the Quality Toolbox,* PICSIE Books, 2005

Mike Rother, *Toyota Kata*, McGraw Hill, 2009

Richard Schonberger, *Best Practices in Lean Six Sigma Process Improvement*, Wiley, 2008

Isao Kato and Art Smalley, *Toyota Kaizen Methods*, CRC Press, 2011

Conrad Soltero and Patrice Boutier, *The 7 Kata*, CRC Press, 2012

31 Kaizen

31.1 The Philosophy of Kaizen

Quality begins with the customer. But customers' views are continuously changing and standards are rising, so continuous improvement is required. Kaizen is dedicated to continuous improvement, in small increments, at all levels, forever. Everyone has a role, from top management to shop floor employees.

Imai believes that without active attention, the gains made will simply deteriorate (like the engineers' concept of entropy). But Imai goes further. Unlike Juran who emphasises 'holding the gains', Kaizen involves building on the gains by continuing experimentation and innovation.

According to Imai there are several guiding principles. These include:

- Questioning the rules (standards are necessary but work rules are there to be broken and must be broken with time)
- Developing resourcefulness (it is a management priority to develop the resourcefulness and participation of everyone)
- Try to get to the Root Cause (try not to solve problems superficially)
- Eliminate the whole task (question whether a task is necessary at all)
- Reduce or change activities (be aware of opportunities to combine tasks).

These are similar to the traditional industrial engineering or TWI job methods approach of 'Eliminate, Combine, Rearrange, Simplify'.

31.2 The Kaizen Flag

The Kaizen Flag is a famous diagram developed by Imai and widely copied and adapted. The flag portrays the three types of activity that everyone in a Kaizen organization should be involved with. These three are 'Innovation, 'Kaizen', and 'Standardization' against level in the organization. In the original, senior management spends more time on 'innovation' (to do with tomorrow's products and processes), a definite proportion on 'kaizen' (to do with improving today's products and processes), but also a small proportion of time on 'standardisation' (that is, following the established best way of doing tasks such as, in top management's case, policy deployment and budgeting). A standard method is the current best and safest known way to do a task, until a better way is found through kaizen.

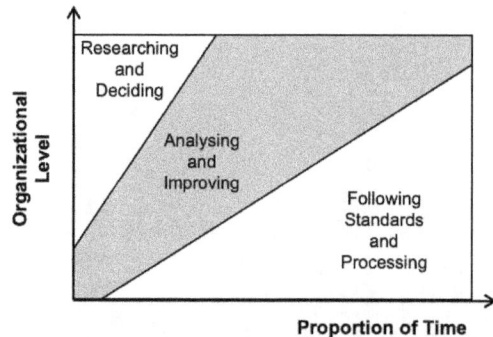

Middle managers spend less time than top managers on innovation, about the same time on kaizen and more time on standardisation. Operators spend a small, but definite, proportion of time on innovation, more time on kaizen, and the majority of time on standardisation.

Kate Mackle, former head of the British Kaizen Institute, explains that innovation is concerned with preventing waste from entering tomorrow's processes, kaizen is concerned with getting waste out of today's processes, and standardisation is concerned with keeping waste out.

The version of the flag presented above has been developed based on Imai's original, but taking into account our experience. Here 'processing' is following the current standard best and safest known way.

Further reading

Maasaki Imai, *Kaizen: The Key to Japan's Competitive Success*, McGraw Hill, New York, 1986

Maasaki Imai, *Gemba Kaizen*, McGraw Hill, New York, 1997

31.3   Kaizen Events

Kaizen events fill the gap between individual, local improvement initiatives and bigger initiatives such as value steam improvement. They are a means to get cross-functional and multi-level teams involved in a Lean transformation. In that respect, kaizen events have a dual role – they make improvements but also to teach and communicate. An important and stimulating aspect of kaizen events is that they are done over a very short period of time, thereby allowing manager involvement that might otherwise not be possible.

What comes to mind when one says 'Kaizen Event' is the 5-day variety. However, 'Mini Kaizens' taking from half a day to two days are a useful variant, have become more popular. What is described below is the full 5-day variety. The one or two variety is essentially the same process but streamlined and downsized with regard to participation.

Most kaizen events are focused on internal processes. But there is another, growing opportunity: the customer-focused kaizen event. Here the focus shifts to solving (or dissolving!) the customer's problems or improving the customer's effectiveness. This means putting yourself in the shoes of the customer. It means redefining the system boundary to include the customer.

Beware! *It is very tempting to rush into a kaizen event.* It may even produce good results and make everyone feel good. But what happens if the process is the wrong process? Then the event is simply rearranging deckchairs on the *Titanic*. So priority is essential. Tackle unstable zones first!

Kaizen events are about 'going for it', about a preference for getting 80% of the benefit now rather than 100% of the benefit but much later, about learning by doing, by trial and error. It is also about involvement. It is about real empowerment to 'just do it' without asking for permission to make every little change. A well-planned and followed through event has a good chance of sustaining its improvements over an extended period. Poorly planned and executed events, however, have frequently slipped back to the original state – and

have given such events a poor name in some organizations.

Today, 'Kaizen Blitz' is well tried in both service and manufacturing companies. The name is used by the US Association for Manufacturing Excellence, but also is an oxymoron since kaizen is continuous but blitz is instantaneous3 In the UK, Industry Forum (IF) has adopted a standard approach for kaizen – referred to as the Master Class process. The IF methodology has spread from automotive to, amongst others, aerospace, metals industry, and construction. Some consulting groups such as TBM and Simpler have developed their own versions. We prefer the term kaizen event. An alternative is 'Jishuken', literally 'autonomous study'.

An appropriate quote to introduce kaizen events is:

> *'Whether you believe you can,*
> *or whether you believe you can't,*
> *you're probably right.'*
> (Henry Ford)

31.4   The Kaizen Event Process

Whatever the format, the following activities have to be worked through: Here follows a proven methodology:

Some weeks ahead of the event:

- Select the area – probably from mapping an end-to-end value stream or from an accumulation of problems. But certainly take the overall 'systems view' of the process, including the customer.

- In service events, give specific consideration to whether the system boundary or problem area should extend to include customer systems. It is important to see the process from the customer's perspective.

- Select an appropriate time for the event – this is more important in an office than a factory because variation is usually larger.

- People from the chosen area need to be warned about the event, and participants sought.

- Measures: Decide on relevant measures for the area and take the measures.

- Team selection: one or more facilitators, front line managers from the area, the event owner, participants from the area, subject matter experts, people from the next most likely area for an event, outsiders. Around 12 is a good number – bigger for bigger areas, smaller for smaller areas.

- Draw up an 'Event Charter' covering Focus and aims, current issues, the event boundary, participation, prior training, dates, catering, health and safety, and whether work will continue in the area while the event proceeds. Also, identify any inventory that must be built up in anticipation of the event.

The event itself: The following is typical for a 5-day event:

- Day 1: Introductions, aims and scope, background – why is the event important, event methodology, basic Lean training including mapping, waste awareness, tools such as fishbone diagram, and if relevant practice on observation timing.

- Day 2: Go to the area and observe, map the routings, time durations, discuss the process with the people. Possibly the customers in some types of service process. Many offices have longer cycle operations so it may not be possible to observe or time all activities, so tagging or simulation may be used. If possible observe several cycles. Begin to generate ideas.

- Day 3: Idea generation, discussion around the maps and formulate priorities and the implementation plan. Discuss with office workers and other shifts. Begin implementation.

- Day 4: The main day for implementation. Try out and adjust. Begin to prepare flipcharts for the presentation on Day 5. Measure results.

- Day 5: A final check and adjust. Document the new process. List follow up items. Prepare an A3 summary sheet. Finish flipcharts for presentation. Present to area managers and directors. Agree next steps. Enjoy the free buffet.

After the event it is necessary to:

- Close off any outstanding points. The persons responsible for doing these mopping-up mini-projects must be identified. The event champion or a line manager MUST follow these up. Kaizen events lose credibility if the list of outstanding topics are never closed down.

- Have a review session every (say) month for a period of (say) 6 months. These may be very short meetings. But they look at the continuing performance of the area and, importantly, record lessons learned. In other words they are 'after action reviews'.

Some lessons learnt about kaizen events

- The workshop itself is the easy part. The harder and longer part is preparation and follow-up. An approximate time split is 40% preparation, 30% workshop itself, and 30% follow-up.

- The participation of managers in events is essential. Without this they will be lukewarm or even critical. Participation also helps overcome the problem of gaining authorization.

- The participation of the supervisor or team leader from the area is essential.

- Moreover, the supervisor should attend one or two events in other areas before it is the turn of his or her area. Think how you would feel if a team descended on your area for a week and produced a 30% productivity improvement. (Not too good – you may be motivated to show that what has been done was not all that good in retrospect.) Ideally, when it is the turn of the supervisor to have a kaizen event in his area, she will already be the most enthusiastic participant – having experienced it elsewhere.

- Kaizen events should be co-ordinated through a Lean Promotion Office (or similar) in relation to a wider Lean implementation programme.

- All participants should have a clear understanding how the particular event contributes to the overall Lean vision or objectives.

- A good facilitator is invaluable. The ability to spot waste and opportunity builds slowly. Take the opportunity to transfer some of these skills.

- Events work better in supportive companies. Do not set expectations too high. Under promise and over deliver.

- Sustainability remains the big issue.

- Kata methodology is recommended.

31.5 Recording the Lessons

Many useful points, both big and small come out of kaizen events. They need to be recorded so they will be available to other parts of the organization. It is a 'drag' to have to write up the lessons but if it is not done the experience will be lost. Several organizations have set up data bases that can be quizzed on an intranet. Remember that 'knowledge management' should ideally include both 'explicit' (factual, hard) and 'tacit' (experiences and soft) information. At a minimum, set up a data base with:

- Name of Event
- Key words
- Participants.

To be able to speak to someone who has been involved in a similar project is the most valuable aspect. Thereafter, the data base could include, short notes, digital photos, value steam maps, sketches, and even voice notes.

Further reading

Nicola Bateman, *Sustainability.... A Guide to Process Improvement*, Lean Enterprise Research Centre, Cardiff University and Industry Forum, 2001.

Sid Joynson and Andrew Forrester, *Sid's Heroes: 30% Improvement in Productivity in 2 Days*, BBC, London, 1996

Anthony C Laraia, Patricia Moody, and Robert Hall, *The Kaizen Blitz: Accelerating Breakthroughs in Productivity and Performance,* John Wiley and Sons, New York, 1999

Siobhan Geary, MSc dissertation on Kaizen Blitz, LERC, Cardiff, 2006.

32 Problem Solving

It has become clear that there are two elements to improvement, namely *continuous improvement* and *breakthrough improvement*. These are two faces of the same coin, both are necessary, neither is sufficient on its own! Thus Juran refers to 'breakthrough' activities, using 'project by project' improvement, to attack 'chronic' underlying quality problems as being different from more obvious problems. Davenport, in the context of business process reengineering, has referred to 'the sequence of continuous alteration' between continuous improvement and more radical breakthroughs by reengineering. And Womack and Jones discuss 'kaikaku' (also called kaizen-blitz, or rapid improvement events) resulting in large, infrequent gains as being different from kaizen or continuous improvement resulting in frequent but small gains.

32.1 Improvement Types

A traditional industrial engineering idea is that breakthrough or major event improvement activities are not continuous at all, but take place infrequently in response to a major change such as a new product introduction or in response to a problem or 'crisis'. But during the past few years, through the 'Kaizen event', we have learned that effective breakthrough should be both proactive and frequent.

More senior management working across a value stream generally drives breakthrough or Flow Kaizen. Incremental or Point Kaizen is led by team leaders, and sometimes by Six Sigma Black Belts working on local issues that have arisen either through value stream analysis (proactive), or from workplace suggestions (reactive).

There are therefore four types of improvement, as shown in the figure. There is, or should be, a place for all four types in every organisation. Kaizen and

kata form the core passive approaches should always continue. However, if all improvement is of the passive, reactive type the company may well slip behind.

Unfortunately, several British factories think they are doing kaizen, but their brand of kaizen is 'passive' or left to chance. Improvements are left to the initiative of operators or industrial engineers or managers: if they make improvements - good. If they don't - 'oh well, it'll happen sometime'. But sometime never comes.

IMPROVEMENT CATEGORIES		
Incremental ('Point Kaizen')	**Breakthrough ('Flow Kaizen')**	**Execution:**
Suggestion schemes; Self-directed teams; Quality Circles; Open Book Mgmt; 5S; Waste awareness	Industrial Engineering; Operations Research; (Some) Six Sigma	Passive/ Enabled
Line stop; Andon; Heijunka; Visual Mgmt; Inventory withdrawal; 'Chalk circles'; Red Tags; Six Sigma projects; Kaizen events	Value Stream Mapping; Supply Chain Development	Driven/ Enforced

Note: An earlier version of figure was shown in *Cause and Effect Lean* (Bicheno, 2002) A similar concept is used in by Hayes et al. *Pursuing the Competitive Edge*, Wiley, 2005.

32.2 Passive Incremental

Passive incremental may also be termed 'reactive'. A reaction takes place in response to a crisis. By contrast, enforced improvement is proactive. 'Crises' are actually engineered and the pressure kept on. For example, Intel brings out a new chip at regular, paced intervals and does not wait passively for technological breakthrough. 3M dictate that

30% of revenues will come from new products every year. This forces the pace.

In some plants, workers take improvement initiatives simply to make their worklife easier. They may never have heard of kaizen. Whilst this is to be encouraged, it must be made easy for workers to incorporate such improvements into standardized work. Team leaders have an important role here.

Passive improvement has been around for many years, and it too is found in two categories - incremental and breakthrough. Classic passive incremental improvement approaches are the suggestion scheme, with or without rewards, and the Quality Circle. Please do not regard 'passive' as somehow inferior.

Suggestion Schemes and Idea Management

Most suggestion schemes fail, but a main reason is mismanagement. Managed well they are powerful resource for continuous improvement. .

Thomas Edison is reported to have said that the way to have great inventions to have many inventions. The same applies to suggestions. Guidelines for better schemes follow:

- First, the attitude. Toyota has the attitude that all suggestions are valuable, so the company is prepared to make a loss on more mundane suggestions to develop the culture of improvement. At the top end of the Pareto the company reckons that the top 2.5% of suggestions pay for the entire reward programme, even though a good number of suggestions at the bottom end are loss-making, taking into account the implementation time. (One is reminded of the classic statement about advertising, 'I waste half of the money I spend, but the problem is I don't know which half'.)

- The 80/20 Principle of Improvement from Robinson and Schroeder says that 80% of performance improvement potential comes from the front line; only 20% from management initiatives. Belief and humility is required.

- Psychological Safety. 'Drive out fear', said Deming. Do employees fear making suggestions that impinge on manager status? Amy Edmondson of Harvard Business School believes this to be widespread. A 'no fears' culture is powerful but must be supported and demonstrated by attitudes from the top.

- Martin Lindstrom believes, amusingly, that 'bureaucratic red tape, bad excuses and corporate bullshit' is widespread and should be countered by a full-time 'Ministry of Common Sense' that is tasked with their removal. Often the opportunity for 'common sense' fall between two sections. Everyone has encountered niggles - form filling, poor web sites, silly signs, KPIs, etc. that, somehow, perpetuate. Many have not been experienced by senior managers. 'Encourage Yelling' says Robinson and Schroeder.

- Discard the suggestion box, and an approval committee that meets monthly. They often prove to be the butt of cynical jokes.

- Suggestions are not just savings. Quality of life, environmental issues, local community are just a few areas where suggestions are welcomed.

- Make it easy to submit suggestions. No bureaucracy. Some organisations (e.g. Virginia Mason hospitals) encourage ideas to be submitted electronically, and have a reminder screen on log-in.

- Acknowledge all – and fast. Toyota also insists that all suggestions are acknowledged within 24 hours and evaluated within a week. Non-acknowledgement and non-recognition have probably been the major reason for suggestions schemes producing poor results and being abandoned.

- Show progress on a visual board, prominently displayed. This should show the stages of progress, from submitted to implemented. Let operators design the board.

- An Ideas, Suggestions, and Problems Solved data base is in place at several companies with multiple sites. Keywords are used. If there is an issue, the first step is to search the data base.

- Where a suggestion is rejected, explain the reasons carefully with empathy. Certainly no hint of criticism.

- Facilitators play an important role. Many ideas are not fully developed and require help from engineers and managers. Time and a procedure must be allowed.

- Leadership, of course, is vital – to support and encourage. By the way, there is an all-too-common sequence whereby leaders are initially enthusiastic but this fades away. Fix a monthly event where senior management attendance is mandatory?

- Give small rewards. Contrary to popular conception, the reward-based suggestion scheme is alive and well at many Japanese companies. At Toyota's US plant, for instance, rewards are based on points and range from $10 (for submission, irrespective) to $10,000. (We disagree with the top end. These can play havoc with teamworking.) However, a high value reward could be shared by a team. One company has a quarterly 'lucky dip' for all suggestions made (not necessarily implemented) with the winner getting a substantial reward.

- Publicise the results.

- Measure the number and locations of ideas and suggestions. Show a measles chart. Set an expectation for submitted ideas.

- Yuso Yasuda has described the Toyota suggestion scheme or 'Kaizen system'. The scheme is co-ordinated by a 'creative idea suggestion committee' whose chairmanship has included Toyota chairmen (Toyoda and Saito) as well as Taiichi Ohno. Rewards for suggestions are given at Toyota based on a points system. Points are scored for tangible and intangible benefits, and for adaptability, creativity, originality, and effort. The rewards are invariably small amounts, and are not based on a percentage of savings. However operators value the token reward and the presentation ceremony itself. Note the contrast with typical Western Suggestion Schemes.

Quality Circles

Team-based Quality Circles are an integral part of the Toyota Production System. At Toyota, QC presentations to senior management occur almost every day. At Japanese companies QCs often meet in their own time. This is also known as Jishuken. There is often both a suggestion scheme and quality circles.

An important point is that QCs are learning events, not just team-based problem solving. QCs are an important way for teams to learn both the tools and the teamworking skills of TPS. This why there is one or more full-time Jishuken coaches. At Toyota, the best QC presentations go forward into regional presentations and may go forward to presentations in Japan. This gains status, and the emphasis is on learning, not on a reward-trip 'jolly'.

Management involvement and support are crucial elements. Edward Lawler has described a 'cycle of failure' for many Western QCs. The following sequence is typical. In early days the first circles make a big impact as pent-up ideas are released and management listens. Then the scheme is extended, usually too rapidly, to other areas. Management cannot cope with attending all these events, and is in any case often less interested. There is no or inadequate coaching and support. In the initial phases, the concerns of first line supervisors, who often see QCs as a threat to their authority, are not sufficiently taken care of in the rush to expand. Some supervisors may actively sabotage the scheme; others simply do not support it. Then, as time goes on, with less support from management and supervision, ideas begin to run out. The scheme fades. And it is said, 'QCs are a Japanese idea which do not work in the Western culture'. (By the way, it was Deming who introduced circles to Japan, albeit that Ishikawa refined the methods).

From the forgoing, for both Suggestion Schemes and Quality Circles there aa few important lessons; (1) not all improvements will pay, but creating the culture of improvement is more important; (2) Give it time, and expand slowly; (3) recognition is important - management cannot always be expected to give personal support, so establish a facilitator or function that can do so; (4) emphasize learning; (5) any rewards are tokens of appreciation, not a 'jolly'; (6) do not underestimate potential opposition; (7) react rapidly to suggestions and (8) give groups the tools, coaching and techniques – often provided by a facilitator - and the time.

32.3   Passive Breakthrough

Many traditional industrial engineering and work-study projects are of the passive breakthrough type, particularly when left to the initiative of the Industrial Engineering department. Of course, IEs also work on enforced breakthrough activities initiated by management or by crisis, but passive breakthrough activities, led by IEs, have undoubtedly been a major source of productivity improvement over years. Many of Taiichi Ohno's activities could be classified as passive breakthrough. (Apparently Ohno was a great experimenter on his own in the dead of night.) But today we recognise that many I.E. (or for that matter Six Sigma) projects done in an elitist way are unlikely to be sustained.

32.4   Enforced Incremental

Kaizen, as practised at Toyota, is the classic here. Waste elimination should not only be a matter of chance that relies upon operator initiative, but is driven perhaps by a Hoshin priority. There are a number of ways in which this is done:

Response Analysis

At Toyota operators can signal, by switch or chord, when they encounter a problem. At some workstations, there are a range of switches covering quality, maintenance, and materials shortage. When an operator activates the switch, the overhead Andon Board lights up highlighting the workstation and type of problem. People literally come running in response. But the sting is in the tail: a clock also starts running which is only stopped when the problem is resolved. These recorded times accumulate in a computer system. They are not used to apportion blame, but for analysis. Thus at the end of an appropriate period, say a fortnight, a Pareto analysis is done which reveals the most pressing problems and workstations. Andon does not necessarily result in line stoppage. If the operator feels that he is too far behind time within the cycle time, he will pull the cord. The situation can often be recovered within the cycle.

Line Stop

A Toyota classic, related to the above, allows operators on the line to pull a chord if a problem is encountered. Again, the Andon Board lights up. Again, the stoppage is time recorded. But the motivation to solve the problem is intense because stopping the line stops a whole section. This means application of the 5 Whys root cause technique. (See later section). Toyota in fact splits the assembly line into sections that are separated by small (one car?) buffers, so line stop only stops that section not the whole line.

Inventory withdrawal

Many will be familiar with the classic JIT 'water and rocks' analogy, whereby dropping the water level (inventory) exposes the rocks (problems). This is done systematically at Toyota. Whenever there is stability, deliberate experimentation takes place by withdrawing inventory to see what will happen. Less well known is that this is a 'win win' strategy: either nothing happens in which case the system runs tighter, or a 'rock' is encountered which according to Toyota philosophy is a good thing. It is not any rock, but the most urgent rock. Deliberate destabilisation creates what Robert Hall has referred to as a 'production laboratory'. However, Toyota is not averse to adding inventory where necessary. (See also Rock-Boat analogy).

Waste Checklists

Toyota makes extensive use of waste checklists in production and non-production areas alike. A waste checklist is a set of questions, distributed to all employees in a particular area, and drawn up by the LPO, asking them simple questions: 'Do you bend to pick up a tool', 'Do you walk more than 2 yards to fetch material', and so on. Where there is a positive response, there is waste. The result is that individuals and teams never run out of ideas for areas requiring improvement.

Kobayashi's '20 Keys' is a classic, long-established methodology and audit. Likewise, the Shingo Prize.

The 'Stage 1, Stage 2' cycle

Toyota's improvement culture or belief stems from the widely held attitude that each completed improvement project necessarily opens up opportunity for yet another improvement activity. For want of a better phrase, Bicheno has termed this 'stage 1, stage 2' (See *Fishbone Flow*) after a list of Lean 'stage 1' activities that lead to 'stage 2' opportunities which in turn lead to stage 1 opportunities, and so on. The list of possible chains is very large, but an example will suffice. Thus setup reduction (stage 1) may lead to reduced buffers (stage 2), which may lead to improved layout (stage 1), leading to Improved visibility (stage 2), leading to improved quality (stage 1), leading to improved scheduling (stage 2), and so on and on.

32.5 Enforced Breakthrough

Active value stream current and future state mapping drive this category of improvement. They generally target a complete value stream. This type must be subject to regular action review cycles and an action plan or master schedule. (Refer to the Mapping Chapter). If a value stream map simply hangs on the wall without an accompanying master schedule it would be classified as passive breakthrough, if at all. Supply chain ('Seeing the Whole') projects would also be classified as enforced breakthrough.

Kaizen events are a special case of enforced breakthrough and are the subject of an earlier section in this Chapter. It is breakthrough because typical events achieve between 25% and 70% improvements within either a week or within a month at most. On the other hand events are typically related to a small area, so are frequently more 'point kaizen' than 'flow kaizen'. It is enforced because the expectations and opportunities are all in place. 'No' and 'it can't be done' are simply not acceptable. Concentrated resources are applied.

Further reading

Alan Robinson and Dean Schroeder, *The Idea-Driven Organization*, BK, 2014

Martin Lindstrom, *The Ministry of Common Sense*, John Murray, 2021

Alan Robinson and Dean Schroeder, *Ideas are Free*, BK, 2004 and 2006

Andy Brophy and John Bicheno, *Innovative Lean*, PICSIE, 2010. (Gives details of Idea Management Systems in several companies)

John Bicheno, *Fishbone Flow*, PICSIE, 2006

32.6 Improvement Cycles

A recognised and understood improvement cycle gives a disciplined framework for the process of improvement. It is of great value to have a standardised approach to improvement in any organization. There are several variants, but all basically similar. The cycles can be used on various levels – from Hoshin or Policy Deployment at the strategic level to value steam implementation, to organizational change (the 'unfreezing, changing, refreezing' cycle is a variation), to training, and to the smallest process change.

Whatever cycle is used, it should be thought of as an overarching approach often used with supplementary tools such as 5 why, root cause problem solving, and force field analysis.

Plan, Do, Study, Act (PDSA)

The widely used PDCA or PDSA cycle has already been described in the Lean Mindset Chapter. In the sections below some alternatives are discussed.

DMAIC

The Six Sigma methodology uses a variation of PDSA known as DMAIC (or Define Measure Analyse Improve Control). This has added several useful points. (See also Section 20.5). You will notice that there is not a one-to-one relationship between PDCA and DMAIC. DMAIC has expanded upon the critical 'Plan' stage.

Define. Define the problem. Sub stages are identify what is important to the customer and scope the project.

Choosing the right project also means not doing an alternative project. An organisation or improvement team has limited time so should select carefully. Use Pareto. Use Cost of Quality analysis. Begin with customer priorities. Be specific on project aims; go SMART (simple, measurable, agreed-to, realistic, and time-based). Six Sigma is strong on financial returns, so a savings estimate should be made. Scoping the project is critical - where are the problem boundaries, and what will be considered outside and inside? Of course, the 'project' will be found within a process, not necessarily a department. Systems thinking is required. Typical tools: SIPOC analysis, Pareto analysis, Cost of Quality analysis, Kano model.

Measure. How are we doing? The sub stages are: determine what to measure and validate the measurement system, quantify current performance, and estimate the improvement target. Six Sigma places strong emphasis on measurement. Find a suitable measure – preferably related to the process customer or output. Six Sigma prefers to use quantitative rather than qualitative data. Think defects per million opportunities. Are current measures appropriate? Define the measure clearly, the sources of the data, the sampling plan. Think validity (is what I am measuring a good indicator - preferably a lead indicator?) and reliability (would another observer get the same result?). Think about appropriate defect classification – for instance record the total number of complaints in a hotel, or by type, by location, by customer? Check the consistency in the way defects are recorded. Also, be clear on the boundary of the process. Typical tools: 7 tools of Quality, MSA.

Analyse. What's wrong? The sub stages are identifying the causes of variation and defects, and providing statistical evidence that the causes are real. Try to get to the root cause. Use the '7 tools' or process mapping. (See separate sections). The majority of tools in this book are useful here. Creative thinking, Benchmarking, QFD, Value Analysis, Design of Experiments, are but a few of the possibilities. Six Sigma places emphasis on statistical validation of results using tests. Typical tools: 7 Tools of Quality, FMEA, Design of experiments (DOE)

Improve. Fix what is wrong. Sub stages are determine the solutions including operating levels and tolerances, then install solutions and provide statistical evidence that the solutions work. Now you have to implement. 'Go to Gemba' and do it. You may use Kaizen or a Kaizen event. You may also have to plan by using project management tools. Typical tools: DOE, poka-yoke, 7 Tools.

Force Field Analysis done with the team should precede implementation.

Control. Hold the gains, and sustain. Sub stages are putting controls in place to sustain the improvements over time, and provide statistical evidence of sustainment. Verify. Measure again. And celebrate with the team. Set up SPC charts. Set new standard operating procedures. Test to see whether gains are real by going back to the old process and forward to the new. Typical tools: SPC, visual management, TPM, Standard Work.

8D Cycle

The 8D Cycle is another improvement cycle methodology, widely used and probably originating with Ford. The '8 D's' are eight **D**isciplines:

1. Form a team
2. Contain the symptom
3. Describe the problem
4. Find the root cause
5. Verify the root cause and select the corrective action
6. Implement permanent corrective action
7. Prevent recurrence, make the solution standard
8. Congratulate and celebrate.

32.7   Root Cause Problem Solving

The emphasis on 'root cause' problem solving is fundamental to the Lean philosophy. It means solving problems at the root rather than at the superficial or immediately obvious levels. But how do you get to the root cause? In the following sections some techniques are examined. But first, we should look at the whole concept of root cause analysis. There is usually more than one root cause, so 'root causes' may be more realistic.

To get to root causes, asking the right questions, and actually establishing a questioning culture is a challenge. As Deming once said, 'If you do not know how to ask the right question, you discover nothing.' For any organisation, questioning is vital. In a fast changing world, expertise cannot reside only at the top. We all need to be more childlike, asking questions to find out, to learn, but also to challenge.

Begin with the question: 'Why is so much Lean training delivered in a classroom setting where participants must sit passively and listen?' Those same participants are then expected to return to the workplace and begin questioning!

Warren Berger points out that, increasingly, answers are less important than questions. Many answers are to be found on the internet, in data bases, libraries, with experts, and with your people if you can only ask the right question. It was not always like this, but many managers still have the outdated mindset that, somehow, they must have all the answers. Schools, unfortunately, remain bastions of uni-directional instruction, and re-gurgitation during tests. That won't do in a Lean and changing environment. Levitt and Dubner say that three of the powerful words a manager can use are 'I don't know'. Many times, managers don't actually know, but simply guess or put forward their opinion in areas outside of their expertise, thus stifling creativity and innovation. But, of course, questions need to followed by action.

There have been great advances in learning, retention, and questioning in recent years. Here we explore some relevant considerations from this extensive field. A few pointers:

- Drive out fear, said Deming. Without this, a questioning culture cannot begin. This cannot be achieved by edict, only by demonstration. Deming also spoke about the 94/6 rule (94% of problems lie with the process; only about 6% with the people.) So questioning should not begin with a people witch-hunt.

- 'God gave you two ears and one mouth'.

- The higher your position the less you should give your opinion and the more you should ask and listen.

- Don't monopolise the conversation. Have round robin sessions that give everyone a chance.

- Open questions rather than closed questions. Remember, that many KPI's are answers to closed questions – How much? How many? On target? – rather than encouraging open questions Why? How?

Instead of giving a Powerpoint presentation on the 7 Wastes or Kanban, try the following questions or provocations in a training program:

- Is one piece flow a bad idea? Why or why not?
- How should you calculate the correct batch size / size of a supermarket / number of kanbans ?
- Determining a bottleneck can be dangerous.
- Is waste sometimes good? Is failure?
- 'Respect is horse shit' (Seddon)
- Why use Hoshin?
- TPS is dangerous to you, to shareholders, to suppliers.
- Why are women vastly under-represented in manufacturing management?
- What are the benefits of doing Lean?
- Lean is a con. It is really about cutting jobs. Toyota uses a lot of temps.
- Standard work means less thinking.

32.8   5 Whys and Fishbone

5 Whys is a well-established tactic, aimed at finding the root cause of a problem. Ask why several times – perhaps 3 to 5 times – successively. Poor customer service? Why? Deliveries are often late. Why late? Inventory is often out of stock. Why out of stock? Often other products have to be made first. There is a queue. Why a queue? Because batches are large and it takes time to process them. Why large? Because changeover time is long. Why is it long? Don't know. It has never been studied. Voila!

Great if this works. Certainly try it. Certainly don't accept the first reason without further probing. Unfortunately in practice there is not often one answer to each why. This leads to an expanding tree that may lead to either an unworkable number of avenues to pursue or the rather vague 'the problem is the people' or 'the problem is management'. So be specific, not general.

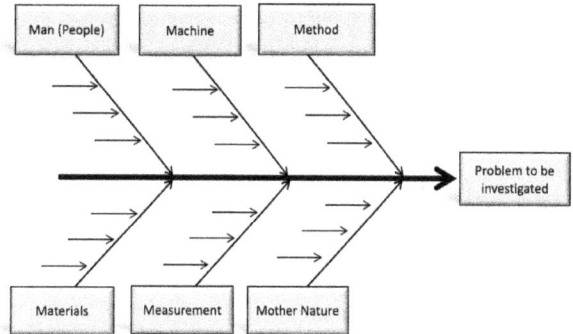

Hence, a few rules for more effective use of the 5 Whys:

- 'People' reasons are not acceptable. No to 'the people (or the culture) is the problem'. Remember Deming's 94/6 rule. Most problems lie with the system or the process, not the people. It is just too easy to blame 'people'. What is causing 'the people' to behave in that way?
- Do not allow any Why to become personal or accusing.
- At each Why stage, prioritise. A rule of thumb: don't allow more than two reasons for every why.
- Home in, not home out. For example: We have unreliable machines. Why so? Allow 'Because we don't have regular maintenance'. Do not allow 'Because we have no TPM'. Further: 'Why no regular maintenance?' Allow 'Because maintenance priorities are not clear'. Do not allow 'Because no one has worked out a TPM schedule'. In each case, the first answer allows one to be more specific, the second answer runs a risk of widening out the reasons.
- Stop when you get to a reason that is beyond your control or frame of reference. Finlow-Bates suggests that there are no ultimate root causes. It just goes on and on. (A delivery failure is due to a van running out of petrol, caused by a leaking tank, caused by a weld failure, caused by quality

of weld, caused by poor material, caused by cost cutting, caused by financial pressures, caused by...)

The 5 Whys and Fishbone or Ishikawa diagrams are closely related: you can depict the outcomes of the 5 Whys graphically by populating the Fishbone, with the starting problem at the head of the fish.

The classic version of the fishbone chart uses the 6M's to systemically understand the root causes that drive the problem: Man (or People, including aspects of skills and training), Machine (the assets you use in the process), Materials (all inputs into the process), Method (the 'how', including questions of SOPs and variation), Measurement (how you capture the output/outcome of a process, including the assessment of measurement-induced variation), and Mother Nature (aspects that are beyond your control).

Example: The Fishbone diagram shown in the TPM Chapter starts with 'Why is OEE low?' Because of breakdowns, idle time, stoppages, low yield, rework, etc. Then you ask 'Why?' again for each, and populate the Fishbone diagram.

Dean Gano, has produced very useful guidelines in his book 'Apollo Root Cause Analysis'. Gano uses a 'Reality Tree' in place of the standard 5 Whys. He states that a problem should begin with a complete definition – a statement of what the problem is, when did it happen, where did it happen, and the significance of the problem. (There are similarities with A3 here.) At each stage there is one or more 'primary effects'. Then answer 'the (primary effect) is caused by.....'. The answer will be an 'Action' (verb plus noun) and one or more 'Conditions' (typically nouns). Effective problem solving should entertain possible causes, from various parties, until the value of the reason is established.

For example, in the earlier customer service example: Statement: There is a problem of unsatisfactory delivery that happens with more complex items towards the end of every month, causing dissatisfaction amongst our most valuable customers'. This is caused by 'complex items out of stock' (action item), 'at month end' (condition). Each of these is explored by questioning or data collection. Then the next stage is 'complex items out of stock' is caused by.....

Another possibility particularly useful in innovation is the Why, What if, and How sequence. Warren Berger points out that this is the natural path of innovation.

- *Why*: Be childlike. Wonder. Step back – particularly from 'knowing'. (Danger 'I already know the best way'). Challenge assumptions. Ask for explanations as to 'why that way?'. Then repeat. Gain deep understanding through direct observation. Remember, most thinking is Kahneman's 'System One' (fast, automatic, non-deep). Think small, advises Levitt and Dubner. Beware of self-styled 'thought leaders'. The Zen principle used by Steve Jobs was 'shoshin', or 'beginners mind'.

- *What if*? Be wild and speculative. Industrial engineers have for decades used (Can we) Eliminate, Combine, Rearrange, Simplify? The TRIZ notion of (can it be made) 'Free, Perfect, Now' is provocative. (Almost every development is along that path, so can it be taken to the limit? Think Skype, Wikipedia.) So too is the concept of 'Ideality' – what would be the ideal? (Not a lawnmower, but very slow growing grass.)

- *How*: The bottom line! Again TRIZ may be useful – particularly the 40 principles. (Examples: Do it the other way around, add a dimension, do it at a different time.)

Keep in mind Deming's '94/6' rule – 94% of problems probably lie with the system, and only 6% with the person.

Thus, 'Why don't you....?' (a partly closed question) is much weaker than 'Is there another way to do that?' or 'What do you think is the cause of...?' (more open questions).

Beware: The 5 Whys can be counterproductive. Avoid suggesting the solution yourself rather than asking others to question, to think out possibilities themselves. This is the essence of the Socratic method – leading to a far more effective, and sustained, solution because it is then their idea.

Finally, Rudyard Kipling's 'Six Honest Serving Men' remains, some 100 years after it was first written, one of the most useful problem analysis tools. The original verse is:

'I knew six honest serving men,

they taught me all I knew;

their names are what and why and when,

and how and where and who'.

Such a simple little verse; so much wisdom – so often ignored!

The six men are a very useful way of defining customers, their requirements and what is really valued.

Further reading

T Finlow-Bates, 'The Root Cause Myth', *TQM Magazine*, 10:1, 1998

Michael Marquardt, *Leading with Questions*, Jossey Bass, 2005

32.9   A3 Problem Solving

The A3 method has grown hugely in popularity amongst Lean organizations in recent years, and with good reason.

A3 refers to the standard sheet of paper – two A4 portrait sheets, side by side. The story is that it was the largest size of paper that can be conveniently faxed.

A3 is:

- A standardised problem-solving methodology incorporating the PDCA cycle.

- A standard report format: Instead of a multi-page report that may come in various formats depending on the whim of the writer, A3 forces the writer to be concise. (Recall the quote from George Bernard Shaw 'I am sorry to send you this long letter – I did not have time to write a short one.') For the reader, another advantage is that he or she knows exactly where to look for the salient points. So, 'don't give me a report, give me an A3'.

- A standard documentation method, and easy filing method.

- A hugely powerful mentoring and coaching approach. (Note that a 'single pass' A3 misses much of the benefit of a full A3, and should probably not even be called 'A3'. The full benefit is only obtained in a multi-pass dialog between mentor and mentee using the A3 format.)

A3 is actually a family of report formats – used for planning, top level budgeting, communication, and problem solving. Here we consider only the generic problem solving type.

The general format of A3 is current state and analysis on the left hand side and future state and implementation plan on the right hand side. Often, along the bottom is space for 'sign off' – for people who have seen or agreed to the analysis.

Throughout an A3, good practice is to use graphs, diagrams, sketches, cartoons etc. and not lengthy text. Lots of text usually indicates a poor A3.

A3 is a hierarchical methodology, homing in on the biggest, most pressing problem. One problem at a time. Then developing a plan to improve the situation – 'countermeasures' rather than 'solutions' because a problem is seldom 'solved'.

An example is shown below.

The standard layout is to have on the left hand side Check and Plan, and the right hand side is Do, Act and again Check. In the following section a standard classic 8 step methodology is explained. A similar methodology is used by Toyota. This methodology can be represented as a funnel – homing in on the 'big issue'.

Headings: The location name and problem type are entered. Type may be, for instance, cost, quality, delivery, layout, schedule.

Step 1: Clarification. Three sub steps: 1A: Background. How the problem arose or developed. 1B: Statement of the problem itself. Statements (or sketches) of ideal condition and current condition. 1C: Containment. Statement of what is being done to contain the problem.

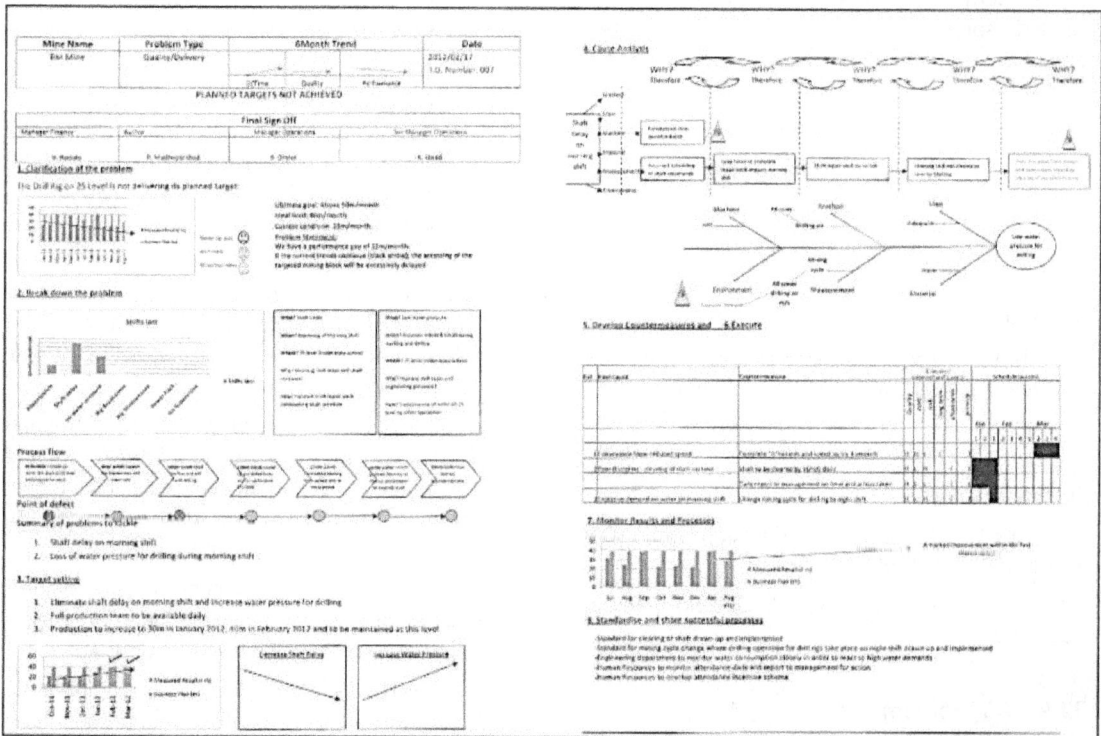

Step 2: Breaking down the Problem. Here 'classic' tools are used:

- Several of the '7 Tools' (Flowchart, pareto, fishbone, correlation diagram). These are often used successively – for instance using pareto to identify the 'big one' then again the 'big one of the big one'.

- 5 of the Kipling 'serving men': What, When, Where, How, Who

- The Process steps. Here the analyst is expected to 'go see', document the steps, then ask at which step the problem first becomes apparent. The problem may then lie in the previous step. So: 1 No; 2 No; 3 No, 4 Yes; so problem source might be step 3.

- Another possibility here is to use the TWI JM approach of writing down the steps, 'Question Every detail' using 'Kipling' and then consider Eliminate, Combine, Rearrange, Simplify.

Step 3: Target Setting. This is a clear statement of the specific problem that has been homed in on. For example: 'Burrs occur on right hand side of all parts, in line 3 during the second shift.' To quote Charles Kettering, American inventor, 'a problem well stated is a problem half solved.' The now-refined problem statement is the outcome of all the steps on the left-hand side and is usually written at the bottom of the left-hand side.

Step 4: Root Cause Analysis. (Often on RHS of the A3.) Here, a standard approach is to use the '5 Whys' for each of Men, Material, Machine, Method, Environment. The 'whys' proceed forward, and 'therefores' backward. For instance: Men: (forward): Lack of skill. Why?: No training. Why? No time. (backward): No time, therefore no training, therefore lack of skill. One of the 'M's sequence should reveal the top few root causes.

Step 5: Develop Countermeasures for each root cause.

Step 6: Execute. Plan the implementation, including who, where, when.

Step 7: Monitor. The countermeasures are an experiment. So a test needs to be devised to see if it works. The results of the test are written here.

Step 8: Standardise and Share: The new method needs to be incorporated into standardized work. When and who. Also shared with other relevant processes.

Sign off: Along the bottom various line managers concerned with the issue should see and sign off the A3. Of course, they could annotate and discuss with the team.

Mentoring: 'It takes two to A3' says John Shook. This means mentoring – perhaps the greatest benefit of an A3 exercise. Having gone through steps 1 to 4, discuss with the mentor. He or she will probe. 'When you went to the gemba, what did you see?'; 'What is the customers view?'; 'What did the operator think?'; 'Can we look at it from a design perspective?' And so on. This will probably lead to another version of the A3. Finally, the mentor and mentee agree. Then proceed to the later steps. Further mentoring may occur. This is actually the 'nemawashi' process of gaining consensus. Discussion eliminates misunderstandings and leads to easier implementation.

So an A3 is not just a problem solving tool, but a developmental tool. A most effective way to grow employees.

A3 need not be restricted to an A3 size paper. J&J company uses a 'rapid response board', set out with A3 steps, on a large whiteboard on wheels. Where a situation arises the board is wheeled to the gemba and the team tackles the problem.

A good A3 should involve systems thinking – taking a balanced viewpoint from several perspectives.

An A3 can be used at different levels. They are used:

- For routine problem solving – point kaizens.
- As a supplement to mapping.
- As a tool and record for kaizen events. (One company places kaizen event A3s on the wall near the area for a standard period of 12 months.)
- As a supplement to policy deployment.
- As a test to evaluate a new employee.

Further reading

John Shook, *Managing to Learn*, LEI, 2008

Durward Sobek and Art Smalley, *Understanding A3 Thinking*, CRC Press, 2008

32.10 OODA Loop

Observe-Orient-Decide-Act is a sequence devised by Col. John Boyd of USAF drawing on air combat experience. For Boyd, OODA is about agility – meaning the ability to rapidly change orientation in response to what is happening externally – especially in what we have referred to as VUCA times.

OODA is a more rapid, continually adjusting, problem methodology as befits its origins in air combat. By contrast PDSA involves experimental cycles usually of a longer duration – although in the case of a mentor/mentee coaching process both OODA and PDSA would give frequent and rapid feedback. OODA is belatedly but increasingly favoured in dynamic environments and in rapid adjustment cycles such as in agile software and product development.

OODA is sometimes shown as a 4-stage cycle like PDSA, but in fact has feedback loops back to Observe from all three other stages. OODA is an attractive model for 'Fix It Now', Immediate Kaizen and for Directed Improvement. Why? Because OODA is

- A rapid decision process, not a scientific experiment.
- Rapid feedback allows adjustment.
- Dynamic. The decision evolves as changes take place.
- It follows the sequence of how people actually decide in the short term.

- Starting with Observe fits well with the Lean 'Go see' requirement.
- At a strategic level, Observe and Orient nicely implies looking at the developing external situation.

In short, OODA is the opposite of top-down command and control, where analytical models are built and then tested (by which time the 'landscape' may have changed). This was the by-now well-known problem in software development known as the 'Waterfall' method, and why 'sprints' and 'pivoting' have grown in popularity. These latter concepts are fully compatible with OODA.

Further reading
Chet Richards, *Certain to Win: The strategy of John Boyd applied to business*, Xlibris, 2004

33 Kata

Kata (or Toyota Kata) has begun to have a major influence in Lean since Mike Rother published *Toyota Kata* in 2010. It may even be the most important development in Lean for a decade. Rother defines a kata as a well-rehearsed routine that eventually becomes second nature or habit. The word stems from Karate where basic sequences are rehearsed even by high-Dan black belts such that the actions establish and reinforce pathways in the brain and become automatic or a habit. (Many will have seen the famous movie sequence with Mr. Miyagi: 'wipe on, wipe off'!)

Kata is now a proven methodology in manufacturing, service, healthcare, and government.

The following is an important point at the outset: Kata is not only an improvement approach but is an approach to develop people into orderly, scientific thinkers. To this end Kata, as briefly described below, is not explicitly used by Toyota although the development of scientific thinking certainly is.

By the way: *'For any theory to be scientific, it must be stated in a way that it can be shown to be false as well as true.'* says Tavris and Aronson in *Mistakes were Made but not by me*.

33.1 Types of Kata

The Kata experience has much in common with TWI. (In recent years there have been several joint Kata-TWI conferences.) Kata overlaps with the Gemba and Leader Standard Work approaches, and can fit in well with Hoshin Kanri (Policy Deployment) planning. Hence this section on Kata is placed after Gemba and LSW sections and before the Hoshin Kanri section. Kata also has close links with several other important concepts and theories, amongst them: (a) Small Wins, (b) Habits, (c) System 1 and System 2 (Kahneman) and (d) Mindset (Dwek). (e) Coaching. All of these are discussed in separate sections. In that sense, Kata is a 'meta methodology', combining several forms of best practice.

Establishing Kata aligns with the PDSA incremental experimental method. Rother defines management as *'the systematic pursuit of desired conditions by utilizing human capabilities in a concerted way'*. But Rother has been at pains to point out that Kata is not a tool but one of several ways to ingrain Lean behaviour. It is a teaching or learning routine.

In both Kata and TWI, skills are built up by repetition. Very often learners get it wrong for the first few times and need coaching. But confidence is built through feedback 'at the gemba'. Hence there are unique improvement and leadership routines referred to by Rother as Improvement Kata and Coaching Kata.

There is the realistic assertion that one must have a target condition to know where one is going. With a target condition the direction and first few steps can be attempted. Unlike the assumptions of much of project planning, one is not quite sure or confident about the overall path leading to achieving the target condition. So one proceeds in small steps as with the experimental method. What is the first step? Try it. Does it move you closer? Reflect. Adjust. Avoid blame. What is now preventing us from moving ahead? What is the next specific small step to take? – not some big, vague step like 'reduce inventory', but perhaps 'let us try running the workstation with a container of 8 parts rather than 10'. Small wins build confidence and motivation. Practice builds mindset. The habit is established with each 'que' of going to check.

The **Improvement Kata** is a routine for moving from the current situation to a new situation in a creative, directed and meaningful way. It has four elements:

- Understand the direction
- Grasp the current condition
- Establish the next target condition. A measurable target.
- PDSA toward the target condition

Then repeat, and repeat again. This last step would often require several iterations, or PDSA cycles. Have patience.

One small step at a time, and learning from each step. Don't try to take big steps, containing several smaller simultaneous steps. Why? Because some small steps will work but others may not – but you may not be able to distinguish the successful from the unsuccessful if several initiatives are attempted at the same time. This is really the essence of scientific method – set a hypothesis, test it, reject if necessary. (Of course, a full scientific approach would today (especially in healthcare) require a randomised trial. Although very seldom possible in operations rather than research, do think about the possibility – for instance, with two cells, making a change in one cell but not in the other and observing the difference.

The **Coaching Kata** is a pattern for teaching the Improvement Kata. It is a set of coaching routines to practise in order to develop effective coaching habits. It gives managers and supervisors a standardised approach to facilitate Improvement kata skill development in daily work. The Coaching Kata uses a standard set of five questions that are primarily focused on the leader or coach in an improvement area. The five are:

1. What is the target condition? What is it we are trying to achieve?

2. What is the actual condition now?

3. What obstacles do you think are preventing you from reaching the target condition? Which one are you addressing now?

4. What is your next step? What do you expect to happen? (This is the start of the next PDSA cycle)

5. When can we go and see what we have learned from taking that step?

Feedback and review are integral to both Kata and Hoshin. Remember, Kata is a PDCA / PDSA improvement <u>cycle</u>. Rother suggests that there are four 'Reflection Steps' for each small step carried out in an experimental cycle. The writers of this book believe that the Reflection Steps, if conscientiously carried out, are a principal benefit of Kata. They are...

1. What did you plan as the last step?

2. What did you expect?

3. What actually happened?

4. What did you learn?

Sometimes there is a second coach, whose role is to make sure that the five steps and the four steps are followed, and to give guidance when they are not followed. Rother suggests these steps should form a daily 20-minute coaching cycle!

33.2   Kata and Hoshin

Rother has pointed out that there are two phases to Kata – Planning and Execution. Planning establishes the longer-term vision or strategy. (Hoshin, discussed in Chapter 40, is the Lean approach to deploying the vision and associated KPI's.) A Hoshin cycle applies to an organisation, department, and the associated value streams. Under Hoshin, within each value stream, there will be several processes each of which will have challenges to address in order to meet the higher level Hoshin targets. This then sets up a framework for a whole series of Katas, each working towards their own desirable future states or target conditions. Hoshin is appropriately also called Policy Deployment and this deployment, level by level, establishes the full integrated plan.

Now, having established the target condition for the value stream, and often for a particular process, the Kata Execution phase can begin.

It is good practice to display the hierarchy of Katas on a visual management progress storyboard.

Of course, a Kata approach does not necessarily have to be integrated with Hoshin. It can fit in with other integrated transformation frameworks, with Shingo Prize aims (see Section 3.17), or with a local initiative aimed at, for instance, defect reduction or lead-time reduction.

33.3   Wider Areas of Application

It is interesting to note that Kata has been, and is, used in teaching school kids. This is Kata in the Classroom (KiC). In one intervention with which one of the authors (John) was involved, Kata was used successfully to improve reading with dyslexic children. The teaching assistants found that with the Kata approach they and the kids both learned at an accelerated rate as opposed to traditional methods. The KiC website is inspirational. The potential is huge!

Finally, Rother suggests that we should not 'implement or add on some new techniques, practices, or even principles', but rather seek 'to develop consistent behaviour patterns across the organisation.'

Rother suggests that a change in organisational culture cannot be achieved by classroom training, workshops, bringing in consultants, incentives or reorganisations. Instead, he suggests that we should learn by doing. He is specific that training and doing should not be separated: 'To practice the improvement and coaching katas, students apply them in actual situations at actual work processes. In this manner your experimentation will be real, not theoretical.' He advocates not a change, but a gradual shift in organisational culture. This sentiment is exactly in line with Anders Ericsson's ideas on 'Deliberate Practice'. (More on this is given in the later section 39.2 on The People Trilogy.)

In summary, Kata is a small scale experimental approach. Sir Terry Leahy, Tesco's former CEO had a similar approach: 'When creating a new offer, the critical aim – and basic building block of success – is to win custom, not create a perfect process... much better to get cracking by creating a simple process that you can build on and perfect as you go along. '

Further reading

Rose Heathcote and Daryl Powell, Improve Continuously by Mastering the Lean Kata, *The Lean Post*, December 9, 2020

Mike Rother, *Toyota Kata*, McGraw Hill, 2010

Mike Rother, *The Toyota Kata Practice Guide*, McGraw Hill, 2017

Mike Rother and Gerd Aulinger, *Toyota Kata Culture*, McGraw Hill, 2017

Sarah Williams, *Coaching non-literary TAs with Kata*, MSc Lean dissertation, University of Buckingham, 2017

Anders Ericsson, *Peak: Secrets from the New Science of Expertise*, Bodley Head, 2016

34 Holding the gains

Juran taught us how important it is to 'hold the gains' after making a process improvement. Yet often too little attention is devoted to this aspect of the improvement cycle. Improvements quickly degrade, and the process gradually goes to its original state. We call this problem 'backsliding'.

This section deals with its causes and prevention.

34.1 Backsliding

No improvement reaches 100% (by definition, as Lean is an ongoing effort – so it is moving target). Equally, no effort ever slides back to zero (as there is always some residual benefit, e.g. training). So what is backsliding?

Backsliding means that a process improvement slides back towards its original level of performance, so that the initial investment in making that improvement would not be justified. In other words, the firm would have been better off not investing time and resources into improving the process in the first place.

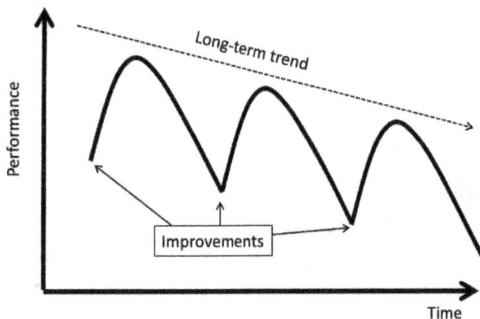

There are many root causes for backsliding, but first and foremost, humans are creatures of habit. So there is a strong tendency to revert back to the 'old ways'. It is for this reason that process improvement needs to be managed, during AND after the change.

There are many terms in use: holding the gains, avoid backsliding, or sustainability. Unfortunately, 'sustainability' can mean very different things:

- Some see it in terms of long-term viability, generally with an environmental or ESG perspective

- Some see a dynamic nature in project sustainability to do with strategy, technology, finance. This type of sustainability is one of the great issues in management, never mind Lean. Ask GE or GEC/Marconi or ICI. In their book *Creative Destruction*, Richard Foster and Sarah Kaplan report that of the 500 top US companies in 1957, 37% survived to 1997, and of those only 6% outperformed the stock market.

- Some see it simply as lasting change, which is the way in which we will use it here.

We believe that, like perpetual motion, there is no such thing as 'self-sustainability'. The Second Law of Thermodynamics, (or Entropy) sometimes called the supreme law of the universe, says that unless you put energy into a system it will run down, degrade into disorder and, eventually, death (as in no energy). The natural state is chaos! The same applies to Lean project sustainability. But there are greater risks – without the right sort of energy the system will degrade very rapidly. The amazing story of Wiremold is a case in point. After 12 years of hugely successful Lean transformation the company had become one of the Lean showpieces in North America. It was written up in *Lean Thinking*. Yet three years after being taken over, many of the measures of performance had declined to what Bob Emiliani (who wrote a case study on the success of the company) describes as 'batch and queue'.

One view of project sustainability is simply 'Doing a Cortes' – that is burning his boats so that his men had no choice but to adapt their old-world ways to the new world. The equivalent may be an option in a time of real crisis but is not really available to most.

34.2 The Failure Modes of Lean Implementations

Over the years, we have seen many implementations of Lean – initially in automotive, then in manufacturing in general, and more recently in service and healthcare operations. Many of these initiatives were successful initially, but all too often these were not sustained over a longer period of time. In the following section, we will outline, from our own personal experience, why these implementations have failed. An older survey of the leading 1,000 Canadian manufacturing companies in 2007 revealed that 'backsliding to old ways of doing things' and 'lack of implementation know-how' were by far the greatest obstacles to Lean.

Senior Management Respect and Support

The first failure mode of Lean implementation relates to senior management support and buy-in. While many would like to believe that Lean can be implemented 'bottom-up', by implanting a few tools on the shop-floor, then rolling it out to the entire organisation, this is a myth. Implementing Lean very soon requires changing not just the layout of the facility or lines, but also changes in the work organisation and 'culture'. Beginning with senior managers themselves, this means having true 'respect' for all. If senior managers have this already, then great. If not, several gemba walks and participation in improvement events will often be necessary before Lean properly can begin. Invert the organizational triangle. Also required is a careful review of KPI's aligned to purpose. ('Tell me how you will measure me and I'll tell what I will do.') Behavioural principles will need to be developed and made the norm. (See Chapters 10 and 13). Responsibilities, rewards and incentives, and very often pay will need review. Changing the role of front line managers is key. TWI would often be a good foundation. Confidence and security need to be built. An open letter to all employees explaining the plans for Lean would be a good start. Even better (essential?) would be active participation.

The CEO, of course, is crucial. Not that he or she needs to know the detail of Lean tools, but the person should have a belief in Lean so obstacles (including some people) can be removed.

Perhaps the best way to raise senior manager commitment is for the senior managers to feel the customer experience, first hand. This cannot be delegated to some 'mystery shopping' type team. Follow a selection of actual orders from origin of the demand to use of the product or part in practice. Spend time in the call centre actually listening. Talk face to face with users and suppliers.

Finally, it has been said with some justification, that unless each member of the senior management team possesses their own well-worn steel-capped safety shoes, Lean is doomed!

Failure to hit the 'Bottom Line'

Dan Jones and many others have observed that unless progress is reasonably quickly translated into increased sales, freed-up cash, lower unit costs, and/or reduced capital expenditure, interest from top management quickly wanes This failure can result from one or more of the following:

- Failure to follow through improvements. Waste reduction is futile if not followed through. For instance, setup reduction must translate into smaller batches and better flow. Movement reduction should be followed by kanban card removal and inventory reduction. Quality improvements must be followed by buffer stock removal. On and on. (In fact this is the theme of John Bicheno's book 'Fishbone Flow')

- A failure in accounting methods. As we shall see later, inventory reduction can lead to worse results on Profit and Loss if traditional standard costing is used.

- KPI-driven cost reduction initiatives in the name of Lean that with time lead to increased costs due to defects, safety, morale and customer loyalty issues.

Whilst the bottom line is important, Lean should not be confused with an initiative solely to improve shareholder value. Lean must have benefits for customers, employees, managers, community, the environment and shareholders.

Dealing with Competing Initiatives and Initiative Overload

In many organisations we have seen multiple improvement programmes over time sometimes run in parallel. Such initiative overload leads to confusion ('Is all the good work we have done so far no longer valid?') to apathy or sitting-it-out ('Why should I take part in Six Sigma: in two months time we will do something else anyway..'), to open resistance ('These new programmes don't change anything: within a few weeks everything will back to where it was').

So how do you deal with 'competing initiatives'? An important point to remember is that most improvement approaches have similar goals: value enhancement, lead time reduction, reduction in defects or variability, and ultimately, cost reduction. The problem is not *where they want to go*, but *how to get there*.

When introducing a new initiative, it is hence vital to make people understand how it fits in with the existing strategy or tactics. The name is important, as many perceive 'Lean' to be a competitor to 'Six Sigma', whereas in fact they can be compatible. It is not by chance that, say, Unipart doesn't call its production system 'Lean', but the 'the Unipart Way'.

Lean, Six Sigma or Lean Six Sigma?

We now know that Lean and Six Sigma can be made to work well together. However, they are not the same! They are two very different concepts, with very different strengths.

Consider this analogy: Lean is like the Public Health Engineer, Six Sigma is like the surgeon: both want to improve the health of the population, yet the way they go about it is very different! The Public Health Engineer will see to providing clean drinking water, a working sewage system and efficient garbage collection. He provides the environment or framework, and indirectly saves hundreds of lives every day. The surgeon on the other hand is called in to solve a particular issue, and does so in a single high-profile project (the operation) using his specific instruments and skills. Overall, society needs both. What does this mean – do not do Six Sigma before you understand the end-to-end process! Start with Lean, develop a complete understanding of value, and the value stream, then pull in Six Sigma as and when you need it.

Beware. Many so-called Lean Six Sigma initiatives touted by consultants and trainers are simply Six Sigma training programs with a smattering of Lean. If anything they should be the other way around!

Toyota does not talk Six Sigma. But the roots of TPS are very much with Total Quality Control (TQC), having won the Deming Prize decades ago. Interesting is the word 'total' that implies everyone and every process - certainly not only specialist 'belts'.

Lean and Six Sigma are complimentary in many aspects: Lean sets the philosophical background of value-focused thinking, Six Sigma provides a powerful toolkit to address specific 'hard nuts' and problems that have been identified. It is important to understand this distinction! Six Sigma has a focus on reduction of variation – an important concept – and on the elimination of defects where conventional Lean tools are not effective.

Thus, Six Sigma – as a tool for variability reduction and tough problem clarification – fits very well into the wider umbrella of Lean. One issue where they differ is where to start: Lean starts with analysing customer value and understanding demand and capacity. This is the big picture. Six Sigma, by contrast, homes in on a process, typically measuring its performance in terms of opportunities (defects). Be aware of the fact that Six Sigma has a strong methodology (DMAIC), but can also be very inflexible, and most importantly lacks the strategic perspective that Lean can provide.

Also, Six Sigma has a rigid training regime ('green belts' who are trained in basic statistics, and 'black belts' who receive several weeks of training and need to complete a certified improvement project). This can be useful as it creates a common set of skills, but it can also be elitist! Lean only works if the ownership for improvements rests at worker and team leader level, and not with a select number of 'belts'.

In particular, be very cautious of a 'Lean Six Sigma Black belt'. The very name would suggest mastery of field that is still developing – a contradiction in terms. Worse, the name may place such people on a pedestal – an anathema to Lean!

With time, some of the original companies that championed Six Sigma have begun to back down. (Is it the S curve again?). GE is a classic example. Others, like 3M (according to Klein) have found that Six Sigma has inhibited innovation. Yet others have trained too many black belts. (Some is good, so more must be better!). They have then found that there are insufficient high-level projects. Redundancy or de-motivation result.

Finally, and appropriately, Lean Six Sigma and Six Sigma itself has no agreed body of knowledge, curriculum, or certification. Thus, like an MBA, it is not the title that is important but where you took it. Frankly, some 'black belts' are a complete con!

In summary, use Six Sigma as pull, not push.

Operational Excellence and Agile

Operational excellence (OpEx) is a term that has emerged strongly over the past half dozen years. It is often used as a surrogate for Lean. There is even an operational excellence society! Maybe it is an improvement on the word Lean and is more acceptable to those who have experienced Lean failure. If so, fine.

But 'excellence' is a strange word. As the quality guru Phil Crosby pointed out in the 1980's, it has no real meaning. What is 'excellent'? If it is an aspiration, then it fits in with Lean. If it is an assertion of present status, then it is misleading. And has 'operational excellence' another unique approach, another body of knowledge, something different to offer from Lean? We doubt it, but would be delighted to discover any real differences.

Likewise, 'Agile' was for a decade or so used as another approach in operations. But we fail to identify any meaningful difference to Lean, except perhaps for Seru cells. Agile proponents talk about postponement, flexibility and strategic inventories. But these are features of Lean. Today, 'Agile' is less used in a manufacturing context but is strongly found in software development. Fine.

Abusing Lean as Short-term Fix

Lean is not primarily a cost reduction strategy (!), but unfortunately often is used to achieve exactly that. Certainly not **L**ess **E**mployees **A**re **N**eeded! More specifically, two common mistakes are to set out to use Lean to reduce inventory, and to set out reduce headcount. Inventory reduction and headcount reduction will frequently be outcomes of a Lean initiative but should not be the aim.

Inventory is a common focus as it is visible on the shop-floor, it is easy to measure, and it is a direct operating expense. So often it becomes the focus of improvement programmes, with disastrous consequences. Inventory MAY be there for good reasons:

- To buffer against internal uncertainty (defects, breakdowns, variation)
- To buffer against external uncertainty (demand fluctuations, supply, quality)
- To buffer against imbalances in the capability of the facility
- To temporarily isolate unstable zones in a value stream with buffers.

This is shown in the 'water and rocks' analogy (see figure). So when inventory is drastically reduced without solving the underlying issues, many problems surface at the same time, a fire-fighting frenzy erupts, and within a short time the initial process and inventory levels are restored.

The Lean way is to gradually reduce inventory level, to expose one problem first, solve it, then expose the next, and so on. Bill Sandras of PCI refers to this as 'one less at a time' implementation. Inventory reduction becomes a means of identifying problems, not a goal in its own right.

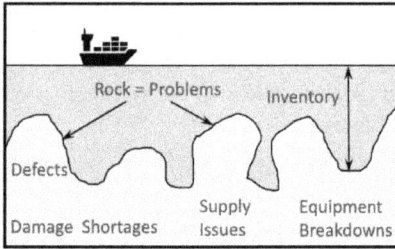

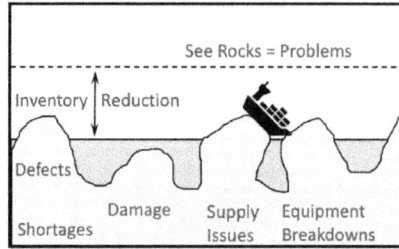

Headcount reduction has similar dangers. Labour has a direct bearing on productivity, and also generally is the most significant variable cost. So any reduction yields direct 'bottom-line' benefits. This brings a great temptation to lay off any labour that has been saved by Lean. However, doing this even once means that Lean will be perceived as a headcount reduction tool within your operation, and no one will 'improve themselves out of a job'. So a better way is to use natural attrition. Better still, improve the process, then use the 'spare' labour as a kaizen team initially, until you acquire more business for your firm to soak up the excess labour.

The cycle is: improve process, which results in better quality and lower cost, which increases market competitiveness, which increases business, which requires more labour, etc. It should be a virtuous cycle of growth, not one of reduction!

As Dan Jones says: *'Doing it to them for me'* does not work!'

Misaligned Performance Measures

'You get what you measure'. In fact everyone, from CEO to shop-floor worker, will act so as to look good on his or her personal performance measures. Performance measures drive personal behaviour, and this is important to understand.

Three brief points: First, Goodhart's Law: 'When a measure becomes a target, it ceases to be a measure'. (For instance, the British in India sought to improve health by paying for dead rats. Enterprising Indians began to breed rats.)

Second: Give preference to measuring the process over measuring the person. This point comes from

Deming and the classic red bead game. In the game, operators are powerless to change the process but get the blame for poor results. (By the way, have you ever complained to a call centre operator about poor service? It's probably not their fault.)

Third: A point from John Seddon. Begin with purpose, derive the necessary measures that support purpose, that in turn drive method. Too often, the starting point is to dream up KPI's that then de facto influence the purpose resulting in misalignment between purpose and method.

See Chapter 16 on Accounting and Measurement for more detail.

Lack of Ownership

Process improvement can be dictated, either by external consultants or by adopting a corporate template 'how things ought to be done'. But imposed improvements run the risk of lack of ownership. In some cultures, there is a strong resistance to being told what to do. The ownership of improvements needs to reside at process level, and workers need to feel that they have a stake in the future state. This is a particular problem when bringing in external consultants that make very good changes to the process, but which are often not sustained because they are not 'owned' by the workforce. Team involvement in any process improvement is vital, and the process ownership issue should never be neglected.

Keep the Momentum!

Lean does not support itself: a 'self-sustaining Lean culture' is a myth that is often propagated. Lean requires continuous support (and pressure) from the top – clarifying the direction and leading by example. Complacency is a great danger, and one that Toyota is most afraid of. Having a clear need to improve in order to ensure survival is a great motivator. Once you have reached the status of being an 'industry benchmark', such motivation is hard to maintain. Then other goals need to be defined, such as becoming environmentally friendly for example. So keep the momentum alive!

34.3 Sustaining Improvements

Sustainability is a word much used in present times, yet also one that has many meanings. In the sections below we will refer to 'sustainability' to mean 'sustaining process improvement', as opposed to environmental sustainability.

Sustaining Improvements and Tools

A large number of organizations have failed to produce the desired results from the direct and prescriptive application of Lean tools. The tools themselves have been proven to work in many situations. The difference must then be in how the tools were applied, their appropriateness, but not the tools themselves. Spear and Bowen state that observers of Lean often confuse the tools and techniques with the system itself. They point to the paradox of the Toyota Production System (TPS) that relates to a very rigid framework of activities and production flows coupled with extremely flexible and adaptable operations. This paradox is partially explained by the authors' revelation that Toyota actually practices the *scientific* method in its operational activities. Plan Do Study Act is the principle mechanism for this scientific approach. Tools and techniques are thus treated as hypotheses to be tested in the particular situation at hand. If the results are unfavourable the tools must be modified. Organizations without this understanding often fail to allow for local factors influencing the successful application and sustainability of tools and techniques. Nakane and Hall also studied TPS and came to a similar conclusion. They found companies that merely implement the techniques without developing the people and culture and hence fail to fully realise the expected gains. Emiliani agrees, calling the latter 'Fake Lean'. The point is that Lean is a system of tools and people that need to work together.

Concepts such as 5S or value steam mapping are seen as short-term exercises instead of systems – for visual management and creating a new concept, respectively.

A Systems View on Sustaining Improvements

Systems thinking is a way of viewing and interpreting the universe as a series of interconnected hierarchies and interrelated wholes. Within organizational systems there are both technical and social interactions and interrelationships that govern the output of the system. The famous Tavistock research amongst miners (See 10.1), illustrated that both technical and social aspects need to be considered if a new system (in their case long wall mining) was to be successful and sustained. The 'socio' side involves understanding the system of mutually supporting roles and relationships, both formal and informal, within the organization.

A related 'systems' aspect on sustainability is discussed by Senge who talks about feedback loops. Feedback loops are beginning to be understood in natural and eco systems but also exist in human organizations. Change generates antibodies that automatically grow to fight the change. This is like Newton's Third Law – for every action there is an equal and opposite reaction. The antibodies need to be managed or the fever will take hold. Those not in favour of change may need to be neutralised. So identify the antibodies as early as possible. 'Inject' them. Antibodies that continue to react need to be moved out decisively and quickly. This is the state of 'quasi stationary equilibrium' described by Kurt Lewin that led to his diagnostic technique known as force-field analysis. For both Senge and Lewin the most important lesson from this realisation is that it is preferable to reduce the restraining forces before increasing the driving forces. In other words, time spent up front on preparing for change, means less time spent later sorting out problems. Or, to quote Frank Devine, 'if people help to plan the battle, they are less likely to battle the plan'.

Sustaining Improvements and Feedback

Another stimulating view using feedback loops, and concerning how improvement efforts degrade is given by Repenning and Sterman. They talk about an 'improvement paradox' that managers face – the vast and expanding number of tools available but the inability to make effective use of the tools. Their model sees 'capability' (machines, processes, people) eroding over time. Managers are, of course, concerned with this erosion and have two ways to counter it. One way is to 'work harder' (like cutting jobs), the other way is to 'work smarter'. Working harder yields quick results but not very dramatic results. Working smarter (say with Lean) is more of a risk. It takes time to yield results, but the results are often more substantial, although they sometimes fail because it is a new area. The problem is that these two are not independent. Working harder can drive out time to work smarter. A problem is that, because working harder yields short-term results, it is often the course of action that is sought whenever there is a crisis. If management is not very careful with priorities, if they do not 'reinvest' in working smarter with the longer view in mind, all working harder efforts will fail. A feedback loop develops – the capability gap grows, leading to more pressure to work harder. On the other hand, working smarter can gradually close the capability gap, meaning less time is needed for working harder and even more for working smarter. (The feedback diagram was shown in Section 23.3)

Many people concerned with Lean transformation will recognize the wisdom of this analysis. It is Occam's razor for sustainability – bad 'improvement' drives out good.

34.4   Keeping the Momentum

In the earlier Change section of the book, the tendency for managers to give up too early was identified. Sustaining improvements begins at the top. Managers send out signals about their commitment – verbal, but even more importantly, non-verbal. The 'watchers' continually watch the manager's behaviour and 'signals' of their commitment, and, as a result, will become sceptics or converts. What happens when the chips are down: Are workers fired? Are defectives shipped? Are schedules maintained? Is Lean training abandoned? Strongly linked to this is measures, and the priority of measures tracked by managers. ('Everybody knows that tons per day is what really counts'.) It is obvious that measures need to support the ongoing Lean initiative. Unfortunately this obvious point is often either neglected or not sufficiently thought through.

Bob Emiliani has pointed out that, surprisingly, gaining executive buy-in is not something new in performance improvement. He cites a book written by Knoeppel in 1914 much of which is applicable today. This accords closely with our experience. Why are so many top managers so hesitant, so that Lean efforts start, falter and re-start? Some reasons are:

- They are focused on finance in the case of caretaker managers, or on new product development in the case of owner-managers. Operations is low priority.

- They are risk-averse to concepts that they don't fully understand. Owner-managers have made their money by means other than Lean. Why risk it?

- They see Lean as a shop floor thing, not as Lean enterprise. Lean is cost reduction, but the path to growth is via marketing.

- They see Lean as unproven in their industry, even though they accept it as a great success in automotive. This is particularly the case in process industry, having for example, fixed vessel sizes.

- They have just bought a big ERP system, (or IoT or AI) and any conflict with this is to be avoided. The ERP/IT folks 'know what they are doing'. A sunk cost bias permeates: 'We can't abandon our investment.'

- Consultants have to bear much of the blame for presenting a tool-based, partial view.

These are difficult and often valid points. Put yourself in a CEO's shoes to appreciate the issues.

Momentum and Staff Turnover

Researchers into self-directed work teams have found that these teams simply do not work when staff turnover is greater than about 30% per year.

They are always in Tuckman's 'forming' and 'storming' stages, never progressing to 'norming' or 'performing' stages. The same thing is very likely with Lean transformation. A particular problem with 'the great resignation'.

Momentum and Motivation

The sustainability of tools is related to the degree to which people are motivated to use them. Recall some classic theories of motivation. Herzberg's motivator-hygiene theory says that hygiene factors such as pay and conditions can de-motivate but not motivate. Only motivators, such as recognition and personal satisfaction actually motivate. And Maslow talked about the Hierarchy of Needs. This suggests that a foundation of trust and support is necessary, but sustainability requires interest and involvement.

Deming spoke about the necessity to 'drive out fear' as one of his famous 14 points. Surely psychological safety is a pre-requisite for sustainability. Fear about the short term, and trust, remains one of the prime concerns of employees in Western organizations. 'So, if I do all this Lean stuff, will I really retain my job?' Forget the issue of long term (company) survival so often voiced by management – it is short term personal survival that is of far more concern. Stephen Covey, as one his 7 Habits of Highly Effective People, discusses the 'Win-win or walk away' habit. Both sides must win. A way must and can be found, or else both parties should walk away. Covey believes that without this fundamental principle there can no sustainability – in business, in personal life, or in society. Reject TINA (there is no alternative); embrace TEMBA (there exist many better alternatives – just find them).

Finally, on motivation, the excellent diagnostic booklet *Analysing Performance Problems* by Mager and Pipe, suggests that several questions need to be cleared before getting down to motivational issues. These issues include: has training been adequate?, is what is expected clear?, has sufficient time been allowed?, and have adequate resources been provided?. Only then should you ask about the motivational issues: Is performance punishing? ('He is good. Give him that extra work'), is non-performance rewarding? (for instance, letting others do the work and being rewarded by more free time), and does it make a difference? (for instance, will anyone notice or will there be any recognition?).

Of course, this is very like Deming's 94/6 rule – 94% of problems are the system, about which only managers can do things. So be very cautious of labelling someone a 'concrete head'!

Momentum and Discipline

For Hirano the concept of sustainability is dependent upon discipline and in the context of 5S this means 'making a habit of properly maintaining the correct procedures'. Without good discipline the 5S system will not be maintained and the workplace will revert to chaos. The need for discipline is not restricted to the 5S's but is also essential in all aspects of business according to Hirano. In the classic Japanese definition of 5S the fifth S or pillar is *Shitsuke* or Discipline. (Refer to the 5S Chapter). Hirano firmly believes that management and supervision must teach discipline and that problems with discipline arise when management fails to correct lapses as they occur. The workplace 'faithfully reflects the attitudes and intentions of managers, from the top brass to the shop floor supervision'. The art of correcting another person is also emphasized and the need for compassion is said to be key. The person correcting another must also acknowledge his or her own failings. This particular aspect of discipline has a cultural slant that is highlighted by the description of the worker being criticised thanking the critic for their correction followed by a bow of acknowledgement. Jeffrey Liker refers to this in his

14th Toyota Way principle, calling it Hansei (Reflection). This is, alas, a scenario seldom seen in the West.

Conditions for Sustained Improvements

Rosabeth Moss Kanter of Harvard says there 5 factors on the sustainability of change:

- **Success.** People feel happier and perform better when there is a feeling of success. And vice versa. And attitude drives performance. There is a feedback loop. So managers must project confidence. War leaders know this.
- **Hard Work.** It is hard work to keep it going. This is entropy. Without it, the system runs down.
- **Emphasis on the team not the individual.** In the West we love heroes, but actually teams are more fundamental for long term survival. Teams need to be mentored ad developed.
- **Many small wins, rather than the occasional big win.** Small wins keep up enthusiasm, and certainly add up. Certainly a TPS trait. Management needs to continually recognise small wins. (See The People Trilogy in Section 39.2)
- **Attitude to failure.** Everyone fails from time to time, but what is crucial is the attitude to failure: punish or treat as part of learning? (Kantor's Law is that : everything dips in the middle (referred to as the 'valley of death' in NPD)

In 'The Village Effect', Susan Pinker quotes several references that demonstrate the positive effects of face-to-face contact on productivity, work satisfaction, and (although she does not use the term) failure demand. Zappos, the shoe retailer, is a case in point. Although no face-to-face contact takes place between call centre operators and customers, staff are allowed to talk amongst themselves and to take as long as required to give customer exactly what they require. 'Delivering WOW through service'. For service organisations,

Pinker quotes, 'Eliminate waste in everything but staffing, and let employees make some decisions.'

Give employees short breaks, allow and encourage them to talk, to gossip, to share experiences.

This leads not only to sustainability but to growth. Military intelligence officers know that a situation is only dangerous when there is both capability and intention. Both are necessary; otherwise there is no danger. The same goes for sustainability – there must be both the capability (time, resources) and the intention (determination, drive, and insistence). Ukraine as a case study?

Two theories from change management seem relevant. 'Cognitive Dissonance' says that people try to be consistent in attitude and behaviour. Thus if a change is out of kilter with prevailing attitudes it will fail. The 'psychological contract' says that there is an unwritten implicit set of expectations (covering, for instance, a sense of dignity and worth) which if breached will lead to disruption and implementation failure. A related theory is that of 'the norm of reciprocity' which is what is given needs to seen as equitable with what is received. Not just money, but behaviour in general. Relations, both at work and personal, cannot be sustained without this balance. The root of many industrial relations issues and strikes?

Single and Double-Loop Learning

Chris Argyris', of Harvard, theory of single and double loop learning is particularly pertinent to Lean implementation and sustainability. Use the analogy of a thermostat: the thermostat makes continual adjustments to maintain the temperature (single loop learning), but does not question whether the temperature is appropriate for prevailing conditions (double loop learning). According to Argyris, many senior managers are excellent at single loop learning, but poor at double loop learning. This is because they have been successful throughout their career, at lower levels, but when faced with wider challenges, they fail. Moreover, they then tend to blame others.

A way around this is self-reflection and constructive feedback criticism. Set up scenarios for important interventions and get constructive, honest feedback from senior colleagues about how you come across. It is not what you say, but how you say it.

To summarize this section, there is no self-sustainability; it requires ongoing efforts in the areas of processes and systems and people. And managers, through their control of the systems, and adaptation to changing circumstances, bear much of the responsibility for the failures of sustaining process improvement.

Further reading

Fraser Wilkinson, *Sustainability of 5S*, MSc Dissertation, Lean Enterprise Research Centre, Cardiff Business School. The author is grateful to Fraser for pointing out several of the concepts discussed here. See also Hervé Duval and Fraser Wilkinson, *Towards Excellence: The Change Agent's Handbook*, Neilson, 2022

Nicola Bateman, *Sustainability*, Lean Enterprise Research Centre, Cardiff Business School, 2001

Peter Senge, *The Dance of Change*, Nicholas Brealey, London, 1999.

Schaffer, R.,H., and Thompson, H., A., *Successful Change Programmes Begin with Results*, Harvard Business Review, Jan-Feb 1992.

Nakane, J. and Hall, R. W., 'Ohno's Method – Creating a Survival Work Culture', *Target* Vol 18, No 1.

Thomas Choi, 'The Successes and Failures of Implementing Continuous Improvement Programs', in Jeff Liker (ed), *Becoming Lean*, Productivity Press, Portland, 1998

Michael Lewis, 'Lean Production and Sustainable Competitive Advantage', *IJOPM*, Vol 20, No 8, 2000

Spenser Johnson, *Who Moved My Cheese?*, Vermillion, London, 1998

Three excellent little books by David Hutchens, *Shadows of the Neanderthal: Illuminating the Beliefs that Limit our Organizations (1999); The Lemming Dilemma (2000); The Tip of the Iceberg (2001)*, Pegasus Communications

Bob Emiliani, *Real Lean*, Volume 1, Centre for Lean Business Management, 2007

Jeffrey Pfeffer, *What Were They Thinking?*, Harvard, 2007

Nelson Repenning and John Sterman, 'Nobody Ever Gets Credit for Fixing Problems that Never Happened: Creating and Sustaining Process Improvement', *California Management Review*, 43:4, Summer 2001

Joan V Gallos (ed), *Organization Development*, Jossey Bass, 2006. This 'blockbuster' text contains articles by virtually every significant writer in the OD field.

Susan Pinker, *The Village Effect: Why Face-to-face Contact Matters*, Atlantic, 2014

Douglas Stone and Sheila Heen, *Thanks for the Feedback,* Portfolio, 2015. (This uncomfortable book should be read by all who give and receive feedback!)

Tracey and Ernie Richardson, *The Toyota Engagement Equation*, McGraw Hill, 2017

Amy Edmondson, *The Fearless Organisation*, Wiley, 2019

DESIGNING FOR FLOW

Without good design and design practice, the potential of Lean will not be realised. Of course, without good customer-responsive and process-responsive design all factory and office operations are waste. Over the past two decades Lean Design concepts have extended into Agile including service, software, and start-up.

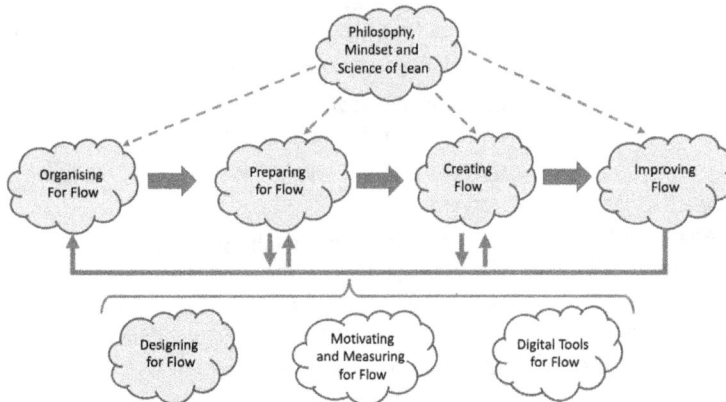

35 Lean Product Development

It can be argued that product development will become the dominant industry competence within the next decade. The reason for this prediction is that there is much more opportunity for competitive advantage in product development than anywhere else.

Good new product management is essential in Lean operations because up to 90% of costs may be locked in after the design and process planning stage, yet these stages incur perhaps 10% of cost. The time taken to bring a new design or product to market is where much of the competitive edge is gained or lost. And, the earlier a problem is detected the less expensive it is to solve. The new product development (NPD) and new product introduction (NPI) area is where leading Lean companies are increasingly competing.

The benefits of applying Lean to product development were first documented by Clark and Fujimoto's seminal study of product development processes in the automotive industry. Much like in manufacturing, they noticed a distinctive set of practices and organisational features that enabled Japanese companies to outperform their Western counterparts. Lean manufacturers tended to also have a Lean product development organisation.

As in manufacturing, cost, speed and quality are important criteria, but these three take on a different perspective: **Cost** ('how much does the development cost overall?', as well as 'how much does one unit cost?'), **speed** (how quickly can we get a product into the market, or 'time-to-market'), and **quality** (how many defects need to be rectified post product launch, e.g. in the form of costly recalls). The priorities for each of these will depend on the product characteristics. Targets for these objectives are typically determined and prioritised by management, whether consciously or not, and should be oriented toward achieving specific financial and or strategic goals of the firm. For innovative, fashion-driven products time will be more critical, for commodities or utilitarian products cost will be more important. Beware, however, of simply trying to copy Toyota's approach to NPD. Instead, a selection of tools is needed that matches the product characteristics and strategic objectives.

While it would be desirable for firms to excel on all of these aspects of performance, there is a growing body of literature that suggests that there are trade-offs that occur between these performance dimensions (see Figure below). In light of this, some authors have recently suggested that the goal of management should be to bring these trade-offs out into the open so that they may be made consciously within the project to maximise profitability or other performance criteria as appropriate.

In this section we will first give a brief overview of how to balance the multiple considerations and wastes in NPD, then illustrate with several variants of product development, before introducing the tools for each respective performance criteria.

Further reading

Kim Clark and Takahiro Fujimoto, *New Product Development Performance,* Harvard Business School Press, 1991

35.1   Four Objectives and Six Trade-offs

In their ground-breaking work on accelerated new product development, Smith and Reinertsen identified four objectives (Development Speed, Product Cost, Product Performance, and Development Programme Expense) as being central to the management of new product development.

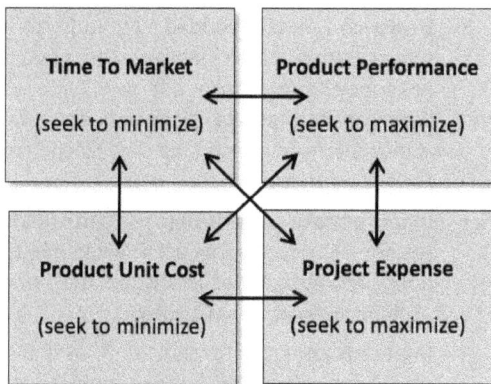

Source: Adapted from Smith and Reinertsen (1998)

These four areas interact in six ways. Smith and Reinertsen believe that it is necessary to quantify the trade-offs since every new product introduction is a compromise that needs to be understood and managed.

1.   Development Speed and Product Cost. Rationalising and improving a design through part count, weight analysis, part commonality, DFM, and value engineering can save future costs. But they take time, thereby delaying the introduction of the product and possibly losing market share.

2. Development Speed and Product Performance: Improving performance can make it more attractive to customers thereby improving future sales through a larger market, a higher price, and a longer product life. These improvements take time and may sacrifice initial sales and initial market share. The 'first mover' advantage may be lost.

3.   Development Speed and Development Programme Expense: This is the traditional 'project crashing' trade-off from classic project management. Most projects have 'fixed' costs such as management and overhead that accumulate with time. On the other hand, within limits, adding extra resources decreases project duration but costs more. Is it worthwhile spending more to finish earlier? There are non-linear effects – digging a trench with six men does not take one sixth of the time it takes with one man.

4. Product Performance and Product Cost: Adding or redesigning a feature may improve performance but at what product cost? What marginal performance are customers prepared to pay for?

5. Product Cost and Development Programme Expense: By spending more on development, say through value engineering, we may be able to reduce cost. Is it worth it?

6. Development Programme Expense and Product Performance: Improving a design and improving performance may result in improved sales. But improving performance may involve additional cost. In a less complex way, Mascitelli suggests a 'least discernible difference test' which is to ask whether customers will pay a penny more for a feature that is being considered. There is a conceptual maximum number of satisfied customers that reduces on the one hand due to reduced benefits and on the other hand due to price increases.

Similarly, Smith and Reinertsen suggest that a spreadsheet model be developed to quantify these six relationships. Remember to use the time value of money, trading off immediate project costs against discounted future sales (essentially using

Net Present Value (NPV)). Quantifying the six relationships forces marketing, design and engineering to think carefully about additions and rationalisations. Such a sensitivity analysis can be used as a powerful management tool, as it creates a visual prioritisation of performance objectives. Based on such NPV data, one can illustrate the effects of questions such as 'how much does one month delay cost?', or 'if you miss unit cost by 3%, what will this do to profitability?', or 'what does missing a features or performance specification mean for sales?' Playing with such scenarios will focus everyone's attention on the truly important factors.

However, there are no fixed rules to be followed – as Michael Cusumano and Kentaro Nobeoka, show in their comparisons of Japanese approaches to car development between 1980 and 1990, the answers to these trade-offs change with time and environment.

Further reading

Michael Cusumano and Kentaro Nobeoka, *Thinking Beyond Lean*, The Free Press, New York, 1998

Preston Smith and Donald Reinertsen, *Developing Products in Half The Time*, Van Nostrand Reinhold, New York, 1991

Ronald Mascitelli, *Mastering Lean Product Development*, Technology Perspectives, 2011

35.2 Wastes in New Product Development

Many professionals would like to do their professional work but spend inordinate amounts of time on frustrating secondary work. (An estimate of waste of time, often shocking, can be obtained by activity sampling done by the professionals themselves.) A priority, then, is to maximise the time that designers spend designing, or engineers spend engineering.

Waste awareness, as in manufacture, is an excellent point of departure. Allen Ward, in his seminal book on the Lean Product and Process Development, that is strongly based on Toyota design principles, gives three categories of

'knowledge waste'. First, Scatter (that disrupt flow through poor communication barriers, and inappropriate complex tools – Ward illustrates this with FMEA or QFD). Second, Hand-off waste (that result from the separation of knowledge, responsibility, action, and feedback. Third, 'Wishful Thinking' waste. This includes discarded knowledge and making decisions without data or thinking – this is partly what Reinertsen describes in his trade-off model – see above.

Here we attempt our own list, with inspiration from one of the great gurus of Lean Design, Ron Mascitelli.

- **Sorting and Searching**. Basically, 5S in design and NPD. In office and documents,

- **Inappropriate targets**. These lead to either cutting corners where targets are too tight, or to loafing where they are too lax. The latter is 'Parkinson's Law' – work expands to fill the time available.

- **Underload and Overload**. An important managerial task is to load level the work. If not done, the results are the same as inappropriate targets. Kingman's equation is even more relevant! (See 'The Science of Lean', Chapter 4)

- **Inappropriate prioritising** – particularly resulting in designs that are shelved due to policy changes. Note: This is not the same as 'bookshelving' – see below.

- **Interference.** From 'dropping in', (e mails, socialising, noise, etc.) Rules need to be established to allow for thinking time.

- **Inappropriate trade-offs**. See Reinertsen, above.

- **Excessive part proliferation**. This results from not using a standard set of, for example, fasteners or components but 'starting from a blank sheet of paper'. Also not building on appropriate previous designs.

- **Presence.** At meetings where 90% of the time a person has no role.

- **Waiting** – for decisions, for stage gates, for tests, for data, etc. This is particularly important for critical resources, where flow needs to be maintained, and appropriate time buffers used.

- **Starting too late; stopping too early**. NPD needs to be end-to-end – from customer need to well into product life.

- **Inappropriate involvement**. Omitting or delaying the involvement of key functions such as marketing, production, manufacturing engineering, tooling, quality, packaging, distribution.

The following three not only waste time and resources on rework, but are compounded when learning and recording is not built in.

- **Lack of feedback** – resulting in a low learning rate.

- Not recording **lessons learned**.

- **Mistakes, defects and errors**.

The following four waste gaps are a set. The 'Service Gaps' (see Zeithaml et al.) model is useful here. They talk about the gap between what is actually wanted and what is thought to be wanted, the gap between what is wanted and what is specified, the gap between specification and performance, and the gap between actual performance and what is said about performance.

- **Co-ordination**. A good design is holistic. Optimizing the parts does not necessarily optimise the whole. A very important idea for the lead designer.

- **Communication.** All participants need to have the same, clear, goals.

- Ill-defined product requirements.

An effective, and relatively quick, way to reduce all these wastes is, first, to recognise their presence, and, second, to collectively work out actions for each professional in the group. Many designers value their creativity and individuality – so bureaucratic rules don't work. However, voluntary participation does work, particularly if it makes their life easier.

An amusing, but also serious view of wastes is Huthwaite's 'Ings': Tracking, training, tooling, certifying, monitoring, validating, documenting, inspecting, reworking, and many others....

Further reading

Ronald Mascitelli, *The Lean Product Development Guidebook*, Technology Perspectives, 2007

Allen Ward, *Lean Product and Process Development*, LEI, 2007

Bart Huthwaite, *The Lean Design Solution*, Institute for Lean Innovation, 2011

Valerie Zeithaml and Bitner, *Services Marketing*, McGraw Hill, 2008

Norbert Majerus, *Lean-Driven Innovation*, CRC Press, 2016

35.3 Toyota's Approach to Product Development

Toyota's approach to new product development is based on a mixture of techniques related to cost and lead-time reduction, as well as quality assurance. In their study of Toyota, Clark and Fujimoto found several 'best practices': high levels of supplier engineering, overlapping product and process engineering, strong communication mechanisms, strong in-house manufacturing capability, wide task assignments for engineers and the heavyweight project manager system. These closely mirror the Lean principles, but applied to new product development. Cusumano also published a list of Lean product development practices based on Honda's model that reinforced these findings and additionally noted Honda's skilful use of computer aided design tools. This bundle of concepts became widely accepted as 'Lean product development' and rapidly diffused beyond the automobile producers into the manufacturing industry in general. The following features draw on both Allen Ward and on Morgan and Liker.

First, let us make a general point. Putting in front-end effort on project clarification, working concurrently and meticulously (even if much slower) to avoid sub-system technical conflict is thoroughly worthwhile. You want to minimise the number of post launch problems. The tortoise and the hare.

Ward, and Sobek, start with a useful pneumonic, LAMDA – the product developer's version of PDCA. Look, Ask, Model, Discuss, and Act. (Notice this – much time on finding out from understanding customer's needs, and modelling and discussing alternatives, before starting actual design work.)

- **Chief engineers** – sometimes referred to as 'Heavyweight project managers'. These are not project managers in the conventional administrator sense but, as Ward calls them, Entrepreneurial System Designers (ESD). Moreover, they are experienced ENGINEERS, not managers. Their task is both holistic (integrating all parts) and end-to-end (from need to use). Thus if an ESD brings a product to market on time but the product itself fails in the market, he has failed. These chief engineers have only a small staff but work through functional managers using their influence, reputation and considerable experience to avoid the many delays so common in traditional product development. The chief engineer or ESD has such strong influence on the final product that it internally often becomes known as 'Mr. Ohashi's car'. ESD's also 'represent customers' – not relying only on market survey but uncovering needs that customers have not yet articulated. (See, for example, notes on Ideal Final Result in TRIZ). As such they are responsible for specification, cost targets, layout, and major component choice in order to make sure that the product concept is accurately translated into the technical details of the vehicle.
- **Functional managers are responsible for developing 'towering expertise'** in their own areas – maybe engines, suspension, or

controls. They bring state-of-the-art solutions into new products. Functional staff are as much researchers as designers, so they enjoy high status and professional development in their own area. In new product development they work for their functional engineer, not for the project manager. The latter needs to negotiate for their time but be concerned with integration. The ESD, however, signs every drawing. Integral with the use of functional expertise are the following:

- **Set based design**. The concept here is to keep options open as late as possible. There are 'sets' of options for the various system elements, and these are gradually narrowed down as the design clarifies. As a result, there are less 'stage gates', but broader 'milestones'. Between the milestones there is considerable individual flexibility. Concepts are gradually narrowed using 'Concept Screening' techniques. Possible 'solution sets' are explored in parallel, but once a particular solution is decided upon it is frozen unless a change is absolutely necessary. This is similar to the Lean concept of postponement - delaying freezing the specifications until the last possible moment.
- **Bookshelving.** Starting with sets may sound wasteful. Not so, if unused designs, and basic research, are bookshelved for future use. This also allows rapid new product development. It is a form of modularity.
- **Trade-off curves**, are developed by the functional experts. Examples may be strength against thickness, number of cycles against type of alloy, noise level against insulation thickness. Sets of choices are quickly established. Having trade-ff curves helps the ESD and the engineer to make appropriate the trade-offs, as described by Reinertsen, above.
- **Check sheets**. This is the simple but powerful idea of recording experiences systematically as a project proceeds. What

works and what does not. As a result the wheel is not re-invented. Expertise does not walk out the door when a person leaves. Next time a similar product or sub-system is stated, start with what was learned last time.

- **In-house tooling and manufacturing engineering.** Alas, a skill set that so many have outsourced. Outsourcing may seem cost efficient, but remember product features are easy to copy, but how to make them, and how to make them fast, is not. Good new product development rotates staff from design to manufacturing engineering. For example, prototypes are built by regular manufacturing engineers, so that they experience what it takes to produce this product at full volume. Virtual modelling has an increasing role.

- **Concurrency (or cross-functional teams).** Quite a well-accepted idea is to work concurrently on stages rather than 'over the wall' (for example, research to design to engineering to production). So, multi-discipline teams work together. The chief engineer is the facilitator. While car design is proceeding, engineering and die production also proceed. During the early concept stages, engineering makes from 5 to 20 one-fifth scale clay models. The engineering team begins full-scale clay modelling at intermediate stages as well as at final stage, unlike other car manufacturers who only make half size models during early stages. This enables tool and die designers to begin work. They too use engineering check sheets, built up from experience, about what can and cannot be done. Difficulties are fed back immediately to the design team.

  Today much use is made of 3D 'walk in' virtual reality computer simulation and displays – as for example by BARCO

- **Project levelling.** Bring the Heijunka concept into new product development. This means careful thought on time phasing. Traditional critical path software, even using the resource levelling feature, is seldom good enough. Set based design, bookshelving, and functional development can all be used.

- **Project flow.** Avoiding hold-ups by critical resources whilst waiting for other stages, is an important role for the chief designer's team. A leaf can be taken from Lean Construction where the 'Last Planner' methodology aims to do just this by developing checklists for other functions before critical activities are due to start.

- **Visibility.** The good Lean principle of visual management is even more important in product development. Toyota uses an 'Obeya' (Big Room) for each new product where all activities and progress is shown on charts. Co-ordination meetings are held in the Obeya. A hierarchy of charts are on display from overall concept to sub system. There are progress boards and A3 problem solutions. Who is doing what where is monitored. Problems are highlighted in daily, short, stand-up meetings. Increasingly, ideas from Agile and SCRUM software design are found. See below for more on Obeya.

- **Supplier involvement.** A critical decision, by the chief engineer is what to insource and what to outsource. See the Supply chain section. Clark and Fujimoto found that Japanese companies tended to sub-contract out much larger fractions of the engineering work to a group of suppliers with whom they had developed close relationships. This practice allowed projects to be kept compact and simplified the amount of internal project coordination required which, in turn, contributed to shorter lead times and higher development efficiency. In addition, since it was the suppliers who were to eventually manufacture the parts anyway, this practice allowed them to develop specialised knowledge and design the components themselves with their own manufacturing capabilities in mind, lowering the cost of components. This is also known as 'open spec'. A seat must fit into the space, but you design the seat.

- **Front loading.** The later in the design process a problem is fixed, the more effort is required, hence the more expensive and lengthy fixing the problem becomes. Front-loading aims to address this pulling key decisions forward, whist retaining set-based flexibility. The early identification and solving of problems can help reduce development time and cost, and frees up resources to be more innovative in the marketplace. According to Thomke and Fujimoto, front-loading can be achieved by (1) project-to-project knowledge transfer, which leverages previous projects by transferring problem and solution-specific information to new projects; and (2) rapid problem-solving that leverages CAD and other simulation technologies to increase the overall rate at which development problems are identified and solved.

Further reading
James Morgan and Jeffrey Liker, Designing the Future, McGraw Hill, 2019

36 Tools for Lean NPD

36.1 Design Thinking

A significant lesson about Lean NPD is spending sufficient time up front clarifying the purpose and uncertainties. In other words, before sitting down in front of the CAD system there is a lot of thinking to do. Westrick and Cooper extend the Double Diamond approach discussed below, to two diamonds in the exploration phase and two in the execution phase. We will illustrate this with moving overseas – something both the authors have done. Instead of ordering a container and hoping for the best...get the family together (don't do this yourself!), face-to-face, and...

Explore:

- What don't we know?: How much space, is there going to be at the destination; what appliances (and clothes) will be compatible; what are prices at the destination; how long to get there, etc. Home in on the crucial questions. Find out.

- What are possible solutions? Take all or some; air, sea or both; Risks and costs? Home in on the solutions.

Execute:

- Detail options? Packing options; Movers? Insurance? Packing order? Select the most appropriate. Write specs, sign contract.

- Production. What should be monitored?

Cooper and Westrick state that only when the Exploration phase is complete can a 'Promise' be given. Before that we just don't know. Steve Jobs was a master here – only announcing products when he was confident of launch date with all uncertainties having been worked through.

Furr and Dyer propose a very similar four stage approach for the Exploration phase: Insight, Problem, Solution, Business Model.

Insight is gained by questioning, observing, networking, experimenting. 'Problems' focuses on the 'job to be done', not the solution – Levitt's famous 'holes not drills' story. Look at customer 'pain points'. The result is the value proposition. Solution involves prototyping the 'minimum awesome product(s). Business Model involves validating the go-to-market strategy – pricing, customer acquisition and cost structure.

In manufacturing the realisation has grown that being truly Lean requires beginning at the design stage. It is often too late when products arrive at the shop-floor manufacturing stage – too many wastes are already built in. A poorly designed product can never fully be compensated for by excellent manufacturing.

Design Thinking is different from operations thinking. Roger Martin explains this well by citing James March (of 'The Behavioural Theory of the Firm' fame) who stated that a firm might engage primarily in *exploration* (seeking new knowledge) or *exploitation* (seeking payoff from existing knowledge or refinement of the knowledge). The former is the realm of Design Thinking, the latter Operations thinking. Operations have been the traditional area of Lean Thinking. Systems Thinking encompasses both areas. Today, most Western organisations cannot compete, in either manufacturing or service, unless they embrace exploration or design thinking.

The British Design Council has for years used the 'Double Diamond' approach to design. This is a two stage approach. The top diamond is about Discover and Define, the bottom Diamond is about Develop and Deliver. This is roughly equivalent to exploration and exploitation, or to open thinking and closed thinking, to design thinking and operations thinking. Yet another view is that the top diamond is concerned with heuristics and the lower diamond with algorithms. The Double Diamond is shown below.

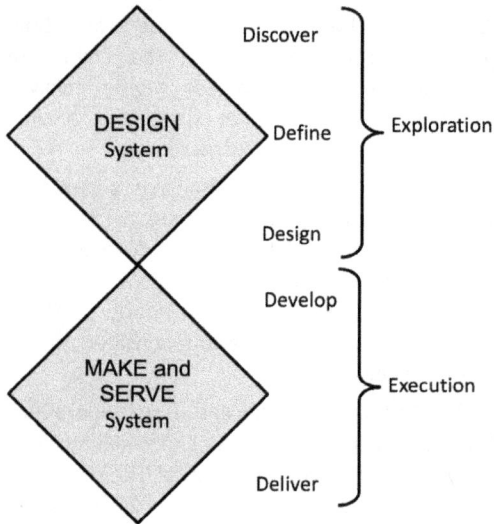

Design Thinking and Lean Thinking both harness the creative skills of employees but do so in different ways. Design thinking is much more open. There is a blank sheet of paper to begin. Lean Thinking is about creativity within given parameters – developing ways in which a given product or service can be better made and delivered.

Design thinking cuts through the traditional barriers that frequently exist between industrial design and operations, between R&D and product and service design, between service designers and customers, and between those that design the service and those that deliver the service. Design thinking is therefore a natural extension of Lean Thinking.

Design Thinking is about moving towards 'Experiment First, Then Design' rather than Design then trial. There are great similarities with the Eric Ries' 'Lean Startup'. Design authority Ron Mascitelli tells about making a wooden table, varnishing it, and then discovering problems with the varnish: far better to test the varnish on a sample of the wood first. Likewise in software or service design, just do enough to test and get feedback. Perhaps pivot. In other words, learning!

The Double Diamond figure is derived from the Design Council model, and has similarities to the problem solving funnel used within Lean, the knowledge funnel used by Roger Martin, and in Value Engineering.

The figure shows stages of evolution, perhaps of a new service or product, perhaps an improvement, moving through four stages. The stages are frequently not uni-directional. Many recursions take place. The figure can be related to several concepts discussed throughout this book. Note: In this figure, the diamonds overlap. Some think this is a bad idea.

The problem area is 'discovered'. This may involve several of the following:

- o Visiting the gemba for direct observation;
- o Understanding customer needs;
- o Defining value for the clients (there may be several);
- o Questioning the system boundary;
- o Demand analysis
- o A 'Painstorm' – identifying customer's greatest pain points (used by Intuit)

The Define stage may involve

- o Homing in on the real issues as in the left side of an A3;
- o Defining the purpose;

The top diamond is explored, by for instance:

- o Generating alternatives via creative thinking techniques such as 3P
- o End to end thinking;
- o Benchmarking;
- o Finding contradictions as in TRIZ
- o Examining the process, not the person;
- o Keeping options open rather than closing them down too early, as in set based design

Develop: here the defined area is explored, by for instance

- o Lean analysis tools, including mapping;
- o Muri and Mura;
- o Kaizen events;

- o Idea management;
- o A3 analysis;
- o Pareto analysis;
- o Root cause analysis;
- o 5 why thinking;
- o SIPOC;
- o Six Sigma tools for variation reduction;

Deliver: Methods and tools include

- o Leader standard work;
- o Visual management;
- o 5S;
- o Standard work;
- o Detail waste reduction;

We may note that:

- Not all problems or situations progress through all four stages, nor should they. Rather, there is evolution from top to bottom as understanding develops and experience is gained. Take planning an overseas journey: once there was considerable uncertainty. Now you book your flight on-line from home. The top stages can be progressed through very rapidly. For effective design, there is therefore a need to understand current customers, current technology, and current service delivery practice.

- Systems Thinking is highly relevant in the top three areas of discover, define, and develop

- Design thinking is most relevant in the top diamond, but Lean Thinking also plays a role.

- Both Daniel Pink and Roger Martin discuss 'heuristics' and 'algorithms'. Both make the point that competing on heuristics rather than algorithms is already a necessity for work, especially in the West. A heuristic sets the general course, but allows adaptation. For instance 'keep going up' is a heuristic that will get you to the top of a

mountain – if not to the summit, at least to a localised peak. An algorithm is more specific. It provides much more detailed instruction: 'walk 100m, turn right'. An extreme case of an algorithm is computer code. Heuristics are found in the explore stage, algorithms in the develop and deliver stage. They overlap in the refine stage. Heuristics are more applicable in professional services and interactive services. Algorithms are more applicable in transactional service. Pink makes the point that extrinsic motivators MAY be applicable with algorithmic work, but that intrinsic motivators are the only successful type in heuristic work.

- You should only attempt 'algorithmic' control when the system is routine. Parts of some manufacturing jobs are like this, but virtually no service job is completely algorithmic

- Lean thinking is most relevant in the lower diamond. Much of lean thinking has been too narrowly defined, being limited to the 'deliver' stage only. This is 'Fake Lean' leading to 'Lean is Mean' accusations, and to a disrespectful use of employees whose opinions are not sought despite being on the front line.

- Industrialised working and traditional Lean thinking (emphasising a high degree of standard work) is NOT appropriate in open ended, exploratory situations. Design thinking allows variety to be designed into processes.

- There will be more standard work as one progresses from top to bottom. In the top diamond, standard work may only be appropriate in outlining the main stages. At the bottom of the lower diamond many tasks (but not all) will have standard work. (Note: Standard work is NEVER fixed in stone. See the 'Preparing for Flow' Chapter.)

- There may be different starting and end points. Some situations are clear and can start at the develop stage. But beware, defining a problem too narrowly may be what the late Ackoff called 'resolving' the problem rather than 'dissolving' it, by systems or design thinking. Other situations may carry the 'solution' too far – reducing the 'solution' to algorithm status (too closely specified standard work?) when a heuristic solution would be more appropriate.

Further reading

Marc Strickdorn et al, *This is Service Design Thinking*, BIS Publishers, 2010

Roger Martin, *The Design of Business*, Harvard, 2009

Roger Martin, 'The Innovation Catalysts', *Harvard Business Review*, June 2011.

Ronald Mascitelli, *Mastering Lean Product Development*, Technology Perspectives, 2011

Thomas Lockwood (ed), *Design Thinking: Integrating Innovation, Customer Experience, and Brand Value*, Allworth Press, 2010

Katherine Radeka, *The Shortest Distance Between You and Your New Product*, (revised 2nd edn.) Chesapeake, 2017

36.2 Phase Gates

The 'Phase Gate approach, where a NPD project is divided into phases, separated by gates (at which decision makers decide to go, kill, hold, or recycle), has been around for some decades. This is similar to the 'Waterfall Method' where each phase is completed before the next begins. The intent of the process is for the gate reviews to serve as a means to inform the leadership of project status and build confidence in the project as spending and financial commitments escalate through the development cycle. In the phase gate process, the rationale for requiring executive sign-off for increased spending levels is that executives can then manage the financial exposure of the company by restricting spending or cancelling risky projects. Reality is often different. The project may

be required due to regulation, or the sales revenue is needed to meet growth objectives. Cancelling a project can involve loss of 'face'. Many (all?) have sunk cost bias – a reluctance to throw away all that expenditure. So even though the phase gate system was instituted to manage financial risk, the basic control mechanism—cancelling the project—is rarely a feasible option and there is tremendous pressure on the review committee to move the project forward.

36.3 Obeya

Cooper and Westrick point out that despite dramatic advances in technology, the most effective way to create teamwork is to work face-to-face as a team on tasks of mutual importance. This can't be achieved by simply demanding cooperation or putting everyone together. This is where a face-to-face collaboration tools such as team-based project planning (vertical value stream mapping), team boards, all in an 'Obeya Room (or 'big room') or 'Design studio' become necessary.

An Obeya room should not be used only for reviews. Rather, documents and plans placed around the walls should be regularly updated and visited frequently. The purpose is team working, not a display or a review room.

Further General Reading on NPD and Design

Kim Clark and Takahiro Fujimoto, *New Product Development Performance,* Harvard Business School Press, 1991

Durward K. Sobek II, Allen C. Ward and Jeffrey K. Liker, 'Toyota's Principles of Set-Based Concurrent Engineering', *MIT Sloan Management Review* Winter 1999, Vol. 40, No. 2, pp. 67–83

James Morgan and Jeffrey Liker, *The Toyota Product Development System,* Productivity, 2006

Allen Ward, *Lean Product and Process Development*, LEI, 2007

Allen Ward and Michael Kennedy, *Product Development for the Lean Enterprise*, Oaklea Press, 2003.

Lawrence P Leach, Lean Project Management: Eight Principles for Success, Advanced Projects, 2006

Stefan Thomke and Takahiro Fujimoto 'The Effect of 'Front-Loading' Problem-Solving on Product Development Performance' *Journal of Product Innovation Management* Vol. 17 No. 2, p. 128-142, 2000

Rob Westrick and Chris Cooper, *Winning by Design*, Simpler, 2012

Donald Reinertsen, *The Principles of Product Development Flow,* Celeritas, 2009

Stefan Thomke and Donald Reinertsen, 'Six Myths of Product Development', *Harvard Business Review*, May 2012, pp 85-94

Gwendolyn Galsworth, *Smart Simple Design Reloaded*, Visual Lean, 2015

Trevor Owens and Obie Fernandez, *The Lean Enterprise: How Corporations can Innovate like Startups*, Wiley, 2014

James Adams, *Good Products Bad Products*, McGraw Hill, 2012

36.4   Quality Function Development

Quality Function Deployment (QFD) is a 'meta' technique that grew in importance in both product and service design. Its use seems to have declined of late. It is understood by the authors that Toyota no longer uses it. QFD is a meta technique because many other techniques described in this book can or should be used in undertaking QFD design or analysis. These other techniques include several of the 'new tools', benchmarking, market surveys, the Kano model, the performance - importance matrix, and FMEA. Customer needs are identified and systematically compared with the technical or operating characteristics of the product or service. The process brings out the relative importance of customer needs which, when set against the characteristics of the product leads to the identification of the most important or sensitive characteristics. These are the characteristics that need development or attention. Although the word 'product' is used in the descriptions that follow,

QFD is equally applicable in services. Technical characteristics then become the service characteristics.

Perhaps a chief advantage of QFD is that a multidisciplinary team all concerned with the particular product carries it out. QFD acts as a forum for marketing, design, engineering, manufacturing, distribution and others to work together using a concurrent or simultaneous engineering approach. QFD is then the vehicle for these specialists to attack a problem together rather than by 'throwing the design over the wall' to the next stage. QFD is therefore not only concerned with quality but with the simultaneous objectives of reducing overall development time, meeting customer requirements, reducing cost, and producing a product or service which fits together and works well the first time. The mechanics of QFD are not cast in stone, and can easily be adapted to local innovation.

The first QFD matrix is also referred to as the 'house of quality'. This is because of the way the matrices in QFD fit together to form a house-shaped diagram. A full QFD exercise may deploy several matrix diagrams, forming a sequence that gradually translates customer requirements into specific manufacturing steps and detailed manufacturing process requirements. For instance, a complete new car could be considered at the top level but subsequent exercises may be concerned with the engine, body shell, doors, instrumentation, brakes, and so on. Thereafter the detail would be deployed into manufacturing and production. But the most basic QFD exercise would use only one matrix diagram that seeks to take customer requirements and to translate them into specific technical requirements.

36.5 Value Engineering and Value Methodology

Value engineering and value methodology (VE/VM) has traditionally been used for cost reduction in engineering design. But the power of its methodology means that it is an effective weapon for quality and productivity improvement in manufacturing and in services.

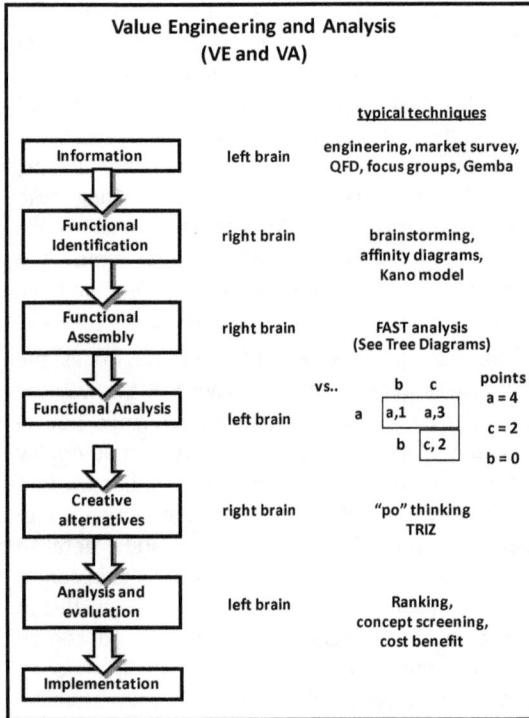

Value Engineering and Analysis (VE and VA)

The term value methodology (VM) recognises this fact. The first step in any VE/VM project is Orientation. This involves selecting the appropriate team. and training them in basic value concepts. The best VE/VM is done in multidisciplinary teams. 'Half of VE is done by providing the relevant information,' says Jaganathan. By this he means that clarity of communication about customer (internal or external) is half the battle, particularly if customer needs have changed without anyone taking notice.

VM proper begins by systematically identifying the most important functions of a product or service. Then alternatives for the way the function can be undertaken are examined using creative thinking. A search procedure homes in on the most promising alternatives, and eventually the best alternative is implemented. One can recognise in these steps much similarity with various other quality techniques such as QFD, the systematic use of the 7 tools of quality, and the Deming cycle. In fact these are all mutually reinforcing. VM brings added insight, and a powerful analytical and creative force to bear.

Value engineering was pioneered in the USA by General Electric, but has gained from value specialists such as Mudge and from the writers on creative thinking such as Edward de Bono. Today the concepts of TRIZ are most relevant. The Society of American Value Engineers (SAVE) has fostered the development.

VM usually works at the fairly detailed level of a particular component or sub-system, but has also been used in a hierarchical fashion working down level by level from an overall product or service concept to the detail. At each level the procedure described would be repeated. Like many other quality and productivity techniques, VM is a group activity. It requires a knowledgeable group of people, sharing their insights and stimulating one another's ideas, to make progress. But there is no limitation on who can participate. VM can and has been used at every level from chief executive to shop floor.

What appears to give value management particular power is the deliberate movement from 'left brain' (linear) analysis to 'right brain' (creative) thinking.

Effective problem solving requires both the logical step forward and the 'illogical' creative leap.

Functional analysis

Functional analysis is the first step. The basic functions or customer requirements of the product or service are listed, or brainstormed out. (Right brain thinking.) A function is best described by a verb and a noun, such as 'make sound', 'transfer pressure', 'record personal details' or 'greet customer'. The question to be answered is 'what functions does this product/service undertake?' Typically there will be a list of half a dozen or more functions.

Customer Requirements	Importance	Percentage importance	Components			
			Beef	Bun	Lettuce	Ketchup
Taste good	6	46	23 .5	11.5 .25		11.5 .25
Provide nutrition	2	15	10.5 .7	4.5 .3		
Appeal visually	1	8	2.4 .3	1.6 .2	2.4 .3	1.6 .2
Value for money	4	31	15.5 .5	15.5 .5		
		100%				
Overall influence		%	51.4	33.1	2.4	13.1
Cost (%)		%	62	30	20	8
Value index		Influence/cost	0.83	1.1	0.12	1.6

There is a temptation to take the basic function for granted. Do not do this; working through often gives very valuable insights. For instance, for a domestic heating time controller, some possible functions are 'activate at required times', 'encourage economy', and 'supply heat when needed'. The example shows a hamburger design. Pair wise comparison or points distribution may be used to weight the functions or requirements. In pair wise comparison, each function is compared with each other function, and 1 point is given to the most important of the two, or zero points if the functions are considered equally important. This gives the relative importance weighting column.

Adding up the scores gives the relative weightings These relative weightings need to be converted to percentages such that the sum adds up to 100%. Now the components of the product are listed as columns in the matrix. See the figure. Then the importance of each component to each function is estimated and converted to a percentage of total cost. In the example, the function 'taste good' is estimated to be influenced 50% by the beef and 25% each by bun and ketchup. The influence is written in the bottom left hand corner of each cell.

The weighted influence (i.e. the weight x the influence) is written in the top right of each cell. The overall influence of each component is the sum of the top right hand cell entries, and is written in a row below the matrix. Then the cost of each component is estimated, and written in a row. The last step is to calculate a value index, which is the influence % divided by the cost %. Ratios less than one are prime candidates for cost reduction. Ratios substantially greater than one indicate the possibility of enhancing the feature. Back to the right brain.

Creativity

Now the creative phase begins. This is concerned with developing alternative, more cost effective, ways of achieving the basic functions and reducing costs of the most important components. Here the rules of brainstorming must be allowed - no criticism, listing down all ideas, writing down as many ideas as possible however apparently ridiculous. Various 'tricks' can be used; deliberate short periods of silence, writing ideas on cards anonymously, sequencing suggestions in a 'round robin' fashion, making a sketch, role-playing out a typical event, viewing the scene from an imaginary helicopter or explaining the product to an 'extra-terrestrial'. Humour can be an important part of creativity. See also TRIZ, later.

A particularly powerful tool is the use of the de Bono 'po' word. This is simply a random noun selected from a dictionary to conjure up mental images that are then used to develop new ideas. For instance the word 'cloud' could be used in conjunction with the design of packaging where the basic function was 'give protection'. The word cloud conjures images of fluffiness (padding?), air (air pockets?), rain (waterproof?), silver lining (metal reinforcement?), shadow (can't see the light, leads to giving the user information), cloud is 'hard to pick up' (how is the packaging lifted?), wind (whistling leading to a warning of overload?), moisture (water/humidity resistant? water can take the shape of its container – can the packaging?), obscuring the view (a look inside panel?), and so on. Do not jump to other 'po' words; select one and let the group exhaust its possibilities.

Analysis and evaluation

Now back to the left brain. Sometimes a really outstanding idea will emerge. Otherwise there may be several candidates. Some of these candidates may need further investigation before they can be recommended. (In the above example, is it feasible or possible to introduce some sort of metal reinforcement?). Beware of throwing out ideas too early - the best ideas are often a development from an apparently poor idea. So take time to discuss them. In some cases it may be necessary for the team to take a break while more technical feasibility is evaluated or costs determined, by specialists. There are several ways to evaluate. Pairwise comparison with multi-discipline group discussion is good possibility. Another possibility is to write all ideas on cards, then give a set of cards to pairs of group members, and ask each pair to come up with the best two ideas. Then get the full group to discuss all the leading ideas. Yet another is to draw up a cost-benefit chart (cost along one axis, benefits along another). Ask the group members to plot the locations of ideas on the chart. There is no reason why several of these methods cannot be used together. Do what makes the group happy - it is their project and their ideas.

Implementation

Implementation of the most favourable change is the last step. One of the benefits of the VM process is that group members tend to identify with the final solution, and to understand the reasons behind it. This should make implementation easier and faster.

Further reading

Kaneo Akiyama, *Function Analysis*, Productivity Press, Cambridge MA, 1991

G. Jaganathan, *Getting More at Less Cost*, Tata McGraw Hill, New Delhi, 1996

See also, J Jerry Kaufman and Roy Woodhead, *Stimulating Innovation in Products and Services with Function Analysis and Mapping*, Wiley, 2006. This gives a detailed description of FAST (Function Analysis System Technique) modelling.

See the SAVE International website. www.value-eng.org

36.6 Design for Manufacture (DFM) and Design for Assembly (DFA)

Design for manufacture (DFM) is a key 'enabling' concept for Lean manufacture. Easy and fast assembly has an impact right through the manufacturing life of the product, so time spent up front is well spent. A wider view of DFM should consider the cost of components, the cost and ease of assembly, and the support costs.

Cost of Components should be the starting point. Much will depend upon the envisaged production volume: for instance, machined components may be most cost effective for low volumes, pressings (requiring tooling investment) best for middle volumes, and mouldings (requiring even higher initial investment but low unit costs) best for higher volumes.

Other considerations include

- Create variety as late as possible
- Design for no changeover or minimal changeovers
- Design for minimum fixturing

- Design for maximum commonality (Group Technology)
- Design to minimise the number of parts

Complexity of Assembly

Boothroyd and Dewhurst have suggested a DFA index aimed at assessing the complexity of assembly. This is the ratio of (the theoretical minimum number of parts x 3 seconds) to the estimated total assembly time. The theoretically minimum number of parts can be calculated by having each candidate part meet at least one of the following:

- Does the part need to move relative to the rest of the assembly?
- Must the part be made of a different material?
- Does the part have to be physically separated for access, replacement, or repair?

If not theoretically necessary, then the designer should consider the physical integration with one or more other parts. And why 3 seconds? Merely because that is a good average unit assembly time. Once this is done, then Knight Boothroyd and Dewhurst suggest further rules for maximum ease of assembly. These include:

- Insert part from the top of the assembly
- Make part self-aligning
- Avoid having to orient the part
- Arrange for one-handed assembly
- No tools are required for assembly
- Assembly takes place in a single, linear motion
- The part is secured immediately upon insertion

Boothroyd and Dewhurst now market a software package to assist with DFM. They suggest that for both DFA and Design Complexity (see below), not only should there be measurement and monitoring of one's own products, but that the measures should be determined for competitor's products as well. This is a form of benchmarking. Targets should be set. Such measures should also be used for value engineering.

Continuous improvement is therefore driven by specific targets, measures, and benchmarks, and not left to chance. It should be possible to create design and assembly indices for each subassembly, to rank them by complexity, and Pareto fashion to tackle complexity systematically. Further, it should be possible to determine, from benchmarking competitor products, the best of each type of assembly and then to construct a theoretical overall best product even though one may not yet exist in practice. This is a form of Stuart Pugh's 'Concept Screening' method.

Assembly Support Costs should be considered at the design stage. This includes consideration of:

- Inventory management and sourcing
- The necessity for new vendors
- A requirement for new tools to be used
- A requirement for new operator skills to be acquired
- The possibility of failsafing

More recently C Martin Hinckley has estimated that assembly defects are directly proportional to assembly time. To this end he has developed so-called Quality Control of Complexity that is a straightforward way of estimating assembly time. Details are given in his book.

Assembly alternatives can now be considered relatively easily for their impact on assembly defects due to mistakes.

Further reading

W. Knight, G. Boothroyd and P. Dewhurst, *Product Design for Manufacturing and Assembly*, T&F India, 2020.

Karl Ulrich and Steven Eppinger, *Product Design and Development*, McGraw Hill, New York, 1995, Chapter 3

C Martin Hinckley, *Make No Mistake!*, Productivity Press, Portland, 2001

36.7 Modularity and Platforms

In order to save development cost, there are essentially three ways how to cut down: first, to increase the 'component carry over' by using components from the previous model (although this might not always be a possibility, in particular in high-clockspeed industries where technology moves on). Secondly, a firm can choose to adopt a modular product architecture that allows for flexibility in sourcing and customisation. Thirdly, one can create product platforms, which each contain multiple end products. Here development cost is saved by creating larger economies of scale for the 'basic design'. We will discuss the latter two in turn. Also see Cusumano and Nobeoka in their book on 'multi-project management' for more details on the benefits of modularity and component carry over.

Modularity

Modularity essentially means that (a) a 'one-to-one mapping' between components and functions exists, and (b) that interfaces are standardised: in computers, for example, the hard drive only has the function to store data. It is plugged into a standard slot, and the interface it connects to is also standardised. You can essentially use any hard drive you like. This is different in 'integral' products, where one component is connected to multiple functions: for example, the brake system in a car is there to slow the vehicle down but also links to ABS-ESP systems, that apply the brakes without the driver requesting it, in order to keep the vehicle on the road.

Modularity can be used as a means for outsourcing, but also for product customisation. This long-established form of customisation simply involves assembly to order from standard modules. Examples are legion: calculators or cars having different appearance but sharing the same 'platform', aeroplanes, and many restaurant meals. Pine lists six types: 'Component sharing', where variety of components is kept to a minimum by using Group Technology, Design for Manufacture, 'Component swapping' (cars with different engines), 'Cut-to-fit modularity' (a classic example being made to order bicycles), 'Mix modularity', combining several of the above, and 'bus modularity', where components, such as on a hi-fi are linked together. Baldwin and Clark take this further, believing modularity to be a fundamental organising principle for the future. Thus today Johnson Controls makes the complete driver's cockpit for Mercedes, and VW runs a truck factory using not only the modules of suppliers but their human operators also.

Gilmore and Pine (1997) have gone on to state that there are four approaches to module customisation (See Lean Supply Chain Section 29.5). 'Collaborative customizers' work with customers in understanding or articulating their needs (a wedding catering service), 'adaptive customizers' offer standard but self-adjusting or adapting products or services (offering hi-fi, or car seats which the customer adjusts), 'cosmetic customizers' offer standard products but present them differently (the same product is offered but in customer specified sizes, own-labels), and 'transparent customizers' where customers take on the customisation task themselves often without them realising (providing the right blend of lubricant to match the seasons or the wear rate).

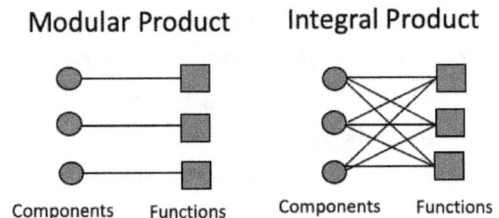

Modular Product   Integral Product

Components   Functions   Components   Functions

Johnson and Bröms give a description of Scania trucks' approach to modularity. Four basic modules – generate power, transmit power, carry load, house and protect driver – have been developed as modules to meet various environmental conditions encountered around the world. A matrix has been developed for parts and modules. These remain standardised until an improvement takes place, but are used 'Lego brick' style to act as the foundation for any new model. Scandia builds to order using the matrix.

Also sometimes the German term 'Baukastensystem' is used to describe modularity, which refers to the inter-changeability of parts.

Platforms

A product platform is a design from which many derivative designs or products can be launched, often over an extended period. So, instead of designing each new product one at a time, a product platform concept is worked out which leads to a family of products sharing common design characteristics, components, modules, and manufacturing methods and technology. This in turn leads to dramatic reductions in new product introduction time, design and manufacturing staff, evaluation methods such as FMEA, as well as inventory, training, and manufacturing productivity; in short, Lean design.

There are similarities to the Modularity concept and GT (group technology), but product platforms go far wider. Product platforms are found from calculators (e.g. Casio) to Cars (VW / Audi). The Apple Macintosh uses the platform of a common operating system (MacOSX) and common microprocessors (the Intel Duo or Apple's own) for a variety of computers. Notice the similarities with 'The Essential Paretos', described in the 'Strategy and Deployment' section of this book.

Further reading

Carliss Baldwin and Kim Clark, Managing in an Age of Modularity', *Harvard Business Review*, Sept-Oct, 1997, pp 84-93

Marc Meyer and Alvin Lehnerd, *The Power of Product Platforms*, Free Press, New York, 1997

Behnan Tabrizi and Rick Walleigh, 'Defining Next Generation Products: An Inside Look', *Harvard Business Review*, Nov-Dec 1997, pp116-124

David Robertson and Karl Ulrich, 'Planning for Product Platforms', *Sloan Management Review*, Summer 1998, pp 19-31

H Thomas Johnson and Anders Bröms, *Profit Beyond Measure*, Nicholas Brealey, 2000.

See the ECR Journal. www.ecr.org

36.8   TRIZ

TRIZ is a family of techniques, developed originally in Russia, for product invention and creativity. It is superb for innovative product design, and for production process problem solving. TRIZ is a Russian acronym for the theory of inventive problem solving. In 1948, the originator of TRIZ, Genrich Altshuller, suggested his ideas on improving inventive work to Stalin (a big mistake!), and was imprisoned in Siberia until 1954. His ideas once again fell into disfavour and only emerged with perestroyka. The first TRIZ ideas reached the U.S. in the mid 1980s. TRIZ is already linking up with Lean in Policy Deployment and QFD, and with Six Sigma in Design for Six Sigma.

The fundamental belief of TRIZ is that invention can be taught. All (?) inventions can be reduced to a set of rules or principles and that the generic problem has almost certainly already been solved. The principles, relying on physics, engineering, and knowledge of materials can be learned. A TRIZ team uses the basic principles to generate specific solutions. Here, only a brief overview or flavour of some of the 40 principles can be attempted. TRIZ is bound to, and deserves to, become better known. We hope this will be a stimulant to you to acquire some TRIZ publications.

Darrell Mann has summarized TRIZ into five main elements.

Contradictions: TRIZ believes that the world's best innovations have emerged from situations where the inventor has sought to avoid conventional trade-offs. For example, composite materials that are strong and light. TRIZ uses a matrix to identify which of the 40 principles are most likely to apply in any contradiction.

Ideality: TRIZ encourages problem solvers to begin with the Ideal Final Result and work backwards, rather than moving forward from the current state.

Functionality: This is an extension of value methodology principles. (See earlier.)

Use of Resource:. TRIZ encourages making best use of any resource that is not being used to its maximum potential. 'Lemons into lemonade'.

Thinking in Space and Time: Don't just think about the current state in the present, but also about the past and future, and about wider states (supply chains?) and narrower states (sub processes?). All hugely relevant to Lean!

A partial list of some of the 40 inventive problems includes: partial or overdone action (if you can't solve the whole problem, solve just a part to simplify it), moving to a new dimension (use multi layers, turn it on its side, move it along a plane, etc.) self-service (make the product service itself, make use of wasted energy), changing the colour (or make it transparent, use a coloured additive), mechanical vibration (make use of the energy of vibrations or oscillations), hydraulic or pneumatic assembly (replace solids with gas or liquid, join parts hydraulically), porous material (make the part porous, or fill the pores in advance), thermal expansion (use these properties, change to more than one material with different coefficients of expansion), copying (instead of using the object use a copy or a projection of it), thin membranes (use flexible membranes, insulate or isolate using membranes), regenerating parts (recycle), use a composite material. This is a powerful list - just reading them can stimulate ideas.

Altschuller emphasises thinking in terms of the 'ideal machine' or ideal solution as a first step to problem solving. You have a hot conservatory? It should open by itself when the temperature rises! So now think of devices that will achieve this: bimetallic expansion strips, expanding gas balloons, a solar powered fan.

A general methodology comprises three steps: First, determine why the problem exists. Second, 'state the contradiction'. Third, 'imagine the ideal solution', or imagine yourself as a magician who can create anything. For example, consider the problem of moving a steel beam. Why is it a problem? Because it cannot roll. The contradiction is that the shape prevents it from rolling. So, ideally, it should roll. How? By placing semi-circular flanges on the T sections. Finally, invention requires practice and method. Altschuller suggests starting young and keeping one's mind in shape with practice problems. Also keeping a database of ideas gleaned from a variety of publications.

Many TRIZ ideas require some technical knowledge, or at least technical aptitude. Therefore it will not work well with every group. However, it is most useful for designers, technical problem solvers, persons involved with QFD, and for implementation of Lean manufacturing (particularly the technical issues).

Further reading

G. Altschuller, *And Suddenly the Inventor Appeared*, Technical Innovation Centre, Inc., Worcester MA, 1996

Darrell Mann, *Hands on Systemic Innovation*, CREAX, 2002

Darrell Mann, *Hands on Systemic Innovation for Business and Management*, IFR Press, 2004

Karen Gadd, *TRIZ for Engineers*, Wiley, 2011

37 Agile Development

37.1 The Idea of Agile Development

Development techniques that quite closely relate to lean can be found in the methods associated with the Agile software development movement, which challenges the traditional incremental and waterfall approaches. Instead, it promotes adaptable and responsive ways of working in self-organising teams. Techniques include SCRUM, and SCRUM-ban, an adaptation of Kanban for software development.

The Agile methodology – especially in software development – is different from the waterfall methodology. Instead of up-front, detailed specifications, Agile progresses through short cycles that allow adjustment to changing conditions.

37.2 The Agile Manifesto

Two decades ago a group of software developers proposed a new approach to software development - the Agile Manifesto and the Four Values. Since that time the manifesto has not only been widely adopted amongst software developers but has spread and been adapted to many situations – work and play, private and public, service and manufacturing. We believe the concepts are highly relevant, not only in software development. Simply replace the word 'software' with your main business task, and 'project' with 'transformation'. The manifesto is:

- Our highest priority is to satisfy the customer through early and continuous delivery of valuable software.

- Welcome changing requirements, even late in development. Agile processes harness change for the customer's competitive advantage.

- Deliver working software frequently, from a couple of weeks to a couple of months, with a preference to the shorter timescale.

- Business people and developers must work together daily throughout the project.

- Build projects around motivated individuals. Give them the environment and support they need, and trust them to get the job done.

- The most efficient and effective method of conveying information to and within a development team is face-to-face conversation.

- Working software is the primary measure of progress.

- Agile processes promote sustainable development. The sponsors, developers, and users should be able to maintain a constant pace indefinitely.

- Continuous attention to technical excellence and good design enhances agility.

- Simplicity--the art of maximizing the amount of work not done--is essential.

- The best architectures, requirements, and designs emerge from self-organizing teams.

- At regular intervals, the team reflects on how to become more effective, then tunes and adjusts its behavior accordingly.

There are also the 4 Values:

- Individuals and interactions over processes and tools.

- Working software over comprehensive documentation.

- Customer collaboration over contract negotiation.

- Responding to change over following a plan.

As the influence of the Agile Manifesto grows, and as VUCA becomes the norm, both Lean Leadership and Lean Organisations will need to adjust. No doubt both AI and RPA will have increasing roles. The heralding of a 'New Lean'?

Further reading

The Agile Manifesto for Agile Software Development: http://agilemanifesto.org/

Mary and Tom Poppendieck, *Leading Lean Software Development*, Addison Wesley, 2010

37.3 SCRUM and Sprints

Sutherlands' 'Scrum' technique, which was originally utilised for software development projects has also become popular. Scrum has a similar methodology of focussed activity called 'sprints' to move the new product development forward utilising a cross functional team.

Essentially, quoting Sutherland, 'Scrum is based on a simple idea; whenever you start a project, why not regularly check-in, see if what you are doing is heading in the right direction and if it is actually what people want.' Activities between meetings are called 'Sprints' – a short planning exercise followed by a short (one week?) phase of execution.

At the beginning of each Sprint, a cross-functional team selects items (customer requirements) from a prioritized list. They commit to complete the items by the end of the Sprint. Every day the Team gathers briefly to re-plan its work to optimize the likelihood of meeting commitments. Visual management boards are usual.

The sprint methodology as used with software development is widespread. However, now, Sprints are becoming more widespread outside of software and into Design and even marketing and banking. There is much in common with Kaizen Blitz 5 day events, except that Sprints have more frequent reviews. Usual steps are Target, Sketch, Decide, Prototype, Test. There are also similarities with Lean Startup (See next section).

Further reading

Ken Schwaber and Jeff Sutherland, *The Scrum Guide*. The Scrum Alliance.

Jeff Sutherland, *SCRUM*, RH books, 2014

Jake Knapp, *Sprint: How to solve big problems and test new ideas in just five days*, Bantam, 2016

37.4 Kanban in Software Development, Service and NPD

As opposed to manufacturing, Kanban cards are used differently in software development (for example in SCRUM) and frequently used differently in service. Both in manufacturing and in software or service, kanban is a visual aid to the status of the system (or item or job), but in manufacturing kanban is used as a pull or authorization signal. In software an accumulation of kanbans, each associated with a job, indicates an overload or issue for discussion. In other words, this has similarities to an andon cord.

As with manufacturing kanban, the use of kanbans improves flow through limiting the amount of work in process (WIP). Reducing WIP reduces lead time (as per Little's Law), and improves quality because detection time is reduced. A kanban board improves work visibility with all the attendant advantages.

The same principles apply in service for routine work. For instance, kanban can be used for the progression of purchase orders, recruiting, monthly accounting activity, budgeting, and student enrolment. The same concepts can be used in Lean in new product development.

In Agile software development work is monitored by a kanban board. Typically one board per team. Stages track projects on a whiteboard as they move through development. Typical stages are New Work, Analyse, Develop, Test, Deployment, Done. Some variants use two stages for all stages except the first and last. These two are 'Doing' and 'Done'. Kanban cards – typically 'Post-Its' - each representing a job are located in columns under each heading. Kanbans in the 'Done' columns show the queue of work waiting for the next stage. All the kanbans together indicate the total WIP.

Each job has a kanban card. Cards progress across the board as stages are completed. A card would contain details such as name, customer, release date, possibly a priority coloured sticker. Other visuals can be added as required – for instance a coloured sticker for quality problem and another for a specification change.

Unlike most manufacturing kanbans, software or service does not necessarily use a FIFO (first in, first out) sequence. Some jobs may be fast tracked. Others may be delayed by customer approvals. Yet others may have specific completion dates.

Another difference is that in manufacturing a kanban would be used to pull similar sized batches from the previous stage. In software and service, most jobs differ in length of time.

Almost certainly there is a 'WIP Limit' for each stage. This indicates the target maximum number of jobs for each stage. (Where two columns are used for a stage the WIP Limit applies to both columns in a stage.) The WIP Limit for each stage does not, and usually is not, the same for each stage. If the number of kanban cards under a column (or two columns) reaches the WIP Limit , the previous stage does not stop work as with a manufacturing kanban. Rather, a problem is highlighted and the team needs to discuss suitable actions such as work reallocation.

Deciding on WIP Limits is a judgment call. There is no kanban formula, as with manufacturing loops. Rather, start conservative, monitor, and then reduce by trial and error. 'One less than last time' as PCI's Bill Sandras says.

CONWIP (Constant work in process – see Chapters 26 and 27) is a good thing to consider. Here as a job is completed, another job is allowed into the fist (Analyse) stage. Such as system more or less controls overall lead time, although not as exact as with manufacturing due to jobs of different length and job leapfrogging. CONWIP has the nice feature that jobs automatically tend to accumulate just where you want them to – in front of the bottleneck.

Often, there will be a known Bottleneck stage. If so, the TOC principles of protecting the bottleneck (and Identify, Exploit, Subordinate, Elevate, Repeat all apply – see Chapter 26.). For such cases it is useful to have two columns in the stage before the bottleneck so that the queue in front of the bottleneck can be monitored. There should always be a job in front of the bottleneck – 'an hour lost at the bottleneck is an hour lost for the whole system.)

Many software development kanban boards include a 'Rush' or 'Expedite' row. Cards in this row always enjoy priority. But, as with manufacturing priority jobs, one must be strict on the number of jobs allowed to be expedited. (Or else, soon, every job ends up in this row.) A good rule is not to allow (say) only one or two kanban cards in the entire expedite row. Good (essential?) practice is to have team members update the board in real time as stages are completed, and for the whole team to meet at the board once per day facilitated by the team leader. Similarities with Leader Standard Work should be adopted. (See Chapter 9.)

37.5   Lean Software and DevOps

The concepts behind Agile Development and Lean Operations are very compatible. The 2018 book *Accelerate* is a superbly written and researched study of what it takes for effective software delivery. The point is made that almost EVERY organisation now relies on software and hence software delivery performance. The authors summarise their work in 24 capabilities covering Continuous delivery, Architecture, Product and process, Lean management and reporting, and Cultural issues. The detail and research findings relating to these capabilities make for essential reading by all involved with IT.

It is noteworthy to observe how many established Lean concepts are embodied in these capabilities. These include small batches, work-in-process limits, early detection of problems and rapid feedback, visualisation, experimentation, lean measurement, decentralised and empowered teams, and emphasis on transformational leadership. From the Lean Startup, the concepts of minimum viable product and pivoting are embodied.

Further reading

Nicole Forsgren, Jez Humble, Gene Kim, *Accelerate: Building and Scaling High Performing Technology Organizations*, IT Revolution, 2018

38 Lean Start-Up

A 'startup', according to Eric Reis, is 'a human institution designed to create a new product or service under conditions of extreme uncertainty'. Unlike traditional organisations, startups should expect, indeed welcome, failure where 'failure' results in learning and 'pivoting'(i.e. changing direction). This links build, measure, learn into a rapid experimental loop. The method tracks the validity of the hypotheses upon which the product or software design is founded, as it develops. Experiments need to be falsifiable, and if and when they fail, root causes are sought. 'There is no such thing as a failed experiment'.

A widespread use of experiments is now routine at Amazon, Google and others. A good experiment requires careful design including clear hypothesis, alternatives, randomised selection, and appropriate sample size. This is made possible by these companies that can experiment with large numbers of customers at low cost. However, an experiment can be much more simple using the concept of the 'minimum viable product'. The aim is to develop a real, tangible product just sufficiently for it to be evaluated in a test market – not a market survey. Waste is reduced by not over-committing resources to projects or products that are likely to fail. 'Fail often, fail fast.'

Revealing and then killing a non-viable product whilst 'pivoting' to a viable alternative is revealed as good thinking. The idea is that this will allow for rapid market feedback based on tangible innovations, not opinion surveys.

Reis explains that The Lean Startup has five key principles:

1. Continuous Innovation
2. Startup as atomic unit of work. (Teams that can experiment with new concepts)
3. The Missing Function. (A new organizational discipline or function is needed)
4. The Second Founding (A startup is like starting a new company)
5. Continuous Transformation. (Do all the above continually, not as a one-off.)

It essentially is a translation of many of the lean principles into an entrepreneurial setting, where often there are no established processes at all. Key tools here are the business model (or lean) canvas (which resembles an A3), and the Build-Measure-Learn loop (which follows the PDSA logic). Accountability is a fundamental point – although the focus tends to be longer term, accountability and rewards, whether via stock-options or bonus, are a strong feature.

Interestingly, when Reis described the Lean Startup concepts to Toyota their reaction was to accept that although their production system was excellent, their new product innovation process was lacking.

In 2017 Reis expanded his ideas in *The Startup Way*. The aim here was to apply Startup principles to large organisations and to tackle the ramp-up problem Reis believes that 'the modern company' has rapid experiments at its core and is one where 'every employee has the opportunity to be an entrepreneur.' (Echoes of Ricardo Semler and Semco?) Instead of functional silos there are cross-functional teams. Instead of managers and subordinates, there are leaders and entrepreneurs. Instead of meeting short-term targets the emphasis is on longer-term achievement. Startups must be integrated throughout the organisation. Note the difference between this and the earlier 'Skunk works' concept where a separate unit was established.

It is interesting to note the strong emphasis on Customer problems. Womack and Jones' first Lean principle is understanding customer value, but alas this is not always followed through. The

Startup Way gives real focus here, testing customers habits, beliefs and preferences by using minimum viable products and experiments.

The Minimum Viable Product: Like the Wright brothers, break the problem down into components, each of which can be tested. Avoiding 'analysis paralysis' – in short, keep it moving forward. Readers will notice similarities with the Kata approach described in several sections of this book.

Further reading

Ries, E. (2011). *The lean startup:*. Penguin Random House.

Blank, S. (2013). Why the lean start-up changes everything. *Harvard Business Review*, 91(5), 63-72.

Reis, E. (2017).*The Startup Way*, Penguin Random House

Nathan Furr and Jeff Dyer, *(2014), The Innovator's Method : Bringing the Lean Startup into Your Organization*, Harvard Business School Press

Stefan Thomke, (2020), *Experimentation Works: The surprising power of business experiments*, Harvard Business Review Press, 2020

MOTIVATING AND MEASURING FOR FLOW

Back to people in a Lean Organisation: How they are lead, how culture is created and maintained, how functions are aligned, and how organisational processes and people are measured.

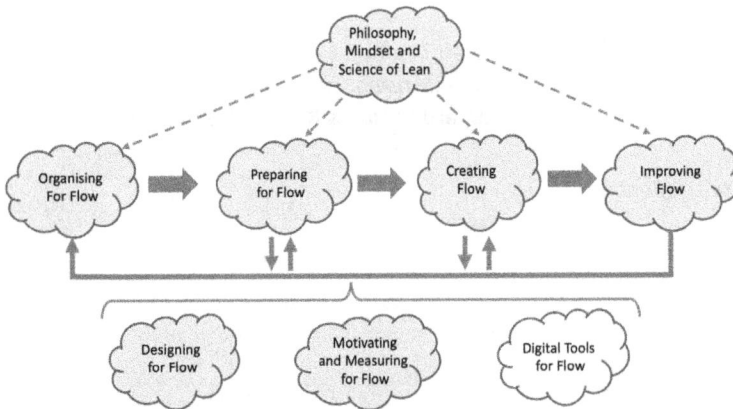

39 Leading a Lean organisation

To begin, change happens from leadership which in a Lean-aspiring organisation is founded on the Gemba principle. This involves going to the Gemba, observing the process (Genbutsu) and collecting the facts (Genjitsu). All first-hand, direct.

The Gemba might be a customer site, a workplace, a design centre, a website, a call centre, a supplier, or a logistics provider. Whilst a CEO can't do this him- or her-self for every Gemba, (although some should be sampled), such behaviour should be expected from every level.

39.1   People and Change in Lean

For too long we have lived with Tayloristic so-called 'Scientific Management' that separates thinking from doing. Now, says Dan Jones, it is time to replace it with management by science.

It was Deming who said that most problems lie with the process not the person (so don't blame the person first), that there needs to be a consistent message, that there is a need to 'drive out fear', that barriers that prevent improvement and prevent 'pride in work' need to be removed. This is the prime task for every manager – to facilitate, not to 'check-up'. The challenge remains to this day: how do you successfully implement change in a process that consists of both people and machines? It is often easy to change the layout, move machines, and redesign material flows. Changing the people that operate this process is far from easy. Manufacturing and service operations alike are socio-technical systems, where human beings and physical equipment need to work in harmony to create the desired outcome. It is aligning this 'social system' with the technical that is the challenge when implementing change.

One of the most striking examples of aligning social-technical systems was NUMMI, short for New United Motor Manufacturing Incorporated. When Toyota approached GM about a possible joint-venture for the US market, GM offered one of its worst plants in Fremont, California, as manufacturing location. The plant had one of the worst quality and productivity records of all GM plants, and was the scene of numerous labour disputes. It had been closed in 1982, but reopened in 1984 as joint Toyota-GM plant under the name of NUMMI. Now under Toyota leadership, many of the former workers (and union leaders) were rehired. Teamworking began. Pride in work was restored. Quality at source became paramount even if this meant stopping the line. Within two years the plant became the most productive plant within GM, much to the embarrassment of Roger Smith (then GM CEO). GM largely failed to learn from this tremendous opportunity to see Lean in action, and instead focused on automation. NUMMI was eventually closed during the global

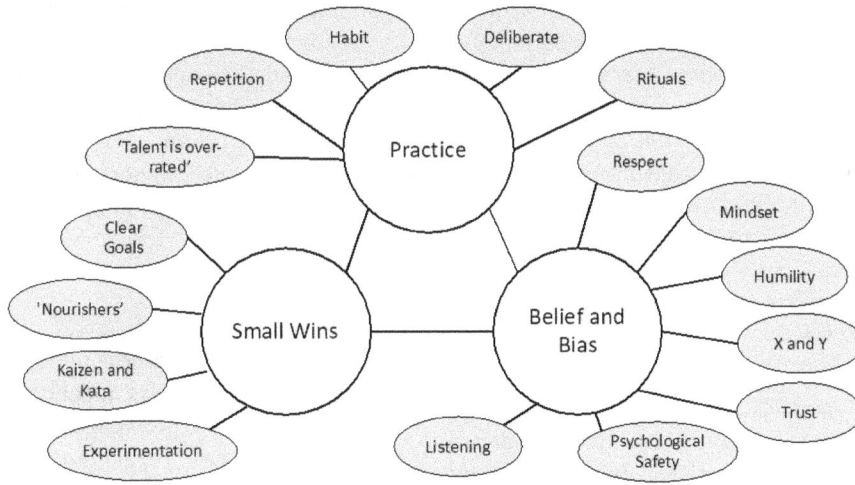

financial crisis in 2010, but reopened again the same year to produce TESLA electric vehicles.

In this section we will look into some useful models for change.

39.2   The People Trilogy

There are three inter-related concepts of particular relevance to people aspects of Lean transformation. They are the concepts of **Deliberate Practice** (closely linked to Kata and TWI), **Small wins motivation** (closely linked to Kaizen), and **Belief and Bias** (closely linked to Respect and Humility). These three mutually reinforce each other. They form a set, the combined power of which is significant for Lean transformation. All three are necessary.

We know now that effective learning and training for Lean requires practice and repetition. One off instruction – and particularly classroom instruction without practice simply does not work in a Lean context. It is soon forgotten, if indeed it was learned in the first place. As Benjamin Franklin said almost 300 years ago, '*Tell me and I forget, teach me and I may remember, involve me and I learn*'.

'Small Wins' is the essence of Kaizen and Continuous Improvement. (Kaizen is continuous

change for the better). Many small wins add up to a big win. Of course, there may be occasional 'Kaikaku' or breakthroughs but many such innovations rest on combining several previous smaller gains. Steven Johnson calls this 'the adjacent possible'. Thus, the iphone combined developments in the web, micro-processors, glass, music, memory chips and more. The implementation of small wins is a powerful feedback motivator.

Belief in people's potential is the essential third component, creating the climate for Practice and Small Wins to flourish.

(Deliberate) Practice

Two stories about practice: Gary Player, one of only 5 golfers (and the only non-American) to win The Career Grand Slam (Masters, PGA, US Open, British Open) said, '*Yes, I am lucky. And, you know what, the more I practice the luckier I get*'. Then there is the tale of the lost tourist in New York City who enquires how to get to Carnegie Hall, '*Practice, man, Practice!*' is the response. Malcolm Gladwell in his popular book *Outliers* discusses the '10,000 hour rule for Mastery'. Quoting a string of famous people including The Beatles, Mozart, Bill Gates, and many sportspeople, Gladwell proposes that it is hours of practice that is a large determinant of success. *'We do owe something to parentage and patronage.... But they are invariably the beneficiaries of hidden advantages and extraordinary opportunities and cultural legacies that allow them to learn and work hard...in ways others cannot'.* Although it might not necessarily take 10,000 hours to become a Lean master, certainly a Lean Six Sigma Black Belt with a 40-hour course and a project under his belt would not come close.

It is not just practice that is needed but deliberate practice. Deliberate practice, as described by Anders Ericsson involves observation, constructive feedback and correction. Mozart did not just practice but was coached by his father – a talented teacher. Practice is necessary but not sufficient and the extent of practice depends on the field of endeavour. So, a coach or tutor is required. Even the best tennis players retain coaches.

Repetition

We all know that repetition is necessary for improvement. This is not something new. For centuries the church has relied on weekly or daily repetition to reinforce religion. Repetition is the premise of TWI. TWI's effectiveness is embedded in the repetition and practice over the 10 hour (two hours per day for 5 days) class. ('Continue until you know that they know'). These are discussed in a separate section on TWI in this book. In Steve Spear's Shingo award winning book 'The High Velocity Edge' he gives examples of repetition combined with scientific method – for example Admiral Rickover's continual insistence on questioning and uncovering things that are unknown.

Habits

Aristotle is reputed to have said, *'We are what we repeatedly do. Excellence, then, is not an act, but a habit.'* The effectiveness of habit is

something that is becoming established in Lean – Leader Standard Work, Yamazumi, 5S, A3's, Lean scheduling – all emphasize regularity. Most effective habits are not only regular but also involve small actions. See below. Establishing good habits is very important in Lean. (Habit is discussed several times in this book, See 2.4 and Chapter 17)

Rituals

Schwartz, in a HBR article refers to 'rituals' at Sony, where daily walks, meetings, and periods when e mails are prohibited, are compulsory. The US Army now regularly uses After Action Reviews (AAR's) . As the name suggests an AAR is conducted as soon as possible after every action or exercise. It is conducted by a trained facilitator almost invariably in the field. Status or rank is downplayed, but personal criticism is not allowed. The phases are: What did we set out to do? What went right? What went wrong? What can we learn and how can we do better next time? The effectiveness of AAR's is discussed by David Garvin of Harvard in his book *Learning in Action*. Garvin warns that AARs fail where facilitation skills are inadequate. AAR's have lots of similarity with A3 mentoring described by John Shook. Focus on the problem, not the person. Direct observation is required. Fact based, not opinion based.

Small Wins

Recent years have revealed the power of small and 'varied wins' motivation. In a seminal 1984 article, Karl Weick said; *'By itself, one small win may seem unimportant. A series of small wins at small but significant tasks, however, reveals a pattern that may attract allies, deter opponents, and lower resistance to subsequent proposals. Small wins are controllable opportunities that produce visible results. Once a small win has been accomplished, forces are set in motion that favour another small win. When a solution is put in place, the next solvable problem often becomes more visible. This occurs because new allies bring new solutions with them and old opponents change their habits.'* (A crucial quote for Lean transformation!)

More recently, Teresa Amabile and Steven Kramer's momentous work at Harvard Business School has elaborated on the power of small wins on 'positive inner work life'. Small wins are shown to be the most powerful motivating factor, but need to be supported with 'catalysts' (for instance clear goals, providing resources and time) and 'nourishers' (for instance, respect, and encouragement). But 'setbacks' (like small losses and negative leader behaviour) can overwhelm small wins. An enthusiastic medical doctor, Robert Maurer, explains the power of small wins and kaizen with reference to the human brain. Humans find small changes far less threatening. Large changes provoke fear that automatically restricts access to the cortex (for safety and survival). But failure often results. Small changes bypass the amygdala giving access to the cortex. Success is more likely. Hence ask small questions, take small actions, solve small problems, and bestow small rewards. (This seems similar to Kahneman's System 1 and System 2 brain concepts.)

All these give justification for Rother's Toyota Kata concept. Small wins, with PDSA and learning. Kata is discussed at length in Chapter 33.)

Small wins is also the essence of 'The Lean Startup' methodology. Here, instead of spending huge amounts of time on lengthy project definition and specification, an experimental approach is used which tests out 'minimal viable products'. Where the small test product succeeds it is gone ahead with; where it fails it is abandoned. A low risk and learning methodology. Fail fast and learn. The small wins idea is absolutely integral to learning with Experiments as used by Google, Amazon, Microsoft and now many others. These organizations conduct literally hundreds of experiments each month (See previous Chapter).

As an aside, why was Eisenhower chosen as supreme allied commander for D-Day? He had very little battle experience against the huge experience of Patton, Montgomery, Bradley. Well, some say he was chosen because of his excellent consensus building skills. Also, humility and respect. He made progress through splitting the vast requirements into 'small wins' packages that everyone could agree on.

Belief and Bias

What VS Mahesh calls 'Pygmalion' and Kahneman and many others calls 'Confirmation Bias' has long been known. We selectively seek out information that confirms our beliefs, and tend to ignore information that contradicts our beliefs. Margaret Heffernan calls this 'wilful blindness'. We all have 'filters' and build on flimsy evidence. This is a type of cognitive bias that everyone has. So, for example, Israeli drill sergeants are told that one group comprises specially selected achievers and other group comprises the less able. The groups, however, unbeknown to the sergeants, were randomly selected. Nevertheless the 'superior' group performs much better. So do randomly selected maths students. A self-fulfilling prophesy.

The distinguished psychologist Carol Dwek classifies people according to a 'fixed mindset' or 'a growth mindset'. (Actually a continuum.) People with a fixed mindset think their intelligence is static, a fixed trait. They avoid challenges, deflect criticism, and feel there is no point in effort. By contrast, those with a growth mindset embrace challenges, work hard to improve, and learn from criticism and feedback. Intelligence is not fixed, but can grow. Countless 'under-achievers' (Churchill, Branson, many sportspeople) have demonstrated this through determination. As Henry Ford said, *'Whether you think you can or whether you think you can't, you're absolutely right.'* The growth mindset is captured in Dwek's word 'Yet'. The attitude is that a person can't do it yet, but will be able to with effort and support. The point is a growth mindset can be learned! And taught. A good teacher motivates by giving constructive feedback, and by linking effort to achievement. Praise effort rather than success.

Of course, to give genuine constructive and specific feedback one must believe in the potential of the mentee. One must be aware of confirmation bias. George Davidson, former Manufacturing Director at Toyota South Africa, when asked about the aim of TPS simply said 'To create thinking people'. In other words, change their mindset.

Listening and Respect go hand in hand. Genuine listening implies respect and vice versa. It begins with the recognition that the person doing the job is the real expert about that job.

Humility is required. The sub-title of Edgar Schein's excellent book is instructive: 'The gentle art of asking instead of telling'. Very hard for most people, including the authors of this book. But remember, you never learn from telling. Schein makes an early point about how annoying it is to be told something you already know by someone who assumes you are ignorant. He tells of examples from the Deepwater gulf spill and from the Columbia and Challenger shuttles where information that could have prevented the disasters was known but not listened to. A climate of both feeling safe to tell, and the ability to be listened to, is required. Not easy with a powerful boss.

This is best summarised by the important concept of *Psychological Safety*. This is the lack of fear that bringing bad news to the boss will be treated positively not negatively. As Amy Edmondson of HBS explains the concept as 'People are not hindered by *interpersonal* fear' and where 'they fear holding back their full participation *more* than they fear sharing a

potentially sensitive, threatening or wrong idea'. So people realise that their job may be lost due to economic or company competitiveness, but not through highlighting defects and mistakes. It is vital for leaders and managers to cultivate the characteristics of trust, respect, humility, listening, and psychological safety in any Lean-aspiring organisation. *'Approach problems as a joint collaborator'* and *'replace blame with curiosity'*, says Laura Delizonna. (See also Section 20.3 on Mistakes)

Margaret Heffernan tells of how threatening and how common is 'wilful blindness' amongst senior people from all walks of life. An ostrich mentality is far from unusual. So is Groupthink Heffernan praises the former CEO of British Airways who appointed an official 'corporate fool' who had a licence to speak up and challenge. Apparently, the Catholic Church, for several hundred years, had a person whose task was to challenge any proposal for sainthood.

Bringing the People Trilogy Together

The three factors of the trilogy are mutually reinforcing. When brought together they form a powerful system for the softer side of Lean Transformation. A common theme is that training and doing should not be separated. This theme is echoed by TWI, by Mike Rother, and by many in the field of Learning. (See Chapter 33)

Between Repetition and Small Wins.

Repetition and practice need to be deliberate and coached with a goal in mind. But small wins along the way are vital to retain momentum. The linkage might explain the disenchantment with week-long Kaizen Events that has set in. Whilst changes can be dramatic, they are often not sustained. Why not make the small, non-threatening changes as opportunities arise, coupled with experimentation as suggested by Rother's Kata methodology? Rother explains that whilst the 'target condition' might be known, the route to get there is uncertain. Many small steps, some of which will fail but from which we will learn, is the way to go. According to Rother 'Because the improvement kata is a set of behavioural guidelines, it is something that we learn through repeated practice. It takes conditioning to make behavioural routines become second nature, and consequently a lot of Toyota's managerial activities involve having people practise the improvement kata with their guidance. For team leaders and group leaders, this teaching occupies more than 50 percent of their time, and for higher-level managers it can also occupy up to 50 percent.'

David Mann's thesis on 'Creating a Lean Culture' combines Daily Accountability, Leader Standard Work, Visual Controls, and Discipline. Daily means repetition. Leader standard work, visual controls and discipline together imply directed small wins becoming the norm. Specifically, the rapid problem solving and feedback that these four result in, stimulate culture change.

Some may wonder if Skinner's classic work on behaviour modification is appropriate here – linking repetition with small wins. Alfie Kohn, in Punished by Rewards page 6, wrote (somewhat unfairly?) that Skinner '...could be described as a man who conducted most of his experiments on rodents and pigeons and wrote most of his books about people'. More recently a phrase, and several books, discuss Lab Rats as becoming a form of work that is beginning to appear, but such work is definitely Non-Lean!

In line with expectancy, Skinner talked about positive reinforcement (such as praise) and negative reinforcement (such as punishment or withdrawal). Both types increase the probability of behaviour modification. Behaviour is modified by future goals. He discussed, amongst many other theories, Continuous Reinforcement whereby every time a specific action takes place the person receives a reinforcement. This method is effective because it quickly establishes a link between the behaviour and the reinforcement.

Skinner held that people (and rats!) don't just respond to stimuli, they respond to patterns of stimuli. It is the pattern of stimuli rather than the stimulus itself that is important. This is profound - a one off incentive (or reinforcement) will not be effective. Initially, to establish a desired behaviour, reinforcement should be 'fixed' (at a regular time, or following a given achievement), but then, once established, reinforcement should be variable (with time or achievement) in order to sustain the change. However, there must be 'contiguity' – in other words as short an interval as possible between the behaviour and the reinforcement. (An annual Christmas bonus will do nothing to affect behaviour in mid-year!).

Between Repetition and Belief.

Gladwell wrote of the 10,000 hour rule for mastery. But two comments: The 10k rule really only applies to world-leading performance, and practice without belief – for however long - will fail.

Mike Rother, discussing Kata as an improvement approach, emphasized the duo of an 'improvement kata' and a 'coaching kata'. Both are necessary.

Carol Dwek's examples of people moving towards a growth mindset show a determination to get there, a belief that it is possible, as well as sustained practice.

Geoff Colvin says about deliberate practice: 'It is an activity specifically designed to improve performance, often with a teacher's help; it can be repeated a lot; feedback on results is continuously available; it's highly demanding mentally, whether the activity is purely intellectual, such as chess or business-related activities, or heavily physical, such as sports; and it isn't much fun'. For people who have been guided through a successful A3 problem solving exercise, including the frustration of having to repeat the analysis in order to get to 'root cause', that sounds just about right!

Between Small Wins and Belief.

These are mutually necessary. Mindset can be learned. It has been said that Toyota achieves excellent results with average people, but many others achieve mediocre results with excellent people. Although we feel that this is rather insulting to Toyota people, the sentiment is clear. Take an excellent person and put her in an organisation that does not believe in using or growing her talents, and her results will disappoint. But talent CAN be developed....

Mike Rother claims that 'We have misunderstood why Toyota is more successful than other organisations in achieving the challenges (target conditions) it sets for itself. It is not primarily because Toyota people have greater discipline to stick with a plan or experience fewer problems, as is often thought. Rather, they spot problems at the process level much earlier, when the problems are still small and you can understand them and do something about them.' (The opposite of the HiPPO syndrome: highest paid personal opinion.)

This however is no easily accomplished task. Steve Spear describes how Dallis, a successful auto-manufacturing manager, upon joining Toyota is developed as a Toyota manager through a painful process of being mentored. Dallis learns to see, understand and solve many small problems at several Toyota locations before being released into the position he was hired for. 'Dallis spent 12 weeks learning about the importance of observation as the basis for improvement and of using the scientific method of being clear about expectations before making changes and following up to observe the results of those changes.'

Further reading

Teresa Amabile and Steven Kramer, *The Progress Principle: Using Small Wins to Ignite Joy, Engagement, and Creativity at Work*, Harvard, 2011

Geoff Colvin, *Talent is Overrated*, Nicholas Brealey, 2008

Daniel Coyle, *The Talent Code: Greatness Insn't Born, It's Grown*, Arrow, 2010

Laura Delizonna, 'High Performing Teams need Psychological Safety', *Harvard Business Review*, 24 August 2017

Carol Dwek, *Mindset: The new psychology of Success*, Random House, 2006

Amy Edmondson, *The Fearless Organisation*, Harvard Business School Press, 2019

David Garvin, *Learning in Action*, Harvard, 2000

Malcolm Gladwell, *Outliers: The Story of Success*, Penguin, 2009

Margaret Heffernan, *Wilful Blindness*, Simon and Schuster, 2011

Daniel Kahneman, *Thinking, Fast and Slow*, Allen Lane, 2011

David Mann, *Creating a Lean Culture*, Second edition, CRC Press, 2011

Robert Maurer, *One Small Step Can Change Your Life: The Kaizen Way*, Workman, 2004

Robert Maurer, *The Spirit of Kaizen: Creating Lasting Excellence One Small Step at a Time*, McGraw Hill, 2013

Edgar Schein, *Humble Inquiry: The Gentle Art of Asking Instead of Telling*, Berrett-Koehler, 2013

Steven Spear, *Chasing the Rabbit*, McGraw Hill, 2009, and the later edition, *The High Velocity Edge, 2010*

Karl Weick 'Small Wins: Redefining the Scale of Social Problems,' *American Psychologist*, January 1984.

39.4 Lean Leadership

In Chapter 3 (Section 3.11), Steven Spear's widely quoted views of 'The DNA of TPS' were outlined. To repeat, Spear maintained that there were rules at the heart of Toyota. These are, to summarise, Standard work, Clear

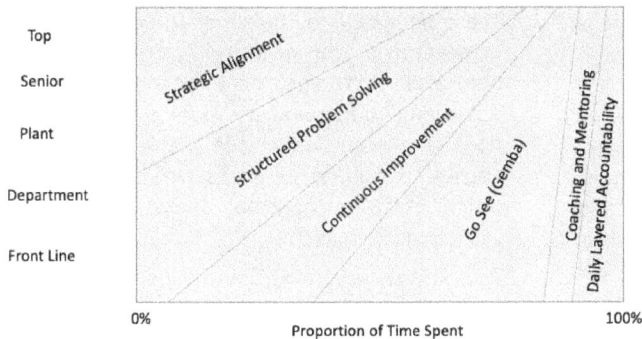

Strategic Alignment
Structured Problem Solving
Continuous Improvement
Go See (Gemba)
Coaching and Mentoring
Daily Layered Accountability

Top
Senior
Plant
Department
Front Line

0%   Proportion of Time Spent   100%

we propose the figure above following Imai's famous 'Kaizen Flag' (See Section 31.2)

To emphasize the critical role of management influence below the C-suite, a study by researchers from University of Edinburgh, London Business School and University of North Carolina found that individual plant managers are a key determinant of auto assembly plant productivity. The difference in productivity (Hours Per Vehicle) between a manager in the bottom quartile of manager influence and a manager in the top quartile was 30%(!!) And further, that plant manager experience has a major influence on new model introduction productivity – for each year that a manager spends at a plant productivity (in HPV) increases by about 1.6%.

Further reading

Torbjörn Netland, Daryl Powell, Peter Hines, 'Demystifying Lean Leadership', *International Journal of Lean Six Sigma*, 11(13),2019

Soledad Giardili, Kamalini Ramdas, Jonathan W. Williams, ' Leadership and Productivity: A Study of US Automobile Assembly Plants', *Management Science*, April 8, 2022

communication, Value Stream thinking, and application of Scientific Method. These are not very different from the later Lean Leadership ideas of David Mann: Leader standard work, Visual controls, Daily accountability process, and Leadership discipline. (See Section 9.1)

Netland et al, based on Spear, and their own research, maintain that there are 6 critical aspects to Lean Leadership. These are:

1. Go and see (The Gemba mindset as discussed in Chapter 6)
2. Daily layered accountability (Where, daily, problems and challenges are reported in a hierarchical series of meetings from front line to top management, with responses and communication flowing downward. See Section 9.1)
3. Structured problem solving. (Often using PDSA, A3 – but see Chapter 32)
4. Continuous Improvement (Kaizen. See Chapters 30 and 31)
5. Coaching (and Mentoring. See Section 9.2)
6. Strategic Alignment. (Essentially Hoshin or OKR. See Chapter 40)

More recently, Netland maintained that lists such as these six, although satisfactory, tend to ignore situational factors and in particular at what managerial level failures occur. As a result

39.3   Creating the Lean Culture

The word 'culture' is a great word, and also one that is greatly misused! Scholtes describes organizational culture as the day-to-day experience of the ordinary worker. 'Culture' has become the great fallback word for why Lean is not working as it should. 'It is the culture'. There is now also a book on 'Toyota Culture'. First, let us say that we support Scholtes' scepticism about the word, and go along with his suggestion that you substitute the phrase 'current behaviour' instead of 'culture'. But let us make a few points about Culture or Current Behaviour:

- Culture is something that you learn day by day, not by going on an outward bound course or by reading a book about moving cheese. 'Act into a new way of thinking', not 'Think into a new way of acting'.

- Do you ever hear about successful sports teams having 'cultural' problems? Seldom. Why? Because the team as a whole and all the members individually know exactly what the aim is, exactly what they need to do to get there, in detail. It is the coach who has to make these clear.

- Don't allow the 'culture' excuse. Instead, use the 5 Whys. If there is an issue and you give 'culture' as the reason it is a dead end. This is not to deny that there are cultural issues, but what is causing it? At Toyota, when using fishbone analysis, the 'M' of Men, of the 6 M's is not allowed!

- Psychologist Frank Devine talks about the non-negotiables, the 'limit testers' and the 'watchers'. Management must first make clear the non-negotiables – whether safety, attendance, quality, punctuality, development or whatever. There will be the 'inner committed' about whom you don't have to worry. But there are also the limit-testers who push the boundary to see if management really means what they say. The watchers watch the reaction of managers to the limit testers. If the managers give way, just a little, the downward spiral begins.

These points can all be summarized by a word – management. Not necessarily top management but also first line, face-to-face, every day management. Remember the statement 'the shop floor is a reflection of the management'. That applies to cultural issues as well. If you accuse others of being 'concrete heads', it may be a reflection on yourself.

Typical activities from team leader to CEO, in a Lean-aspiring organisation, are given in the table.

Level	Frequency	Typical activities
Team Leader	Several times per day at Gemba	Review problems, Set tasks
	Daily, with team, at Gemba or at bottleneck	Morning meeting: yesterday, today. Review charts, Problems, tasks, training, briefing, improvement, target inventory
Supervisor	Daily, with team leaders	Review with Team Leaders. Production tracking, Staff reallocation, Kaizen and training activities.
Section manager	Daily, with supervisors	Review KPI's, problems, point kaizens, progress
Value Stream Manager	Weekly with section heads and others e.g. quality, accounting	Review value stream KPI's, kaizen event plans, VSMs
Plant manager	Weekly with section managers and value stream managers	Review value stream KPI's, progress, problems
Vice President	Monthly with plant managers	Review plant and value stream KPI's and progress.

Although Lean often involves revolutionary change, culture change is evolutionary. Day by day. And because, inevitably, managers leave, coaching future managers on their attitudes to day by day interaction with subordinates needs to be continually done. Arguably, there is no more important a task.

So, what makes a 'Lean' culture? Basically all people, from CEO to junior, share two related characteristics, both related to Learning: humility and respect. See the Organization for Flow section.

Skills for Managers and Leaders

Leadership remains a very hot topic with hundreds of books available. In the West Leadership has assumed mythical significance – get the right top person and your problems are over. Yes, leaders are important, but be cautious of the hype surrounding leaders – at least in a Lean environment.

- You may know who the current Toyota president is but he is hardly a figure of the legendary status of Jack Welsh, Steve Jobs, or Larry Bossidy. Lawler and Worley point out the wealth of research studies that highlight the importance of continuity of both leadership and management. To rely on one leader is risky as numerous cases have shown.

- The Harvard case study, *Jack Smith: Becoming a Toyota Manager*, comes as a shock to many. Smith is recruited into Toyota with an impeccable background both academic (MSc and MBA) and high level management experience. Yet he spends his first three months on the shop floor. He learns that the team leaders are generally better than him at problem solving, he gains credibility with operators, he learns what the scientific method really means, and his eyes are opened to the hundreds of small scale improvements that are possible even in one of the best plants in the world. He learns humility. And Toyota learns about him – before 'turning him loose' as a senior manager.

- Rosenzweig's book, *The Halo Effect*, is also sobering on leadership. Many high profile, legendary, leaders fail when the situation changes. Rosenzweig points out that one can always find good things to say about leaders of successful companies, and bad things to say about leaders of unsuccessful companies. But sometimes it is the same person in different circumstances.

So an aspiring Lean company needs to pay a lot of attention to developing its managers. Lawler and Worley, whilst not taking specifically about Lean organizations, but rather about organizations that need to be continually adaptive to change, make a number of suggestions:

- Whilst job descriptions are out (because they are wedded to the past), person descriptions are in. A person description lists the knowledge and skills that each manager already has but also needs to develop. The needs are based on how the organization sees its future. The person descriptions should be searchable within the organization on a data base.

- But, the organization should not direct managers to learn required skills. 'People need to be responsible for their own careers and employability'. This is not to say that the organization does not sponsor development. There is nothing as deadly as people forced to attend Lean 'education'.

- Whilst training should not be directed by the organization, it should be available on a just-in-time basis, and rewarded appropriately.

- Organizations need to think about how jobs can be made more stable, whilst giving suitable rewards. So many Lean transformations have failed to realize their potential because of manager turnover. This may mean, for example, flatter organizations, more fluid job titles, a reward structure not based on position, and many parallel career paths.

This fits well with Lean. Working for a Lean company should be seen as a huge career boost. No organization can guarantee jobs, although they should commit clearly to nobody losing their job as a result of improvement.

40 Hoshin Kanri or Policy Deployment

First, Hoshin is not about developing high-level strategy. It is about the effective deployment of a given strategy throughout an organisation and ensuring that the whole organisation is aligned to support the strategy. In other words, it is about the 'how' of strategy deployment, not the 'what' of the strategy. Russell Ackoff talked about doing the right thing, doing things right, and the danger of doing the wrong thing right. (See on Ackoff in Section 10.2). Thus there should be clear separation between corporate strategy and Hoshin. The development of strategy is a huge field in itself, certainly not limited to Lean organisations. (There are many publications on strategy development. We recommend 'Good Strategy, Bad Strategy' as an excellent lead into the what, followed by Hoshin or OKR for the how.) In Lean the strategy is sometimes referred to as 'True North'.

A critical, and distinguishing, feature of Hoshin is engagement and participation in the development of deployment plans – projects, tactics, and improvements – that are necessary to achieve the overall strategy. This involves identifying what is necessary to be done, no less and no more. The combination of Strategy, Hoshin, and Kaizen is summarised by the figure below adapted from Cowley and Domb. At each stage of deployment PDSA is required. It is often said that Hoshin requires a much longer time to develop, through participation, but a much shorter time to execute than old-style MBO but is much more effective.

Hoshin Kanri (or simply Hoshin) is the Japanese term for Policy or Strategy Deployment. The term derives from the helmsman of a ship. Thus, the captain may determine where the ship is headed and set an arrival time target, but all functions need to be subservient to the goals. Navigation must determine the route (and adjust for weather). The engine room needs to ensure appropriate propulsion capability. And so on. At lower levels there will be necessary supporting

activities such as catering and deck cleaning. The Hoshin process seeks to translate the top-level goals into appropriate aligned measures for the entire organisation. Policies (or strategies) are deployed to achieve an aim. The strategies are brought about by tactics (or projects). Tactics are, in turn, brought about by various processes or deliverables. These in turn produce results.

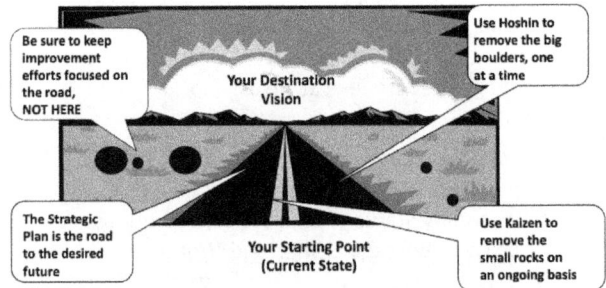

Adapted from Cowley and Domb 'Beyond Strategic Vision'

A quote from Churchill during WWII helps clarify:

'You ask, what is our policy? I can say: It is to wage war, by sea, land and air, with all our might and with all the strength that God can give us….. You ask, what is our aim? I can answer in one word: It is victory, victory at all costs, victory in spite of all terror, victory, however long and hard the road may be; for without victory there is no survival….'

Following this, tactics could then be specified by theatre: first The Battle of Britain, then North Africa, Italy, Burma, Europe, and finally Japan. Processes (or Deliverables) would be all the (high level at this stage) activities necessary to achieve these - involving the USA, supporting Russia, securing supply lines, finance, ramping up war production, building and training resources. Results could be specified in terms of achieving the tactics against time horizons and costs.

There would be much discussion and participation on the tactics and processes, although not about the top-level strategy. Then the Processes would be deployed to a second level. Here, each main process becomes a sub-strategy. The sub-strategy of 'Supporting Russia' could involve tactics (or projects) of organising convoys, allocating navy resources, securing armaments and vehicles, and so on. The processes would be the activities involved in, for example, convoys.

Thereafter implantation of the convoy sub-strategy is thoroughly discussed. Participation and ideas from those with convoy expertise is vital, before deployment of the plan. Now there would be greater detail and plans for specific ships, sailings, crew, navy support vessels. The broad concept is shown in the figure below.

40.1   The Hoshin Process and Catchball

Referring to the figure, the 'catchball' analogy from netball is frequently used. In netball, the ball is passed between players on the same side to gain the best positional advantage before being sent over the net to the other side. The analogy is about firming up the goals and alternatives before passing them on. Sub-strategies are broken down into shorter term challenges. At the same time, unconventional approaches to attaining the goal are discussed. Detail is worked out in a participatory methodology using the X matrix – or sometimes a series of A3's – or both. In addition, a series of X matrices are sometimes displayed in an 'Obeya' room. (Both A3 and Obeya are discussed briefly in a section below and in the chapter on Problem Solving). Of course, plans require review and change. PDSA is necessary.

The deployment process is sometimes referred to as 'The Big W'. Imagine beginning with the desired

strategy at the top left of the W. The strategy is thrown down to the level below for implementation development. The resulting proposals are then returned to the top level for comment, adjustment and approval. Some changes are made, and then returned to the level below. The adjusted proposals are then returned to the top level. Once again comment and adjustment take place and returned to the level below. Fine tuning takes place before returning the proposed actions to the top level for final approval. (This is also known as 'Nemawashi'.)

At the implementation level there should be emphasis on developing people through (according to Isao Yoshino) assigning people to teams, allowing flexibility in instructions, encouraging people to think creatively, listening and discussing, checking progress and giving advice or help when necessary. Further, in line with psychological safety, tolerating failure is a means to learn valuable lessons. Participation encourages development as well as 'buy-in'. As Jack Stack of Open Book Management states, 'People support what they help create', and Frank Devine (see Engagement Section) says 'If people help to plan the battle they won't battle the plan.'

40.2   The Hoshin Matrix

The Hoshin Kanri process identifies goals, initiatives, and owners at each level. Benefits of using the process include; it can be used to refine the sub-strategies through participation, and it helps break down objectives into manageable parts that people can start to work on immediately. The measurement section (of an X matrix or A3) gives employees a way to see how incremental improvements can address both short and long-term needs. It fosters cross – collaboration by giving everyone the same view of success. It is an effective communication tool to monitor progress and quickly flag if roadblocks start to appear.

PD uses the 'outcome, what, how, how much, and who' framework. A Policy

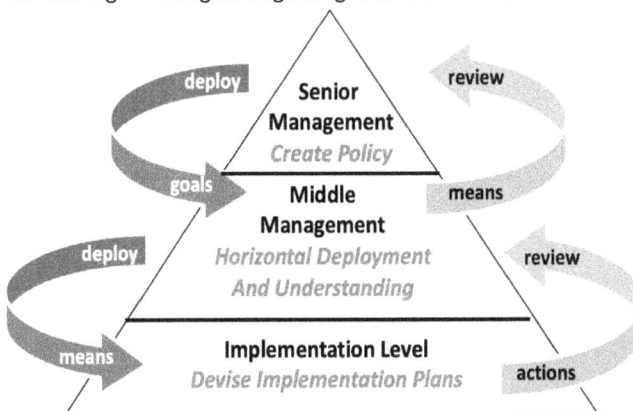

Matrix (X Matrix) is useful here. See the figure. At Board level, a visioning process covers the key questions of what is required by the system, (the purpose and the design), what is to be achieved (e.g. reductions in lead time), how is it to be done (e.g. extend Lean manufacturing principles), and by how much (e.g. all areas on 5S by year end). Specific quality and productivity goals are established. Then, the 'who' are discussed. Normally there will be several managers responsible for achieving these objectives. Appropriate measures are also developed.

The PD plans are cascaded in a Tree Diagram form. This cascading process is also different to most traditional models. In traditional models, cascading plans come down from the top without consultation, and there is little vertical and especially horizontal alignment. In PD, people who must implement the plan design the plan. The means, not just the outcomes, must be specified. And there are specific and ongoing checks to see that local plans add up to overall plans. The matrix is used to assure horizontal alignment.

As the plans are cascaded, projects at one level become the aims at the lower level.

A final stage in the cycle is the Hoshin Review where achievements against plan are formally rolled up the organization. This uses visual results where possible. Exceptions are noted and carried forward. Hewlett Packard does this very formally once per quarter, 'flagging up' (by yellow or red 'flags') problem areas. Intel uses, against each Hoshin, a classification showing highlights, lowlights, issues, and plans. Again, root causes are identified. At Unipart in the UK, a policy deployment matrix like the one shown can be seen in each work area. Staff are able to reconcile what they are doing with the wider organizations aims.

Correlation between Aims and Projects	What projects are needed to achieve the Aims?	Correlation between Projects and Deliverables
What are the Strategic Objectives?	Projects Aims ⨉ Delivery Results	What are the project deliverables?
Correlation between Results and Aims	What financial and other benefits are expected?	Correlation between Deliverables and Results

Some key tools are part of the Hoshin process:

Ringi is a system of decision making used in Japan. 'Rin' means submitting a proposal to one's superior and receiving his approval. 'Gi' means deliberation and decisions. The ringi system is almost always preceded by nemawashi.

Nemawashi is a process of informal discussion and consultation before the formal proposal relating to the ringi is presented. It may be seen as a process of horizontal communication.

Hansei or reflection is an important aspect. Look back and is learn. The future is uncertain, although the destination is clear. Treat every unexpected event as an opportunity to learn and to adapt. Of course, it is similar to the study stage in Deming's PDSA cycle.

So PD is in essence an expanded form of 'team briefing' but requires written commitment, identification of goals, the setting of measures, and discussion at each level. In Western companies, top management sometimes spends much time on corporate vision but then fails to put in place a mechanism to translate the vision into deliverables and measures, at each level in the organization. Hoshin may go some way to explaining why in better Japanese companies the decision-making process is slower, but implementation is much faster and smoother.

Speaking at the 2018 European Lean Educator conference, Isao Yoshino, former Toyota executive in charge of Hoshin, gave the key characteristics of Hoshin-Kanri as follows:

- Employee engagement. Both top-down and bottom-up.

- Focus on the current 'big issue' and prioritise.

- Setting a clear target and expectation. A numerical target or concrete milestone.

- The process must match the result. (A good result with a poor process is mere luck.)

- Fact-based rather than assumption-based. (Including Gemba, 5 why)

- Regular review (PDSA process).

- People development.

- Not hesitating to bring bad news.

Once the goals have been set for the year, various teams across the organisation apply problem solving techniques such as A3, Kaizen, and PDSA to move towards the goals. A fundamental requirement of Hoshin Kanri is the requirement to have a monthly review process where each project or initiative is tracked against set milestones. This ensures that potential roadblocks are identified early. Good Hoshin involves three levels: 1. Tracing and correcting; 2. Researching why things did not work out; and 3. Learning how to improve the system itself. In other words, there is both single and double loop learning as explained by Argyris. (See Section 34.4)

Visuality is important. Clear X matrices (which show goals, processes, and measures) or Planning A3's should be shown and updated at every group meeting place. These show the clear link between the group's targets and initiatives and the overall corporate strategy.

At the end of each year a comprehensive assessment of the organisation's progress is carried out. This may result in some of the key goals and time-lines changing for the coming year. If all goals are achieved, something is wrong. Likewise, if no goals are achieved something (big) is wrong.

A critique: Hoshin is most suitable in businesses that have stable operations. In a fast-changing business such as IT project work, or in a VUCA environment, Hoshin may be less suitable. There is an analogy with the rejection of the 'waterfall' method in many IT projects and the adoption of agile approaches (Sprint? Scrum?). This leads onto the growing adoption of OKR, as outlined in a section below.

Further reading
Michael Cowley and Ellen Domb, *Beyond Strategic Vision: Effective Corporate Action with Hoshin Planning*, BH, 1997 (A book that gives an excellent overview of strategy with Hoshin.)
Thomas Jackson, *Hoshin Kanri for the Lean Enterprise*, Productivity Press, 2006
Yoshino

41 Measuring Performance

41.1 A Good Measurement System

First, we need a definition of measurement. A good definition, due to Douglas Hubbard is, 'A quantitatively expressed reduction of uncertainty based on one or more observations'. This 'reduction of uncertainty' is important – a 'measure' does not have to be precise, but reduction of uncertainty is valuable. A useful thought, building on Hubbard's definition is that Lean is a system to reduce uncertainty. The less the uncertainty, the less the waste in capacity, time, and inventory.

Hubbard maintains that measures should start with defining the decision dilemma. The direction, the trade-offs. Only when this is clear can we begin to define the relevant variables to be measured.

Several KPI's and visual management boards don't do this. Instead they begin by collecting, and often beautifully displaying, information on a 'nice to know' basis but without thinking through how the measures will be used. If KPI's and measures are unlikely to affect any decision they are waste! This thought should apply to 'Dashboards', Hoshin displays, daily meeting boards, and idea boards.

'You cannot fatten the calf by weighing it'. At the same time, an effective measurement system is one of the most powerful tools for Lean transformation. Measures should:

- Provide short-term indicators of problems – and show when action is required.
- Be part of a feedback loop of surfacing and resolving problems.
- Show learning or capability of the process or people, and what or who needs attention.
- Focus on improving performance.

'A science is as mature as its measurement tools', said Louis Pasteur (as quoted in Dean Spitzer). Is it not time for Lean to develop more maturity?

Three basics are:

- **Goodhart's Law:** When a measure becomes a target it ceases to be a measure.

- **Measures not Targets**. Measures help you to decide what to do. But Targets are often associated with rewards, punishments and motivation and thereby encourage deviant behaviour. The many examples from the British Health Service illustrate – from ignoring patients that have passed the target wait-deadline to removing wheels from hospital trolleys so they don't count as patients waiting on trolleys. Moreover, when targets are associated with rewards, often ever bigger rewards have to be given. Targets were a Deming pet-hate. Motivational measures (or targets) frequently result in cheating, but informational measures can assist improvement.

- **'What gets rewarded gets done'** says Michael LeBoeuf but better is Spitzer's statement, **'You get what you measure'**. Think about it, and beware!

The Process, not the Person

Deming spoke about the 94/6 rule – 94% of problems can be traced to the process or system, but only 6% to the person. But often it is the person that is measured, not the process. Start with the assumption that it is the process that is broken and most times you will be right. Almost everyone has experienced negative measurement – errors, cost overruns, lateness – and almost everyone has responded by negative emotions – blame, threats, defensiveness. Most of this can be avoided if you start with the process not the person – and that therefore the manager, not the subordinate, needs to correct the process. To repeat, an important insight from John Seddon: Begin with purpose, derive the necessary measures, that in turn drive method. Too often, the starting point is to dream up KPI's that then de facto influence the purpose resulting in misalignment between purpose and method.

Sins of Measurement

Michael Hammer's '7 Deadly Sins of Performance Measurement' are a salutary list. Briefly, with Lean transformation examples, they are: Vanity (measures that are aimed at making the manager look good – profits due to price not productivity); Provincialism (measuring within the department not the value stream); Narcissism (measuring from your point of view, not the customer's – for example, delivery performance against promised date not customer's request); Laziness (assuming one knows what is important to measure – for instance, cost when delivery performance is more important to the customer); Pettiness (measuring only a small part – delivery on time, but not in full); Inanity (measuring without thought of the consequences for example, prioritizing OEE – OEE improves but schedule attainment decreases and batch sizes increase); Frivolity (not being serious – 'we can't stop the line to look at problems').

The Cycle

Dean Spitzer says measurement should be thought of as a cycle: Plan (think decisions, as above), Select, Collect, Analyse, Interpret, Decide, Commit, Take action, Review. All these stages are subject to error and variation. Please specifically consider possible errors and their consequences in each of these stages, or do a PDSA on each stage by writing down the expectations and then reviewing them during the next cycle.

The Keys to Good Measurement

Setting a KPI out of thin air and believing it will make a difference is naïve! Spitzer says there are four keys to measurement success:

1. **Context.** Effective measurement can only occur in a positive, supportive context. This is the culture that surrounds the measurement – supportive or critical, process or person. An unfavourable measure is an opportunity not a threat. We want to surface issues, not suppress them.

2. **Focus.** Measure the right thing, then measure it right. Pareto. Derive many of the measures from participative policy deployment, not sucked out of the air. As Nassim Taleb says, 'It is important to be aware that the following is fallacy: The more information you have, the more you are confident about the outcome.'

3. **Integration.** There must be an integrated system or cycle for measurement, as above.

4. **Interactivity.** Measures need to be acted on in real time. Perhaps a daily meeting around the Communications Board. It is as much a social process as a technical process. Performance against measures should be reviewed level by level and escalated where necessary.

Useful guidelines for practical Lean measurement

- Little's Law, discussed in 'The Science of Lean' is an efficient and robust way to assess lead time, and to test the validity of data on WIP and throughput.

- The Rule of Five: 'There is a 93.7% chance that the median of a population is between the smallest and largest values in any random sample of five from that population'. Useful and efficient for lead time, quality, customer satisfaction and a host of other measures relevant to Lean.

Further reading

Douglas Hubbard, *How to Measure Anything*, Wiley, 2014

Dean Spitzer, Transforming Performance Measurement, AmaCom, 2007

Nassim Taleb, *Fooled by Randomness*, Random House, 2005

Richard Rumelt, *Good Strategy, Bad Strategy*, Profile Books, 2011

41.2   OKRs

The Objectives and Key Results (OKRs) framework has become a popular, and simplified – but not necessarily simple – alternative to Hoshin. Introduced by Andy Grove at Intel and subsequently introduced to Google in 1999 by John Doerr (who worked with Larry Page, Alphabet co-founder) whose book is *Measure What Matters*. Amazon, Google and Oracle remain enthusiastic.

Start with one Objective, or goal. For a team, this could be derived from corporate objectives, and could be broad. The point is, it is simply stated and easy to remember by all. Note that an objective should not be confused with a slogan.

Then, a small number – two or three, absolute maximum of five, specific key results (KRs) are set that directly relate to the objective. For a team, quarterly is usual. These are SMART (specific, measurable, actionable, reachable, time limited). Clear, Yes or No results. If all key results are achieved, this would indicate that they have been incorrectly set.

Objectives are the *what* statement, and key results are the metrics that relate to the *hows*. There should be clear transparency between objectives and results – probably in line with Andy Grove's outlook as an engineer.

OKRs work with a CFR (Conversations, Feedback, Recognition) methodology. This is a key feature, bringing some of the tasks of traditional Human Resources to line managers - not dissimilar to Blanchard's One-minute manager concepts. In his book, John Doerr points out the similarity with Amabile and Kramer's concepts in *The Progress Principle* of Catalysts (OKRs) and Nourishers (CFRs). (Refer to section 39.2 on Amabile in Small Wins). Recognition, of course, shows Respect.

As with Hoshin, there is a cascade. Begin with the broad and long-lasting Mission statement and Company values. These are cascaded down by level, perhaps company, department, team, individual – from longer-term to short-term. The cascade is not introduced as a 'big-bang' but gradually, say from two levels to eventually reaching the team and individual.

Where we have observed Hoshin and OKR, it would seem to us that Hoshin is more participative but slower and more detailed. (Bureaucratic?). OKR is more top-down and shorter. CFR, however, makes OKR more human. We see no conflict with Lean or Agile.

Further reading
John Doerr, *Measure What Matters*, Portfolio Penguin, 2017

41.3   Deming's and Shewhart's Counsel

A quotation from W Edwards Deming's famous book, *Out of the Crisis*, serves as a salutary warning on measures: 'Rates for production are often set to accommodate the average worker. Naturally, half of them are above average and half below. What happens is that peer pressure holds the upper half to the rate, no more. The people below the average cannot make the rate. The result is loss, chaos, dissatisfaction, and turnover.'

Deming illustrated his frustration with managers and measures with his famous red bead game. Six volunteers draw 50 beads at a time from a container having red and white beads, using a paddle. The reds are defects. The participants are urged to produce fewer defects. Of course there is variation between the participants, but it is out of their control. The 'good' performers are praised, the 'bad' ones given a warning. Some improve ('warnings work!'), but some don't and are fired. 'Managers don't understand variation', said Deming. Do you?

This amusing game nicely illustrates 'regression to the mean'. If you get a high reading this time, there is a very good chance that you will get a lower reading next time. And, a low reading will very likely be followed by a high reading. Hence, managers 'learn' never to praise 'good' performance , but always to criticise 'poor' performance. It works!.......

Shewhart's Insight

Shewhart, Deming's teacher, saw measurement having three elements, the data, the human observer, and the conditions. Note that all three are subject to variation. Everyone filters (or interprets) data according to their own bias and background. We all implicitly use models, mental or written, good or bad – and they are uncertain. Since we are dealing with uncertainties in data, observation, and interpretation we should use control charts to assist in understanding the variation – whether special cause or common cause. And we should try to improve on the model and understand the system via Plan Do Study Act.

Variation is important in measurement. 'Drowning in a river of average depth 3 feet', and 'The next person to walk through the door will have more than the average number of legs.'

It would also be useful, in setting measures, to be aware of the Cynefin framework (See Section 4.9). If you are in a chaotic or complex domain variation and uncertainty may be so high as to make measurement and forecasting difficult to interpret.

Further reading

W Edwards Deming, *Out of the Crisis*, Cambridge, 1986

Walter Shewhart, Statistical Method from the viewpoint of Quality Control, Dover, 1986

41.4   The Basic Lean Measures

Arguably, there are four basic or prime measures for Lean. Each of them encourages 'all the right moves'. Each can be implemented on various levels from cell to plant, even supply chain. They are also a set, to be looked at together.

Lead time. Measuring lead-time encourages inventory reduction, one-piece flow, reduction of flow length, and waste reduction. The measure is best done end-to-end from receiving dock to dispatch. Next best is to track only work in process lead-time. A variation on this measure is to track 'Ohno's Time Line' – the time between receiving an order and receiving payment, expressed in $ per hour. This is particularly good since it includes transaction processing time, and puts the emphasis on cash flow.

Customer Satisfaction. Following the first Lean principle, monitoring customers is a basic requirement. If failure is indicated here, this has to be the first priority. Do get this measure from customers, not internally from shipments or marketing. An obvious question is – who are your customers, Final or intermediate? Answer: Both. Sample them across all relevant dimensions – cost, quality, delivery as basics, but note also soft measures such as the RATER framework: reliability, assurance, tangibles, empathy, responsiveness. (See Zeithaml and Bitner, *Services Marketing*, 2006).

Schedule Attainment. An internal measure of consistency. Schedule attainment is the ability to hit the target for quantity and quality on a day-to-day basis line-by-line or cell-by-cell – not weekly for the plant. Again track the distribution. Compare the best with the worst, and seek opportunities not blame. If you have a Heijunka system this is straightforward. Of course, if the schedule is out of line with customer demands, the measure is a waste of time.

Inventory Turns, and 'SWIP to WIP'. Inventory turns is an established measure. An alternative is days of inventory. Better is to break it down into raw material, WIP, and finished goods days. Why? Because WIP is fully under your own control, raw materials and finished goods are not fully under own control. SWIP is standard work in progress inventory, so measuring the variation between what should be and actual is useful.

QCD(MMS): QCDMMS is an acronym for a set of measure categories widely used in Lean organizations and displayed at each line or area.

Quality. Internal scrap, rework, and first time through – expressed in parts per million. 'First time through' percentage is parts entering minus parts scrapped or reworked at each stage. Because rework can happen several times this measure can be negative.

Cost. Typically a productivity measure – units per person per week. Usually not a monetary value. OEE performance may be shown here.

Delivery performance. Inbound from suppliers, outbound to customers. QOTIF. (Quality, OnTime in Full) A delivery that is not 100% perfect, on time, and in full scores zero.

Morale. Absenteeism, suggestions or improvements are indicators. Possibly make use of an attitude audit.

Management. Communications, extent of cross training, attendance at shop floor meetings.

Safety. Accidents, Unsafe acts and audit of unsafe conditions.

Further reading

Richard Schonberger, *Best Practices in Lean Six Sigma Process Improvement*, Wiley, 2008. This excellent text contains a sobering view and comparison of company inventory turns (including at Toyota), and on metrics and 'Improvement gone wrong'.

41.5   Short Interval Tracking and Control

SIT / SIC allows companies greater agility to plan work, people and equipment in order to maximise the use of resources, aid decision making and respond to issues effectively. SIT is a process for driving improvements on the production floor during each shift. The shift is split into short intervals of time e.g. four hours, within which the production employees and support staff use data to identify and implement improvement actions. These actions may be countermeasures to address a gap between actual and target performance, or actions to improve current performance. SIC is in essence a form of Kaizen as it encourages teams to work together to achieve regular, incremental improvements to the manufacturing process.

SIC works in tandem with the daily Gemba meeting. It engages and supports the production team to address problems which are likely to cause them to miss their shift targets. Crucially SIT enables the team to react at an early stage, to minimise damage and implement containment measures while the root cause is being identified. At the meetings the team should focus first on the performance since the last interval. Where targets are not being met, they should prioritise and implement corrective actions; if this is not possible, they should escalate the problem for assistance and direction. Lastly, they should look ahead to the next interval for any potential problems.

Finally, to make it work consider these points:

- Perhaps two SIC meetings per shift?
- Meetings should be focused around a cell board
- Meetings should be less than 10 minutes.

42 Lean Accounting

It is interesting to note, as Michel Baudin has done, that few Japanese or Toyota texts discuss management accounting. As Ohno is reported to have said, Costs do not exist to be calculated; costs exist to be reduced. Cost accounting is waste; cost reduction is not.

First of all, one needs to distinguish between 'Lean accounting', and 'accounting for Lean'. Lean accounting tries to minimise the number of transactions and the efficiency of the process; accounting for Lean tries to improve decision making to enable Lean operations. We will cover both.

David Cochrane and Thomas Johnson, amongst others, have made the point that many companies are now managed the wrong way around. They start with measures or targets, then work out the physical solutions (the 'hows' and the 'whats'). By contrast, becoming Lean should start with the purpose, derive 'hows' and 'whats', and then choose to reinforce achievement.

There are few points to remember before reading this section about Lean accounting. Strong reasons why 'Accounting for Lean' gained prominence is (firstly) because traditional accounting and costing sends out contradictory messages about Lean progress, and (secondly) because traditional accounting systems were essentially backwards looking (i.e. only reporting on past performance, but giving few (if any) real pointers how to improve in the future. Accounting for Lean is undoubtedly a major improvement over the status quo, but cannot be used for Financial Accounting where GAAP requirements are necessary. Accounting information is always descriptive, not prescriptive. Even though Accounting for Lean will provide much better information, it is important to understand that financial performance is an emergent outcome of the relationships among the organisations' parts. As Thomas Johnson points out, managers who strive to improve financial results by encouraging their staff to chase financial targets will invariably achieve worse results than those who help improve the system that generates these results! As Deming pointed out, managers should not use financial targets to control financial results, instead, manage the relationships that produce these results.

Nonetheless, accounting is a vital instrument to control the organisation, not least because of the legal requirements and shareholder accountability requirements. It is against this backdrop that you should read this chapter.

With Lean, 'bean counters' should become 'bean growers'.

Further reading

Thomas Johnson, Management by Financial Targets isn't Lean, *Manufacturing Engineering*, December 2007, p 1-5

Johnson, T., Kaplan, R.S. 1987. *Relevance Lost - The Rise and Fall of Management Accounting,* Harvard Business School Press, Boston

David Cochrane, 'The Need for a Systems Approach to Enhance and Sustain Lean', in Joe Stenzel (ed), *Lean Accounting: Best Practices for Sustainable Integration*, Wiley, 2007

Brian Maskell, *Making the Numbers Count*, Second edition, CRC Press, 2009

Gloria McVay et al, *Accounting in the Lean Enterprise*, CRC Press, 2013

Nicholas Katko, *The Lean CFO*, CRC Press, 2014

42.1 Warnings and Dilemmas

While the benefits of Lean are generally obvious to the Operations people, they are far from obvious to the traditional Accounting world. Hence a few warnings and dilemmas that one needs to be aware of:

Much of the 'conflict' between traditional and Lean thinking on accounting and measures derives from a fundamental difference in assumption about the system. Traditionalists believe that departments, functions and parts are separate and that improving the parts will lead to improving the whole. Lean thinkers, by contrast, take an end-to-end, or value stream view. Thus a traditionalist might automate a warehouse, or favour speeding up a machine, but a Lean thinker would ask about eliminating the warehouse or slowing the machine. This fundamental difference in viewpoint leads to other differences:

- Inventory is seen an asset in our current accounting systems – so its reduction can appear unfavourable on the Balance sheet.

- Stopping work because there is too much inventory or is not needed for a while will mean that budgeted activities will not take place. Activities 'absorb' overhead, so that by not carrying them out means that the overhead will not be absorbed and there will be an unfavourable variance. There will be under-recovery. Unfavourable variances, in turn, show up on the profit and loss (or income) statement.

- Overproduction, at least in the short term, may generate positive variances and increase the book profit. However, cash flow is likely to decline. If profit is seen as more important than cash, this is an issue.

- Two products are made – one with high labour content and high contribution, the other with high automation, low labour and low contribution. As overhead is allocated, the high labour, high contribution product may turn into a loss maker. It may then become a candidate for outsourcing. If this happens, the overhead will now have to be allocated to the low contribution product, eventually also driving it out of the business.

- Saving operators as a result of Lean activity may be a dilemma. If people's jobs are threatened, they are unlikely to participate in improvement. Even though an assurance has been given that 'no-one will lose their job as a result of improvement', no saving is made until a person actually leaves. This can be managed in a situation of growth or where there is labour turnover. However, there will be a delay before the saving reaches the 'bottom line'. If there is no growth or where there is small labour turnover the dilemma is worse. Moving people to an 'indirect' category will create an unfavourable variance in that category. Thus, many claimed savings are 'fake'. (In a low growth scenario it may be dishonest to say that no-one will lose their job due to improvement.)

- If supplies can be acquired at a discount this will generate a positive variance. But what if that means that delivered batches will be bigger and more inventory will need to be stored?

- When labour is reduced, skills and training are lost – but this goes uncosted. It is 'good'. But Lean should be about growth. With growth, those skills are more valuable – and much less expensive than if acquired from scratch.

- A cell is implemented. The previous system had process layout. The cell is more labour-intensive but lead time is slashed. So a huge reduction in lead time is a little more expensive. Competitiveness and delivery performance is much improved, but the financials are unfavourable – at least in the short term.

- Through poka-yoke and self inspection it is possible to slash the number of inspectors. Inspectors are 'indirect' because they work in several departments. Overhead goes down but the standard cost in the area may increase

- 'Kaizen results don't show up on the bottom line!'. Of course they don't! Actual savings are only made when people actually leave or less material is purchased. A statement like the opening one reflects the view that Lean is about cost reduction. In fact, it is about growth and competitiveness.

- There is invariably a lag between actual performance and the financials.

Accounting for Lean is a developing field. After over a century of little change the basic assumptions of accounting are at last being questioned in the light of Lean and Theory of Constraints. We need to distinguish between Financial Accounting that is required for tax and shareholder purposes and is subject to GAAP, and Management Accounting that is used for decision-making. Accounting for Lean falls into the second category.

In some ways, what has happened in Lean manufacturing is beginning to happen in accounting in Lean environments. Lean manufacturing lifted the focus from the activity to the value stream. End-to-end performance became much more important than the efficiency of an individual operator or machine. It is the non value adding steps between operations that get the focus. Economies of scale were important pre-Lean. But with Lean, economies of flow and time are more relevant. Similarly with accounting for Lean: not the person, machine, or department but the end-to-end value stream matter. More was better, and producing more, irrespective of demand, was rewarded with positive variances and greater apparent profit. Lean (and TOC) has begun to show the fallacy of this non-systems view.

What should Accounting for Lean give us?

- More relevant information for decision-making. More relevant means the ability to identify factors and products that are becoming uncompetitive, and where there are potential opportunities for improvement.

- Positive support and evidence for doing the right things – fast, flexible, flow. For reducing inventories and lead times, for improving quality, and for improving delivery performance.

- Financial numbers that are able to be understood by non-accountants without having to go through several days of education. Develop 'Plain English' profit and loss statements that exclude variances, show actual operations profit, and have additional lines that show changes in overhead, labour and inventory.

- A simplified system that cuts waste and unnecessary transactions. A Lean accounting system needs to be a minimalist system – tracking only the absolute minimum transactions with the lowest frequency possible.

- A system that highlights when to take action, as importantly when not to.

- Guidance on medium term product costing and target costing.

Although accountants, planners and managers probably may not like it, recall that Ohno said that an aim of Lean / TPS should be to make the system so simple and visible that there would be little need for complex controls. Real Lean must cut overhead! Ohno also said: *'Excess information must be suppressed!'*

What should Accounting for Lean NOT give us?

- Evidence that implementing Lean is exactly the wrong thing to do. The earlier warnings are illustrative.

- Product costing on a month-by-month basis. There is a Western obsession with detailed product costing brought about by the belief that costs can be controlled by the financials. They cannot. Only productivity improvement can make a difference. Variances often encourage game playing managers who thereby spend inordinate time on manipulating figures rather than focusing on improvement. Plant and machines are sunk costs. These costs cannot be changed in the short term, only manipulated. In fact, there is no such thing as the true product cost, at least in the short-term.

- Detailed variance analysis. Variances are tracked in detail against standards, resulting in for example labour efficiency variances, volume variances, material usage variances, and purchase price variances. Variance analysis is almost pure waste. Worse, it can generate non-Lean behaviour. Many non-accountants do not understand where 'unfavourable' negative variances come from. (In fact, they are based on assumptions and forecasts about future operation levels.) But they learn that overhead is absorbed as labour and machine hours accumulate, and they do not want to be caught with unfavourable variances. This encourages overproduction. The point is, what can a manager do about an unfavourable variance in the short term? Answer: almost nothing favourable for Lean. Senior managers need to ponder that one.

- Being 'precise' but late (and worse, expensive) is far worse from a Lean perspective from being approximate but fast.

Maskell makes the point that Lean should not be regarded as a short-term cost cutting strategy, but rather as a long term competitive strategy. Cutting waste creates opportunity for growth, and accountants have an important role to help identify what is to be done with freed up capacity. Use marginal costing? Certainly. But standard costing? Often inappropriate.

42.2 The Box Score

Brian Maskell's 'Box Score' has become popular. Maskell is a strong advocate of organising by value stream, and each value stream has a box score. This is a more appropriate set of measures than the Balanced Scorecard, at least for value streams. The intention is that the box score format allows the easy and relevant presentation of measures. There are three main sections: within each section, a small but relevant set of measures are chosen:

Performance:

- Productivity (e.g. units / person)
- Lead time (Dock to dock)
- Shipment (e.g. first time through, OTIF)

Capacity (for both people and machines)

- Productive time, non-productive time, available time (%)

Financials (in $, but note: no overhead allocation)

- Revenue, Materials, conversion costs, profit

Conversion costs are made up of direct labour, machine depreciation, and facilities costs allocated on (say) square metres. Material costs are the direct costs of material received. Of course, 'profit' is contribution. But knowing that makes some other analyses possible – such as a contribution per bottleneck minute ranking.

Box score performance is tracked month by month and enables a good overall view of Lean implementation progress.

The box score is easy to set up when there is a clear value stream. If there are shared resources, a simple way must be found to allocate the cost of the shared resource between streams – on a weekly or monthly basis; certainly not by a method that involves lots of data collection.

42.3 Target Costing, Kaizen Costing and Cost Down

This final section brings together many of the tools presented in earlier sections. The concept of Target Costing is well established in Lean. The idea is simply that pricing begins with the market:

Target cost = Market price - Target Profit.

So, instead of the price being derived from cost plus profit, the cost is derived from market factors. Target costing is done in anticipation of future demand. In fact, the price may create the demand. Target costing begins with the customer's needs. A customer may in fact want to buy holes not drills, or 'power by the hour', not an aircraft engine.

It is proactive, not reactive. It is a tough system, because there can be no compromise on the target cost. There are variations - for example in the aircraft industry and in Formula 1 there is the target weight.

According to Cooper and Slagmulder, target costing has the cardinal rule 'The target cost of a product can never be exceeded'. Unless this rule is in place a target costing system will lose its effectiveness and will always be subject to the temptation of adding just a little bit more functionality at a little higher price. There are three strands to target costing: allowable cost, product level target cost, and component target costs.

Much of the following material on the three strands is derived from Cooper and Slagmulder.

Allowable cost is the maximum cost at which a product must be made so as to earn its target profit margin. The allowable cost is derived from target selling price - target profit margin. Target selling price is determined from three factors: customers, competitive offerings, and strategic objectives.

The price customers can be expected to pay depends importantly upon their perception of value. So if a new product or variant is proposed, marketing must determine if and how much customers are prepared to pay for the new features. The position on the product life cycle is important. An innovative lead product may be able to command a higher price.

Customer loyalty and brand name are influential. Then there are the competitive offerings: what functions are being, and are anticipated to be, offered at what prices.

Finally there are strategic considerations as to, for example whether the product is to compete in a new market, and the importance of market share.

Target profit margin is the next factor in determining allowable cost. There are two approaches, according to Cooper and Slagmulder. The first uses the predecessor product and adjusts for market conditions. The second starts with the margin of the whole product line, and makes adjustments according to market conditions.

Product Level Target Costing begins with the Allowable Cost and challenges the designers to design a product with the required functionality at the allowable cost. Sometimes the design team will not know the real allowable cost, but will be set a target which is considered to be a difficult-to-

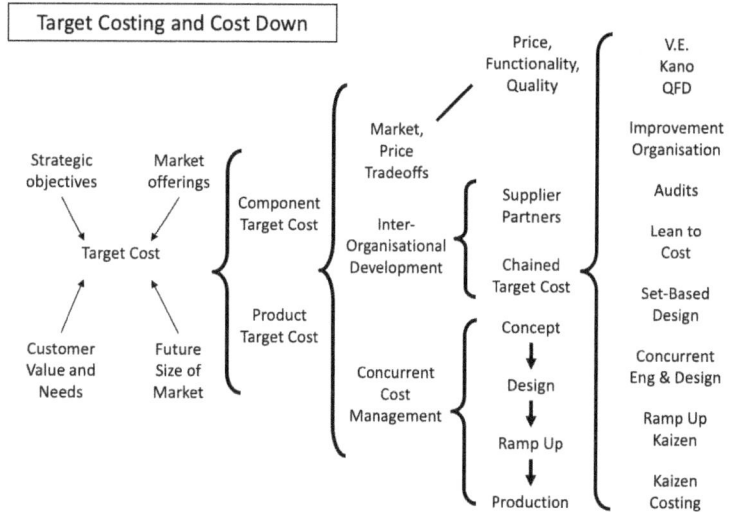

Target Costing and Cost Down

Strategic objectives → Target Cost ← Market offerings
Customer Value and Needs → Target Cost ← Future Size of Market

Component Target Cost / Product Target Cost:
- Market, Price Tradeoffs — Price, Functionality, Quality — V.E., Kano, QFD, Improvement Organisation
- Inter-Organisational Development — Supplier Partners, Chained Target Cost — Audits, Lean to Cost, Set-Based Design
- Concurrent Cost Management — Concept → Design → Ramp Up → Production — Concept, Design, Ramp Up Kaizen, Kaizen Costing — Concurrent Eng & Design

achieve challenge, for motivational reasons. A useful concept is the Waste Free Cost. This concept, also found in value engineering, is the cost assuming that all avoidable waste has been taken out. Another guiding principle is the 'cardinal rule' that cost must not be allowed to creep up: if an extra function is added, there must be a compensating cost reduction elsewhere. The process of moving in increments from the current cost to the target cost is referred to as 'drifting' and is closely monitored. Once the target cost has been achieved, effort stops: there is no virtue in achieving more than is required.

Component target costing aims at setting the costs of each component. This is an important strategic consideration because it involves the question of supplier partnership and trust.

The figure shows a hierarchy of approaches and tools. There are three routes to addressing component and product target costs.

The first is through market-price trade-offs, involving negotiations between designers and marketers and between OEM and suppliers, on the sensitivity of price, functionality and quality. Core tools here are the Kano model, QFD, increasingly design for Six Sigma, and centrally, value engineering. The design concept of the four objectives and six trade-offs is also important. All of these are discussed in earlier separate chapters.

The second is inter-organizational development. This involves working with supplier partners to achieve cost down. These methods include most of this book. Supplier aspects are discussed in the Supply Chain chapter - see particularly the supplier association and purchasing association sections. Chained target costing extends this pressure, or cooperation, further upstream along the supply chain.

Each company along the chain is expected (or forced to?) participate by a level-by-level process. Audits play a part here - for example Ford uses an audit tool to assess suppliers and uses activity sampling to identify the extent of cost down opportunity. Toyota uses their supplier support centre. When waste is identified it is either helped to be removed or expected to be removed. Ford uses a confidential costing system, called Lean to Cost, to translate the identified waste into money terms.

The third area is Concurrent Cost Management. This can take place both, internally or with immediate suppliers. The idea is to address costs at each level, from concept to production. These levels were once addressed sequentially, but are now increasingly being done concurrently. Concurrent engineering ideas are used. Of particular note is the Toyota 'set based' methodology that gradually homes in on the specifications whilst allowing flexibility and innovation until quite late into the process. Ramp up is an important stage aimed at reducing problems before full scale production of the new product begins. Once the product goes into production, three other actions may follow:

1. Further variants may be launched from the base product or platform at strategic intervals, to maintain competitiveness by either adding functionality or to pass on advances in technology, or to pass on price reductions.

2. Further value engineering (sometimes referred to as value methodology after the initial launch) may take place at regular intervals. One Japanese company aims to do a value analysis on each of their continuing consumer electronics products once per year. The aim is to either reduce cost or improve functionality. (See Section 36.5 for more detail on value methods and engineering.)

3. 'Kaizen costing' is undertaken. Kaizen costing is the post-launch version of target costing, and aims to achieve target cost levels at specific points. Kaizen costing is not really costing in the conventional Western sense. A Western way is to track variances. How feeble! The kaizen way is to target productivity improvements in people, materials, methods, and machines - as identified by audits, benchmarks, waste analysis, mapping, and activity sampling - in specific periods of time. What the paperwork says about the variances does not matter - what matters is the real tangible improvements in productivity.

Kaizen costing targets three areas: the method or facilities, the product, the overheads. Method is targeted by both the Policy Deployment process focusing on cost down initiatives, level by level, and by local initiatives carried out by the team with or without help from Lean Promotion Office or OEM staff. A typical improvement would be a cell re-balance as explained in the Layout and Cells section of this book. The product is targeted by value engineering. Overheads are targeted using Information value stream mapping and Brown paper mapping.

Further reading

Robin Cooper and Regine Slagmulder, *Target Costing and Value Engineering*, Institute of Management Accountants / Productivity Press, 1997

Robin Cooper and Regine Slagmulder, *Supply Chain Development for the Lean Enterprise*, Institute of Management Accountants / Productivity Press, 1999

Robert Kaplan and Robin Cooper, *Cost and Effect*, Harvard Business School Press, 1998

Shahid Ansari et al, *Target Costing*, Irwin McGraw Hill, 1997

Joe Stenzel (ed.), Lean Accounting: Best Practices for Sustainable Integration, Wiley, 2007

42.4   Setting up a Lean Accounting System

Some pointers for a Lean accounting system follow:

- Go through the implications of Lean implementation with senior managers beforehand. They need to know and expect the consequences of inventory reduction, and labour and machines changes on Profit and Loss, Balance Sheet and particularly cash. But also incorporate lead times, defect rates, and customer satisfaction alongside the financials.

- Highlight changes in cash flows. For costing, it is money going into and out of the value stream that is of prime importance, not what happens along the route.

- Work towards direct costs. Rather than trying to 'solve' the overhead allocation problem by some 'elegant' procedure such as Activity Based Costing (ABC), set an objective to decentralise overhead functions such that they can be directly associated with cells or product lines. So for example have schedulers, quality, maintenance, purchasing, and training associated with particular products.

- One of the authors, Bicheno, lives near a river and had a flood in the kitchen. A new kitchen was installed at great cost. Since the cost of the kitchen needs to apportioned to meals it is now too expensive to eat at home! (This story emanates from John Darlington.)

- If you must allocate overhead (Why?) at least allocate in a way that supports Lean – a good way is allocation based on lead-time, not on labour hours or activities.

- Better, have a general overhead pool for all overhead that is not directly associable with a product or service.

- As far as possible, cost by end-to-end value stream. Avoid transfer costs between sections of the value stream. The more indirect costs that can be associated with a value steam, the better.

- Eliminate variance reporting. Few understand it. Spend time on cost reduction, not on variance analysis. In any case variances are based on forecasts and everyone knows that forecasts are wrong, lucky or lousy.

- Eliminate detailed product cost reporting. Instead, do a periodic estimation exercise together with line managers. Look ahead rather than back. Direct cost association helps considerably.

- Use accountants, together with designers and marketers to look at costing alternative materials and features.

- Reduce the number of transactions. Use Demand analysis concepts to take advantage of big repeating SKU's that can be grouped for accounting simplicity.

- Reduce reporting time. As with changeover reduction, do as much prior work as possible prior to period end. Then make adjustments only. Do a Pareto analysis on transaction size – do not delay reporting on many small items that can be carried over to the next period with minimal consequence. Be fast and approximate rather than slow and 'precise'.

- Encourage accountants to think about variation of costs rather than cost variances. Cost variation means looking into the distribution of labour, component, and material costs. What is the spread from worst case to best case. Then, why are the worst cases occurring? This is much like the Six Sigma methodology. Tackle the worst cases. This concept is developed by Johnson and Bröms who maintain that many a product line has been abandoned due to unfavourable average costs that could have been saved by appropriate analysis and pruning.

- Report by exception. Get accountants to think common cause and special cause (SPC). Only report special cause events.

- Reduce the frequency of reporting intervals. Ask what are the benefits and costs of shorter financial reporting intervals. Short-term targets are notorious.

- Clarify the presentation of accounts so all can read them. This means that the word 'variance' should not appear on a statement. Specifically report actual increases and decreases in inventory.

- Record inventory valuations in terms of raw material value only. Do not accrue value. Do not show 'deferred labour and overhead' as costs that have been accrued into inventory.

- If the company has constraint resources (and most do), focus costs around these constraints. Calculate contribution per constraint minute. Know what the opportunity cost of an hour lost or gained at a constraint will be, and get the accountants to cost it.

- Get accountants to participate on the assembly and evaluation of Future State maps. There should be a parallel value stream maps that examine the financing periods (time to pay suppliers, time to finance operations, time to get in cash). In other words, end-to-end cash flows or cash turns – not just inventory turns.

Further reading

Richard Schonberger, *Let's Fix It!*, Free Press, 2001, Chapters 4 to 7

Orest Fiume, 'Lean Accounting and Finance', *Target*, Fourth quarter, 2002

Jean Cunningham and Orest Fiume, *Real Numbers*, Managing Times Press, 2003

Jim Huntzinger and Robert Hall, Measurement Conundrums, *Target*, v23 n4, Fourth Issue, 2007

H Thomas Johnson and Anders Bröms, *Profit Beyond Measure*, Nicholas Brealey, 2000.

John Darlington, *Notes on Costing*, MSc Lean Enterprise, University of Buckingham, 2014

Brian Maskell and Bruce Baggalay, *Practical Lean Accounting*, Productivity, (Second Edition), 2012 (N.B: Not first edition!)

Joe Stenzel (ed), Lean Accounting: Best Practices for Sustainable Integration, Wiley, 2007

Gloria McVay et al, *Accounting in the Lean Enterprise*, CRC Press, 2013 and 2017. (Comprehensive, not only on the financials.)

DIGITAL TOOLS FOR FLOW

The digitalisation of the way we live and work is progressing rapidly, affecting nearly if not all aspects of our societies. Digital technologies are ubiquitous in our day and age. While there is much hype behind many of these technologies, nonetheless it is without question that most will become integral parts of our manufacturing and service operations in future.

The main point to remember with any technology though is that technology is a tool, not a solution. All too often technologies are seen as 'silver bullets' that will resolve all problems in a process. This was the case with early MRP systems in the 1980s, with fancy ERP systems in the 1990s, and now with AI. It never works. Technology always is a means to an end, not an end in itself. They can support process improvement activities as part of lean transformation, but they are not standalone solutions. It is important to bear that in mind when assessing the merits of any given technology.

In this section we will briefly describe the main digital technologies and what capabilities they bring. As we tackle each chapter, we will point out how the respective technologies may link to lean transformations. This is a very dynamic space so we will focus on explaining the core concepts, rather than attempting to cover all possible use cases.

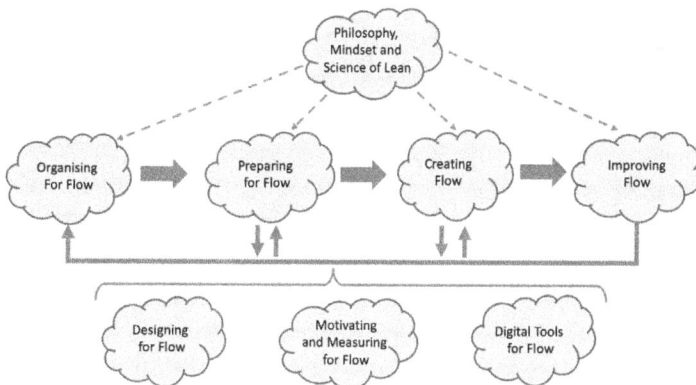

43 Making Sense of the Digital Transformation

43.1 Amara's Law

A common fallacy is to assume that just because a technology provides a certain capability, that it will be adopted. This is known as 'technological determinism' and often drives the hype behind new technological advances. In reality, of course, the process by which new technologies are adopted is just as much a question of economics, as well as social desirability.

A good mental model think about new technologies was defined by Roy Amara, a technologist who worked on technology forecasting. He stated that we commonly overestimate the impact of a technology in the short run, while we underestimate its impact in the long run. One can illustrate this law in the famous hype cycle, which is promoted by Gartner.

What the hype cycle shows is that the prospect of a new technology fuels the hype and leads to inflated expectations. Once the economics of actually putting these technologies into action come to play, however, many of these technologies disappear because they are not viable. This is the trough of disillusionment. Those technologies however that are both economically viable, and socially acceptable or desirable, will reach the plateau of productivity, where will they unfold their true potential. What these will entail cannot be predicted and will often co-evolve as technologies are being implemented. It is for this for this reason that Amara suggested that we tend to underestimate the impact of a technology in the long run. Think about AI, for example. When deep learning was developed by Geoff Hinton in 2012, no one would have predicted that machine learning would support decisions across all industry sectors in the way it already does today.

Amara's Law and the hype cycle are good mental models to make sense of any new technology, as all technologies will follow the hype cycle in one way or another. What will determine whether they will be adopted in the end are three important questions: (1) technological capability, or could we do it?; (2) economic viability, or would we do it?; and (3) social desirability, or should we do it? Technologies that are successful in the long run will be able to answer all three.

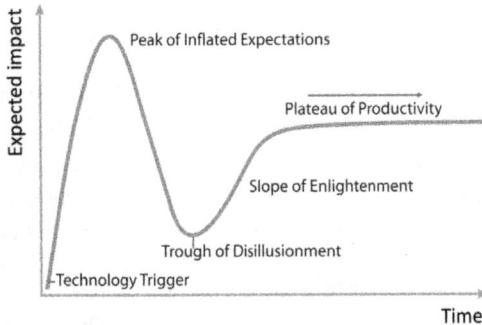

A sobering case comes from Stanley McChrystal, former Commander-in-chief of Allied Forces in Afghanistan. The Allies had all the technology – the digital command structure. Yet the Taliban for a while were 'running rings around' the allies. Why? Flexibility and decentralisation! As McChrystal says, 'Efficiency remains important, but the ability to adapt to complexity and continual change has become an imperative.'

43.2   Digitisation or digitalisation?

While digital technologies are easy to observe in action, the question what digitalisation actually entails is surprisingly hard to answer concisely. The distinction between digitisation and digitalisation is raised here, which is a helpful way to understand what transformation actually is taking place.

Digitisation refers to the substitution of one part or aspect of the process with a digital artefact. For example, replacing a visual pressure gauge with a digital sensor that feeds that signal into an electronic surveillance system. In this case the process flow remains largely intact, while only a specific aspect is changed from an analogue to a digital tool.

Digitalisation on the other hand implies a reengineering of the entire process, or even the business model, on the back of the capabilities that digital technologies offer. For example, using autonomous drone and machine learning to enable a predictive maintenance regime of industrial equipment, which is a fundamentally different process to preventive maintenance operations that rely on human inspections.

We will explore the digital technologies and how they can support lean implementations in more detail below. Across all of these, however, there are common mechanisms that are worth pointing out.

These include a cluster of mechanisms that *augment operational execution* in terms of speed and precision of execution, and as flexibility in space and time. Furthermore, there is a second cluster of mechanisms that *augment decision-making* through visibility and feedback from the process, engagement of the workforce and prevention of mistakes.

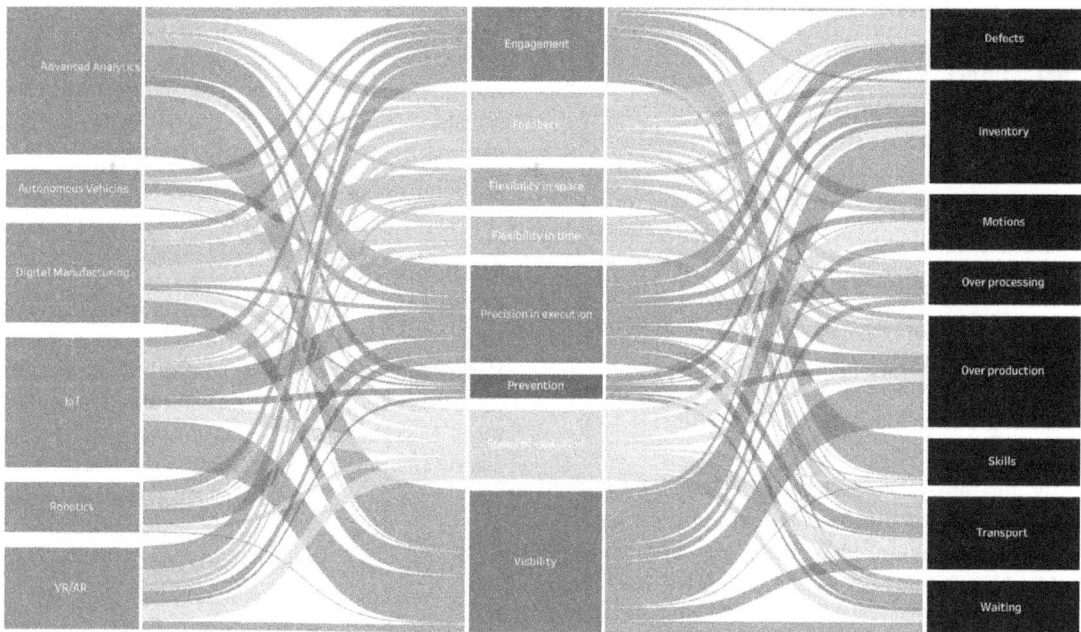

Using these mechanisms, Cifone et al have been able to plot the connections between the main digital technologies and the wastes in manufacturing, see figure. (Figure used with permission.) This will change according to context, but nonetheless highlights the main mechanisms how digital technologies can indeed support lean implementations. An while these digital technologies are powerful indeed, it is important to remember that technologies are a means to an end, not an end in itself!

Further reading

Cifone, F.D., et al. 2021. 'Lean 4.0': How can digital technologies support lean practices? *International Journal of Production Economics*, *241*, p.108258.

Paul Leinwand and Mahadeva Matt Mani, 2021. Digitizing Isn't the Same as Digital Transformation. *Harvard Business Review,* March 26.

Schwab, K., 2017. The fourth industrial revolution. Currency.

44 The Digital Toolbox

44.1 Industry 4.0

Industry 4.0 is a concept that was launched in Germany in 2011 to describe ways in which the German manufacturing sector could remain competitive in future. The main thesis of this report was that investments in 'cyber-physical systems' was needed to achieve this. In other words, the idea is to couple the physical and digital worlds in order to create ubiquitous connectivity of assets, materials, and customers. Being able to 'see' the physical process in a digital way in real time allows for much better and faster control, which in turn increases efficiency.

Later, the term was used to inspire Klaus Schwab's vision at the World Economic Forum of a 'fourth industrial revolution' (4IR). His thesis is that the digital technologies we see emerging will lead to another industrial revolution, following steam, electricity and electronics (the latter in the most simple way).

The key technologies linked to industry 4.0 vary a lot, yet commonly include AI, 3D printing, the internet of things (IoT), autonomous vehicles, augmented and virtual reality. We will discuss these, and others, next.

44.2 AI and Machine Learning

The term artificial intelligence (AI) was coined in 1956 by computer scientist John MacCarthy for a workshop in Dartmouth, MA, that brought together many of the leading computer scientists at the time. The main objective of all AI research is to develop machines that are able to perform tasks intelligently, ideally at the same level of a human. An AI system would perceive its environment and take actions that maximize its chance of achieving its goals.

There are broader definitions of AI too, seeking to develop self-conscious machines that can display cognitive skills. This is known as 'artificial general intelligence' and remains the subject of science fiction movies. In fact, current AI systems are almost all 'narrow AI', which have been set up and trained for a single purpose: they are able to recognise faces, to do machine translation, or to recommend the next move to watch on Netflix. This is changing with modern architectures, like transformers, which are able to deal with multiple data inputs and can solve more complex tasks.

Let us introduce the key concepts.

Machine Learning

Machine learning is a subfield of statistics that dates back to the 1980s. The core idea is for an algorithm to extract ('learn') patterns from existing data, in order to make a prediction about new data. Most AI systems are based on machine learning algorithms, which fall into three basic categories:

1. Supervised learning: here the algorithm learns like a human. It makes a prediction on data, and is corrected if needed by providing the right answer. For this a 'labelled' dataset that contains the right answers for the training of the algorithm. Typical applications include regression (estimation of a parameter, say the value of a house or the right order quantity), and classification (say whether or not a customer should be granted a loan, or whether a tumour is malicious or not).

2. Unsupervised learning. Here the data is 'unlabelled' so does not contain the right answers. Instead, the algorithm considers all available data at once and looks for patterns (clusters). Typical applications are recommender systems, and outlier detection systems like spam filters.

3. Reinforcement learning. In this case no training data is needed, instead the algorithm 'plays' repeated iterations in a set environment. The algorithm learns by receiving a reward signal how well it has done, and then updates its strategy accordingly. Reinforcement learning is used for games, like AlphaGo, but also for protein folding in drug discovery.

So far, the large majority of AI systems in use are based on regression, classification and clustering algorithms, while much of the attention has been placed on the newer algorithms called 'deep learning'.

Deep Learning

Contrary to the name, 'deep learning' is not a type of learning but a class of algorithms. These are based on large artificial neural networks, which in essence try to emulate how the human brain works. This idea dates back the 1950s, yet it was only with recent increases in computing power and data availability that they became viable. The main breakthrough for Deep Learning came with Geoff Hinton's backpropagation idea, which allowed neural networks to learn from their mistakes (supervised learning). Yet deep learning can also be used for unsupervised and reinforcement learning.

All modern AI applications that deal with images and language are based on deep neural networks. For image recognition, we use convolutional neural networks (CNNs), for natural language processing we use transformer architectures that make use of a new concept called 'attention'. This idea allows the network to consider all data at the same time. Transformers are computationally very intensive, but provide a general-purpose architecture that can be used for many different purposes, not just text and speech. See below.

Another interesting class of deep learning algorithms are so-called generative adversarial networks (GANs), which comprise of a reinforcement learning and a trained discriminator network. The former comes up with new solutions, say images, and the latter tries to decide whether it is fake, or not. In essence, they are playing a continuous Turing test until the discriminator is satisfied that the new content is 'real'. This type of architecture is used to generate new content, such as images or text, and often is referred to as 'deepfakes'.

Multi-modal and general-purpose AI

Multi-modal AI systems use several data inputs, such as text and images. Hence they can deal with more complex tasks, such as turning text into images, or describing the content of an image or video. Famous examples include DALL-E or Google's Imagen picture generators. More broadly, multi-modal AI systems will become more common for most tasks, as being able to use multiple data sources generally improves the quality of the prediction.

As we progress with using multiple data sources, future AI systems are likely to become 'general-purpose', meaning that they can deal with tasks that they were not explicitly trained for, as are current 'narrow' AI systems. The more AI can progress towards this objective, the more it will displace human activity in the workplace. Put differently, the real impact AI is likely to have on the future of work still lies ahead of use. Seminal studies by Oxford scholars Frey and Osborne estimate that 47% of all jobs can be automated. Most of these are not in the factories or cabs of trucks, but in offices. Low-level sales, administrative and support staff roles are the most likely to disappear with increasing use of AI systems.

Further reading

Mike Wooldridge, *The Road to Conscious Machines: The Story of AI,* Pelican Books, 2021

Frey, C.B. and Osborne, M.A., 2017. The future of employment: How susceptible are jobs to computerisation?. *Technological Forecasting and Social Change*, 114, pp.254-280.

44.3   Process Mining

A framework of how to use advanced analytics and machine learning for process improvement is called 'process mining'. The idea here, as shown in the figure below, is to convert all the daily activities across processes into an 'event log'. Here, all activities are captured as individual action, and are recorded and timestamped. This becomes the raw material to be 'mined' in the next step. Next, this data is analysed using statistical tools in order to derive insights how the process operates, and how to improve it. Two aspects are of importance here: 'variants', whereby a standard process is executed

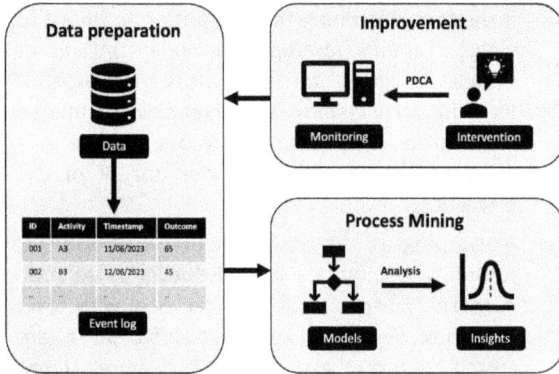

in a slightly different way, for example because the customer has chosen a given option; and 'deviations', which occur when the standard process is not followed.

Based on these insights how the process currently operates, and how it performs against key KPIs, predictive models can suggest improvements, such as identifying high-performance configurations, or highlight potential quality or control problems.

The remaining cycle will then follow a standard PDCA logic, resulting in continuous monitoring and review of the process.

Further reading

Wil van der Aalst, *Process Mining: Data Science in Action*, Second edition, Springer, 2016

44.4 3D Printing or Additive Manufacturing

Commonly referred to as '3D printing', the idea of additive manufacturing (AM) is to build up parts sequentially by depositing layer by layer. This is fundamentally different from traditional 'subtractive' manufacturing, where the material is taken away by cutting, drilling and milling in order to create a part.

Additive manufacturing is not a new technology at all, as it has been around as 'rapid prototyping' since the 1980s. With key patents expiring in recent years, it has seen a major wave of innovations. Modern 3D printers can now create plastic and metal parts to support industrial production.

The key advantages of 3D printing are the absence of costly tooling, which means small lot sizes are possible, and the ability to geometrically freeform parts with few restrictions. In many ways, for small lot sizes or even single parts, 3D printing is a very lean way of manufacturing. A main application, in future, is likely to provide a lean spare parts supply that does not require stock holding.

The downside of 3D printing is that its build volume is limited by the machine itself. Thus, it essentially operates as a small-batch production process, which requires frequent set-ups for larger volume production. This limits the application of AM in producing standard parts, as it cannot compete on unit cost against tool-based manufacturing.

Further reading

Baumers, M. and Holweg, M., 2019. On the economics of additive manufacturing: Experimental findings. *Journal of Operations Management*, 65(8), pp.794-809.

44.5 Internet of Things, RFID and RLTS

The (industrial) internet of things (IoT) embodies the idea of cyberphysical systems by seeking to connect physical assets with the internet. Applications include sensors that can transmit their location and other data in real-time, often referred to as Real-Time Location Systems (RLTS). These will often use radio frequency identification (RFID) tags or WIFI-based connected sensors. An example are sensors in aircraft engines that submit their readings in real time to the maintenance base, where the engine's status is monitored, and maintenance cycles are planned based on that. This concept is called 'predictive maintenance' and relies heavily on real time data from the asset in question.

Other applications include replenishment triggers, which could for example order new coffee beans automatically if the level in the coffee maker is low.

Overall, IoT really is more of an enabler of process improvement by providing real-time information about the process in question. It provides visibility and feedback, which in turn improve the decisions one can take about the process in question.

44.6   Autonomous vehicles

Autonomous vehicles (AVs) are not new at all, as automated guided vehicles (AGVs) for example have been used to organise the material flows in manufacturing for many years. What is new here is to couple autonomous vehicles, like drones and robots, with AI systems so that they can share the same space as humans, for example by flying overhead or using the roads alongside regular traffic. Key innovators like Boston Dynamics are now able to develop robots that can be 'co-bots' and work alongside humans in warehouse and manufacturing settings. Regulation is still a major roadblock for autonomous drone delivery, as is social acceptance.

44.7   Augmented, mixed and virtual reality

Augmented reality refers to overlaying the actual image with a digital one, which is being used very successfully to reduce picking errors in warehousing, remote assistance, and training. Virtual reality is a fully immersive experience, where the user only sees the digital images and interacts with them. It is used in product development and drug discovery. Mixed reality is a medium consisting of immersive computer-generated environments in which elements of a physical and virtual environment are combined.

In a lean context, a major application is to provide guidance and instruction to the user, avoiding mistakes and preventing accidents.

44.8   Digital twins

Digital twins are, in effect, a digital replication of a real-world process. Its ancestor is the discrete-event simulation that has been used to simulate and improve processes. Digital twins do the same, only that they are able to use real-time data from the process to show what is happening in the process. They allow for elaborate simulations and predictions, and thus are a very useful tool in the unstable parts of the value stream. In a lean context, they can also be merged with value stream mapping quite easily.

44.9   The Metaverse

The metaverse is the idea of creating a virtual world in which users can interact through their avatars. Although still in its infancy, many firms are already exploring ideas to hold virtual meetings not on Zooms or Teams, but by using fully digital environments in which all participants interact on equal footing. Big tech is pushing this idea, with Meta leading the pack. Already we are seeing services being offered in the Metaverse, there are even real-estate agents trading virtual houses and land. Social acceptance of such virtual worlds may be slow, or may never fully materialise, yet it is possible to imagine a world where businesses operate in such virtual worlds, meaning that lean improvements could well be happening in both the physical and virtual worlds!

44.10 Cloud Computing

Cloud computing refers to platform-based services that offer computing, storage, and other value-added services. Many providers now offer to provide IT infrastructures via the internet, thus pooling resources and lowering the barriers to entry. Key considerations are not only cost and capabilities, but also security of data and continuity of service in case of disruptions. Like IoT, cloud computing is a general enabling technology in the context of lean.

44.11 Quantum Computing

Quantum computing seeks to exploit quantum-level concepts such as superposition and entanglement in order to develop more powerful computers. There are many different ways how to implement quantum computing that have been demonstrated, yet challenges remain with regard to stability and scaling. If successful, quantum computing will provide a greatly advanced computing capability, but only for specific applications. A central implication of quantum computing could be the need to rethink encryption, as Shor's algorithm promises to break our current factor-based encryption once quantum computing can be scaled. Other applications include molecular-level simulation in drug discovery, as well as general optimisation. In the lean context it thus is a general enabling technology.

Further reading

Segars, A.H., 2018. Seven technologies remaking the world. MIT Sloan Management Review, 58(3).

Manyika, J., Chui, M., Bughin, J., Dobbs, R., Bisson, P. and Marrs, A., 2013. Disruptive technologies: Advances that will transform life, business, and the global economy. McKinsey Global Institute.

Warnings!

From General Stanley McChrystal (Allied commander in Afghanistan, reflecting on the failure of allied forces despite overwhelming technical and IT superiority) 'The more visible something is, or the easier it is to communicate, the greater the temptation to control'

From Toyota: Simplify and reduce waste BEFORE automating!

45 What's Next?

At the very end of a comprehensive coverage of lean tools that have been developed starting with Kiichiro's Toyoda jidoka idea that is a century old by now, it seems appropriate to speculate a little. Much of the lean toolbox was developed prior to the computing era, or at least, at times where both data and computing power were limited resources.

As artificial intelligence applications are increasingly able to use several types (modes) of data as inputs, AI systems may one day become continuous improvement agents in their own right. It does not take much to imagine giving this or future editions of the 'Lean Toolbox' and the literature it is based on to train an AI agent in process improvement. Being able to predict patterns and using multiple data sources will allow them to take on more complex tasks, and more importantly, complete tasks they were not explicitly trained for.

This in turn will make them able to become even more ubiquitous than they already are. First and foremost, this raises fundamental questions about the future of work, and how society will deal with an increasing displacement of humans from the workplace, and what place 'work' will play in our lives in future. These questions were raised by Keynes nearly a century ago and seem more relevant today than ever before. It seems appropriate to end this book with his words (Keynes, 1930):

'I look forward, therefore, in days not so very remote, to the greatest change which has ever occurred in the material environment of life for human beings in the aggregate. But, of course, it will all happen gradually, not as a catastrophe. Indeed, it has already begun.'

A Lean Chronology

1700's Shopkeepers in England hang standard symbols for various trades, to help with illiteracy.

1780s – 1790s Development of what is today called standard ops and quick changeover by Royal Navy enabling them to deliver a broadside twice as fast as the French or Spanish Navies

1797 Maudslay builds the world's first precision metal screw cutting machine. This was the 'parent' machine of the machine tool industry.

1809 Maudslay and Brunel (father of Isambard) set up the first mechanised production line that produced 160k pulleys per year with 10 men, for the Royal Navy – previously done with inferior quality by 110 men

1859 Smiles publishes 'Self-Help' – a book that inspires Sakichi Toyoda. The only book on display at Sakichi's birthplace.

1871 Denny, a Scottish shipbuilder, asked his workers to suggest methods for building ships at lower cost

1893 Taylor begins work as a 'consulting engineer'.

1896 Pareto publishes law of economic distribution

1898 Taylor begins his time studies of shovelling of iron

1904 Cadillac begins building cars using interchangeable parts

1906 Oldsmobile builds first car with multiple parts coming from external suppliers

1908 Ford Model T

1909 Frank and Lillian Gilbreth study bricklaying. Beginnings of motion study.

1911 Wilson Economic Order Quantity (EOQ) formula

1913 Ford establishes Highland Park plant using the moving assembly line

1922 Gantt 'The Gantt Chart: A Working Tool for Management'

1925 Stuart Chase, 'The Tragedy of Waste', Macmillian

1925 'Mass Production' phrase coined by Encyclopaedia Britannica

1926 Henry Ford 'Today and Tomorrow'

1927-1930 Mayo and Roethlisberger studies at Hawthorn Plant of Western Electric

1929 Sakichi Toyoda sells the rights for a quick-change shuttle to Platt Brothers UK for £100k and establishes a car business.

1931 Shewhart. 'Economic Control of Quality of Manufactured Product' Van Nostrand. First book on SPC and PDCA

1934 Maynard coins the term 'Method Study'

1936 An engineer at General Motors coins the term 'automation'. Toyota sells first car. The name 'Toyota' adopted because it can be written in Japanese with 8 pen strokes (8 is a lucky number in Japan). Toyoda requires 12 strokes. Kiichiro Toyoda visits USA, especially Ford, and starts 'just in time'.

1937 Establishment of Toyota Motor (Toyoda Loom Works established 1922)

1940 TWI (Training within Industry) programme begun by US military sets out 3 key tasks for supervisors: Job Instruction, Job Improvement, Job Relations. Introduced into Japan in 1949.

1942 Juran: Reengineering procurement for Lend Lease (90 days to 53 hours)

1943 Toyoda hospital established. Now known as Kariya Toyota hospital.

1943-44 Flow production of bombers at Boeing Plant II and Ford Willow Run

1945 Shingo presents concept of production as a network to JMA. Also identifies batch production as the main source of delays

1947 Vickers sets up a 'pulse line' to make the Viscount aircraft

1948 Deming first sent to Japan. Lectures on waste as being the prime source of quality problems.

1949 Juran first goes to Japan

1950 Eiji Toyoda visits Ford's River Rouge plant. Impressed by Ford's suggestion scheme.

Ohno visits in 1956. Ohno learns about pull from supermarket chain Piggly Wiggly.

1950 Ohno begins work on the Toyota Production System following strikes. First use of a U-shaped cell at Toyota. TWI introduced into Toyota during early 1950s.

1951 Deming Award established in Japan

1951 Juran 'Handbook of Quality Control' (first edition). Includes cost of quality, Pareto analysis, SPC. (Fifth edition published 1999)

1954 Frank Woollard, 'Principles of Mass and Flow Production' (Republished by Emiliani in 2009)

1955 First use of Andon lights.

1956 First sea container shipment

1961 Shingo devises and defines 'poka-yoke', book published in 1985

1961 Ishikawa devises Quality Circles, and first are set up in 1962. Juran introduces the concept in Europe in 1966.

1961 Feigenbaum, 'Total Quality Control', McGraw Hill

1963 Toyota South Africa plant established

1969 First microchip designed at Intel by Ted Hoff.

1971 Mudge, 'Value Engineering: A Systematic Approach', McGraw Hill

1974 Skinner 'The Focused Factory', Harvard Business Review.

1974 First commercial bar code scan – with Wrigley's gum

1975 Orlicky, 'Material Requirements Planning', McGraw Hill

1975 Burbidge, 'The Introduction of Group Technology', Heinemann – lays down cell design principles

1978 APICS MRP Crusade

1978 First articles on 'Just in Time' appear in US magazines.

1980 NBC television screens 'If Japan Can, Why can't We'. Kawasaki opens factory in USA running 'Kawasaki Production System', based on TPS.

1981 Motorola begins a methodology called 'Six Sigma'

1982 Deming 'Quality, Productivity and Competitive Position' MIT Press and 'Out of the Crisis', MIT Press - contains his 14 point plan.

1982 Schonberger 'Japanese Manufacturing Techniques', Free Press

1982: Hewlett Packard video on 'Stockless Production' shown at APICS conference and widely in USA

1983 Hall, 'Zero Inventories', Dow Jones Irwin

1983 Monden, 'Toyota Production System', Ind Eng and Management Press

1984 Goldratt 'The Goal'

1984 Hayes and Wheelwright, 'Restoring our Competitive Edge', Free Press (Second edition. 'Pursuing the Competitive Edge', 2005)

1984 Kaplan 'Yesterday's Accounting Undermines Production' HBR and 1987 Kaplan and Johnson 'Relevance Lost: The Rise and Fall of Management Accounting'

1985 Shingo: 'SMED', Productivity (But note that quick change methods and technology were in use at Ford River Rouge in the 1930s – now on display in Ford Museum.)

1986 Imai 'Kaizen – The Key to Japan's Competitive Success'

1986 Goldratt and Fox, 'The Race'

1987 Baldridge award established.

1987 Davis in 'Future Perfect' makes first mention of Mass Customisation.

1987 Boothroyd and Dewhurst 'Design for Assembly'

1988 Nakajima 'Introduction to Total Productive Maintenance'

1988 Ohno, 'Toyota Production System', Productivity

1988 Motorola wins Baldridge Award. Winners are required to share their knowledge so Six Sigma becomes more widely known.

1988 Akao introduces QFD into manufacturing

1989 Ohno and Japanese Management Association, 'Kanban – Just in Time at Toyota', Productivity Press.

1989 Shingo Prize established

1989 Camp 'Benchmarking: The Search for Industry Best Practices', ASQ Quality Press

1990 Stalk and Hout: 'Competing against Time', Free Press – sets out 'time based competition'.

1990 Hammer 'Reengineering Work: Don't Automate, Obliterate' Harvard Business Review, and 1994 Hammer and Champy 'Reengineering the Corporation'

1990 Pugh 'Total Design', and 1981 Concept Selection

1990 Womack and Jones, 'The Machine that Changed the World', Rawson

1990 Schonberger, 'Building a Chain of Customers', Free Press

1990 Quick Response initiative started by WalMart

1992 EFQM award established

1993 Hajime Ohba becomes general manager of Toyota Supplier Support Centre, and begins teaching TPS to US companies, many of them outside automotive.

1993 Pine, 'Mass Customisation', Harvard

1994 AME begins promotion of 'Kaizen Blitz' (Book by Laraia, Moody and Hall published in 1999)

1994 Altshuller, First English translation of book about TRIZ

1996 Womack and Jones 'Lean Thinking', Simon and Schuster

1997 Christensen, 'The Innovator's Dilemma', (and 2003, 'The Innovator's Solution).

1996 Hopp and Spearman, 'Factory Physics', Irwin

1998 Suri 'Quick Response Manufacturing', Productivity Press

1999 Rother and Shook, 'Learning to See', Lean Enterprise Institute

1999 Spear and Bowen, 'Decoding the DNA of the Toyota Production System', Harvard Business Review

1999 Lean Enterprise Research Centre, Cardiff Business School establishes the first MSc degree entirely devoted to Lean. (The programme moves to Buckingham University in 2012.)

2000 Johnson and Bröms, 'Profit Beyond Measure', Nicholas Brearley

2001 Hinckley, 'Make No Mistake!', Productivity

2001 Schonberger, 'Let's Fix It!', Free Press

2001 The Agile Manifesto is proposed.

2002 Jones and Womack, 'Seeing the Whole', LEI

2003 Seddon writes of 'failure demand and value demand' in 'Freedom from Command and Control'

2003 Schmenner, 'Swift Even Flow' as a service differentiator

2004 Liker, 'The Toyota Way', McGraw Hill

2004 Lee, 'The Triple A Supply Chain', Harvard Business Review

2004 Holweg and Pil, 'The Second Century', MIT Press

2004 Maskell and Baggaley, 'Practical Lean Accounting', Productivity Press

2005 Gershenfeld, 'FAB: The Coming Revolution on your Desktop', Basic Books, explains personal 'fabrication laboratories'

2005 Dinero, 'Training Within Industry', Productivity Press – a rediscovery of TWI principles that were the foundation of TPS

2005 Dassault builds the first aircraft (the Falcon) to be designed entirely in a virtual environment, cutting tooling and manufacturing time in half.

2005 Womack and Jones, 'Lean Solutions', Simon and Schuster

2005 Steve Blank, 'Four Steps to the Epiphani', (start of Lean Startup movement)

2006 Toyota overtakes Ford in cars sold. Honda car sales in USA approach Ford levels.

2006 Morgan and Liker, 'The Toyota Product Development System', Productivity

2007 Ward, 'Lean Product and Process Development', LEI, published posthumously.

2008, Wallace Hopp, 'Supply Chain Science', Waveland

2008 Shook, 'Managing to Learn', LEI (On A3 problem solving.)

2008 Toyota overtakes GM in vehicle sales to become the world's largest car company

2008 Schonberger, 'Best Practices in Lean Six Sigma Process Improvement: A Deeper Look', points out the winners and losers in long term inventory turn trends – Toyota shown to be a poor performer on this measure

2009 GM goes into Chapter 11 bankruptcy

2009 Spear, 'Chasing the Rabbit', McGraw Hill

2010 Toyota closes NUMMI in Fremont CA, Tesla opens on the same site that same year.

2010 Rother, 'Toyota Kata', McGraw Hill

2010 Robert (Doc) Hall, 'Compression', CRC Press

2011 Ries, 'The Lean Startup', Portfolio Penguin

2011, Mascitelli, 'Mastering Lean Product Development', Technology Perspectives

2012 Liker and Convis, 'The Toyota Way to Lean Leadership', McGraw Hill

2013 Edgar Schein, 'Humble Enquiry', Canongate

2014 Poppendiecks (Mary and Tom), 'The Lean Mindset', Addison Wesley

2014, First Shingo Prize awarded to a UK Company

2015 Radjou and Prabhu, 'Frugal Innovation', The Economist

2016 ISO Standard on Lean and Six Sigma

2217 DDMRP is proposed by Carol Ptak and Chad Smith

2021 Christoph Roser, 'All About Pull Production', AllAboutLean.

2022 GE advocates Lean as part of its corporate turnaround

2022 Deepmind develops multi-modal AI systems capable of supporting general process improvement tasks

2030 Toyota aims for most of its vehicles to be non-fossil fuelled.

Abbreviations

3P – Production Preparation Process

3T's – Time, Transparency, Trust (in a supply chain context)

4V's – Variety, Velocity, Variability, and Visibility (in a supply chain context)

5S – Sort, Straighten, Sweep, Standardise, Sustain. Or in Japanese: Seiri, Seiton, Seiso, Seiketsu, Shitsuke. See also CANDO.

8Ds – A problem-solving approach to identify, correct and eliminate recurring problems.

80/20 – Pareto principle, whereby 80% of the effect is caused by the top 20% of the root causes

85/15 Rule – Deming estimated that 85% of problems are due to common causes and only 15% of due to special causes. He changed this later to a 94/6 ratio.

94/6 Rule – see above.

A3 – A problem solving tool presenting an issue on an A3 paper template

AAR – After Action Review

ABC – Activity-based Costing

ABC-Analysis – also referred to as 80/20 or Pareto chart

AI – Artificial intelligence

AM – Additive manufacturing (3D printing)

ANN – Artificial Neural Network (AI)

APS – Advanced Planning and Scheduling Systems

AS/RS – Automatic Storage and Retrieval System (warehousing)

ATO – Assemble-to-Order (e.g. the Dell model)

ATP – Available to Promise (MRP)

BOM – Bill of Materials (product structure tree)

BNR – Bottleneck Rate

BSR – Buyer-Supplier Relationship

BTO – Build or Make-to-Order (syn. MTO)

BTS – Build to Stock (same as MTF/MTS)

CANDO (other way of naming the 5S) – Clean, Arrange, Neatness, Disciple, Ongoing improvement

CI – Continuous Improvement

CONWIP – Constant Work-in-Process

COPIS – a version of SIPOC that starts with the customer (Six Sigma).

CPFR – Collaborative Planning, Forecasting and Replenishment

CPM – Critical Path Method

CRT – Current Reality Tree (root cause analysis)

CT – Cycle Time

CTB – Critical to Business

CTQ – Critical to Quality

DBR – Drum Buffer Rope (how to schedule a bottleneck)

DDMRP – Demand-Driven MRP

DFM/DFA – Design for Manufacture or Assembly

DFSS – Design for Six Sigma

DL and DANNs – deep learning/deep neural networks (AI)

DMAIC – Define, Measure, Analyse, Improve, Control/Check (Six Sigma)

DMADV – Define, Measure, Analyse, Design, Validate (or Verify) (Six Sigma)

DPMO – Defects per Million Opportunities (Six Sigma)

DOWNTIME – 8 Wastes (Defects, Overproduction, Waiting, Non-essential process capability, Transport, Inventory, Motion, Employees not used effectively)

DRP – Distribution Resource Planning

EBQ – Economic Batch Quantity (simpler version of EPQ)

EDI – Electronic Data Interchange

EI – Employee Involvement

EOQ – Economic Order Quantity

EOS – Economies of Scale

EPE – Every Product Every

EPEI – Every Product Every Interval

EPOS – Electronic Point of Sale data (e.g. barcode)

EPQ – Economic Production Quantity (EBQ which considers production rate)

ERP – Enterprise Resource Planning (e.g. SAP, Oracle, or BAAN)

ETO – Engineer (or Design) to Order

FMEA – Failure Mode and Effect Analysis

FTL – Full truck load (deliveries)

FRP – Finite Resource Planning (ERP system with a TOC module)

FTT – First Time Through

GT – Group Technology

ISO – International Organization for Standardisation (ISO 90001 for Quality Management, ISO 14001 for Environmental Management)

JCM – Job Characteristics Model

JI – Job Instruction (TWI)

JIC – 'Just in Case'

JIS – Just in Sequence

JIT – Just in Time

JM – Job Methods (TWI)

JR – Job Relations (TWI)

KPI – Key Performance Indicator

LCL – Lower Control Limit (SPC)

LSL – Lower Specification Limit (process capability)

LT – Lead Time

LTL – Less-than-full Truck Load (logistics)

ML – Machine Learning (AI)

MPS – Master Production Schedule (MRP)

MRO – Maintenance, Repair and Overhaul

MRP – Materials Requirements Planning

MRPII – Manufacturing Resource Planning

MSA – Measurement Systems Analysis

MTBF – Mean Time between Failures

MTF – Make-to-Forecast

MTO – Make-to-Order (syn. BTO)

MTS – Make-to-Stock

MTTR – Mean Time to Repair

MVP – Minimum Viable Product (Lean Startup)

NPD – New Product Development

NPI – New Product Introduction

NRFT – Not right first time

NVA – Non Value-adding

NNVA – Necessary Non Value-adding

OEE – Overall Equipment Effectiveness

OKR – Objective and Key Results

OODA – Observe-Orient-Decide-Act

OTD – Order to Delivery (order fulfilment process)

OTIF – On Time, In Full (delivery)

OPT – Optimized Production Technology (TOC scheduling software)

PCE – Process Cycle Efficiency

PD – Policy Deployment

PDCA – Plan, Do, Check, Act ('Deming or Shewhart Cycle'), also known as PDSA

PDSA – Plan, Do, Study, Adjust

PERT – Project Evaluation and Review Technique

PFEP – Plan for Every Part / Patient

PWC – Practical Worst Case

QCC – Quality Control of Complexity

QFD – Quality Function Deployment

QCD – Quality, Cost, Delivery (often added: S for Service, F for Flexibility, M for Morale, S for Safety, E for Environment)

QCDMMSE – see above.

RCCP – Rough-Cut Capacity Planning (feedback loop that turns MRP I into MRP II)

RCM – Reliability Centred Maintenance

RFID – Radio Frequency Identification

RIE – Rapid Improvement Event, other term used for kaikaku or kaizen blitz

RPA – Robotic Process Automation

RRS – Runners, Repeaters, Strangers (scheduling)

RTLS – Real-time Location and Sensing Systems

SCM – Supply Chain Management

SIPOC – Suppliers, Inputs, Process, Outputs, Customers (Six Sigma)

SMED – Single Minute Exchange of Dies

SKU – Stock Keeping Unit

SOP – Standard Operating Procedure

S&OP – Sales and Operations Planning

SPC – Statistical Process Control

SRM – Supplier Relationship Management

SWIP – Standard Work in Process

TIMWOODS – Original 7 Wastes: Transportation, Inventory, Motion, Waiting, Overproduction, Overprocessing, Defects, often with added new Skills waste

TOC – Theory of Constraints

TQC – Total Quality Control

TQM – Total Quality Management

TPM – Total Productive Maintenance

TPS – Toyota Production System

TWI – Training within Industry

UCL – Upper Control Limit (SPC)

USL – Upper Specification Limit (process capability)

VA – Value Analysis

VE – Value Engineering

VM – Value Methodology

VMI – Vendor Managed Inventory

VMR – Vendor Managed Replenishment

VSM – Value Stream Mapping

VUCA – Volatility, Uncertainty, Complexity, Ambiguity

WORMPITS – Original 7 Wastes: Waiting, Overproduction, Rework, Motion, Processing (inappropriate), Inventory (excess), Transportation, often with added new Skills waste.

Index

Concepts

11 step TPM...118

25 Principles...12

3 T's Supply Chain.......................................222

3C's (Concern Cause Countermeasure) 84

3D Printing...326

3P..137

4 C's...70

4 N chart..158

4 Objectives, 6 Trade-offs.............................271

4 V's of Toyota Supply..................................223

4M plus I..238

5 Whys..251

5S...78

5S case...235

5S sustainability..267

6 Big Losses...34, 115

6 Honest serving men...................................250

6 Ms...302

7 Deadly Sins..309

7 G's...53

7 Tools of Quality.......................................247

7 Wastes..16

8D Cycle...250

8 Wastes..16

94/6 (Deming) 308

A3 problem solving......................................253

AAR (After Action Review) 293, 295

ABC (Activity Based Costing) 316

ABC inventory...167

Accounting...313

Action plan...71, 158

Active listening...55

Activity sampling...95

Additive manufacturing................................325

Adjustment...97

Agile..263

Agile Development.......................................289

Agile Manifesto...289

AGVs..326

AI..324

Allowable cost...317

Amara's Law...321

Amazon..292

Amplification (Demand) 147, 200, 219

'An hour lost..'..196

Andon..247

APICS..4

Appreciative inquiry.......................................61

Area layout...122

ASCM...176

ASQ...1

Assemble to order.......................133, 150, 189

Audits..80

Augmented reality.......................................327

Automation...5, 8, 18, 311

Autonomation..8

Autonomous vehicles...................................326

Autonomy...67

Availability..115

Backsliding..260

'Ballet not hockey'.......................................164

Basic Lean measures....................................311

Batch 185

Batch size calculation..................................215

Bathtub curve...114

Baudin's RRS...164

Behavioural standards....................................73

Belief and Bias..297

Benchmarking...12

Bias..44

Bills of material (BOM) 174

Black belt..109

Blockages...170

Blocked....................................31, 155, 170

Blocked and starved.........................156, 181

Boeing...57

BOMs...198

Bottleneck shifting....................................181

Bottlenecks.................................157, 178, 184

Boundaries..65

Box Score..316

Brain research.....................................255, 294

Breakthrough...247

Brown paper map.......................................141

BTO...165

Bucket brigade...131

Buffer and safety inventory.......................193

Buffer portfolio..40

Buffers...40, 171, 184

Build-to-order...164

Building Blocks..183

Bullwhip effect...224

Business model generation.......................274

Cadence..94

Call centre...20, 33, 53

CANDO..77, 79

Capacity.......................................32, 34, 40

Cash...148, 176

Catchball...305

Categorization 164

Cathedral model..75

CEDAC...114

Cells..120

Cell algorithms..128

Cell balancing..127

Cell flow diagram.......................................124

Cell timing...130

Chaebol..230

Chaku-Chaku...133

Change...70

Changeover..96

Chart type...85

Checklists...106

Chief engineer.....................................272, 274

CI...75, 171

Clear...47

Climate change...27

Coaching..59

Coaching Kata...258

Coefficient of variation................................35

Cognitive bias..103

Combination chart......................................132

Communications board................................84

Competing initiatives.................................262

Complex..47

Complexity...102, 111

Complicated...47

Compression...26

Concurrency..275

Condition appraisal....................................117

Condition monitoring.................................119

Conditions for sustainability......................268

Confirmation bias..45

Constraints..176

Consuming the forecast.............................212

Contradictions...287

Contribution analysis..................................38

Control limits...211

CONWIP...184, 195

CONWIP and Agile.....................................291

Cost accounting..310

Cost reduction......................................14, 19, 233

Countermeasure..84

CoV (Coefficient of variation) 33

CPFR..................................220, 231, 233

Creativity...283

Critical WIP...19, 20

Culture..89, 302

Cumulative Flow diagram...83

Current state..71

Current state map..143

Customer..12

Customer requirements.....................40, 107, 133

Cycle time...31

Cynefin..45

Day by the hour...208

Days of cover...150

DBR...196

DDMRP...198

Decoupling..198

Dedicated assets..229

Defects......................................33, 49, 99, 103

Delay...22

Deliberate Practice...................................295, 322

Delighter...101

Dell..124, 161

Demand amplification map..................................148

Demand analysis.....................................161, 163

Demand forecasting..225

Demand uncertainty..................................39, 222

Demand variation..162

Deming's 85/15 (or 94/6) Rule.............................252

Deming's Counsel..310

Dependent events..176

Design for Assembly.................................112, 284

Design for Manufacture....................................284

Design Thinking...277

DevOps..287

DFSS..108

Digital..29

Digital Lean..321

Digital mapping...158

Digital twin.......................................160, 173, 327

Digitalisation..322

Digitisation..322

Direct costs..319

Direct observation......................50, 99, 158

Discipline...........................57, 77, 265

Disruptive technology.....................................229

DMAIC..107, 249

DNA of Toyota..25

Doing a Cortes..260

Double Diamond..278

DPMO...109

Drum Buffer Rope..196

Dual sourcing...226

EBQ/EOQ.............................177, 211, 213

Effectiveness.....................31, 58, 66, 113

Efficiency......................6, 14, 31, 312, 322

Empowerment.......................19, 22, 58

Enablers...74

Energy waste...19

Engagement........................22, 72, 74, 301, 304

Environmental sustainability...............................27

EOQ/ EBQ............................177, 211, 213

EPEI...208, 216

EPOS...232

Ergonomics...136

ERP..321

Erratic demand...164

Excess information..315

Experimentation...43

Experiments..292

Exploit..179

External activities..96

Extrinsic motivation.......................................63

Failure demand..................11, 21, 33, 102, 162

Failure modes of Lean.....................................261

Fake Lean..64, 263

Farmers...76

FAST..283
Feedback............................64, 67, 265
Feedback diagram.............................154
FIFO lanes.................................196, 208
Fill rate..40
Final assembly............................120, 174
Financials 55, 107, 109, 312
Financial map....................................148
Fishbone 116, 251
Flow..11, 13
Flow efficiency.................................6, 15
Flow Kaizen Groups............................238
FMEA.......................................247, 278
Force Field..70
Functional analysis.....................279, 283
Future state...............................71, 154
Future state map...............................143
Gannt chart..................................37, 152
GANs...325
GE...108, 282
Gemba..52
Gemba walk...52
Genbutsu...294
Genchi Genbutsu..................................52
Glenday sieve.....................................165
Goodhart's Law..................................308
Google..292
Group Technology................................112
Groupthink..........................102, 234, 295
Habit...6
Halo effect..44
Hansei.......................................265, 303
Harder or Smarter? 266
Hawthorne works..................................52
Heijunka.......................................83, 205
Heuristics...279
Holding the gains...............................260

Honda...24, 273
Hoshin......................................303, 305, 307
Hot Stove..51
House of Lean.......................................8
Human resource map............................150
Humility............................14, 50, 51, 58
Hypothesis..24
Iceberg model......................................71
Idea Management................................245
Ideas...........................7, 13, 48, 61, 72
Improvement......................................235
Improvement cycles............................248
Improvement events.....................242, 259
Improvement hierarchy........................237
Improvement kata...............................257
Improvement types..............................244
Inappropriate systems...........................19
Incremental improvement.....................244
Individual improvement........................237
Industry 4.0........................29, 187, 324
Information....................2, 12, 19, 286, 312
Information flow map...........................144
Initiative......................74, 242, 260
Innovation....................250, 261, 277, 285
Internal changeover.............................214
Internet of Things (IoT) 29
Intervention theory..............................61
Inventory..29
Inventory as an asset..........................314
Inventory fill rate................................41
Inventory optimisation.........................161
Inventory trade-off curves.....................41
Inventory turns..............................31, 308
Inventory withdrawal...........................247
IoT..............................29, 172, 325
Jack Smith case..................................235
JCM...66

Jidoka..100

Jishuken...241

Job breakdown.............................89, 92

Job characteristics.............................66

Job methods........................91, 92, 105

Job relations......................................93

Job rotation..68

Job safety..93

Job shop layout................................121

Kaizen......................................235, 240

Kaizen events.............................241, 243

Kaizen flag..240

Kaizen groups...................................238

Kamishibai..54

Kanban..188

Kanban and RRS................................167

Kanban card calculation...................192

Kanban for software.........................290

Kanban in Agile.................................290

Kanban limitations............................194

Kanban rules.....................................188

Kanban types....................................188

Kano model......................................100

Kata...59, 257

Kata in the classroom.......................259

Kata and TWI....................................257

Kawasaki..4

Keiretsu..228

Key points...................................88, 106

Kingman equation...............................32

Kipling analysis.................................253

Kitting...204

Kobayashi's 20 keys..........................248

KPI-driven...261

KPIs..146

Labour (empty) 20

LAMDA...274

Layout..120

Lead time..31

Lead time map..................................150

Leader standard work.........................89

Leadership.................9, 50, 91, 298, 300, 301

Leading..59, 294

Lean and Six Sigma...........................262

Lean Principles....................................10

Lean product development................270

Lean promotion office.......................236

Lean Six Sigma..................................236

Lean startup......................................292

Lean, TOC and Factory Physics..........182

Learning..14, 23

Learning to See Maps........................141

LEI...9

Less employees are needed 263

Less than last time............................263

Level and chase demand....................161

Level scheduling...............................201

Levelling projects..............................275

Line Stop...247

Listening...55

Listening and humility.......................298

Little's Law..36

Load...32

Logistics..233

Lumpy demand.................................164

Machine learning..............................324

Maintenance.....................................114

Maintenance and design...................119

Make to Stock (MTS) 164

Mapping...140

Mapping changeovers.........................96

Mapping in the digital age.................159

Mapping warnings............................157

Market price trade-offs.....................317

Master scheduling 167, 175

Matrix layout method..................................123

McChrystal warning..................................322

Measures..................................264

Measurement..........................63, 170, 308

Measurement cycle..................................309

Meetings..................................59

Mentoring..................................59

Metaverse..................................327

Milk rounds..................................233

Minimum feasible batch..................................203

Minimum viable product..................................292

Ministry of common sense..................................245

Minor stops..................................115

Mistakes..................................58, 102

Mistake demand..................................34, 161

Mix and Demand changes..................................204

Mixed model balancing..................................133

Mixed model scheduling..................................202

Moderators..................................68

Modularity..................................286

Motion waste..................................17

Motivation..................................63

Moving lines..................................135

MRP..................................145

MRP and DDMRP..................................198

MRP and ERP..................................174

MTBF..................................115

MTO..................................165

MTS..................................165

MTTR..................................115

Muda..................................2, 23

Muda, Muri, Mura..................................2, 62, 78

Mura..................................2, 23, 35

Muri..................................2, 23 35

Nemawashi..................................306

New wastes..................................18

New product development..................................270

Normal demand..................................165

NPD..................................270

NUMMI..................................294

NUMMI..................................68

NVA..................................15

Obeya..................................275

Obstacles..................................258

Occam's razor..................................264

OEE..................................31, 114

OEMs..................................231

Office kanban..................................195

Offshoring..................................261

OKRs..................................310

OODA loop..................................255

Open Book Management..................................305

Open spec..................................275

Operating expense..................................176

Operational excellence..................................263

Operators and cells..................................125

OpEx..................................261

Organising..................................236

Outsourcing..................................37, 273, 283

Overhead..................................319

Overload..................................14

Overprocessing..................................18

Overproduction..................................17

Overproduction and cost..................................314

Ownership, lack of..................................264

P-Q analysis..................................37,122

Pacemaker..........................38, 172, 200, 202, 236

Pareto's 80/20 rule..................................37

Part levelling..................................168

Partnership..................................12, 226, 227

'Parts not wholes'..................................64

Parts Paretos..................................39

PDCA..................................23, 172

PDSA............................23, 25, 63, 87, 92, 306

People Trilogy....................................295

Perfection..............................9,11,99

Perspectives...................................65

PFEP..204

Phase gates...................................280

Picking orders.................................205

Pitch time..............................31, 95

Planned cycle time..............31, 42, 82, 93

Platforms......................................287

Point kaizen...................................238

Poisson distribution....................41, 128

Poka-yoke...............................97, 104

POLCA..197

Policy Deployment.............................304

Pollution.......................................20

Pooling...............................211, 226

Postponement..................................211

Predictive maintenance........................326

Problem cards...................................84

Problem solving................................244

Problems with change............................72

Process...12

Process batch..................................178

Process cycle efficiency........................16

Process mining.......................160, 325

Process rate variation..........................32

Process variation..............................162

Product kanban.................................188

Production kanban....................183, 187

Production preparation.........................137

Project layout.................................121

Psychological safety...................57, 298

Pull...................................11, 187

Pulse lines....................................135

Purpose...10

QCC...112

QCD, QCDMS.....................................311

QFD....................................101, 281

Quality..100

Quality Circles................................246

Questioning..............................12, 55

Queueing dynamics.............................170

Queues..33

Quick Response Manufacturing..................197

Quality filter diagram.........................147

Quoted lead time.....................193, 195

Rabbit chase..................................126

RACI..90

Raku-raku.....................................137

RCM..119

Red Bead Game.................................310

Reducing utilization..........................163

Reductionist....................................63

Regularity......................................12

Repetition....................................296

Repetitive scheduling.........................210

Resource efficiency.......................6, 15

Respect...50

Response Analysis..............................247

Rewards..246

Rework..175

Ringi..306

Risk...226

Rituals..296

Rock boat analogy.............................264

Rogers curve....................................76

Root Cause....................................250

RPA...................................160,286

RRS....................................38, 164

Rule of Five...................................309

Runners, repeaters, strangers..........38, 164

Runner routes.................................204

S-curve.......................................236

S&OP..144, 175

Safety...80

Safety stocks...174

SAVE..282

Saving operators...................................314

Scheduling approaches..........................173

Scheduling batches................................213

Scheduling categories............................166

Scheduling comparisons.........................200

Scheduling general.................................170

Scheduling lines.....................................201

Scientific management....................26, 294

Scientific method.....................................43

Scrap...175

SCRUM........................273, 286, 290

Self-inspection......................................104

Senior management...............................261

Sensei..60

Sequence dependent C/over................217

Seru..122

Seru cells..133

Service Systems Toolbox..............22, 102

Service wastes...22

Set-based design...................................274

Setup (changeover)..........115, 177, 192, 211

Shainin methods....................................111

Shared resources...........................156, 182

Shingo Prize..75

Short interval tracking..........................312

Short term...263

Signal kanban.......................................190

Simulations..60

Single card Kanban...............................188

Single point lessons.................................84

Six Big Losses.......................................116

Six Sigma..102, 107

Six Sigma and Lean...............................110

Six Sigma and Toyota............................111

Skill...66

Skills for Managers...............................303

SKUs...211, 215

SLP..124

Small wins............117, 257, 268, 295, 296, 298

SMART kanban.....................................191

SMED...96

Single and Double Loop Learning.........268

Socio-technical systems...........................62

Socratic method..............................25, 250

Sony..90

SOPK (Deming) 45

SOPs..87

Sort...79

Spaghetti diagram.................................146

SPC...107

Sprints..290

Stability...165

Stable and unstable zones.........155, 170, 172, 187

Staff turnover..266

Stage 1-Stage 2 cycle............................248

Standard work...87

Standardise...80

Starvation, starved resources...............170

Statistical fluctuation............................176

Storyboards...83

Suggestion schemes..............................244

Suggestions....................................82, 243, 245

Supermarket...................................185, 210

Supplier selection..................................230

Supplier association...............................226

Supplier partnership..............................228

Supplier relations..................................227

Supply chain...220

Supply chain buffers................................41

Supply chain enemies............................222

Supply chain kaizen.................................238

Supply chain mapping.............................153

Supply chain risk....................................226

Supply chain uncertainty........................224

Sustainability...260

Sustaining improvements....................81, 265

SWIP..311

Synchronous rules..................................178

System 1 / System 2................................44

Systems..19, 62

Systems thinking....................................265

Takt and pitch time.................................202

Takt time..87, 94

Target changeover time...........................219

Target cost..316

Target costing..313

Task identity..66

Team meetings...86

Tesco...221

Theory of Constraints..............................176

Thinking process.....................................179

Throughput..32, 177

Throughput accounting............................180

Tight kanban..168

TIM WOODS..16

Time line...141, 143

TOC...176

TOC batch sizing.....................................213

TOC Improvement...................................179

TOC/FP/Lean...182

TOM..114

Tom Sawyer...80

Tool mindset...6

Toyota..........................2, 54, 96, 235, 237, 246

Toyota history..2

Toyota QC's..246

Toyota supply...223

Toyota Way...8, 25

TPM...78, 160

Trade-off curves.....................................274

Training within industry.............................92

Transfer batch..178

Transformation..7

Transport waste................15, 16, 40, 114, 180

Triple-A Supply Chain..............................222

TRIZ..287

True North...10

Trust..74

Trust in supply chain...............................229

Tugger...167, 189, 192

TWI...87, 92

Types of maps..141

Ubuntu..51

Uncertainty..224

Uncoordinated sales...............................162

Unfreeze..70

Unnecessary Demand..............................162

Unstable zones.......................................155

USAF...255

Utilization..32

Variable demand batch sizing...................214

Value..11, 14

Value demand..22

Value engineering...................................282

Value methodology..................................282

Value stream...11

Value stream Improvement.......................238

Value stream scheduling..........................201

Variance (accounting) 311, 312

Variance analysis....................................315

Variation.....................................14, 102, 107

Virtual cells..134

Virtual queue...................183, 193, 206, 208

Virtual reality...326

Visual management......................11, 81, 102, 304

VMI...167, 232

Volatility...45

VSM...158

VUCA..27, 45

Waiting...17

Wal-Mart...221

Waste checklists....................................248

Water and rocks analogy.......................264

What gets measured..............................308

Wheel (scheduling)........................203, 206

Window analysis.....................................90

Window layout.......................................185

WIP..20, 32

Work combination chart....................96, 129

Work team...238

Wrong thing right...................................301

X-matrix..306

Yamazumi..130

Yet (Dwek)...298

Yield management..................................161

Zero Quality Control..............................104

People

Ackoff...304

Adams...281

Åhlstrom and Modig...................................8

Amabile..76

Amabile and Kramer...............................300

Anderson...39

Argyris..268

Bateman...243, 269

Baudin...138

Bennett...48

Berger...55

Bhote...113

Bicheno..51, 60, 239

Blastland..48

Box...7

Boyd..255

Boylon...164

Bradley..119

Bria...76

Brophy...248

Chapman...15

Checkland...63

Cho..24

Christensen..231

Christopher..220

Churchill...304

Churchman...65

Cifone..323

Clark and Fujimoto.................................271

Cochrane..7, 313

Cohen..102

Coletta...138

Colvin..299

Conrad and Rooks..................................212

Cooper and Slagmulder.........................318

Cooper and Westrick..............................277

Cowley and Domb..................................304

Crosby...164

Cunnngham..320

Cusumano and Nobeoka........................272

Darlington.......................................165, 320

de Treville..66

Deming.......................................16, 24, 102

Dettner...179

Deuse..172

Devine..75, 265

Doerr...310

Duggan..157, 183

Dwek...297

Dyer..229

Edmondson.................................245, 269

Egan...51, 61

Emery..62

Emiliani...66

Eriksson...259

Fiume..320

Ford.............................10, 87, 96, 297

Forrester..149

Found...28, 73

Frei...103

Frey and Osborne..............................325

Furr and Dyer.....................................277

Gadd...288

Gall..65

Galsworth...81

Garvin..296

Gawande...106

Geary...243

Gilmore and Pine...............................286

Gladwell..77, 299

Glenday...169

Goldratt..178

Graupp...93

Grief..86

Grout..105

Hackman..66

Hales..39

Hall..4, 27, 90

Hallinan..107

Hammer..146, 309

Hartmann...23

Hattingh...23, 60

Heathcote..27

Heathcote and Powell.........................259

Heffernan...297

Hennessey...76

Hinckley..102

Hines..71

Hirano..81, 267

Holweg.......................................4, 64, 233

Holweg and Pil.............................154, 169

Hopp.......................................15, 31, 227

Hopp and Spearman.....................171, 183

Hubbard..309

Huntzinger and Hall...........................320

Huthwaite..273

Hyer..138

Imai...1, 54, 210

Jackson...307

Jobs..303

Johnson..86

Johnson and Bröms.............................287

Johnson, Thomas.................................313

Joiner..102

Jones...154, 294

Joynson..243

Kahnemann...300

Kaplan and Cooper.............................318

Kato and Smalley................................239

Kaufman and Woodhead......................284

Keyte and Locher................................146

King..123

Klein...107

Knapp...290

Knight, Boothroyd and Dewhurst.......285

Kotter...72

Krafcik..5

Lee...233

Levitt...10

Lewin..62

Lewis, Michael.....................................269

Lewis, Sarah..61

Liker...8

Lindstrom..248

Luyster..212

MacCarthy...................................324

MacDuffie...5

Mackle..240

MacLeod and Clark........................74

Mager and Pipe.............................77

Mahesh..297

Majerus.......................................273

Makumbe.......................................60

Mann......................................54, 287

Marquardt.....................................56

Martin and Osterling....................144

Martin, Roger...............................280

Mascitelli.............................272, 280

Maskell..313

Maurer..300

McChrystal..................................323

McIntosh.......................................97

McVay...313

Meyer and Lehnerd.......................287

Monden......................................4, 169

Morgan and Liker.........................273

Muther..124

Nakane and Hall...........................269

Nash and Poling...........................144

Netland, Powell and Hines............301

Nicholas......................................139

Niederstadt....................................91

Norman...86

Ohno......................3, 7, 16, 87, 171, 315

Oldham...66

Page...48

Pampanelli.....................................28

Pfeffer..269

Pil..64

Pink...63

Poppendiecks...............................290

Pound...43

Pound and Spearman....................183

Ptak..199

Reinertsen.............................170, 213

Reis..293

Repenning and Sterman................154

Richardsons................................269

Richter..172

Robinson and Schroeder...............245

Rosenzweig....................................59

Roser.............................157, 181, 200

Rother................10, 59, 72, 138, 257, 299

Russell..56

Sandras.......................................263

Schein......................................51, 61

Scheinkopf..................................180

Schmenner......................................1

Scholl...139

Scholtes...................................51, 73

Schonberger.............4, 139, 239, 312

Schwab.......................................325

Schwartz.....................................296

Seddon....................................34, 51

Senge....................................154, 265

Shingo..............................4, 96, 104

Shook....................................9, 255, 296

Sibbert..86

Simchi-Levi.................................222

Smalley..183

Smith and Reinertsen...................271

Snowden.......................................46

Sobek and Smalley......................255

Sobek, Ward and Liker.................280

Soltero and Boutier.....................239

Spear....................................25, 300

Spearman..............................31, 43, 89

Spitzer.......................................309

Stalk and Hout...146

Stanier...60

Stenzel...319

Stoller..6

Stone and Heen...269

Strickdorn...280

Sutherland..290

Swink...134

Taleb...309

Taylor..89

Thomke..44, 293

Tompkins...138

Trist...62

Trivedi...28

VanderAalst..326

Wallace and Stahl...176

Ward...20, 273

Watanabe..10

Weick...296

Weisbord..62

Welsh...303

Wheeler...113

Whitmore...59

Wickens..87

Wilding..223

Wilkinson...269

Willats..172

Williams...259

Willmott...117

Womack...5, 54, 154

Wooldridge..324

Yin...134

Yoshino..307

"Human Lean" –

A companion book to "The Lean Toolbox"

This book, The Lean Toolbox, covers most of the essential tools and techniques for Lean operations. It also covers some of the essential 'people' concepts. However, the people or human aspects of Lean encompass a vast and expanding array that is beyond the scope of The Lean Toolbox. Hence, 'Human Lean' is a companion sourcebook covering topics that are either not included in The Lean Toolbox or where further detail is considered beneficial.

"Human Lean - A Sourcebook for Head, Heart, Hands, Health, and Habitat" by John Bicheno and Noel Hennessey, is written in the same style as The Lean Toolbox. The main sections are: The Human Dimensions of Lean; Antecedents and Myths; Established Lean Practices to Managing People; Eight Models of People at Work; Systems, Systems Thinking, SocioTech and Complexity; Psychological Aspects; Engagement and Applications; Problems and Problem Solving; Decisions, Mistakes and Insight; Learning; Leadership; Teams; Organisations; Ergonomics and Job Safety.

Human Lean won the "Contribution to Knowledge" prize at Lean Business Ireland Awards 2022.

(PICSIE Books, 2022, ISBN 978-0-9568307-8-4, 313 pages).

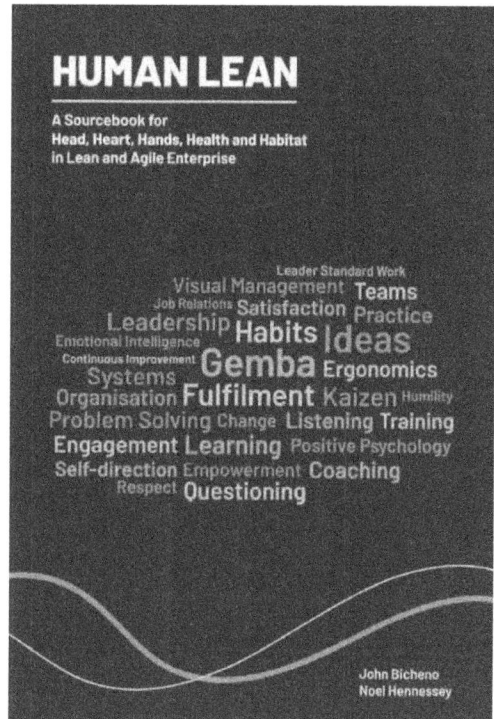